Pro Tools | First

Fundamentals of Audio Production

Avid Technology, Inc.

Published by Rowman & Littlefield
An imprint of The Rowman & Littlefield Publishing Group, Inc.
4501 Forbes Boulevard, Suite 200, Lanham, Maryland 20706
www.rowman.com

6 Tinworth Street, London SE11 5AL, United Kingdom

Library of Congress Cataloging-in-Publication Data available

ISBN 978-1-5381-4384-1 (paperback)
ISBN 978-1538-1-4385-8 (e-book)

About Avid
Avid delivers the most open and efficient media platform, connecting content creation with collaboration, asset protection, distribution, and consumption. Avid's preeminent customer community uses Avid's comprehensive tools and workflow solutions to create, distribute and monetize the most watched, loved and listened to media in the world—from prestigious and award-winning feature films to popular television shows, news programs and televised sporting events, and celebrated music recordings and live concerts. With the most flexible deployment and pricing options, Avid's industry-leading solutions include For more information about Avid solutions and services, visit www.avid.com, connect with Avid on Facebook, Instagram, Twitter, YouTube, LinkedIn, or subscribe to Avid Blogs.

CONTENTS

Acknowledgments

First and foremost, I'm honored to be able to work closely with my colleagues at Avid Technology. You're aware of Avid as the company behind Pro Tools, so you won't be surprised that Avid is made up of dedicated pros, all of them experts in their fields. I work with the training team, and you'll never find a more dedicated group. Special thanks to Kathy Ann McManus, Jason Plews, Bryan Castle, Tim Mynett, Mary Torgersen, Jolene See, and everybody in the worldwide training team. My colleague and friend, Shilpa Patel, helped immensely by tech-editing this book and keeping me accurate on the technical details—special thanks to her. Thanks also to John Dalangin for copy editing the manuscript. Thanks to Alex Brooke, my right-hand man in delivering training at home here in Japan and throughout the Asia-Pacific region. Without all their support, this book would not be possible, and working with them is always a pleasure.

Next, thanks to the worldwide community of Avid Learning Partners (ALPs): a network of schools and teachers committed to offering the highest level of Pro Tools training and certification to their students. Books are one thing (and many of them helped with the creation of this one), but these dedicated and highly-skilled educators bring their material to life for students, performing such important work, and empowering the next creative generation. My gratitude goes to you all for the job you do every day!

In this book, four professionals donated their time to be interviewed, lending their diverse perspectives to the topics covered. Thanks go to Steven Saltzman, Mario De Jesus, Jeff Miyahara, and Scott Weber for taking time from their busy professional days to lend a hand.

Family and friends—the support structure we all need to get through late nights and rough patches. The people I have in my life make me an exception that proves the rule of Karma, and without them, this book would never have become a reality. All my love goes to my wife, Junko, and our daughter, Sachiko.

Finally, this book is written for *you*. May you use what you learn here to create something wonderful.

Andy Hagerman

About the Author

Andrew Hagerman has been a professional musician and teacher for the majority of his 50+ years. Beginning his musical life at the early age of eight as an aspiring tubist, Andy continued his studies at the prestigious Northwestern University in Chicago, Illinois. During his time there, MIDI and computer music were in their infancy, and Andy recognized the usefulness of these new technologies in aiding the creative process. He had a unique opportunity to learn these tools as they were being created and refined, and his quest for the best in audio and music technology ultimately led him to use and teach Avid's Pro Tools.

Andy has accumulated a variety of experience as a performer, composer, arranger, and producer, including a stint as a musician for Walt Disney productions and composer and arranger on a wide range of music projects and post-production works. As an educator, he began teaching at Full Sail University in Winter Park, Florida, where he rose to the position of Associate Course Director of Advanced Audio Workstation Studies. in 2005, he joined the training team at Avid Technology as Training Services Manager for the Asia-Pacific region (with his office based in Tokyo Japan, where he resides today). During this period, he has authored numerous books on music and audio production and continues to create content to inspire the next generation of creative professionals.

INTRODUCTION

Welcome to Pro Tools | First

First of all, congratulations on becoming a Pro Tools user. Pro Tools is the professional audio production standard, and your decision to learn it—starting with Avid's introductory Pro Tools | First version—is a step in the right direction. Before we get into the details, let's discuss this book a bit, so that you can make the most of your learning experience.

What Is Pro Tools, *Exactly*?

In the world of modern audio production, there are several software products that fall into the category of *Digital Audio Workstation* or "DAW". In very rough terms, think of a DAW's role in audio production similar to a word processor—you can use a word processor to create new documents, change sentences, tweak font colors, and more. Then, when you're done, you can export your work as a PDF file that others can easily view. DAWs are like that—they allow users to record audio, create music, make all kinds of changes and tweaks to it, and when done, to export the finished work in a format that other people can listen to. Because DAWs can do all of that, it should come as no surprise that they have become a key part of the professional production world.

When Avid says that their DAW, Pro Tools, is the industry standard, you can believe it. You'll find Pro Tools at all levels of audio production, from modest software-only systems that anyone can use, all the way up to high-end hardware and software systems (with advanced features and price tags to match) that produce Hollywood blockbuster films. It's worth mentioning, though, that Avid didn't make Pro Tools the industry standard—it was the industry's overwhelming choice to use Pro Tools that earned it that coveted spot. As you go through this book, you'll see why pros have chosen Pro Tools, and how learning to use it puts you in very good company.

About This Book

In 2015, Avid introduced a new, free version of their powerful Digital Audio Workstation called Pro Tools | First. While it's true that this product is feature-limited and primarily designed to be a "Try it, Before You Bbuy it" version of Pro Tools, it's also a great way to learn the basic tools and workflows that people have used to create some of the world's most famous audio. That's the goal of *Pro Tools | First: Fundamentals of Audio Production* (the first official Avid book on this product)—to give you a solid foundation in audio production that can take you anywhere you want to go in the world of audio production or music creation.

Who This Book is Written For

Essentially, this book is geared towards beginners with little or no experience in working with a DAW. When it comes to audio production, the assumption will be that everything here is new, so basic key terms and concepts will be described in plain English as we go along.

Don't worry if you're not a formally trained musician, or if you really haven't dealt with digital audio before. The beauty of Pro Tools—and computer music in general—is that even those without formal training can express their creativity! Of course, any general music or audio knowledge that you bring to the table is an added advantage, but it's certainly not a requirement for this book.

However, Pro Tools (including Pro Tools | First) is a *deep* program, and even this introductory version of the software has more features than could fit in a single book. Hence, due to limited space, it's assumed that you understand the basic ins and outs of your computer (Mac or Windows). Don't worry too much, though—you will only need general computer knowledge to use Pro Tools, such as locating, launching, and closing programs and files.

Book Structure

At its heart, audio production is a progressive process. From creation to delivery, it's the result of many small steps taken in order. *Pro Tools | First: Fundamentals of Audio Production* is laid-out to mirror that creative process—from set up, to the recording process, editing and mixing, and then creating your final files:

- Chapters **1** and **2** focus on the basics of digital audio and how to get started with Pro Tools | First. You'll learn here what's important (and what's not) regarding digital audio, what to look for in a system, how Pro Tools' windows are laid out, and how to open and play a project.
- Chapters **3** and **4** deal with the basic concepts of working with audio. We'll start by talking about how audio can be imported into a system, and then how to edit it using a few fundamental tools.
- Chapter **5** is where we will discuss how to record audio. Recording audio in Pro Tools isn't difficult, but the devil is in the details. Here, you will learn how to smoothly record your audio performances.
- Chapter **6** discusses MIDI—**M**usical **I**nstrument **D**igital **I**nterface—and how it relates to music composition within the Pro Tools environment. In this chapter, you'll learn how to set up software synthesizers and get up and running with music creation.
- Chapter 7 continues the topic of editing (which started in Chapter 4), exploring more advanced editing Tools, and how you can apply them to audio and MIDI clips.
- The last block of chapters introduces the complex topic of mixing. Beginning in Chapter **8**. In this chapter, you'll learn the importance of signal flow in the mixing process in general, and basic signal flow in Pro Tools in particular. You'll also learn how to create a rough mix, and how to export your final mix in a format that could be listened to outside of the Pro Tools software.
- Chapter **9** deals with a family of audio effects called *dynamic-based* effects—things like compressors and expanders that are essential processors to the mixer's craft. Don't worry if these terms aren't familiar; we'll go through these essential effects in detail and show you how professionals use them

to take their mixes to the next level. Want to reduce noise or add punch to your song? You'll learn how to do that here.

- Finally, in Chapter **10**, we'll talk about a different kind of plug-in family known as *time-based* effects. In this chapter, you'll learn how to add ambiance to your mix with reverb and delay using the same techniques that the pros use.

Because this book is laid out sequentially according to the production process, you'll be able to follow along from the very start of a project through completion. However, if you're interested in some areas more than others, feel free to read the book out of order and concentrate on those sections that interest you most—this book will work that way as well.

Interspersed within each chapter, you'll find short hands-on-tutorial exercises. Each brief exercise will give you a chance to explore the concepts and techniques being discussed and hear the results. At the end of each chapter will be review questions, so that you can test yourself and make sure that you've understood the main points of the chapter.

The images in this book are captured from a Mac system. Don't worry though—nearly all Pro Tools windows are laid out similarly on Mac and Windows computers, so this is not a problem. In rare cases where the windows are not the same, both Mac and Windows images will be shown.

Conventions and Symbols

Here are some of the text conventions and symbols that will be used in this book:

- Menus will be capitalized.
- Key commands will be capitalized.
- Key combinations will be indicated by a plus (+) sign. For example, if you are directed to hold down the SHIFT key and the CONTROL key, this would be indicated by SHIFT+CONTROL.
- Key commands (key combinations that are accompanied by a mouse click will appear as a dash (-). For example, if you need to click while holding the SHIFT key, this would be indicated by SHIFT–click.
- File hierarchy will be indicated by a forward slash (/). For example, a bass.wav file within the Audio folder within the Loops folder would be indicated by Loops/Audio/bass.wav.
- Menu hierarchy will be indicated by a greater than symbol (>). For example, the TO SELECTION menu item within the TRIM CLIP menu within the EDIT menu would be indicated by EDIT>TRIM CLIP>TO SELECTION.

Pro Tools works equally well on Mac and Windows systems, but some shortcut keys are different:

- The CONTROL key on a Mac system is equal to the START ( ) key on a Windows system.
- The OPTION key on a Mac system is equal to the ALT key on a Windows system.
- The COMMAND (⌘) key on a Mac system is equal to the CTRL key on a Windows system.

- The RETURN key on a Mac system is equal to the ENTER key on a Windows system.
- Throughout this book, you'll see a few symbols that bear mentioning:

When you see this information icon, look here for additional information or tips and tricks.

This exclamation point icon will call out information on things to watch out for, from common mistakes to major problems to avoid!

System Requirements and Download Media

Before we dive into Pro Tools, it's important that you have the right computer for the job and have the files that you need to go through the exercises in this book.

System Requirements

The first thing to do is to make sure that you have a computer that can run *P*Pro Tools | First, including the right operating system. The good news is, Avid has a website that lets you know exactly what you need to run any given version. Just go to: **https://avid.secure.force.com/pkb/articles/Compatibility/Pro-Tools-First-System-Requirements** to get an up-to-date list of the different Pro Tools | First versions and their system requirements.

For those of you who are technically-minded, the Avid compatibility documents page is a great page to bookmark. This information will be invaluable, as you grow in your use of Pro Tools over the years! Here's another link that covers system requirements for *all* versions of Pro Tools: https://avid.secure.force.com/pkb/articles/compatibility/Pro-Tools-System-Requirements

We'll discuss specifics on how to put together a complete Pro Tools system in Chapter 1. Regarding your computer, here are a few things to consider:

- A **Windows** or **Macintosh** system with an internal Hard Drive or Solid-State Drive for running the appropriate operating system and the Pro Tools | First application.
- An optional **external hard drive** for storing media files. Though Pro Tools | First saves most of its files on your system hard drive, having an external hard drive—a dedicated storage for things like sound libraries, audio clips, and your final mixes—can be quite useful. As you move from Pro Tools | First*t* to other versions of Pro Tools, having a dedicated audio hard drive will become more important as your sessions get bigger and your local storage needs grow.
- While you need one computer monitor to use your system on a basic level, adding an optional **second monitor screen** can be very useful, allowing you to see more of your project at one time.

- Monitor **speakers** or high-quality **headphones.** Since you'll make your creative choices based on what you hear, this might be the most important component of your system. We'll discuss this more in Chapter 1, but put simply, the goal of the speakers in a Pro Tools system is to make sure that your work will sound as good in the real world as it does in your studio!

Download Media

This book includes tutorial files that you should download before beginning your studies. Here are the steps:

1. Go to **https://textbooks.rowman.com/PTFirst2021dwnld**
2. Download the **PTFirst_2021_Exercises.zip** file to your computer

When you extract the downloaded .zip file, you can place the extracted files anywhere you like, but if you have an external hard drive dedicated to audio files, it is recommended that you extract them to that drive. Since you'll be referring to those files throughout the course of the book, make sure that you can easily find and access them.

Becoming Avid Certified

This ***Pro Tools | First*** book is designed for teaching and learning the basics of audio production using Pro Tools' free version. As an introduction to DAW use, it can stand on its own. For those looking to learn beyond the basics, Avid has designed an extensive learning series, including Avid Learning Partner schools and various levels of official certification. Avid offers programs supporting certification in areas, including Media Composer, Sibelius, Pro Tools, Worksurface Operation, and Live Sound.

The Avid Learning Partner Program

Avid has partnered with several excellent academic and professional training institutions worldwide called Avid Learning Partners, or **ALPs**, which offer a range of official courses taught by Avid Certified Instructors. After taking courses at one of these ALPs, you can take certification exams, and be listed on Avid's website as a Pro Tools certified User, Operator, or Expert. Studying at an Avid Learning Partner and gaining your official certification can give you a great start on your professional journey.

To locate an Avid Learning Partner near you, visit **https://www.avid.com/education/find-an-avid-learning-partner**

Curriculum and Certification Levels

Avid Offers three levels of Pro Tools Certification:

- Avid Pro Tools **User Certification**, comprising the 101 and 110-level courses
- Avid Pro Tools **Operator Certification**, comprising the 201 and 210-level courses
- Avid Pro Tools **Expert Certification**, comprising the 310-level courses

User Certification

Pro Tools User Certification covers the essential tools of a basic Pro Tools system. User certification begins with the Pro Tools 101 course, followed by the Pro Tools 110 course (for students pursuing **Avid Certified User: Pro Tools** certification), or the Pro Tools 130 course (for students pursuing **Avid Certified User: Pro Tools for Game Audio** certification).

Avid's 100-level courses and User certification is primarily focused on thoroughly understanding Pro Tools software. By the end of these courses, you'll be able to easily use many of Pro Tools' features with confidence.

Figure A Avid Certified Pro Tools User training paths

Much—but not all—of the information covered in the Pro Tools 101 book is also covered in this book. If you are taking this Pro Tools | First course at an Avid Learning Partner (and if you pass the exam at the end of the course), you may be eligible for a shortened PT101 course if you choose to pursue User Certification.

Operator Certification

Operator Certification builds upon the fundamentals learned in the 100-level courses. The 200-level courses that will lead to this higher level of certification explore features exclusively available on Pro Tools | Ultimate software and advanced hardware systems. In these courses, you will gain a deeper understanding of the Pro Tools features that you learned in the 101 and 110 courses (as well as new features) and learn how to apply them in professional Music or Post-Production work setting.

User certification is a prerequisite for becoming Operator certified and begins with the PT201course. After the PT201 course, students may take the PT210M course (in order to become **Avid Certified Operator: Pro Tools | Music** certified), and/or the PT210P course (in order to become **Avid Certified Operator: Pro Tools | Post** certified).

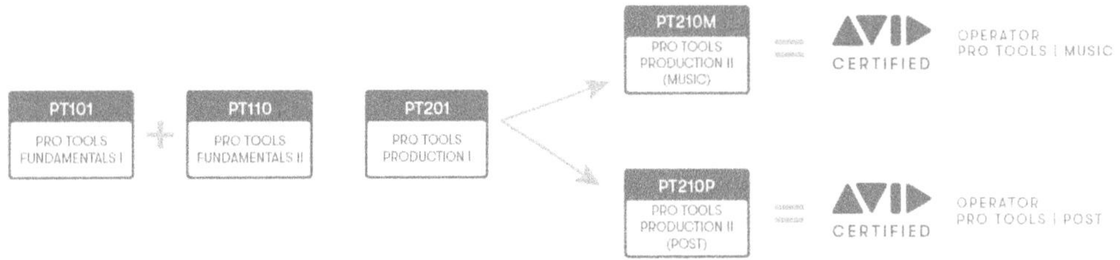

Figure B Avid Certified Pro Tools Operator training paths

Expert Certification

Pro Tools Expert Certification is aimed towards existing professionals, offering training at the highest technical and operational level. Whereas the 100-level focuses on Pro Tools' features and the 200-level teaches how to apply those features in a professional workflow, the 300-level refines those workflows, so that students can work in the most efficient way possible, meeting the demands of today's fast-paced and high-stakes professional scenarios. In addition to certification exams similar to those at the 100- and 200-level, Expert certification involves extensive hands-on testing, requiring rapid responses in order to earn certification.

Operator Certification is a prerequisite for becoming Expert certified. Students can take the PT310M course (in order to become **Avid Certified Expert: Pro Tools Music** certified), or the PT310P course (in order to become **Avid Certified Expert: Pro Tools Post** certified).

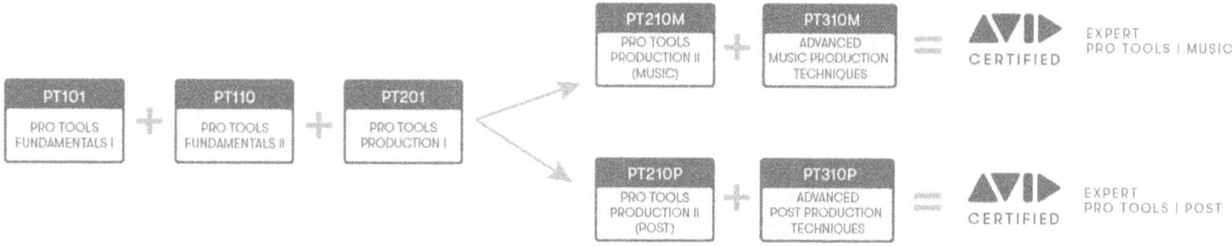

Figure C Avid Certified Pro Tools Expert training paths

Avid Certified. Real Skills. Proven.

Through the Avid Learning Series, you can learn what you need know to be successful in a wide variety of media careers. From your first project to high-end professional work, Avid's courses will teach you the skills you need to stand out in the competitive world of professional audio. The Avid certification that you earn through these courses will demonstrate to the world that you've mastered those skills, a powerful advantage as you begin—and continue—your professional life.

To learn more about Avid official training, please check out Avid's official webpage at **https://www.avid.com/learn-and-support#Learn-from-Avid**. There, you can find more detailed information on the different courses available, find an Avid Learning Partner, and see the worldwide list of Avid Certified Users, Operators, and Experts. If you're a teacher who is interested in joining the Avid Learning Partner team, you can learn more about the ALP program here: **https://www.avid.com/education/avid-learning-partner-program**.

CHAPTER 1

Getting Started

Welcome to the world of Pro Tools, and congratulations! Throughout its decades-long history, Avid's Pro Tools has established itself as a leader in audio technology and preeminent Digital Audio Workstation (DAW) worldwide. Whether you're new to audio production or an experienced producer looking to learn about Pro Tools, this book can give you the information you need to confidently begin using this industry-standard production tool.

Pro Tools can be found in virtually every facet of the audio industry: from music production for streaming services to surround sound for movie soundtracks. You'll find people of all types using Pro Tools in bedroom studios, full-fledged recording and mixing facilities, and massive dub stages working on the next Blockbuster film. The skills you will learn here at the beginning of your journey can take you all the way to the top of the professional audio world. Welcome to the party!

We'll start by talking about sound—how it exists in the physical world and the digital domain. We'll also talk about how digital audio technology has evolved over the years, giving us the current powerful tools that we enjoy today. This history discussion will lead us to Digital Audio Workstations: What are they? How do they work? What can be done with them? And why Pro Tools?

Media Used: Pro Tools First—Fundamentals of Audio Production—Chapter 1 (Low Roar).ptx

Duration: 45 minutes

GOALS

- Understand audio basics
- Learn how audio is digitized
- Understand the evolution of music technology
- Configure an audio production system
- Install Pro Tools I First
- Open and play a Pro Tools I First Project

Audio Basics

Any discussion of audio production is incomplete without first understanding the nature of *sound*. Once you understand the different aspects of audio in the real world, it's then critical to learn how sound is converted into digital audio.

Waveform, Frequency and Amplitude

The three most critical parts of the audio that you hear are **waveform**, **frequency**, and **amplitude**. Let's look at each of these aspects.

Waveform

Waveform is, perhaps, the most recognizable part of a sound. It refers to the *shape* of a sound. For example, here is a picture of a sine wave with its distinctive smooth shape:

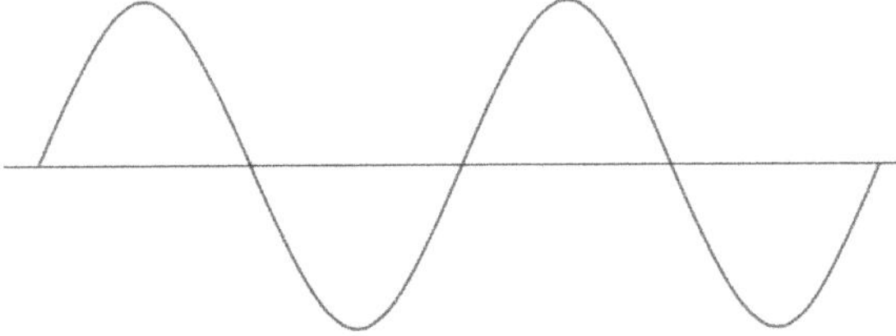

Figure 1.1 A Sine Wave

And here is a picture of a square wave . . .

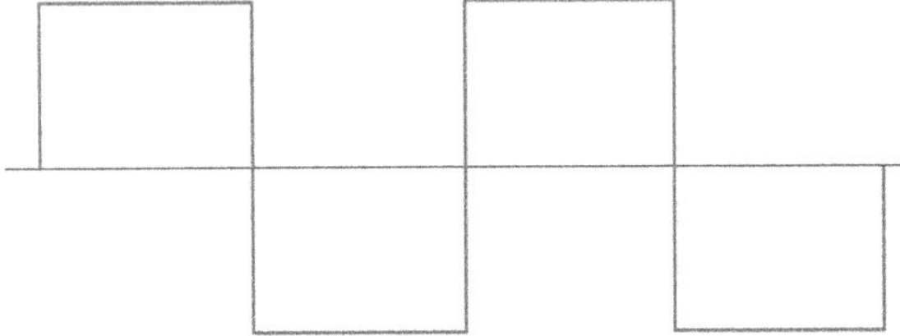

Figure 1.2 A Square Wave

And a triangle wave . . .

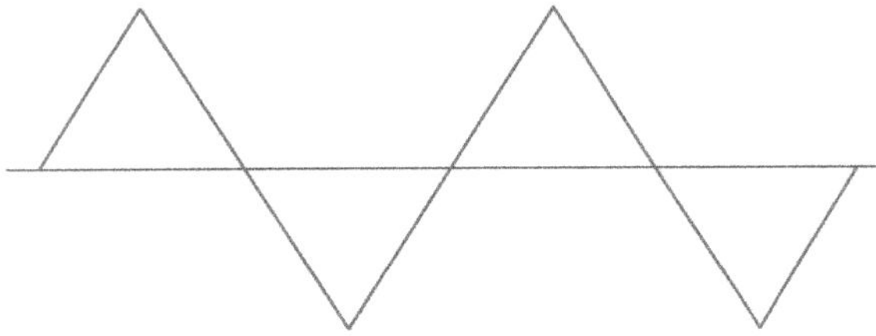

Figure 1.3 A Triangle Wave

You'll see here that even though the waveforms have different shapes, they share a few common features. For example, whenever we look at a waveform graph (which is what these images are), there is a horizontal line in the middle of the graph, which indicates zero energy. A silent waveform would appear as a straight horizontal line following this line:

Figure 1.4 A Silent Waveform

You'll also note that in each case (except for the silent audio), the waveform line begins by ascending from the zero line. Since all sounds in the real world require energy, you'll see this same behavior in all naturally-occurring audio waveforms.

This energy will reach its peak, and then go back down to the zero line. This part of the audio waveform—energy going up and then coming back down—is called the *compression* phase of an audio waveform. The term comes from the fact that air pressure (or the pressure of whatever medium the sound is passing through) increases in this part of an audio wave.

Because sound has a natural back-and-forth motion (since its energy comes from something vibrating), its energy will then drop below the zero line into negative territory. Here again, it will have a (negative) peak and return to the zero line. This is called the *rarefaction* phase of an audio waveform.

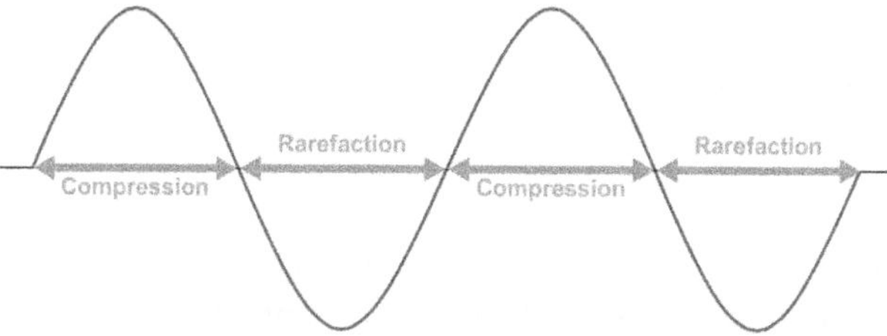

Figure 1.5 Compression and Rarefaction in a Sine Wave

In the natural world, sound never immediately stops. As the energy making the sound stops, the waveform will quickly settle down back to the zero line and silence. This is easy to see with a brief sound, like the snare drum hit shown in Figure 1.6, a brief burst of audio energy quickly settling back down to silence.

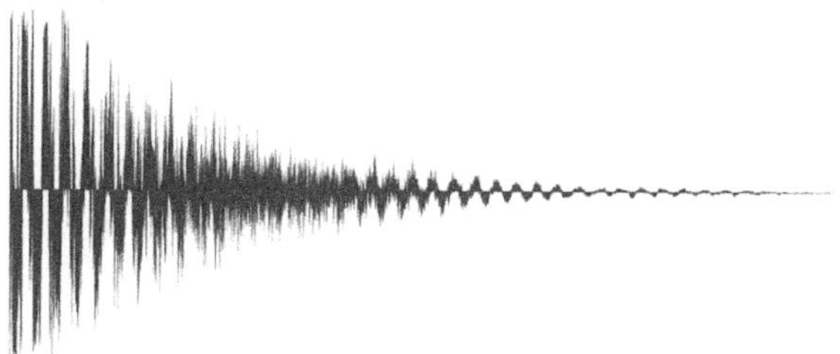

Figure 1.6 A Snare Drum Waveform

We now understand what a waveform *is*, but how is it perceived? As it turns out, a sound's waveform is critically important—the shape of the audio waveform represents the tone or *timbre* of the sound. For example, a sine wave is a very simple and pure sound, quite different from a square wave of the same pitch and loudness. As sound waves become more complex, their waveforms become more complex as well, as you can see with this waveform of a human voice:

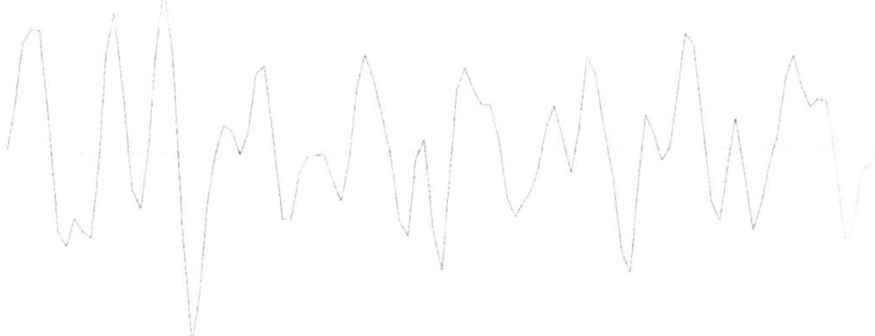

Figure 1.7 A Detailed Look at the Waveform of a Human Voice

Even though the waveform is highly detailed, it still follows the same general compression>rarefaction structure as every other sound you hear every day (though you can see that within each compression or rarefaction phase, there can be multiple peaks and dips). In the real world, no two sounds are exactly alike (every sound-producing object vibrates differently), so every waveform has a distinctive shape.

Frequency

When we refer to the frequency of a sound, we're talking about that sound's *pitch*. High-pitched sounds have a high frequency value, and low-pitched sounds have a low frequency value. On the surface, understanding frequency is a very simple and straightforward matter, but let's dig a little deeper into the science behind the sound.

An understanding of frequency builds upon our previous discussion of what a waveform is. As you've already learned, waveforms have a compression phase followed by a rarefaction phase (followed by another compression phase and another or rarefaction phase, and so on until the sound ends). One period of compression followed by one period of rarefaction is called a *cycle*.

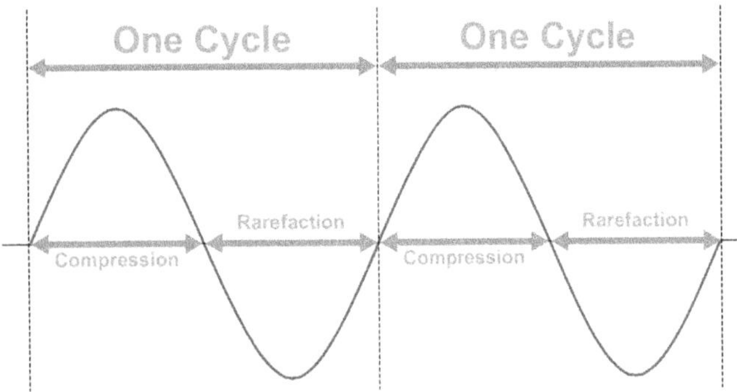

Figure 1.8 Compression and Rarefaction Phases and their Relationship to a Waveform's Cycle

So far, the waveforms that we've looked at represent very short amounts of time (most of the images you've seen in this chapter represent only a single cycle, which translates to an imperceptibly brief sound). Any sound of a significant duration has many cycles. Frequency is measured in cycles per second, in units called Hertz (Hz). A lower-frequency sound has fewer cycles per second, and therefore a lower Hertz value. A higher-frequency sound has more cycles per second and a higher value.

Here is how a low-frequency sound compared to a high-frequency sound might appear. Note that in this case, both waves are sine waves—they have similar waveforms—and the only difference between them is the number of cycles that each has in a given amount of time.

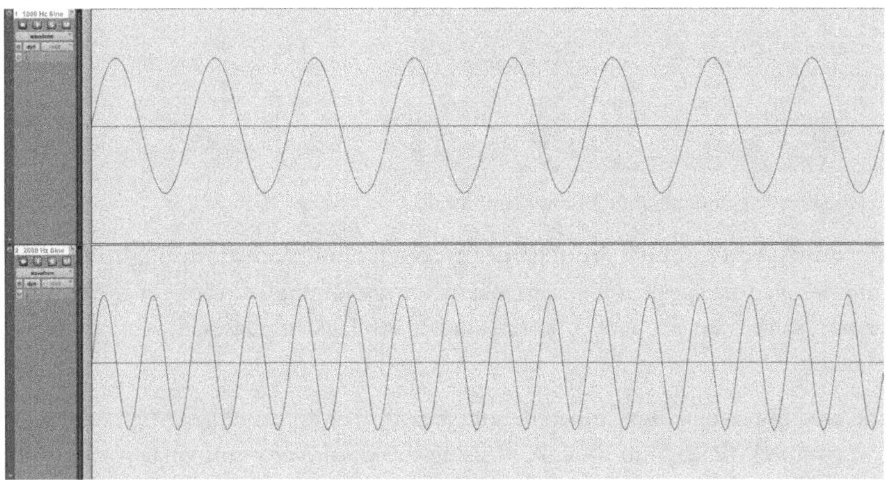

Figure 1.9 A Lower-frequency Sine Wave (top) Compared to a Higher-frequency Sine Wave

Different animals can hear different frequencies. That's how a dog whistle works—it makes a loud sound at a frequency that dogs can hear, but human beings cannot. A human being's frequency range is generally considered to be 20 Hz up to 20,000 Hz (or 20 *kilohertz*, represented by the abbreviation *kHz*).

Although a hearing range of 20 Hz to 20 kHz is often quoted for human beings, it really doesn't apply to everyone. As we age, and depending on our listening habits, humans generally lose high-end frequency sensitivity over time. In general, our sensitivity to frequencies above 10 kHz begins to decrease significantly, beginning in our 30s.

Amplitude

Amplitude, like frequency, is pretty easy to recognize visually in a waveform. *Amplitude* refers to the energy level of a sound and is visually represented in a waveform by its height. Sound with a greater amplitude will be a taller waveform, and lower-amplitude waves will be shorter.

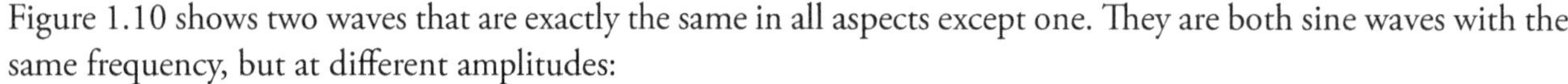

Figure 1.10 shows two waves that are exactly the same in all aspects except one. They are both sine waves with the same frequency, but at different amplitudes:

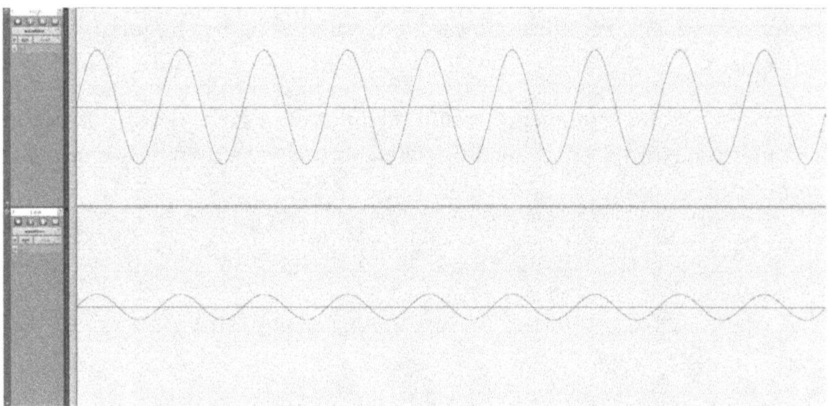

Figure 1.10 The Bottom Waveform has the Same Frequency, but a Lower Amplitude

Amplitude can be affected in many ways—you can hit a drum harder or softer, blow more air through a tuba, or turn up the volume and send more voltage to a speaker. No matter how energy is supplied though, the result is the same: Waveforms with greater amplitude have stronger compression and rarefaction phases, moving more air, and can be heard over greater distances.

There are a few terms that could be used in place of amplitude, like *volume*, *gain*, or even *voltage* (when talking in terms of an audio signal going to a speaker). Be careful, though, of using the word *loudness* if what you're really talking about is *amplitude* (especially when talking to professionals!). Loudness deals with how sound is perceived, and the human ear is more sensitive to some frequencies than others. This means that two waveforms with identical shapes (for example, two sine waves) and amplitudes, but with different frequencies, could be perceived by people as having different levels of loudness.

For those who want to learn more about the difference between amplitude and loudness, and the details of how we perceive sound at different frequencies, a great place to start is with a graph called the *Fletcher-Munson curve.* You can learn more about it here: https://en.wikipedia.org/wiki/Equal-loudness_contour.

Just as the unit of measurement for frequency is Hertz, amplitude has its unit of measurement called a *Decibel* (dB). And just as humans have a frequency range of hearing, there is also a range of Decibels (or dynamic range) that we can withstand as well. The maximum human dynamic range is from 0 dB (which is silent) up to 120-130 dB, after which sound becomes painful. Again, this range, often called the threshold of hearing to the threshold of pain, varies from person to person.

Audio in the Digital Domain

Now that you know how sound operates in general, let's explore how it works in the digital world.

Warning: this section includes some math and science! Don't worry though—what you've already learned about sound will put this in perspective and understanding these basic ideas will help you be a stronger audio producer in the long run!

Frequency and Sample Rates

The term *sample* is used in a number of ways in the audio world. When we use this word relating to the basics of digital audio, a sample can be defined as an instantaneous measurement of an audio signal. A sample measures one thing only, and that is the amplitude of the audio at a specific moment in time.

A single sample is nowhere near enough information for us to record or reproduce a sound. What's needed is a number of samples, spaced evenly in time in order to re-create (or create) a sound properly. Figure 1.11 shows a sine wave with each sample marked. Individually, a sample represents only an amplitude value, but together they can represent a complete waveform!

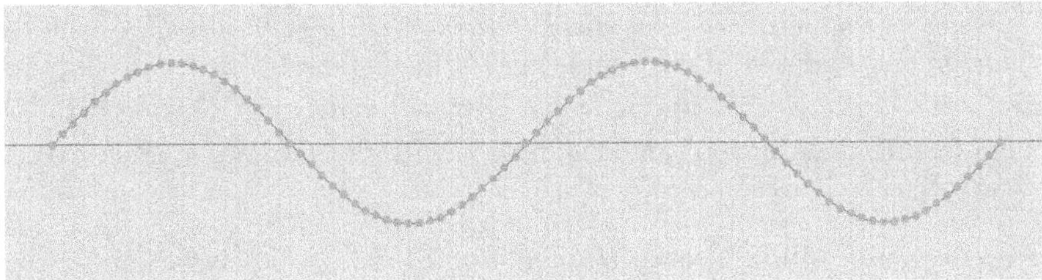

Figure 1.11 Each Red Circle Represents a Sample in this Digitally Generated Sine Wave

The number of samples used per second is called the *sample rate*. Now, here's where it might get a little confusing—sample rates are measured in Hertz and Kilohertz, just like frequency! Here are some different sample rates that are popularly used:

- 44.1 kHz (44,100 samples per second)
- 48 kHz (48,000 samples per second)
- 88.2 kHz (88,200 samples per second)
- 96 kHz (96,000 samples per second)
- 176.4 kHz (176,400 samples per second)
- 192 kHz (192,000 samples per second).

But what is the right sample rate for you to use? If you go on the Internet and search this topic, you'll find a wide range of opinions. Let's talk a little bit about the math behind sample rates, so you can make your best choice.

Sample rate theory finds its roots from a mathematician named *Harry Nyquist,* who is one of the fathers of digital audio and the inventor of a rule called the *Nyquist theorem*. Put simply, the Nyquist theorem states that in order to accurately record or reproduce a sound, the sample rate must be at least twice the highest frequency of that sound. In other words, you need at least one sample in each compression phase, and one sample in each rarefaction phase.

A sine wave with a sample rate like the one in Figure 1.11, since it doesn't break the Nyquist rule, can be accurately recorded and played back. However, if there are less than two samples per cycle when recording, something interesting happens: Instead of the correct frequency being recorded, a lower frequency is created—this is called *foldback* or *aliasing*. Figure 1.12 shows an example of what can happen when you break the Nyquist rule (too few samples), with the blue waveform being what would be actually recorded.

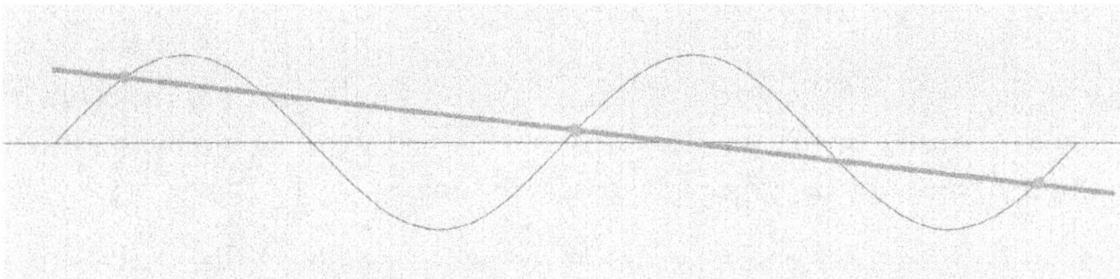

Figure 1.12 Breaking the Nyquist Rule

If you do the math, considering that the highest frequency that a human can hear is 20 kHz, and we need at least two samples per cycle, then a 44.1 kHz sample rate should be more than enough, right? Well, there's one more piece to this puzzle: When sound is recorded digitally, there is a small amount of distortion in the frequencies very near the Nyquist frequency (the frequency that is ½ of the sample rate, or the highest frequency that can be accurately recorded). When recording at 44.1 kHz, you're working with a Nyquist frequency of 22.05 kHz (44.1 divided by 2). In some cases, this high-frequency distortion can be audible—especially with sounds that have a lot of high frequency content, like cymbals.

If you record at 96 kHz though, you're working with a Nyquist frequency of 48 kHz, which is well above the audible range. And if you record it 192 kHz, your Nyquist frequency is way up at 96 kHz. In both cases, the distortion near the Nyquist frequency is still there, but it's so far out of the human hearing range that it doesn't become a problem. While some professionals can hear a difference between 44.1 kHz sample rate audio and 48 kHz audio, most cannot hear a difference between 48 kHz and 192 kHz. So, when it comes to sample rates, more is not necessarily better!

Bit Depth and Dynamic Range

As you just learned, each sample is a digital measurement of only the amplitude of a sound in an instant of time. As with all computer data, this measurement consists of ones and zeroes—the number of those ones and zeros in a sample is something that we call *bit depth*. In the audio production world, the most common bit depths are 16-bit and 24-bit.

Maybe it's easiest to think of it this way: if you're using bits to measure the height of a waveform, using more bits will allow you to measure greater heights. Higher bit depths will allow you to record with a greater dynamic range. Here's an easy formula for you to use: each bit will give you approximately 6 dB of dynamic range, so a 16-bit audio has a maximum dynamic range of 96 dB (16x6) while a 24-bit audio has a maximum dynamic range of 144 dB (24x6).

When it comes to which bit depth to use, the answer is straightforward. As you learned earlier in this chapter, the maximum dynamic range of a human being is 120 to 130 dB. A 16-bit audio doesn't have more than 96 dB. However, with a 144 dB dynamic range, 24-bit audio can record everything that you can hear and more. Yes, a 24-bit audio file will be 50% larger than a 16-bit file of the same duration, but the increased dynamic range will be a major benefit in most situations.

The Impact of Sample Rate and Bit Depth Choices on File Size

The choices you make regarding sample rate and bit depth will have an effect on how much you can do with your Digital Audio Workstation. The more samples or the more bits that you use, the more numbers will be stored on a hard drive or processed by the CPU. In practical terms, higher sample rates and bit depths translate into fewer tracks and plug-ins before your system maxes out.

Regarding sample rates, don't go overboard—use the one that gives you the best sound. In my professional work, I work with Sessions that use sample rates up to 96 kHz, but very rarely beyond that. Regarding bit depths, however, 24-bit is a standard production choice. The goal is to make sure that the audio you're using in production captures everything that you want to hear, even if your final product will be at a lower sample rate or bit depth.

For those interested in diving deeper into the science behind digital audio, here are two great resources: First, check out *digido.com*—this website, run by world-famous mastering engineer Bob Katz, discusses a wide range of topics relating to digital audio, mixing, and mastering. For the brave, I'd recommend a book called *Principals of Digital Audio* by Ken Pohlmann. Now in its sixth edition, it goes *deep* into the math and physics of digital audio.

DAWs and Pro Tools: An Introduction

Now that we've talked a bit about sound and how it's digitally converted, let's take a look at the evolution of modern audio production, the DAW phenomenon, and Pro Tools in particular.

A Brief History of Audio Technology

To really appreciate where we are today, we need to take a look at where we came from:

Before the Revolution

Before digital audio came on the scene, audio was recorded on magnetic analog audio tape. It was common to see 2-inch wide tape being used on massive machines that could record up to 24 tracks. Both the tape recorders and the tape was very expensive. If you wanted to edit it, you used a razor blade to cut the physical tape. Any mistake you made when you cut that tape was permanent!

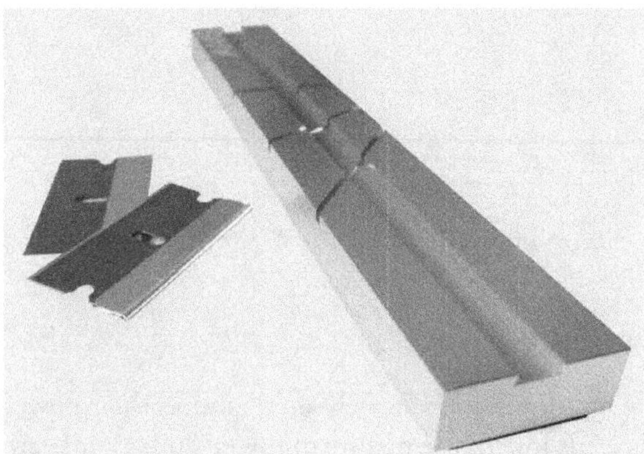

Figure 1.13 Razor Blades and a Splicing Block—State-of-the-Art Editing Tools in the Analog Tape Age!

Drum Machines and Samplers

Digital audio started small—brief chunks of sound (like drum hits, often called drum *samples*) began to gain popularity in the mid-1980s. It was right around this time that the company *Digidesign* came out with a product called *Sound Designer*, which allowed ordinary people to create their own sampled hits and build their personal sound libraries.

MIDI Steps In

Around this time, a different kind of technology was introduced called *MIDI*. MIDI (which stands for **M**usical **I**nstrument **D**igital **I**nterface) allowed people to record musical performances, and then later have them played back by synthesizers. The devices that could record, edit, and play back MIDI data were called MIDI *sequencers*. This was before personal computers became popular, so sequencers in those days were dedicated hardware devices.

Digital Audio Recorders: The Hard Drive Replaces Tape

The next evolutionary step in digital audio was the move from recording single brief segments of sound to recording longer multiple audio signals. This is when the first digital audio recorders came on the scene. Digidesign introduced its digital recorder, called *Sound Tools* which was advertised as a "tapeless" studio system. By this time, these kinds of computer and hardware systems began replacing analog tape decks.

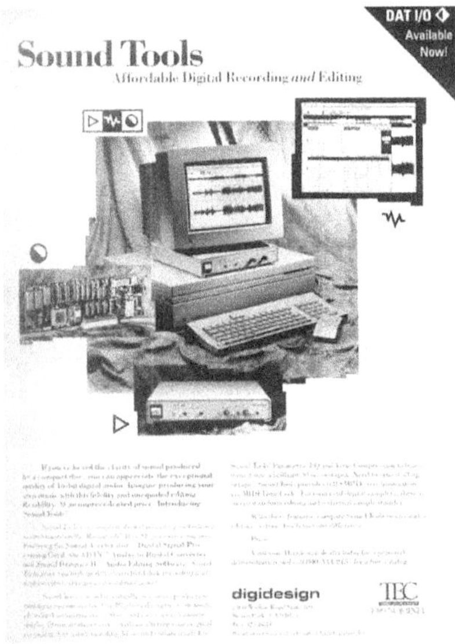

Figure 1.14 An advertisement for Digidesign's Sound Tools—a Game-changer at the Time

Digital Audio Workstations: The Computer Stands on its Own

In 1991 Sound Tools became *Pro Tools*. Computers were now becoming more widely used, and as their power grew, so did the power of the Pro Tools software. Editing tools were added, the quality of digital audio hardware improved, and the cost of building a high-end professional facility decreased substantially. In 1994, Digidesign merged with another company called Avid Technology (itself a leader in the video production world).

During this time, MIDI sequencer systems and digital audio systems were still separate devices. However, in the late 1990s, MIDI sequencers started adding digital audio features, and digital audio products started adding MIDI functionality. In 1999, Pro Tools added MIDI and became a full-blown Digital Audio Workstation. Now, music and audio production can be done on a single system, from the first MIDI notes of a composition to the final audio mix!

Digital Audio Workstations: What Are They?

So, now, we finally have a comprehensive music and audio production tool, in the form of the modern Digital Audio Workstation (DAW). Let's take a closer look at a DAW.

Sessions and Projects

DAWs generally have "master" files—files that bring together all the different media elements you need for your work. In the case of Pro Tools, you can go two ways: As a rule, if you're working on media that resides in your local hard drive, that master file is called a *Session* file. If your work resides in the cloud, the master file is called a *Project*. Session files and Project files are actually fairly small files themselves, but they are important because they are the master files for your work, and enable you to interact with the media that you use.

Clips vs. Files

When you record audio into Pro Tools (or any modern DAW), a file will be created. That file will not be part of your Session file, but rather a separate audio file. So how do you access that recording when using Pro Tools? Pro Tools can access audio files through visual objects in the software environment called *clips*. A clip represents (or "points to") an audio file on your hard drive.

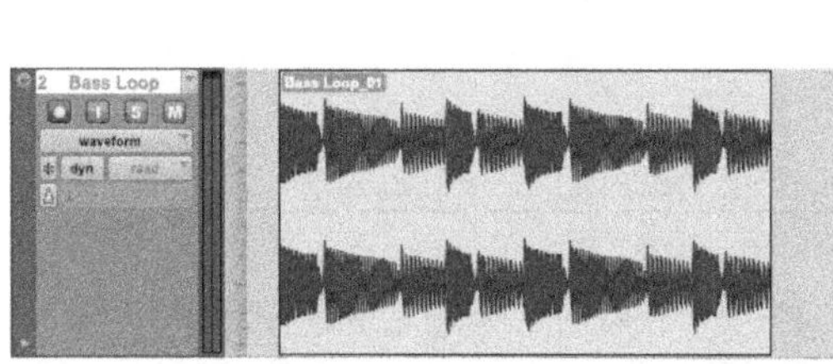

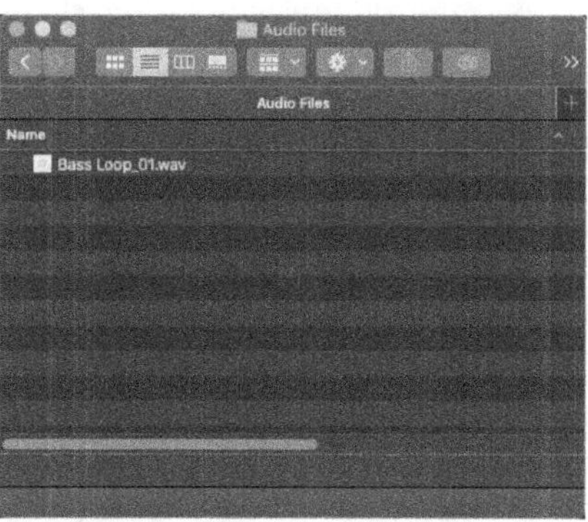

Figure 1.15 An audio clip in Pro Tools, and its Corresponding Audio File.

Non-Linear, Non-destructive

Working with clips has many advantages, and one of the first that you'll discover is that you can move clips earlier or later on the Pro Tools timeline and position them anywhere you want. An environment like this, in which you have the ability to manipulate multiple elements independently on the timeline, is commonly described as being *nonlinear*.

Another great advantage of clip-based DAWs is that you can *non-destructively* edit your audio. This means that you can change the start and end times of clips (removing audio from your project's timeline), and since you're not operating on a file directly, no data is lost. If you don't like an edit you've just done, you can try something different or undo what you did with no damage done to the original audio.

Real-time Processing

Back in the days of tape, if you wanted an effect to be added to a sound, you had to record with that effect. In the early days of digital audio, since computer power was relatively low, we needed to render out brand new files of processed audio. These days, the majority of the effects that you use in your Session are running in real time. Not only does that mean that your effects are non-destructive, but if you want to change a particular effect's settings in real time, you can do that easily.

Why Pro Tools?

There are a number of DAWs on the market, but it is Pro Tools that the industry has chosen to be their standard. Let's take a look at why so many pros have chosen Pro Tools.

What Pro Tools Can Do

Pro Tools is true to its digital audio roots, and throughout its evolution, audio quality has been its priority. Avid audio hardware captures and plays back audio with high fidelity, and audio processing (done within the Pro Tools software) preserves a clean signal, allowing professionals to get the best possible results.

But audio is not all that Pro Tools can do—Pro Tools has many powerful MIDI functions as well, which means that you can compose music, record live performances, and edit and mix MIDI and audio together, all in one software environment. And if you can read music notation, there's great news for you—you can view MIDI data as traditional notation, as well as in a "piano roll" view.

You'll learn more about MIDI in Pro Tools in Chapter 6.

There's a word you'll hear thrown around when talking about audio production: *workflow*. This refers to a series of steps or features that are used to get a job done. The better-designed those features are, the smoother and more efficient your workflow will be. When it comes to recording, editing, and especially mixing, Pro Tools' workflow features are top of the line.

When working in audio post-production (audio for television or film), deadlines are ***tight*** and time is of the essence. It is in this kind of work where having a smooth, efficient, and *fast* workflow is especially important. Not only does Pro Tools give post-production professionals everything they need to do their job; advanced tools, like Dolby Atmos processing (which allows sounds to move freely in a three-dimensional space), can be done seamlessly within the software.

Pro Tools Versions

There are three kinds of Pro Tools: Pro Tools | First, Pro Tools, and Pro Tools | Ultimate. Though they are priced differently, and have different levels of features, the skills that you learn with Pro Tools | First can be used with the most advanced Pro Tools | Ultimate systems. Let's take a look at how the different versions compare:

- **Inputs and outputs**–the more inputs and outputs you have, the more individual audio signals you can record and play back. Pro Tools | First will let you record up to four signals at a time, Pro Tools supports up to 32 separate audio input or outputs, and Pro Tools | Ultimate maxes out at a whopping 192 channels of input and output.
- You learn more about **tracks** in this book (starting in Chapter 2). The more tracks you can work with, the more complex your Project or Session can get. The number of tracks in Pro Tools | Firstt is relatively small, progressively increasing as you upgrade to Pro Tools and Pro Tools | Ultimate. You'll learn specific track types and the numbers you can use in Chapter 2.
- With Pro Tools | First, there is a limit of three cloud-based **Projects** that you can work on at a time (and unlimited local Projects, something we'll talk about later in this chapter). Pro Tools and Pro Tools | Ultimate provide for unlimited cloud-based Projects, as well as the ability to work with **Sessions** that are stored on your local hard drive(s).
- You can work on **stereo** mixes in Pro Tools | First and Pro Tools, but for **Surround** mixing, Pro Tools | Ultimate is required.

As you might expect, features get more powerful as you upgrade—upgrading to standard Pro Tools from Pro Tools | First will give you access to numerous new tools and features, and upgrading from Pro Tools to Pro Tools | Ultimate will take you even further.

Pro Tools: The Industry Standard

Since its earliest days, Digidesign and Avid have played a leading role in the world of digital audio, and Pro Tools has been their flagship DAW. Pro Tools has given audio professionals what they need to get the job done and has earned its place as the industry standard. You'll find Pro Tools in studios of all kinds all over the world, and the skills you learn here can take you anywhere you want to go in the industry.

What Makes Up a Pro Tools System?

Pro Tools, or any DAW, is a key part of any audio production system, but it's not the *only* part. Many different components work together to make a complete audio production system.

The Heart of Your DAW: The Computer

Your computer is the cornerstone of your Pro Tools system. Pro Tools software can run on Windows or Mac, on a desktop computer or a laptop, but it's important to have the right kind of power to make the most out of it.

CPU

Your computer's **C**entral **P**rocessing **U**nit (or CPU) will do everything; from mixing to real-time effects processing and more. The more power your CPU has, the more powerful your Pro Tools software can be.

RAM

In addition to CPU power, your computer's **R**andom-**A**ccess **M**emory (or RAM) plays an important role in how your Pro Tools system will perform. RAM serves as a short-term memory for your CPU, and here again, more is generally better. Pro Tools | First requires a minimum of 4 GB of RAM to run, but Avid recommends at least 8 GB.

Hard Drives

Just as tape-based recording studios relied on magnetic audio tape as a storage medium in the old days, DAWs rely on hard drives to store their audio. Since Pro Tools | First is limited as to where projects can be stored (something we'll talk more about later in this chapter), you may want to use an additional hard drive for storing things like final mixes and sound libraries. When you graduate to Pro Tools or Pro Tools | Ultimate, you'll be able to create local Sessions anywhere you want on your hard drive(s), in addition to cloud-based Projects, at which point hard drives will play a more important role.

The two factors when choosing a hard drive for Pro Tools are *size* and *speed*. A larger-capacity hard drive enables you to store more minutes of audio data, higher-resolution data, or both. Most recording studios don't deal with gigabytes of storage, but rather multiple terabytes of hard drive space. It's also important that the data can be retrieved quickly, so the speed of the drive is very important. Avid recommends drives that have a minimum rotational speed of 7200 RPM if they are traditional hard drive, or the use of SSD drives.

Beginners might be tempted to use their computer's internal system drive for all their audio tasks, which works for smaller jobs. However, at a certain point, your system drive won't be able to do all its normal system work and meet the demands of Pro Tools. For that reason, it's highly recommended to use an external hard drive dedicated to audio data when using Pro Tools | First. You can store your sound libraries and mixes in the hard drive, and as you move into other versions of Pro Tools, you'll also use it to store your Sessions and recordings.

Not to be Overlooked: Mice, Trackballs, Keyboards

Technical specifications aside, it's important to have a comfortable work setup, as most producers tend to spend long hours at their computers. Make sure that your keyboard is comfortable to type on, to avoid wrist fatigue. Choosing a mouse or trackball is a matter of personal preference, but it's worth noting that trackballs generally take up less desk space, and so are commonly seen on professional recording studio desks.

There's no single right answer for what to use. Choose what is comfortable and what will stand up to many hours of use, and you'll be glad you did in the long run.

Getting Audio In, Getting Audio Out: Audio Interfaces

Your computer probably has a built-in microphone and speakers, but these won't be good enough for any kind of serious work. To get high-quality audio in and out of your computer, you need to use an audio *interface.* The good news is that there are a lot of choices, and you won't need to break the bank.

Computer Connections

Audio interfaces can connect to your computer in different ways, such as USB, Thunderbolt, and FireWire. As a general rule, the faster the connection between the interface and the computer, the more channels of input and output or the higher quality audio you will be able to play and record. Since Pro Tools | First*t* only supports four channels of inputs and outputs, even a fairly modest USB Interface should suffice.

Analog Audio Connections

The number of inputs that your interface has is important, and your needs will determine what you should purchase. If you're working by yourself and only recording one instrument at a time, a single stereo input is probably just fine. If you want to record multiple musicians at the same time, however, you'll need more channels of input.

As you've already learned, the maximum number of inputs supported by Pro Tools I First is 4. Pro Tools supports up to 32 channels, and Pro Tools I Ultimate supports up to 192 channels.

The *kinds* of inputs your interface has is important, and you'll want to make sure that the gear you purchase can accommodate the kinds of devices you want to attach to it:

- **Line level** inputs are generally used for connecting devices, such as synthesizers, drum machines, and audio and video media players. Line inputs usually use a quarter-inch phone connector.
- **Microphone** inputs are used to connect microphones to your interface. These generally use 3-pin XLR type connectors. Some microphones require a bit of extra voltage to be carried through that cable, called *phantom power*, which is sometimes labeled as "48v" on an interface. If your microphone requires phantom power, make sure that your interface can supply it.
- If you want to record a guitar or bass, you'll want to make sure that your interface has a **DI** (Direct Input), also sometimes called an "instrument" input. This is where you will plug your instrument in. DI inputs also use a quarter-inch phone connection.

The types of outputs on your interface is also important. Monitor speakers (something we'll talk about later in this chapter) commonly use quarter-inch or XLR connectors. Make sure that your audio interface supports the same connection as your speakers. A headphone output is also convenient to have.

Digital Audio Connections

Many audio interfaces, including entry-level models, include digital audio inputs and outputs of some kind. Digital inputs are commonly used to receive signals from other digital devices, and digital output will often go to speakers that have digital inputs. Digital audio formats include coaxial S/PDIF, optical S/PDIF, ADAT optical, or AES/EBU. Here again, make sure you have the kinds of connections that your digital peripheral gear (if you have any) requires.

The topic of digital audio connections is beyond the scope of this book but is covered in detail in other courses of the Avid Learning Series.

Hearing the Real Mix: Monitors

In order to hear Pro Tools and do your audio production work, you're going to need speakers. Not just any speakers, but *studio monitor* speakers. Monitor speakers are different than normal consumer-level speakers. The good news is, you don't need to spend a lot of money to get good quality monitors.

What to Look for in Monitor Speakers

When it comes to studio speakers, there's sometimes a bit of confusion about what to look for. Some people look for speakers that make music sound fantastic, but that's not really the job of *monitor* speakers. The goal of a good monitor speaker is to give you an honest reproduction of your recordings and mixes, without the enhancements common with consumer-level speakers. It's only when you can hear your mix with all its imperfections that you can fix problems, so that your work will sound great on a wide range of playback systems in the real world.

Case in point: for decades, Yamaha NS-10M speakers were many professionals' choice, and even though they've been out of production for years, they can be found in many studios today. They were never particularly expensive (even now, you can find used ones online for a few hundred dollars, even though they are still in demand by pros) and were originally designed to be home bookshelf speakers. Did they sound especially great? No—their value as studio monitor speakers was that they were so *average* that they effectively represented an average playback system. If your audio work sounded good through those speakers, they'd sound pretty good *anywhere*.

Figure 1.16 A Pair of (used) Yamaha NS-10M Speakers

Here are a few things to look for in monitor speakers:

- **Frequency response:** As a general rule, you'll want an even frequency response over the audible frequency range, meaning that the speaker won't artificially boost or cut any frequencies. Most speaker manufacturers will publish a frequency response chart, and the flattest shape between 20 Hz and 20 kHz is the goal. A flat frequency response will not only give you accurate representation of your mix, but it is also less fatiguing to listen to over long durations.
- **Size:** If you're working in a small room, you don't need huge monitor speakers. On the other hand, if you've got a large studio, small speakers will not provide the power that you need. Shop around for speakers designed to match the size of your production room.
- **Ports:** Some speakers have a hole in the back of their cabinet called a *port*, which allows air to flow out the back of the speaker, generally enhancing low frequencies. Ported speakers need some space. As a rule, the back of the speaker should be at least about 1 meter (or about 3 feet) away from the wall behind them. If you have a small production studio and cannot position your speakers that far from the wall, it might be better to choose non-ported speakers.

Speakers Versus Headphones

Headphones can be useful tools but they can't completely replace your monitor speakers. With monitor speakers, some of the sound coming from the left speaker will be heard by your right ear and vice versa, which doesn't happen with headphones. What you hear can also change when sounds from the left speaker and the right speaker interact with each other in the air, and this can significantly affect your mix. With headphones, the left and right channels are completely isolated and separated by your head, so this interaction can't occur.

However, headphones can be an important tool for audio production. Just as with studio monitor speakers, look for headphones with an even frequency response.

The construction of headphones is also important:

- Most headphones on the market are called *closed-back*. Basically, this means that the outer cover of the headphone is solid and does not allow sound to pass through. If you're listening to music and you don't want to bother the people around you, you need closed-back headphones. Similarly, when you're recording things like vocal performances, you don't want your microphone to pick up what's being played in the headphones, so closed-back headphones are a good choice for recording.
- *Open-back* headphones on the other hand, have an outer case that allows sound from the speaker to pass through. Due to their more accurate sound reproduction, most professional mixing headphones (as opposed to recording headphones) have an open-back design.

Figure 1.17 A Sennheiser HD650 Open-back Professional Headphones

Great Resources

As you put together your system, you might have some questions. Here are a few places to get up-to-date answers.

Avid's Compatibility Documents

Avid maintains a list of system requirements for all the kinds of Pro Tools, which it updates as new versions are released. To find out what you need to run Pro Tools | First, go to **http://avid.force.com/pkb/articles/Compatibility/Pro-Tools-First-System-Requirements**. For all levels of Pro Tools (including Pro Tools and Pro Tools | Ultimate) go to **http://avid.force.com/pkb/articles/compatibility/Pro-Tools-System-Requirements**.

Knowledge Base

Avid also has a database called "Knowledge Base," where you can search for information on a variety of technical topics. To access it, just go to **https://www.avid.com/search#t=KB&sort=relevancy**.

In-Application Help

Once you've installed Pro Tools | First (we'll talk about installation next), you'll find that there are helpful resources within the Pro Tools software itself. From the HELP menu, you can search topics based on keywords, or access Pro Tools online help and support.

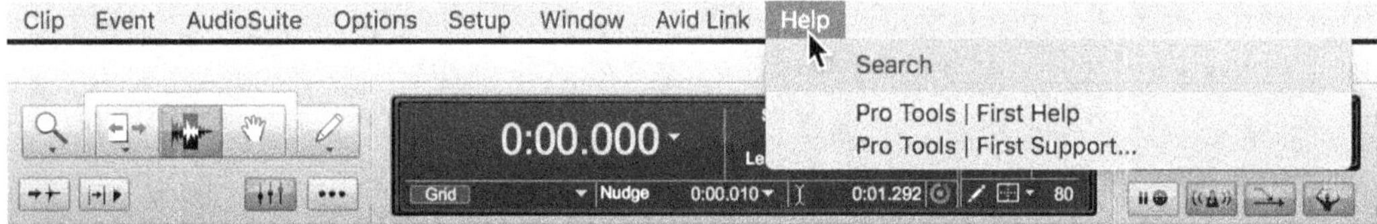

Figure 1.18 Pro Tools | First's HELP Menu

Installing Pro Tools I First

Now that you've got a system that can run Pro Tools | First, let's get the software downloaded and installed.

Installing Pro Tools I First

To get the installation process started, just go to **https://my.avid.com/get/pro-tools-first**. In the screen shown in Figure 1.19, you'll see that you need to sign into your Avid Master account if you have one or create a new Avid account if you don't.

If you have an Avid account, just click the SIGN IN button. If you don't have an Avid account already, here are the steps:

1. Click the CREATE AN ACCOUNT button, as shown in Figure 1.19.

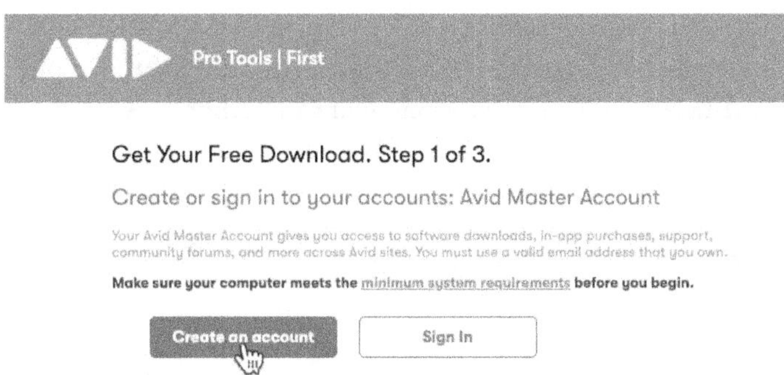

Figure 1.19 Step 1 of 3

2. Enter your first name, last name, country, email address, and password. Make sure to let the internet know that you're not a robot, before you hit the SUBMIT button!

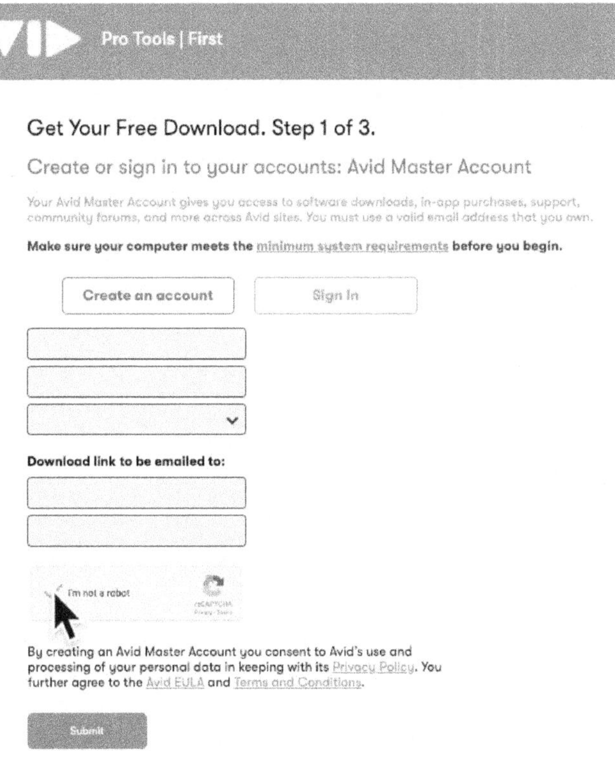

Figure 1.20 Entering Your New Avid Account Information

Your password must be between 8 and 32 characters in length. It must contain at least one uppercase letter, lowercase letter, and number.

Pro Tools | First uses PACE Anti-Piracy software protection for authorization. You can authorize either your computer (no iLok required) or a 2nd- or 3rd-generation iLok USB key (available for purchase separately). In either case though, you will need to have an iLok Account.

3. If you don't already have an iLok account, you can easily create one by just clicking the CREATE NEW ILOK ACCOUNT checkbox. If you already have an iLok account, you can type that name and click the SUBMIT button. (You'll then see another screen where you can authorize Avid to deposit the license.)

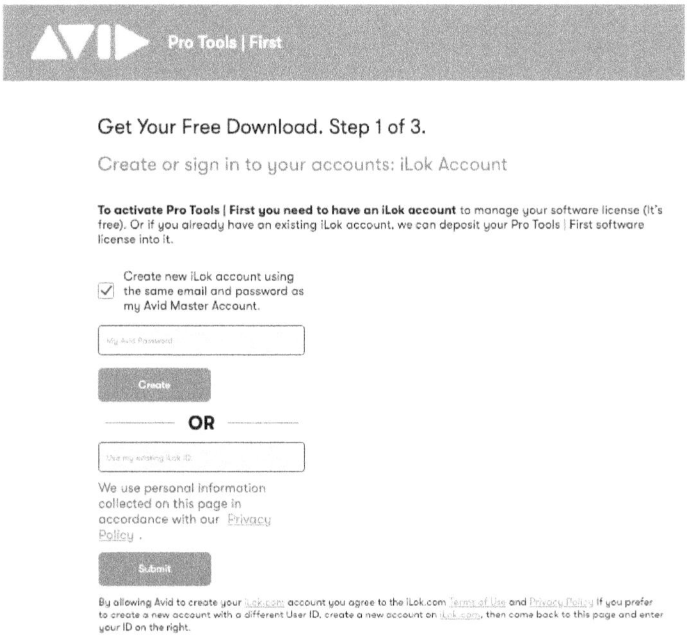

Figure 1.21 Entering Your iLok Account Information

4. In step two of this three-step process, you'll be asked to give Avid a little bit of information about your background and what kind of work you're doing. Once you're done with that, click the EMAIL MY DOWNLOAD LINKS button

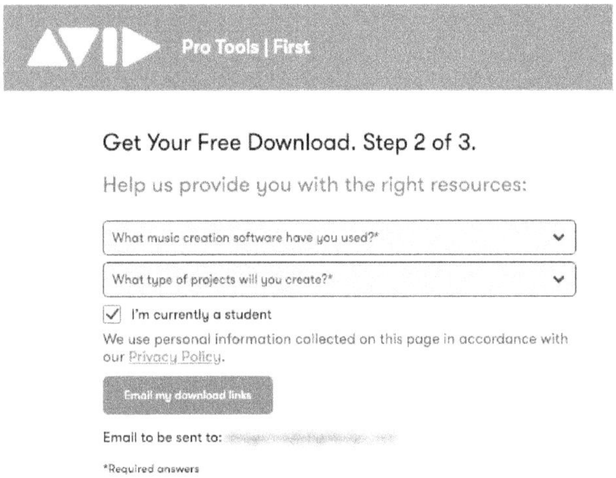

Figure 1.22 Entering Some Background Information

5. In step three, just check your email. You should have gotten a message from Avid that looks something like Figure 1.23. Just click the download button and the software will be downloaded to your computer.

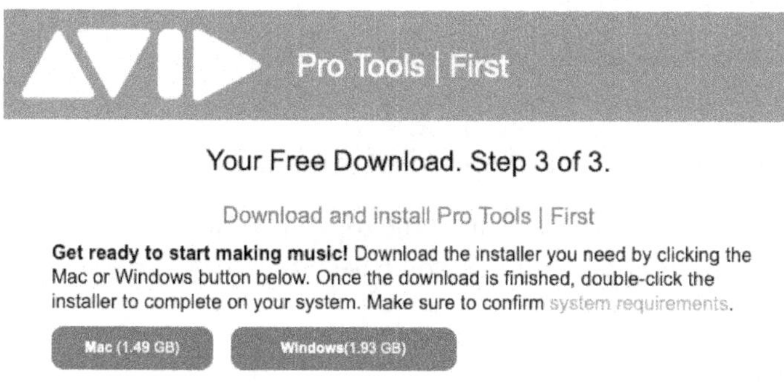

Figure 1.23 Ready to download your Pro Tools Software!

6. Just launch the installation program and follow the directions as you go along. During the installation process, a pop-up window will appear where you will be asked to enter your Avid account, email address, and password.

iLok Protection

In the process of getting your Pro Tools | First software, you had to create a PACE iLok account. Pro Tools | First and the plugins that come with it require licenses, and Avid uses PACE anti-piracy software to manage those licenses. PACE can place your licenses on your computer (requiring no extra hardware), or on an iLok USB key.

Figure 1.24 A 3rd-Generation iLok Key

Many industry manufacturers also use the PACE iLok system, and iLok keys are a common fixture in many studios. An iLok can hold hundreds of authorizations for all of your iLok-enabled software. After a software license is placed on an iLok, you can use the iLok to authorize that software on any computer.

To learn more about PACE and iLok, go to: www.ilok.com.

Avid Link

When you install Pro Tools | First, another application called *Avid Link* is also installed. Avid Link is a useful utility which will allow you to manage your software licenses, keep up to date with the latest versions, and more. When you start to use collaborative Projects, Avid Link will help you communicate with collaborators and enable you to connect with larger forums called *Lounges*.

If you're working on a Mac computer, you can open Avid link from the menu bar icon. On Windows machine, you can open it from the taskbar icon or from the Start menu. There is also a mobile version of Avid Link that you can download from the Apple App Store or from Google Play, which will keep you connected with your editing community even when you are not sitting at your desktop computer.

Software Updates

One of the central functions of Avid Link is to manage your licenses and upgrade them easily:

1. After launching the Avid Link application, click the *Profile* icon at the top left corner to get to the Sign-In page, and enter the email address and password that you have set up for your Avid account.

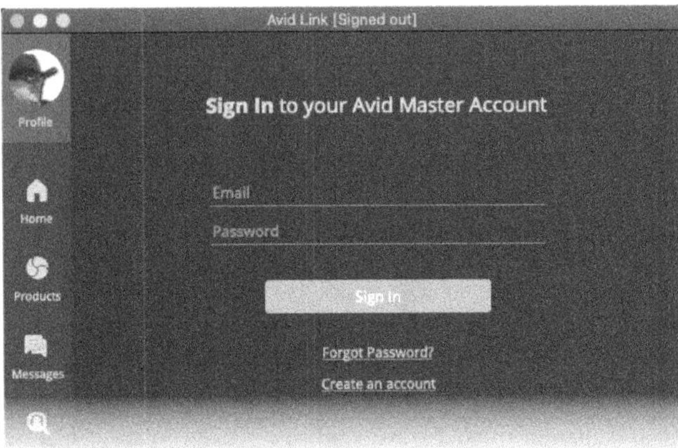

Figure 1.25 The Avid Link Sign-In Page

2. Click the *Products* icon (on the left-hand side of the window) to see a list of all your Avid licenses (this list can take a little while to populate as Avid Link synchronizes with your Avid account). On the right-hand side of each item, you'll see a grey button that allows you to open the application (if your license is up-to-date) or an orange button allowing you to update your license.

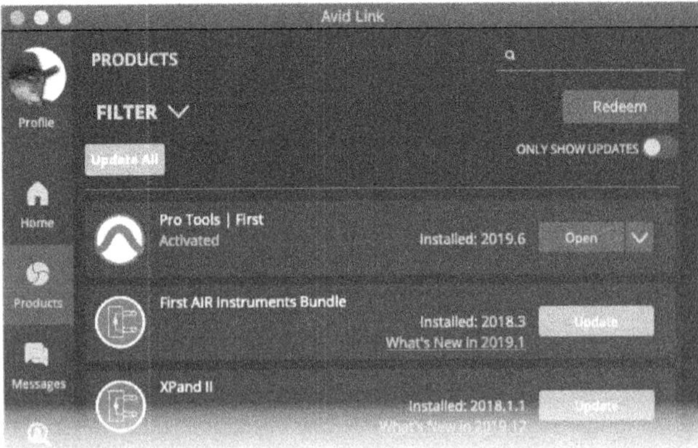

Figure 1.26 The Avid Link Products Page

Finding Installation Information

Before we leave the topic of installing your software, here are a few helpful resources:

- Pro Tools | First Installation Guide: *http://akmedia.digidesign.com/support/docs/Pro_Tools_First_Installation_Guide_12.8_97874.pdf.*
- Pro Tools installation Knowledge Base page: http://avid.force.com/pkb/articles/en_US/How_To/Pro-Tools-Installation

Opening and Playing a Pro Tools I First Project

Pro Tools | First is installed and ready. Now, let's go through the basic steps of opening and playing a Project.

What is a Project?

Pro Tools allows users to work in one of two basic ways: *Sessions* and *Projects*. Let's take a look at these one at a time:

When users choose to create a *Session*, they're creating a master file that will refer to other media (audio or video files) that can exist anywhere on the user's hard drives or local networks. When working with Sessions, the amount of audio they can use is limited only by the amount of their local storage, and they can organize their files any way they like. Hence, Sessions are a common choice, especially for large jobs.

Projects are similar to Sessions in many ways, but Projects are generally used for cloud-based or collaborative work. Storage for cloud-based Projects is limited by how much storage you have in your Avid Cloud Storage plan. Because your files are in the cloud, though, your data wouldn't be deleted if a hard drive crashes, so in that sense the data is more secure. Also, Projects are very easy to work with—you can just launch the Project and get to work without thinking too much about where files are stored on your hard drive (there are some files that are copied to your hard drive while you work with the Project, but Pro Tools does this automatically).

For the general Pro Tools community, most work is done using Sessions. If users specifically want cloud backup or collaborative tools, they'll create a Project instead. Now here's the tricky part: ***Pro Tools | First*** is limited to Projects, whereas Pro Tools and Pro Tools | Ultimate can work with Sessions or Projects. But there's a way to work in Pro Tools | First that will help us work around the normal limitations of Project.

When a Project is Not a Project

While it's true that Pro Tools | First can only work with Projects, it *can* do something that will come in useful—create a *local* Project, which is a hybrid between a Session and a cloud-based Project. Like a normal Project, Pro Tools | First will manage the location of the media files that you work with, making it easy and convenient to use. However, in the case of a local Project, media will not be stored in the cloud in any way, and therefore will not take up any cloud storage space. In that sense, it's like a Session.

It's also worth noting that Pro Tools | First is limited to three cloud-based Projects, but unlimited local Projects. For that reason, the exercises that we'll use in this book will be with local Projects as opposed to more traditional cloud-based Projects.

All versions of Pro Tools come free with 1 Gigabyte of cloud Project storage. If you need more space, you can increase it with a paid plan. To learn more about Project Storage options go to: https://www.avid.com/cloud-plans.

Opening a Project

Opening a Project is simple and straightforward:

Signing In

1. Click on the Pro Tools icon to launch the Pro Tools | First software according to the conventions of your computer's operating system.
2. If you're not already logged into your Avid account, you will be prompted to do so at the beginning of the launch process.

Depending on your Internet connection, this box might appear blank for a short time. Be patient, end it will eventually fill in as shown in Figure 1.27.

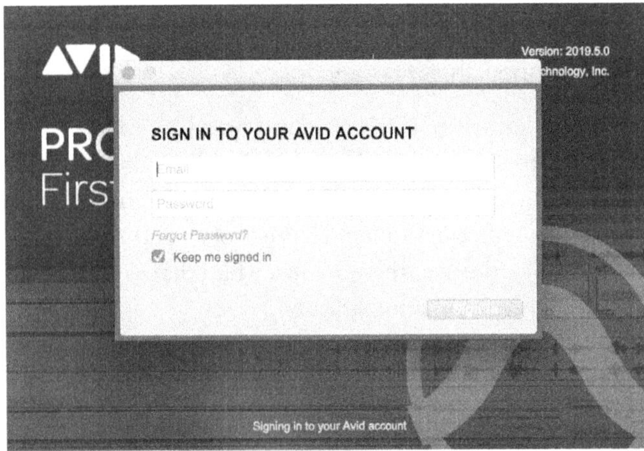

Figure 1.27 Signing Into Your Avid Account

If you want to skip this step next time you launch Pro Tools | First, just click the KEEP ME SIGNED IN check box!

Choosing a Project

Once launched, Pro Tools | First will present you with the *Dashboard* window. In the upper left-hand corner, you'll see your Avid account name and how much cloud storage you're using. Here, you can create a new Project or open an existing one:

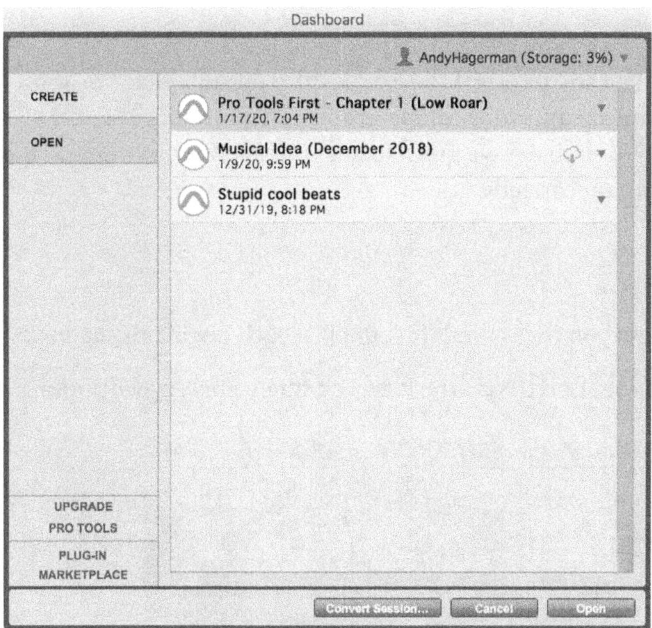

Figure 1.28 The Dashboard Window

3. We'll talk more about creating a new Project in Chapter 2, so for now, just click the OPEN tab. A list of available Projects will appear (if you are new to Pro Tools | First, this list will be empty, since you haven't created any Projects yet).

In the main area of the Dashboard window's OPEN tab, you'll see a list of Projects that you've previously created and can work with (In this example, I've got three Projects that I can open). The color of the circular Project icons means the following:

- A grey Project icon represents a local Project
- A blue Project icon indicates a traditional cloud-based Project

You'll notice that in the second Project on my list (as shown in Figure 1.28), on the right side, there is a small cloud icon. This indicates that the media that this Project needs has not been copied to a local cache (If I open that one, the media would automatically be downloaded, or I can click on the cloud icon to manually transfer it).

4. Select the Project in the list that you want to open by clicking the list item. (Don't worry if you don't have any Projects created yet—you'll learn how to do this in the hands-on exercise in this chapter.)
5. Click the OPEN button and your Project will appear.

OR

5. Alternately, you can double-click any Project that you want to open in the list, and your Project will appear.

Playback Engine and Hardware Setup

At this point, your Project is open and might already be ready to play. However, it's also possible that Pro Tools | First isn't configured to use the audio interface you connected to your computer (or for your built-in inputs and outputs, if that's what you're using to hear Pro Tools). No problem—a quick look at the *Playback Engine* and the *Hardware* dialog boxes will make sure that things are set up correctly.

The Playback Engine Dialog Box

When making sure your Pro Tools system is ready to go, you must check first the Playback Engine dialog box:

1. From the SETUP menu, choose PLAYBACK ENGINE. The Playback Engine dialog will appear.

Figure 1.29 Opening the Playback Engine Window

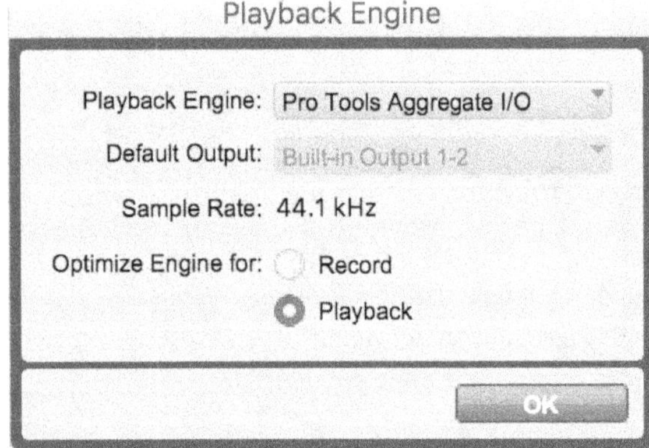

Figure 1.30 The Playback Engine Window

2. In the *Playback Engine* field, choose the hardware that is attached to your speakers or headphones.

On Mac-based systems, Pro Tools creates a new Playback Engine called the *Pro Tools Aggregate I/O*. If you want to use your Mac's built-in input and output together, that is the engine you must choose.

3. If your audio interface supports more than two channels of output, you can choose the pair of connections going to your speakers in the *Default Output* field. In Figure 1.30, this field is grey because I only have two outputs.

4. Your Playback Engine can be optimized for either recording or playback (we'll talk more about what that means in Chapter 5, when we talk about the recording process). For normal playback and mixing, click the PLAYBACK radio button.
5. To close this dialog box, click the OK button.

The Hardware Dialog Box

Once you've chosen your audio interface in the Playback Engine dialog box, you can then configure it from the *Hardware* dialog box.

1. From the SETUP menu, choose HARDWARE. The Hardware dialog box will appear.

Figure 1.31 The Hardware Window

2. The Hardware dialog box will appear differently depending on the interface connected to your computer. Whichever way it appears, you can still configure the specific properties of your connected audio interface hardware. In Figure 1.32, since I've chosen the Pro Tools Aggregate I/O as my playback engine, the Mac operating system's audio devices window is open, displaying Pro Tools Aggregate I/O.

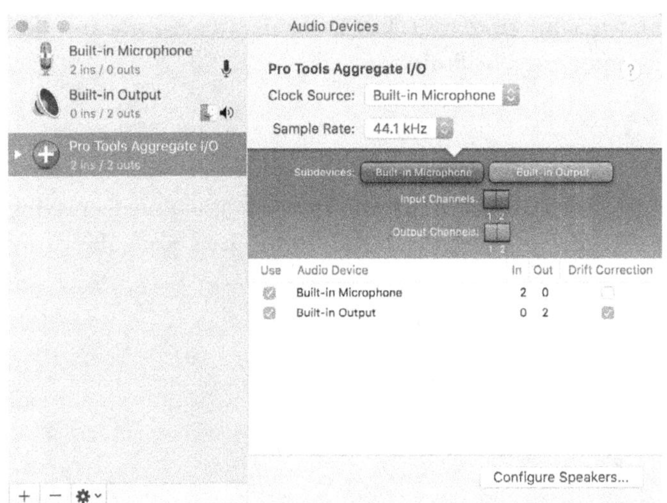

Figure 1.32 The macOS Audio Devices Window, Showing the Pro Tools Aggregate I/O

Basic Pro Tools Operation

Your system's put together, your software is installed, and you're ready to begin. The window that you're looking at in Figure 1.33 is called the *Edit* window, and the colored blocks are the audio and video clips that we discussed earlier in this chapter. Depending on the Project you open, the details of those clips will be different, but the overall look of the window will be the same.

Figure 1.33 The Edit Window

In Chapter 2, you'll learn the Pro Tools | First Graphic User Interface (or GUI) in detail. To close out this first chapter, let's go through some of the basic ways to play and hear your Project.

Starting and Stopping Playback

At the top of the Edit window are different buttons and tools. One cluster will show some familiar media playing icons called *Transport* controls, as shown in Figure 1.34. To play your Session, just click the green triangular PLAY button.

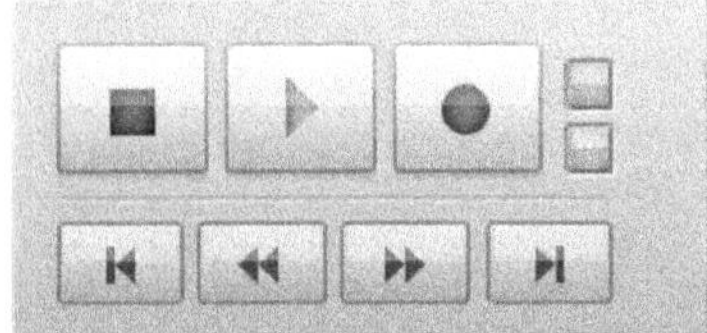

Figure 1.34 The Edit Window's Transport Controls

Alternately, you can press your keyboard's SPACEBAR to start and stop playback.

As your Project plays, you will see a vertical line traveling from left to right. This is commonly called the *play line*, or *playback cursor*, or *timeline insertion*, which indicates where are you are in the song. You will also see large green numbers at the top of the Edit window, which shows you where the playback cursor is located in time.

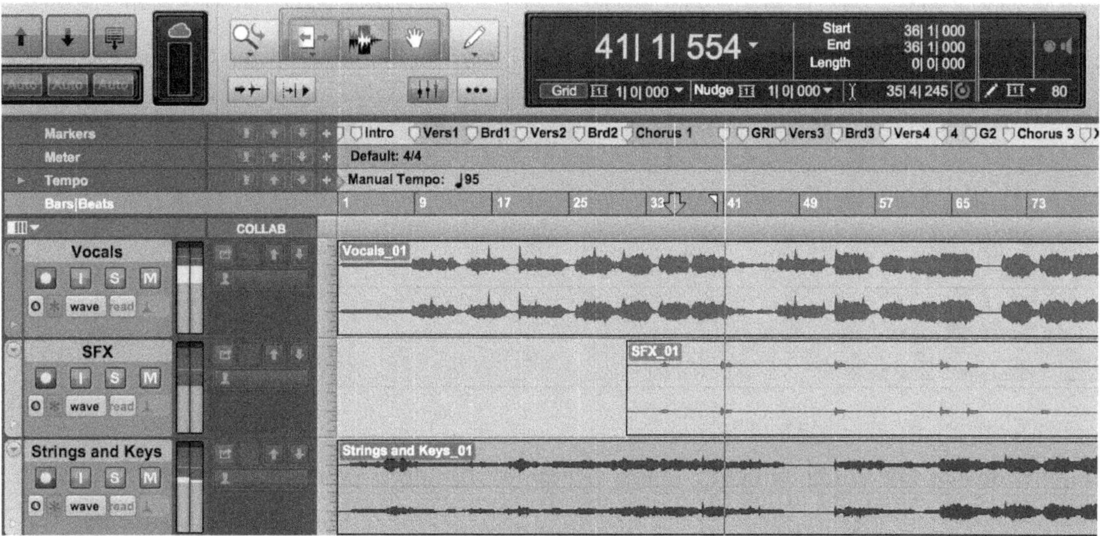

Figure 1.35 The Playback Cursor

On the left-hand side, you'll see volume level meters showing the volume level of each individual row (each row is a *track*, which we'll talk more about in Chapter 2).

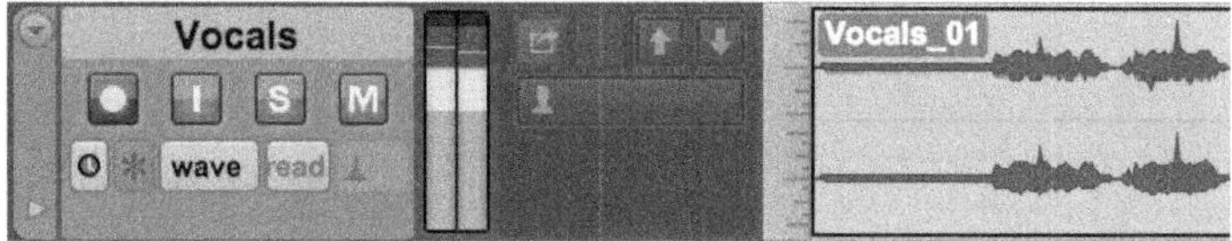

Figure 1.36 A Track Called Vocals and its Level Meters

To stop playback, just press the square STOP button right next to the play button (or press the SPACEBAR).

Setting a Playback Start Point

One of the great advantages of DAWs over tape is the ability to navigate instantly to any location in your work. With Pro Tools, you can do this in several ways:

At the top of the Edit window just below the edit tools are four horizontal strips labeled *Markers*, *Meter*, *Tempo*, and either *Bars|Beats* or *Min:Secs*. These are called *Rulers*, which not only mark the passage of time in the Edit window, but can also allow you to start playback anywhere you want. Just click at the point in time where you want playback to begin. A small blue arrow icon will appear on the Bars|Beats or Min:Secs ruler, indicating where playback will start once you click the PLAY button or hit the SPACEBAR.

Figure 1.37 Edit Window Rulers

You can also choose a position where you want playback to start by typing a number in the Main Counter field (the large green numbers near the top center of your edit window). Just type the number of the place (in Figure 1.38, I'm typing bar 32). You can confirm your number by pressing the RETURN key (Mac) or the ENTER key (Windows), and the blue arrow icon will move to that position, indicating that playback will start at that point.

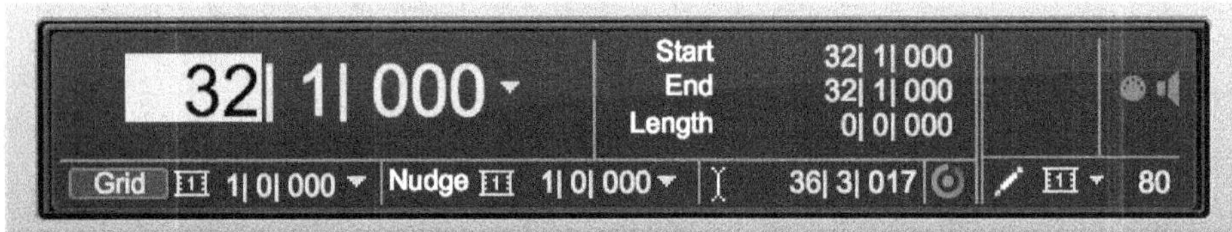

Figure 1.38 Typing a location into the Main Counter

Here are two shortcuts that you will find useful when navigating your Project's timeline:

- To get back to the beginning of your timeline, just press the RETURN key (Mac) or the ENTER key (Windows)
- To go to the end of your timeline, just press the RETURN+OPTION keys (Mac) or the ENTER+ALT keys (Windows)

Closing a Project and Quitting Pro Tools | First

To close an open Project, just to go the FILE menu and choose CLOSE PROJECT.

Quitting Pro Tools | First follows the normal conventions of software.

Hands-On Exercise 1.1: Basic Playback

Now it's time to have a little hands-on practice where you will launch Pro Tools | First, open a Project, and do some basic playback:

Signing In and Opening a Project

1. Launch *Pro Tools | First* and sign into your Avid Account.
2. In the Dashboard window, click the OPEN tab. If you're just starting out with Pro Tools | First, your Project list will be empty, as shown in Figure 1.39.

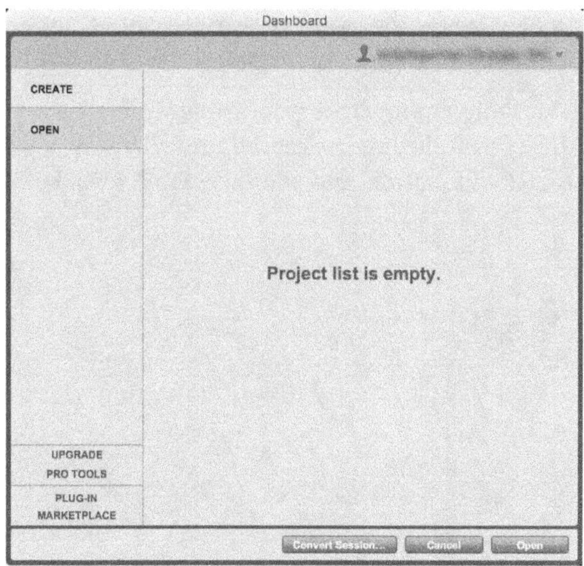

Figure 1.39 Your (currently empty) Project List

3. The first Session you will open will be converted from a Pro Tools Session that you've downloaded with the materials for this book. Click the CONVERT SESSION button and a file browser window will appear.

Figure 1.40 The CONVERT SESSION Button

4. Navigate to the folder named *Pro Tools First—Fundamentals of Audio Production—Exercises/ Pro Tools First—Fundamentals of Audio Production—Chapter 1 (Low Roar)*. Inside that folder you'll find a number of files including one called *Pro Tools First—Fundamentals of Audio Production—Chapter 1 (Low Roar).ptx*. Double-click this file to create a new local Project.

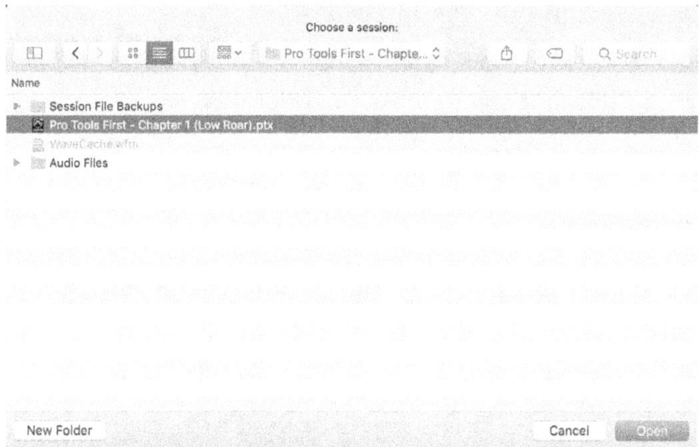

Figure 1.41 Locating the Session that you want to Convert

5. The name of your Project doesn't need to be the same name as the Session that you're converting. Name your new Project *Pro Tools First—Chapter 1 (Low Roar).*

6. In the next window, you will be able to choose your Project's properties (something we'll talk more about in Chapter 2). In this case, choose LOCAL STORAGE and deselect the BACKUP TO CLOUD check box. When you're done click the CREATE button, and your new Project will be created and opened.

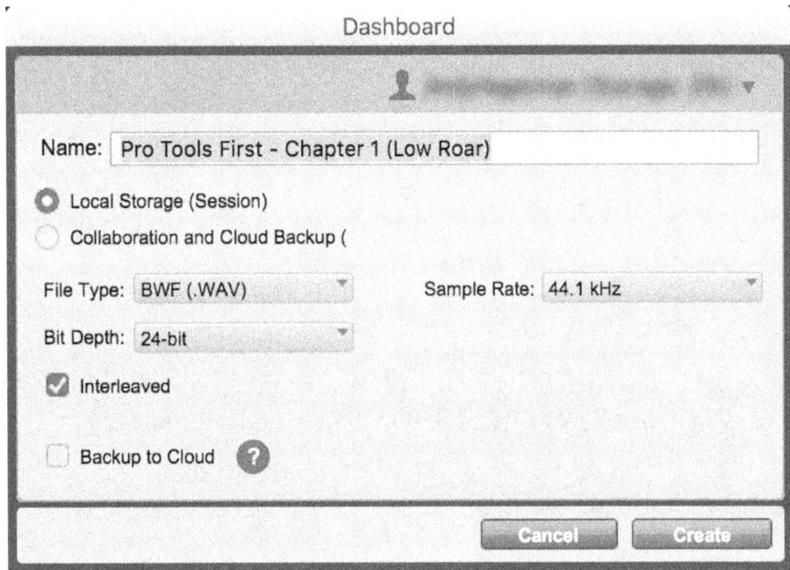

Figure 1.42 Choosing your Project's properties

Throughout this book, when you convert a session, you may see a Session Notes dialog box, saying that "Some inputs or outputs may have become inactive because your audio hardware device has changed." This is a message that often appears when a project was created on a different system from the one it is being opened on. You can safely click the NO button, after which your project will be created. You *may* need to change some if your input or output settings in order to hear your project.

7. Just for practice, let's close the Project. Go to the FILE menu and choose CLOSE PROJECT. The Dashboard window will appear again, except this time you'll see your new local Project in the list. Re-open your new Project from the Dashboard window.

Setting Up the Playback Engine and Hardware

8. In the Playback Engine dialog box, check to make sure that you have the correct audio interface selected.

9. If necessary, go to the Hardware dialog box to make sure that your audio interface is configured correctly as well.

Playing a Project

10. Start playback of your Project by clicking the PLAY button or pressing the SPACEBAR. You should be able to the Project play—if you can't, there might be something misconfigured in the Playback Engine or Hardware dialog boxes.
11. After listening for a while, stop playback.
12. Click on a ruler just before the vocals begin (the vocals start to sing at around measure 9). Don't worry if you're not precisely positioned where the vocals start—just choose somewhere before the vocals begin.

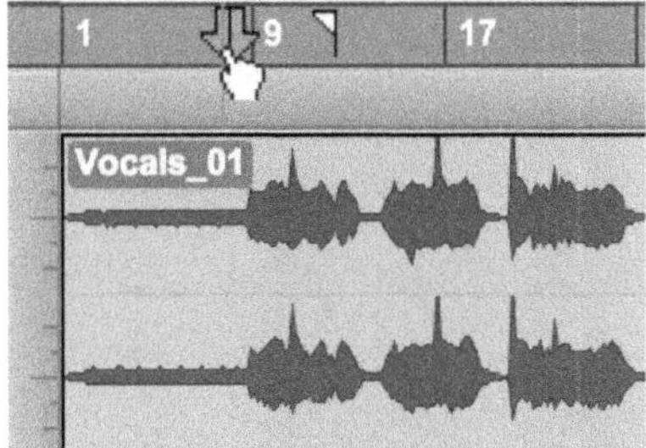

Figure 1.43 Moving Playback to Just Before the Vocals Start

13. Play your Project for a while before stopping playback.
14. Move the playback cursor exactly to bar 53 by typing the value *53|1|000* in the counter. Remember that you will need to press the RETURN key (Mac) or ENTER key (Windows) to confirm your entry.

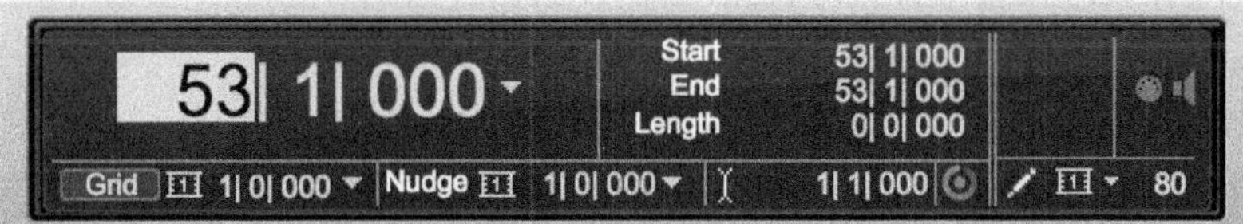

Figure 1.44 Moving playback to Measure 53

15. Quickly go back to the beginning of the timeline by pressing the RETURN key (Mac) or ENTER key (Windows).

Quitting Pro Tools I First

16. Quit Pro Tools | First. This concludes the hands-on exercise.

Review Questions

1. What is a *waveform*? What does a sound's waveform indicate?

2. What is an audio waveform's *cycle*?

3. What does *frequency* mean?

4. What is the audible frequency range of a human being? Is it the same for everyone?

5. What does *amplitude* mean?

6. What's the highest frequency that a sample rate of 96 kHz can accurately record and reproduce?

7. What is the dynamic range of 16-bit audio? What is the dynamic range of 24-bit audio?

8. What are the three different levels of Pro Tools (hint: The first one is Pro Tools | First)?

9. What is the difference between a cloud-based Project and a local Project?

10. Projects can be opened from the ________________ window.

CHAPTER 2

Creating Projects and Tracks

This chapter will cover a lot of new ground: from creating a new project and understanding Pro Tools' windows (and how to make the most of them), to creating new tracks. Mastering these fundamentals is an important step on the road to Pro Tools mastery!

Media Used: Pro Tools First—Fundamentals of Audio Production—Chapter 1 (Low Roar).ptx

Duration: 45 minutes

GOALS

- Create a new Project
- Understand the layout of Pro Tools' main windows
- Customize Pro Tools' GUI to suit your production style
- Understand different track types
- Create and manage your Project's tracks

Powering Up Your Hardware

When computers and audio interfaces are turned on or off, they will sometimes send a spike of voltage from their outputs. If your speakers are on at the time, that voltage spike will sound like a loud pop or thump. Over time, these pops and thumps will wear out your speakers. So, here is a cardinal rule among professional and semi-professional studios of all kinds:

Your monitor speakers should be the last thing you turn on when starting up your system, and the first thing that you turn off when shutting it down.

This might sound like a picky detail, but when professional studios spend significant money and time on their setups, they want to make sure their gear is properly taken care of. Making sure that speakers aren't inadvertently damaged by power on/off voltage spikes is considered basic professional etiquette, and it's a good habit to get into from the start.

Creating a Project

In Chapter 1, you opened a Project. Now, let's create a new one from scratch. There are a number of ways that you can approach this.

Creating a Blank Project

Let's start off by creating a blank Project—in other words, a Project that has no tracks in it:

1. Launch Pro Tools | First. The Dashboard window will appear. Click the CREATE tab if it isn't already selected.

OR

1. If Pro Tools | First is already open, from the FILE menu, choose CREATE NEW. The Dashboard window will appear with the CREATE tab already selected.

The shortcut to create a new Project is COMMAND+N on a Mac or CTRL+N on a Windows computer.

2. We won't be creating a Project from a Template in this case, so make sure the CREATE FROM TEMPLATE check box is unchecked, as shown in Figure 2.1.

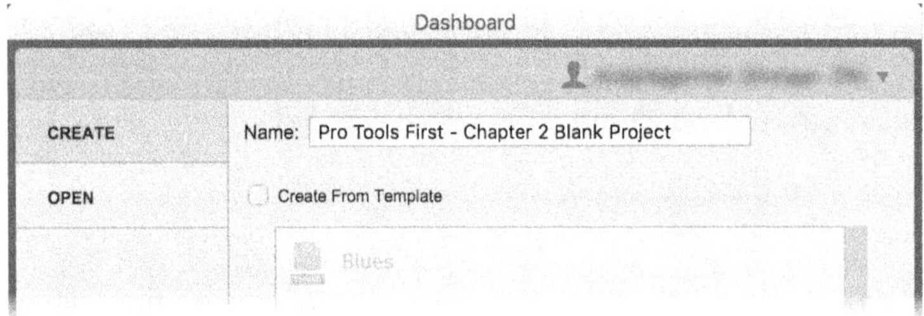

Figure 2.1 Naming Your New Project

3. Name your project descriptively—the default name of *Untitled* won't tell anybody what your Project is about!

4. Checking the BACKUP TO CLOUD check box at the bottom of the Dashboard will back up all your Projects in the cloud.

Figure 2.2 Unchecking the BACKUP TO CLOUD Check Box

5. Click the CREATE button, and your project will be created.

If a Project is already open before you created a new one, you'll be given the option of saving or not saving your work before the new one is created.

Here's what you'll get: You'll see the Pro Tools Edit window just as you did in Chapter 1, but in this case, there are no tracks or clips (yet).

Figure 2.3 A New Blank Project

Creating a Project from a Template

Here's another way to create a new project—from a *Template*. A Pro Tools template is a preconfigured set of tracks, and when you create a new Project from a Template, you're not starting with an empty Edit window.

Creating a Project from a Template is similar to creating a blank project with only a few differences:

1. Just as when creating a blank project, you'll need to get to the Dashboard window, and click the CREATE tab.
2. In this case, please make sure the CREATE FROM TEMPLATE check box is *checked*. You will see a list of templates that you can choose from, as shown in Figure 2.4.

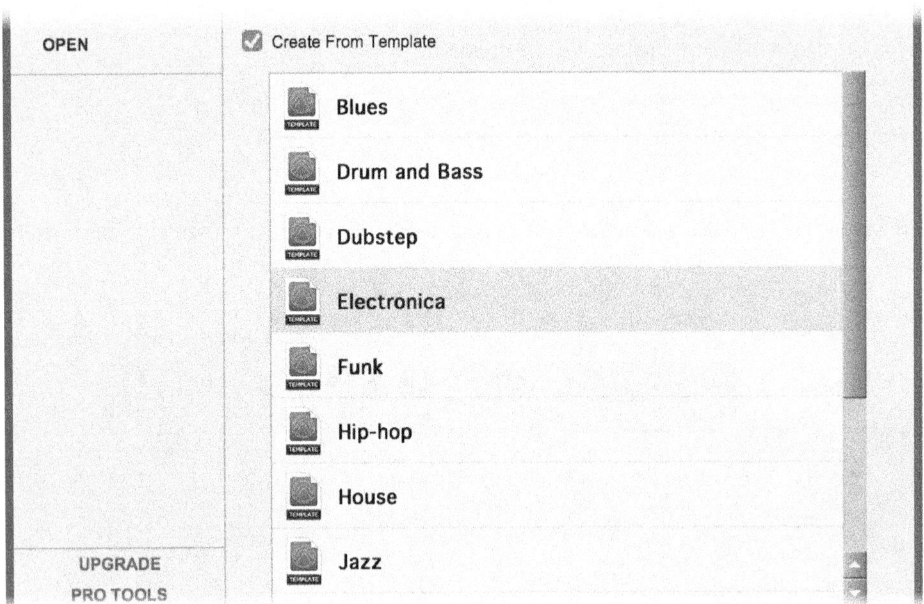

Figure 2.4 Templates to Choose From

3. Click on the desired template for your project (in Figure 2.4, I've chosen *Electronica*).
4. Even though Pro Tools will populate the name field with the name of the template that you choose, you must get into the good habit of naming all your projects descriptively.

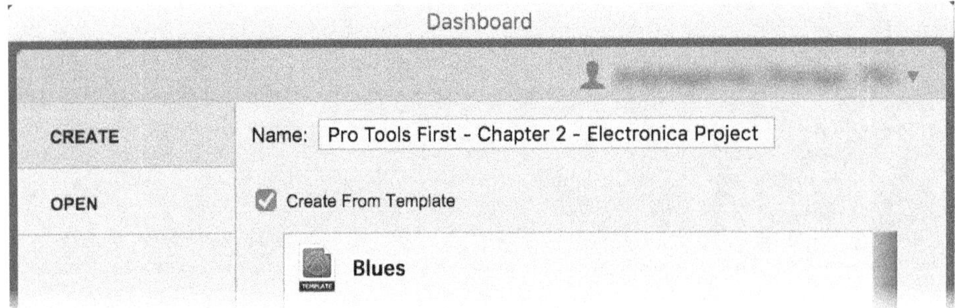

Figure 2.5 Always Name Your Projects!

5. In this case, I'll choose to create a cloud-based project by clicking the BACKUP TO CLOUD check box, as shown in Figure 2.6.

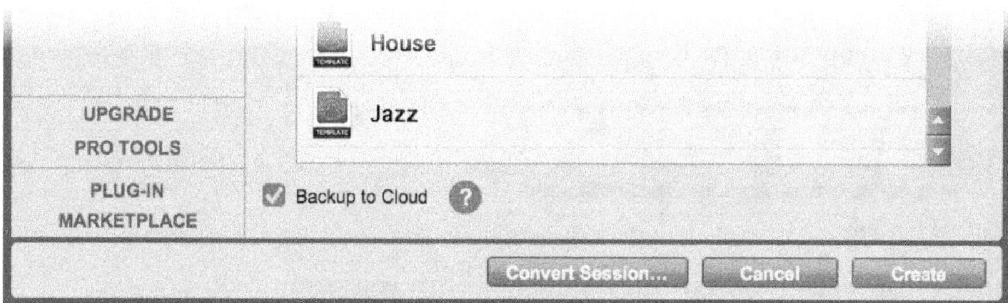

Figure 2.6 Checking the BACKUP TO CLOUD Check Box

6. Click the CREATE button, and your project will be created.

When you create a project from a template, your project will come preloaded with tracks that you can play with, instead of a blank Edit window. Different Templates will give you different tracks, so experiment!

Figure 2.7 A New Project Created from the Electronica Template

Creating a Project from a Session

Another way that you can create a new project preloaded with tracks is to convert a session created in Pro Tools or Pro Tools | Ultimate into a ***Pro Tools | First*** Project. You've done this already in the exercise in Chapter 1, but let's quickly review those steps here:

1. From the Dashboard window, click the CONVERT SESSION button at the bottom of the window. A file browser window will appear.

Figure 2.8 The CONVERT SESSION Button

2. Navigate to the folder that contains the Pro Tools Session file that you want to convert. The Session file will have a .ptx file extension. Double-click it to create a new local Project.
3. In the next window, you will be able to choose your Project's properties. Choosing LOCAL STORAGE radio button will create a local Project (which you can back up to the cloud if you click the BACKUP TO CLOUD check box at the bottom window. A local project will not enable any collaboration tools—if you want to collaborate with others (which you'll learn more about in Chapter 7), choose the COLLABORATION AND CLOUD BACKUP radio button.
4. Click the CREATE button, and your new Project will be created and opened.

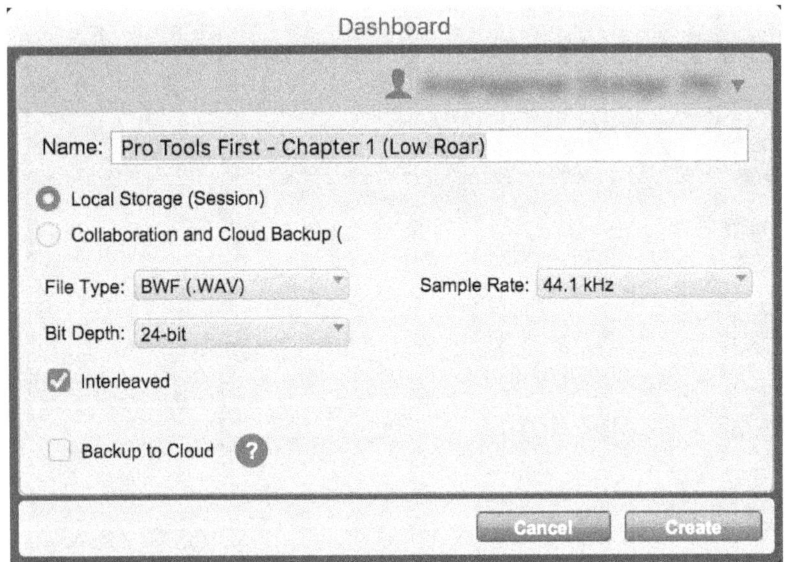

Figure 2.9 Properties For Your New Project

Saving a Project

If there's a rule about saving your work, it's to do it early and often! In fact, every time you've done something that you don't want to lose, you should think about saving your Project. Here are two ways:

1. From the FILE menu, choose SAVE.

OR

1. Here is a useful shortcut for saving your work: COMMAND+S (Mac) or CTRL+S (Windows).

Deleting a Project

Pro Tools | First supports up to three cloud-based Projects and unlimited local Projects. From time to time, when you're finished working on one of your Projects, you might want to remove it from your Project list. Here's how you can delete a Project:

1. The Dashboard window will show all your active Projects, and at the right side of each Project is a small triangular icon. Clicking this icon will reveal a pop-up menu.

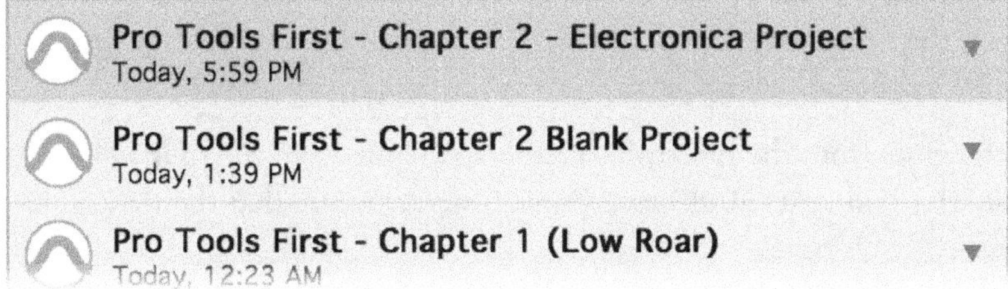

Figure 2.10 The Projects List

2. In the pop-up menu shown in Figure 2.11, you can do a number of important things, including the BACKUP TO CLOUD option, which will change a local Project into a cloud-based Project with collaboration tools (Un-checking this item in a cloud-based Project will change it into a local Project). delete a project, choose DELETE from the pop-up menu.

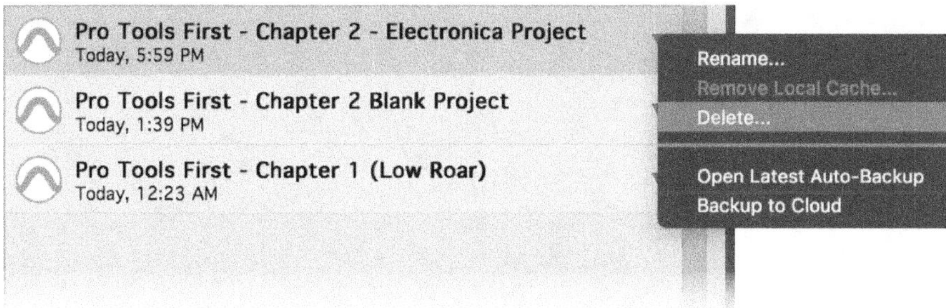

Figure 2.11 Deleting the Electronica Project

3. Finally, you'll see a dialog box that will ask you to confirm your choice to delete the Project. Click the DELETE button to permanently delete the Project.

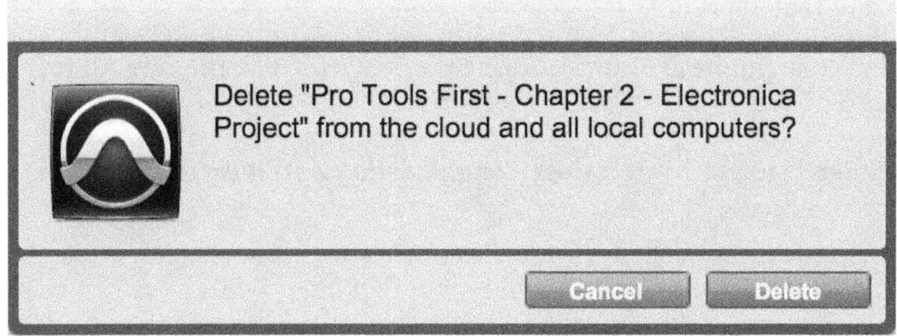

Figure 2.12 Are You Sure You Want to Delete the Project?

Hands-On Exercise 2.1: Creating a Project

Now, it's time to practice creating Projects in different ways and deleting them.

Creating Projects

1. Create a blank project named *Pro Tools First—Chapter 2 Blank Project*. This will be a local Project, so make sure that the BACKUP TO CLOUD checkbox is *unchecked*.
2. When you create a new Project, the Project will open. Since we don't need this one just yet, go to FILE>CLOSE PROJECT. The Dashboard will reappear.
3. Create another new Project, this time from the Electronica template, named *Pro Tools First—Chapter 2—Electronica Project*. This will be a cloud-based Project, so make sure that the BACKUP TO CLOUD check box is *checked*.

When you're done, your Dashboard window's Project list should look like Figure 2.13 (assuming that you've also completed the exercise in Chapter 1).

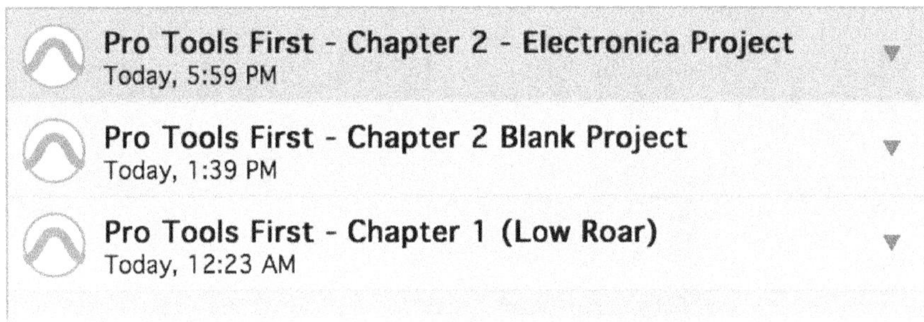

Figure 2.13 Your Three Projects

Deleting a Project

On second thought, we really don't need the Electronica project, and it's taking up one of our only three cloud-based Projects. Let's delete it.

4. Remember, you can delete a Project by clicking the triangle icon to its right and choosing DELETE from the pop-up menu that appears.
5. Pro Tools will ask you to confirm that you really want to delete the Project. Click the DELETE button to confirm your choice.

Now, your Dashboard window should look like Figure 2.14. If it does, congratulations—this exercise is over!

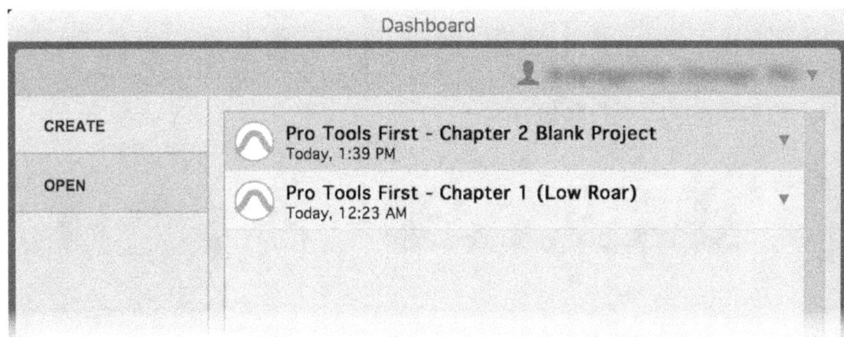

Figure 2.14 Your Two Projects

The Main Pro Tools Windows

As with any software, you have to understand the Graphic User Interface (GUI) of Pro Tools | First to make the most of it. Let's look at its main windows and learn how you can customize them to suit your personal style.

The Edit Window

The Edit window is where many professionals do most of their work. It's where you will import your media, arrange your clips, and (as the name suggests) do your editing. It may look complex at first, but if you break it down to its component parts, it's pretty easy to get around.

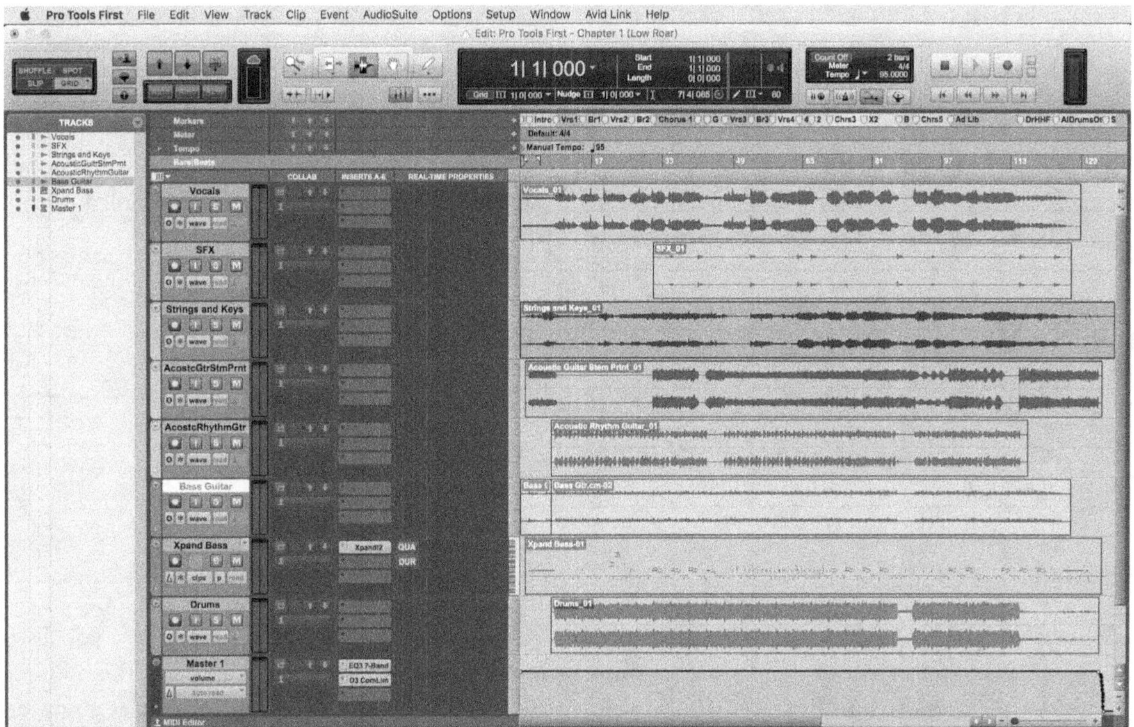

Figure 2.15 The Edit Window

Edit Window Toolbar

At the top of the Edit window, you'll see a row of buttons and icons, collectively known as the *Edit window toolbar*. Here, tools are arranged in clusters according to their function.

Figure 2.16 The Edit Window Toolbar

In this chapter, we will discuss the Edit window toolbar by naming its clusters and describing them in general terms. Don't worry—throughout the book, you'll learn how to use these tools in detail!

Edit Mode Buttons

The tool clusters typically at the far left of the toolbar are the *Edit Modes*. You'll learn more about these modes in Chapters 3 and 4, but for now, just know that you have four of them: *Shuffle*, *Slip*, *Spot*, and *Grid*.

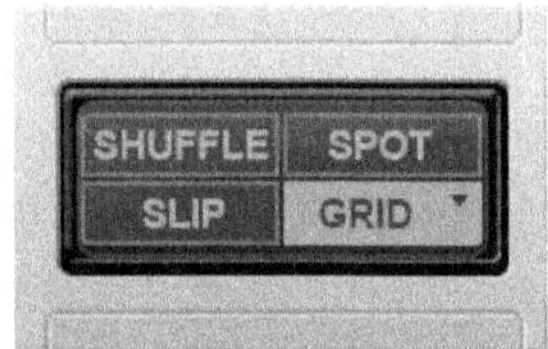

Figure 2.17 The Edit Modes

Edit Tools

Edit Tools are grouped together in the cluster shown in Figure 2.18. From left to right at the top are the *Zoomer Tool*, *Trim Tool*, *Selector Tool*, *Grabber Tool*, and *Pencil Tool*. At the bottom, you have a feature called *Tab to Transient*, then *Insertion Follows Playback*, a shortcut to the *Mix Window*, and *Quick Buttons*.

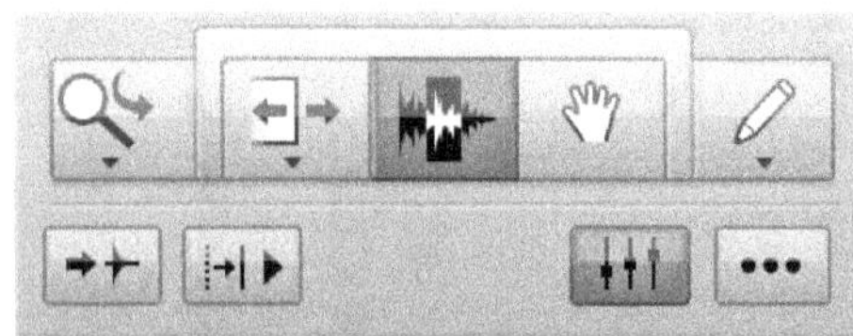

Figure 2.18 The Edit Tools

Counter and Edit Selection

The *Counter and Edit Selection* section will give you some very important information. On the top left, you'll see the *Main Counter*, which tells you exactly where your timeline insertion is on your project timeline. This counter can show position in either the Bars|Beats or Min:Secs time scales, and you can change this display at any time by clicking the downward-facing triangle to the right of the location number.

To the right of the Main Counter, you'll see *Edit Selection* indicators, which will tell you the start, end, and duration of any selection you might have made on the timeline. The bottom row of the Counter and Edit Selection section has a collection of indicators as well, including *Grid* values, *Nudge* values, and some MIDI settings (which we'll talk more about in Chapter 6).

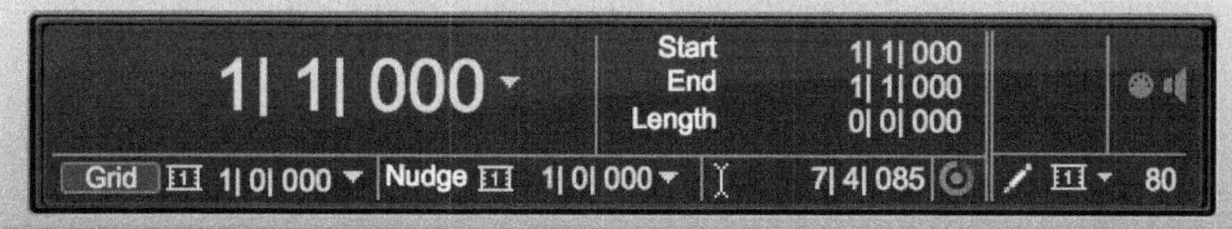

Figure 2.19 The Counter and Edit Selection Section

MIDI Controls

Next on the list are the *MIDI Controls*. We'll talk more about MIDI in detail in Chapter 6, but for now, just know in this section you can set things, like tempo and meter.

Figure 2.20 MIDI Controls

Transport Controls

You've already worked with the *Transport Controls* cluster in Chapter 1. On the top row are the *Stop*, *Play*, and *Record* buttons, and also two small squares that will tell you if a track is record-armed or is in Input Only monitoring mode.

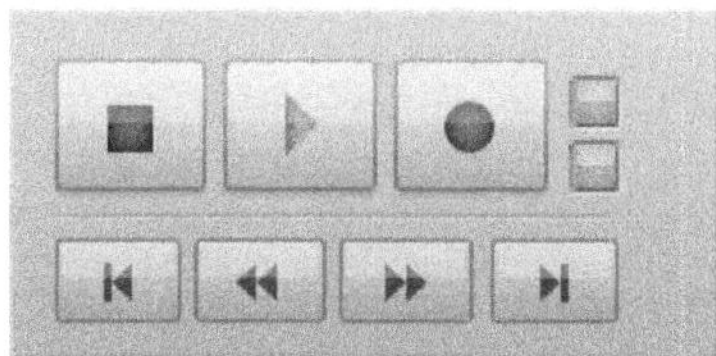

Figure 2.21 Transport Controls

Output Meters

On the far right, you'll see your Project's *Output Meters*. This will show you the total level coming out of the outputs that you chose in the Playback Engine dialog box.

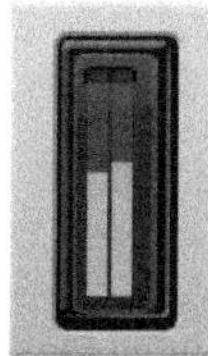

Figure 2.21 Output Meters

Collaboration Controls

Last but not least are the *Collaboration* tools. In Figure 2.23 you're looking at a local Project, which is not connected to the cloud, so these tools are not available and are greyed out. With *Collaboration and Cloud* Backup-type Projects, however, they will be active and will allow you to invite collaborators, chat with them, and share tracks. The meter with the cloud icon on top of it indicates how much of your total cloud storage is used by cloud-based Projects.

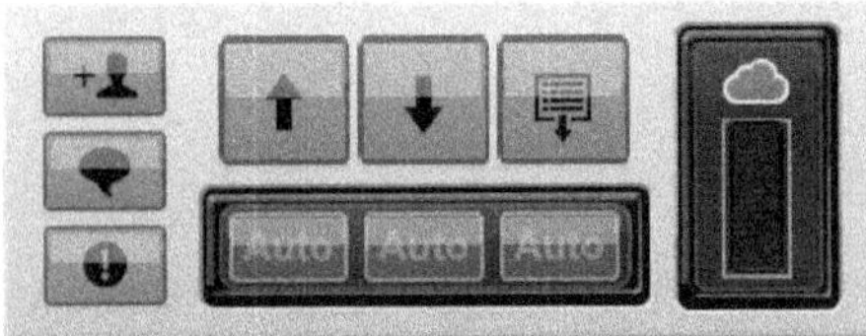

Figure 2.23 Collaboration Tools

Rulers

Just below the Edit Window Toolbar you'll find another horizontal strip subdivided into four segments called *Markers*, *Meter*, *Tempo*, and either *Bars|Beats* or *Min:Secs*. These are your Project's *rulers* and will measure and mark the passage of time in a number of different ways.

Figure 2.24 Rulers

Tracks List

The column on the left-hand side of the Edit window is called the *Tracks List*. This column will show you a list of all the tracks of any kind in your Project, in the order that they appear in the main area of the Edit window. Here, you can also show, hide, or rearrange your tracks (things you'll learn to do later in this chapter).

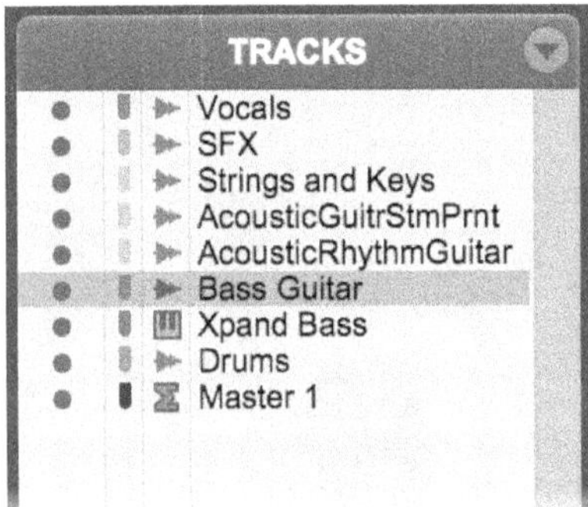

Figure 2.25 The Tracks List

Changing Tracks List Width

You can customize your Edit window by changing the width of your Tracks List. Just move your cursor to the right border of the Tracks List, and your cursor will change appearance as shown in Figure 2.26. Resize your Tracks List by dragging left or right to suit your needs.

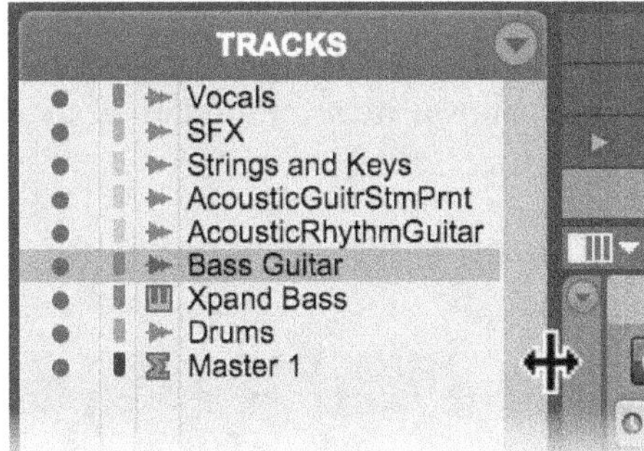

Figure 2.26 Resizing the Tracks List

Many professionals try to keep their track names as short as possible for two reasons: First, short track names can appear in each track without being abbreviated. Second, if you have short track names, your Tracks List can be narrower, giving you more room in your Edit window for other things.

Tracks and Clips

In the main part of the Edit window, you'll see a number of horizontal strips, as shown in Figure 2.27, with names like Vocals, SFX, Strings and Keys, and so on. Each one of these rows is a *Track*, and the colored blocks on the strips are called *Clips*. The number of tracks in your Project, and the number of clips on each track vary depending upon the requirements of the work that you're doing.

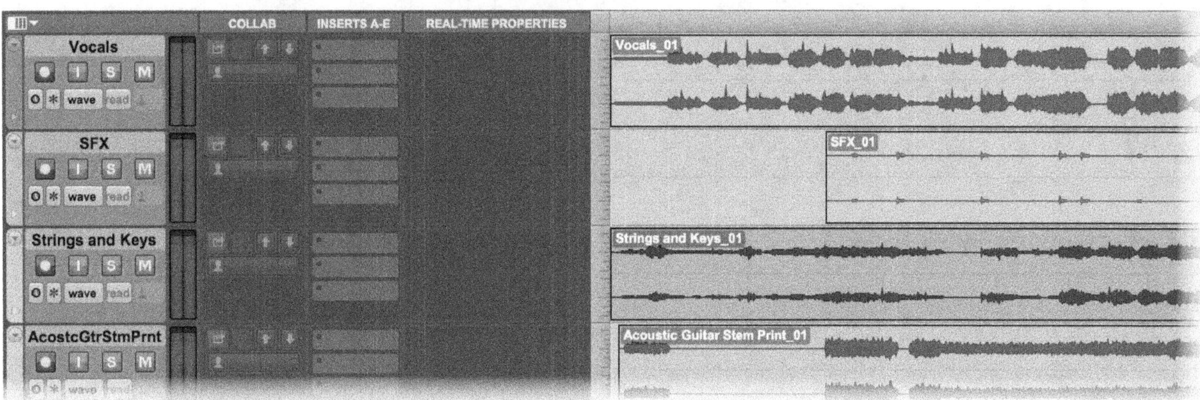

Figure 2.27 Tracks and Clips

Edit Window Views

So far, the elements that you have looked at are always shown in the Edit window. Now let's talk about elements of the Edit window that you can show or hide—the *Edit window Views.*

Perhaps the most straightforward way to change your Edit window Views is to go to the VIEW menu and choose EDIT WINDOW VIEWS. From there, you'll see a list of things that you can show or hide in your Edit window. These include *Comments, Instruments, Inserts A-E, Inserts F-J, Sends A-E, Sends F-J, I/O, Real-Time Properties,* and *Track Collaboration* (if the Project is a *Collaboration and Cloud Backup* type). Shown items are indicated by a checkmark, and as you'll see in Figure 2.28, Inserts A-E and Real-Time Properties are shown.

Figure 2.28 The VIEW>EDIT WINDOW VIEWS Menu

The Edit window Views appear as columns in each one of your tracks as you can see in Figure 2.29.

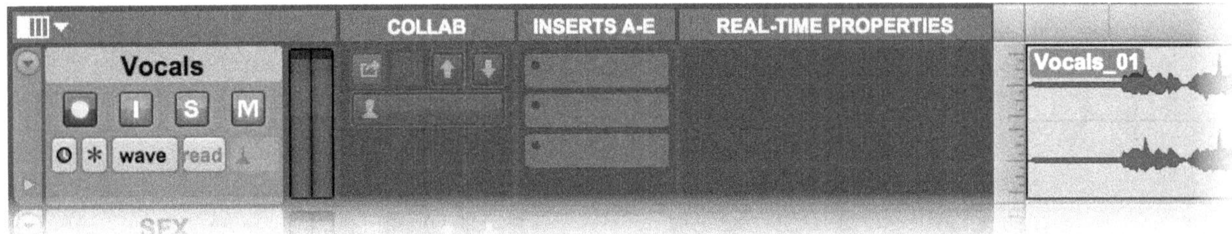

Figure 2.29 Shown Edit Window Views

If there is an Edit window View column that I don't want to see, I simply need to make sure that it is not checked in the VIEW>EDIT WINDOW VIEWS menu list. For example, if I want to hide my Real-time Properties column, I just go to VIEW>EDIT WINDOW VIEWS and un-check REAL-TIME PROPERTIES, as shown in Figure 2.30. As a result, the columns in each track will immediately change.

Figure 2.30 Hiding the Real-Time Properties Edit Window View

Here's another way that you can show or hide Edit window Views: Click on the small white icon at the top left corner of the tracks as shown in Figure 2.31. Clicking this icon will reveal a list similar to the one that you have seen in the VIEW menu, with columns that are shown indicated with a check box. Any changes that you make in this list will immediately be reflected in the columns of your tracks.

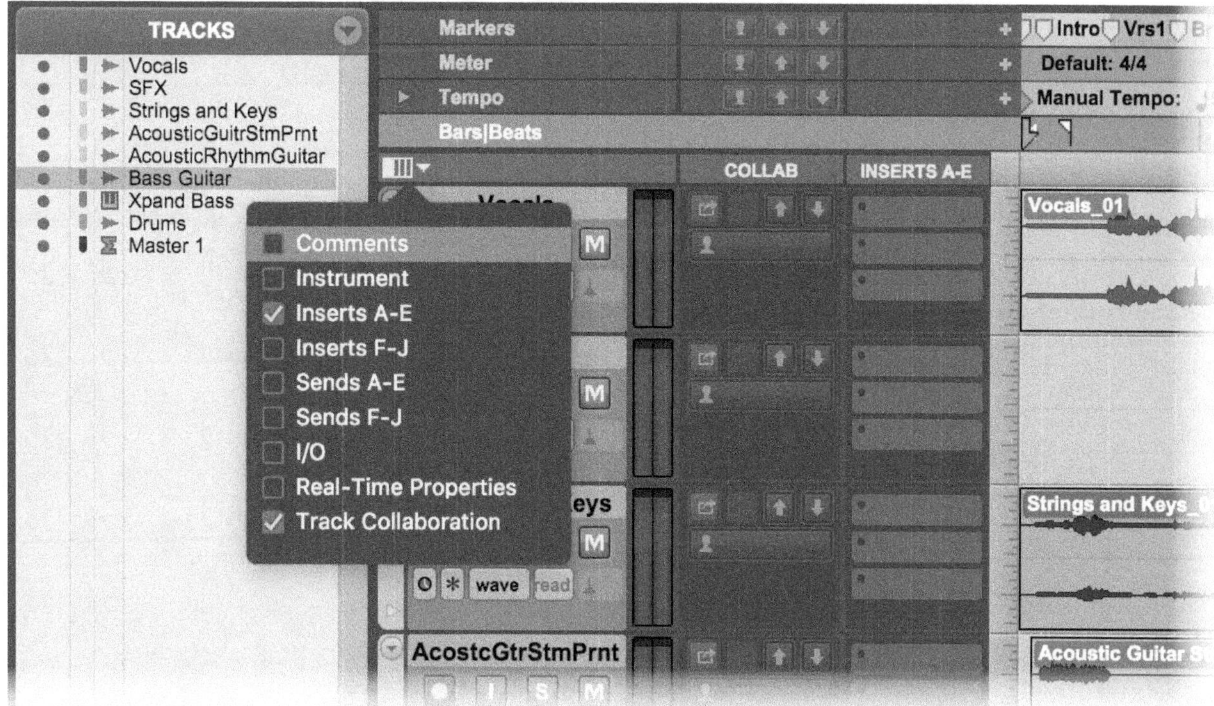

Figure 2.31 The EDIT WINDOW VIEW Selector

You can also open Edit window View check box menu by right-clicking on the heading of any Edit window View column.

You can hide any Edit window View by OPTION-clicking (Mac) or ALT-clicking (Windows) on the heading of any Edit window View column.

If there is one Edit window View that goes under-utilized, I think it's the Comments view (and I know many professionals who would agree!). In this Edit window View, you can type detailed information about a track, which can be valuable information for collaborators and other engineers that might work on your Project. It's also an easy way of keeping good records, so if there's something you don't want to forget about this, track write it down in the Comments view.

If you've looked at the Edit window in other versions of Pro Tools, you've probably noticed two things missing: The first is a column on the far right side of the Edit window, similar to the tracks list. This is called the *Clips List*, which is where you can see all the clips in your session and manage them in different ways. There's also a section at the bottom of the Tracks List called *Groups*—these are for your Edit Groups—which allows you to edit multiple tracks at the same time. These two useful sections are not included in Pro Tools | First, but you will see them in Pro Tools and Pro Tools | Ultimate.

The Mix Window

The process of combining multiple individual tracks into a final cohesive product is called mixing. Though it's certainly common to do some mixing in the Edit window, Pro Tools has a window dedicated to this process, appropriately called the *Mix Window*.

There are three easy ways to get to the Mix window from the Edit window:

- In the Edit window, click the MIX WINDOW button, as shown in Figure 2.32.

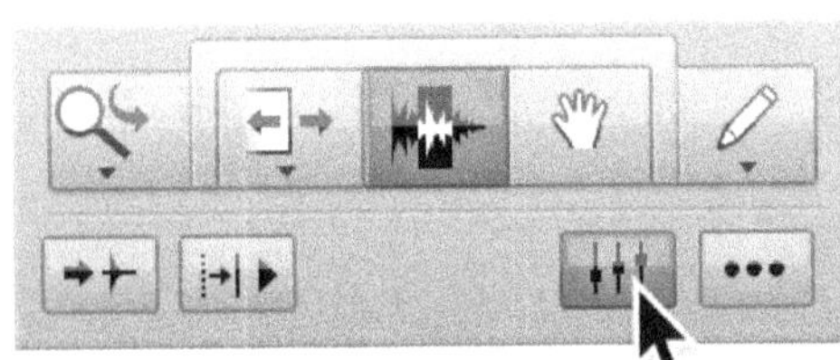

Figure 2.32 The MIX WINDOW Button

- From the WINDOW menu, click MIX
- Moving from the Edit window to the Mix window and back again is something that you'll do many times, so memorizing the shortcut will be useful. The shortcut to toggle between the Mix and Edit windows is COMMAND+= (Mac) or CTRL+= (Windows).

Once you open the Mix window, you'll see something that looks a bit like Figure 2.33. The Mix window is a bit simpler than the Edit window and will be familiar-looking to anyone who's ever sat behind a mixer. Each of the vertical strips in the Mix window represents a Track, in the same order as they appear in the Edit window (Tracks are listed from top to bottom in the Edit window, and from left to right in the Mix window).

Figure 2.33 The Mix Window

Mix Controls

At the heart of the Mix window, you'll find various mix parameter controls, as shown in Figure 2.34.

Working from the top to the bottom:

- The circular knobs, called *pan knobs*, will help you position your track's sound
- The four square-shaped buttons below the pan knobs are used to enable the track for recording, enable or disable *TrackInput*, *solo*, and *mute* for the track
- Finally, the vertical slider controls the volume level for each individual track

Figure 2.34 Basic Mix Controls

Tracks List

Just as there is a Tracks List in the Edit window, there is also one on the left-hand side of the Mix window. It operates in the same way as the Edit window's Tracks List and can be resized in the same way, as well.

Changes made in the Mix window's Tracks List will be reflected in the Edit window, and vice versa.

Mix Window Views

Like the Edit window, the Mix window has its own *Mix window Views*, which can be shown or hidden depending upon your needs. These Mix Window Views are *Instruments*, *Inserts A-E*, *Inserts F-J*, *Sends A-E*, *Sends F-J*, *EQ Curve*, *I/O*, *Comments* and *Track Collaboration*. Just as in the Edit window, there are two ways to show or hide any of these Mix window Views:

- From the VIEW menu, go to MIX WINDOW VIEWS, and then choose what you want to see from the menu. Shown items will be indicated by a checkmark.

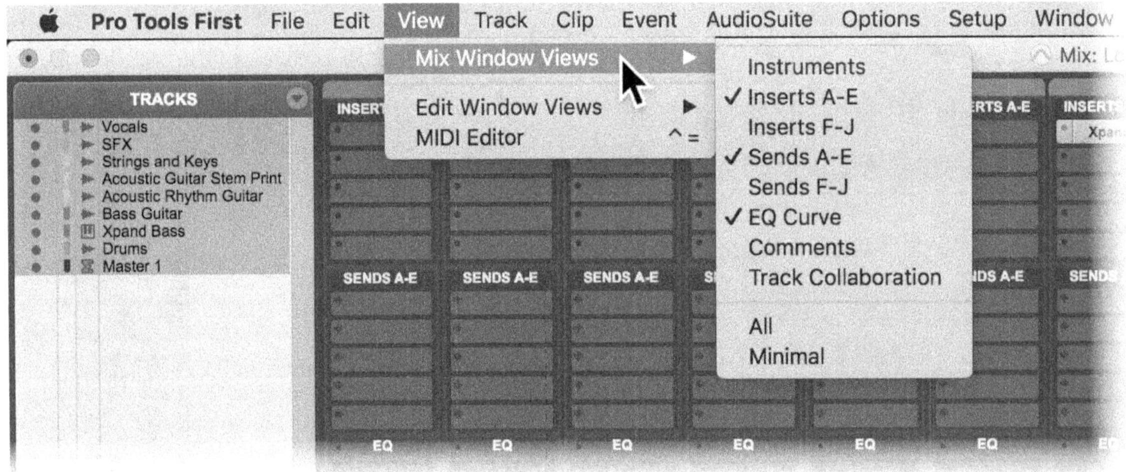

Figure 2.35 The VIEW>MIX WINDOW VIEWS Menu

- At the bottom left corner of the Mix window, you'll find a small white icon, as shown in Figure 2.36. Clicking this icon will reveal a list of elements that can be shown or hidden.

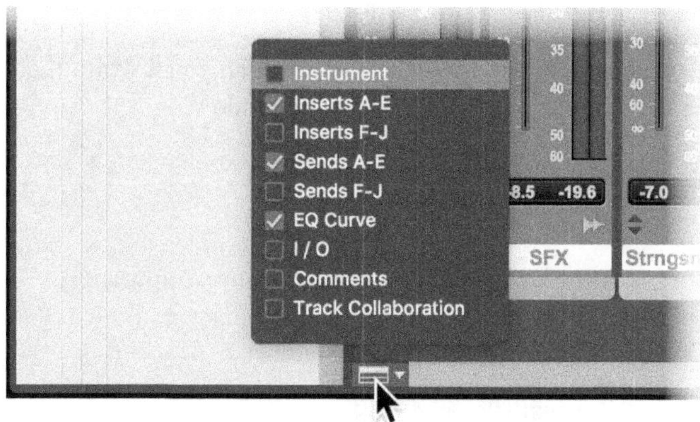

Figure 2.36 The MIX WINDOW VIEW Selector

- Whereas Edit window Views appear as columns to the left side of each track, in the Mix window, Mix window Views will appear as rows for each Track. In Figure 2.37, Inserts A-E, Sends A-E, and EQ Curve Mix window Views are shown.

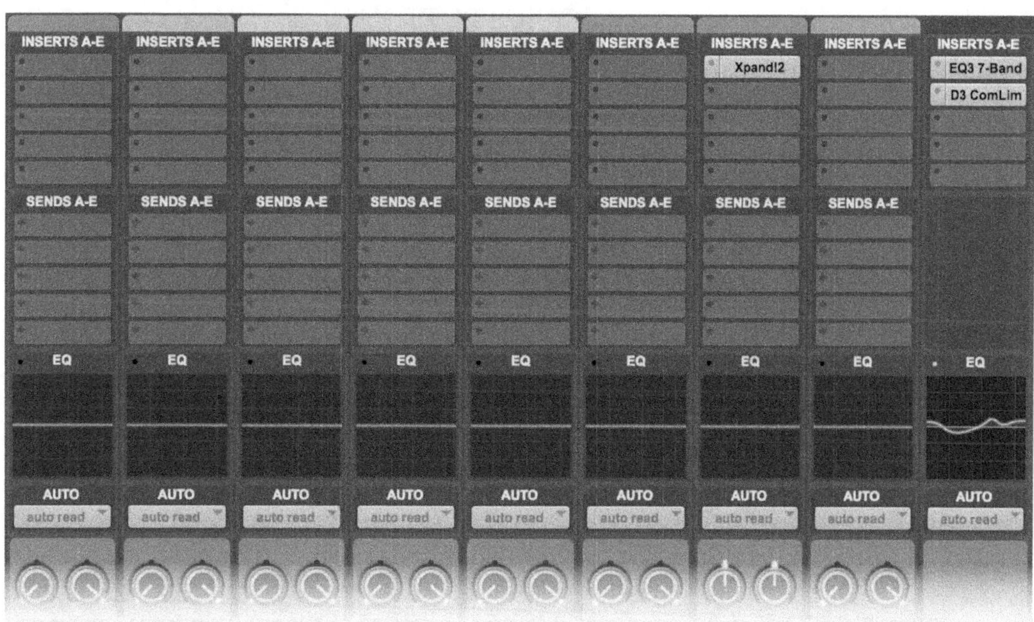

Figure 2.37 Three Mix Window Views—Inserts A-E, Sends A-E, and EQ Curve

You can also reveal Mix window View check box menu by right-clicking on the heading of any Mix window View on any track's channel strip.

You can hide any Mix window View by OPTION-clicking (Mac) or ALT-clicking (Windows) on the heading of any Mix window View on any track's channel strip.

The Transport Window

While the Edit window and the Mix window are the most important environments in which you'll work, there are a few other windows you should understand. Next, let's take a look at The *Transport* window.

There are two easy ways to show or hide the Transport window:

- From the WINDOW menu choose TRANSPORT
- The shortcut to show or hide the Transport window is COMMAND+1 (on your computer's numeric keypad) on a Mac computer, or CTRL+1 (on your computer's numeric keypad) on a Windows computer

You must use the numeric keypad of your keyboard (usually located on the right-hand side of the keyboard) to perform the shortcut for opening and closing the Transport window. Using the number keys at the top of your keyboard won't work. There are many uses for the numeric keypad in the various versions of Pro Tools, so you'll usually see keyboards with numeric keypads in professional studios.

- The QUICK BUTTONS button gives you easy access to some commonly used windows, including the Transport window. Just click the QUICK BUTTONS button and a list of options will appear, as shown in Figure 2.38. Windows that are shown will be indicated by a blue button. Click the TRANSPORT button, and the Transport window will appear.

Figure 2.38 The QUICK BUTTONS Button

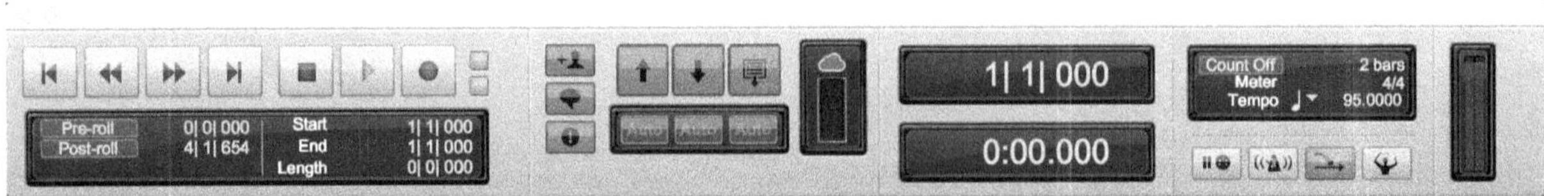

Figure 2.39 The Transport Window

You've seen most of these controls before in the Edit window, so let's go through them quickly:

Playback and Record Controls

On the left-hand side of the transport window, you'll find controls similar to the ones that you saw in the Transport Controls cluster of the Edit window. On the top from left to right, they are *Return to Zero*, *Rewind*, *Fast Forward*, *Go to End*, *Stop*, *Play*, and *Record Enable*. Below these buttons, on the left-hand side, you'll see *Pre-roll* and *Post-roll,* which are important in the recording process (We'll talk more about these in Chapter 5). On the right, you will see indicators showing your timeline selection (Start, End, and Length), displaying what is selected on the Edit Windows timeline.

Figure 2.40 Playback and Record Controls

Collaboration Tools

From left to right, the next tool cluster you'll see are the Collaboration Tools, which mirror the same tools in the Edit window.

Figure 2.41 Collaboration Tools in the Transport Window

Counters

In the Edit window's Counter section, you can choose to see the passage of time either in Bars|Beats *or* Min:Secs, but not both. However, in the Transport window you'll see *both* of these Time Scales. The top display (called the Main Counter) will mirror the Counter in the Edit window. The bottom display (called the Sub Counter) will show the other time scale.

Figure 2.42 Main Counter and Sub Counter

MIDI Controls

Next are the Transport window's MIDI Controls, which mirror the MIDI Controls in the Edit window.

Figure 2.43 The Transport Window's MIDI Controls

Meters

Finally, on the far right of the Transport window, you'll find an Output Meter mirroring the Output Meter in the Edit window.

Figure 2.44 The Transport Window's Output Meter

The System Usage Window

The System Usage window is a useful diagnostic tool which shows you how hard your computer is working. You can open or close the System Usage window by going to the WINDOW menu and clicking SYSTEM USAGE (at the bottom of the menu).

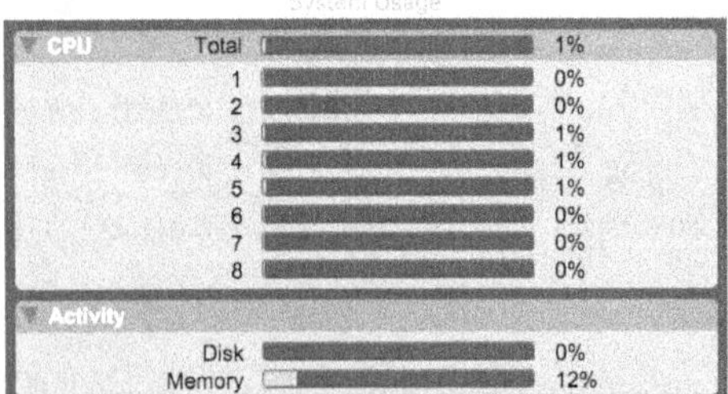

Figure 2.45 The System Usage Window

The System Usage window is pretty simple, but very important. At the top of the window you'll see a number of rows in the *CPU* section. Each of these rows equals one of your computer's processors. The graphs and percentage values that you see on the right-hand side will tell you how hard the processors are working on Pro Tools' real-time processes. In general, the goal is to keep these meters from hitting 100% (as you can see, in this case, there's no problem).

The *Activity* section at the bottom will show you two important things: The *Disk* meter will show you how much throughput is being used by your hard disk during playback. The *Memory* meter will tell you the percentage used by your computer's RAM. In both cases, again, we want to avoid getting anywhere close to 100%.

If you're not seeing this kind of detail in your System Usage window, it might be because either the *CPU* view or the *Activity* sections is collapsed. To expand the view of either sections, click the triangular icon next to the word CPU or Activity—the triangle icon will then point downward, and you will see the detail shown in Figure 2.45.

Window Management

Before we move on from our first discussion on Pro Tools' Graphic User Interface, here are a few useful tips to help you get around smoothly:

- As mentioned before in this chapter, the keyboard shortcut for quickly toggling between the Mix and Edit windows is COMMAND+= (Mac) or CTRL+= (Windows). This is a great shortcut to remember, as you'll be switching between these windows frequently in the course of your work.
- The Transport window and the System Usage window fall into a category called floating windows. You'll use these and other floating windows as you go through this book, and sometimes, your desktop can get pretty cluttered with them. Of course, you *could* close and then show them one at a time, but here's another way to do it: From the WINDOW menu, choose HIDE ALL FLOATING WINDOWS. All these floating windows will move behind the Mix or Edit window. If you go back to the WINDOW menu and click HIDE ALL FLOATING WINDOWS again (unchecking that menu item), all your floating windows will come back in the same position they were before.

Professional Pro Tools users will show and hide floating windows frequently, so it's no surprise there's a shortcut for this. On a Mac, it's CONTROL+OPTION+COMMAND+W, and on a Windows computer, it is CTRL+START+ALT+W.

- You can arrange your open windows in a lot of different ways. From the WINDOW menu, choose ARRANGE and a menu will appear, as shown in Figure 2.46. This can be useful if you want to see a bit of your Edit and Mix windows at the same time.

Figure 2.46 The WINDOW>ARRANGE Menu

Menu Structure

At the top of the Pro Tools' Edit or Mix windows, you'll find a number of menus. While it's not important to memorize everything in these menus at this point, it *is* important to get a sense of what each menu covers:

Figure 2.47 Pro Tools | First's Menus

- The FILE menu follows most of the common conventions of any software, allowing you to open and close Projects, save, and so on. Here, you can also import audio and MIDI and export your final mixes.
- In the EDIT Menu, you'll find tools for cutting, copying, pasting, and other common operations— again, similar to other software you may have used. Towards the bottom of this menu, you can also access other editing processes that we'll discuss during the course of this book.
- You've already seen a bit of the VIEW menu. The only menu item that we haven't covered is the MIDI EDITOR, which we will go into when we discuss MIDI in Chapter 6.
- If it relates to the creation, duplication, or deletion of tracks (and more), you'll find it in the TRACK menu.
- The CLIP menu can be thought of as a sibling of the EDIT menu. It is here where you can do more advanced clip-based editing and processes.
- EVENT: here is a simple rule—if it has anything to do with time or with MIDI, look first in the EVENT menu.
- When we start to discuss more about mixing and how to use plugin effects, you'll learn that these effects fall into two types: Real-time and file-based. In the AUDIOSUITE menu, you can find your file-based effects.
- Here's another menu memorization trick— if it can be turned on or off, you can find it in the OPTIONS menu (think "O" for "On", "O" for "Off", and "O" for OPTIONS).
- The SETUP menu is where you go to configure how things will behave. You've done this already in the Playback Engine and Hardware dialog boxes—this menu will enable you to configure other aspects of your Pro Tools system, as well.
- The WINDOW menu is an easy one to describe: it's used to show or hide a window, very similar to other software you've probably used.
- The AVID LINK menu allows you to access various areas of the Avid Link application without leaving Pro Tools. It's useful for collaborative workflows, to check software versions and make purchases, or to check out and see what's happening in the Avid Lounges.

- Finally, the HELP menu is where you go to search for information on a topic by keyword, or access Pro Tools online help and support pages.

When I teach courses, there are usually a few students— great and enthusiastic students—who will try to memorize every item in every menu. Here's a bit of friendly advice: Most experienced professionals haven't done that level of memorization! I suggest that the important thing to do, at this point, is to understand the overall structure of the menus. Memorizing what's important to you will come in time.

Hands-On Exercise 2.2: Customizing the Pro Tools GUI

If you've been following the hands-on exercises in this book, you should have one Project called *Low Roar* from Chapter 1 and one blank Project that you've created earlier in this chapter. Let's open up the *Low Roar* project and practice getting around the software environment:

1. If it isn't already open, open up the *Pro Tools First—Fundamentals of Audio Production—Chapter 1—Low Roar* Project you created in Chapter 1. If Pro Tools, isn't running, launch ***Pro Tools | First*** and open the Project from the Dashboard. If ***Pro Tools | First*** is already running, go to FILE>OPEN PROJECT and open the Project from the Dashboard window

Change Main Counter

Let's start off by changing the way that we view time in this project. At present, as shown in Figure 2.48, your counter shows time in terms of *Bars|Beats|Ticks* (this is a Time Scale we'll talk more about when we discuss MIDI in Chapter 6). Let's change it to show time in minutes and seconds.

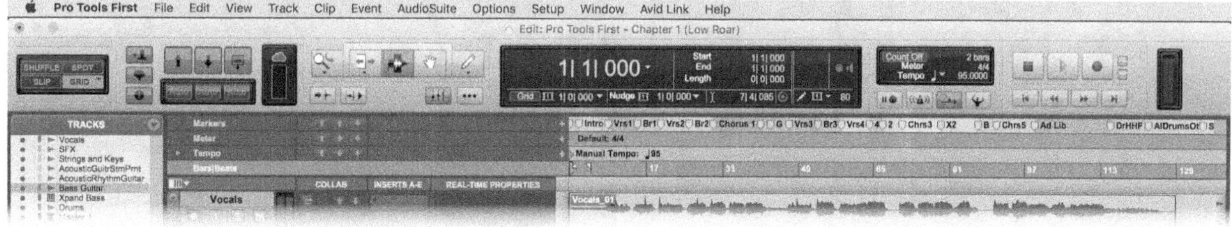

Figure 2.48 Your Counter Showing Time in Bars, Beats, and Ticks

2. In the Counters section of the Edit window, click the downward-facing triangle next to the main counter and choose *Min:Secs* from the pop-up menu, as shown in Figure 2.49.

Figure 2.49 Changing Your Counter To Min:Secs

Note that three things have happened:

- The Edit window's Counter has changed its Time Scale from Bars and Beats to Minutes and Seconds.
- In the Rulers area, the Bars|Beats ruler has changed to Min:Secs.
- In the Transport window, the Main Counter and Sub Counter have flipped—now the Main Counter shows Minutes and Seconds, and the Sub Counter shows Bars and Beats.

Show or Hide Edit Window Views

3. Now, let's change your Edit window Views. If you haven't made any changes to the Low Roar Project, the Edit window Views that will be displayed are Track *Collaboration*, *Inserts A-E*, and *Real-Time Properties*. Let's hide *Track Collaboration* and *Real-Time Properties*, and instead show *I/O* and *Comments* (in addition to the already shown *Inserts A-E*).

Here's a tip: If you're following these steps, you've created a local Project, and therefore won't be able to hide the Collaboration Edit window View from the VIEW menu. In this case, you'll have to use one of the other methods we've talked about in this chapter.

When you're done, your Edit window should look like Figure 2.50.

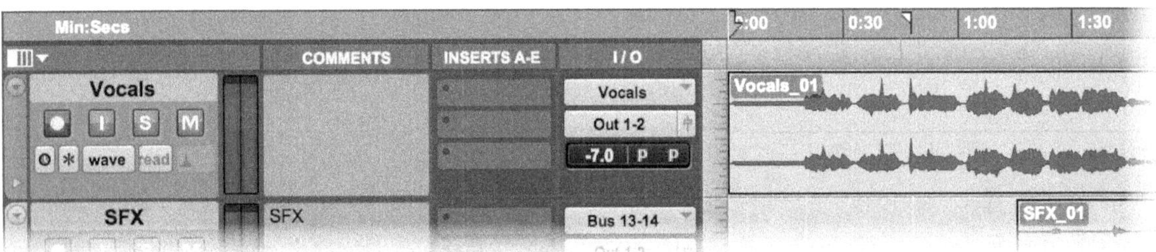

Figure 2.50 New Edit Window Views

Change Main Windows

Next, let's do a little window management:

4. Using any method, switch from the Edit window to the Mix window.
5. Since the Mix window doesn't include any transport controls (but the Transport window *does*), show the Transport window.

Show and Hide Mix Window Views

Now let's customize your Mix Window Views.

6. Show Inserts A-E, EQ Curve, I/O, and Comments. When you're done, your Mix window should look something like Figure 2.51.

Figure 2.51 Your New Mix Window Views

7. Next, switch back to the Edit window. Note that the Transport window, being a floating window, will not close when you change to the Edit window.

8. Finally, from the QUICK BUTTONS button, close the Transport window (Hint: Any shown windows button will appear blue in the QUICK BUTTONS menu, as shown in figure 2.52).

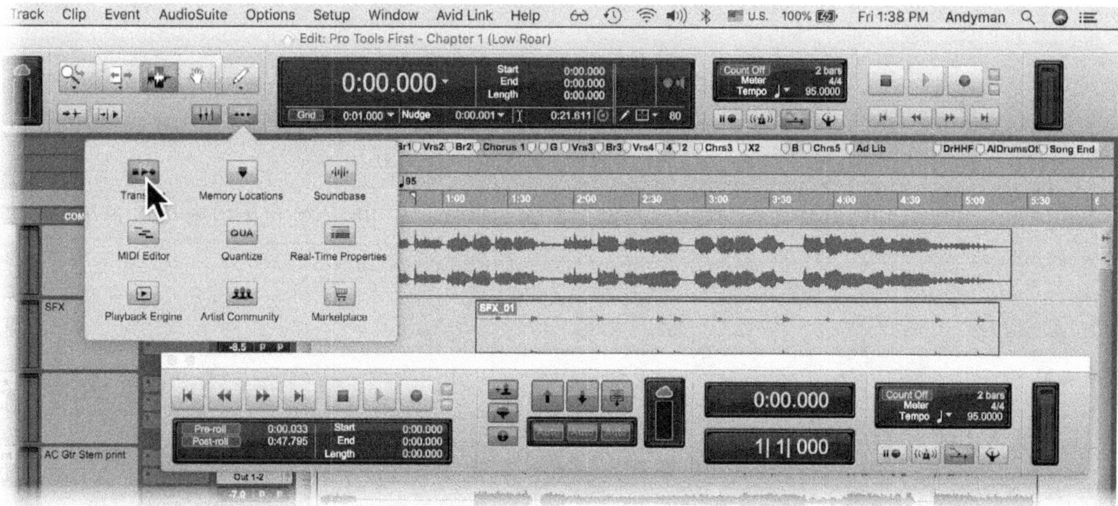

Figure 2.52 Closing the Transport Window from the QUICK BUTTONS Menu

9. You're all done! Just one more thing to do: Save your Project.

Introduction to Tracks

Earlier in this chapter, you created a blank Project. Now, it's time to put some tracks in that Project! Let's talk a bit about the different track types in Pro Tools | First and how to use them.

Track Types

This book will talk about the five different track types available in *P*Pro Tools | First: *Audio*, *Auxiliary Input*, *MIDI*, *Instrument*, and *Master Fader*.

Audio

Audio Tracks are the foundation upon which Pro Tools stands. All audio clips, if they're going to be heard in your session, will reside on an Audio track. When you are recording audio, the audio that you record will be on an audio track.

In the Mix window or Tracks List, Audio tracks can be visibly identified by a waveform icon, as shown in Figure 2.53.

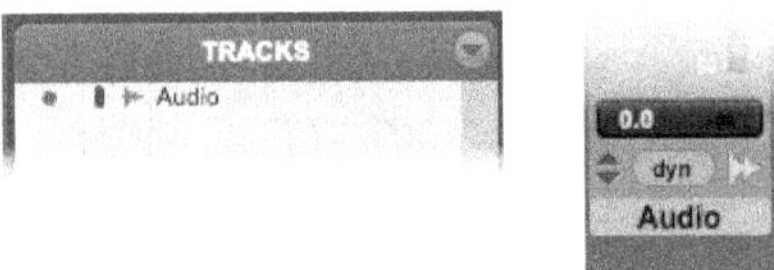

Figure 2.53 Audio Track Icons in the Tracks List and Mix Window

In Pro Tools | First, the maximum number of Audio Tracks is 16. In Pro Tools, the maximum is 128, and in Pro Tools | Ultimate, the maximum is 1024 Audio Tracks (768 of which are audible at any given time).

Auxiliary Input

Auxiliary Input Tracks (commonly called *Aux Tracks* for short) are like Audio tracks, with one important difference: An Auxiliary Input Track cannot hold audio clips. While it might seem strange to have a track that can't hold any clips, Aux Tracks play several important roles that you'll learn about later in this book.

In the Mix window or Tracks List, Auxiliary Input Tracks can be visibly identified by an arrow icon, as shown in Figure 2.54.

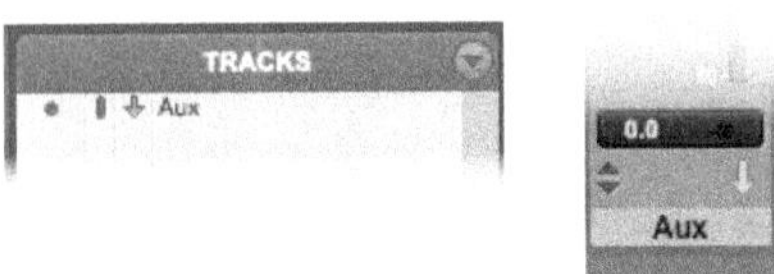

Figure 2.54 Aux Track Icons in the Tracks List and Mix Window

In Pro Tools | First, the maximum number of Auxiliary Input Tracks is 16. In Pro Tools you have a maximum of 128 Aux Tracks, and in Pro Tools | Ultimate, you have a maximum of 512.

MIDI

MIDI Tracks are one of two track types where you can put a MIDI clip and also record MIDI data from a MIDI Instrument. A MIDI track is a very simple and basic track and cannot be heard on its own—it's commonly used in combination with an Auxiliary Input Track.

In the Mix window or Tracks List, MIDI Tracks can be visibly identified by a small circular MIDI plug icon, as shown in Figure 2.55.

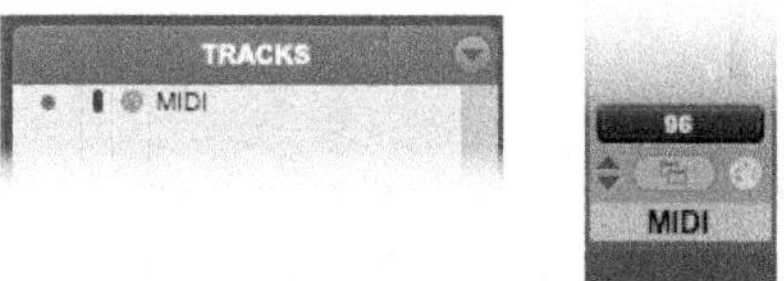

Figure 2.55 MIDI Track Icons in the Tracks List and Mix Window

In Pro Tools | First, you have a maximum of 16 MIDI Tracks. In Pro Tools or Pro Tools | Ultimate, you have a maximum of 1024 MIDI Tracks.

Instrument

Instrument Tracks are the other kind of track where you could put a MIDI clip or record MIDI. This track type can be thought of as the combination of a MIDI Track and an Auxiliary Input Track, allowing MIDI to be heard in a single track.

In the Mix window or Tracks List, Instrument Tracks can be visibly identified by a keyboard icon, as shown in Figure 2.56.

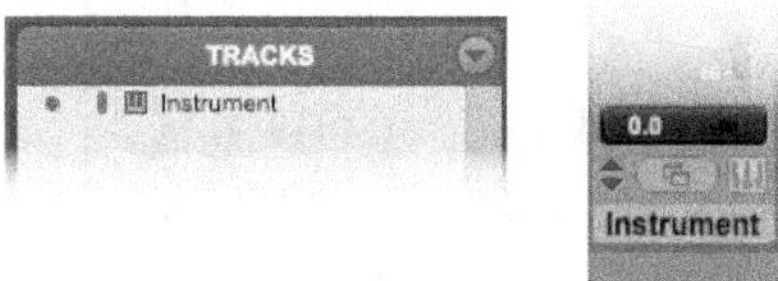

Figure 2.56 Instrument Track Icons in the Tracks List and Mix Window

In Pro Tools | First, you have a maximum of 16 Instrument Tracks. In Pro Tools or Pro Tools | Ultimate, you have a maximum of 512 Instrument Tracks.

Master Fader

Master Faders are a powerful tool, especially when you're mixing. Like Auxiliary Input Tracks, Master Faders cannot hold clips, but are used to control the level of an output. Master Faders are frequently underused or even misused, so we'll pay special attention to this track type and on how to use it, when we discuss the mixing process.

In the Mix window or Tracks List, Master Fader Tracks can be distinguished by the Greek letter Sigma (Σ), which means sum in mathematical terms, as shown in Figure 2.57.

Figure 2.57 Master Fader Track Icons in the Tracks List and Mix Window

In Pro Tools | First, you have a maximum of 4 Master Fader Tracks. In Pro Tools or Pro Tools | Ultimate, you have a maximum of 64 Master Fader Tracks.

Mono vs. Stereo

In Pro Tools | First, Audio Tracks, Auxiliary Input Tracks Instrument Tracks, and Master Faders can be either *mono* (meaning that they only have one input) or *stereo* tracks (which have two input channels—a left side and a right side) In the case of Audio Tracks, mono audio clips can only be put on a mono track, as shown in Figure 2.58.

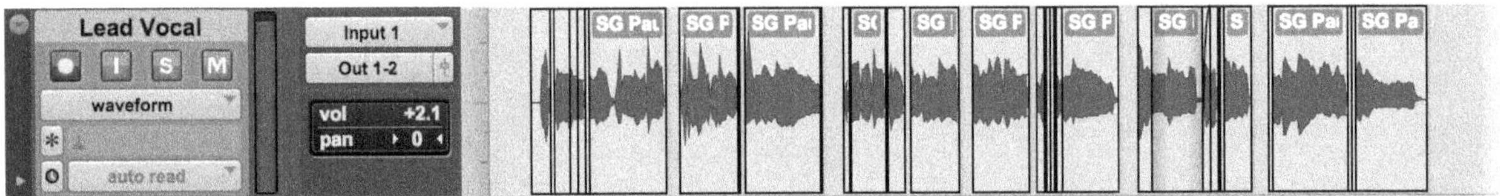

Figure 2.58 The Lead Vocal track is a Mono Audio Track. Note the Single Waveform in the Clips.

If the audio file that you want to use in your Project includes a left side and a right side, the clip you must put into your Project should be a stereo clip, which would be put on a stereo audio track, as shown in Figure 2.59.

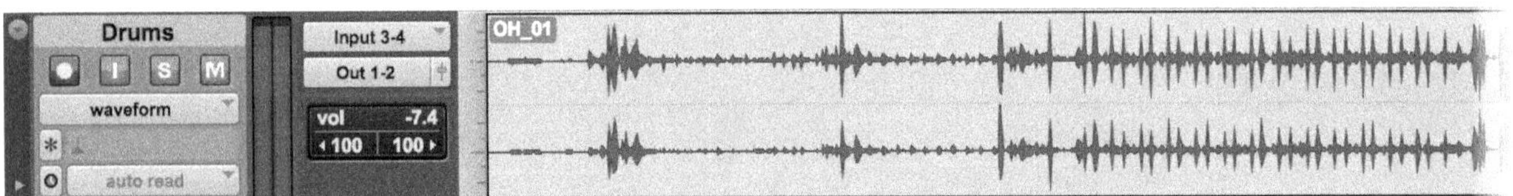

Figure 2.59 The Drums track is a Stereo Audio Track. Note the Two Sets of Waveforms in the Clip (the top one is for the left side and the bottom is for the right).

Since MIDI on its own makes no sound, a MIDI track is in neither mono nor stereo.

Pro Tools | First and Pro Tools are limited to mono and stereo tracks. On the other hand, Pro Tools | Ultimate supports a variety of multichannel track types, including Ambisonics surround tracks and Dolby Atmos 7.1.2 tracks.

Creating New Tracks

Making new tracks is fairly straightforward and, as with many things in Pro Tools, there are a number of ways that you can do it:

1. From the TRACK menu, choose NEW.

OR

1. There's also a shortcut for creating new tracks. On a Mac, it's SHIFT+COMMAND+N, and on Windows, it's SHIFT+CTRL+N.

The *New Tracks* dialog box will appear, as shown in Figure 2.60. The process of creating tracks works well if you work from left to right:

Figure 2.60 The New Tracks Dialog

2. Next, choose how many tracks you want of a given track type. In this case, I'll choose 3.

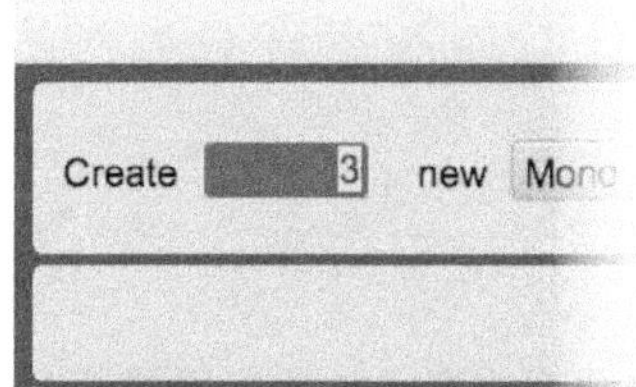

Figure 2.61 How many tracks do you want?

3. You'll need to choose whether your new track(s) will be mono or stereo (in other words, whether it will have one input or two inputs). Click the TRACK FORMAT menu button to reveal your choices as shown in FIGURE 2.62. In this case, I'll choose mono.

Figure 2.62 Choosing Between a Mono or Stereo Track Format

Here's a neat little shortcut that will allow you to toggle through the stereo or mono options: Press and hold the COMMAND key (Mac) or CTRL key (Windows) and press either the Left or Right Arrow keys.

4. To choose what *kind* of track you're going to create, click on the TRACK TYPE menu button to reveal the drop-down menu shown in Figure 2.63. In this example, I'll create Audio Tracks.

Figure 2.63 Choosing the Track Type

There's also a shortcut to cycle through the different track types: Press and hold the COMMAND key (Mac) or CTRL key (Windows) and press either the Up or Down Arrow keys.

5. All tracks that you create have a *timebase*—the way that they view the passage of time. Tracks can be either sample-based or tick-based. In Pro Tools and Pro Tools | Ultimate, MIDI and Instrument tracks are tick-based by default, and all other tracks are sample-based by default. For the purpose of this book, we'll choose these more common track defaults, so in this case, I'll choose samples from the TRACK TIMEBASE menu, as shown in FIGURE 2.64.

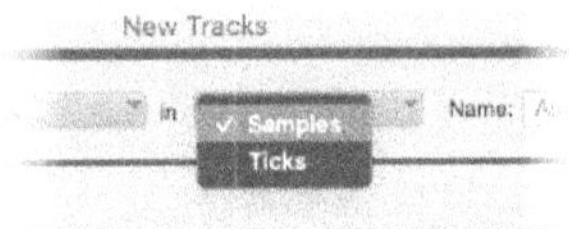

Figure 2.64 Choosing the Track Timebase

6. The importance of naming your tracks cannot be overstated. Without a descriptive name, who can tell what kinds of clips (for example, Vocal, Bass, or Effects) are on the track? Just like powering your system on and off correctly, naming your tracks and Projects descriptively is basic etiquette, and a good habit to get into from the start. There are a number of ways you can name a track—one way is to name it as it is created in the New Tracks dialog box. In this case, I'll name my track *Vocal*, as shown in Figure 2.65.

Figure 2.65 Choosing the Track Name

7. You've done all the hard work—Now, just click the CREATE button, and your new track(s) will be added to your Project. Figure 2.66 shows the results: we have three mono Audio Tracks named Vocal 1, Vocal 2, and Vocal 3 (since in this case we were creating multiple tracks, Pro Tools added the number after the name).

Figure 2.66 The New Tracks

Adding Multiple Tracks

In addition to creating single tracks or multiple tracks of a single type, you can create multiple tracks of *multiple* types in a single operation:

1. At the right side of the New Tracks dialog box, you'll see button with a plus (+) symbol. This is the ADD ROW button, which when clicked will add a new row, allowing you to create a new kind of track.

Figure 2.67 The ADD ROW Button

2. You can do this a number of times, and as shown in Figure 2.68, I will create three mono Audio Tracks (named *Vocal 1*, *Vocal 2*, and *Vocal 3*), one mono Audio Track (named *Guitar*), two stereo Audio Tracks (named *Music 1* and *Music 2*), one stereo Aux Input Track (named *Reverb*), and one stereo Master Fader (named *Master*). When I click the CREATE button, all of these tracks will be created in the order that they appear in the New Tracks dialog box.

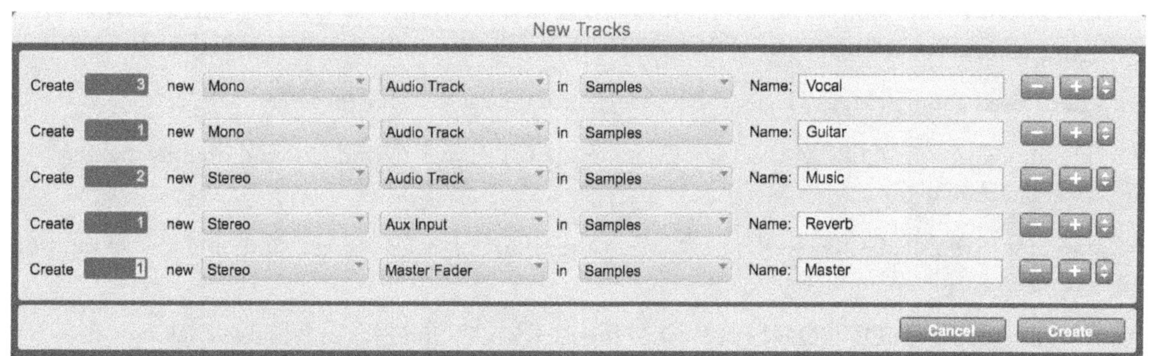

Figure 2.68 Creating Multiple Tracks At Once

3. If you want to rearrange the tracks' order before they're created, just click and hold on the MOVE ROW button, as shown in Figure 2.69. A blue box will appear around that row, and from there, you can drag and drop this row to rearrange the order of the tracks as needed.

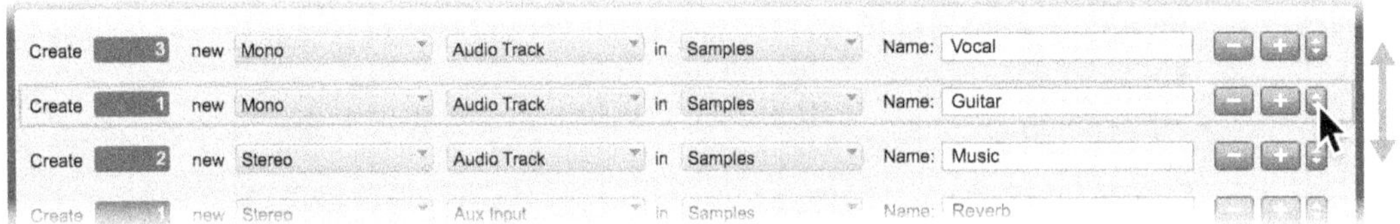

Figure 2.69 Moving the Guitar Track Up or Down in the List of Tracks to be Created

Adding New Tracks Like the Previous

In the course of their work, audio professionals will create a lot of tracks, and anything that makes the process even a little easier can be a huge benefit. Here's one more shortcut that can help when it comes to creating tracks.

You'll notice that in the Tracks List (in either the Edit window or the Mix window), there is a bit of blank space under the last track. There's also always a bit of blank space at the bottom of the Edit window's tracks, and on the far right of the Mix window's tracks.

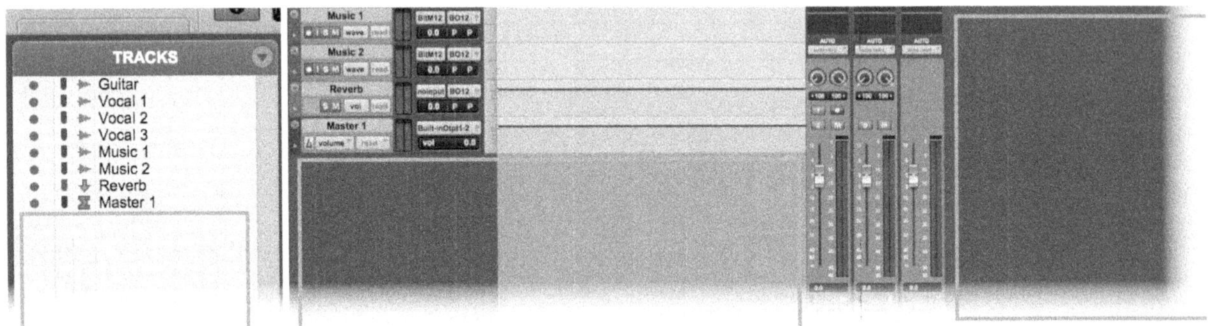

Figure 2.70 Blank Spaces for Creating New Tracks

Here is the shortcut: double-clicking in any of those blank areas will create a track just like the last track you've created. Put in context: In the example we just finished earlier in this chapter, the last track that I created was a stereo Master Fader. Double-clicking in any of these blank areas will create a second Master Fader.

But what if I don't need another Master Fader? That's where modifier keys come into play:

- Holding down the COMMAND key (Mac) or the CTRL key (Windows) and double-clicking will create an Audio Track
- Holding down the CONTROL key (Mac) or the START key (Windows) and double-clicking will create an Auxiliary Input Track
- Holding down the OPTION key (Mac) or the ALT key (Windows) and double-clicking will create an Instrument Track
- Holding down the SHIFT key and double-clicking will create a Master Fader Track

And as if this wasn't cool enough, holding down multiple keys will create multiple new tracks. For example, if I hold down COMMAND+CONTROL (Mac) or CTRL+START (Windows) and double-click, a new Audio Track and Aux Track will be created.

Selecting Inputs and Outputs

Once tracks have been created, make sure that you can hear them (and if you're recording, make sure the signal will go to it properly). That's where a track's *inputs* and *outputs* come into play. Setting your tracks' inputs and outputs is easy to do if you know where to look.

Let's start in the Mix Window—you can set a track's input and output from the I/O (which stands for *Inputs/Outputs*) Mix window View. Here's what the I/O View looks like in the Mix window:

Figure 2.71 The Mix Window's I/O View

At the top is the *Input Path* selector. Clicking on this will allow you to choose where your signal is coming from. As you go through this book, you'll deal with setting up inputs in a number of different situations, but for an audio track that's just playing an audio clip, you can have any setting (or even *No Input*, as shown in Figure 2.71).

Below the Input Path selector is the *Output Path* selector, which will allow you to choose where a given track's signal is going. For now, let's keep things simple: If you want to hear a track out of your speakers, just click the output button and choose the output that is connected to your speakers (the one that you've chosen as the *Default Output* in the Playback Engine dialog box).

In the Edit window, the I/O View can look a little bit different depending upon the height of the track (changing track height is something you'll learn to do later in this chapter). For example, if the track height is set to small, the Input and Output Path selectors are side-by-side with the Input selector on the left and the Output selector on the right, as shown in Figure 2.72.

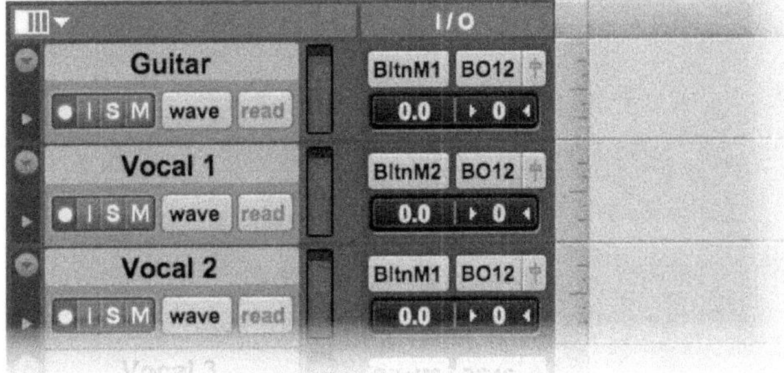

Figure 2.72 The Edit Window's I/O View with Track Heights Set to Small

If the track is a bit taller, the Input and Output Path selectors may appear similar to what you saw in the Mix window, with the Input selector on the top and the Output selector on the bottom, as shown in Figure 2.73.

Figure 2.73 The Edit Window's I/O View with Track Heights Set to Medium

Managing Your Tracks

Before we go into the last hands-on section in this chapter, here are a few ways that you can work with the tracks you create:

Selecting Tracks

Selecting a track is easy to do—here are three ways:

- In the Tracks List (in either the Mix or Edit window), click the name of the track that you want to select
- In the Edit window, click the track name of the track that you want to select
- In the Mix window, click the track name of the track that you want to select

No matter how you do it, the result will be the same: the name of any selected track will be highlighted in the Tracks List, the Edit window, and the Mix window, as shown in Figure 2.74.

Figure 2.74 The Guitar Track is selected. This is how it appears in the Tracks List, Edit Window, and the Mix Window.

Showing and Hiding Tracks

Sometimes you want to see all the tracks in your project, but other times you want to show or hide visual tracks. It's easy to do this in Pro Tools: In the Tracks List, in either the Mix or Edit windows, you'll find a small circle to the left of each track name.

Figure 2.75 All Tracks Shown

In Figure 2.75, you'll see a dark circle to the left of each of the track names, meaning that all the tracks are visible in the tracks area of the Edit window.

In order to hide a track, just click the small dark circle in the row of the track that you want to hide. The circle will turn to light grey, and the track will be hidden in the tracks area of both the Edit and Mix windows. In Figure 2.76, the Guitar Track has been hidden.

Figure 2.76 Hiding the Guitar Track

Another way to hide a track is to right-click the track name (in the Track List, Edit window tracks area, or Mix window track area). A menu will appear—choose HIDE from that menu.

Hidden tracks are still audible. When you hide a track, you're simply removing it from view, not from your mix.

In order to show a track that has been hidden, just click the light grey circle next to the track name. The circle will turn dark grey, and the track will be visible.

Now that you know how to select a track, here's another way you can show or hide tracks. Clicking on the Tracks List pop-up menu button (the small circular button at the top right corner of the Tracks List) will reveal a menu of track-related operations. From here, you can show or hide any tracks that you have selected.

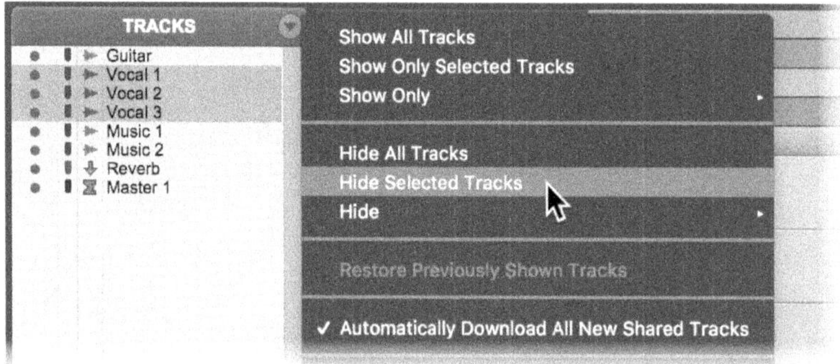

Figure 2.77 The Tracks List Pop-Up Menu

Changing Track Order

At some point, you'll want to re-order your tracks after you've created them. This also can be easily done. Here are three ways:

- In the Tracks List, click and drag the track name of the desired track up or down. A yellow line will indicate where the track will be placed once you let go of the mouse.
- In the Edit window tracks area, click and drag the track name of the desired track up or down. A yellow line will indicate where the track will be placed once you let go of the mouse.
- In the Mix window tracks area, click and drag the track name of the desired track left or right. A yellow line will indicate where the track will be placed once you let go of the mouse.

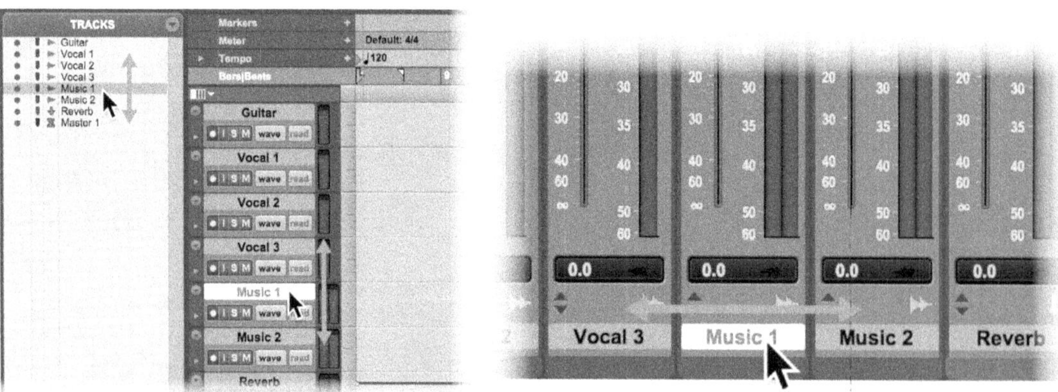

Figure 2.78 Moving Tracks

Changing Track Height

Not only can you change the track order to suit your taste, but you can also change individual track heights as well. For example, if you've got a lot of tracks and you want to see most of them in your Edit window, you might want to set them relatively small. On the other hand, if you want to take a closer look at a track's waveform, making the track taller will give you that visibility. Here are a few ways to change your track height:

1. Click in the area immediately to the left of the desired track's clip area (called the *Vertical Zoom Scale*), as shown in Figure 2.79.

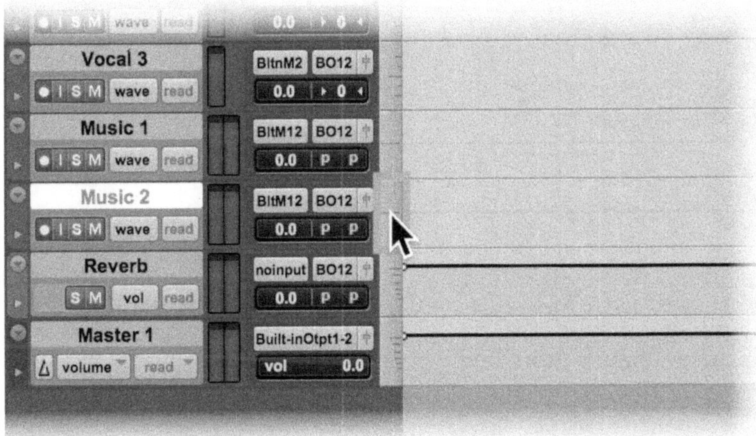

Figure 2.79 Changing the Music 2 Track's Height

2. A menu will appear, giving you a choice of different track heights for the track, with the currently selected height indicated with a checkmark. Just choose the track height you want, and the track height will be changed.

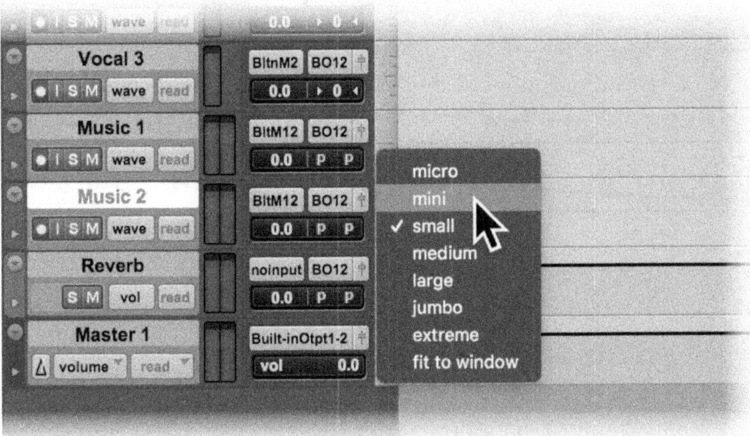

Figure 2.80 Changing the Music 2 Track's Height from SMALL to MINI

You can also click the Track's Pop-Up menu (the small circular icon to the left of each track name). Depending upon the current track height, different menus will appear. From here, you can choose the desired track height as shown in Figure 2.81.

Figure 2.81 Changing the Music 1 Track's Height from the Pop-Up Menu

This might be the easiest way: Just move your cursor to the bottom boundary of the track that you want to resize. A double arrow icon will appear (as shown in Figure 2.82). Just click and drag up or down to your desired height.

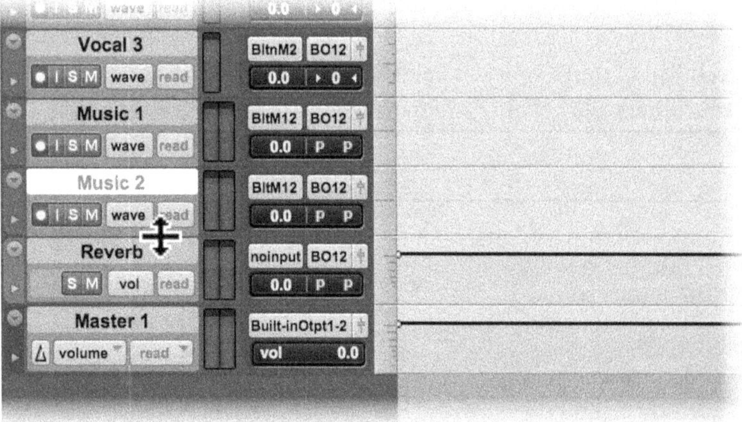

Figure 2.82 Resizing the Music 2 Track's Height

There's also a shortcut for changing track height—Just hold the CONTROL key (Mac) or START key (Windows), and press the UP or DOWN ARROW keys to change the height of any selected tracks.

Changing Track Color

As your session gets larger with more tracks, organization becomes increasingly important, and color-coding your tracks is a great way to keep things in order.

At the bottom and top of each track channel strip in the Mix window, and at the far left of each track in the Edit window, you'll see a colored tab. Just double-click on this tab to reveal the Color Palette window, as shown in Figure 2.83.

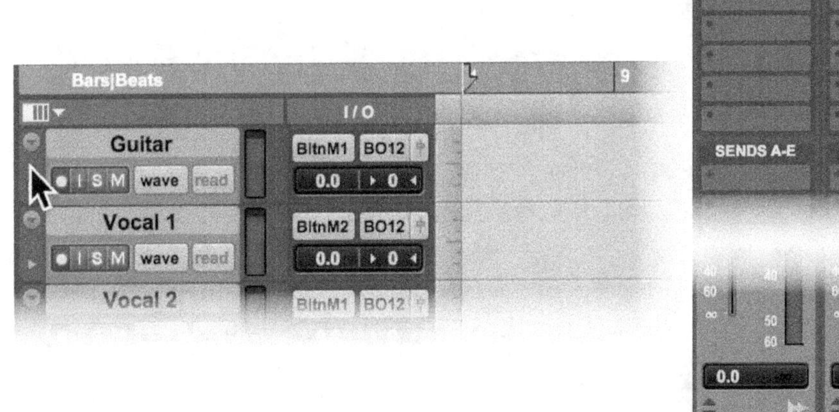

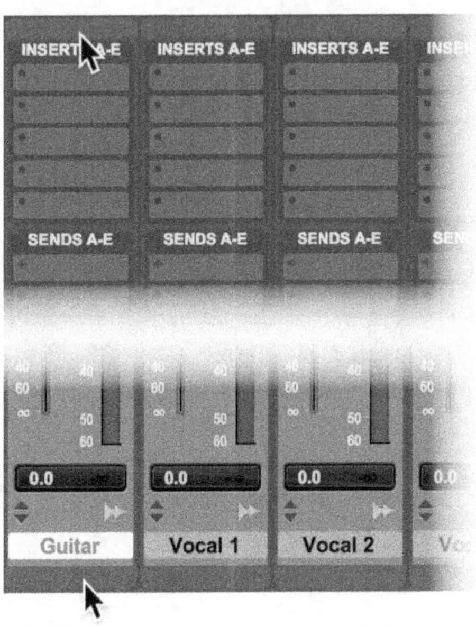

Figure 2.83 Track Color Bars

If you want, you can also open the Color Palette window by going to WINDOW>COLOR PALETTE. The Color Palette window will open, and from there all you need to do is click the menu button in the upper left of the Color Palette window and choose TRACKS, as shown in Figure 2.84.

Figure 2.84 The Color Palette Window

Next, just choose the desired color tile in the Color Palette window, and any selected tracks will change to this color. As you can see in Figure 2.85, I've changed my Guitar track to orange.

Figure 2.85 Changing the Color of the selected Guitar Track

But wait, there's more! If you want to change the entire track strips color, just click the APPLY TO CHANNEL STRIP button, which would then extend the track color through the entire channel strip. From there you can adjust the brightness and saturation of the colors to suit your tastes, as I have done in Figure 2.86.

Figure 2.86 Applying Track Color to the Channel Strip

Renaming Tracks

While naming your tracks is very important, you don't have to do it when the track is being created, as we have done so far in this chapter. If you want to name a track after it's been created (or rename a track), it's easy to do. Here are two ways:

1. Double-click the name of the track whose name you want to change.

OR

1. In the Mix window or the Edit window, right-click the name of the track whose name you want to change. In the menu that appears, choose RENAME, as shown in Figure 2.87.

Figure 2.87 Changing Track Name

2. In the dialog box that appears, you can type a new name for the track (and/or comments for that track). If you've gotten to this dialog box by double-clicking the track name, you can navigate to the PREVIOUS or NEXT tracks with the appropriate buttons at the bottom of the dialog box. To confirm your change, click the OK button.

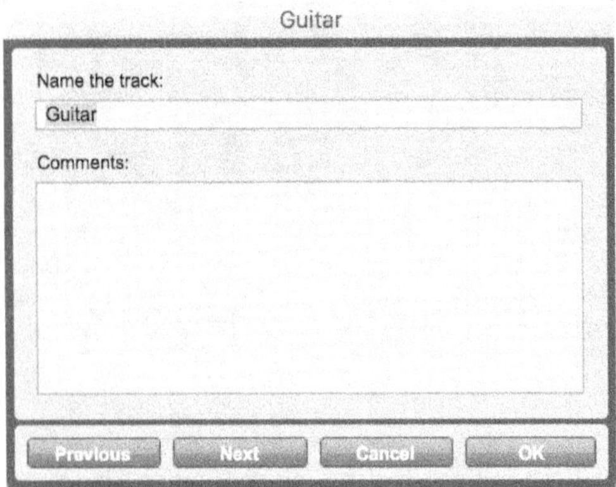

Figure 2.88 The Track Name Dialog Box

Muting and Soloing Tracks

Sometimes, you don't want to hear a given track in your mix, or you want to hear it in isolation, without other distractions. That's where the MUTE and SOLO buttons come into play:

When a track is soloed, that track will be the only one heard—all non-soloed tracks will be silent (or *muted*). In order to solo a track, click the S button in the Edit or Mix window as shown in Figure 2.89.

Figure 2.89 Soloing a Track in the Edit Window (with different track heights) and the Mix Window

Multiple tracks can be soloed at a time.

A track that is muted will *not* be heard. In order to mute a track, just click the track's M button in the Mix or Edit window, as shown in Figure 2.90.

Figure 2.90 Muting a Track in the Edit Window (with different track heights) and the Mix Window

Here are two useful shortcuts: SHIFT+S will toggle the Solo on or off on any selected tracks. SHIFT+M will toggle the Mute on or off on any selected tracks.

Deleting Tracks

Finally, deleting tracks is easy to do—perhaps *too* easy. As a general rule, deleting in Pro Tools is usually not doable. That means that when you delete a track, it's gone forever, so make doubly sure that you really don't need that track before you delete it!

Deleting a track will also clear your Project's Undo History, which means you cannot undo the deletion of a track, and you can also cannot undo anything you did before deleting the track! It's one more reason to think before you delete.

That being said, here's how you can delete a track.

- From the TRACK menu choose DELETE. All selected tracks will be deleted.

OR

- Right-click on the track name of a track and choose DELETE from the menu that appears. All selected tracks will be deleted.

Hands-On Exercise 2.3: Making Tracks

In this hands-on exercise, you're going to add some new tracks to the blank Project that you created earlier:

Open an Existing Project

1. Open the blank project that you created in Hands-On Exercise 2.2. If you were following the steps, the project would be called *Pro Tools First—Chapter 2 Blank Project.*

Create New Tracks

2. Next, add the following tracks in this order:
    - One Mono sample-based Audio Track named *Sax*
    - One Mono sample-based Audio Track named *Guitar*
    - One Mono sample-based Audio Track named *Bass*
    - Three Stereo sample-based Audio Tracks named *Audio* (the default name for an Audio Track)
    - Two Stereo sample-based Master Faders named *Master* (the default name for a Master Fader Track)

You can create them one at a time if you want, or do them all in one operation, as shown in Figure 2.91.

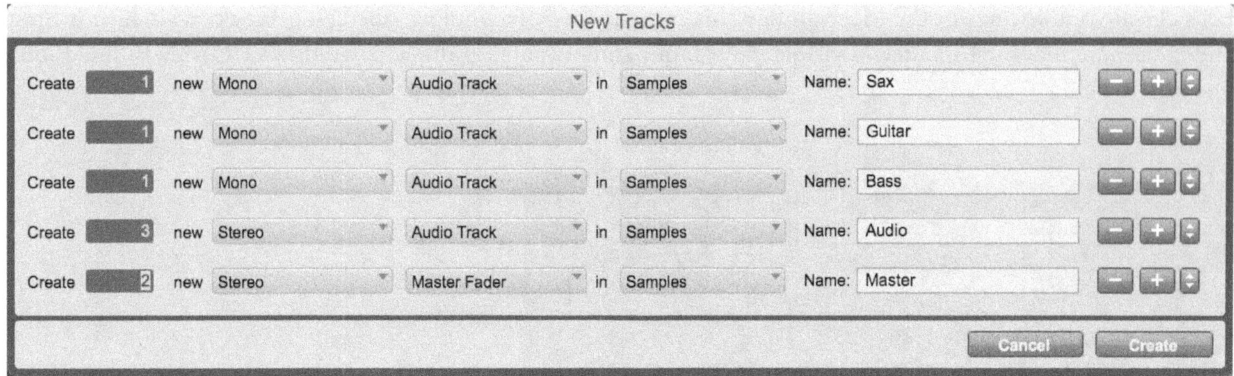

Figure 2.91 Creating the Tracks in One Operation

When you're done, your Edit window screen should look like this:

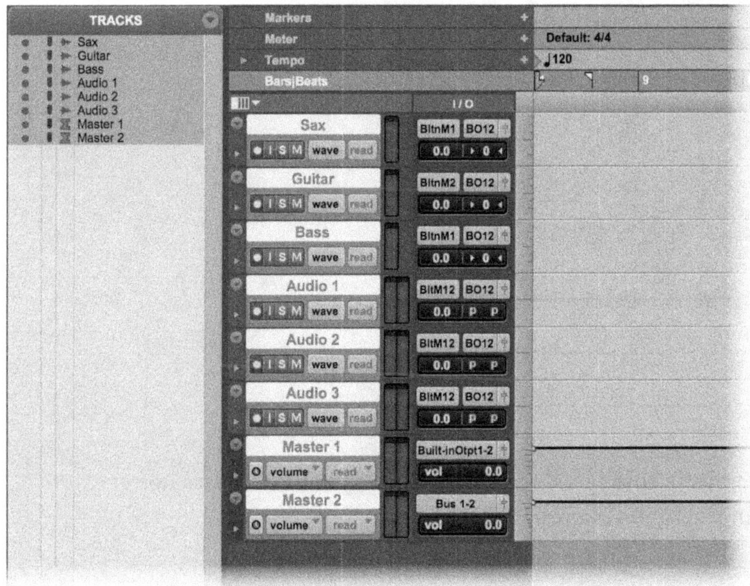

Figure 2.92 The New Tracks in Order

Set Inputs and Outputs

3. In this particular case, since we're not going to be recording to any of these tracks, set the input of all of the Audio Tracks to NO INPUT.

Note that the two Master Fader Tracks have no inputs, only outputs. That's not a bug; Master Faders only control the level of the assigned output, without the need for an input.

4. Set the output of all the Audio Tracks and the first Master Fader Track to the same output that you have selected in the Playback Engine dialog box as your Default Output.

Let's check your settings in the Mix window this time. If the Mix window isn't being shown, switch to it now, and make sure that the I/O View is visible. Your input and outputs (in the Mix window's I/O view) should look like Figure 2.93.

Figure 2.93 Inputs and Outputs as they Appear in the Mix Window

Renaming Tracks

5. The three stereo Audio Tracks are just named *Audio 1*, *Audio 2*, and *Audio 3*. That's not very descriptive, so let's name them in the following order:
   - *Audio 1* renamed to *Trumpets*
   - *Audio 2* renamed to *Keys*
   - *Audio 3* renamed to *Drums*
   - Also, rename the *Master 1* track to *MAIN OUT*

When you're done, your Mix window should look like Figure 2.94.

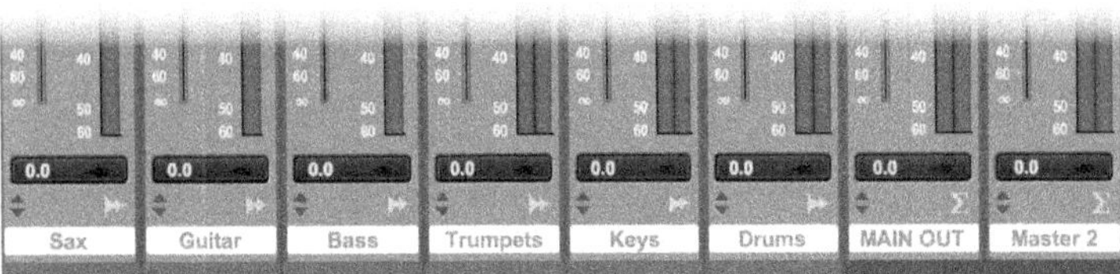

Figure 2.94 Renamed Tracks

Delete a Track

You're almost done. As it happens, we don't need a second Master Fader at this time, so let's delete the track called *Master 2*.

6. From the TRACK menu, or by right-clicking the *Master 2* Track name, delete the *Master 2* Track.

Make sure that the Master 2 track is the ONLY track that is selected. No matter what method you choose, deleting tracks will delete all selected tracks (and it's not undoable)!

Your final track list should be:

- Sax (Mono Audio Track)
- Guitar (Mono Audio Track
- Bass (Mono Audio Track
- Trumpets (Stereo Audio Track)
- Keys (Stereo Audio Track)
- Drums (Stereo Audio Track
- MAIN OUT (Stereo Master Fader Track)

Save a Project

Before we leave this chapter, let's save your work.

7. From the FILE menu, choose SAVE.
8. From the PRO TOOLS FIRST menu, choose QUIT ***PRO TOOLS | FIRST***. This concludes the exercises for Chapter 2.

Review Questions

1. When turning on your system, what device should always be turned on last?
2. What is the difference between creating a blank Project and creating a Project from a Template?
3. What are Pro Tools' two main windows?
4. What are the two different ways that you can show or hide Edit window Views? How about Mix Window Views?
5. How can you show or hide the Transport window?
6. What are the two Time Scales that you can view in the Edit window's counter?
7. What is the difference between an Audio Track and an Auxiliary Input Track?
8. What is the shortcut to create New Tracks?
9. How can tracks be shown or hidden from the Tracks List?
10. True or False: Tracks cannot be renamed after they are created, so it's very important to name them before you create them.

CHAPTER 3

Importing Audio

In Chapter 2, you created a blank Project into which you created a few new empty tracks. Now it's time to put some audio clips in your tracks. In Chapter 3, you'll learn how to import audio into your Project in different ways.

Media Used: Pro Tools First Fundamentals of Audio Production—Chapter 3 (Mambo).ptx, Pro Tools First—Fundamentals of Audio Production—Chapter 3—Audio for Import

Duration: 45 minutes

GOALS

- Learn how to make the best decisions about the kind of audio files to use in your Project
- Learn to import audio to a new track from the FILE menu
- Learn to import audio from your computer's file browser window
- Learn to import audio using Soundbase
- Learn to search for audio by keyword

Considerations Prior to Import

In Chapter 1, you learned about sample rates and bit-depth, and how they relate to frequencies and amplitude that can be recorded and played back. Choosing the right kind of audio specs for your Project is important, and something that is best decided early in the production process.

When creating a blank Project or a Project from a template, your sample rate and bit-depth are automatically set. When you convert a Session to a Project, you will have the ability to choose your desired sample rates and bit-depth settings.

Sample Rate and Bit Depth

As a general rule, larger files will use more CPU and consume more hard drive space. That translates to fewer minutes of audio, and fewer tracks and effects (since your CPU is crunching larger amounts of data). The choices that you make regarding sample rate and bit-depth will affect file size. Here are some pros and cons:

- Regarding sample rates, more is not always better. Consider this: a file with a sample rate of 176.4 kHz includes four times as many samples as a file with an identical length of time, but with a sample rate of 44.1 kHz; meaning that the 176.4 kHz file is four times as large as the 44.1 kHz file (assuming that the bit-depth of both files is the same). Yes, a higher sample rate will give you more accurate higher frequencies, but after a certain point, that difference is inaudible. It's good advice not to go overboard with your sample rates.
- Choosing the right bit-depth for your Project is an easier choice to make. The two most commonly used bit-depths are 16-bit and 24-bit. At any given sample rate, choosing 24-bit will be 50% larger then choosing 16-bit. That little bit of additional file size will give you significant benefits—16-bit audio falls short of giving you all the dynamic (amplitude) range that a human being can perceive, but 24-bit audio gives you more than enough.

When choosing the sample rate and bit-depth of your Project, don't feel limited by what the final output will be. In many cases, professionals will record, edit, and mix at sample rates and bit-depths greater than those of their final mix. These higher specs are what often give us better results, even if we will be reducing sample rates and bit-depths when we export our final work.

Audio File Formats

The next choice to make is the audio files' format. In all versions of Pro Tools, you have two choices: WAV or AIFF. As a general rule, WAV files are the popular choice, for a number of reasons. First, WAV files are more common than AFF files and are therefore more broadly compatible. Secondly—and this next bit means more to post-production than to music production—the kind of WAV file that Pro Tools uses is called a ***Broadcast Wave Format*** (or BWF). These BWF files can include additional information in the file that is useful in professional post-production workflows (in other words, production for some sort of video medium).

WAV and AIFF files are both uncompressed PCM (Pulse Code Modulation) files. As such, there is no difference in sound quality between the two formats.

You can import compressed audio formats like MP3 files—Pro Tools will convert the file to the format that you have selected for the Project.

Split Stereo versus Interleaved

The only remaining choice you'll need to make when converting a Session to a Project is whether your audio files will be Interleaved or not. But what does that mean?

- If the Interleaved check box is left *unchecked* when you create your Project, clips on stereo Audio Tracks Will refer to two files—one file for the left channel's output and one file for the right channel's output.
- If the Interleaved box is *checked*, clips on stereo Audio Tracks will refer to a single file. That single file will comprise both left and right channels.

The decision on whether to use interleaved files or not will not affect sound quality, hard drive usage, CPU workload, or Pro Tools workflow. The only significant difference—and this applies to Pro Tools and Pro Tools | Ultimate more than it does Pro Tools | First—is the number of files that you will have in your Session's Audio Files folder. Choosing interleaved files will generally mean that you will have fewer files to keep track of.

Importing Audio

There are a number of different ways that you can import audio into a Pro Tools | First Project. Let's start with a couple of simple and direct ways:

Importing Audio from the File Menu

1. From the FILE menu, go to IMPORT. A file browser window will open.

There's a shortcut to get to the file browser window. On a Mac, it's SHIFT+COMMAND+I. On a Windows computer, it's SHIFT+CTRL+I.

2. Navigate to the folder and file that you want to import. In the example shown in Figure 3.1, I will be importing the *Chapter 3—Guitar 1.wav* file into a Project that already contains some blank tracks.

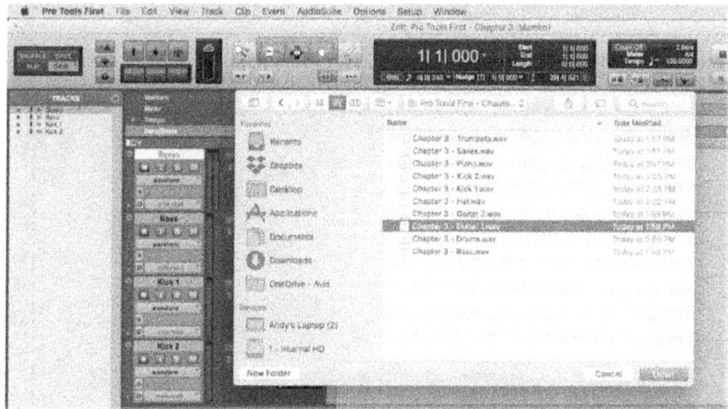

Figure 3.1 Importing a Guitar Audio File

3. Click the OPEN button.

The file that you chose will be imported into a new track. Note that the track name follows the name of the file that was imported. Also note that the clip has been placed at the beginning of the timeline, as shown in Figure 3.2

Figure 3.2 The imported Guitar File

Importing from a File Browser

You can also import audio into a Project using your computer's file browser, and this method actually gives you a bit more flexibility:

1. Open your computer's file browser (Mac Finder or Windows Explorer) and navigate to the file that you want to import.
2. Drag the file from the browser into Pro Tools' Edit window. There are a few ways to do this that will give you different results:
   - If you drag a file from the browser window into the Tracks List, a new track will be created, and the clip will be placed at the beginning of the timeline (the same result as if you imported the file using the FILE>IMPORT method).
   - If you drag from the browser into a blank area in the Edit window's track area (where there are no tracks), you will see an outline where the file will be deposited, as shown in Figure 3.3. Once you drop the file, a new Audio track will be created with a clip where you dropped the file.

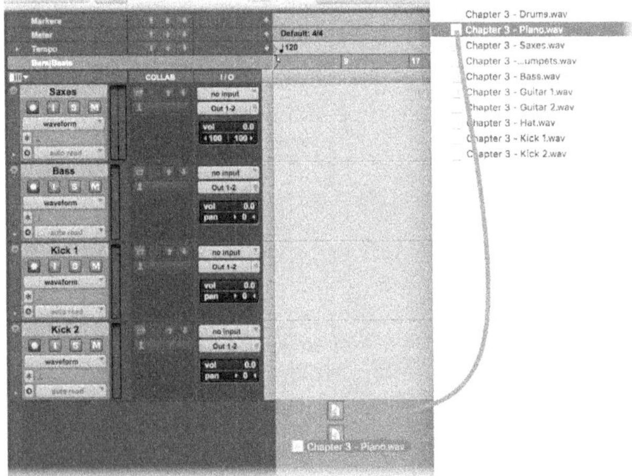

Figure 3.3 Creating a New Track and a Clip Where the File is Dropped

- If you drag a file onto an existing track, you will see an outline where that file will be deposited once the mouse is released (as shown in Figure 3.4). Once the mouse is released, a new clip will be placed on the track, this time without a new track being created.

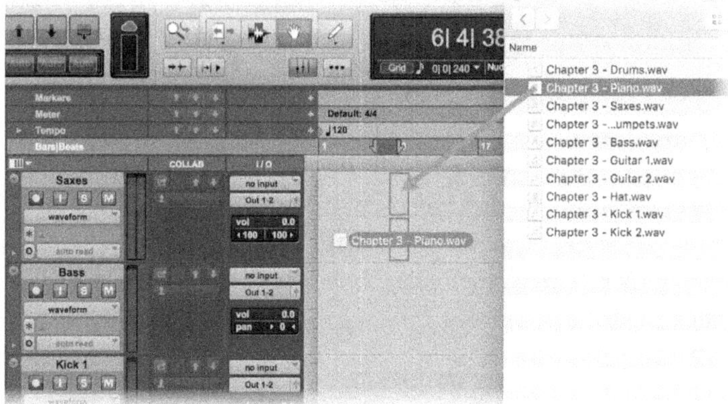

Figure 3.4 The imported Piano File

Here's something to watch out for: mono audio files cannot be dropped onto stereo Audio tracks. If you drag a stereo audio file (a file that has two channels) onto multiple mono tracks, two separate mono clips will be created on two mono tracks.

When you import audio into a Project in Pro Tools I First, that imported audio is copied to a location on your local hard drive where Pro Tools I First manages its Projects. On a Mac, the location is *Users/[your user name]/Documents/Pro Tools/Project Cache*. On a Windows computer, the location is *[your user name]/My Documents/Pro Tools/Project Cache*.

In Pro Tools and Pro Tools I Ultimate, there is an additional way to import. With those other versions of Pro Tools, you can drag from a file browser window into the Clips List, importing the audio without creating any tracks or placing the clip on the timeline of any existing track. Because Pro Tools I First does not have a Clips List, this method of importing is not available.

Whether you're using the FILE>IMPORT menu or dragging from a file browser window, you can import multiple audio files at the same time. When importing from the FILE>IMPORT menu, dragging multiple files to the Tracks List or to an empty area in your Edit window tracks area, multiple tracks will be created with each clip aligned vertically. Multiple files can be dragged to existing tracks as well but be careful: stereo files will be split if you try to drop them onto mono tracks.

Hands-On Exercise 3.1: Importing Audio

Now it's your turn to import some audio into a Project:

The materials that I created for this exercise (and for some editing practice in Chapter 4) were something that I whipped up, with guitar tracks from a friend and Avid colleague, Alex Brooke. We hope you enjoy it!

Create a New Project

For this exercise, you're going to convert a Pro Tools session into a Pro Tools | First local project.

1. Launch Pro Tools | First.

OR

1. If Pro Tools | First is already running, click FILE>CREATE NEW.
2. In the Dashboard window, click the CONVERT SESSION button.
3. Navigate to the folder that contains this book's downloaded exercises and open the *Pro Tools First—Fundamentals of Audio Production—Chapter 3 (Mambo)* folder. In that folder, there's a single Pro Tools session file called *Pro Tools First—Fundamentals of Audio Production—Chapter 3 (Mambo).ptx.* Select that session and click the OPEN button.
4. You will be asked to set up your new Project. Choose these settings:
   - Local Storage (Session)
   - File Type = BWF (.WAV)
   - Sample Rate = 96 kHz (if 96 kHz is not available in your system, choose any other sample rate)
   - Bit Depth = 24-bit
   - Interleaved = Enabled (checked)
   - Backup to Cloud = Disabled (unchecked)

When you're done, your Project settings should look like Figure 3.5.

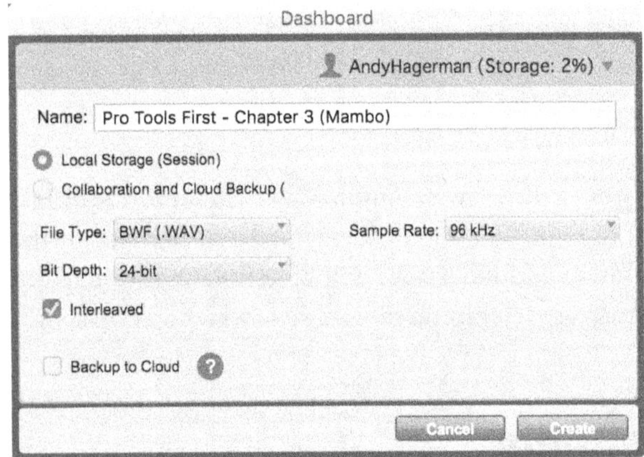

Figure 3.5 Settings for Your New Project

5. Click the CREATE button, and your Project will be created.
6. Let's adjust the Edit window to suit our purposes:
   - Hide the Track Collaboration (COLLAB) Edit window View.

- In the Edit Tools cluster, make sure that the Grabber Tools is selected, as shown in Figure 3.6 (you'll learn more about how to use Edit Tools in the next chapter, but for now, you'll use this tool to move clips on the timeline).

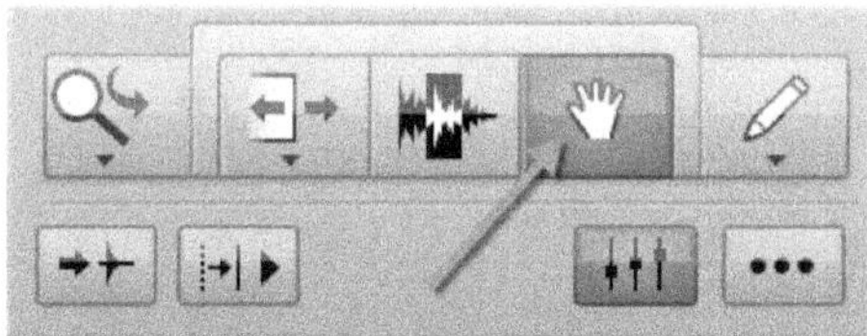

Figure 3.6 The Grabber Tool Selected

- In the Edit Modes section, make sure that SLIP mode is selected, as shown in Figure 3.7 (you'll also learn about Edit Modes in the next chapter, but for now, just understand that this mode will allow you to position clips freely).

Figure 3.7 Slip Mode Selected

When you're done, your Edit window should look like Figure 3.8:

Figure 3.8 Ready to Go!

Import Audio from the File Menu

Let's start with the drums:

7. From the FILE>IMPORT Menu, import the *Chapter 3—Hat.wav* and *Chapter 3—Drums.wav* files. You will find these two files in your downloaded exercise materials folder in a subfolder called *Pro Tools First—Chapter 3—Audio for Import.*

You can import these two files separately or together.

When you're done, two new tracks will be created under your last selected track (if you're following the steps in this exercise, before you imported these files, the Saxes track was selected). Your Edit window should look like Figure 3.9.

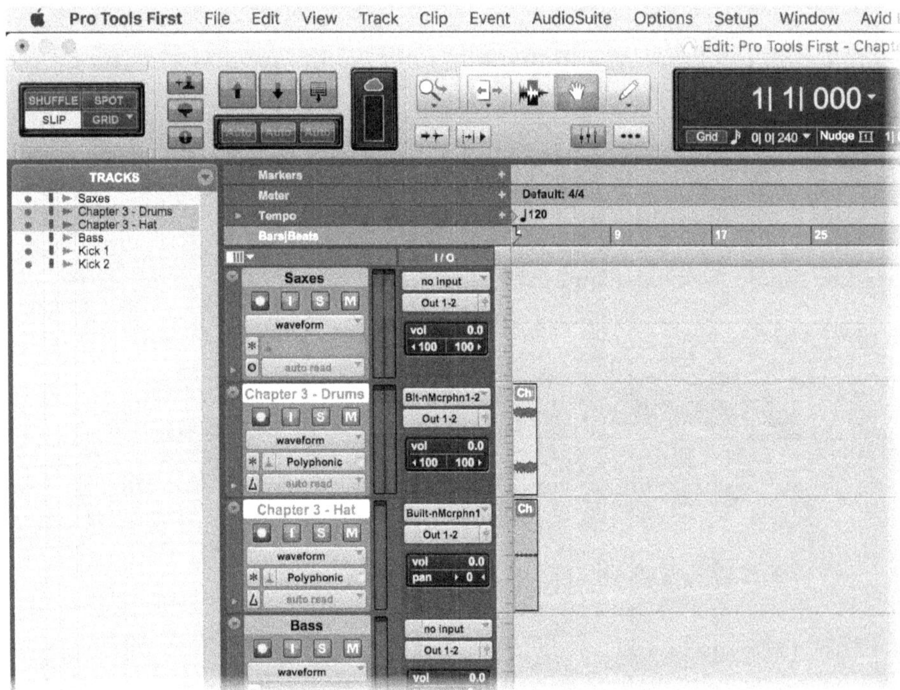

Figure 3.9 After You've Imported the Two Drum Tracks

Drag Audio from the File Browser

You'll see in your Project that there are two kick drum tracks, named *Kick 1* and *Kick 2*. Let's get some clips on those tracks.

8. Launch your computer's file browser window, making sure that you can see both the browser window and Pro Tools' Edit window at the same time, similar to what's shown in Figure 3.10. Navigate to the downloaded exercise materials folder, and from there to a subfolder called *Pro Tools First—Chapter 3—Audio for Import.*

9. Select Chapter 3—Kick 1.wav and Chapter 3—Kick 2.wav, and drag those files into the Edit window, so that the clip outlines are placed on the Kick 1 and Kick 2 Audio tracks, as shown in Figure 3.10. It's no problem if the clips aren't at the beginning of the track.

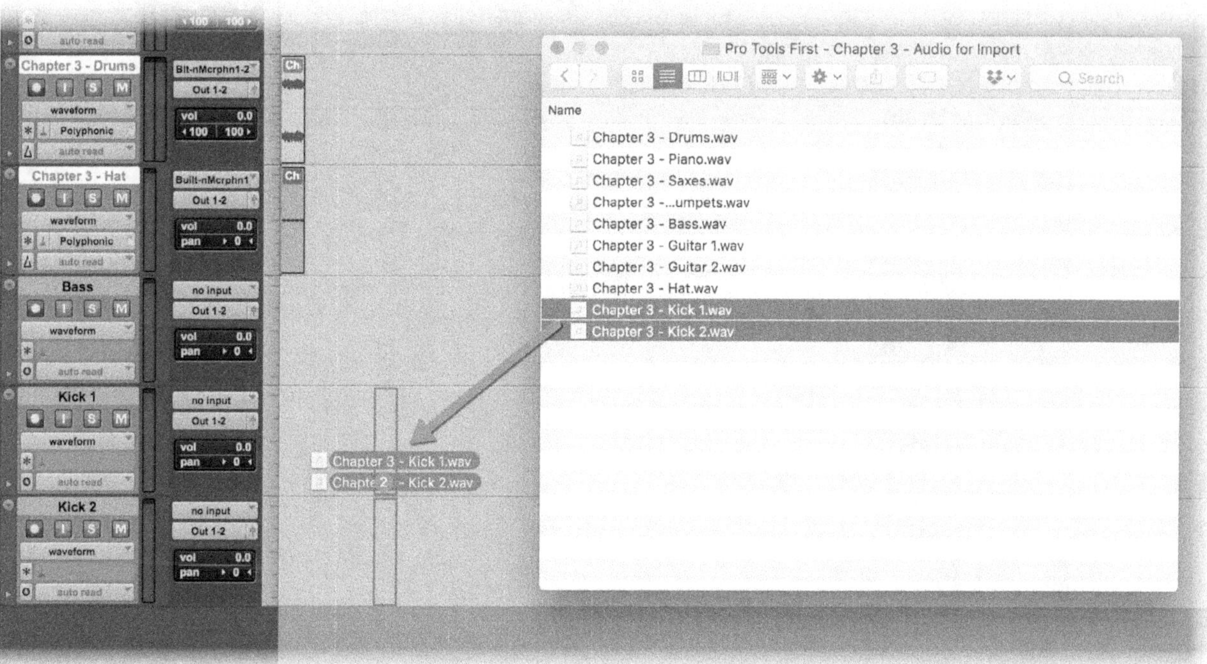

Figure 3.10 Dragging Kick Files to Your Tracks

10. It's likely that your clips are not at the beginning of your timeline. If so, they aren't lined up with the other drum clips, so you'll need to line them up. Just click the Grabber Tool and drag the clips, so that they move to the very beginning of the timeline, as shown in Figure 3.11.

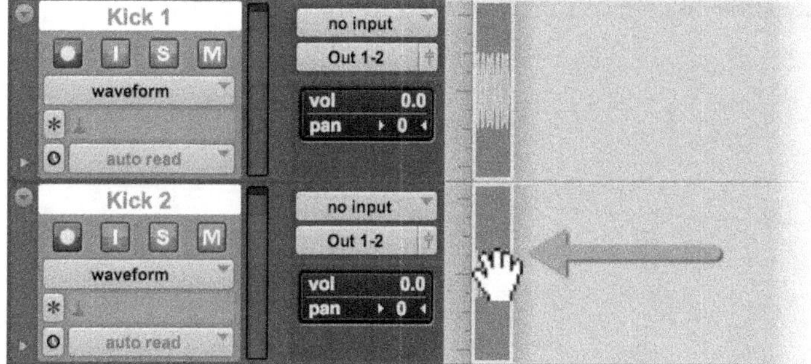

Figure 3.11 Positioning the Kick Clips to the Beginning of the Timeline

When you're done, your Project's Edit window should look something like Figure 3.12:

Figure 3.12 All of Your Drums Imported

Project Clean-Up

11. Let's do a little bit of cleanup. Re-order your tracks, so that they read from top to bottom:
    - Saxes
    - Bass
    - Chapter 3—Drums
    - Chapter 3—Hat
    - Kick 1
    - Kick 2
12. Rename the following tracks:
    - *Chapter 3—Drums* renamed to *Drum Kit*
    - *Chapter 3—Hat* renamed to *Hi Hat*

When you're done, your Edit window should look like Figure 3.13

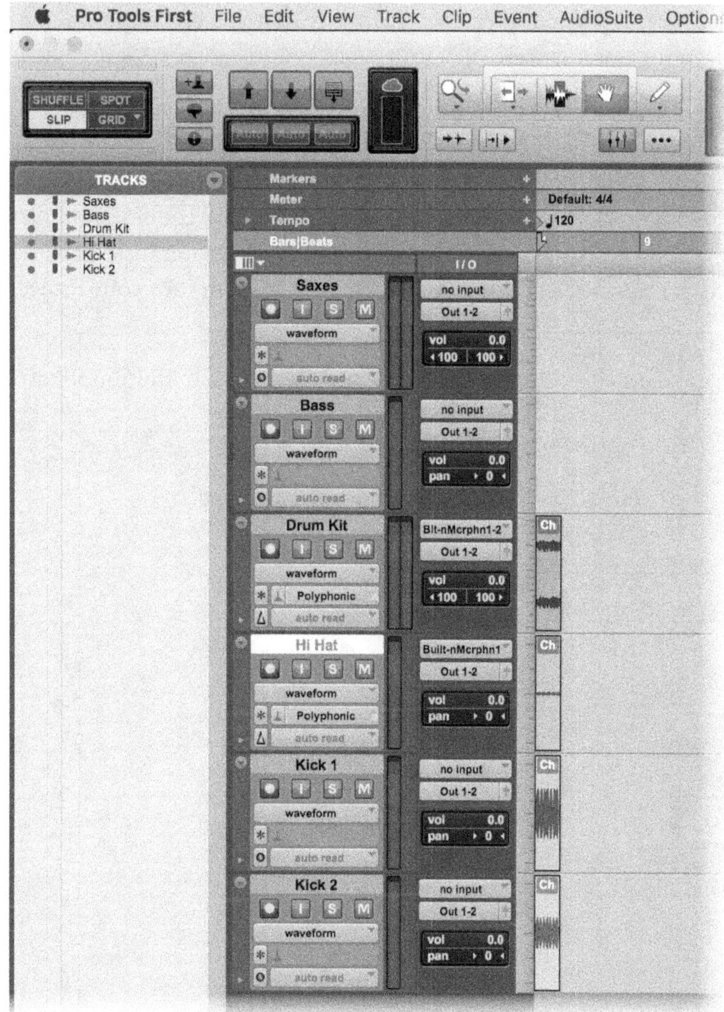

Figure 3.13 Your Tracks, Reordered and Renamed

13. Now let's have some fun. From the OPTIONS menu, turn on LOOP PLAYBACK.
14. Click any clip to select it. Note that when you select a clip, a corresponding area in the Bars|Beats ruler is also selected.
15. Press the SPACEBAR to begin playback. You should hear all four tracks together (you can test this by individually soloing each track). If you're not hearing any of these tracks, check to make sure that the track's output is set correctly. If the outputs look like they're correctly set, go to SETUP>PLAYBACK ENGINE to make sure that the Playback Engine and Default Output settings are configured to match your audio hardware.
16. You're done with this hand-on exercise—before you move on, make sure to save your work!

The Workspace/Soundbase Browser

While dragging audio files from your computer's operating system is certainly one way that you can import audio, searching for the file you want can be pretty painful. For example, if I search for "vocal" in my Mac's Finder window, I'll see PDF files, videos, emails—everything with the word "vocal" in it! Fortunately, there's another way to locate files that's customized for Pro Tools—the Workspace and the Soundbase.

Think of the Workspace as similar to your computer's file browser but designed specifically for use within Pro Tools. From the Workspace browser, you can quickly find audio files, sessions, and other Pro Tools-related files without any of the distractions that commonly come with using a generic file browser. The Soundbase browser is a further customized version of the Workspace, set up to easily find audio files and get them into your Project or Session.

In Pro Tools | First, while you don't have the Workspace available, you have its customized version, the Soundbase. Let's look at what you can do with it:

Opening the Soundbase Browser

Opening the Soundbase is very easy:

- From the WINDOW menu, choose SOUNDBASE, as shown in Figure 3.14.

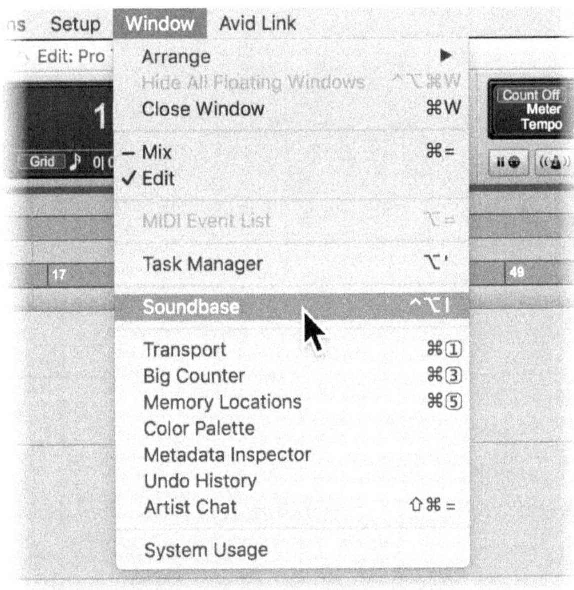

Figure 3.14 Opening the Soundbase Window

OR

- Press the SOUNDBASE button from the QUICK BUTTONS menu

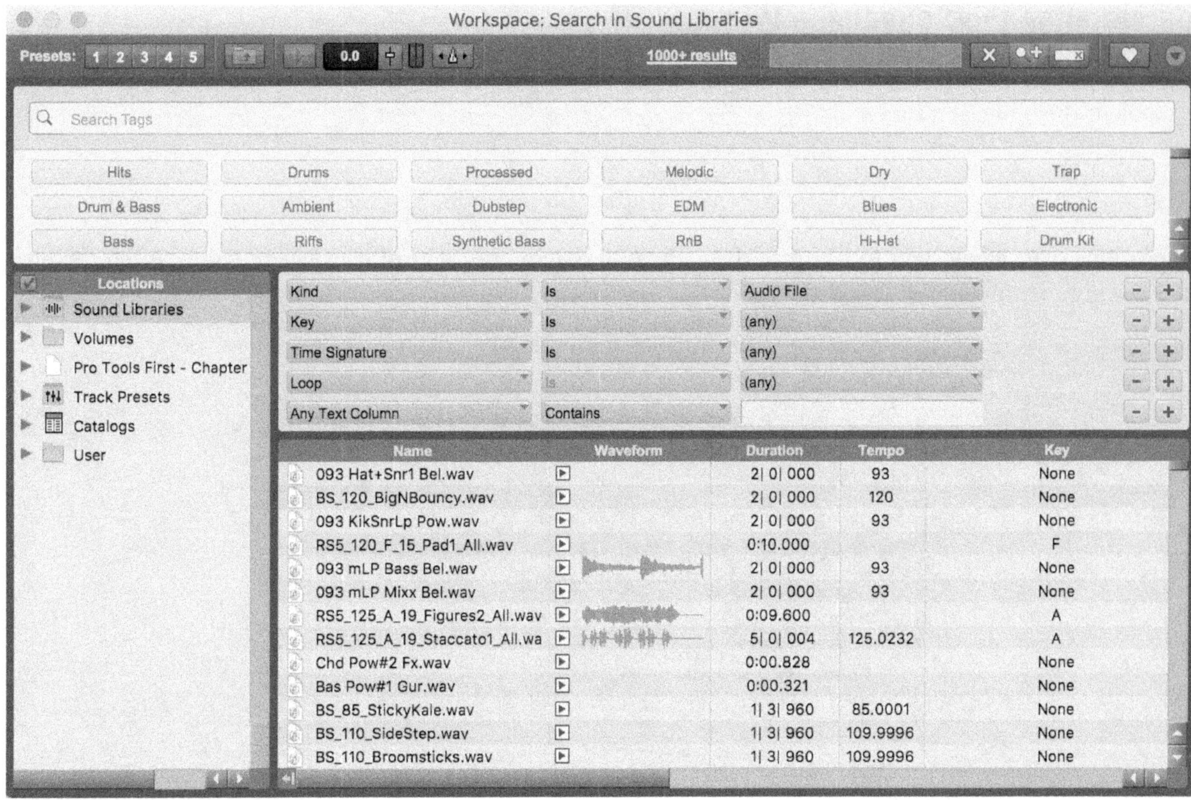

Figure 3.15 Opening the Soundbase Window from the Quick Buttons

OR

- Press CONTROL+OPTION+I (Mac), or START+ALT+I (Windows)

The Soundbase window will appear, as shown in Figure 3.16:

Figure 3.16 The Soundbase Window

Understanding the Soundbase Window

The Workspace/Soundbase window is broken into four primary parts, plus some useful tools at the top of it. Let's take a look at them one at a time:

The Locations Pane

The Locations pane allows you to navigate through your system and control over where you'll search for files. There are a number of items in this list:

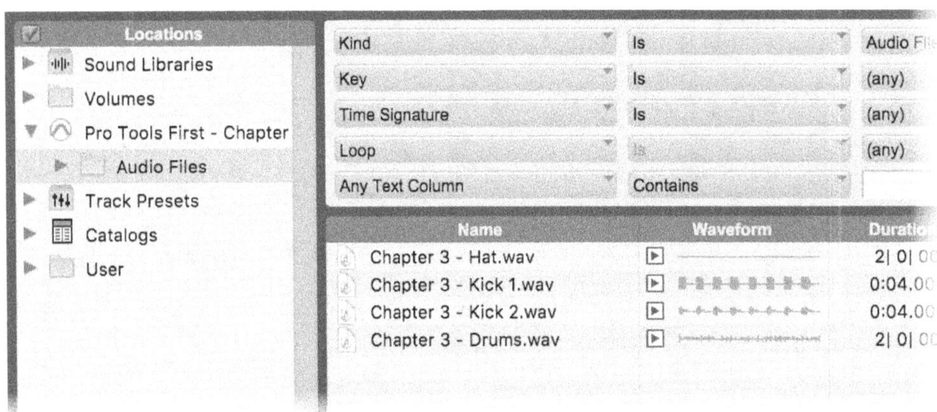

Figure 3.17 The Soundbase Window's Location Pane

- **Sound Libraries:** This item gives you quick and easy access to any folders that you designate as locations for your sound libraries, in addition to the sound libraries that are automatically installed when Pro Tools | First is installed. You'll learn how to customize Soundbase by adding your own sound libraries to this searchable area later in the chapter.

Sound libraries are collections of sounds for different purposes. For music producers, they might be a collection (either purchased or compiled by the user themselves, or both) of drum hits, bass loops, phrases, and more. For a Pro Tools user who is focused on audio for film, sound libraries would contain things like footstep sounds, sound effects, atmospheric sounds, and other commonly used audio segments. As you grow in your Pro Tools experience, you'll build your own libraries and perhaps buy some from third parties—the Soundbase makes it easy to quickly search your ever-growing collection!

- **Volumes:** Clicking on the disclosure triangle next to the Volumes item will display all of your attached hard drives (including your internal hard drive), enabling you to navigate to specific locations, similar to a traditional computer's file browser.
- The next item will be named after your Project and will allow you to see the individual audio files imported or recorded into your Project, as shown in Figure 3.18.

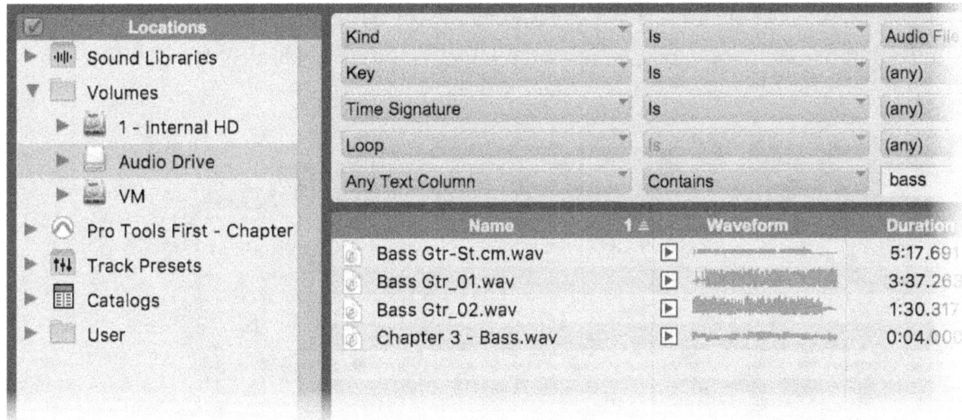

Figure 3.18 Showing Your Project's Audio Files

- **Track Presets:** Let's say that you customize a track with plug-ins, sends, and more. Pro Tools lets you save that track as something called a Track Preset, which you can easily recall again in a future Project. The topic of Track Presets is beyond the scope of this book, but when you do create them, they will be accessible from here.
- **Catalogs:** This is another topic that is beyond the scope of this book, but simply put, Catalogs are a collection of file aliases, allowing users to set up quickly searchable folders of their favorite sounds.
- **User:** Disclosing this item will give you quick access to your Desktop, Documents folder, and your User folder.

At the top of the Locations pane, you'll see a check box in the upper left-hand corner called the SEARCH CHECKED button. When this button is dark grey, any search you do will be limited to your selected location. For example, in Figure 3.19, my search is limited to my Audio Drive.

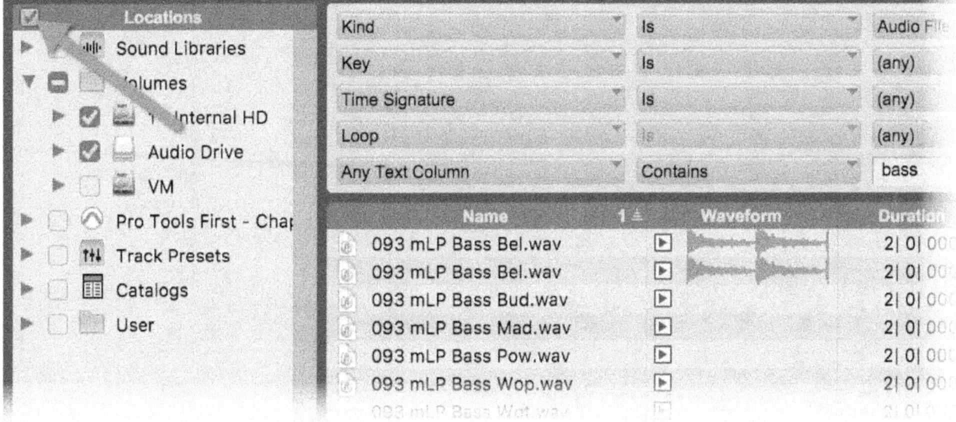

Figure 3.19 Searching For Bass files in the Audio Drive

When you click the SEARCH CHECKED button, it will turn green. Now, you can search multiple locations simultaneously. You can choose the locations that you want to search by clicking the appropriate check box. In Figure 3.20, I am searching in my Audio Drive and my internal hard drive.

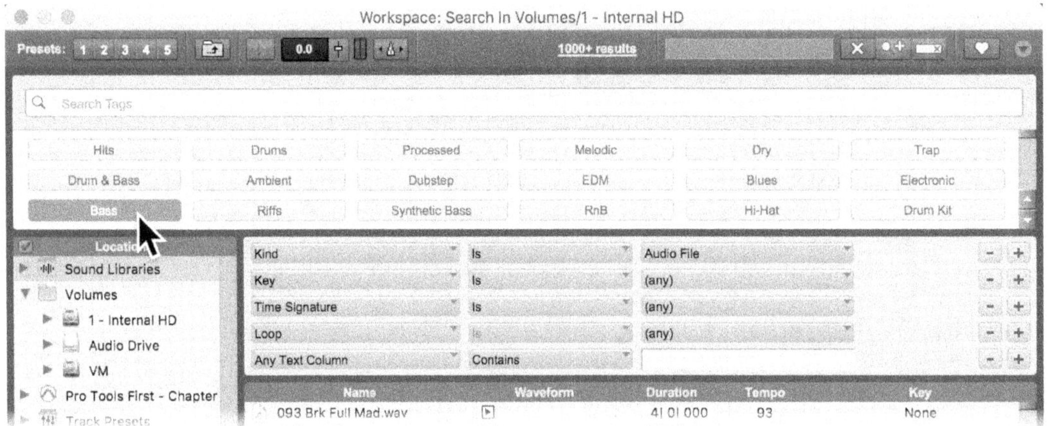

Figure 3.20 Searching for Bass files in the Internal Hard Drive and Audio Drive

The Tags Pane

At the top of the window, you'll see a large section with named buttons. Each of these buttons refers to a *tag* (something you'll learn about later in this chapter), which allows you to quickly search for files that are "tagged" with a keyword.

Here's how you might use this section in a workflow: Let's say that I want to search for just the right bass file. I'll click on the button with the word "Bass" as shown in Figure 3.21.

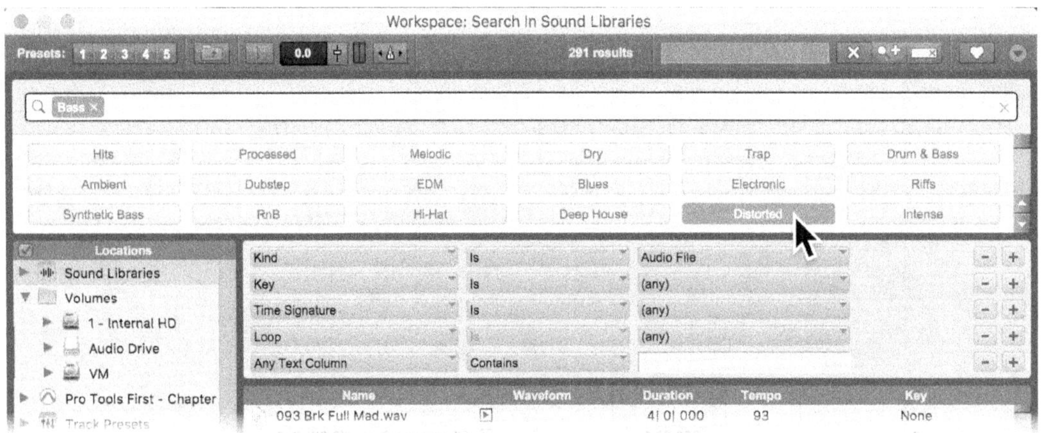

Figure 3.21 Searching for Files That Are Tagged with the Key Word "Bass"

You'll see in Figure 3.22 that the names on the buttons have changed. What you will now see are all of the remaining searchable tags for any files that are also tagged with the keyword "Bass", refining your search. Now let's say that I want a distorted bass, so I'll click the button with the word "Distorted".

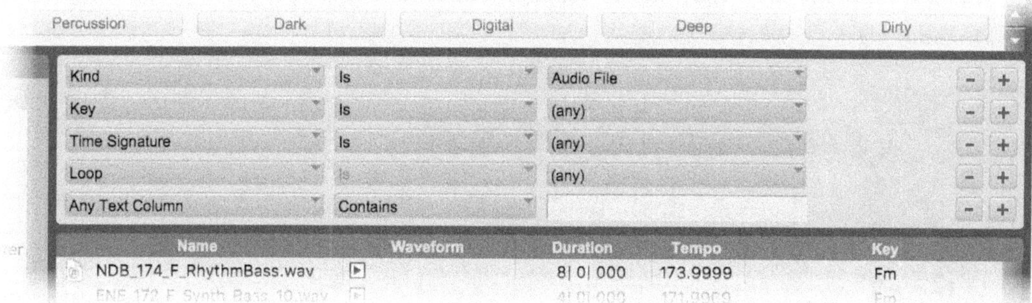

Figure 3.22 Refining the Search . . .

Again, the search will be narrowed down, and the buttons will be renamed accordingly. In the case of this example, your search results would only show files that have *both* "Bass" and "Distorted" tags. Using these searchable tags, it's easy to find just what you were looking for.

Tags must be manually applied to audio files. With the sound libraries that are installed with Pro Tools I First, that work has already been done for you. However, you can add your own tags and make this workflow even more powerful! You'll learn more about how to add your own tags later in this chapter.

The Advanced Search Settings Pane

Below the Tags pane are some additional ways that you can filter your searches. By default, you can filter your search by the *Kind* of file, *Key*, *Time Signature*, whether the file is a *Loop* or not, or by *Any Text Column* (if you're searching by name, here's where you would generally type it). When you open the Soundbase window, your advanced search settings will be set to limit any search results to only show audio files, as shown in Figure 3.23.

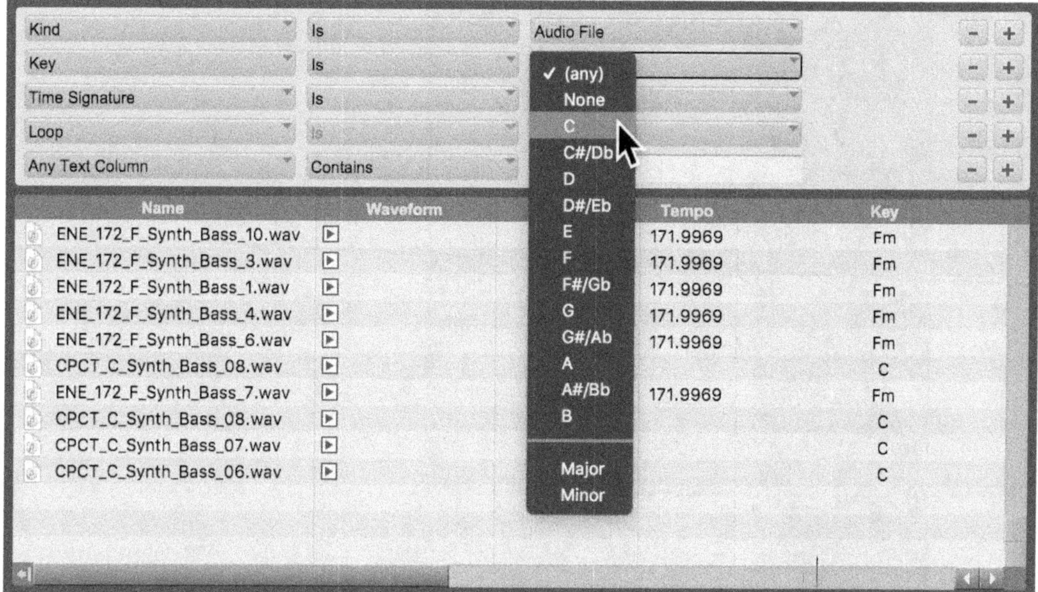

Figure 3.23 The Advanced Search Settings Pane

You can change any filter criterion anytime you want. In Figure 3.24, for example, I'll add another filter to my search, looking only for audio files in the key of C.

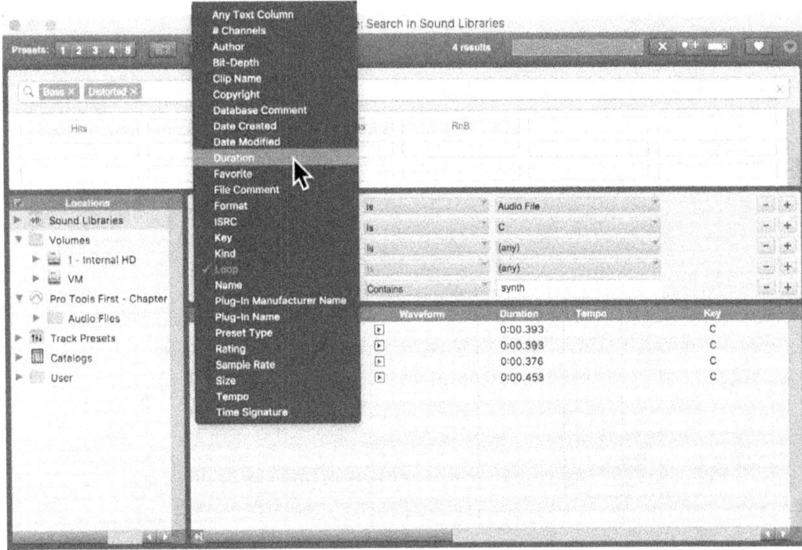

Figure 3.24 Refining a Search to Add Key Restrictions

If five different search filters aren't enough for you, you can add a row of criterion by clicking a plus (+) button on the right hand side of the Advanced Search section, or if you want to remove a row, just click the minus (-) button.

If you want to change one of the filters, just click on the SEARCH COLUMN SELECTOR menu button to change your search type. Figure 3.25 shows me changing the row from filtering by Loop to filtering by Duration.

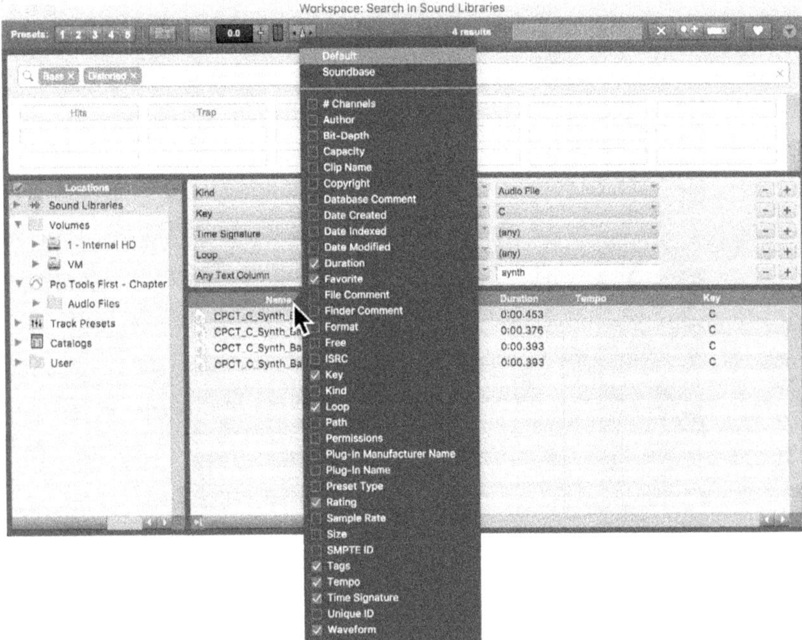

Figure 3.25 Changing a Search Type

The Browser Pane

The Browser pane (directly below the Advanced Search Settings pane) will display the contents of any folder that you navigate to in the Locations Pane, or the results of any search. There's a lot of information that is shown in this area in addition to file names. For example, in the Waveform column, you will see a graphic representation of the audio's waveform; in the Tempo column, you'll see the tempo that the audio was originally recorded at, file comments, and more.

You can change what a column is showing by right-clicking in the column heading, which will reveal a list of options for you to choose from, as shown in Figure 3.26. Column types that are already shown in the Browser pane are indicated with a checkmark.

Figure 3.26 Changing a Column in the Browser Pane

Don't worry if there's not enough space in your window to see all the columns that you want to see: You can use the scroll bar at the bottom of the Browser pane to navigate left or right.

The Toolbar

Last but not least are the buttons and tools at the top of the browser. Let's take a look at each, moving from left to right:

Figure 3.27 The Soundbase Window Toolbar

You have five user-defined preset Soundbase window layouts in that you can store. When you get the window just right, showing and hiding what suits a particular workflow, you can save the window layout as a preset for easy recall later. Just hold the COMMAND key (Mac) or CTRL key (Windows) and click on the numbered VIEW PRESET button where you want to store your layout. After that, any time you want to recall that layout, just click the corresponding VIEW PRESET button (no modifier key needed).

Figure 3.28 View Presets

The folder icon to the right of the VIEW PRESET buttons (called the PARENT FOLDER button) will go up one level when you are in a directory's subfolder. For example, if you are in a folder with a path of AUDIO/DRIVE/SOUND EFFECTS/FOOTSTEPS, clicking the PARENT FOLDER button once will move up one level to the AUDIO/DRIVE/SOUND EFFECTS folder.

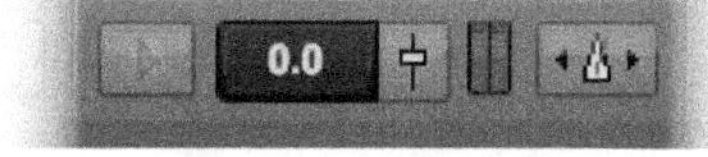

Figure 3.29 The Parent Folder Button

Any selected file can be listened to before you import it into your Project. Workspace/Soundbase *Preview Controls* will allow you to preview audio files within the browser in a number of different ways.

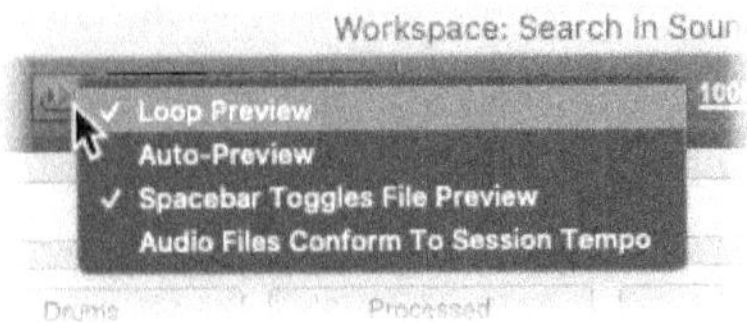

Figure 3.30 Preview Controls

On the leftmost side of the preview controls, the PREVIEW button icon will start and stop playback of the audio file that is selected in the Browser pane. If you right-click this button, you'll find that you have some preview options:

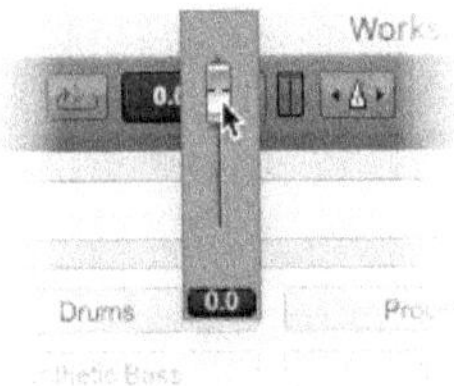

Figure 3.31 Preview Options

- **Loop Preview:** When this option is selected, your previewed file will play and repeat endlessly until you press the PREVIEW button again to stop playback. This is especially useful for previewing phrases that will repeat in your Project, like drum loops.
- When the **Auto-Preview** option is selected, selecting a file (by clicking it in the Browser pane) will automatically begin the preview process. To stop preview, click the PREVIEW button.
- **Spacebar Toggles File Preview:** When this option is enabled, pressing your computer's spacebar will start and stop preview of the selected file (just as your spacebar starts and stops playback in the Edit and Mix windows.
- **Audio Files Conform to Session Tempo:** This is *cool.* When enabled, any previewed audio file will automatically match the tempo of the currently open Project, even if the file was recorded at a different tempo. This enables you to listen to your audio at the right tempo before you import it.
- Right next to the PREVIEW button is your *Preview Volume* display and control. This shows you the level of your previewed audio's playback, which can be changed by clicking and holding on the display or the fader button to the left of the display. A fader will be revealed, as shown in Figure 3.32. Continuing to hold down your mouse, drag the fader up or down to reach the desired preview volume (the value in the preview volume display will change as you make your adjustments). The small meter to the right of the control will indicate the output level of your previewed audio as it plays.

Figure 3.32 Changing Your Preview Volume

- To the right of the preview volume control, the AUDIO FILES CONFORM TO SESSION TEMPO button mirrors the option of the same name that you saw previously in the Preview button menu. You can enable or disable this option by clicking the button—if the button is colored green, the option is enabled.

On the rightmost side of the toolbar are the *Search Tools*:

Figure 3.33 Search Tools

- The *Search Field* is where you can type in a word to search if you are *not* using any of the advanced search features. If you are using advanced search features, then this field will be grey and inaccessible as shown in Figure 3.33.
- The *X* button will cancel any search in progress and clear any advanced search criteria. The button will then turn into a magnifying glass, indicating that a standard search (which you'll learn about later in this chapter) can be done, and the search field next to it will be accessible.
- The button with a Magnifying Glass and a Plus Sign will enable or disable the Advanced Search Settings and show or hide the window's Advanced Search Settings pane.
- The button with a Tag icon will enable or disable the Tags pane of the window.
- The *Heart* button will filter the Files shown in the Browser pane to show only files that you've tagged as favorites.

Finally, in the rightmost corner of the browser window is a circular button. Clicking this will display the Browser pop-up menu, giving you access to browser-related options.

Soundbase Workflows

Now that you know a bit about the different parts of the Soundbase, the workflow of searching, previewing, and importing audio is probably starting to become apparent. By way of example, here are a few ways that I could search for the right guitar audio file.

Basic Search

Let's start off with a basic simple search. To do this, simplify the Soundbase to operate just like a basic Workspace browser:

1. First, I'll click the X button to clear any searches that might be in progress. Note that this button will change to a magnifying glass. At the same time, the Advanced Search Settings will be deactivated, and the search field at the top of the window will become active, indicating I'm ready to search, but this time without any Advanced Search Settings applied.

Figure 3.34 Deactivating Advanced Search

2. Next, I will also hide the Tags pane by clicking the TAGS button. At this point, Soundbase has been reduced to a Workspace browser. From this point, searching will be easy.

Figure 3.35 Deactivating the Tags Pane

You might notice at some point that the Browser pane's color has changed from green to blue. When the rows in that section are green, that's an indication that a search is in progress. When the rows are blue, that means it's operating as a basic file browser (but still with the benefits of preview tools, etc.).

3. Type a keyword into the search field.
4. In the Locations pane, choose the volume that you want to search. Note that the results you see in the Browser pane will change according to your search location.

One easy way to search your entire system is to choose "Volumes" in the Locations pane. All attached drives will be included in your search.

Advanced Search

When you search by keyword only, the kinds of results that you'll see in the Browser pane might be more than what you're actually looking for. For example, if I search the word "guitar" on my system, I'll see all kinds of different files, all of which have relevance to Pro Tools in some way, but may not be the kind of file I'm looking for. Fortunately, the Advanced Search options will help you narrow in on exactly what you're looking for.

1. In order to re-enable the window's Advanced Search features, click the ADVANCED SEARCH button, as shown in Figure 3.36. The button will be displayed with a blue color, and the Advanced Search Settings Pane will appear.

Figure 3.36 Re-activating the Advanced Search Pane

2. Since I am looking for an audio file, I'll make sure that in the Advanced Search Settings Pane, in the *Kind* row, the only type of file that will be included in the results is an audio file (conveniently, this is set by default).
3. By default, the *Any Text Column* row is at the bottom of the pane. This is a convenient place to type what I'm looking for, in this case, guitar.

The ***Any Text Column*** **search filter will only show results that have a given word in any of their columns (including comments, Project name, etc.). If you want to limit your search only to files that have that word in their file** ***name*****, change the** ***Any Text Column*** **search criterion to** ***Name*****.**

Your search results are still determined by your setting in the Locations Pane. As shown in Figure 3.37, in my case, I'm only seeing results found in the Audio Drive hard drive. Additionally, my search is being refined with the Advanced Search features, so that I'm only seeing audio files with the word "guitar" in any of the columns.

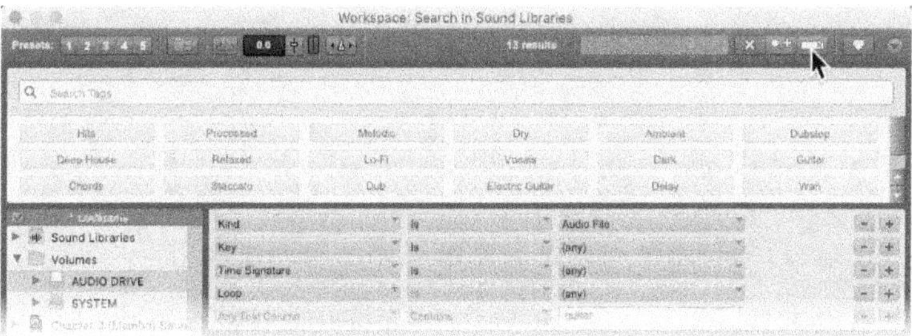

Figure 3.37 The Search Results

Searching by Tag

Finally, you can search by file *Tags*. Currently, the only tagged files you're likely to have in your system are part of the installed sound libraries, but later in this chapter, you'll learn how to add your own tags and sound library locations, making this way of searching even more effective.

1. At the top of the window, click the TAGS button to reveal the Tags section of the browser, if it isn't already visible (when the Tags pane is visible, this button will appear colored blue). At this point, the browser effectively becomes Soundbase again.

Figure 3.38 Showing the Tags Pane

2. You can start your search in two ways:

   - Click the button named for the tag that you want to search (in my case, the GUITAR button)

   OR

   - Type a keyword that you want to search in the Search Tags field at the top of the Tags Pane. Pro Tools will *auto-complete* as you type, based upon the tags available.

3. You can further refine your search by adding more tags to the search criteria.

Figure 3.39 shows the results—*three* different kinds of filtering working together:

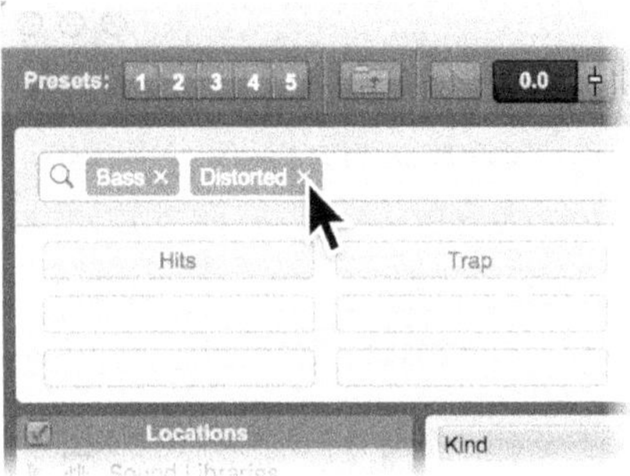

Figure 3.39 Search Results!

- In the Locations pane, only files in the Sound Libraries locations will appear as results in the Browser pane.

AND

- In the Advanced Search Settings pane, only audio files will be shown as results in the Browser pane.

AND

- In the Tags pane, only files that have both a *Guitar* and an *Electric Guitar* tags will be shown as results in the Browser pane.

So, only audio files in the Sound Libraries with Guitar and Electric Guitar tags will show up in your search!

One more thing: In order to remove a Tag from the SEARCH TAGS field, just click the X in the desired tag, as shown in Figure 3.40.

Figure 3.40 Removing a Tag

Previewing

Once the Browser pane shows you the files you want (either by searching or by navigating to the desired folder), you'll probably want to preview some before you commit to importing them.

1. Select the file that you want to preview.
2. Click the PREVIEW button.

OR

2. Click the small Waveform Preview button (to the left of the waveform waveform), as shown in Figure 3.41.

Figure 3.41 Another Way to Preview from the Start of a File

OR

2. Click at the desired location within the waveform display (as shown in Figure 3.42), and preview will begin at the point where you clicked.

Figure 3.42 Previewing from the middle of a file

Regardless of how you preview your file, your preview will follow the options that are selected in the PREVIEW button menu. Again, to get to this menu, just right-click on the Preview button, or choose the options from the Browser pop-up menu.

As you learned already, you can adjust the volume of your previewed file by adjusting the preview volume controls. Clicking the AUDIO FILES CONFORM TO SESSION TEMPO button will ensure that any musical phrases that you preview will be played in the tempo of your current Project, regardless of their original tempo! These two features are huge timesavers; a computer's file browser cannot perform these functions.

But the news gets even better. You can preview audio in the Soundbase browser while your Project is playing. For example, you could start a looped selection in your Edit window (the phrase will play repeatedly), and then go into Soundbase. If the AUDIO FILES CONFORM TO SESSION TEMPO button is green, any previewed musical phrase will play back in the same tempo as your Project. It will even wait until the downbeat to start play back, so that your phrases are aligned properly!

Of course, not all audio files are musical phrases, so not all files should change according to the tempo of your Project. Not a problem, though—Pro Tools will analyze the files in your browser before you preview, looking for a recognizable pattern of transients (rapid changes in amplitude, like drum hits). If Pro Tools finds a pattern, it will assume that the file is a musical phrase and can conform it to the Project tempo. If there is no pattern (as would be the case in a single drum hit), Pro Tools will determine that the file is not a musical phrase and will play it at its original speed, regardless of the AUDIO FILES CONFORM TO SESSION TEMPO setting.

In order for this workflow to work the way you want, your Project's tempo must be set correctly. This is something you will learn more about in Chapter 6, when we talk about MIDI.

Importing

You searched for your audio and previewed a few of your options, and now you're ready to import your choice into your Project. This process is very similar to importing from your computer's file browser window.

1. Position your cursor in the Browser pane, over the name or icon of the file that you wish to import. Your cursor will turn into a small hand icon as shown in Figure 3.43.

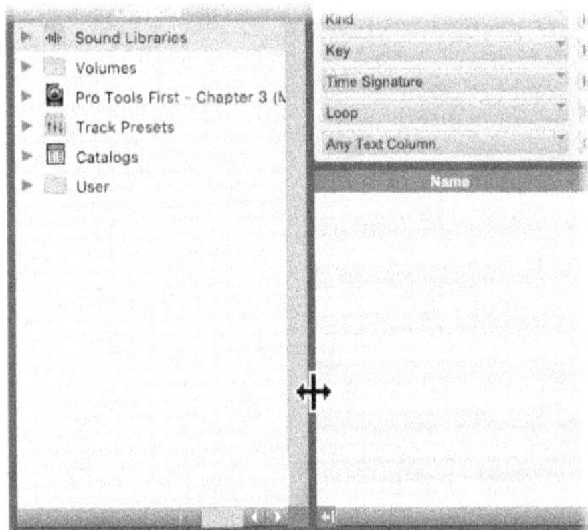

Figure 3.43 Ready to Drag

2. Now, you're ready to drag your audio into your Project, and just like dragging from your computer's browser window, there are a number of different ways you can do it:
   - If you drag a file from the Soundbase window into the Tracks List, a new track will be created, and the clip will be placed at the beginning of the timeline (the same result as if you imported the file using the FILE>IMPORT method).
   - If you drag from the the Soundbase window into a blank area in the Edit window's track area (where there are no tracks), you will see an outline where the file will be deposited. Once you drop the file, a new Audio track will be created with a clip where you dropped the file.
   - If you drag a file onto an existing track, you will see an outline where that file will be deposited once the mouse is released. Once the mouse is released, a new clip will be placed on the track, this time without a new track being created.

Similar to importing via your computer's file browser, in Pro Tools and Pro Tools I Ultimate, there is an additional way to import from the Workspace or Soundbase. Dragging from the browser window into the Clips List will import the audio, but without creating any tracks or placing a clip on the timeline of any existing track. Because Pro Tools I First does not have a Clips List, this method of importing is not available.

Hands-On Exercise 3.2: Importing from the Soundbase Browser

You now know how to make the best use of the Soundbase. Now, let's use it to choose the best Guitar part for Mambo.

This exercise assumes that you've already completed exercise #3.1. The Project should already have four imported files (Drum Kit, Hi Hat, Kick 1, and Kick 2), and also be in loop playback mode.

Setting Up

1. From the WINDOW menu, open the SOUNDBASE.
2. Select any clip in the Edit window and press the SPACEBAR. Since you are in LOOP PLAYBACK mode, your selected area on the timeline will play back repeatedly.
3. In the Soundbase window, navigate to your downloaded exercise file, and from there, to the *Pro Tools First—Chapter 3—Audio Files for Import* folder
4. Make sure that the AUDIO FILES CONFORM TO SESSION TEMPO button is green, indicating that the option is enabled.

Importing a Guitar Part

5. Preview both the *Chapter 3—Guitar 1.wav* and *Chapter 3—Guitar 2.wave* files while the loop plays. If you need to adjust the volume of the preview, you can do that with the Preview Volume controls.
6. Once you've chosen your preference, drag the file into the Tracks List, creating a new track with the clip at the beginning of the timeline.

Importing Other Tracks

7. Import the *Chapter 3—Trumpets.wav* file to a new track. If necessary, use the Grabber tool to position the clip at the beginning of the timeline.
8. Import the *Chapter 3—Piano.wav* file to a new track. If necessary, use the Grabber tool to position the clip at the beginning of the timeline.
9. Import the *Chapter 3—Saxes.wav* file to the *Saxes* Track. Use the Grabber tool to position the clip at the beginning of the timeline.
10. Import the *Chapter 3—Bass.wav* file to the *Bass* Track. Use the Grabber tool to position the clip at the beginning of the timeline.

Cleaning Up

Let's build good habits and clean up the Project.

11. Rename the *Chapter 3—Guitar* (1 or 2) track to *Guitar*.
12. Rename the *Chapter 3—Trumpets* track to *Trumpets*.
13. Rename the *Chapter 3—Piano* track to *Piano*.
14. Reorder the tracks to be:
    - Saxes
    - Trumpets
    - Piano
    - Guitar
    - Bass
    - Drums
    - Hi Hat
    - Kick 1
    - Kick 2
15. Once you've reorganized your tracks, you're done with this hands-on exercise. Make sure to save your work before moving on!

Customizing the Soundbase

Before we leave this chapter, let's look at some ways that you can customize the Soundbase window and improve your workflow.

Changing the Soundbase Window

Let's start with a few ways that you can change the look of the Soundbase window:

- When you place your cursor at the boundary between the Locations pane and the Browser pane, as shown in Figure 3.44, it will turn into a double arrow icon. Click and drag this boundary to give you the space you need in either pane.

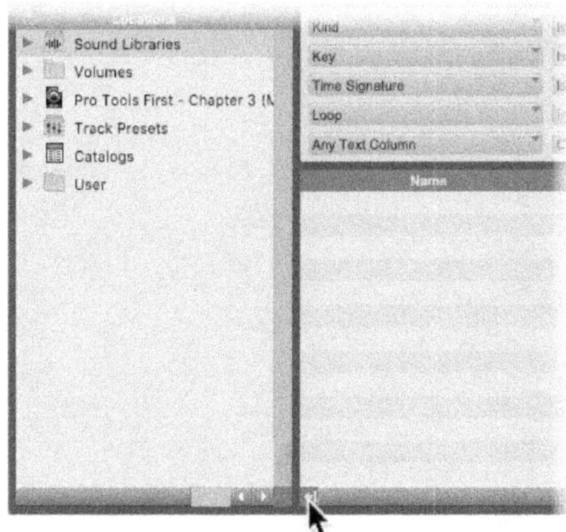

Figure 3.44 Adjusting Boundaries

- You can hide the Locations pane by clicking the small arrow icon in the lower left-hand corner of the Browser pane (as shown in Figure 3.45). This can be useful in giving you more visible information in the Browser pane. You can re-show the Locations pane by clicking the icon again (the arrow will appear the same but change direction).

Name	Waveform	Duration	Tempo	Key
093 mLP Bass Bel.wav		2| 0| 000	93	None
093 mLP Bass Bel.wav		2| 0| 000	93	None
093 mLP Bass Bud.wav		2| 0| 000	93.0004	None
093 mLP Bass Mad.wav		2| 0| 000	93.0004	None
093 mLP Bass Pow.wav		2| 0| 000	93.0004	None
093 mLP Bass Wop.wav		2| 0| 000	93.0004	None
093 mLP Bass Wot.wav		2| 0| 000	93	None
80s Dance Bass Synth 06.caf		0:02.098		None
80s Dance Bass Synth 07.caf		0:02.098		None
Alternative Rock Bass 01.caf		0:08.788		None
Alternative Rock Bass 02.caf		0:08.812		None
Alternative Rock Bass 03.caf		0:02.727		None
Alternative Rock Bass 04.caf		0:02.727		None

Figure 3.45 Hiding the Locations Pane

- Browser pane columns can be resized by moving your cursor to a column boundary. Your cursor will turn into a double arrow icon, after which you can drag your column widths as desired.

It's common for Pro Tools users to want to see more detail of the audio file in the Waveform column. Elongating the Waveform column will give you this extra detail.

- Columns can also be re-ordered. Just move your cursor over any column name, and it will turn into a hand icon, as shown in Figure 3.46. Just drag and drop the column to the desired location—a thick black line will indicate where the column will be deposited once the mouse is released.

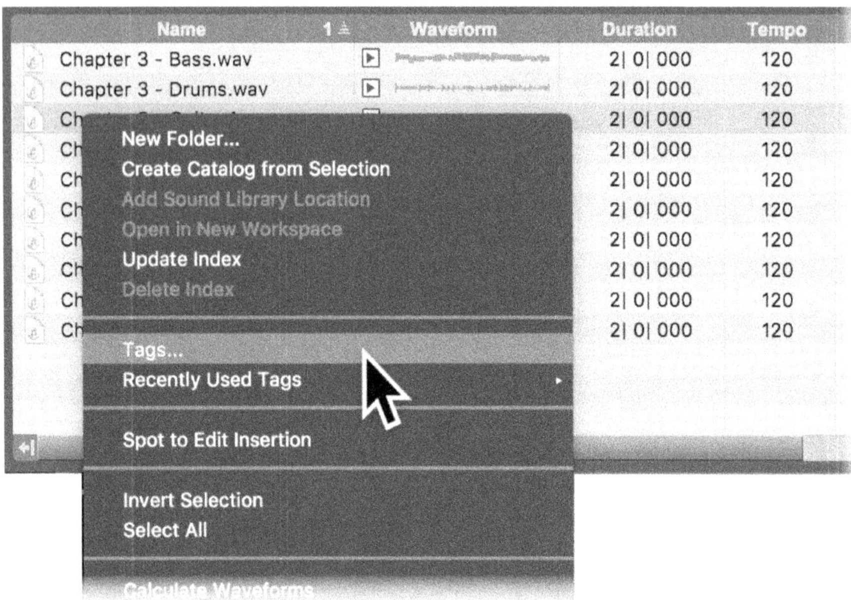

Figure 3.46 Moving Columns

- Finally, as with many windows, the Soundbase can be resized by moving your cursor to any corner of the window and dragging it accordingly.

As you have seen throughout this chapter, there are a lot of elements in the Soundbase window, and different elements will apply to different kinds of work. Earlier in this chapter, you saw the VIEW PRESET buttons (in the upper left-hand corner of the window), and now you can take full advantage of them. Just hold the COMMAND key (Mac) or the CTRL key (Windows) and click on the VIEW PRESET number button where you want to save your settings. Clicking the button again any time after that (with no modifier key needed) will recall the window size and layout.

Tags

You've already seen how searching by tag keyword can speed up the process of finding files that you want to bring into your Project. As you gain experience and collect files of your own that you frequently use in Projects, you'll want to expand your collection of searchable tags. Indeed, there are some professional careers, like sound design for movies or video games, that work with sound libraries so extensively that the ability to quickly find files is essential to getting the job done on time. For many kinds of work, the effort that you'll spend setting up your tags is time well spent and will save you much more time down the road.

Adding a tag to a file is a pretty straightforward process:

1. In the Soundbase window, right-click a file that you want to add a tag to. A menu will appear.
2. Choose TAGS from the menu, as shown in figure 3.47.

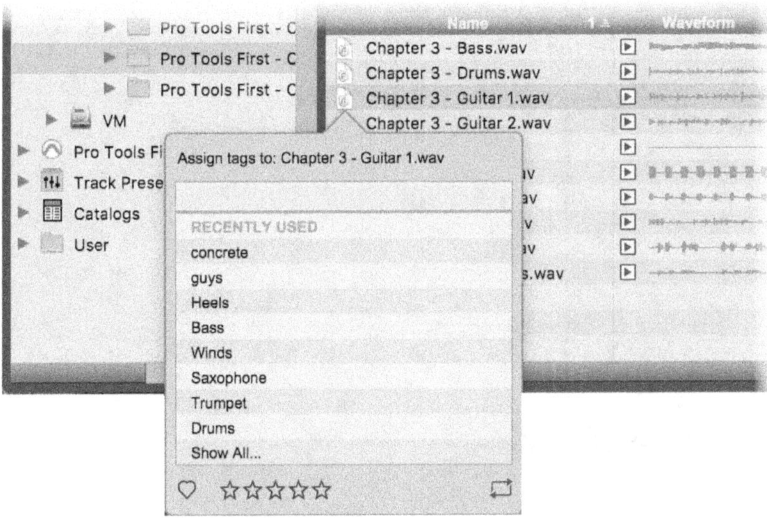

Figure 3.47 Right-Clicking the File to be Tagged

3. The window that appears, called the Assign Tags popover window, will show you a list of recently used tags. At the top of this window is a field showing all of the tags that the file currently has. In this case the *Guitar 1.wav* file has no tags.

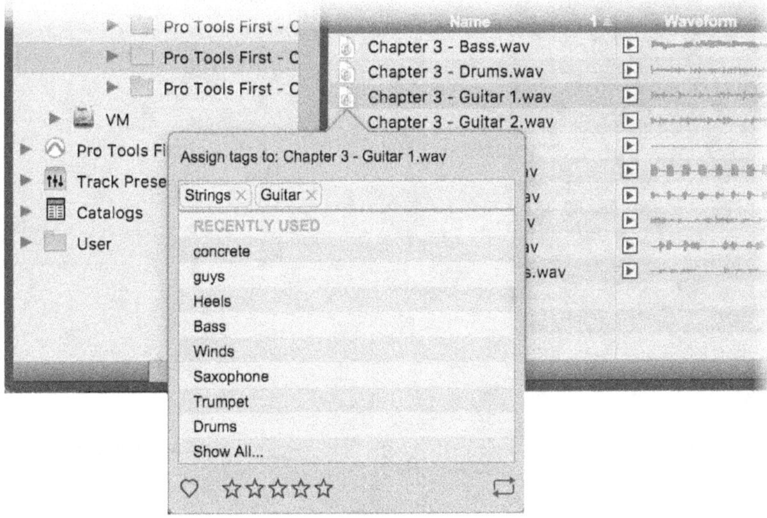

Figure 3.48 The Assign Tags Popover Window

4. Click the RECENTLY USED list item that you want to add as a tag. If you don't see what you want on the list, click the SHOW ALL... list item at the bottom of the popover window.

OR

4. Type a tag in the top Tags field.

Files can have multiple tags, and the more tags a file has, the more ways that you can search for it. I'm going to add two tags in this example. As shown in Figure 3.49, the file now has two tags: *Strings* and *Guitar*.

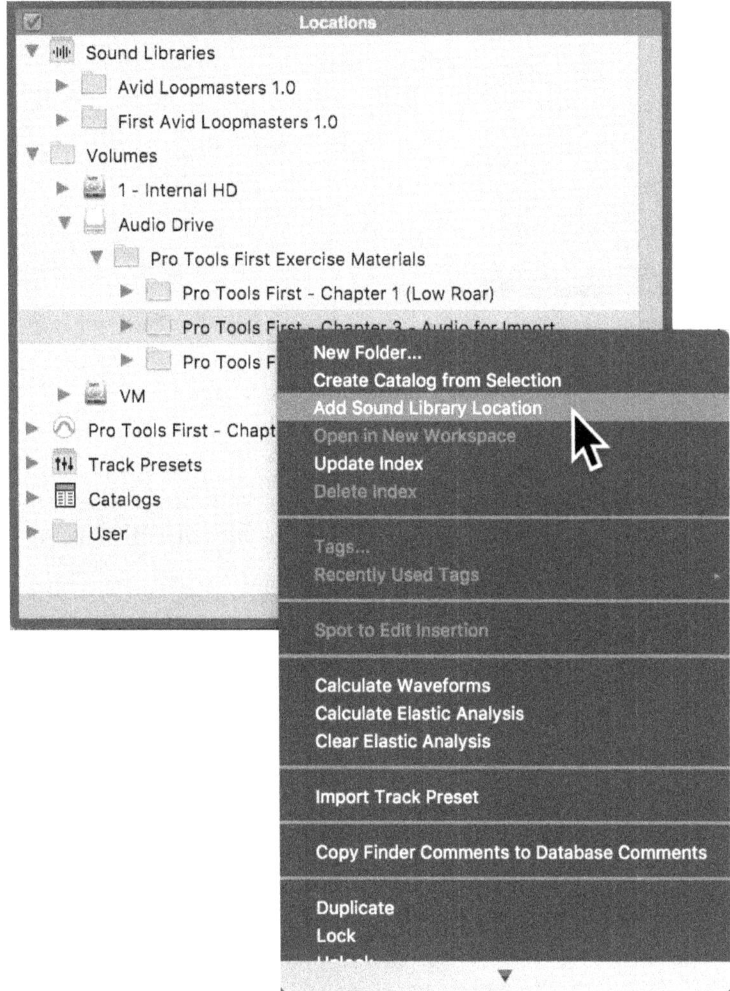

Figure 3.49 The Tagged File

At the bottom of the Assign Tags popover window, you'll find a series of icons. These are additional ways that a file can be tagged:

- On the far left-hand side is a heart icon. Clicking this icon will tag a file as a *favorite*. Files tagged as favorites are indicated by a blue heart in the Assign Tags popover window.

As you learned earlier in this chapter, you can limit your search results to favorites by clicking the heart icon at the top right-hand corner of the Soundbase window.

- You also have the ability to rate a file from one to five stars. Star ratings are indicated by blue stars (a 3-star rating, for example, would show 3 blue stars at the bottom of the Assign Tags popover window).

You can search by rating in the Advanced Search Settings pane. Just change any column selector button to RATING, and then adjust the additional settings in the row to refine your search.

- You can also tag a file as a loop. This is commonly done for drum loops or other repeating phrases. Just click on the rectangular Loop Icon in the bottom right-hand corner of the Assign Tags popover window (files that are tagged as loops will show this icon in a blue color).

You can limit your search to show only loops by changing the criterion in the Advanced Search Settings pane, in the Loop row, to "Set".

Setting Sound Libraries

As mentioned before, Pro Tools | First installs its own sound library, and the folder that contains those files is automatically added to the Sound Libraries Location. Your own tagged files will likely be saved in different folders. However, you'll typically want to be able to search your custom tagged files and the Pro Tools | First sound library at the same time. That's where adding a folder to the Sound Libraries location can come in handy.

1. In the Locations pane, navigate to the folder containing the tagged files that you want to add to your Sound Libraries location.
2. Right-click the folder, and a menu will appear.
3. Select ADD SOUND LIBRARY LOCATION from the menu (as shown in Figure 3.50), and the folder will be added to the Sound Libraries.

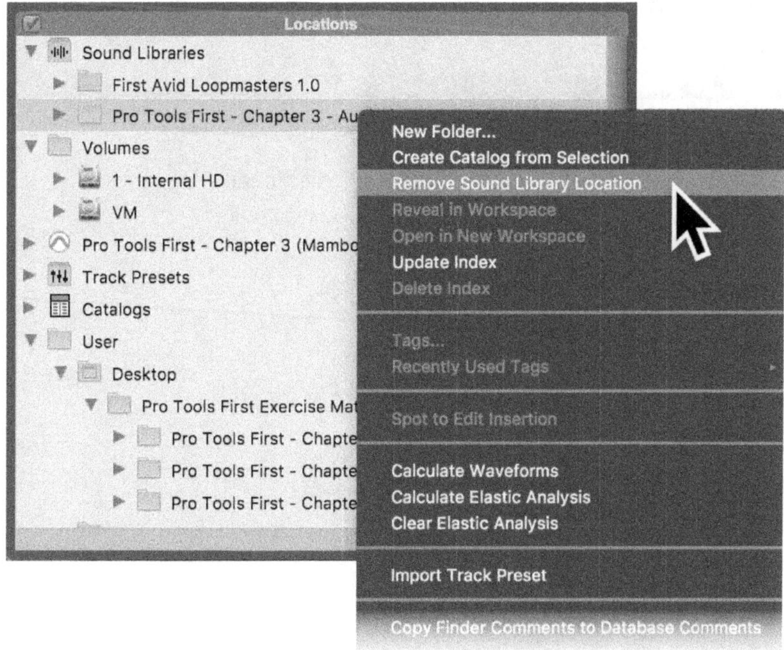

Figure 3.50 Adding a Folder to the Sound Libraries Location

You can see which folders are part of your Sound Libraries by clicking the disclosure triangle to the left of the Sound Libraries in the Locations pane. In my case, I've added the Pro Tools First—Chapter 3—Audio for Import to my Sound Libraries location. Now, when the Sound Libraries menu item is selected, tags will show up for the *First Avid Loopmasters 1.0* folder and the *Pro Tools First—Chapter 3—Audio for Import* folder.

To remove a folder from the Sound Libraries locations, just right-click the desired folder in the Sound Libraries and choose REMOVE SOUND LIBRARY LOCATION from the drop-down menu (as shown in Figure 3.51), and the folder will be removed.

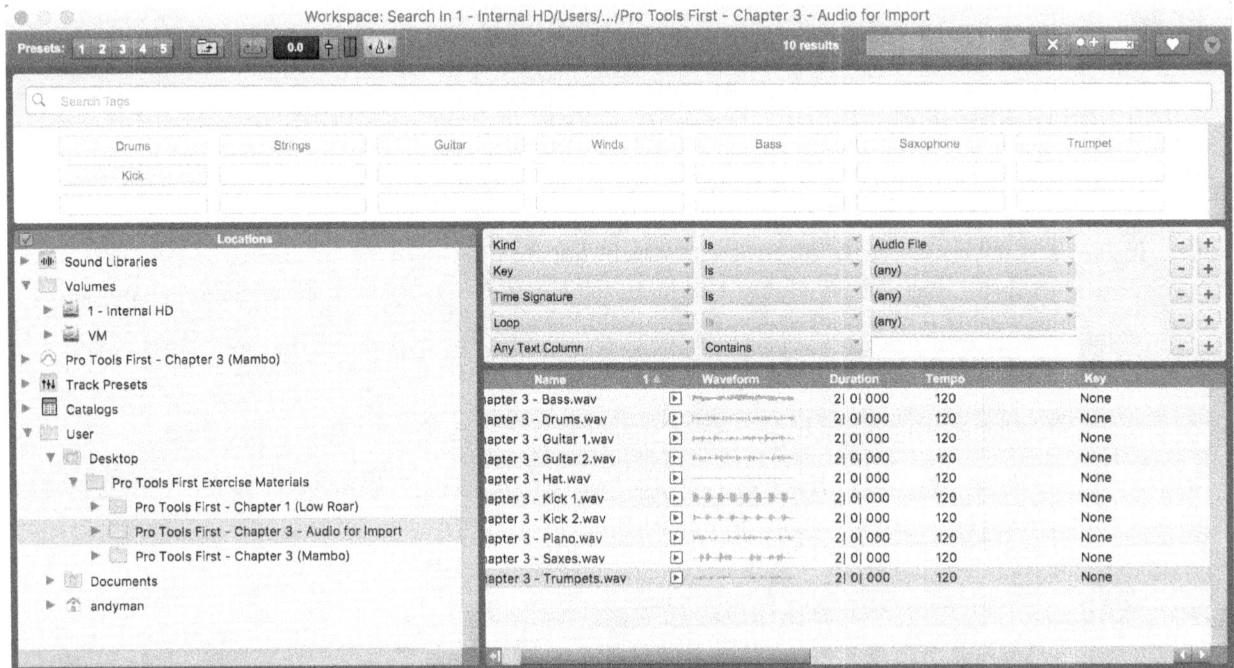

Figure 3.51 Removing a Folder from the Sound Libraries Location

At no time during this process were any files copied, moved, or deleted. The Sound Libraries is simply a collection of folder aliases that you can add to as your sound libraries grow.

Hands-On Exercise 3.3: Tagging Files

To wrap up this chapter, you're going to create tags for the files in the ***Pro Tools* | *First*—** *Chapter 3—Audio Files for Import* folder. At the end of this exercise, we'll even throw in a neat little trick that you can use to make your searches even more effective.

Setting Up

1. Using the Soundbase window, navigate in the Locations pane to ***Pro Tools* | *First*—** *Chapter 3—Audio Files for Import* folder. In the Browser pane, you should see 10 files:
    - Chapter 3—Bass.wav
    - Chapter 3—Drums.wav
    - Chapter 3—Guitar 1.wav
    - Chapter 3—Guitar 2.wav
    - Chapter 3—Hat.wav
    - Chapter 3—Kick 1.wav
    - Chapter 3—Kick 2.wav
    - Chapter 3—Piano.wav
    - Chapter 3—Saxes.wav
    - Chapter 3—Trumpets.wav

Adding Tags

2. Let's start with the largest groups—Winds, Strings, and Drums:
    - Assign the Tag "Winds" to the following: *Chapter 3—Saxes.wav* and *Chapter 3—Trumpets.wav*
    - Assign the Tag "Strings" to the following: *Chapter 3—Bass.wav*, *Chapter 3—Guitar 1.wav*, and *Chapter 3—Guitar 2.wav*
    - Assign the Tag "Drums" to the following: *Chapter 3—Drums.wav*, *Chapter 3—Hat.wav*, *Chapter 3—Kick 1.wav*, and *Chapter 3—Kick 2.wav.*
3. Now let's add a little bit more detail to a few of the files:
    - Add the Tag "Bass" to the following: *Chapter 3—Bass.wav*
    - Add the Tag "Guitar" to the following: Chapter 3—Guitar 1.wav, and Chapter 3—Guitar 2.wav
    - Add the Tag "Saxophone" to the following: *Chapter 3—Saxes.wav*
    - Add the Tag "Trumpet" to the following: *Chapter 3—Trumpets.wav*

- Add the Tag "Kick" to the following: *Chapter 3—Kick 1.wav*, and *Chapter 3—Kick 2.wav.*

4. Let's see what you've created: Make sure that the Tags pane is being displayed as shown in Figure 3.52. You should see eight different searchable tags:
   - Drums
   - Strings
   - Guitar
   - Winds
   - Bass
   - Saxophone
   - Trumpet
   - Kick

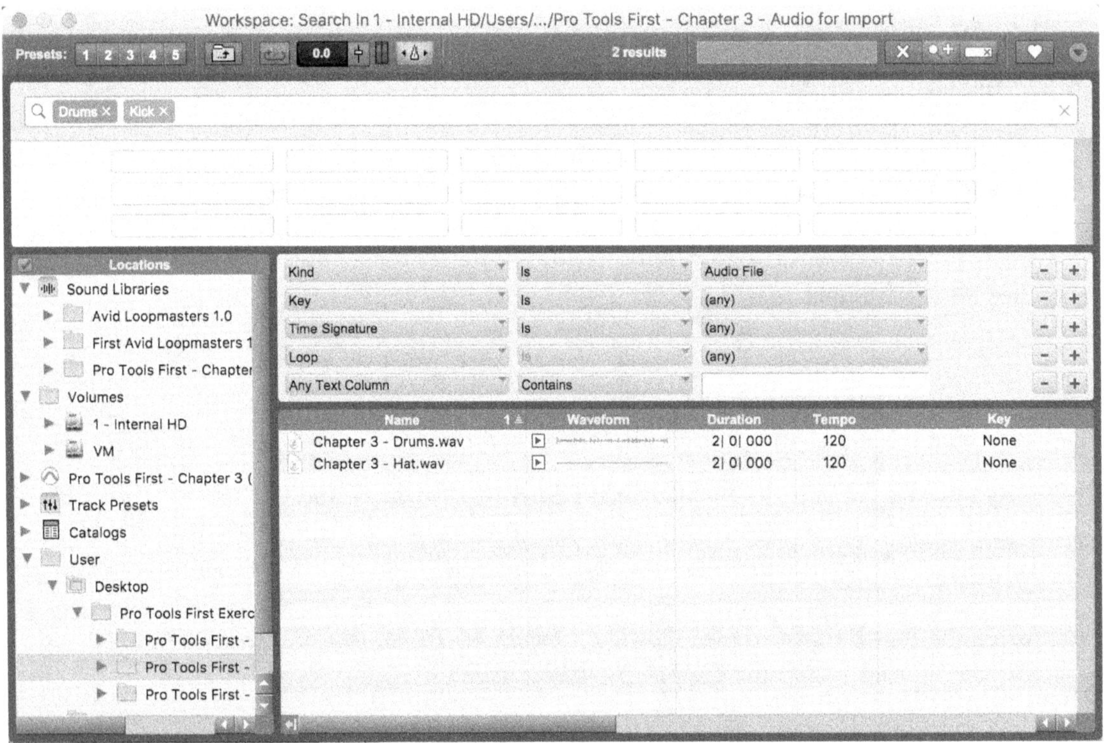

Figure 3.52 Your Searchable Tags

5. Click the *Strings* tag button. If you've assigned your tags correctly, the Tags pane will now show only show tag buttons for files that also have the Strings tag: *Guitar* and *Bass*. You'll also see in the Browser pane that the three files that have a *Strings* tag are displayed.
6. Click the *Bass* Tag button to further refine your search. A single file (*Chapter 3—Bass.wav*) will appear in your Browser pane.

7. Clear your search by clicking X in each tag in the SEARCH TAGS field. All the TAG buttons for this folder will reappear.

A New Way to Search by Tags

At this point, you've cleared all of the tags from your search. Here's the trick that I promised earlier:

8. Click the DRUMS tag button. You'll see that there is another tag—Kick—that's associated with at least some of the files that also have the Drums tag.

If I were to click the KICK tag button, only two files would appear in the Browser pane: Kick 1 and Kick 2. Those are the only files that have both a Drums tag *and* a Kick tag. But what if I want to see only the files that have the Drum tag and specifically do *not* have the Kick tag?

9. Hold down the OPTION key (Mac) or ALT key (Windows) and click the KICK tag button.

The Kick search tag will not appear as blue, but grey, which indicates it is excluding from the search results all Drums-tagged files that *also* have a Kick tag. As a result, you will see that the two Kick drum files have been removed from the search results, as shown in Figure 3.53.

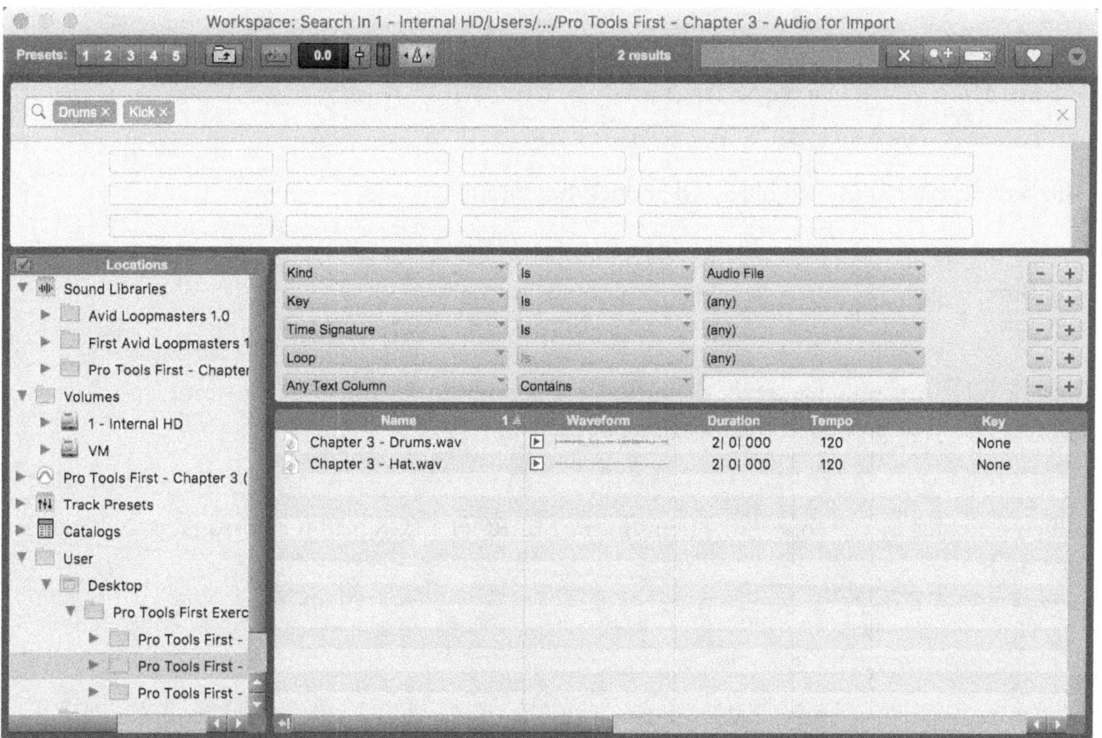

Figure 3.53 Files that Have a Drums Tag but Not a Kick Tag

You can also invert the search at any time (turning the search name from blue to grey, or from grey to blue) by holding the OPTION key (Mac) or ALT key (Windows) and clicking the SEARCH TAGS field entry that you want to change.

Well done! This concludes the exercises for chapter 3.

Review Questions

1. What two audio file formats are supported? Of the two, which sounds better?

2. What is the difference between interleaved files and non-interleaved?

3. True or False: It is possible to import audio to an existing track in your Project from FILE>IMPORT.

4. What will be the result if a file is dragged from your computer's file browser window into the Tracks List?

5. What does the small checkbox at the top left-hand corner of the Soundbase's Locations pane allow you to do?

6. What is a *Tag*? How can a file be Tagged?

7. The Browser pane is colored blue—what does that mean?

8. The Browser pane is colored green—what does that mean?

9. True or False: An audio file can be previewed at any point in the file (in other words, you don't have to start your preview at the beginning of the file).

10. When searching by tags, one of the items in the SEARCH TAGS field is colored grey—what does that mean?

CHAPTER 4

Editing Audio

You've created a project, made your tracks, and imported some audio to work with. The next step in the production process is editing—the adjusting, tweaking, and moving of elements in a project to a point where it's ready to be mixed. In this chapter, we'll focus on the basics of the editing process.

Media Used: *Pro Tools | First*—Fundamentals of Audio Production—Chapter 4a (Mambo Part 1).ptx, Pro Tools First—Fundamentals of Audio Production—Chapter 4b (Mambo Part 2).ptx

Duration: 45 minutes

GOALS

- Understand the components of a recording setup, and make the best choices for your needs
- Learn about the "big three" editing tools—Trim, Selector, and Grabber
- Learn how the Edit Modes work and when to use them
- Learn how to navigate your Project by zooming and scrolling

What is Editing?

To best understand just what exactly editing is, and how it's evolved over the years, it might be a good idea to step out of the audio realm. Since you're holding a book in your hands, let's see how editing has changed in the world of words.

Not as long ago as you might think, books and letters were written by hand or on the typewriter. Typewriters, the current technology at that time, were mechanical devices that placed ink on paper, but they didn't have an undo button for correcting mistakes. Editing back in those days involved all sorts of creative techniques–from painting over typographical errors with liquid paper, cutting and taping sections of pages together, to just giving up on trying to fix it, wadding up the paper and starting again. It was a time-consuming and expensive process, and even in the best cases, it didn't work all that well.

Coincidently, at the same time, audio studios were recording to magnetic tape, which posed some of the same kinds of editing problems. For example, if a musical note or phrase was wrong, it would have to be recorded over, and the engineer needed to have lightning-quick reflexes to make sure that only what was needed to be replaced was recorded over. It was literally "Cut and paste" process—the audio tape was cut with a razor blade and a block of metal, and different strips were then taped together. To make matters even worse, all these editing methods were destructive, so if a mistake was made, it couldn't be undone. Often, it was just best to go back to the beginning and start all over again.

Computers made their mark first in the publishing world, starting off by replacing typewriters, and opened new editing possibilities. Made a mistake? Delete it. Want to move a sentence? Cut and paste it. Change font size, change text to color—The sky was the limit!

And maybe that's the best way to think of audio editing in the modern age: DAWs are to audio what a word processor is to text. Starting with the simple process of cut, copy, and paste, the modern-day DAW can let you do just about anything: from reversing an audio file, to inverting its phase, to changing its amplitude, and more.

In normal production, the editing phase of production generally comes after the acquisition of audio (either through recording or by importing audio files) and before the mixing process. Different kinds of work involve different kinds of editing–for example, the way you edit a musical piece differs from the way you edit dialogue for a movie–but the essential tools that you learn in this chapter will work in all kinds of situations.

Careers in Editing: An Interview with Steven Saltzman

Up to this point in the book, the concepts and techniques you've learned are essential skills for any kind of work you can do in the audio world. There are many kinds of professional paths that will open up for those who are especially interested editing audio. There are professionals who focus specifically on different fields, such as music editing for pop songs to music, effects, and dialogue editing for TV and movie production, and much more.

But what kind of jobs are out there? What kind of skills does one need to be successful as a professional audio editor?

Steven Saltzman, AMPAS, MPSE, MPEG, is a music editor, composer and educator based in Los Angeles, CA. He holds a Bachelor of Music degree in composition and film scoring from Berklee College of Music, and is an Avid Certified Pro Tools instructor. He has been editing music for film and television for the past twenty years, including movies like Ghost Rider and The Revenant. A recipient of a Golden Reel Award for music editing, Steven is also a new member of the Academy of Motion Picture Arts and Sciences. He is also a member of the Motion Picture Editors Guild and the Society of Composers and Lyricists, and sits on the board of the newly formed Entertainment Industry Professionals Mentoring Alliance (EIPMA). In addition to teaching, lecturing and presenting workshops, Steven has also written a great book on the topic of music editing called "Music Editing for Film and Television," published by Routledge (**https://www.routledge.com/Music-Editing-for-Film-and-Television-The-Art-and-the-Process/Saltzman/p/book/9780415817578**).

Steven and I have known each other for a few years, so I thought I might touch base with him to get answers to these questions straight from the source:

Figure 4.1 Steven Saltzman

AH: So, Steven, what kinds of editing-centric jobs are out there for people entering the professional field?

SS: There are so many different visual and audio media that require audio editing—it's almost an endless list. My work tends to focus on feature films, and there are three main areas of sound work in that medium: dialogue editing, sound effects editing, and music editing, which are the three main parts of an audible sound track the audience hears when watching a movie or TV show. From there, it gets more detailed: There's sound design, sound effects, background effects, Foley, ADR (Automated Dialog Replacement) editing, temp music editing, song editing, and more. Taking this craft of audio editing further, there are many other fields that need sound editing work such as, TV broadcast, webinars, Web-TV, theater, documentaries, independent films, animation, short films, and song recording just to name a few.

AH: And what kind of technical and professional skills are needed for that kind of work?

SS: One must become proficient using Pro Tools because it has the widest reach worldwide. I would encourage you to master its editing tools because in the audio, music and post-production fields, it will be expected that you are a competent Pro Tools operator. To be more specific, you must be proficient working with clips, crossfading, track layout, and session management, so your work can be viewed and understood by another editor or mixer. Beyond the technical learning of Pro Tools or any DAW, if you aim to be an editor, you need to have a clear understanding of what is needed for a particular challenge, workflow, or 'puzzle', and be able to implement it in your DAW.

This learning is built over many years of practice, working with others and starting off with small jobs. When you're editing, step back and listen with critical ears—don't just accept the edit as perfect the first time. I need to practice this all the time! Often, we are misled that speed is looked at as a mastery of one's tools, but in my opinion, this is not necessarily so. I often notice that many experienced editors are not particularly fast, but they do it right the first time. This kind of technical experience combined with professional skills and the ability to build professional relationships in your field are some of the things needed for long-term success.

AH: Let's step back from the technical side for a bit. What kind of personal qualities does somebody going into professional editing need to have? What kind of person can really be successful in this kind of work?

SS: Professional skills involve much more than meets the eye and are usually not taught in any book, but it's your professionalism that will carry you on the long road to success. I would suggest the following: learn to work well with others, listen, be cordial, be on time, and deliver your editing work on time; when you said it would be done, or when the director or producer wants it delivered! Yes, there can be many a late night—or all-night—projects. I sometimes reflect on those times when I was late with my work or late showing up and think, "If I had only managed my work or time differently. . . ." This is all part of learning, and directly affects whether you will be hired again.

Another tip on professionalism is to accept when you don't know something or know how to do something—this is where you need to step back, leave your ego at the door, and either find someone who can do this part of the job or find out how to do it, usually from another editor. This too has come back to bite me, and one learns pretty quickly how to better manage one's commitments and responsibilities!

I've found the type of person who finds success seems have at least most of these qualities; they are calm; their attitude is positive and collaborative; they know their craft; they are friendly (but not too friendly), and they watch their egos and frustrations. I certainly have an ego around my work, and even after all these years, I have had to remember it's not about me, it's about the film or the "product," and making your boss (the director-producer) happy.

AH: You and I both are Pro Tools Certified Instructors, and I know that you're an enthusiastic Pro Tools user. Pro Tools is everywhere in the industry, and nowhere is this truer than in audio post-production, where you work as an editor. Why do you think the professional community has chosen Pro Tools to be the industry standard?

SS: When I started working in audio and purchased my first Pro Tools system, there were already a few digital systems being used in the post-production community. One, I remember, being an IBM-based system called *Waveframe*. It was used mainly for dialogue editing. I worked with it a little, but it didn't seem very intuitive. Coming from the music world and already being comfortable with sequencers, such as *Digital Performer* and *Opcode*, I already had a feel for the track and timeline visual layout. It seems to me since Pro Tools was developed out of MIDI sequencing technology from the music world, it felt comfortable, intuitive, and simple to learn. In post-production, many people that work in this industry are musicians or composers, and this kind of creative feel and connection to the visual (screen layout) is comfortable for them as well.

Additionally, Pro Tools was introduced at the right time. When I started in this field, analog tape-based editing, playback, and recording systems were being used, and digital audio technology was taking over. Pro Tools took on the user workflow and visual interface in a very similar way to old analog editing machines, such as *Steenbeck* and *Moviola*. So, it made sense, and it was comfortable to editors who needed to transition to Digital Audio Workstation systems. At that time, there was a huge learning curve for editors as they moved from analog to digital, and Pro Tools was right there at a reasonable price, waiting for them and growing with their technological needs.

AH: Awesome. Thanks for your time. Any last words of encouragement for the readers?

SS: When you're starting out in this field or just curious and want to get your feet wet, I'd say that Pro Tools, and particularly Pro Tools | First, gives you the most powerful and flexible tools to meet almost any editing challenge. Once mastered, you will be in a good position to embark on a most exciting and fulfilling career path. Learning the technology is only one part of the successful career puzzle, though—additionally, you must learn the language of the kind of work that you're looking to do. Also critical to post-production, music, or any field you choose, is the interpersonal relationships you build through friends and colleagues. The person sitting next to you while you're reading this (if you're in a classroom) may be the next Steven Spielberg, and the friendships you build in high school and college can be lifelong keys to your success. Cherish and nurture them.

Trust. In this and other industries I have worked in over the years, trust is a key part of relationships and success. The Hollywood industry is built around trust. There is so much fear of failure around investments in films, television, and other media, that the power players, all the way down to the editor and directors, need to feel they can trust you. Further, you need to have a solid work ethic, technical skills, people skills are most important, and the ability to develop friendly relationships is crucial. I encourage you to dive in with both feet, learn as much and meet as many people as possible, be enthusiastic, but not arrogant, and be open to wherever your path will take you!

Scrolling and Zooming in the Edit Window

As your Project gets bigger, knowing how to get around Pro Tools | First becomes more important. Navigating in your Edit window falls into two general categories—*scrolling* and *zooming*.

Scrolling

Scrolling in Pro Tools, on a basic level, isn't all that different from scrolling a webpage, except that there is vertical and horizontal scrolling.

- Clicking and dragging on the Vertical scroll bar will enable you to navigate up and down the Edit window. This is the kind of scrolling you'll be doing if you want to see different tracks.

Figure 4.2 The Edit Window's Vertical Scroll Bar

- At the bottom of the Edit window, there is a Horizontal scroll bar that will allow you to shift your view earlier or later in time.

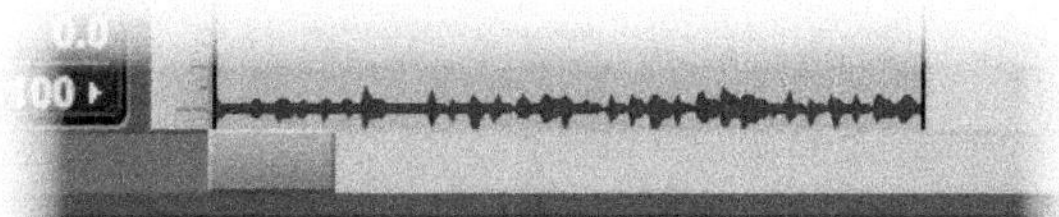

Figure 4.3 The Edit Window's Horizontal Scroll Bar

In the lower right-hand corner of the Edit window, you'll see two pairs of buttons—the first includes up-down triangles, and the other has left-right triangles, as shown in Figure 4.4:

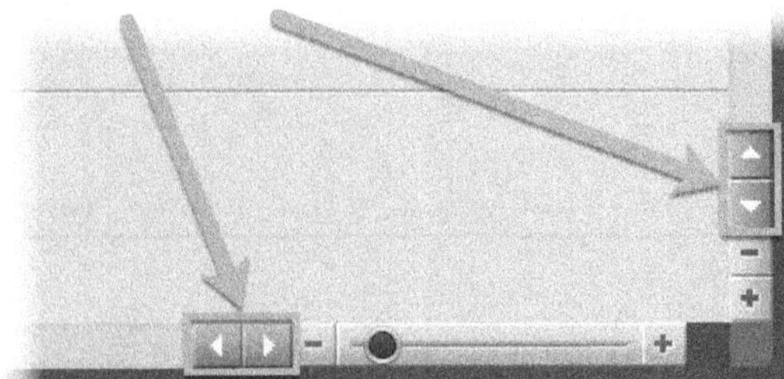

Figure 4.4 Scroll buttons

- Clicking on the upward- or downward-facing triangle buttons on the right edge of the Edit window will scroll your view up or down by a one-track increment.
- Clicking on the left- or right-facing triangle buttons on the bottom edge of the Edit window will scroll your view earlier or later on the timeline (the amount of that shift will depend on your zoom level, which you'll learn about later in this chapter).

If you have a mouse with a scroll bar, you can use this to scroll as well. Using the scroll wheel (with no modifier key) will scroll your Edit window up and down, and by holding the SHIFT key while using the scroll wheel, you can scroll your window left or right (earlier or later on the timeline).

Zooming

Zooming is also critically important, so much so that there is a dedicated Zoom tool just for that purpose. We'll talk about that tool later—for now, let's go through other ways that you can change how much time you're seeing in your Edit window:

In the bottom right-hand corner of the Edit window, there's a small slider—clicking and dragging it will allow you to smoothly zoom out or in (zooming out will show more time in your Edit window, and zooming in will show you more detail in your clips, but less time in the Edit window. At either end of the slider are minus (-) and plus (+) buttons that will incrementally zoom out or in.

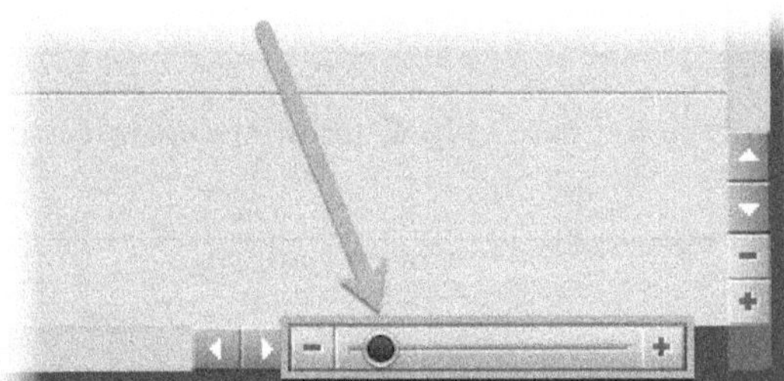

Figure 4.5 Zoom Slider and Buttons

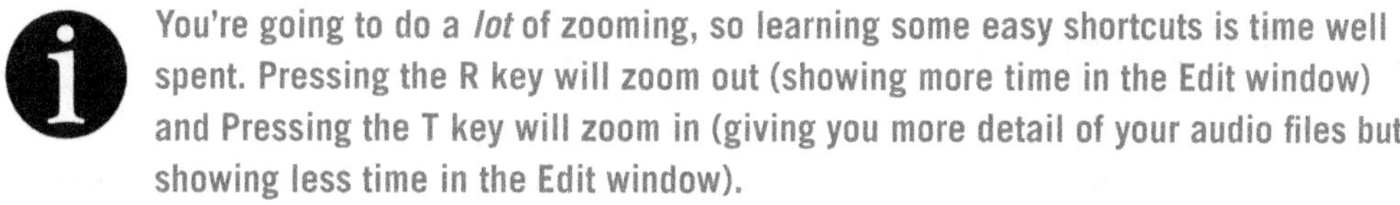
You're going to do a *lot* of zooming, so learning some easy shortcuts is time well spent. Pressing the R key will zoom out (showing more time in the Edit window) and Pressing the T key will zoom in (giving you more detail of your audio files but showing less time in the Edit window).

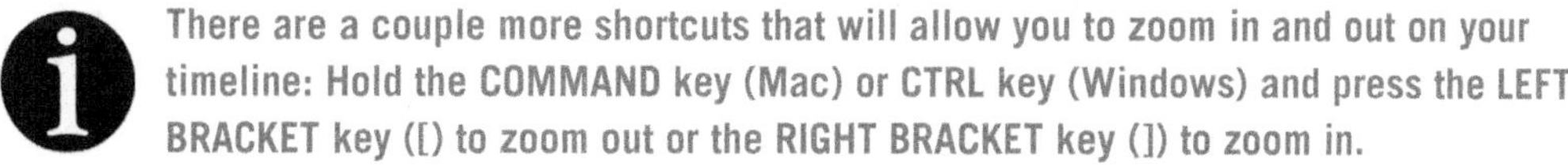
There are a couple more shortcuts that will allow you to zoom in and out on your timeline: Hold the **COMMAND** key (Mac) or **CTRL** key (Windows) and press the **LEFT BRACKET** key ([) to zoom out or the **RIGHT BRACKET** key (]) to zoom in.

Vertical Zooming

Horizontally zooming in or out of the timeline isn't the only way you can zoom—you can also zoom in or out vertically, which can be useful in seeing more detail in your audio files. In the upper right-hand corner of your tracks area, you'll see a button with an audio waveform in it. This is the AUDIO ZOOM IN/OUT button, which will enable you to vertically zoom in on your audio clips. Directly below that button is the MIDI ZOOM IN/ OUT button, which will similarly let you vertically zoom in on MIDI notes.

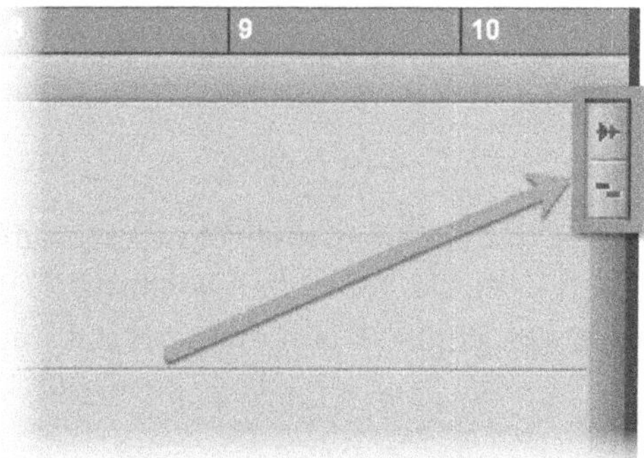

Figure 4.6 The Audio Zoom In/Out Button

Clicking the top half of this button will zoom up vertically on your audio clips, making the audio waveform appear taller. This will not make your audio louder, but it will give you the ability to see low-amplitude sounds more clearly. If you click the bottom half of this button, you will zoom down vertically.

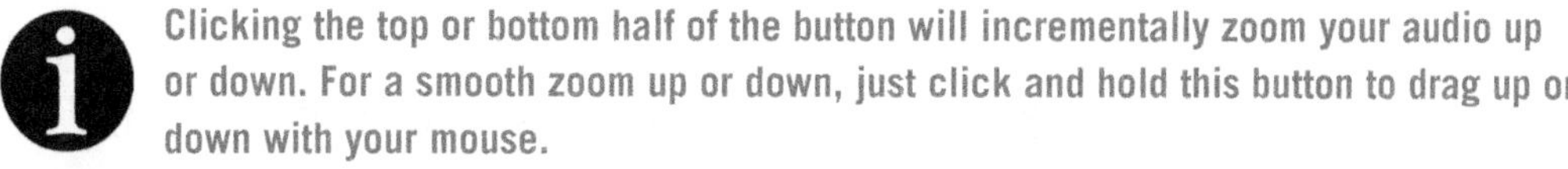
Clicking the top or bottom half of the button will incrementally zoom your audio up or down. For a smooth zoom up or down, just click and hold this button to drag up or down with your mouse.

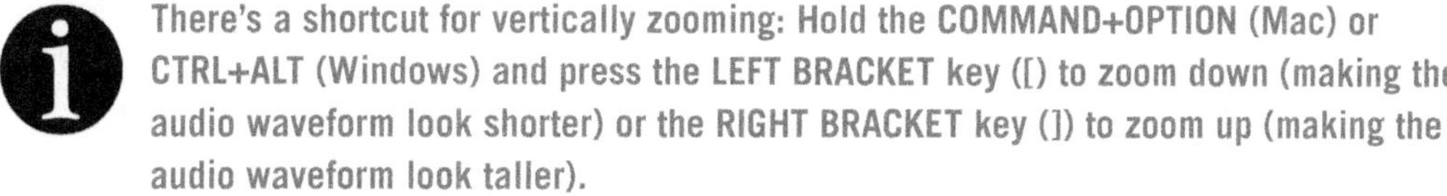
There's a shortcut for vertically zooming: Hold the **COMMAND+OPTION** (Mac) or **CTRL+ALT** (Windows) and press the **LEFT BRACKET** key ([) to zoom down (making the audio waveform look shorter) or the **RIGHT BRACKET** key (]) to zoom up (making the audio waveform look taller).

The Big Three: Trim, Selector, and Grabber

Pro Tools has a wide variety of Edit tools and features, but there are three that stand above the rest: The Trim tool, Selector tool, and Grabber tool. These are at the heart of most of the editing you'll do, so it's important to understand how they work. Let's take a look at these one at a time:

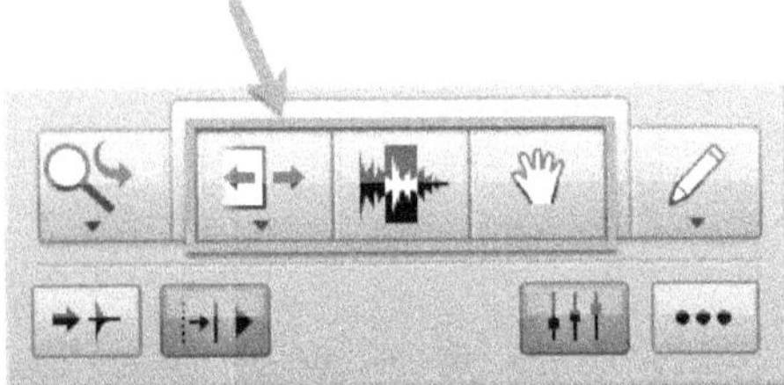

Figure 4.7 From Left to Right: Trim Tool, Selector Tool, Grabber Tool

The Trim Tool

Figure 4.8 The Trim Tool

The Trim tool enables you to adjust the boundaries of clips in your Project. Here is an example of how it might be used in a typical editing workflow: Figure 4.9 shows an audio clip, and as you can see by the waveform, there are four distinct phrases within this clip. Let's say that I want to cut the first two phrases out of the clip—the Trim tool can get the job done.

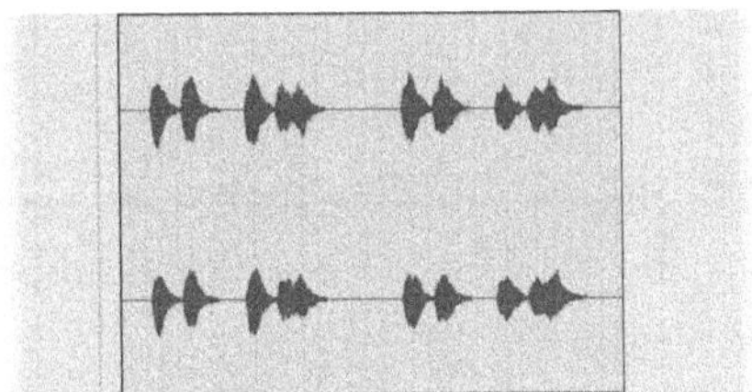

Figure 4.9 A Clip with Four Short Phrases

1. Select the TRIM TOOL in the Edit Window's Edit Tools section, as shown in Figure 4.10.

The Shortcut to activate the Trim tool is the F6 Key.

If you're on a Mac computer and your F1 keys aren't behaving this way, it's probably because your F keys are assigned to different functions. For dedicated Pro Tools computers, you'll want your F keys to change your Edit Modes and tools, and there's an easy way to do it: From your System Preferences, choose Keyboard, and then check the USE F1, F2, ETC. KEYS AS STANDARD FUNCTION KEYS check box.

Figure 4.10 Activating the Trim Tool

2. Move your cursor near the beginning (left) or the end (right) boundary of the clip that you want to trim. Since I want to remove material from the beginning, in this case, I'll move my cursor towards the beginning of the clip. The cursor will become a bracketed icon as shown in Figure 4.11, indicating that I'm ready to trim the clip.

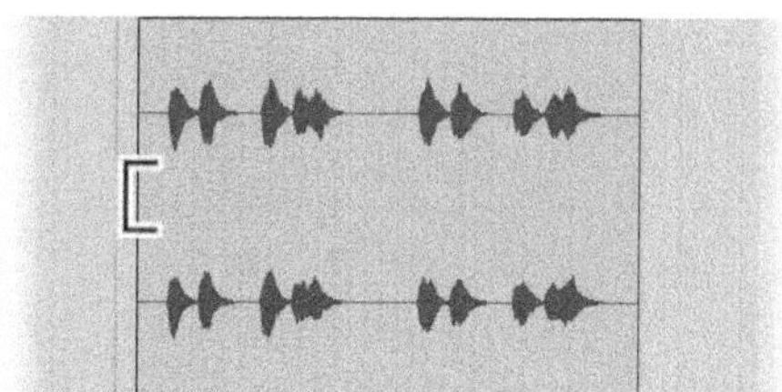

Figure 4.11 Ready to Trim the Beginning of the Clip

There are a few terms that you're likely to hear when you talk about the beginning (left-hand side) or end (right-hand side) of a clip, especially when you're talking to video editors: The beginning of a clip is commonly called the *head*, and the end is often called the *tail*.

3. To trim the clip, I'll just click and drag left or right (in my case, I'll drag towards the right). When you're done, just release the mouse—your clip has been trimmed, as shown in Figure 4.12.

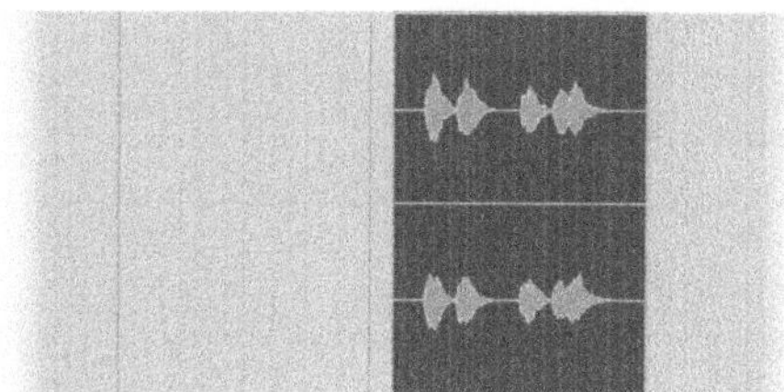

Figure 4.12 The Trimmed Clip

Pro Tools, like most DAWs, is not a destructive editing platform, meaning that even though you might remove audio content from the timeline, no audio data will be permanently deleted. In the example you just saw, if I wanted to show any of the material that I had previously trimmed, all I need to do is click and drag with the Trim tool (in the opposite direction) to reveal what had been hidden.

If you look very closely at the Trim tool button, you'll see a very small, downward-pointing triangle. If you click and hold on the Trim tool button, you'll see a menu of Trim tool variations, including *Standard*, *TCE*, and *Loop*. In this chapter, you'll just be dealing with the Standard Trim tool, but we'll explore the other Trim tools in Chapter 7.

The Selector Tool

Figure 4.13 The Selector Tool

Next to the Trim tool is the *Selector Tool.* The Selector tool is fairly intuitive, and if you've ever written an email or sent a text, you can expect that it operates similarly—using Selector tool, just click and drag anywhere on a track or ruler.

As an example, here's another common scenario: We're looking again at the clip you saw before. Now, instead of cutting the first two phrases and leaving the last two to be audible, I want to cut the second phrase and just have the first, third, and fourth phrases be audible:

1. Select the SELECTOR TOOL in the Edit window's Edit Tools section, as shown in Figure 4.14.

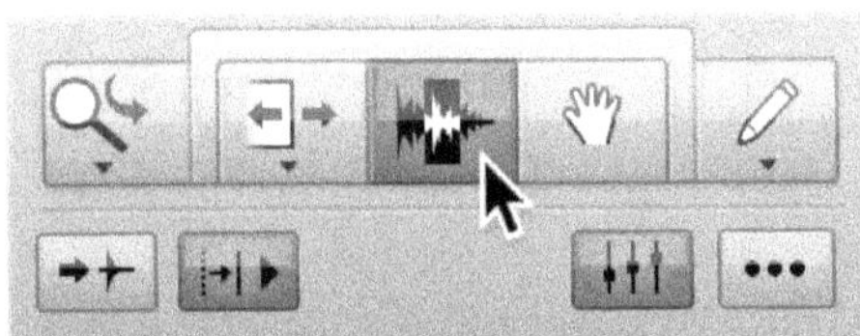

Figure 4.14 Activating the Selector Tool

The Shortcut to activate the Selector tool is the F7 Key.

2. Click and drag over the area that you want to change. Figure 4.15 shows the second phrase selected.

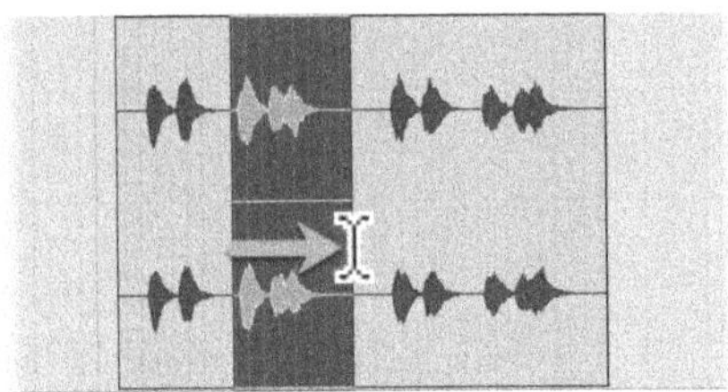

Figure 4.15 The Second Phrase Selected with the Selector Tool

3. Since in this case, I want to remove what I've selected, all I have to do is press the DELETE key, and the section will be removed from the timeline.

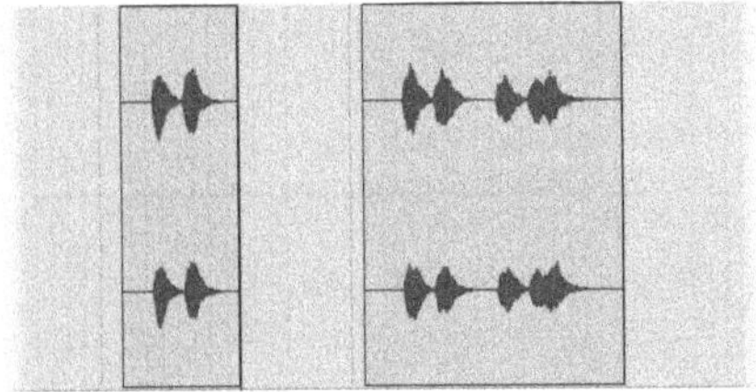

Figure 4.16 The Selected Area Removed

You can also use the Selector tool to select clips or your entire track:

- Double-clicking a clip with the Selector tool will select the entire clip.
- Triple-clicking in a track with the Selector tool will select all clips on that track.

The Grabber Tool

Figure 4.17 The Grabber Tool

The last of the three primary Edit tools is the *Grabber Tool.* Like the Selector tool, it does what you might expect: just click on the clip that you want to move, and drag it left or right to move it earlier or later on your Project's timeline. You can also drag clips up and down to move them to other tracks.

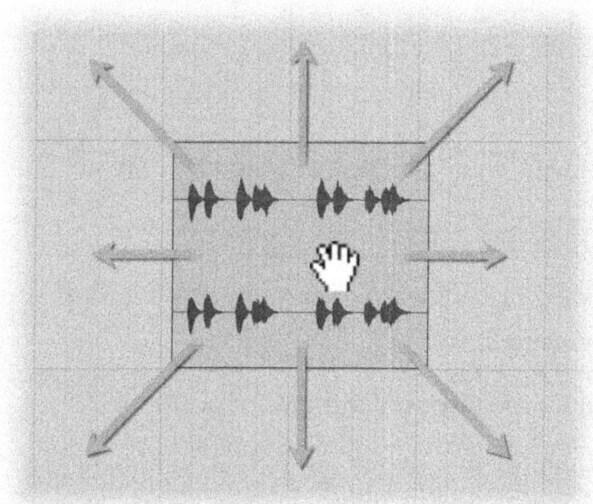

Figure 4.18 Moving a Clip with the Grabber Tool

The Shortcut to activate the Grabber tool is the F8 Key.

Here's a handy little tip: Holding the OPTION key (Mac) or ALT key (Windows) while moving a clip with the Grabber tool will make a copy of that clip. This allows you to move a duplicate clip to a new location while leaving the original clip in its original position.

You can also use the Grabber tool to select clips or name your clips:

- Clicking a clip with the Grabber tool will select the entire clip.
- Double-clicking a clip with the Grabber tool will open the Clip Name dialog box, enabling you to rename a clip.

The Edit Modes

You'll choose your Edit tools—Trim, Selector, or Grabber—based on what you want to do to a clip. There's another choice that you must make, and that is which Edit Mode to use. Your Edit Mode choice will determine how your Edit tools behave.

Figure 4.19 The Edit Modes, with Slip Mode Currently Active

Your Edit Modes are shown at the top left-hand corner of the Edit window. They are *Shuffle*, *Slip*, *Spot*, and *Grid*. The currently active mode is indicated buy a colored field—in the case of Figure 4.18, Slip mode is the currently active mode, so let's start with that one.

Slip Mode

Slip Mode is easy and straightforward. When Slip mode is active, a green field will appear around the word "Slip".

Simply put, when you're in Slip Mode, your tools will move smoothly and freely:

- When using the Grabber tool, you can drag clips forward or backward in time to any location you want. This mode suits fine-tuning the position of clips quite well.
- If you're using the Selector tool, any selection you make can start and end at any point.
- When using the Trim tool, you can adjust the beginnings and ends of clips with a high degree of flexibility.

Shuffle Mode

Shuffle Mode is quite powerful, but requires a little bit of explanation:

In Figure 4.20, you'll see that I have three clips on three different tracks—*Intro*, *Verse*, and *Chorus*. Let's say these three clips are vocal parts of a song. The bottom track (*Song*) is empty, and I'll use this track to assemble a sequence of clips in the order Intro-Verse-Chorus.

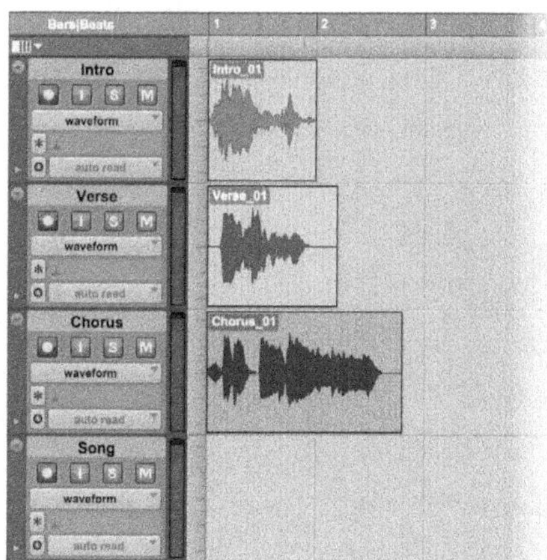

Figure 4.20 Three Sections of a Song, and the Assembly Track

1. First, I'll activate Shuffle Mode by clicking the word SHUFFLE. You'll know that this is the active Edit Mode when the field around the word is colored red.

Figure 4.21 Activating Shuffle Mode

2. The first clip in my sequence of clips is the *Intro_01* clip. I'll drag it from the Intro track down to my Song track. No matter where I drop the clip on the timeline, the clip will place itself at the beginning of it.

3. Next, I'll drag the *Verse_01* clip from the *Verse* track to the *Song* track. I'll place my cursor anywhere after the first clip on the track (which is the Intro_01 clip in this case). No matter where my cursor is on the timeline, the dragged clip will snap to the end of the previous clip with no space between them, as shown in figure 4.22.

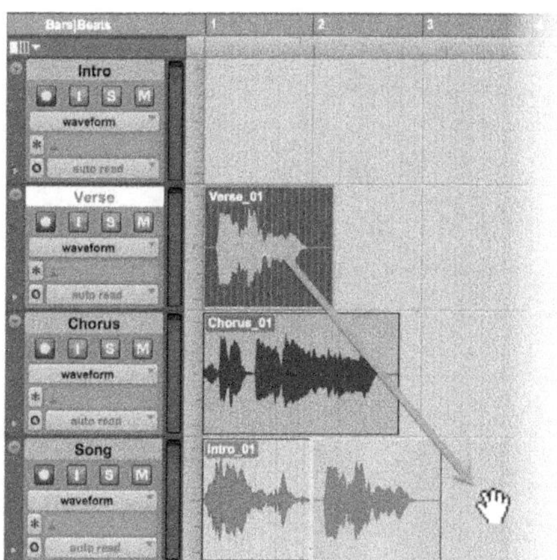

Figure 4.22 Dragging a Clip in Shuffle Mode

4. I'll do the same thing with the *Chorus_01* clip, dragging the clip anywhere behind the last clip on the *Song* track. My result, as shown in Figure 4.23, will be that on the Song track, the dragged clips are back-to-back with no gaps between the clips. This is the basic operation of Shuffle Mode.

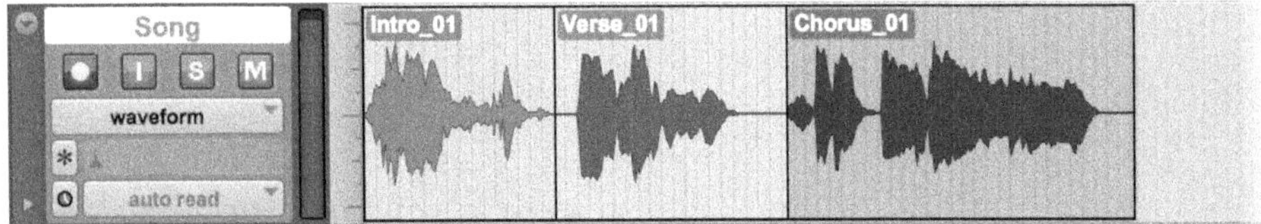

Figure 4.23 The Assembled Song: Intro, Verse, and Chorus

5. But it gets even better: Let's say that I need to re-order the clips (my producer comes in and tells me that he wants the order to be Intro, Chorus, Verse). No problem, I'll just drag Chorus_01 clip earlier in my timeline. As you can see in Figure 4.24, a yellow line will appear to tell me where the dragged clip will be deposited once I release the mouse. In this case, the yellow line between the Intro_01 clip and the Verse_01 indicates that the dragged clip will be inserted between the two.

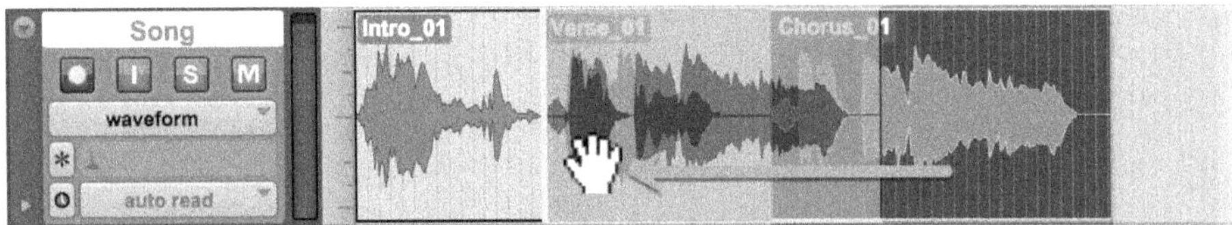

Figure 4.24 Reordering Clips in Shuffle Mode

The Clips have been reordered now into *Intro*, *Chorus*, and *Verse*. There is still no gap, and the *Verse* clip has just moved later on the timeline to make space for the *Chorus* clip to be inserted, kind of like shuffling a deck of cards.

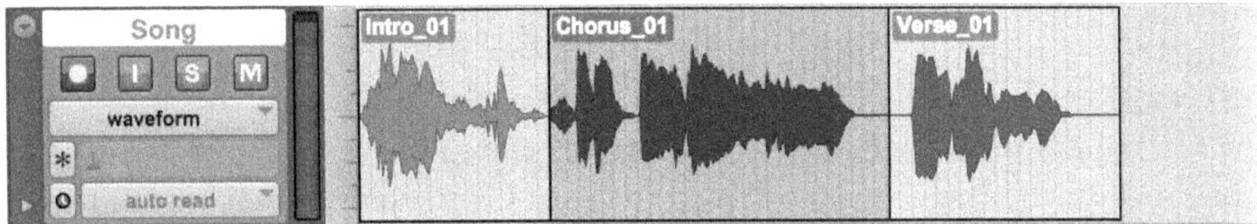

Figure 4.25 The Reordered Clips

Shuffle Mode is certainly powerful, but there are only certain workflows that it's suited for. For a song editor who is dragging together sections of a song (like the example we just covered), it's a great tool. However, if you're using the Trim tool, you must be aware that as you drag it to adjust a clip's boundary, Shuffle Mode will make sure that there is no gap and no overlap between clips, meaning that any edit you make on a track will affect the location of any clips later in the timeline. This behavior makes Shuffle Mode unsuitable for other kinds of workflows, and why it's generally avoided for post-production work.

Grid Mode

Like Slip mode, Grid Mode is straightforward and easy to use:

- If you're using the Grabber tool, as you drag a clip earlier or later on the timeline, it will jump from grid increment to grid increment. For example, if your grid is set to one measure (or one *bar*), any clip that you drag will snap to the nearest bar's first beat.
- Similarly, if you're using the Selector tool, any selection you make will immediately snap to the nearest grid lines. If you make a selection that is exactly one bar long, set your grid value to one bar, and selecting that amount will become very easy.
- When using the Trim tool, adjustments to the beginning or the end of a clip will snap to the nearest grid line.

Let's take a look at Grid Mode in a practical situation using the Grabber tool. In this first scenario, I want to move a clip so that it starts *exactly* on the second beat of the second measure.

1. First, I'll turn on Grid Mode. Click GRID, and you'll see a blue field around the word *Grid,* indicating that Absolute Grid Mode is active (there's another Grid Mode called *Relative* Grid Mode, which we'll talk about next.)

Figure 4.26 Activating Absolute Grid Mode

2. The next thing I'll do is set my Grid *Value*. The grid value that I choose will determine the spacing of the grid lines, and how my clip will snap. The Grid Value is shown immediately below the Counter (as shown in Figure 4.27).

Figure 4.27 The Grid Value

3. Clicking the triangle icon next to the Grid Value will allow me to change the spacing of my grid. In this case, I'll change my grid to a quarter note.

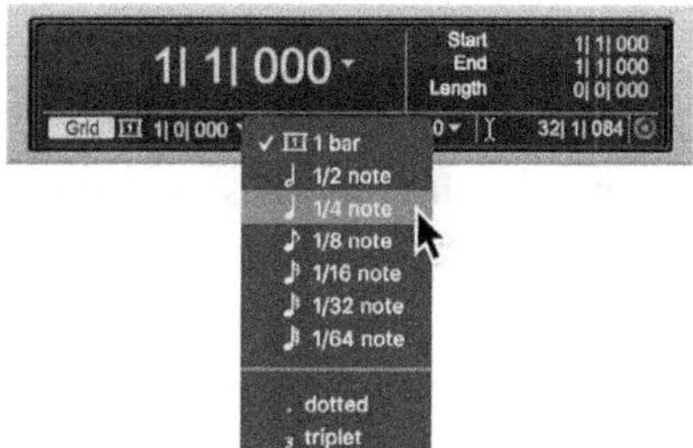

Figure 4.28 Changing the Grid Value

4. When using Grid Mode, you'll probably want to see your grid *lines*. You can show (or hide) these lines by clicking the SHOW GRID LINES button shown in Figure 4.29. When the field around the word *Grid* is green, your grid lines will appear in your tracks area.

Figure 4.29 The SHOW GRID LINES Button

5. From there it's easy—just drag your clip to the desired location. Even if your clip wasn't on a grid line, it will snap to the nearest grid line as you drag. Figure 4.30 shows my clip exactly positioned to bar 2, beat 2.

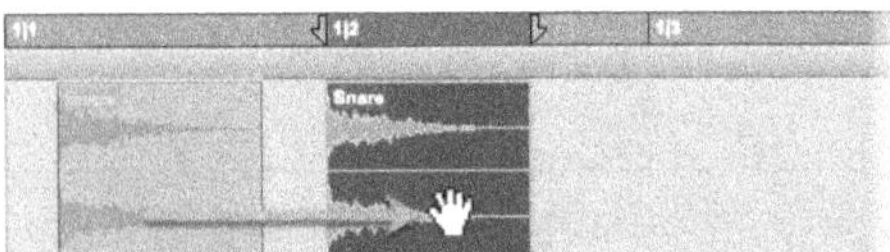

Figure 4.30 Dragging a Clip in Grid Mode

Relative Grid Mode

What we commonly call Grid Mode is more properly called Absolute Grid Mode. There's another Grid Mode available to you called *Relative* Grid Mode.

Here's another scenario: Let's say that I have a snare drum hit that is close to a grid line but not exactly on it. Let's also say that I want to move the clip later in my Project's timeline, but I want to maintain that distance from the grid. That's where Relative Grid Mode comes in:

1. In the Edit Modes section, you'll see a small triangle by the word "Grid". Clicking and holding the Grid Mode button will reveal a menu showing the two different grid modes. I'll change to Relative Grid Mode, and the field around the text will change to a purple color, indicating that I'm now in Relative Grid Mode.

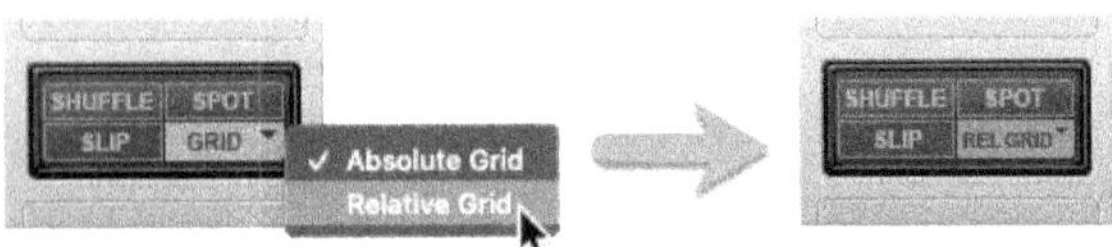

Figure 4.31 Changing to Relative Grid Mode

2. Now when I drag a clip, it won't snap to the closest grid line, but will instead move by the grid amount (in this case my grid is one beat). You'll see that as I move this clip, it maintains the same relative distance from the nearest line, hence the name *Relative* Grid Mode.

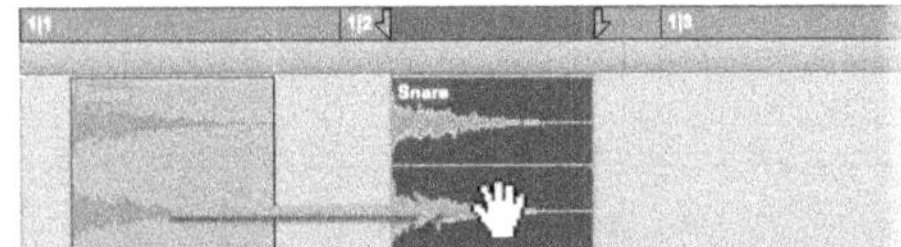

Figure 4.32 Dragging a Clip in Relative Grid Mode

Spot Mode

Last on the list is *Spot* mode. This mode is most commonly used in post-production, though it could be used in any situation. Spot Mode operates by enabling the user to type a specific location for where a clip will be placed.

Let's take a look at how Spot Mode might be used to place a clip at a specific place in the timeline. In this situation, I have imported an explosion sound effect, and the director has told me that it needs to be placed exactly at *1 hour, 1 minute,* and *3.2 seconds.*

1. First, I'll click the SPOT MODE button. An amber color will indicate that Spot Mode is active.

Figure 4.33 Activating Spot Mode

2. With the Grabber tool, click the clip that you want to move. The spot dialog box will immediately appear, as shown in Figure 4.34.

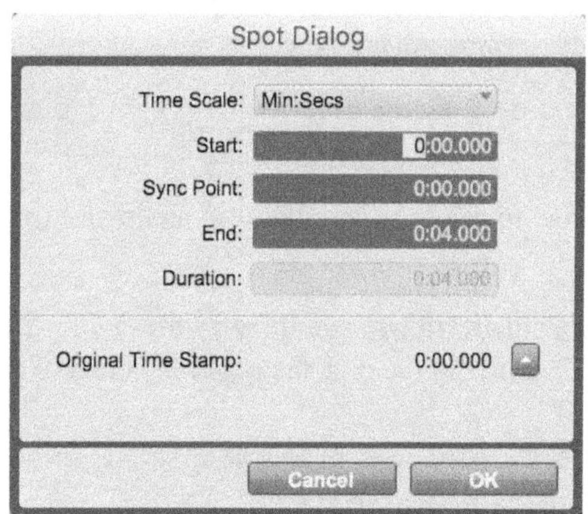

Figure 4.34 The Spot Dialog Box

3. At the top of the Spot Dialog box is the Time Scale, which I can change in Pro Tools | First between Minutes and Seconds (Min:Secs) or Bars and Beats (Bars|Beats).

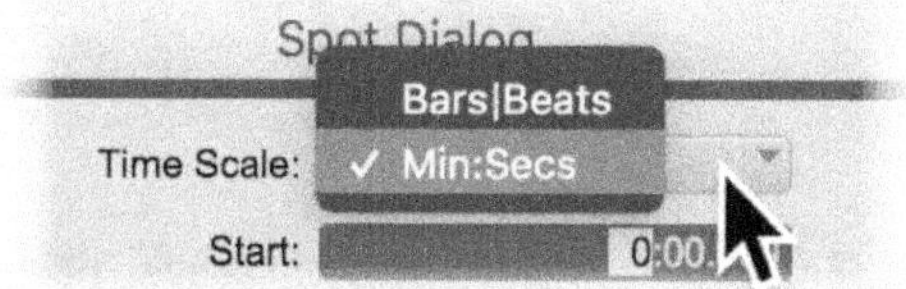

Figure 4.35 Changing the Time Scale

With Pro Tools and Pro Tools | Ultimate, there are additional Time Scales that you can use—SMPTE Timecode, Feet and Frames, and Samples.

4. In the Start field, I'll see the numbered field, with minutes and seconds separated by a colon symbol (:). I'll type 61:03.200. This will place the beginning of my clip at 1 hour (60 minutes), 1 minute, 3.2 seconds.

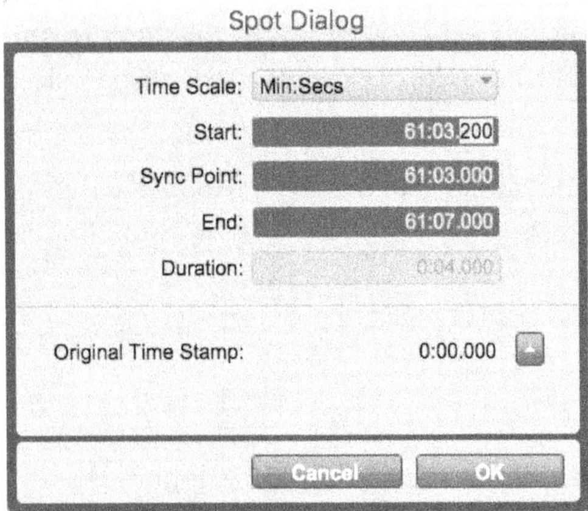

Figure 4.36 Placing the Beginning of a Clip to 1 Hour, 1 Minute, 3.2 Seconds

5. When I click the OK button, the clip will be moved to the location that I typed.

You'll see that there's also a field where I can type an *End* position. If I type the same number (61:03.200), then the *end* of the clip will snap to that position.

You can also align a *Sync Point* to any location that you type. Here's how to create a Sync Point in a clip and use it with Spot Mode:

1. Using the Selector tool, click any position that you want to mark. In my example, it's the beginning of an explosion sound, as shown in Figure 4.37. You will see that the position is marked by a single vertical line.

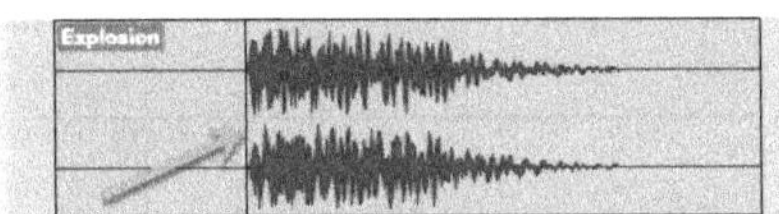

Figure 4.37 Choosing the Right Location for a Sync Point

2. From the CLIP menu, choose IDENTIFY SYNC POINT. A small triangular icon will appear in the clip, as shown in Figure 4.38.

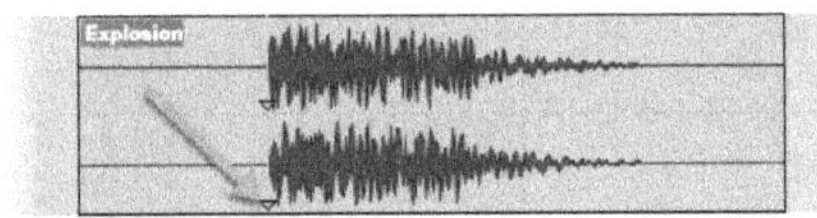

Figure 4.38 The Clip with a Sync Point

Sync Points can be quite useful in a number of situations. Here's a shortcut to quickly create one: Press COMMAND+, (Mac) or CTRL+, (Windows). This will save you a trip to the CLIP menu!

3. Now that you've marked the clip with a sync point, you can type its position in the Sync Point Field of the Spot Dialog box. When you click the OK button, the clip will be moved so that the sync point is at the position that you entered.

There's another way to bring up the Spot Dialog box without going into Spot Mode:

1. Right-click the clip that you want to spot. The clip will be selected, and a menu will appear, as shown in Figure 4.39.

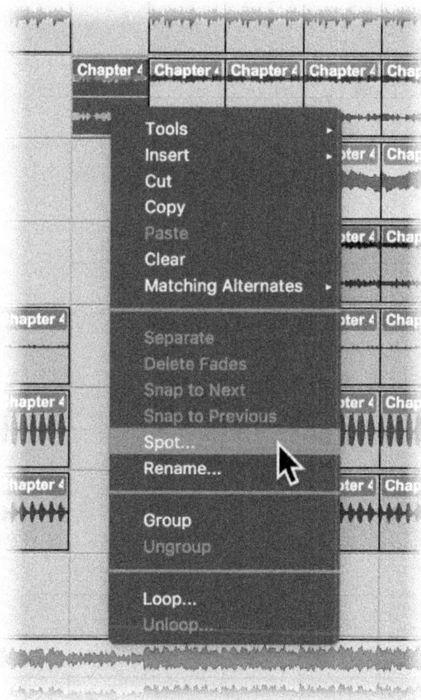

Figure 4.39 Another way to Bring Up the Spot Dialog Box

2. Choose SPOT from the menu, and the Spot Dialog box will appear. This will not change your currently active Edit Mode, and is an easy way to bring up the Spot Dialog box if you only need to move one clip.

Accessing the Edit Modes with F Keys

Changing your Edit Modes is frequently done in many kinds of workflows, so doing it quickly can be a real timesaver. Here are some shortcuts:

- Pressing the F1 key will activate Shuffle Mode.
- Pressing the F2 key will activate Slip Mode.
- Pressing the F3 key will activate Spot Mode.
- Pressing the F4 key will activate Grid Mode. Repeatedly pressing the F4 key will toggle between Absolute Grid mode and Relative Grid mode.

Hands-On Exercise 4.1: Assembling a Song Pt. 1

Now that you understand the basic Edit tools and the Edit Modes, you can do quite a bit. In Chapter 3, you imported a few small loops. Let's take these loops and build something with them.

Getting Started

1. Create a new Project by converting the *Pro Tools First—Fundamentals of Audio Production—Chapter 4a (Mambo Part 1).ptx* session to a local Project. The session is found in the *Pro Tools First—Fundamentals of Audio Production—Chapter 4 (Mambo)* subfolder of this book's downloaded exercise material. You learned how to convert a session to a Project in Chapter 2. Choose any desired sample rate, 24-bit, and do not Backup to Cloud.

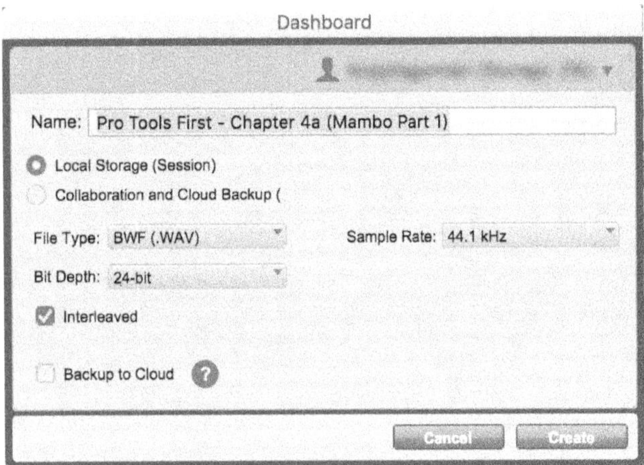

Figure 4.40 Your Project Settings

The Project that will appear includes the loops that you worked with in the previous chapter, plus a *Final Hit* track, and a *Reference* track. As shown in Figure 4.41, the bottom two tracks have been muted—we'll leave it that way for the time being.

Figure 4.41 Your Starting Tracks

Building the First Section

Let's start out by building the first section of the song. Grid mode is going to make it easy:

2. Activate Absolute Grid mode. The color of the Grid mode button be blue (as opposed to purple, which is the color for Relative Grid mode).

3. Just under the Counter display, check that your grid lines are displayed by making sure that the GRID button is highlighted in green (click the GRID button if it is not), and set your grid value to 1 bar, as shown in Figure 4.42.

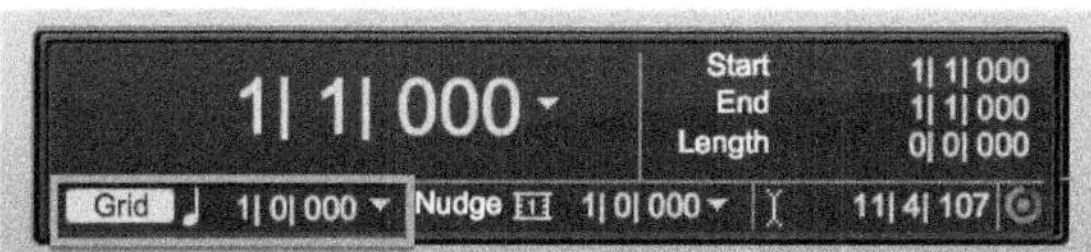

Figure 4.42 Setting Up Your Grid

Editing is a repetitious process by nature, so this exercise is going to require some patience and perseverance!

4. Let's take the Saxes first: Holding down the OPTION key (Mac) or ALT key (Windows) while dragging with the Grabber tool in order to make a copy as you drag, place copies of the Saxes clip at bars 3, 5, 7, 9, 11, 13, 15, 27, 29, 31, and 33. Use the scroll bar to move along your timeline or zoom out, so that you can see more time in your Edit window.

5. Trumpets: Drag the Trumpet clip to measure 19, then drag and copy the clip (by holding the OPTION/ALT key while dragging) to measures 21, 23, 25, 27, 29, 31, and 33.
6. Guitar 1: Drag the Guitar 1 clip to measure 13, then drag and copy the clip (by holding the OPTION/ALT key while dragging) to measures 15, 23, 25, 27, 29, 31, and 33.
7. Guitar 2: Drag the Guitar 2 clip to measure 9, then drag and copy the clip (by holding the OPTION/ALT key while dragging) to measures 11, 13, 15, 19, 21, 23, 25, 27, 29, 31, and 33.
8. Piano: Drag the Piano clip to measure 17, then drag and copy the clip (by holding the OPTION/ALT key while dragging) to measures 19, 21, 23, 25, 27, 29, 31, and 33.
9. Bass: Drag the Bass clip to measure 19, then drag and copy the clip (by holding the OPTION/ALT key while dragging) to measures 21, 23, 25, 27, 29, 31, and 33.
10. Drums: Drag the Drums clip to measure 19, then drag and copy the clip (by holding the OPTION/ALT key while dragging) to measures 21, 23, 25, 27, 29, 31, and 33.
11. Hi-Hat: Drag the Hi-Hat clip to measure 5, then drag and copy the clip (by holding the OPTION/ALT key while dragging) to measures 7, 9, 11, 15, 19, 21, 23, 25, 27, 29, 31, and 33.
12. Kick 1: Drag and copy the Kick 1 clip (by holding the OPTION/ALT key while dragging) to measure 3, 5, 7, 9, 11, 13, 15, 19, 21, 23, 25, 27, 29, 31, and 33.
13. Kick 2: Drag and copy the Kick 2 clip (by holding the OPTION/ALT key while dragging) to measure 3, 5, 7, 9, 11, 13, 15, 19, 21, 23, 25, 27, 29, 31, and 33.

When you're done, your Edit Window should look like Figure 4.43:

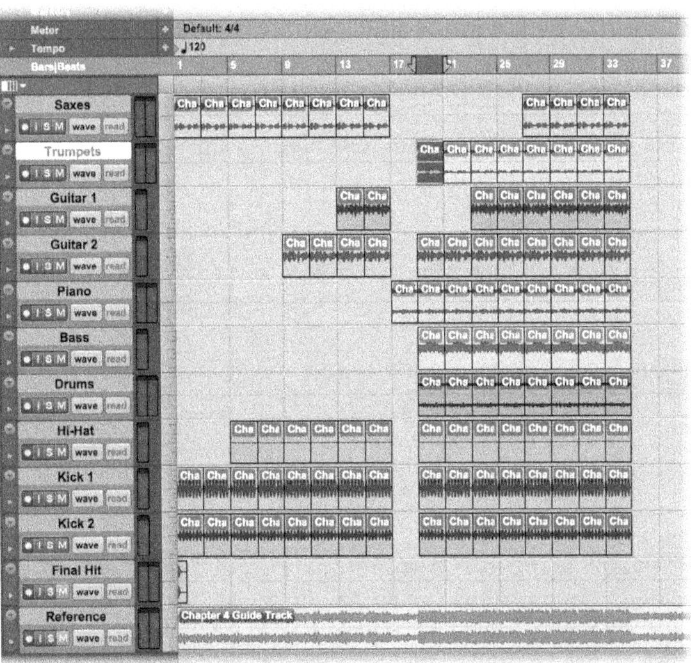

Figure 4.43 Your Assembled Intro

Another way to check your work is to compare it to the Reference track at the bottom of your Project, which is currently muted. Click the SOLO button to turn on solo and then click the MUTE button to turn off muting on that track, and listen to it compared to your assembly.

14. Once you're satisfied with your editing, you're done with this hands-on exercise. Before we move on, make sure you save your work!

More Edit Tools

There are other Edit tools available to you in addition to the Trim, Grabber, and Selector tools—let's take a look at them:

The Zoomer Tool

To the left of the Trim tool, you'll see a magnifying glass-looking icon as shown in Figure 4.44—this is called the *Zoomer Tool.* There are a number of ways that you can use this tool to zoom in and out of your project:

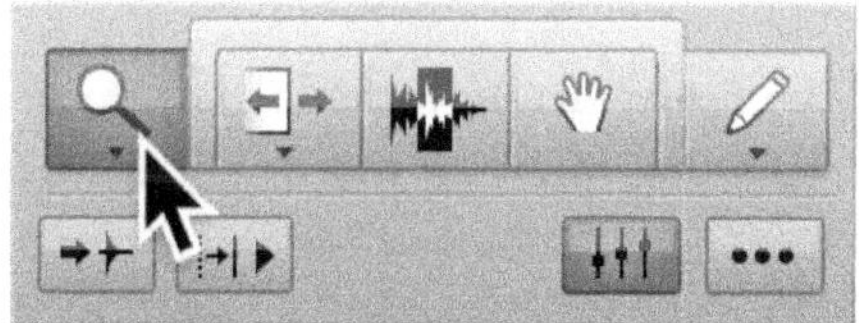

Figure 4.44 The Zoomer Tool

The Shortcut to activate the Zoomer tool is the F5 Key.

- Position the Zoomer tool anywhere on your tracks area and click once—this will incrementally zoom in on your timeline.
- Position the Zoomer tool anywhere on your tracks area while holding the OPTION key (Mac) or ALT key (Windows) and click once—this will incrementally zoom out on your timeline. When zooming out, the magnifying glass will show a minus sign (-).
- If you have a particular area that you want to zoom in on, click and drag over it. As shown in Figure 4.45, a marquee box will appear. Once you let go of the mouse, your view will be zoomed in on that selected area, as shown in Figure 4.46.

Figure 4.45 Zooming in on a Specific Area

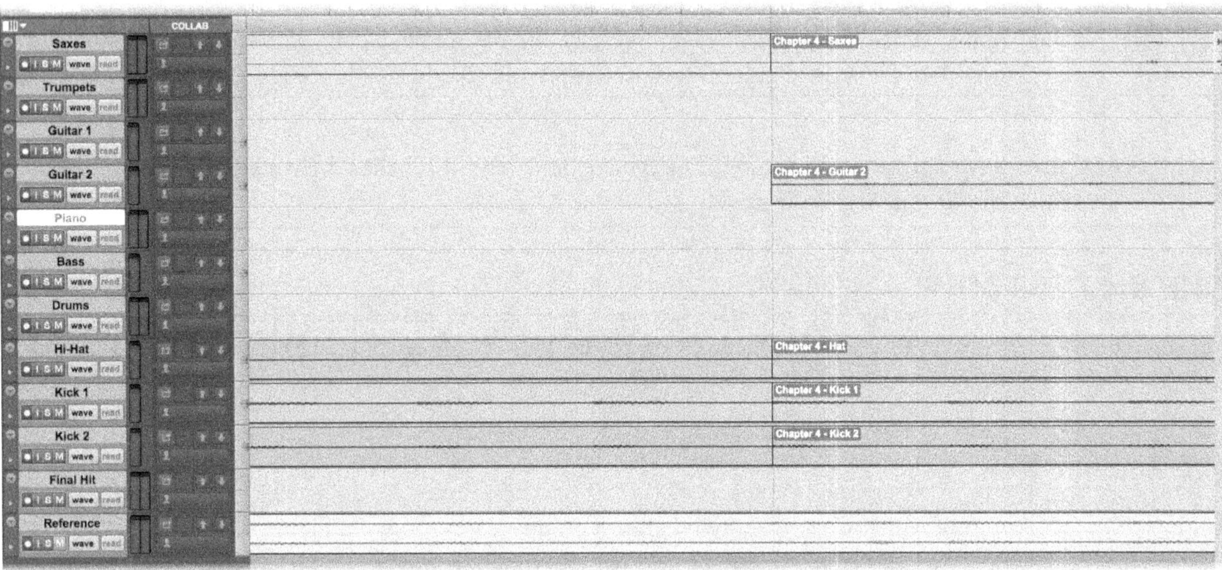

Figure 4.46 After Zooming In

- Double-clicking the Zoomer tool will zoom out your view of the Project to show the longest track in its entirety, as shown in Figure 4.47. This is particularly useful when you want to quickly see your entire timeline.

Figure 4.47 Double-Clicking the Zoomer Tool

- Holding the CONTROL key (Mac) or START key (Windows), click and drag left or right anywhere in your tracks to smoothly horizontally zoom in or out.
- Here's one more: Holding the CONTROL key (Mac) or START key (Windows), click and drag up or down on any track—that track's waveform will vertically zoom (note that this will not change the vertical zoom level of other tracks). Holding CONTROL+SHIFT (Mac) or START+SHIFT (Windows) and dragging up or down on any track vertically will zoom all audio waveforms in your Project.

Single Zoom

The Zoomer tool has one interesting variation, called *Single* Zoom. This is one of those tools that's best shown in a workflow situation:

Let's say that I'm trimming a clip, but I can't see the clip edge in as much detail as I'd like, so I want to zoom in. Normally this would involve switching to the Zoomer tool, zooming in, and then switching back to the Trim tool to continue my work, but Single Zoom takes one step out of the process.

1. Click and hold the ZOOMER TOOL button. A menu will appear, as shown in Figure 4.48. Choose SINGLE ZOOM and the Zoomer tool will change.

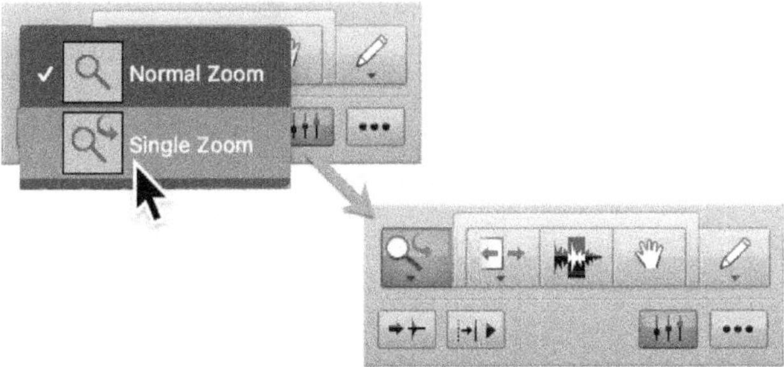

Figure 4.48 Changing to Single Zoom Mode

2. I'm working with the Trim tool, changing a clip's boundary, but I want to zoom in. I will switch to the Single Zoom mode and draw a marquee around the area that I want to see in detail, just as I would with the Normal Zoomer tool.
3. Once I release my mouse, two things will happen: First, I will zoom in on my timeline, and secondly, my active Edit tool will switch back to my previously used tool (in this example, the Trim tool). This means that I can continue trimming my clip, removing one step from the process.

The time saved by using the Single Zoom Tool as opposed to Normal Zoom may seem too small to make any real difference, but many professional editors will tell you differently. Editing sessions can easily involve many thousands of individual operations a day, and if even a small amount of time can be saved on these edits, that saved time can really add up. Many editors choose Single Zoom as their go-to Zoomer tool because it's time-efficient and it makes them a significantly more effective editor.

The Pencil Tool

Just to the right of the Grabber tool, you'll see the Pencil tool, as shown in Figure 4.49. Though it is certainly a tool used for editing, it is most commonly used in MIDI production (which we will discuss in Chapter 6), and during the mixing process (which we will discuss in Chapter 8).

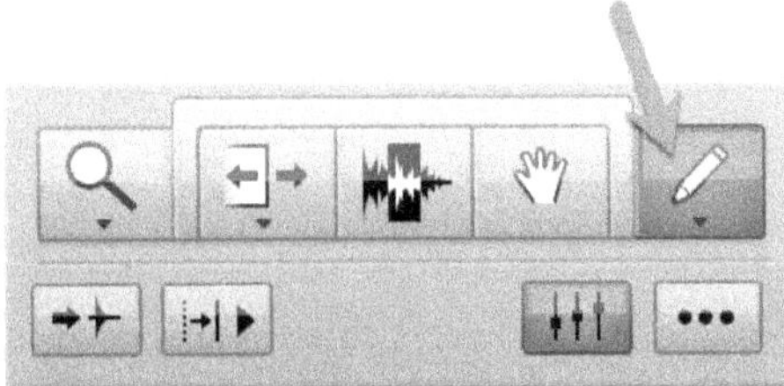

Figure 4.49 The Pencil Tool

The Shortcut to activate the Pencil Tool is the F10 key.

Though the Pencil tool can be used to draw waveforms, this is an extremely tricky (and destructive!) process. Fixing waveforms with the Pencil tool is an advanced editing workflow and discussed at length in other books in the Avid Learning Series.

There are several shapes that can be drawn with the Pencil Tool, which are revealed when you click and hold on the PENCIL TOOL button, as shown in Figure 4.50. They are Freehand, Line, Triangle, Square, Random, Parabolic, and S-Curve.

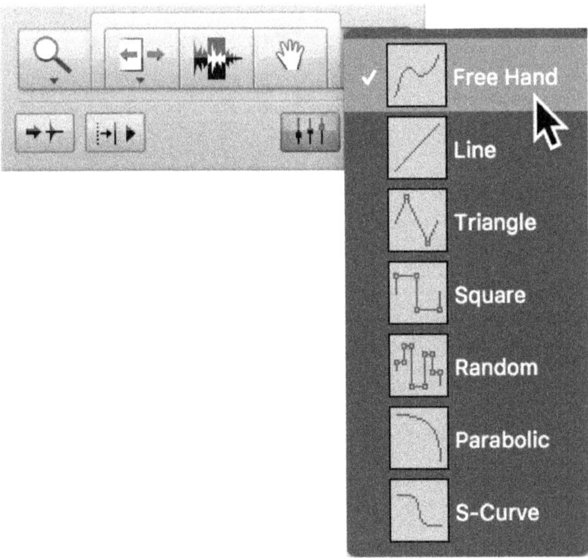

Figure 4.50 Different Pencil Tool Shapes

The Smart Tool

The mark of an accomplished editor is that they can get things done quickly and with minimal effort. Any technique that that removes even a single mouse click can be immensely valuable to a Pro Tools user, and the Smart Tool does that and more. Though it takes a little bit of practice to get used to, when you get comfortable with it, you'll want to use Smart Tool frequently.

To activate the Smart Tool, click the bracket above the Trim, Selector, and Grabber Tools. The bracket and all three tools will turn blue, as shown in Figure 4.51.

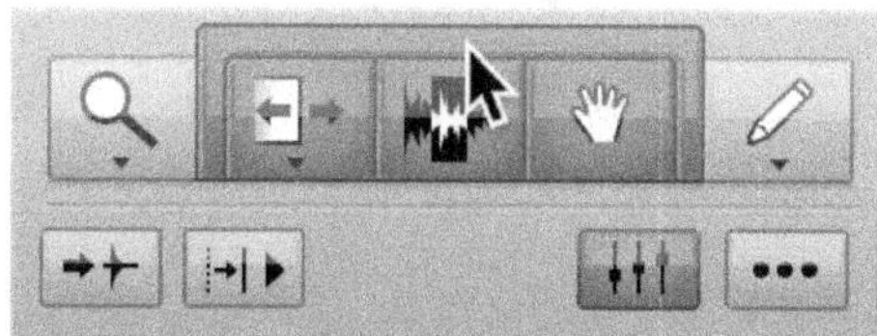

Figure 4.51 Activating the Smart Tool

The Shortcut to activate the Smart Tool is any two- or three-key combination of F6, F7, and F8.

The Smart Tool operates by changing the active tool according to the position of the cursor on a track:

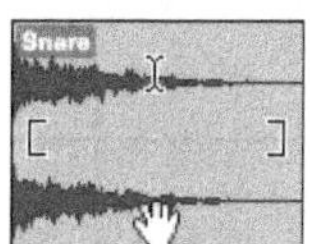

Figure 4.52 Smart Tool Behavior

- If your cursor is in the upper half of a track, the active tool is the Selector tool.
- If your cursor is in the bottom half of the track, the active tool is the Grabber tool.
- If your cursor is at either end of a clip, the active tool is the Trim tool.

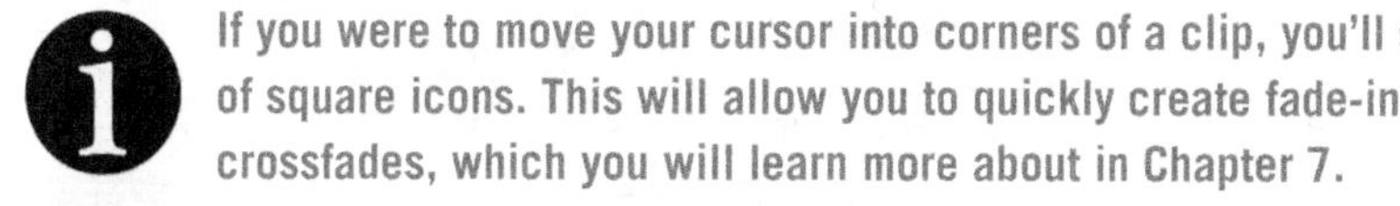

If you were to move your cursor into corners of a clip, you'll see different kinds of square icons. This will allow you to quickly create fade-ins, fade-outs, and crossfades, which you will learn more about in Chapter 7.

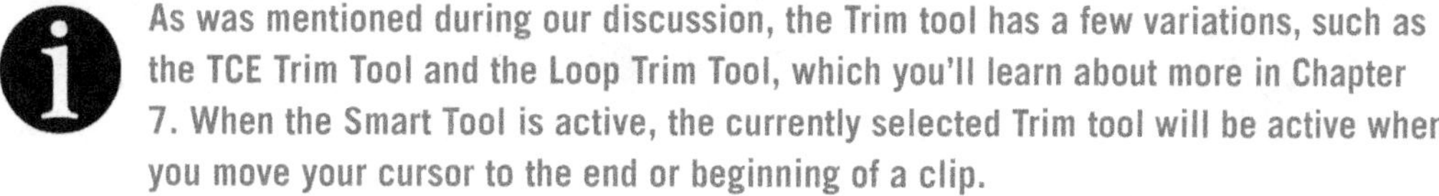

As was mentioned during our discussion, the Trim tool has a few variations, such as the TCE Trim Tool and the Loop Trim Tool, which you'll learn about more in Chapter 7. When the Smart Tool is active, the currently selected Trim tool will be active when you move your cursor to the end or beginning of a clip.

Making Selections and Playing Audio

To edit efficiently, you'll need to be able to quickly make selections and control playback in different ways. In Chapter 1, we touched upon some of these—now let's review and expand on them:

At the top of the Edit window is the Counter, showing me the location of the timeline insertion, and the beginning of any selected area. For example, in Figure 4.53, if I were to start playback, it would begin at measure three. This display not only shows location; you can also type in a value to move the playback cursor to any desired location.

Figure 4.53 The Counter and Edit Selection Section

Immediately to the right of the Counter is an Edit Selection section, which indicates the *Start*, the *End*, and the *Length* of any area that I have selected. Figure 4.53 shows that my selected area starts at Bar 3 and ends at Bar 5, giving it a total duration of 2 measures. You can change any of these values by clicking the desired field and type in a new value. This is useful when you know exactly where you need your selection to begin and/or end.

Perhaps an easier way to make selections is from the Bars and Beats (Bars|Beats) or Minutes and Seconds (Min:Secs) ruler. Just click and drag to create a selected area. This area will then determine your playback, starting at the beginning of the selected area and ending at the end of it. As shown in Figure 4.54, this method of selecting will also select a corresponding area on all your visible tracks. You can drag the blue arrows on either side of the selected area to adjust the beginning or end.

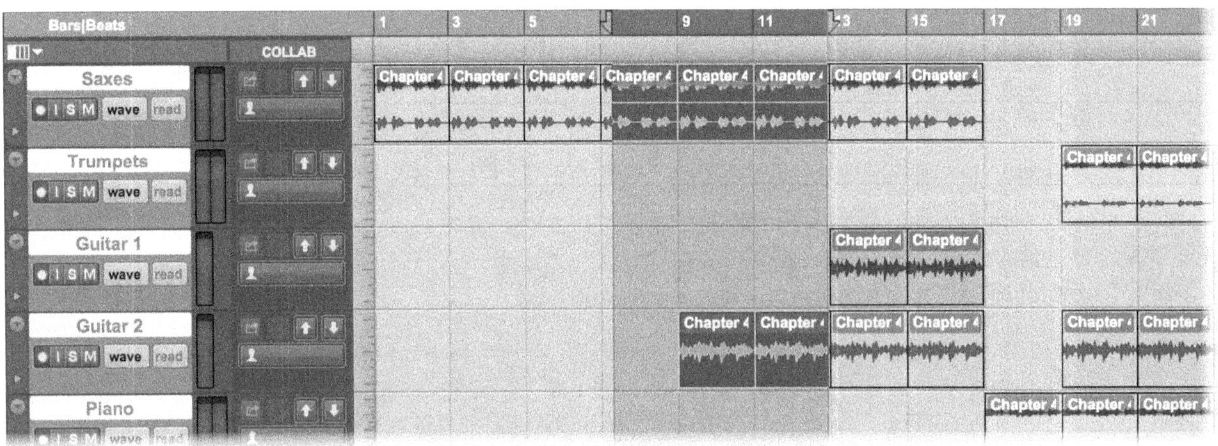

Figure 4.54 Making a Selection on the Ruler

You can also make a playback selection in the *Markers*, *Meter*, or *Tempo* rulers. When a playback selection is made in this way, no corresponding selection will be made on any tracks.

The way that selections are made on the ruler will depend upon your active Edit Mode. For example, if you want to make a selection without any restrictions, choose Slip Mode, but if you want your selected area to snap to a grid, use Grid Mode.

But what if you don't want to have this area selected on *all* your tracks? No problem—the selected area will mirror what is selected on the ruler on any *selected* track. In Figure 4.55, I've deselected that in the Guitar 1 track, and you will see that the selected area has been removed from that track only.

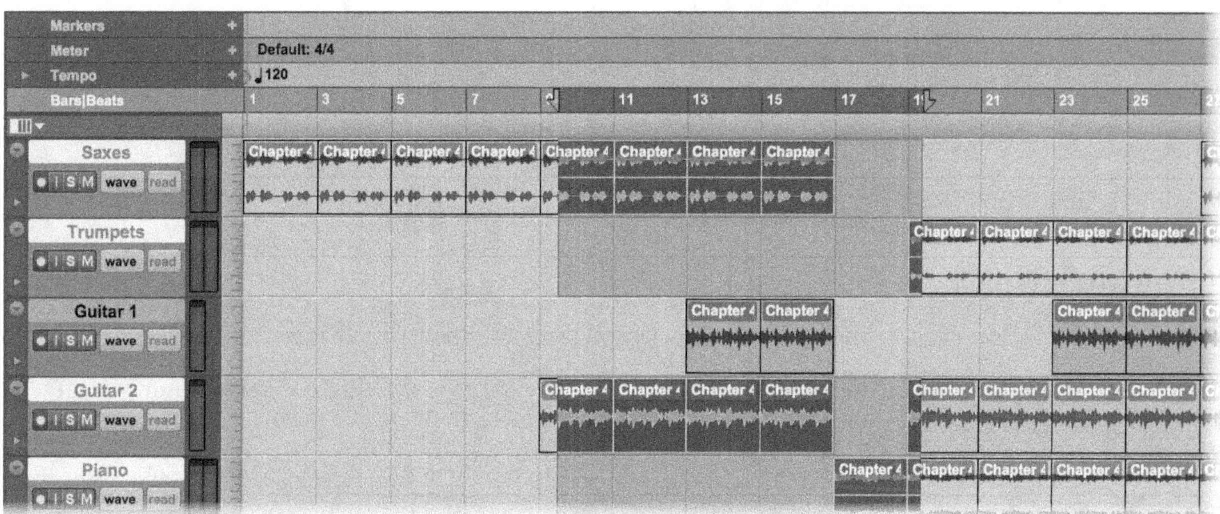

Figure 4.55 Removing a Selection from a Track

To deselect a track that is already selected, hold the COMMAND key (Mac) or CTRL key (Windows) and click on the track name (in the tracks area or the Tracks List). To deselect (or select) all tracks, hold the OPTION key (Mac) or ALT key (Windows) and click on any track name.

Making Selections on Multiple Tracks

There are two easy ways to make selections on multiple tracks:

- Select an area on one track (which will also select the track), then select additional tracks to extend the selection to those tracks as well. Just hold the COMMAND key (Mac) or CTRL key (Windows) and click the track names of desired tracks to add individual tracks or hold the SHIFT key to select a range of adjacent tracks.
- Drag a diagonal box with the Selector tool (as shown in Figure 4.56) by clicking in one corner and dragging diagonally to include other adjacent tracks.

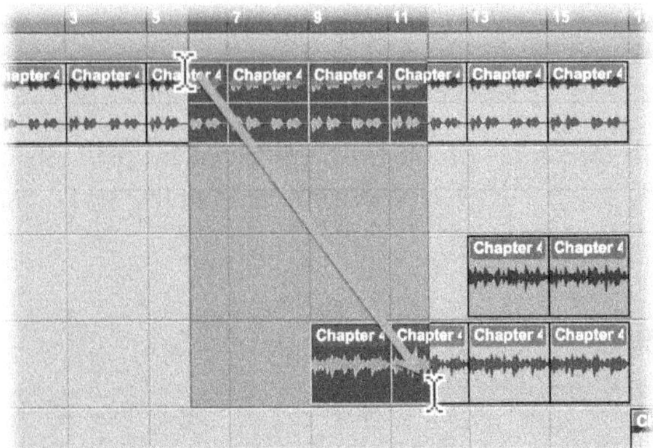

Figure 4.56 Making a Selection on Multiple Tracks

Playing Selections

Once you make a selection, you might want to play it, and there are a few ways that you can do this:

- **Normal Playback:** When Normal Playback is active, playback will start at the beginning of the selected area, and end at the end of the selection.
- **Loop Playback:** With Loop Playback activated, playback will start at the beginning of a selected area, play to the end, and then start again. This will repeat until playback is *stopped*, and is especially useful when working with musical phrases or other segments that need to be heard repetitiously.

Changing your playback mode can be easily done. There are two ways that you can do it:

- From the OPTIONS menu, click LOOP PLAYBACK. A checkmark will indicate that it is active. To change back to Normal Playback mode, just go back to the OPTIONS menu and select LOOP PLAYBACK again, removing the checkmark.

OR

- Right-click the PLAY button in the Transport Controls section (either in the Edit window or the Transport window). A menu will appear allowing you to choose the desired mode, as shown in Figure 4.57.

Figure 4.57 From Left to Right: Normal Playback, Changing Modes, Loop Playback

Pressing the SPACEBAR will start and stop playback according to the playback mode that you're in.

Hands-On Exercise 4.2: Assembling a Song Pt. 2

Before we end this chapter, let's continue your edit of the Mambo Project:

Getting Started

1. Create a new Project by converting the *Pro Tools First—Fundamentals of Audio Production—Chapter 4a (Mambo Part 2).ptx* session to a local Project. The session is found in the *Pro Tools First—Fundamentals of Audio Production—Chapter (Mambo)* subfolder of this book's downloaded exercise material. Choose any desired sample rate, 24-bit, and do not Backup to Cloud.

The Project that will appear includes what you did in the previous exercise, plus a little more work done on it. In a typical workflow, this is the kind of thing that would commonly happens when you work with a collaborator or team of colleagues. It's your job to put on some extra touches.

Editing with the Smart Tool

2. Activate the Smart Tool.
3. Copy any clip on the *Drum* track to start at measure 38. If you're copying by OPTION/ALT-dragging with the Grabber tool in Grid Mode, you can watch the Edit Selection Start field to track the motion of the clip.
4. The Drum clip is a 2-measure long clip. Using the Trim tool function of the Smart Tool (and staying in Grid Mode), trim the first measure off the newly copied Drum clip. The clip will then start at measure 39.
5. Using the Grabber tool function of the Smart Tool, copy the new 1-measure long clip to start at measures 40 through 59. When you're done, you'll have a new, shorter drum loop that starts at measure 39 and ends at measure 59, as shown in Figure 4.58.

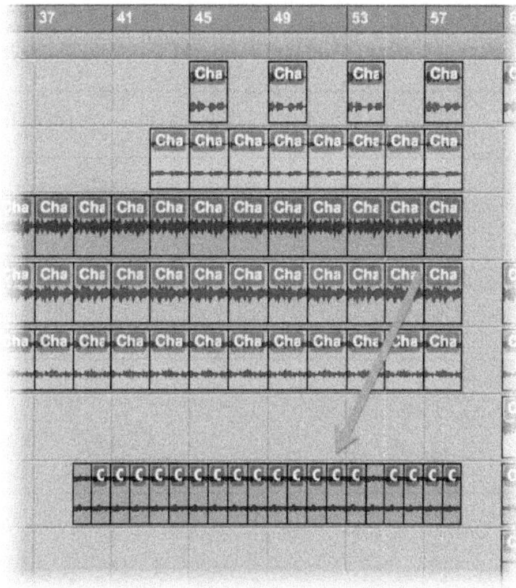

Figure 4.58 Your New Drum Loop

6. To set things up for the next section, horizontally scroll your Edit window, so that you can see the end of the tracks. You'll see that all the clips end at measure 77. Using the Trim tool, trim the end of all the clips (except the clip on the *Reference* track) so that they end on bar 76.

Sync Points and Spot Mode

The last thing to do in this exercise is to end the song with a quick loud note (commonly called a "stinger" in musical circles). The sound we need is on the *Final Hit* track, but there's a problem: The sound doesn't start at the beginning of the clip and doesn't really line up with any Grid line. No problem—the skills you learned with Sync Points and Spot Mode will save the day!

7. Navigate to the beginning of the timeline.
8. Horizontally zoom in so that you can clearly see the details of the clip on the *Final Hit* track.
9. Change to Slip Mode.
10. Using the Selector tool function of the Smart Tool, click at the point in the clip where the sound begins (you might want to solo the track to hear what you're working with). You may need to zoom in extremely close to see the actual beginning of the sound, as shown in Figure 4.59.

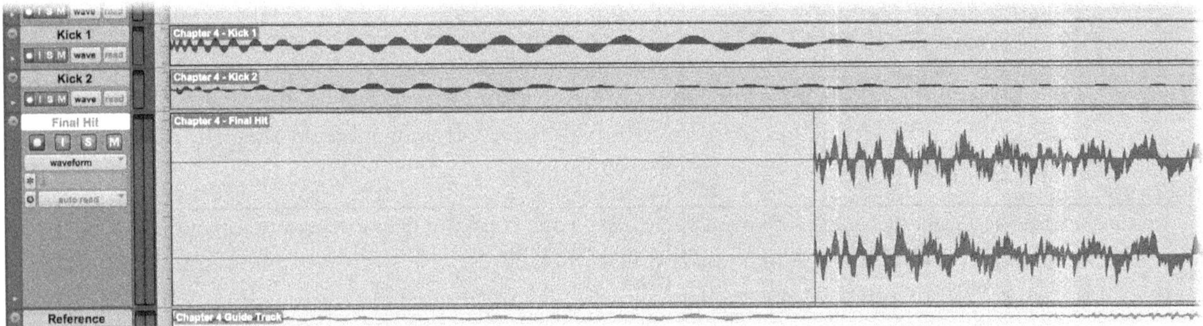

Figure 4.59 Finding the Start of the Sound

11. Create a Sync Point at the position where the sound starts, as shown in Figure 4.60.

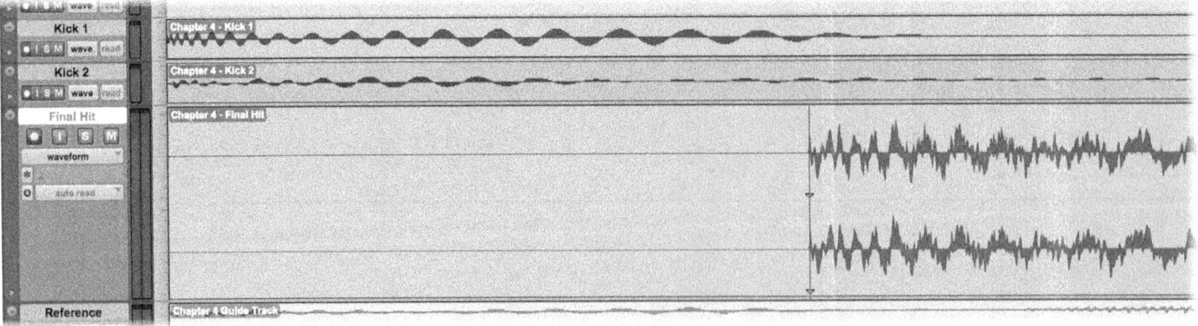

Figure 4.60 Marking the Start of the Sound with a Sync Point

12. Change to Spot Mode. (Can you do it with your F keys?)

13. Click the clip with the Grabber tool function of the Smart Tool to bring up the Spot Dialog box.
14. Spot the Sync Point to the start of measure 76 (76|1|000, as shown in Figure 4.61).

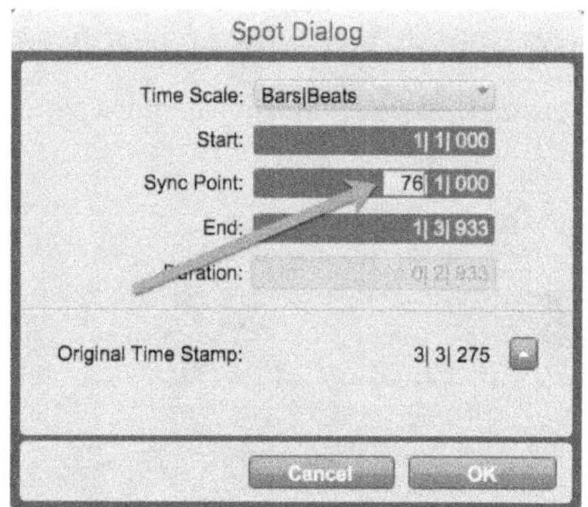

Figure 4.61 Spotting the Sync Point

15. Click the OK button to move the clip.

Since you're zoomed in, it'll look to you as if the clip has disappeared, but in fact, it's jumped to the end of the song, so that its Sync Point is lined up with measure 76.

16. Double-click the Zoomer tool to see your entire project. It should look something like Figure 4.62:

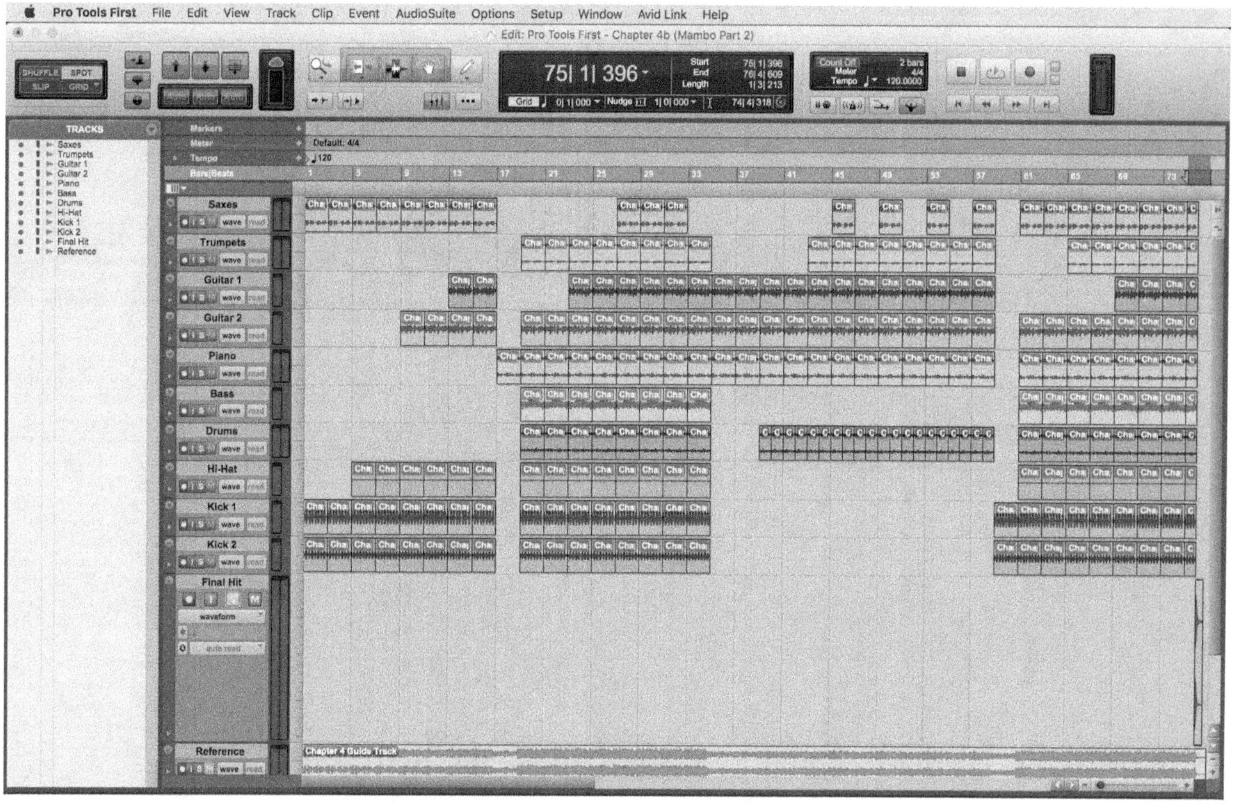

Figure 4.62 Zooming Out to Show the Entire Project

17. Using Single Zoom mode, zoom in on an area towards the end of the song. Note that the active tool will automatically shift back to what you were using before (which, if you've been following the steps, is the Smart Tool)—convenient!
18. Un-mute the *Final Hit* track.
19. In the *rulers* area, make a selection that will allow you to hear enough of your ending to check your work, as shown in Figure 4.63.

Figure 4.63 Selecting the End of the Song

20. Using Loop Playback mode, check the ending. If you're not hearing the result you want, just click and drag the sync point to move it, and re-spot the *Final Hit* clip. This concludes the exercises for this chapter—well done (and make sure you save your project)!

Review Questions

1. What are the different ways to horizontally scroll your Edit window?
2. What is the shortcut for horizontally zooming in the Edit window?
3. What are the different ways to vertically zoom an audio waveform?
4. How can you make a copy of a clip while dragging with the Grabber tool?
5. Which Edit Mode will automatically snap clips end-to-end, with no gap between them?
6. What is the Shortcut to change your Edit Mode to Slip Mode?
7. What is the difference between Absolute Grid Mode and Relative Grid Mode?
8. How can a Sync Point be created?
9. When using the Smart Tool, what is the active Edit tool when the cursor is in the top half of a track (but not near the beginning or end of a clip)?
10. True or False? When a selection is made in the *Bars|Beats* or *Min:Secs* ruler, a corresponding area will be selected on all visible tracks.

CHAPTER 5

Recording Audio

The things you've learned in the previous chapters are some of the most important skills towards becoming a strong Pro Tools user. Sooner or later though, you'll need to move beyond simply importing audio and actually *record* a performance. The ability to record quickly and easily is a key area where Pro Tools really shines, and its flexibility helped it earn its place as a leader in the audio field. This chapter will start you on the road to recording!

Media Used: Pro Tools First—Fundamentals of Audio Production—Chapter 5 (Podcast).ptx, Pro Tools First—Fundamentals of Audio Production—Chapter 5 (Talkback)

Duration: 45 minutes

GOALS

- Create a new Project
- Prepare for recording by setting up a click track, tempo, and signal routing
- Easily execute a basic recording workflow
- Learn how to use other recording methods, such as Loop Record, Punch-in, and QuickPunch recording

What is Recording?

Recording audio is straightforward enough–the goal is to acquire a signal as accurately as possible, with minimal noise, into your recording medium. In fact, from a procedural perspective, that's been the aim since the earliest days of recording, and the process of recording into an older analog system or a modern DAW is quite similar.

Recording audio can take on different forms; from using one or two microphones for a podcast or plugging in a guitar, all the way up to recording full symphony orchestras and dialogue for film. Though all these workflows still follow the goal of recording the highest quality sound into your computer, the skills involved vary significantly. Concepts like microphone placement, recording studio sound treatment, and session management will all come into play in different degrees, depending on the work at hand. Although recording audio can be understood quickly at a basic level, it can take years to master it in different situations.

Careers in Recording: An Interview with Mario De Jesus

Recording audio can lead to employable skills, but this field has changed a bit over time. In the past, a subset of engineers used to work exclusively on audio recording. Nowadays, recording is considered a regular professional skill that many people practice, and aside from recording audio, their work involves other aspects (including composition, editing, and mixing) as well.

Mario De Jesus, known professionally as MarioSo, is a seven-time American and Latin American Grammy-winning recording engineer and producer, whose influential mixing style has been called "the revolutionary sound of the urban music genre." With well over 20 Grammy nominations and counting, Mario has worked alongside artists such as Wisin & Yandel, Jencarlos Canela, Björk, Christina Aguilera, DJ Nelson, DLG, and Ricky Martin.

I thought it'd be great to get Mario's take on recording:

AH: So, Mario, over the years, I'm seeing fewer people who are dedicated exclusive recording engineers, and it seems that recording, though still critical, is becoming a component of other kinds of jobs, rather than a standalone trade. Are you seeing something similar, and if so, where do you think this change is coming from, and where do you think it's going?

MDJ: Yes. Over the years, it's become the job of the producer or beat maker to record the artist's vocals or instruments. Sometimes, the artist or band feels more comfortable that way. I think the reason we are seeing such a fast rise of the Producer/Engineer is because of the information available online for learning, the kind of knowledge used to be learned only in trade schools or by being a recording studio intern. I do expect to see more of this trend as long as the knowledge and tutorials are out there.

AH: From a technical perspective, what are the key skills that make for an excellent recording engineer?

MDJ: Technically, it is your ears. The key to being a great recording engineer is knowing how to capture a great performance. Knowing how to use the gear and operating Pro Tools is ideal, but the real key is knowing how to use your ears to hear that great take. Yes, you should know how to listen for unwanted distortion, but it is not just sonically. You must also learn how to listen for those magic takes and performances. Record that magic. The artist and client will thank you for it.

AH: Of course, it's not just the technical skills that make a good recording engineer, but also the social skills, as well. A huge part of any successful recording session is making sure that the artists are happy and relaxed, while at the same time ensuring the producers are satisfied. Sometimes, that's an easy job; sometimes it's not. What do you think are the personal traits needed to be a successful recording engineer?

MDJ: This comes from just being around the industry: knowing the clients, knowing how to read their vibes, and just being a cool person. Sometimes a recording session will start with a 2-hour conversation about anything. It can be sports, fashion, family, food, anything, but that conversation will set the vibe of the session. When clients feel comfortable, they will have a great recording session. I am a true believer that a great vibe also gets recorded with that magical performance.

AH: I didn't know until recently that you were a student at Full Sail University, where I was a teacher a million years ago, so we have that in common! What would you say are the most important skills you learned in a formal school environment that helped you become successful today?

Figure 5.1 Mario De Jesus

MDJ: Schools like Full Sail are a great place to learn how to use and operate the gear. Having access to that equipment and tools was a huge advantage. After I graduated from Full Sail, I remember being the only studio intern who knew how to recall an SSL and align a tape machine. That knowledge was key, because I would end up becoming an assistant engineer faster than most interns.

AH: Thanks so much for your time! Before we wrap up, any words of wisdom for the readers?

MDJ: I would just quote something one of my teachers told me: "The moment you stop learning, you will become old." Keep learning! The beauty of this industry is that the technology keeps getting better. Learn it, master it, use it, and go capture some magic.

Getting Audio into Your System

As with many things that relate to audio production, if you understand the signal flow behind the recording process, you're more than halfway there already.

Microphones

Let's start off by talking about one of the most commonly used input devices: microphones.

Believe it or not, microphones and speakers are closely related, and are both forms of transducers–devices that convert one form of energy into another. With speakers, an electrical signal is applied to an electromagnet (called a voice coil), which then pushes and pulls a speaker cone, creating a vibration. If you reverse that flow, you have a microphone. With microphones, a vibration goes to a small vibrating component—similar to a speaker's cone—called a diaphragm. The movement of that diaphragm creates an electrical signal.

That electrical signal is then transmitted through the microphone cable to your recording medium, but the voltage coming from microphones is unusably low. To bring up the level of the signal to something you can work with, here are some ways:

- **Microphone Preamp:** One way to solve the voltage issue is to connect the microphone's 3-pin XLR connection to a microphone preamp. The preamp will increase the level of the signal up to a line-level signal, which is then connected to a line-level input on your audio interface.

- **Connecting to an Audio Interface:** Many audio interfaces—particularly those that are popularly used in smaller studios—have built-in microphone preamps, solving the voltage problem. If your interface has 3-pin XLR microphone connections, it's a safe bet that it has an integrated microphone preamp.
- **USB:** USB microphones are also popular choices in smaller situations and arguably the simplest solution for boosting the signal. A USB mic includes not only a built-in microphone preamp, but also a built-in audio interface, converting the real-world sound to digital audio.

There are different microphone types, including *dynamic*, *condenser*, and *ribbon* microphones. Let's take a look at the pros and cons of each type:

Dynamic Microphones

The oldest type of microphone is called a dynamic mic, which has a simple design.

A dynamic microphone works by moving a coil of wire around a magnet (or moving a magnet around a coil of wire), pushing electrons in the wire and creating an electrical current, similar to how an electrical generator works. In the case of dynamic microphones, the diaphragm of the microphone is attached to a metal coil suspended between two magnets. When sound causes the diaphragm to move, the coil interacting with the magnets generates a small electrical current, which is then sent to a microphone preamp (either a stand-alone microphone preamp or one built into your audio interface).

Dynamic Microphones have a few advantages:

- They are generally less expensive than other kinds of microphones. Two of the most popular dynamic microphones, the Shure SM57 and SM58, are only about $100 USD.

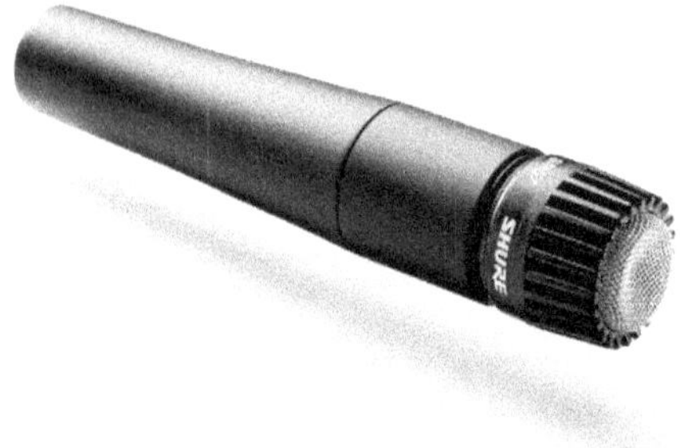

Figure 5.2 The Shure SM57 Dynamic Microphone

- They have a simple design and tend to be very sturdy. Not only can they withstand the occasional knocks and drops, but they are also well-suited to record louder sounds like guitars and drums, and are commonly used in live music stage performances. Classic examples of dynamic microphones, Shure SM57 and SM58 microphones are not only quite affordable, but among the most popular microphones today.

Condenser microphones have some downsides, though; they are typically not the most sensitive type of microphone and will not capture some of the nuances of a performance, particularly in the higher frequencies.

Condenser Microphones

Condenser microphones are also commonly found in recording studios. The way that condenser microphones work boils down to two metal plates, both of which are supplied with a small amount of electrical charge. One metal plate is attached to the diaphragm, while the other has a fixed position, with a small gap between the two plates. As vibrations cause the diaphragm to move, the relative distance between the two plates changes, producing *capacitance*, which generates an electrical signal.

Condenser microphones are typically a little more expensive than dynamic microphones. They also tend to be more delicate due to their more complex construction, meaning you should not put it too close to the kick drum or the guitar amp. However, they can record sound in greater detail and over a larger frequency range. The Neumann U87, perhaps the most coveted microphone in the world, is a great example of a condenser microphone.

Figure 5.3 The Neumann U87 Condenser Microphone

Another thing you should know: Condenser microphones need power. Electrical current must be supplied to the two metal plates, or else their change in relative position will not generate a signal. This power is typically supplied by the microphone preamp or the audio interface that you connect the microphone to, called *phantom power*. If you've got a condenser microphone, just make sure that phantom power is turned on for that connection, and you'll be good to go.

Dynamic microphones don't need phantom power, but most modern dynamic microphones won't be damaged if phantom power is turned on. As a general rule, though, if a microphone doesn't need phantom power, don't turn it on.

Condenser microphones can make a sound when they are plugged in due to their circuitry powering up. Turn down your studio monitors before connecting these kinds of microphones to your preamp or interface.

Ribbon Microphones

Although a ribbon microphone is generally the most expensive kind of microphone you can buy, it is actually the sibling of the humble dynamic microphone. In a ribbon microphone, instead of a coil interacting with magnets (as is the case of a dynamic mic), an extremely thin strip of metal is suspended between two magnets. Also, a ribbon microphone doesn't have a diaphragm—the sound hitting the ribbon causes it to move, generating an electrical current.

If the goal is to capture sound with very high quality and accuracy, it's hard to beat a good ribbon microphone. The ribbon design can capture detail and clarity from very low to very high frequency ranges. They are also well-suited for providing a good reproduction of the area around the microphone, making them very effective recording tools in professional recording spaces and concert halls.

Two things to be aware of, though: First, they are typically on the higher end of the price range (the Royer R-121 shown in Figure 5.4, for example, is over $1,000 USD). Secondly, the thin ribbon—the core of the microphone's design—is very delicate and can be torn by wind or rough handling, rendering the microphone useless.

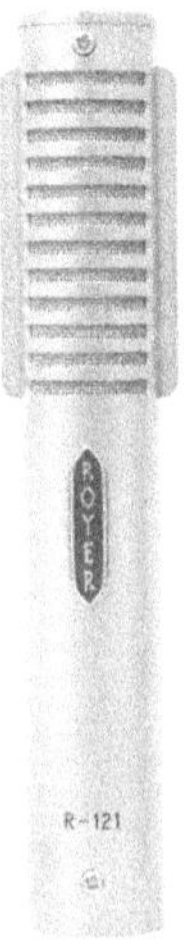

Figure 5.4 The Royer Labs R-121 Ribbon Microphone

With modern ribbon microphones, having phantom power on will usually do no damage (as ribbon microphones don't need phantom power). However, older ribbon microphones *can* be damaged by phantom power—another reason to turn it off (on your microphone preamp or interface) if the connected microphone doesn't need it.

Large Diaphragm vs. Small Diaphragm

When you're shopping for microphones—condenser mics, in particular—you'll find that there are two different types: *Large diaphragm* and *small diaphragm* microphones. As a general rule, a large diaphragm microphone has a diaphragm (the vibrating part that captures the incoming sound) of 1 inch or more in diameter. On the other hand, a small diaphragm microphone has a diaphragm of ½ inch or less in diameter.

As you might expect, small diaphragm microphones tend to be smaller than large diaphragm microphones, but their differences go beyond size:

- **Large diaphragms**, with a larger vibrating area, have a generally higher signal level and lower noise. They are generally less sensitive than small diaphragm microphones, but although they don't record as accurately, they do provide a pleasing warmth in the low frequencies, making them a popular choice for recording vocals.
- **Small diaphragm** microphones tend to be more technically accurate in recording a performance. The small vibrating area is far more responsive, especially to the initial attack (or transient) of sounds, and higher frequency ranges. Small diaphragm microphones are better for recording all the details of a performance, and are commonly used for drums, guitar, piano, and other instruments.

Polarity Patterns

Last, but certainly not least on the list of factors determining your microphone choices, is the microphone's *polarity*—in other words, the directionality of the microphone. Microphones use different polarity patterns, but for the purposes of this book, we'll focus on the three most common: *omnidirectional*, *cardioid*, and *figure 8*:

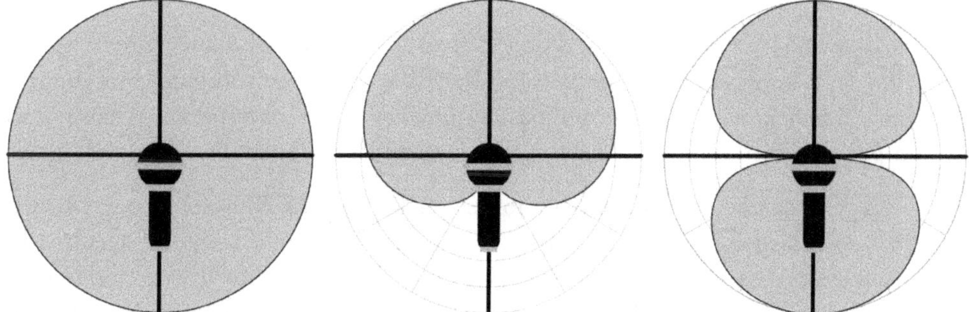

Figure 5.5 From Left to Right: Omidirectional, Cardioid, and Figure 8 Polarity Patterns

- A microphone with **omnidirectional** polarity is sensitive to sound, capturing it in virtually all directions. This kind of design typically gives you the most natural sound and is resistant to plosives (the pop sound that microphones will often pick up with hard "P", "B", and other consonants).
- The most common polarity pattern is called **cardioid**. It's easy to remember because the name of the pattern is derived from its heart (or *cardio*) shape. This kind of microphone "listens" to whatever is in front of it, making it the most directional kind of microphone. Sounds behind it or to the side of it will not be picked up to the same degree as the sounds directly in front of it. For that reason, cardioid microphones are commonly used in live performances. Unlike omnidirectional microphones however, cardioid microphones are susceptible to plosives.
- The last pattern, called **figure 8** (or sometimes *bidirectional*), is equally sensitive to sounds in front of it and behind it, but not to the side of it. Ribbon microphones, as a result of their design, tend to have this polarity. Figure 8 polarity microphones give a clear recording of an individual performer's sound, plus the ambience of the recording space. They are also commonly used in combination with other microphones in more complex and advanced recording situations.

Line Level Inputs

Compared to microphones and all their variations, level signal is a much simpler and more straightforward topic. Line level signals will be used in your studio for connecting devices like microphone preamps, keyboard synthesizers, television monitors, or CD/DVD players to your interface.

Line level signals fall into two different types:

- **-10dBV:** This is the kind of line level signal that you're going to encounter in all consumer level and some professional-grade equipment. Audio interfaces that have line level inputs and outputs are usually of this type.
- **+4 dBu:** Sometimes called *professional* line level, this line level signal is used in high-end professional equipment like mixing consoles, microphone preamplifiers, and other professional grade hardware components, but is rarely used in home studio systems.

DI Inputs

Most guitar and bass amplifiers have line level outputs, in addition to their speaker outlets, allowing the amplifier to be directly connected to a line level input on an audio interface. But what if you want to plug your guitar or bass directly into your interface? Instruments like guitars and basses don't have microphone level signals nor do they have line levels—their output is a bit stronger than microphone level and a bit lower than line level signals.

One way that instrument level signals can be brought into audio devices like mixing consoles through a small hardware called *Direct Injection* (also called a *Direct* or *DI*) box. Without getting into the technical details, a DI box will accept a signal from the guitar or bass (the guitar or bass plugs directly into the box insert), and outputs a microphone level signal that would then go to a mic preamp. These boxes are not expensive and can be very handy to have around. Figure 5.6 shows a DI box that I've had for decades, and it can still get me out of a jam when I need it.

Figure 5.6 An Example of a Simple and Inexpensive DI Box

Many audio interfaces have built-in DI boxes, allowing the user to plug a guitar or bass directly into the interface without any additional hardware needed. Usually these inputs are called *Instrument* Inputs; occasionally, they're called *DI* Inputs.

The Importance of the Recording Space

Recording spaces come in all shapes and sizes, depending upon the kind of recording work being done. If you're only recording line level or instrument level signals directly into an audio interface—for example, playing a guitar or keyboard synthesizer that's plugged into an interface—pretty much any room will do the trick. Recording with microphones, though—that's another story.

Isolating the Microphone

When you see pictures of vocalists singing in a studio, you'll notice that they generally do not hold the microphone with their hands, for two reasons: First, holding a microphone increases the likelihood of the distance changing between the singer (or instrument) and the microphone, as the arm's position naturally changes, which will then result in an inconsistent recording. Secondly, holding a microphone can produce handling noise, and natural movements like adjusting one's grip will also add noise into your recording.

Microphone stands solve the problem of handling noise, and they come in a variety of shapes and sizes, from desktop to standalone mic stands. They free up the performer's hands and provide more consistency and stability when recording. Frequently, microphone extensions called *boom arms* are attached to a basic microphone stand, as shown in Figure 5.7. These boom arm attachments not only extend the height of a microphone stand, but also give more flexibility with microphone placement.

Figure 5.7 A Microphone Stand with a Boom Arm Attached

In basic setups, microphones are attached to the stand by way of a solid plastic microphone clip. These kinds of clips, however, respond to vibrations can be transmitted along the microphone stand to the microphone, which will be picked up as noise. Hence, additional isolation is often used in the form of microphone shock mounts, which suspend the microphone using elastic cords (as shown in Figure 5.8) or springs.

Figure 5.8 A Microphone in a Shock Mount

If you're recording vocals, there's one more item you might consider—a pop filter. Pop filters are designed to minimize *plosives*—the burst of air that accompanies hard consonants like "P" or "B". Pop filters are inexpensive and easy to use; just clip it to your microphone stand and position the circular barrier between the performer's mouth and the microphone, as shown in Figure 5.9.

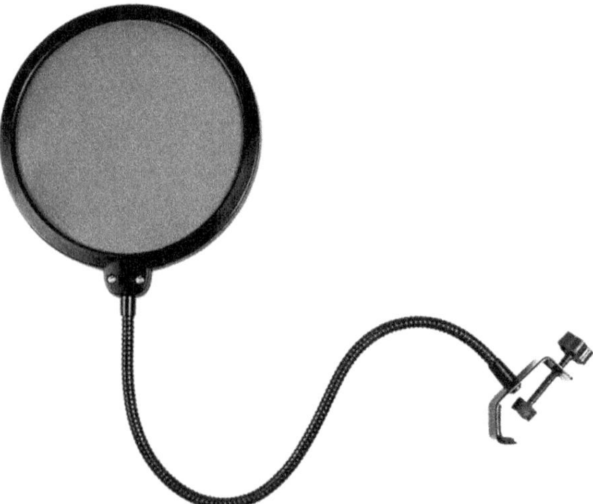

Figure 5.9 A Pop Filter

Sound Absorption

Sound, like light, can be reflected. This means that sounds that you make also produce sound reflections that bounce on nearby walls, and in turn, are picked up by a microphone. Generally speaking, you'll want these reflections to be minimized, so sound absorption panels are applied on walls and other surfaces in the recording space.

Sound absorbers are not tremendously expensive, but they can be a bit difficult from a logistical perspective. Sometimes it's just not practical to put squares of sound-absorbing foam on the walls of a home studio. Fortunately, there are a number of less intrusive alternatives, including small sound-absorbing panels that can be attached to microphone stands, as shown in Figure 5.10 (this setup not only minimizes plosives with a pop filter, but also removes sound reflected from the wall behind the microphone with the sound absorption panel).

Figure 5.10 A Microphone Setup with a Pop Filter and Sound Absorbtion Panel

The Proximity Effect and Your Recording Space

Finally, the size of your recording space matters. If you're recording in a space that's too small, forcing you to be too close to the microphone, something called the *proximity effect* occurs. This is an increase in low frequencies as a sound source gets closer to a microphone. Sometimes, this may be what you want: For example, if you're doing a voiceover for a documentary, a rich, warm low end is a great sound. However, the proximity effect can sometimes create a "muddy" recording, and you need some room to move away from the microphone to remove it.

Microphones with an omnidirectional polarity are not affected by proximity.

As a sound source is a moved farther from a microphone, less of the source and more of the room will be recorded, and the more important sound absorption can be.

Preparing to Record

You have your microphones have and prepared your room. Now, you're ready to record. Let's go through the pre-session checklist:

Meter and Tempo

If you're working on a music project, it's quite common to have performers playing to a *click track*—a track with a steady clicking sound indicating the tempo. For the click track to work correctly though, you need to set up your song's meter and tempo first.

Meter

Without getting too deep into music theory, a song's *meter* (also commonly called *Time Signature*) determines the number of beats in a measure (the first number), and which note value gets one beat (the second number). Most songs that you hear on the radio have a 4/4 meter, meaning that there are four beats in a measure and a quarter note gets one beat. However, many other meters are commonly used as well, and it is your job as a Pro Tools producer to be able to give your musicians the meter that they want.

By default, Pro Tools' meter is 4/4, but if you need to change it:

1. In the MIDI controls section of the Edit window or Transport window, double-click the meter value, as shown in Figure 5.11.

Figure 5.11 Double-Clicking the Meter Value

OR

1. Click the plus (+) button to the right of the word *Meter* in the Rulers area of the Edit window.

Figure 5.12 Clicking the Add Meter Change button in the Meter Ruler

2. In the Meter Change dialog box that will appear, you can choose the location for your meter (in this case, my meter change will happen at measure 1, beat 1, and tick 000—the beginning of my song). Then type in the Meter you want (in this case it's 4/4), and finally you can choose your click value (in this case a quarter note).

In the Meter Change dialog box, you'll see a check box in the upper left-hand corner called *Snap To Bar*. With this enabled, even if you clicked in the middle of a bar, the meter change will be applied on beat 1 of the bar. It is very rare to change meter at any point other than the beginning of a bar, so you can safely leave this box checked.

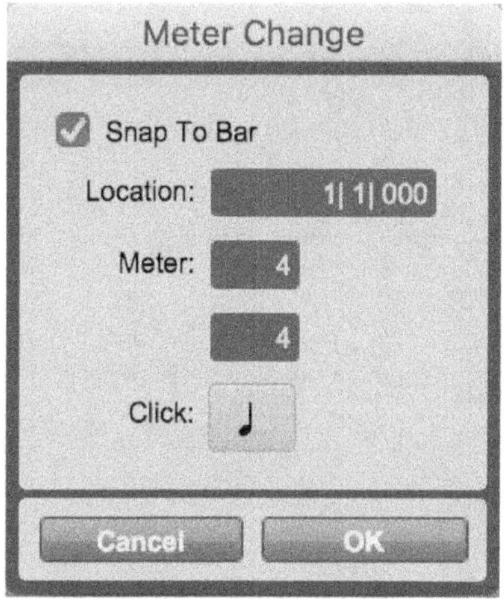

Figure 5.13 The Meter Change Dialog

3. When you're happy with your settings, click the OK button and the meter event will be created.

Though many songs will have the same meter throughout the entire piece, it's not uncommon to have the meter change during the course of a piece of music. By choosing a different location in the Meter Change dialog box, you can create meter changes anywhere on your Project's timeline.

Tempo

Tempo is the speed at which beats are played. In music, tempo is measured in Beats Per Minute, or BPM. By default, Pro Tools' tempo is 120 BPM, but you can set it up to anything you like:

1. In the MIDI controls section of the Edit window or Transport window, click on the tempo field, as shown in Figure 5.14. Just type the tempo value that you want and confirm your choice by clicking the RETURN key (Mac) or ENTER key (Windows).

Figure 5.14 Setting the Tempo from the MIDI controls

OR

1. Click the plus (+) button to the right of the word *Tempo* in the Rulers area of the Edit window.

Figure 5.15 Clicking the Add Tempo Change button in the Tempo Ruler

2. In the Tempo Change dialog box, as shown in Figure 5.16, you can choose the location where your tempo change will start. In this case, it starts at bar 1, beat 1, tick 000—the beginning of my song. In the BPM field, you can type your desired tempo.

Figure 5.16 The Tempo Change DialogClick the OK button, and the tempo change will be applied.

Just as with meter, by choosing a different location in the Tempo Change dialog box, you can create tempo changes anywhere on your Project's timeline.

You can also choose the resolution of your beat. This is typically the same value as the resolution value in your meter selection, but can be changed if needed.

Tempo and Meter Rulers

Once you've made your tempo and meter changes, you can check them by looking at your Meter and Tempo Rulers. Initial meter and tempo settings will be shown at the far left of the ruler. As shown in Figure 5.17, my starting tempo is 120 BPM and my starting meter is 4/4 time.

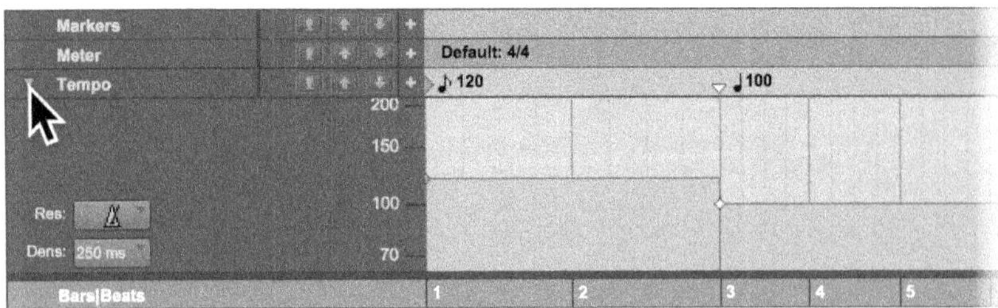

Figure 5.17 The Tempo and Meter Rulers

As mentioned in this chapter already, both meter and tempo changes can happen at any time on your timeline. Figure 5.17 shows a tempo change at measure three from 120 BPM down to 100 BPM. Tempo changes can be shown not only in the ruler but also in the Tempo Editor, which can be shown by clicking the triangular disclosure button to the left of the word Tempo.

Tap Tempo

Sometimes, though, you might not know the number value of a tempo. No problem—just highlight the tempo field, as shown in Figure 5.18, and press the *T* key on your keyboard in tempo. As you tap it, Pro Tools will quickly calculate the tempo of your song.

Figure 5.18 The Tempo Field Highlighted, Ready to Tap the Tempo

The Conductor Track

In the MIDI controls section in either the Edit window or Transport window, you'll see a button that is meant to look like a conductor holding a baton. This is the *Conductor Track* button, which determines how your Project will deal with tempo:

Figure 5.19 The Conductor Track Button

- When the Conductor Track button is enabled (blue), any tempo settings that you've made in the Tempo Ruler will be in effect. For example, in Figure 5.20, the tempo would start at 120 BPM, and then change at measure 3 to 100 BPM.

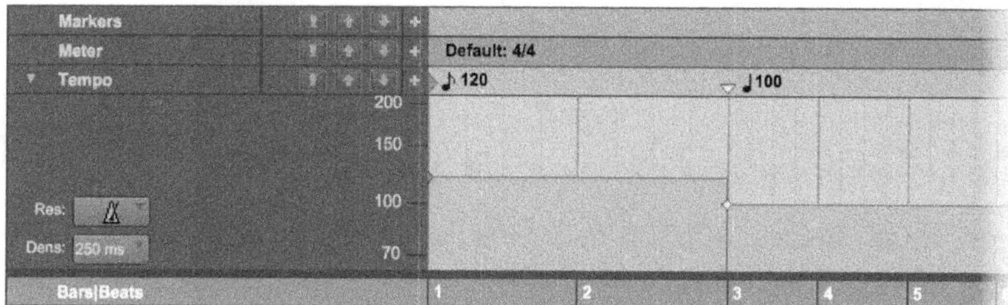

Figure 5.20 Tempo Changes in Effect when the Conductor Track is Enabled

- When the Conductor Track button is disabled (grey), your project will be in *Manual Tempo* mode, and your tempo will simply be the value that is set in the Tempo field directly above the Conductor Track button. Any tempo settings in the Tempo Ruler will be disregarded.

Click Track

Once you've set up your tempo and meter, all that's left is to create the click track itself and set up how it will behave.

Creating a Click Track

The most straightforward way to create a click track is from the TRACK menu: From the TRACK menu, choose CREATE CLICK TRACK.

Figure 5.21 Creating a Click Track

The track type that is created is an Auxiliary Input Track, which will have one plug-in on it called *Click II*. This simple plug-in technically falls under the category of Virtual Instrument (which you'll learn more about in the next chapter), but this instrument simply plays short notes to indicate tempo.

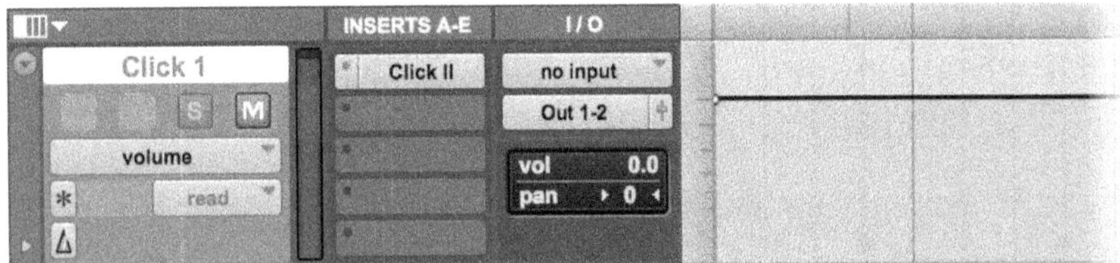

Figure 5.22 A Click Track

Though it's a simple plug-in, there are some ways that you can customize your click:

1. Click on the Click II plug-in's Insert button. (On this track, it is the small box with the C on it, for Click.) The Click II plug-in window will open.

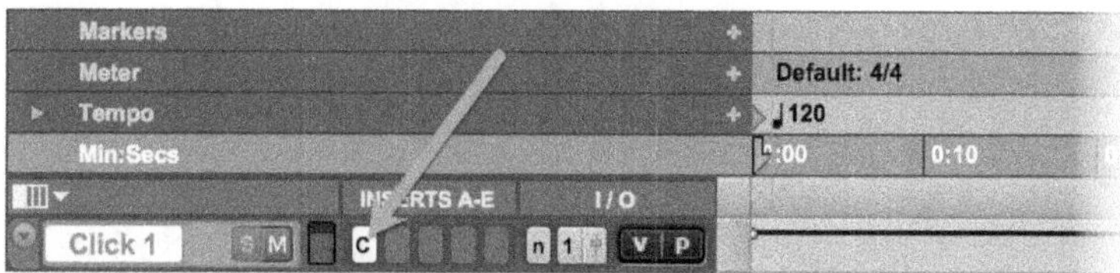

Figure 5.23 Opening the Click II Plug-in

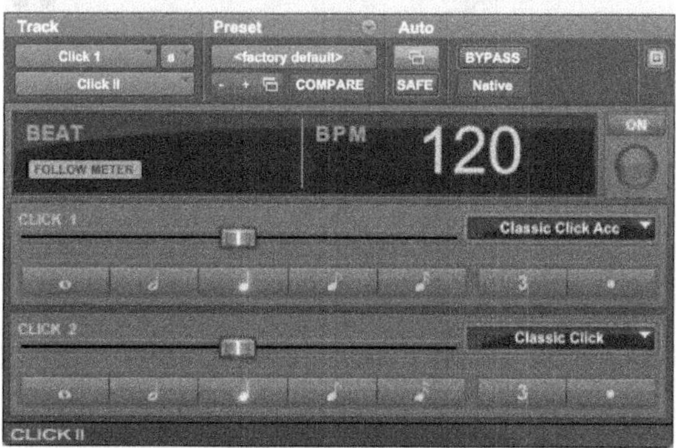

Figure 5.24 The Click II Plug-in Window

2. Adjust the CLICK 1 slider (for each measure's Beat 1) and CLICK 2 slider (for the other beats) to get the best overall volume.
3. If you want different sounds for your metronome, click on the Click Sound selector to the right of either click volume slider (which shows the current sound assigned to the click). A drop-down menu will appear, from which you can choose the best tone for your click. Note that you can set the Click 1 and Click 2 sounds independently.
4. By default, the Click II plug-in will follow the session's meter, but you have the option of selecting any click resolution that you desire for either Click 1 or Click 2. Just click Follow Meter to disable the function and choose the desired click resolutions from the buttons below each volume slider.
5. Finally, a nice little new feature: a visual indicator! If you have difficulty hearing your click in a mix, you can open the plug-in window and watch the click as a flashing light. To turn off the feature, click the ON button above the visual indicator.

Figure 5.25 Visual Tempo Indicator in the Click II Plug-in

6. When you're finished, click on the Close button (a small button in the upper left-hand corner of the window on a Mac, or in the upper right-hand side on a Windows computer). The Click II plug-in window will close.

Click and Countoff Options

Now that the click track is set up, you'll need to choose how it will behave, and you can do that from the Setup menu:

1. From the SETUP menu, choose CLICK/COUNTOFF.

Figure 5.26 Setting Up Your Click from SETUP>CLICK/COUNTOFF

OR

1. Double-click the METRONOME button in the MIDI controls section in the Edit window or Transport window.

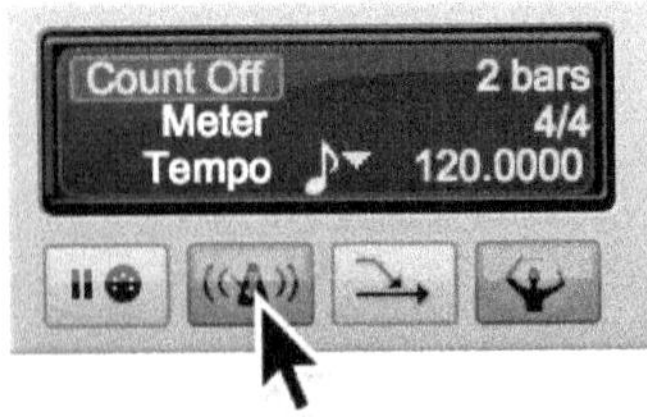

Figure 5.27 Setting Up Your Click from the METRONOME Button

2. The Click/Countoff Options dialog box will appear, where you can choose how your click will behave.

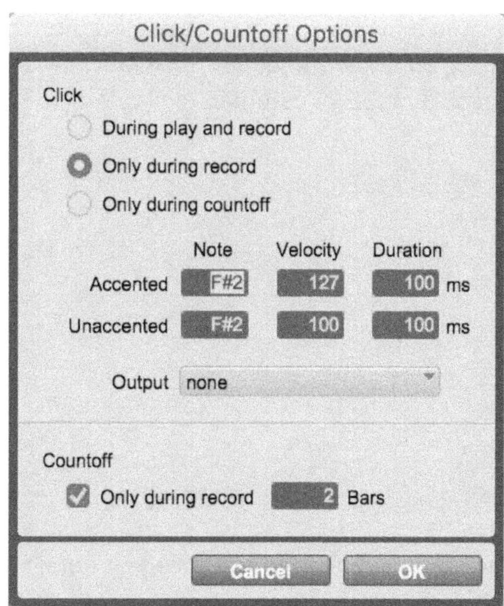

Figure 5.28 The Click/Countoff Options Dialog

3. The Click/Countoff Options dialog box is divided into three sections. At the top, you can choose *when* you will hear a click:

   - **During Play and Record:** With this option selected, you'll hear the click track during playback and when you're recording. Since click tracks are commonly used only during recording, this is not a common choice.
   - **Only During Record:** This is the most common option in most recording situations. When your Project is only playing, and not recording any tracks, the click track will be silent. The click track will only be heard when at least one track is in the process of recording.
   - **Only During Count off:** *Count off* is the number of beats before recording starts, allowing musicians to get comfortable with the tempo before they start recording. With this option chosen, the click will be heard *only* during the count off—once recording begins, the click track will be silent.

4. The middle section, as shown in Figure 5.29, is largely unused these days. This section allows you to choose how MIDI data will be transmitted to an external sound module, creating a click sound. If you're using a click track within Pro Tools and the Click II plug-in, this section can be skipped.

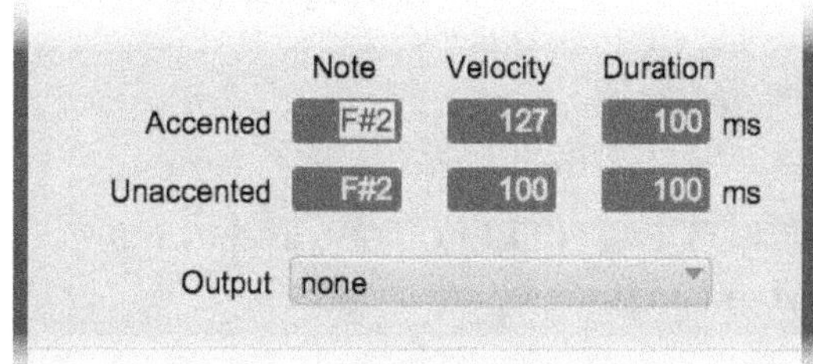

Figure 5.29 MIDI Click Setup

5. As already mentioned, *count off* is the number of beats played in tempo before recording begins. In the bottom section of the Click/Countoff Options dialog box, you can set how many measures of count off you'll hear. Typically, it is only used during recording, so it's common to check the ONLY DURING RECORD check box.

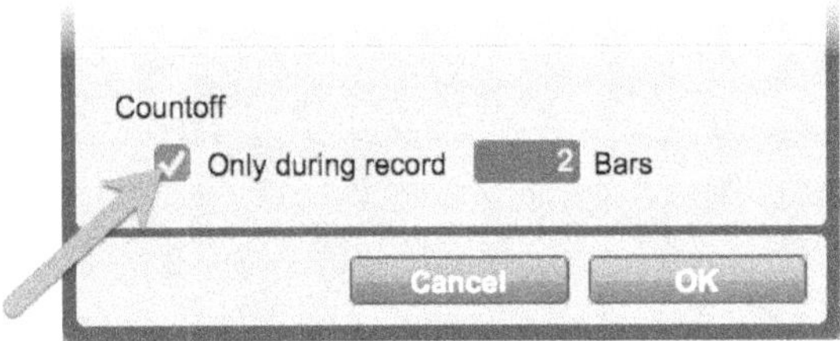

Figure 5.30 Setting Up Your Count Off

6. Click the OK button, and your settings will be applied.
7. There's only one more step, and that is to enable your metronome. There are two ways you can do it:
   - From the OPTIONS menu, you can see the status of your metronome. If your click is enabled, you'll see a checkmark next to the CLICK menu item. If there's no checkmark, just click the CLICK menu item to turn it on.
   - Just click the METRONOME button to activate it, as shown in Figure 5.31. An active click track will be indicated by a blue metronome button.

Figure 5.31 Enabling Your Click

Setting Up I/O for Recording

We're getting close to being ready to record, but before that, we need to choose where your signal is coming from and where it's going:

For this section, you need to see the I/O View in the Edit window (or Mix window). You learned how to show and hide these window views in Chapter 2.

1. On the track on which you wish to record, click the INPUT PATH SELECTOR, as shown in Figure 5.32. Choose the input that corresponds with your audio source.

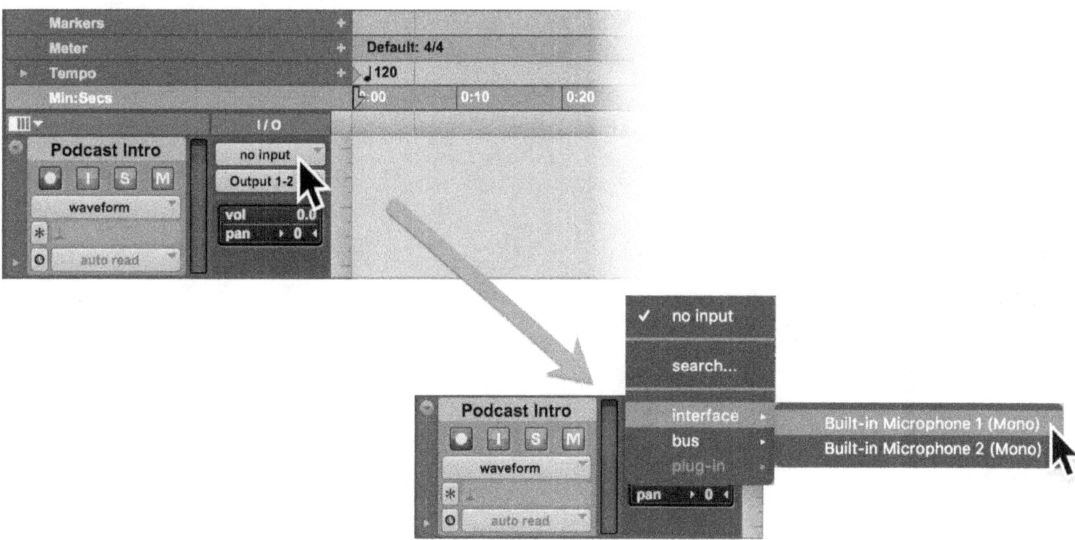

Figure 5.32 Setting your Track's Input

2. Directly below the INPUT PATH SELECTOR is the OUTPUT PATH SELECTOR. Clicking this selector will also display a menu of output options. Choose the path that corresponds to the connection that you'll use for monitoring your Project as you record. In the example shown in Figure 5.33, I'm choosing to route the output of my recorded track to my headphones (Output 1-2).

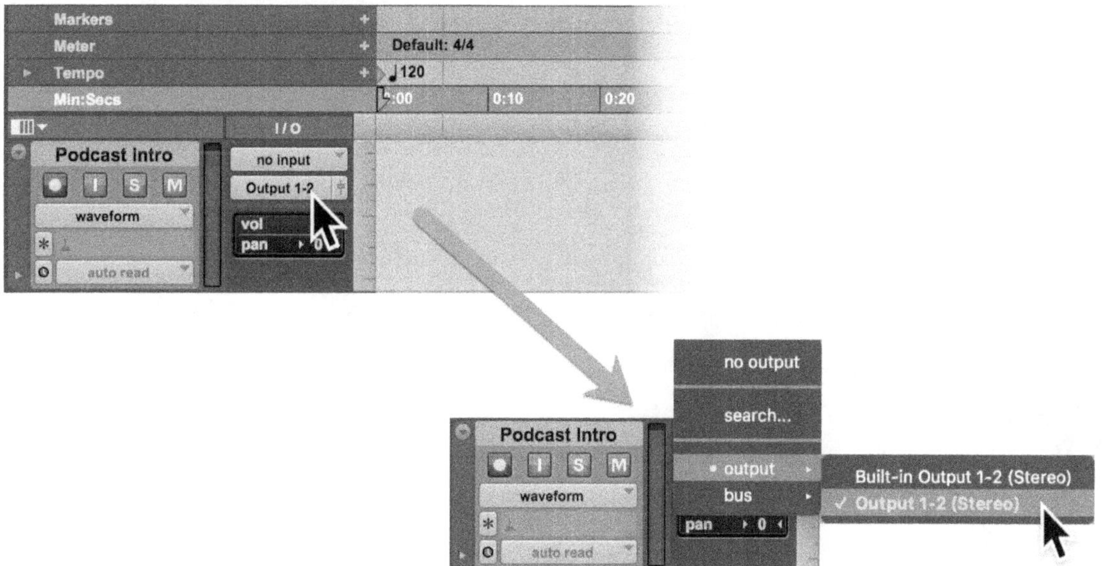

Figure 5.33 Setting Your Track's Output

3. Changing the PAN of the monitor output will shift the output of your recording track left or right. Though this parameter is mostly used when mixing, it can come into play in some recording situations. For example, if I have a person in my studio didn't want to wear the left headphone, I would pan the recording track to the right.

4. You can adjust your monitoring level in a number of ways—here are two: In the Mix window, set the Volume fader on the track that you are recording on, or click and hold on the Volume indicator of the track that you're recording on in the Edit window (a fader will show up, as shown in Figure 5.34. Your settings here will not affect the audio being recorded. Just set so that you and your talent can comfortably hear yourselves.

Figure 5.34 Adjusting Volume in the Edit Window

Using an Output Window

There's another way to view and manipulate essential track-related data. A track's Output window (sometimes called a *tear-away strip*) enables you to adjust many of your track's parameters through a single mixer-like interface. You can launch the Output window from either the Mix window or the Edit window. The Output window is particularly useful when adjusting mix settings in the Edit window.

Click on the OUTPUT WINDOW button to the right of the Output Path selector. (The icon looks like a tiny fader.) The track's Output window will appear. Notice that much of the track-related data you set up earlier in this chapter is shown here, as well.

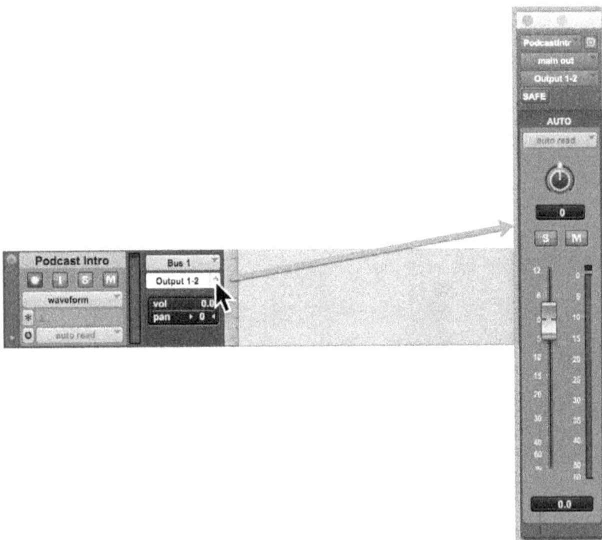

Figure 5.35 Opening a Track's Output Window

You can quickly reset your volume to unity (0.0) or your pan to center (0) by holding the OPTION key (Mac) or ALT key (Windows) and clicking on the volume or pan controls in either the track's display fields or the Output window.

Monitoring During Recording

If you're recording with a microphone, it is very important that the signal from your monitor speakers isn't picked up by the microphone. If that happens, you run the risk of feedback, which can quickly damage your speakers and your hearing. This is easily avoided by turning off your monitor speakers and monitoring your Project through closed-back headphones, but this is an impractical approach in many scenarios.

In order for a producer to listen to their monitor speakers and record multiple performers at the same time, a producer will often use a *cue mix*, which is a headphone mix typically different from the mix that the engineer is listening to, routed out of dedicated outputs through the use of something called a send. You'll learn how this is set up in Chapter 10.

Basic Recording

You're now ready to record!

1. Ensure that you are avoiding any feedback situations—if you're recording with a microphone in the same room as your monitor speakers, turn your speakers off, and ensure that you can hear your mix through closed-back headphones.
2. Check to see if signal is coming to your destination track. There are a number of ways that you can do it, but here's one that has a few additional benefits in various recording workflows: Click the TRACKINPUT MONITOR button, as shown in Figure 5.36 (when this is active, the button will be green). Once TrackInput monitoring is active, the track will have a "live" input, and you'll hear your incoming signal.

Figure 5.36 Enabling TrackInput Monitoring

3. This is a crucial step: Once your track's input is being monitored, the meter on the track will show the level of the signal as it comes to the track. At this point, adjust the *output* of the sound source so that it is strong, but not clipping. Though there are several schools of thought on the perfect recording level, but to start out with, set a target that your levels are in the light green section of the meter, but not in the yellow range.

The changes you make on the output volume and output pan controls will affect the track's output only, not its input level. This means if you're recording an especially loud signal that is clipping (distorting) your input, you'll need to bring down the level of your sound source (instrument, microphone, and so on) rather than the volume fader on the track.

4. Once you're happy with the incoming level of the track, click the TRACKINPUT MONITOR button to disable TrackInput monitoring.
5. Click on the TRACK RECORD ENABLE button to "arm" the desired track(s) for recording. Bear in mind that as soon as the track is armed, its input will be active, so take care to avoid situations that can cause feedback.

Figure 5.37 Record-Enabling a Track

There is a shortcut to record enable a track: Select the track(s) that you want to enable and press SHIFT+R.

6. Recording will start at the position of the playback cursor *or* any selected area on your timeline. Either position your playback cursor where you want recording to begin, or select the area on your timeline where you want to record.
7. Click on the RECORD button in the Transport window or in the Edit window's Transport controls. The Record button will begin to flash.
8. Click on the PLAY button (again, either in the Transport window or in the Edit window's Transport controls). Recording will begin.

There are a number of shortcuts to start recording: Press the COMMAND+SPACEBAR keys (Mac) or CTRL+SPACEBAR keys (Windows), the F12 key, or 3 on your keyboard's numeric keypad.

9. Click the STOP button when you want to stop recording. A new clip will be shown in the track.

After Recording

After you've successfully recorded, you'll want to be able to hear what you've just done!

1. Before you listen to your track, click on the TRACK RECORD ENABLE button (to disarm the track). Otherwise, you will hear signal being inputted to the track, not the clip you've just recorded.
2. Make sure the Record button in the Transport controls section in the Edit window or Transport window is not highlighted.
3. Use the Selector tool to position your playback cursor at the desired position on your timeline.
4. Click on the Play button or press the spacebar. You will hear your newly created track.

Hands-On Exercise 5.1: Basic Recording

Now that you understand basic recording workflows, let's put them into practice. In this chapter's exercises, I've mocked up what might happen in a typical simple recording session: The job today is to record a small bit of voiceover for a podcast. In this situation, the engineer (you) and the producer (me) are in a control room. In a separate recording space is the voice talent (Alex), who is listening to a cue mix on his closed-back headphones.

Alex Brooke is my colleague at Avid, and also the host of Learn Japanese Pod, a podcast for people who want to learn how to speak natural conversational Japanese. Together with his co-host Ami Sensei they also cover topics such as Japanese culture, etiquette, travel tips, and interviews with people who have made their home in Japan. If you want to get a unique insider's perspective of language, life, and culture in Japan, check out Learn Japanese Pod with Alex at http://learnjapanesepod.com/.

Setting Up

The first thing is to create a Project:

1. Create a new Project by converting the *Pro Tools First—Fundamentals of Audio Production—Chapter 5 (Podcast).ptx* session to a local Project. The session is found in the *Pro Tools First—Fundamentals of Audio Production—Chapter 5 (Podcast)* subfolder of this book's downloaded exercise material. You already learned how to convert a Session to a Project in Chapter 2. Choose any desired sample rate, 24-bit, and do not Backup to Cloud.

This is a simple session with four audio tracks. Here they are from top to bottom:

- **Andy Slate:** A *slate* track is often used in different recording scenarios, for different purposes. When recording in situations like this, many producers (myself included) will have a microphone nearby where we can record our notes in the timeline while the performers are being recorded. The performers do *not* hear these notes—it's just for reference, so that we can go back to any sections that are needed. For now, keep this track *muted.*
- **Alex First:** This is a mock-up of Alex's first read of the text. For the purposes of this chapter's exercises, you'll treat this track as a live performance.
- **Alex Punch:** This is a mock-up of some additional recording that will be needed later in this chapter to fix some mistakes that Alex made in the first recording pass. For this exercise, this track should stay *muted.*
- **Podcast Intro:** This is the track that you will be recording to.

Here's the script that we're working from:

So, how difficult is Japanese to learn? Well, that's a great question! I'm glad you asked. And it's a question I get asked a lot, perhaps partly due to the mass of confusing information on the internet about this.

On the one hand, there are a lot of blogs with titles such as "10 Reasons Japanese is Way Easier Than You Think." On the other hand, there are more scholarly articles that put Japanese up there with Mandarin, Cantonese, Arabic, and Korean in terms of difficulty.

And then there's the question of "How do you define difficult?" And who is it difficult for? And . . . I understand if your head is starting to hurt now.

But fear not my friends: As someone who has lived in Japan for 20 years and uses Japanese on a daily basis, perhaps I can offer some personal anecdotes and experience to help answer this question.

But before that . . .

What kind of language is Japanese? Is it similar to anything else?

Short Answer: Japanese is sort of unique . . . ish.

Japanese is an exotic, colorful bird out there in the menagerie of the world languages. It's part of the Japanese-Ryukaan linguistic group, Japanese being the only branch in this family and is spoken by 130 million people. It has a similar grammar structure to Korean and adopts Chinese kanji characters into the writing system.

It's not as widely spoken as English and doesn't have as many speakers as Mandarin, but 130 million speakers is a fair amount of people.

One of the features of Japanese is the written language, which has 3 main scripts. They are Hiragana, the basic syllabary; Katakana, used for foreign words; and Kanji, pictographs or characters imported from China. It's also quite common to see Romaji or Roman letters used in magazines, posters, and books, so things can get a little confusing at times for a student new to Japanese.

So, with the exception of Chinese kanji and the increasing mass of Katakana words, Japanese isn't that similar to other languages.

So, guess where Japanese falls on the scale of difficulty? That's right up there with Arabic and Mandarin.

Ouch.

But don't worry. Let me explain: Japanese isn't all difficult. If I can learn to speak it, you certainly can.

Preparing to Record

If you look at the Project, you'll see that the output of both of Alex's tracks have an output called *Alex's Mic*. Again, this is a simulation of a recording workflow, so in this case, we'll assume that the signal coming from a live performance is coming from Alex's microphone. Next, you'll need to set your recording track's input:

2. Click the *Podcast Intro* track's Input Path selector, and then choose BUS from the menu. From there, choose *Alex's Mic*, as shown in Figure 5.38.

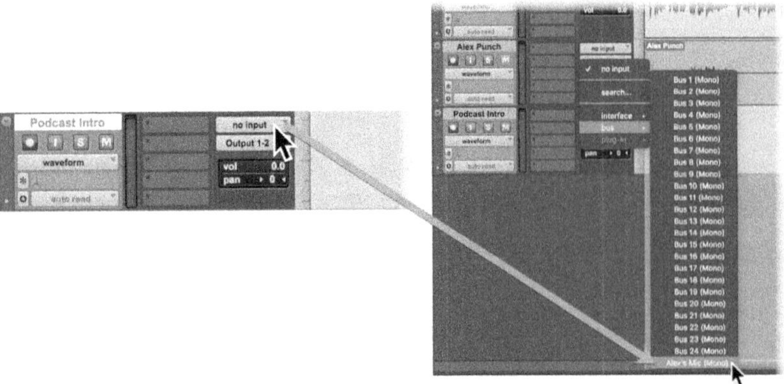

Figure 5.38 Selecting a Recording Track's Input

A *Bus* is a way of routing the output of one track to the input of another track within Pro Tools. You'll learn more about how to use busses in Chapters 8 through 10.

3. Record-enable the *Podcast Intro* track.

Record Voiceover

4. Just to simulate what a producer might say to a performer, I've recorded four *Talkback* audio files in the *Pro Tools First—Fundamentals of Audio Production—Chapter 5 (Talkback)* subfolder in your exercise material folder. Talkback is often used for people in a control room to speak to recording artists in other rooms. Play the *Chapter 5 (Podcast)—Talkback #1.wav* file.

You'll be previewing files during the course of this chapter's exercises. You don't need to preview this within Pro Tools—you can just listen to this file through any media player. However, if you want to preview a file within Pro Tools, I recommend that you do it through the Soundbase browser.

5. In this case, you'll want recording to begin at the start of your timeline. Using the Selector tool, position your playback cursor at the beginning of your Project's timeline (or press the RETURN key (Mac) or ENTER key (Windows) to quickly position the playback cursor at the beginning of your project's timeline).

6. Record a first pass of the entire script. You should hear the voiceover as you see a clip progressively created as you record, as shown in Figure 5.39. Record the entire script in a single pass.

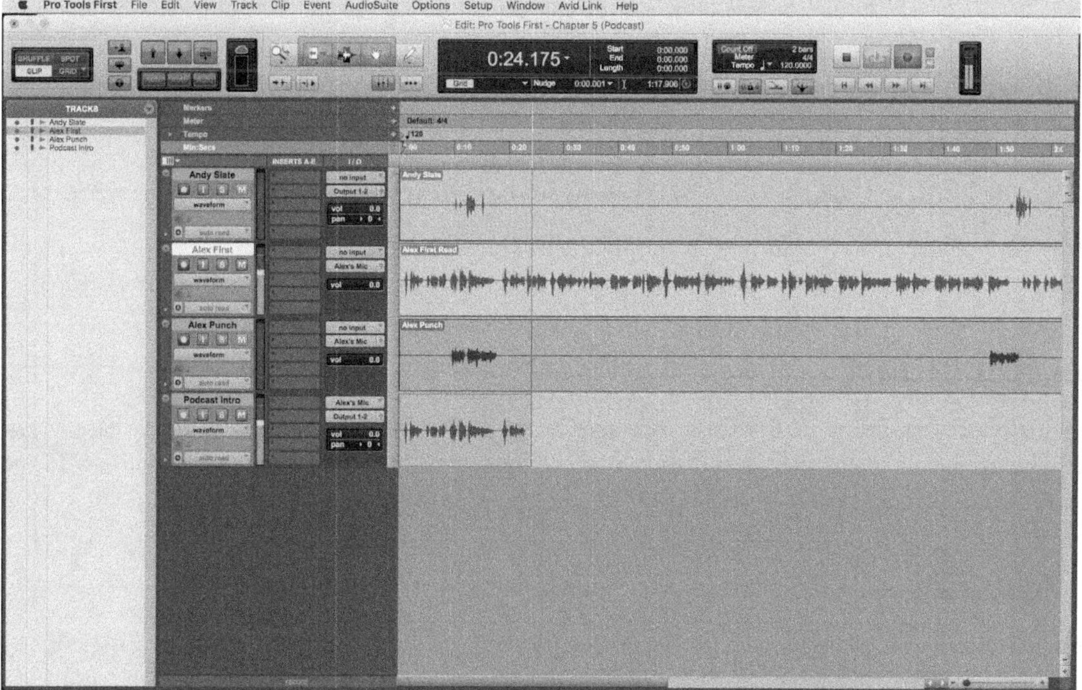

Figure 5.39 Recording in Progress

7. After recording the entire script, STOP playback to stop recording. Your Edit window should look something like Figure 3.40.

Figure 5.40 Your Finished Recording

Review Recording

Before we leave this exercise, you should check your work.

8. Click the TRACK RECORD ENABLE button on the *Podcast Intro* track to disarm the track.

9. Play your session. You should now hear only the newly-recorded audio. If you do, congratulations—you're done! Before we move on, please make sure that you save your work.

Punch-In Recording

Although having a perfect recording take with no mistakes from start to finish is the goal, it rarely happens in real life. That's why producers often take notes during a recording session (or use a slate track as you saw in the previous exercise). Here's where *punch-in* recording comes into the workflow.

Recording Selections

As was mentioned earlier in this chapter, recording will either start at the location of the playback cursor or any selected area on the timeline. This latter method—recording a selected area—can come in particularly handy when you are "punching in" on a section that needs to be re-recorded. When making selections for recording, the beginning of your selection will be where recording starts (called the *punch in* point) and the end of your selection will be where recording ends (called the *punch out* point).

There are a number of ways selections are commonly made for punch-in record passes:

- **Selecting a Range on a Track or on a Ruler:** Using the Selector tool to drag and select a span of time on a track or in a ruler is probably the most straightforward method. Remember that your selection will follow the rules of your Edit Mode. Use Slip mode to have complete freedom in setting start and end points, or Grid mode to make selections that align to a grid.
- **Using Clips to Make Selections:** Single-clicking on a clip with the Grabber tool or double-clicking on a clip with the Selector tool will select that clip in its entirety. If you want to replace an entire clip with a new recording, this is an easy way to make that selection.
- **Making Selections "On the Fly":** You can also make a selection while your Project is playing (or recording). To start a selection, press the DOWN ARROW key, and to end a selection, press the UP ARROW key.

No matter how you make a selection, your selected area will be represented in the Rulers area of your Edit window, bordered on either side by two half-arrow icons (called *Timeline Selection Markers*). If any track is record-enabled in your Project, those icons will be colored red; if not, they'll be colored blue, as shown in Figure 5.41. You can easily adjust either the beginning (punch-in) or end (punch-out) of your selected area by moving your cursor to either icon and dragging it to the desired location.

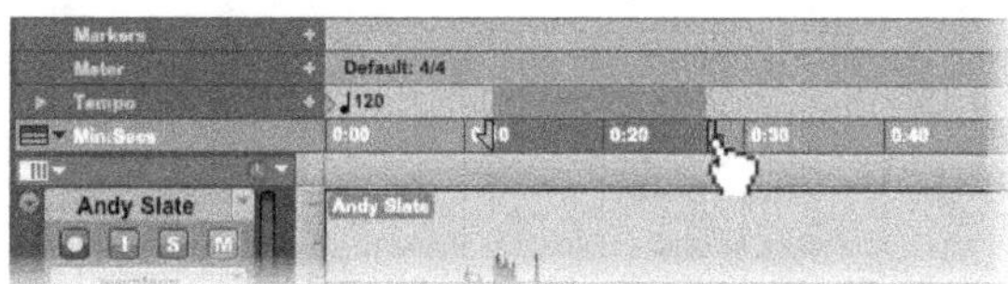

Figure 5.41 Adjusting Your Punch-Out Point

Pre-Roll and Post-Roll

Once you've made your selection for your punch-in recording, you're off to a good start—but there's a potential problem: Both playback and recording will start immediately at the beginning of the selection (or if you have count off enabled, count off will happen, and then playback and recording will start simultaneously). Sometimes, that's not a problem, but frequently, the recording talent will want to hear a bit of the Project before the punch-in, and sometimes a bit of playback after the punch-out. That's where *pre-roll* and *post-roll* come into the workflow.

Pre-roll is an amount of time that you can set for playback to occur before the beginning of the selection, when recording starts. This is useful in giving the performer a sense of tempo, volume, context, and so on. before they will be recorded with the punch-in. *Post-roll* is a similarly user-defined amount of time for playback to occur after the punch-out point before playback is stopped.

There are a number of ways that you can set up a pre-roll and/or post-roll, but for this book, let's go with the most straightforward:

1. Open the Transport window (WINDOW>TRANSPORT).

2. Type in the desired pre-roll amount (in Figure 5.42, I've typed in 3 seconds).

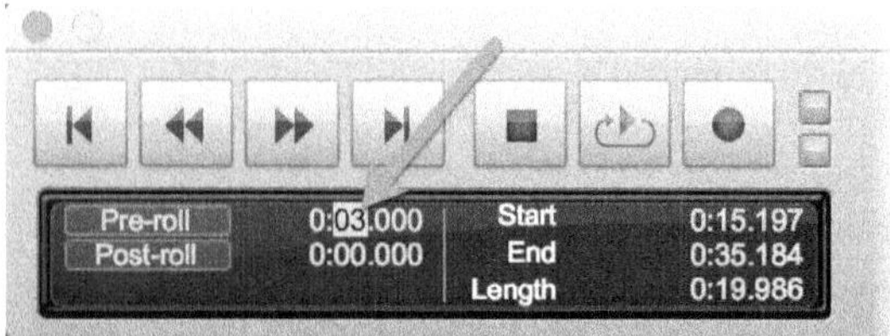

Figure 5.42 Setting Your Pre-Roll

3. Confirm your settings by pressing the RETURN key (Mac) or ENTER key (Windows). The settings will be confirmed, and pre-roll will be activated (an active pre-roll is indicated by the word "Pre-roll" in black text against a green background).
4. If you also want a post-roll, type a value into the post-roll field. Again, you can confirm your settings by pressing the RETURN key (Mac) or ENTER key (Windows).

Figure 5.43 shows both pre-roll and post-roll activated (with a pre-roll value of 3 seconds and a post-roll value of 5 seconds).

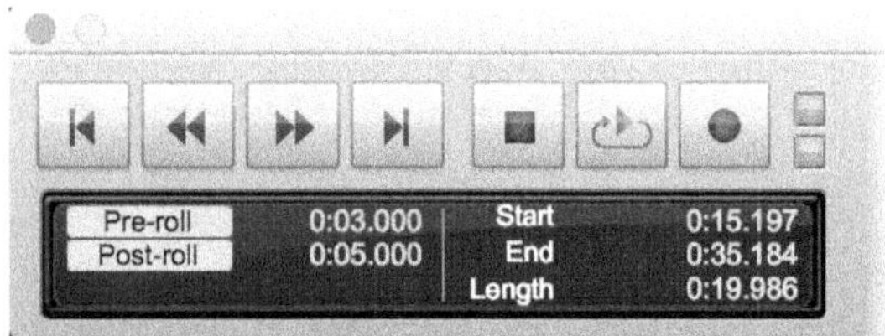

Figure 5.43 Pre-Roll and Post-Roll Set and Active

You can individually activate and deactivate your pre-roll and post-roll by clicking the green PRE-ROLL or POST-ROLL button. When deactivated, the text will be green against a black background. The settings will be retained, however, so you can re-enable either pre-roll or post-roll with one click, without having to type in new values.

Another way to enable or disable pre-roll or post-roll is to go to the OPTIONS menu and choose PRE/POST ROLL, as shown in Figure 5.44.

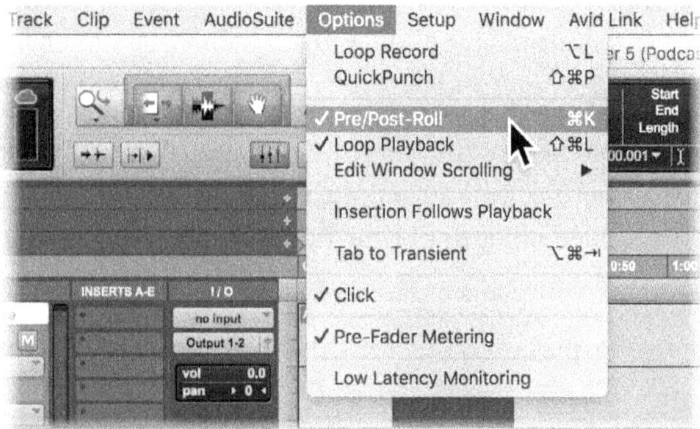

Figure 5.44 Enabling or Disabling Pre/Post-Roll from the Options Menu

The shortcut to enable or disable pre-roll and post-roll is COMMAND+K (Mac) or CTRL+K (Windows).

You can see your pre-roll and post-roll locations indicated in the Rulers area as a pair of flags (the Pre-Roll Flag is to the left of the beginning of the selected area, and the Post-Roll Flag is to the right of the end of the selected area). If the flag is colored amber, the "roll" is active. If it is white, then it's inactive.

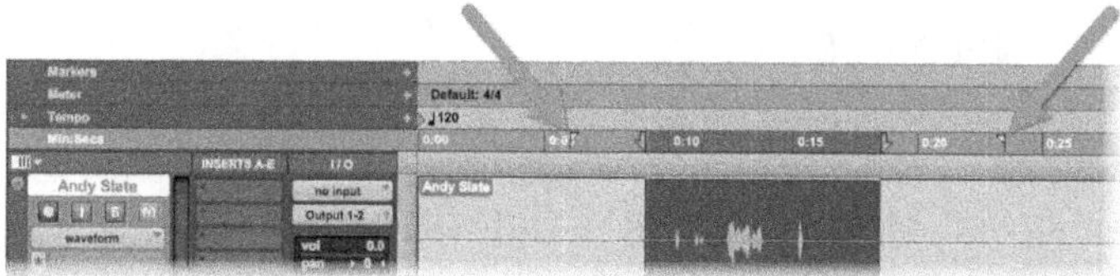

Figure 5.45 Pre-Roll and Post-Roll as they Appear in the Rulers

If you want to change the position of either your pre-roll or post-roll, you *could* type a new value , but in many cases it's easier to move your cursor to the flag that you want to move and just drag it to the desired location, as shown in Figure 5.46.

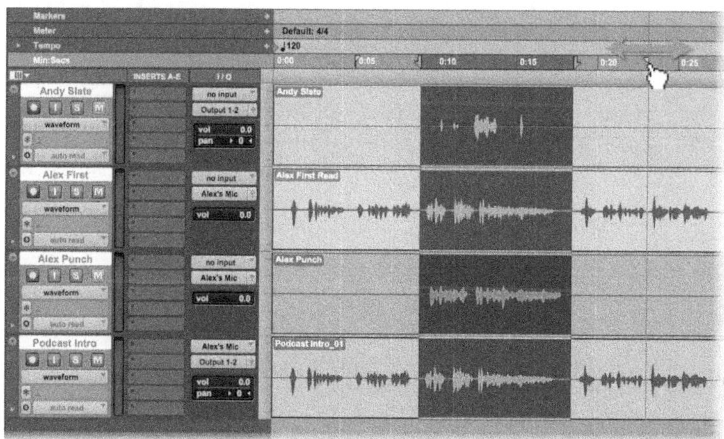

Figure 5.46 Changing the Post-Roll by Dragging

Once you have your pre-roll and post-roll set the way you want them, here's what will happen when you record:

1. Playback will start at the pre-roll position. The artist (and you, the producer) will hear the pre-recorded material.

2. Once the playback cursor reaches the beginning of the selected area, the record-enabled track(s) will begin recording. Your recording subject will then hear only what they are performing during that time (and the playback of any non-record-enabled tracks).

3. Once the playback cursor reaches the end of the selected area, the recording tracks will stop recording. If there is no post-roll enabled, playback will also stop at this point.

4. If post-roll is enabled, then playback will continue until the playback cursor reaches the post-roll location.

QuickPunch Recording

Making a selection and punching in and out is a great way to fix a single problem, but this is a one-shot workflow—if you need to fix another part in the same area, you need to make another selection and record that one as a separate take. Wouldn't it be great if there was a way that you could just punch in and out a number of times in a single recording pass?

QuickPunch recording will do just that, and like punching in and out, the workflow is pretty straightforward:

1. From the OPTIONS menu, choose QUICKPUNCH.

OR

1. The shortcut for activating QuickPunch recording mode is COMMAND+SHIFT+P (Mac) or CTRL+SHIFT+P (Windows)

OR

1. Right-click the RECORD button, and choose QUICKPUNCH from the menu, as shown in Figure 5.47.

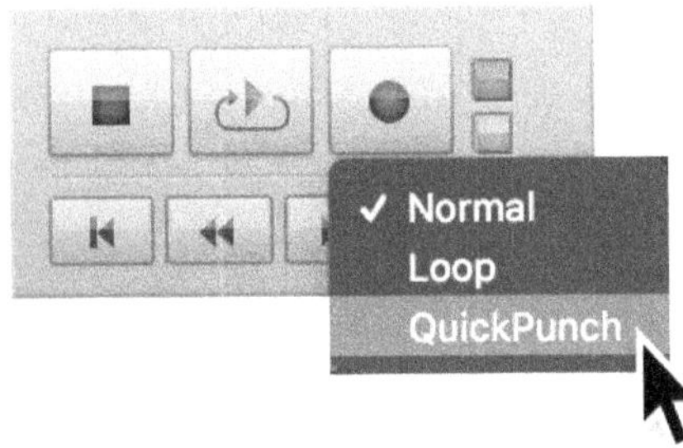

Figure 5.47 Activating QuickPunch Recording Mode

Whichever method you choose, when QuickPunch recording mode is active, you'll see a small letter "P" in the record button.

2. Record-enable the track(s) that you want to record to.
3. Position your playback cursor to a point *before* you want to start your first punch-in.
4. Begin playback (either by pressing the PLAY button or the SPACEBAR key).
5. To start recording, press the RECORD button.
6. To stop recording, press the RECORD button. Playback will continue.

Other ways to begin and end recording that work well for this workflow: Press the COMMAND+SPACEBAR keys (Mac) or CTRL+SPACEBAR keys (Windows), or the F12 key, or 3 on the numeric keypad.

7. You can punch in and out again numerous times—up to 200 times per recording pass!

Here's what you'll end up with: For each punch-in and punch-out, you'll get a new clip on your recording track(s) (in the case of Figure 5.48, I've recorded silence, so that you can easily see each new clip on the timeline). These clips can be moved and edited just like any other clip, and if you've missed the perfect punch-in or punch-out, you can use the Trim tool to adjust the clip boundaries.

Figure 5.48 After a QuickPunch Recording Pass

Hands-On Exercise 5.2: Punching In

After recording Alex's first pass, we'll need to go back and do a little bit of clean-up:

Set Punch-in and Punch-out Points

1. Mute the *Alex First* track.
2. Unmute the *Andy Slate* track.
3. Play back the Project from the beginning. At about 9 seconds is a sentence that reads, "And it's a question I get asked a lot, perhaps partly due to the mass of confusing information on the internet about this." There's a small mistake in that sentence that I've made a note of on the Slate Track. If you are listening to both the recorded first take and my slate track, you'll see that we need to fix something here.
4. Mute the *Andy Slate* track.
5. To get a sense of the kind of direction you might give your recording talent in a real-world situation, play the *Chapter 5 (Podcast)—Talkback #2.wav* file in the *Talkback* subfolder of the *Pro Tools First—Chapter 5 (Podcast)* folder. You *don't* need to play this through Pro Tools.
6. Using the Selector tool in Slip mode, select "And it's a question I get asked a lot, perhaps partly due to the mass of confusing information on the internet about this" on the *Podcast Intro* track. Here's a hint—the selection should start at about 9 seconds and end at about 18 seconds.

Set Pre-Roll and Post-Roll

We told our talent that we would give them pre-roll starting at "That's a great question . . . " Let's set that up next.

7. Set a pre-roll of 2 seconds.
8. Play your Project. You'll hear your playback start from the pre-roll position. If you've set your punch-in correctly, you'll probably hear playback start from somewhere around "I'm glad you asked," which is a little late. Grab the Pre-Roll Flag, and drag it before Alex says, "That's a great question." You'll see a vertical line as you drag, showing you where the pre-roll will begin. Here's a tip: Figure 5.49 shows about where the pre-roll should begin (with a pre-roll value of about 4 seconds).

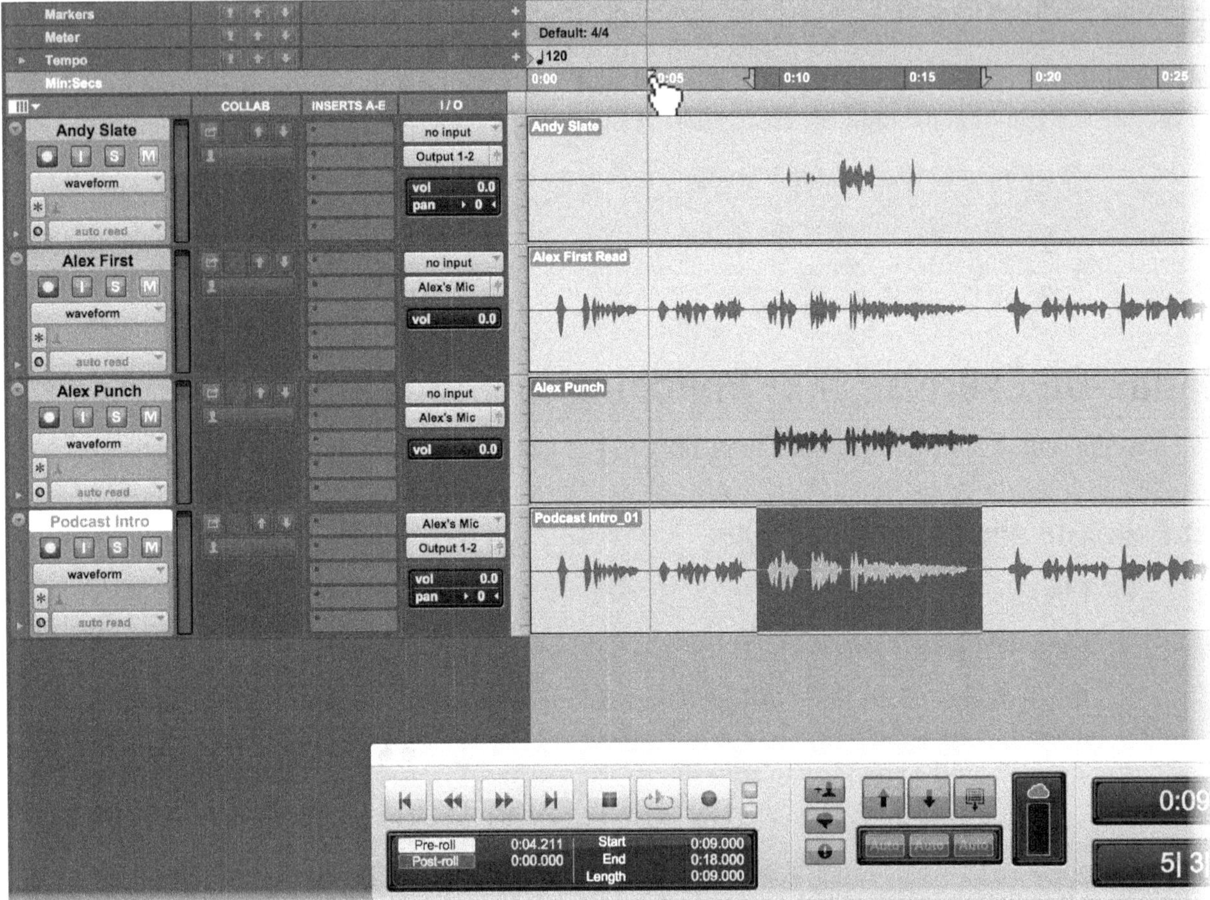

Figure 5.49 Adjusting Your Pre-Roll

9. Set a post-roll value of 10 seconds.

Punch-In

You're all set to fix the selected area:

10. Make sure that the *Alex First* track is muted.
11. Un-mute the *Alex Punch* track (this is the track that has Alex's fixed performance).
12. Record-enable the *Podcast Intro* track.
13. Begin Recording. Playback will start from the pre-roll position, and you will hear the original recording before the play line reaches the beginning of the selected area. Recording will begin at the start of the selected area and end at the end of the selected area. Playback will continue until the post-roll location.

When you're done, here's what you'll get.

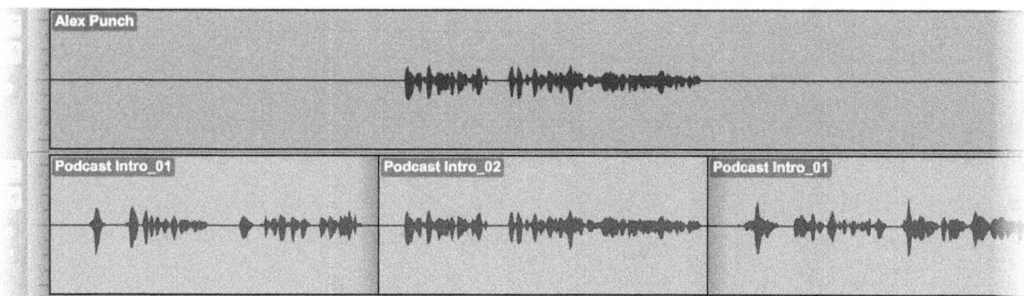

Figure 5.50 After Your First Punch Recording

There's another place in this Project where we can do the same kind of workflow. The steps here will be intentionally minimal—Now that you've done it already, it's time to use your ears!

14. To get a sense of the kind of direction you might give your recording talent in a real-world situation, play the *Chapter 5 (Podcast)—Talkback #3.wav* file in the *Pro Tools First—Fundamentals of Audio Production—Chapter 5 (Talkback)* folder. You *don't* need to play this through Pro Tools.
15. Select the phrase "One of the features of Japanese is the written language, which has 3 main scripts." Use the script that you saw earlier in this chapter to help you locate this on the timeline. (Hint: The selected area should *end* at 1 minute 55 seconds, as the redo of the phrase is longer than the original recording.)
16. Set your pre-roll to start at "It's not as widely spoken as English." The easiest way to do this will be to refer to the script and drag the Pre-Roll Flag (which is still active) to the proper location. To test your pre-roll, just start playback.
17. Disable the post-roll from the Transport window.

Figure 5.51 Ready for Your Second Punch Recording

18. Begin Recording. When you're done, your Edit window should look something like this:

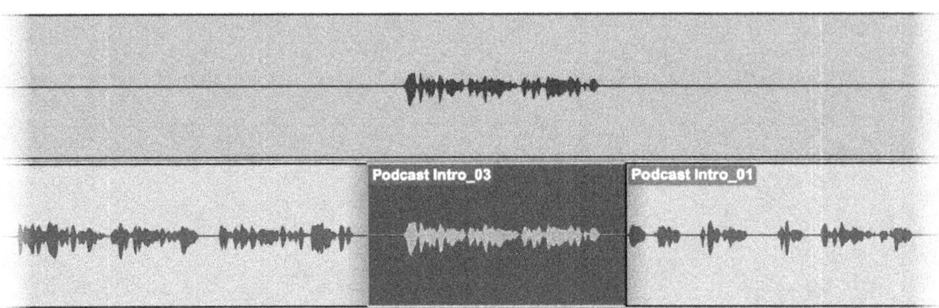

Figure 5.52 After Your Second Punch Recording

QuickPunch

To end this exercise, we're going to use a bit of QuickPunch. This will require a bit of attention to detail as you record. Good luck!

19. To get a sense of the kind of direction you might give your recording talent in a real-world situation, play the *Chapter 5 (Podcast)—Talkback #4.wav* file in the *Pro Tools First—Fundamentals of Audio Production—Chapter 5 (Talkback)* folder. You *don't* need to play this through Pro Tools.
20. If it isn't already on, activate QuickPunch recording mode. When it's active, you'll see a small letter "P" in the record button.
21. Pre-roll and post-roll aren't really needed in QuickPunch, so disable both of those now.
22. Using the Selector tool (or the Selector tool mode of the Smart Tool), move your playback cursor to just before "It's also quite common to see Romanji, or Roman letters . . . " The location on your timeline is at about 2 minutes, 7 seconds.
23. Record-enable the *Podcast Intro* track.

OK, you'll need to do the rest in one single pass, so please read and understand steps #24 through #29 before you start.

24. Begin Playback. You'll hear Alex say, "It's also quite common to see Romaji or Roman letters used in magazines, posters and books so things can get a little confusing at times for a student new to Japanese."
25. Right after you hear the word "Japanese," begin recording. Record the entire phrase "So, with the exception of Chinese kanji and the increasing mass of Katakana words, Japanese isn't that similar to other languages."
26. After you record the word "languages," stop recording, but *don't* stop playback. The timing of the first and the second takes isn't exactly the same, but don't worry if you didn't get your punch-out point just right—just keep going.
27. Continuing playback, you'll hear, "So, guess where Japanese falls on the scale of difficulty? That's right up there with Arabic and Mandarin."

28. After the word "Mandarin," start recording, and only record the word "ouch." After that word, stop recording, but continue playback for a while (the exact amount of time you play isn't important).

29. Stop playback.

When you're done, your track might look like this:

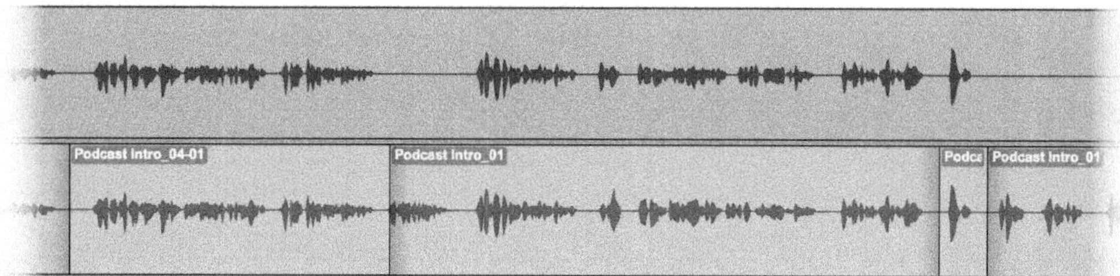

Figure 5.53 After Your QuickPunch Recording

You'll see that the in first punch-in (the part where Alex says, "So, with the exception of Chinese kanji and the increasing mass of Katakana words, Japanese isn't that similar to other languages"), the new performance of the line is a bit shorter than the original recording, and as a result, I "punched-out" too early. I can fix that by using the Trim tool to extend the end of the *Podcast Intro_04-01* clip (your clip name might be slightly different based upon how many takes you've done).

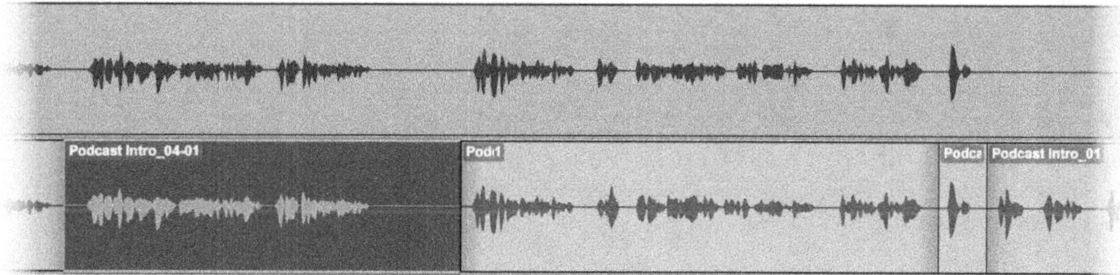

Figure 5.54 Adjusting Your QuickPunch Recording

Once you're happy with your recording takes, and cleaned up your clips as needed, you're all done. Make sure you save your work!

Loop Recording

There's one more way of recording left to discuss before we close this chapter: *Loop Record mode.* With this mode of recording, a selected area is recorded over and over again, saving each take as a separate clip.

Though Loop Record mode is used in a variety of situations, its traditional origins are in music production. Let's say you have a guitar solo over a 16-bar phrase: Loop recording allows the guitar player to record that section over and over, with some good and not-so-good takes. After the recording is done (with multiple takes of the guitar solo), the best take can be chosen (or the best bits of each take can be compiled into a single solo—a process called "comping").

The workflow follows much of what you've done already with normal and QuickPunch recording:

1. From the OPTIONS menu, choose LOOP RECORD.

OR

1. Use the shortcut for activating Loop Record mode: OPTION+L (Mac) or ALT+L (Windows).

OR

1. Right-click the RECORD button, and choose LOOP from the menu, as shown in Figure 5.55.

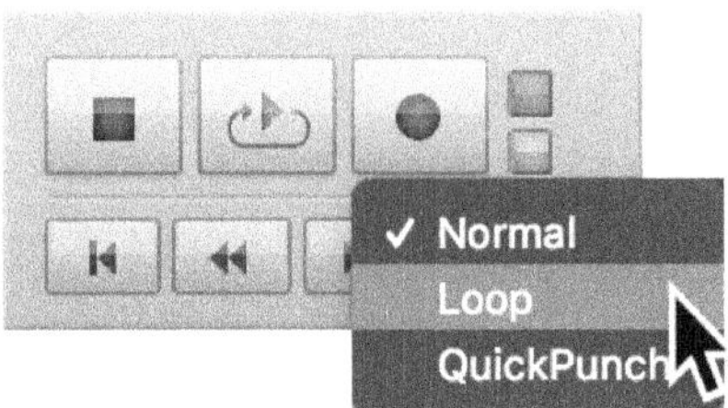

Figure 5.55 Activating Loop Record Mode

Whichever method you choose, when Loop Record mode is active, it will appear as shown in Figure 5.56.

Figure 5.56 Loop Record Mode Enabled

2. Record-enable the track(s) that you want to record to.
3. Select the area that you want to loop.
4. To begin recording, press the RECORD button. If there is a pre-roll set and active, playback will start from the pre-roll position, and recording will start at the beginning of the selected area.
5. Once the end of the selected area is reached, the playback cursor will jump back to the beginning of the selected area, and recording will continue without a pause (pre-roll will not be heard for these subsequent takes.
6. Stopping playback will also stop recording. The clip that you will see on your timeline depends on when you stop recording:
   - **If you stop playback in the first half of your selected area**, the last full loop will appear as a clip that spans your entire selected area.
   - **If you stop playback in the latter half of your selected area**, the current take will appear as a clip that is less than the full span of your selected area.

Choosing Takes

After you've done some loop recording, you'll want to listen to your different takes. There are a number of ways that you can view your takes:

1. Using the Selector tool, hold down the COMMAND key (Mac) or CTRL key (Windows) and click the clip whose alternate takes you want to view.

OR

1. Right-click the clip whose alternate takes you want to view. From the pop-up menu that will appear, choose MATCHING ALTERNATES.

Whichever method you choose, you'll see a list similar to Figure 5.57.

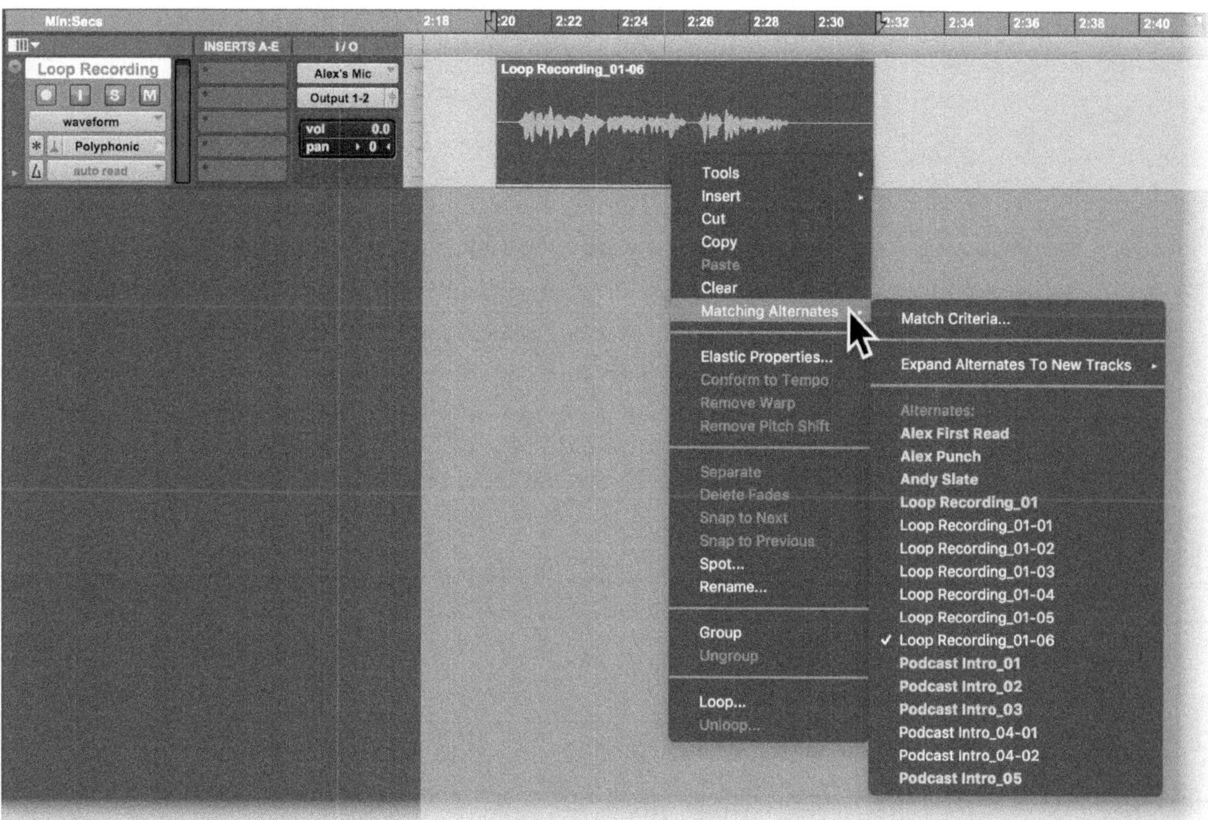

Figure 5.57 A Long Alternate Takes List

In Figure 5.56, you'll see that the list includes clips that are clearly on other tracks (this clip is on a track called *Loop Recording* in the image). It'd be great to filter the unwanted clips from this list, and setting your *Match Criteria* will do just that!

2. In the Alternate Takes pop-up menu, choose MATCH CRITERIA. The Matching Criteria window will appear, as shown in Figure 5.58.

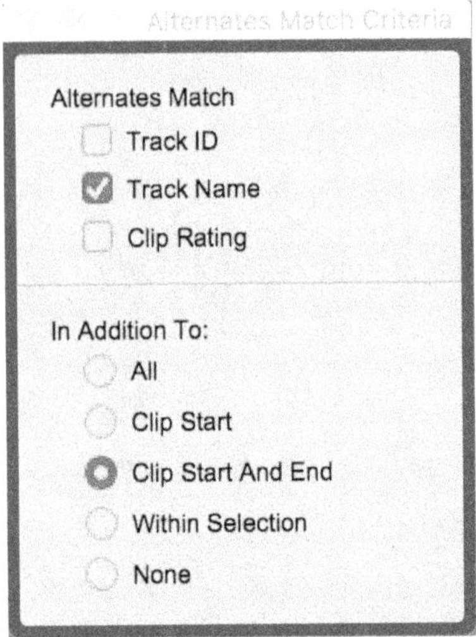

Figure 5.58 The Matching Criteria Window

3. The top section of the Matching Criteria window will allow you to start to filter your clip (by *Track ID*, *Track Name*, or *Clip Rating*). You can choose as many of these as you want, but typically, *Track Name* is a common choice.
4. The bottom section of the Matching Criteria window will enable you to further filter your alternate takes, with an eye towards timing (*Clip Start, Clip Start and End, or Within Selection*). You can choose *All* or *None* of these additional criteria, or any one of the other options. *Clip Start and End* will filter out any incomplete takes. If you *do* want to include the last incomplete take, choose *Clip Start.*
5. Once you set your match criteria, you will see a shorter—and hopefully more relevant—list of alternate takes. In Figure 5.59, you'll see that now I only see takes that are on that track and have the same start *and* end points.

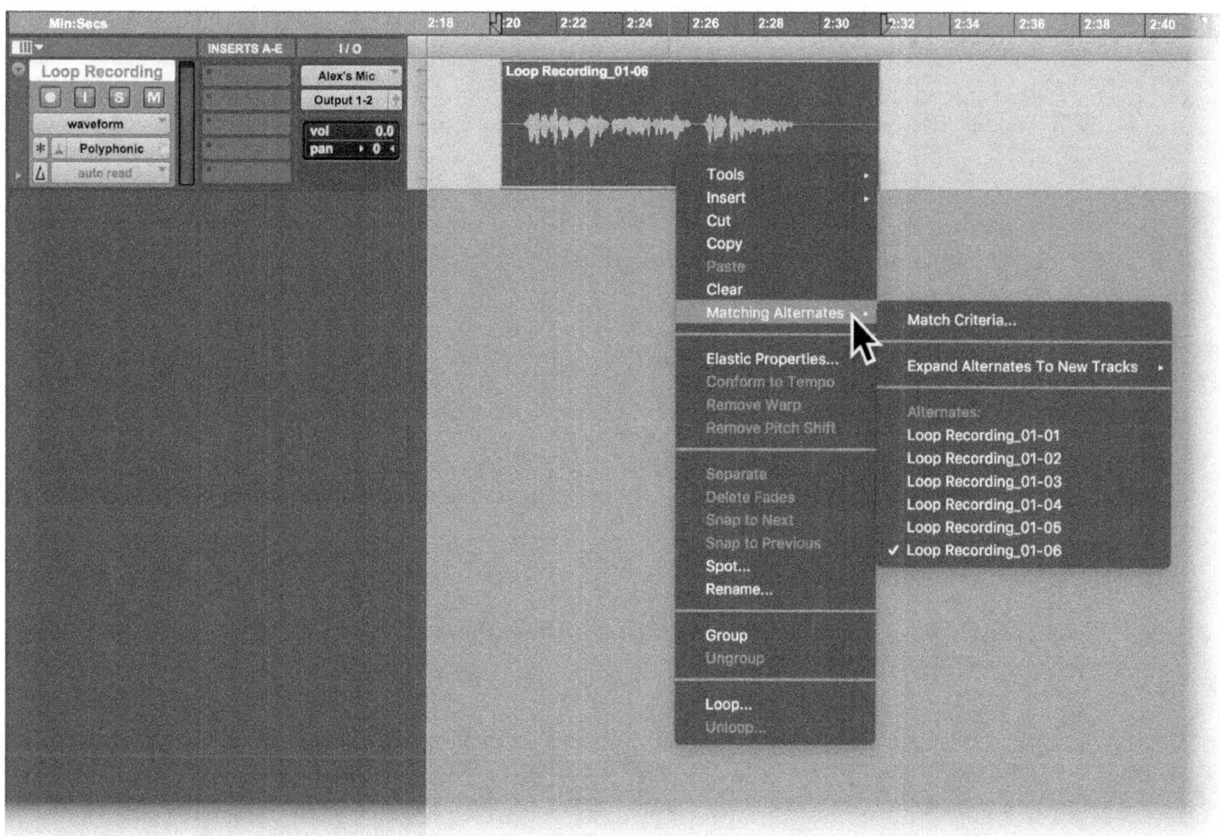

Figure 5.59 A Shorter Alternate Takes List

6. From the (now filtered) list, choose the take that you want to hear, and the clip will be replaced on the track's timeline.

Review Questions

1. What is the difference between a Dynamic and Condenser microphone? Which needs "phantom" power?

2. Which microphone polarity is most resistant to plosives?

3. Which microphone polarity will pick up what is in front of it, but ignore any sounds that are to the side or behind it?

4. The *Proximity Effect* is an increase in _________ frequencies as a vocalist moves closer to a microphone.

5. What kind of track (Audio, MIDI, Aux, etc.) is created when you create a click track from TRACK>CREATE CLICK TRACK?

6. True or False: If your signal coming into a recording track is too high, just bring down the fader in the Mix window, and the audio file that is created will be recorded softer.

7. There are many different ways to begin recording. Can you name at least two?

8. What is pre-roll? What is post-roll?

9. True or False: In order to use QuickPunch record mode, pre-roll *must* be enabled.

10. When I look at my alternate takes (after loop recording), the list is too long and includes clips on other tracks. How can I filter my alternate takes so that I only see the clips that are on the track that I'm working with?

CHAPTER 6

MIDI

MIDI (short for Musical Instrument Digital Interface) is a language that enables keyboards, synthesizers, and other musical devices to interact with each other. Invented in the early '80s, MIDI transformed the music industry, and has since been an invaluable tool for music creation of all kinds.

In the early days of audio and music technology, software could only work with audio *or* MIDI, but not both. Thankfully, with the advent of modern DAWs like Pro Tools, the creative power of MIDI and the advantages of digital audio have now been incorporated into a single powerful platform. In this chapter, you'll learn how to bring MIDI into your Projects.

Media Used: Pro Tools First—Fundamentals of Audio Production—Chapter 6 (Mambo).ptx, Pro Tools First—Fundamentals of Audio Production—Chapter 6 (Mountain King).ptx, Pro Tools First—Fundamentals of Audio Production—Chapter 6—MIDI for Import

Duration: 45 minutes

GOALS

- Set up your MIDI studio
- Use MIDI and Virtual Instruments in Pro Tools | First
- Record and Edit MIDI data
- "Print" MIDI to an audio file

A mastery of music and MIDI is a full course of study in and of itself. For the purposes of this book, we'll focus on the basics of what MIDI is, how it's commonly used in Pro Tools, and the types of MIDI skills that any engineer might call upon when working with a MIDI musician in a studio environment.

MIDI Basics

As with some other topics in this book, in order to understand MIDI, we need to go back to the early days of music technology. In the late '70s and early '80s, many different electronic music manufacturers (primarily focused on keyboard synthesizers) built new, powerful sound-making tools, but designed with specific proprietary ways of working. For example, a keyboard made by a certain manufacturer would be incompatible with a sound module made by another, and therefore both could not be used together.

Enter the National Association of Music Manufacturers (NAMM). Founded in 1901, it was a long-standing professional association well-positioned to break down barriers between manufacturers. At the 1981 NAMM convention, two companies (*Sequential Circuits* and *Roland*) proposed an idea of a way to connect musical devices in a kind of network so that different tools (even those made by different manufacturers) could easily communicate. Its creation was enthusiastically assisted by other forward-thinking companies, mostly based in Japan.

After three years, MIDI was unveiled at the 1984 NAMM convention. This revolutionary standard, adopted by virtually all music manufacturers worldwide, now allows for musical devices of various types and manufacture to be used together in flexible ways.

Digital Music Paper

One thing to remember about MIDI is that it has *no sound* by itself–it is *only* information that controls an instrument. MIDI controls sound-producing devices in much the same way printed music controls musicians. Think of it this way: I'm a tuba player, and if a piece of music is placed before me, I can read certain kinds of information—notes, tempo, dynamics, and so on. When I play the music (and again, a sheet of music produces no sound on its own), I'd be interpreting that information by playing the tuba. Now, my wife plays the saxophone, and if the same music was put in front of her, she would be "controlled" by the same musical information, but in her case, she would play the sax. The printed music that guides both of us has no sound on its own–MIDI works the same way.

Without getting too technical, MIDI data is broken into different types. Here are the most important ones:

- **Channels:** Most MIDI data is assigned to a MIDI *channel.* There is a total of 16 channels in the MIDI protocol. Channels allow for specific MIDI data to be directed to specific devices. For example, a MIDI instrument can have a piano sound assigned to respond to data on one channel and drums to respond to a different channel. This allows a DAW like Pro Tools to send a single stream of data to the instrument, but control both sounds discreetly.
- **Note Data:** Individual notes can be recorded and played back as note data, including aspects such as pitch, timing, duration, and velocity (which we'll discuss later in this chapter). All this information is stored numerically.
- **Continuous Controllers:** There's other non-note data that MIDI can store as well, like volume, pitch change, and expression, which can change smoothly over time, so that notes can get louder and softer and change in pitch during the course of a single note.
- MIDI can also store other messages which affect a song, such as tempo, meter, and key.

How Sound is Created with MIDI

Through the years, different kinds of MIDI setups have evolved. Let's take a look at some of the most common ones.

Controllers and Sound Modules

Remember that MIDI was invented in the early 1980s, at a time when personal computers had barely arrived on the scene. Back then, it was primarily used to connect keyboard MIDI controllers with sound-creating modules. This connection was made with a five-pin DIN connector, as shown in Figure 6.1.

The connection was easy enough–one end of the cable was connected to the MIDI controller's MIDI OUT port, which was then connected to a synthesizer module's MIDI IN port. Many synthesizer devices also had a MIDI THRU port, which allowed the MIDI information to pass through the module to additional sound-generating devices. This allowed a single keyboard controller to trigger sounds on multiple devices.

Figure 6.1 A 5-Pin MIDI Cable

Over the years, MIDI controllers have taken on many forms, moving beyond the initial keyboard style. Figure 6.2 shows some of the alternative controllers of my own studio, including an Akai EWI (Electronic Wind Instrument) and a Moog Theremini (a MIDI version of a theremin). Both these devices create MIDI data; the difference is the ways in which I interact with them as a performer.

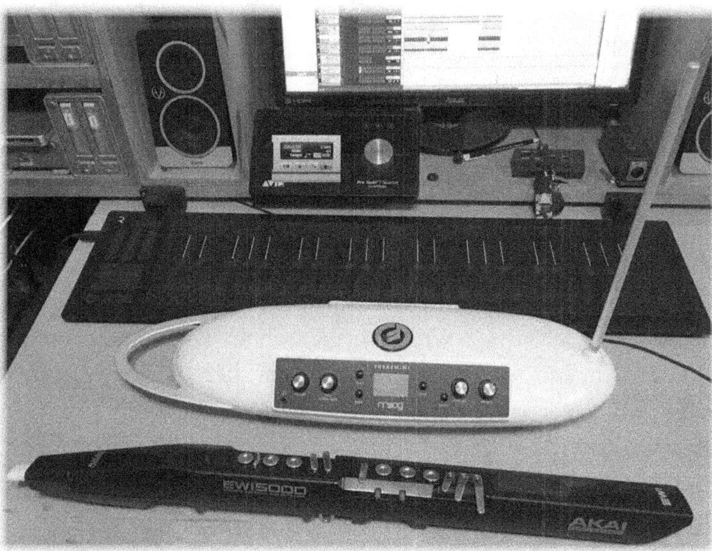

Figure 6.2 Different MIDI Controllers

Virtual Instruments

Due to a number of factors, not the least of which being cost, hardware sound modules are not as common as they used to be. These days, MIDI controllers are still being used, but they are controlling software synthesizers commonly called *Virtual Instruments* (or VIs). Virtual Instruments can be either standalone software applications or operate as plug-ins in a DAW (which is what we'll be working with in this chapter).

Virtual Instruments bring with them a few advantages: First, they're generally less expensive than their hardware counterparts. They're also easy to use within software DAWs, requiring no cabling or mounting into hardware racks. Further, a single Virtual Instrument plug-in can be used multiple times in a single Project—something that can't be easily done with physical hardware sound modules.

With the advent of virtual instruments, the way that MIDI controllers are connected has also changed. Although the traditional 5-pin cable is still around, it is also common for MIDI controllers to be connected to computers via a USB connection. This removes the necessity of having a separate MIDI interface (which is needed for MIDI controllers that don't support USB).

Careers in Music Creation: A Conversation with Jeff Miyahara

Generally speaking, MIDI is associated with music creation of some sort. Of course, composers use MIDI to realize their musical idea (just as they've done with music paper in the past), but there are other careers that relate to MIDI as well, such as arrangers, orchestrators, producers, and transcriptionists.

To give you a sense of how a music producer uses MIDI, I spoke with Jeff Miyahara, one of the world's most successful hitmakers. Based in Tokyo, Jeff is the CEO of J-POP Music Group and CCO of Hitmaker Global Academy in Singapore. He's the creative behind artists like Girls' Generation, SHINee, EXO, Namie Amuro, J-Soul Brothers, Boyz II Men, and over 200 international artists. Jeff has earned impressive awards, including several Japan Gold Disc Awards by the Recording Industry Association of Japan in 2005, 2008, and 2009, as well as Nikkei Entertainment's "Hitmaker of the Year" in 2010.

AH: Jeff, you probably remember the days of music production before MIDI was commonly used. For you, what was the impact of MIDI when it was first introduced?

JM: Oh man. The first time I ever tried MIDI was in 1996—my friend had a copy of Cakewalk on his computer. I believe I tried to create a few MIDI channels and then playback through his Soundblaster audio card, and I actually broke the hardware. That happened to me two times by the way: the second time was when I saw smoke coming from my Korg 1212 I//O back in 1999.

I've been using MIDI extensively since 1999. I grew up playing guitar and singing vocals, and the only way for me to put my ideas down onto a playback-able format was through tape-based Multitrack recorders. It was the first time I connected a MIDI sequencer, and later, using a Mac G3 with Emagic's Logic, I was finally able to fully realize my musical ideas into full songs. I started out using outboard MIDI gear, like the tried-and-true Roland JV1080 and old Kurzweil synth pieces, all connected via a MOTU MIDI Timepiece. Around the same time Cubase and Logic came out with VSTi's (software synthesizer instruments), I quickly made the change from using hardware instruments to software instruments.

MIDI made it possible for me to become my own band, conductor, arranger, and arsenal of musicians. It's enabled someone like myself, with musical ideas but without an extensive amount of musical training and musician friends, to become a professional.

Figure 6.3 Jeff Miyahara

AH: From a technical perspective, what kind of skills are needed to be a successful composer using MIDI and DAWs?

JM: I believe that composing and producing on the computer is similar to playing an instrument. It requires a lot of practice, education, and hours of dedication. Trends change quite drastically, so from the perspective of a songwriter/producer in the pop genre, in order to stay relevant, it's essential to be diverse and open to new ideas.

Technology has come a vast way in the past years as well, and unless you're that 1 percent that makes music so unique, it cannot be replicated by anyone else, I believe embracing new technology in the form of hardware and software is essential to have in your arsenal of creative tools.

AH: I've asked this to some of the other interviewees in this book as well: What kind of personal traits do you think are necessary to be a successful music producer?

JM: Be honest, be smart, be wise, be young, be proactive, be reactive, be loud, be quiet, be hungry, be proud, be humble, be ruthless, be forgiving, be steadfast, be open, and be clean. Be wild, be charismatic, be hermetic, be loving, be selfish, be cultured, be open-minded, be well-traveled, be spontaneous, be gracious, be thankful.

AH: and I have worked on a few projects over the years. Can you walk us through a normal song production process and tell us a little bit about the different kinds of people that are typically involved?

JM: A lot of my music is a collaborative effort. I have up to 12 songs I work on simultaneously within the span of a month. Some of them I work on alone; some of them I write with musical partners like yourself, Andy. I always pay attention to what the client and artist want. This is not always what *I* want to make, but I will find a way to put my artistic fingerprint on it, as well as current creative trends in *anything* I release.

If I have an idea of a rhythm, I will start programming rhythms and eyeball a good tempo before I lay down melodies and chord/riff ideas. If I have a vocal melody or riff I like, I'll usually throw that down as MIDI notes on a synth, or I'll sing it through a simple handheld microphone into Pro Tools. From there, I'll open up Kontakt (a virtual instrument) and start playing with sample libraries and jump on SPLICE to find inspiration samples. I'll let the creative process take control, and usually within 15-30 minutes, I'll have a sketch of either the hook or verse of the song.

I'm a very melodic person, so for me, nailing the vocal melody quickly throughout all sections of the song is more important than stopping everything to find the perfect lyrics for the first line of the verse. Once I've gotten a sketch of what I want to portray to my client and artist, I'll either lay proper male or female vocals with lyrics on the song. By the time my client gets my demo, it'll sound like it's ready to stream on Spotify. I want to WOW them.

I've got a few mix engineers I like to work with, but I like to consider Jon Rezin, Miles Walker, and Satoshi Hosoi my brothers. These guys mix all the big songs that you rock out to on Billboard Top 100, so I know that by the time the first *Mix In Progress* mp3 arrives in my iMessage chat window, it's going to sound amazing. My favorite mastering engineer for the past decade is John Horesco IV. I'm not sure what type of voodoo he's got going on in his studio, but I've never been short of amazed. His masters work on any platform, physical or digital. And we always win.

Bottom line: I've got an amazing team of creatives from songwriters, lyricists, arrangers, musicians, engineers, and A&R's that make the magic happen on a daily basis, 24/365. All across the globe.

AH: There are a lot of DAWs and other music production platforms out there. What made you choose Pro Tools?

JM: Pro Tools is the global standard. If you can use Pro Tools, no matter how big or small the studio, in any country in the world, you can work. My teammates are all over the world: Los Angeles, Atlanta, Tokyo, South Korea, Singapore, Thailand, Taiwan. A lot of us use the same plug-ins and hardware, so we are all listening in a similar environment. Our workflow is seamless, and our track record speaks for itself.

AH: Thanks a lot, man. I really appreciate your time. Any final words of wisdom for the readers?

JM: I always wanted my music to be fascinating and impactful, so I decided to lead a fascinating and impactful life. What's your story?

Setting Up Your MIDI Studio

Before you can record any MIDI data, you'll need to attach your external MIDI device(s) to your system's MIDI interface. (Refer to the documentation that came with your MIDI gear for more information.) Once done, you'll need to set up Pro Tools to recognize that connection.

1. Click on the SETUP menu.
2. Choose MIDI STUDIO. The Audio MIDI Setup window (Mac) or MIDI Studio Setup window (Windows) will appear.

Figure 6.4 Opening the MIDI Studio Setup

The process of configuring your MIDI studio varies a bit between Mac and Windows-based computers. For example, the window you'll use to configure your MIDI devices on a Windows system is called *MIDI Studio Setup*, whereas it's *MIDI Studio* on a Mac.

MIDI Studio Setup on a Mac

The *MIDI Studio* window will give you an overview of the devices attached to your system. Initially, it might show you only your MIDI interface (the device to which you'll attach any external MIDI devices). The next step is to add a device to your system.

The figures in this section are based on my own setup in my home office: I have an M-Audio Axiom 25 connected via USB to my computer. In addition to the Axiom acting as a MIDI device, it also has two MIDI in ports and one MIDI out port, and operates as a MIDI interface.

1. Click on the ADD DEVICE button. A New External Device icon will appear.

Figure 6.5 Adding a New Device (Mac)

2. In the MIDI Studio window, click and hold on the MIDI OUT port of the MIDI interface that is connected to your external device (In my case, the MIDI OUT port of the Axiom 25).
3. Drag with your mouse to the MIDI IN port of your external device. You'll see a line connecting the MIDI interface icon and the New External Device icon.
4. Repeat steps 2 and 3 for the connection from the MIDI OUT port of your external device to the MIDI IN port of your interface, if applicable. In my system, the result is shown in Figure 6.6

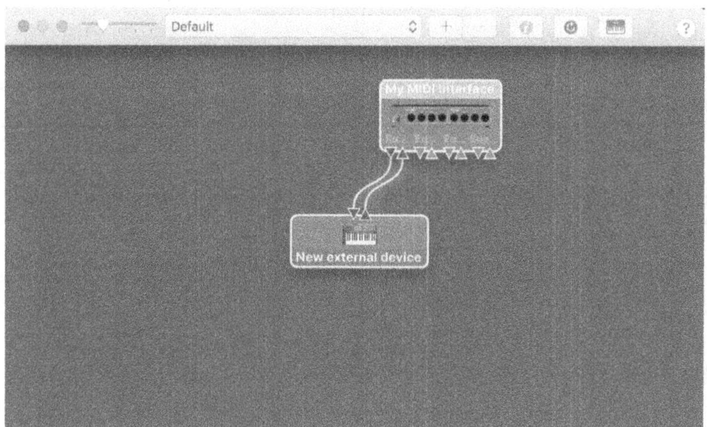

Figure 6.6 Connecting the New Device (Mac)

5. Double-click the New External Device icon. The *New External Device Properties* dialog box will appear, enabling you to customize the connection.

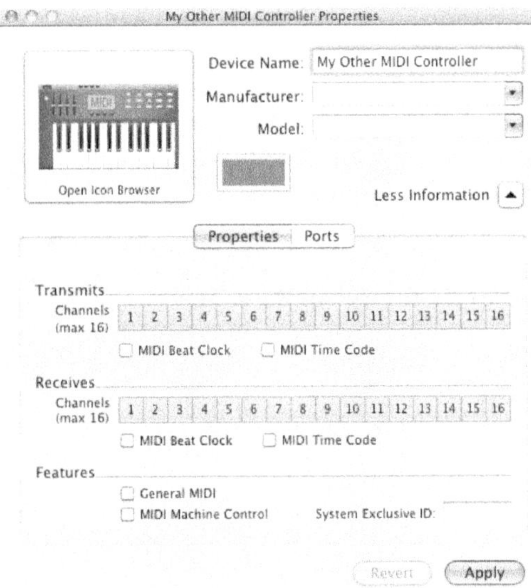

Figure 6.7 The New Device Properties Window (Mac)

6. The top section enables you to type a descriptive name for your device and choose the manufacturer and model that match your gear. If you can't find your manufacturer or model on those lists, just leave the fields blank.
7. Click on the TRANSMITS CHANNELS buttons for the transmitting channels that you want to make available for your device. (Enabled channels will be colored blue.) You can also choose to enable the device to transmit MIDI Beat Clock and/or MIDI Time Code. (Enabled options will be indicated with a checkmark.)
8. Click on the RECEIVES CHANNELS buttons for the receiving channels you want to make available for your device. (Enabled channels will be colored blue.) You can also choose to enable the device to receive MIDI Beat Clock and/or MIDI Time Code. (Enabled options will be indicated with a checkmark.)
9. You can enable your device to operate as a General MIDI device or a MIDI Machine Control device (to control the transport of Pro Tools), or you can assign a System Exclusive ID number (if you have multiple devices of the same model).
10. When you've set up your device, click on the APPLY button. The dialog box will close. When you've created and configured all your external gear, just close the MIDI Studio window.

MIDI Studio Setup on a Windows Computer

Like the MIDI Studio window on a Mac, the MIDI Studio Setup window on a Windows computer enables you to set up your MIDI devices. The steps vary a bit, however:

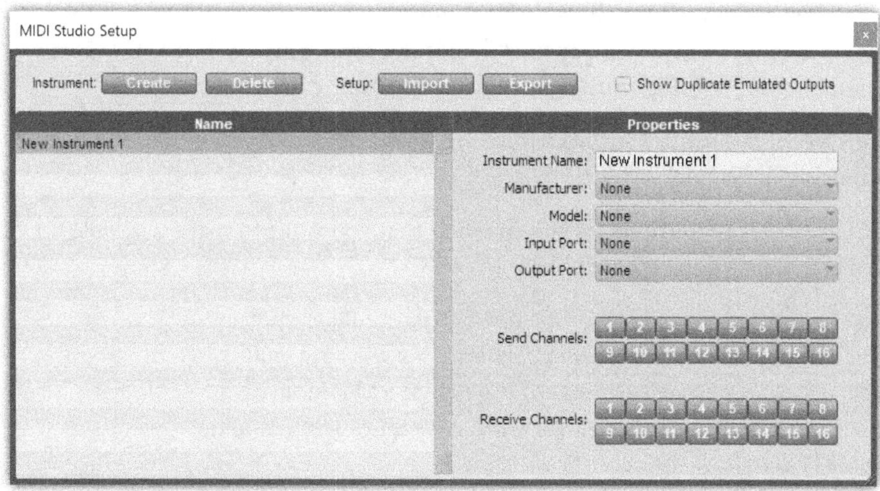

Figure 6.8 MIDI Studio Setup (Windows)

1. Click on the CREATE button. A new device, initially named *New Instrument 1*, will be created.

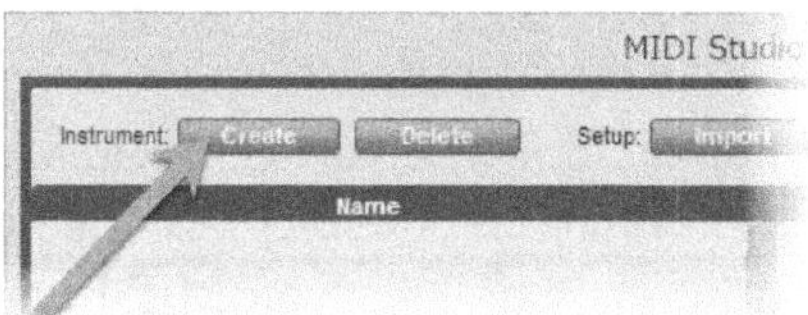

Figure 6.9 Creating a New Device (Windows)

2. The top section of the window's Properties pane will enable you to type a descriptive Instrument Name for your device, and choose the manufacturer and model that match your gear. If you don't see your manufacturer or model, just leave the fields blank.

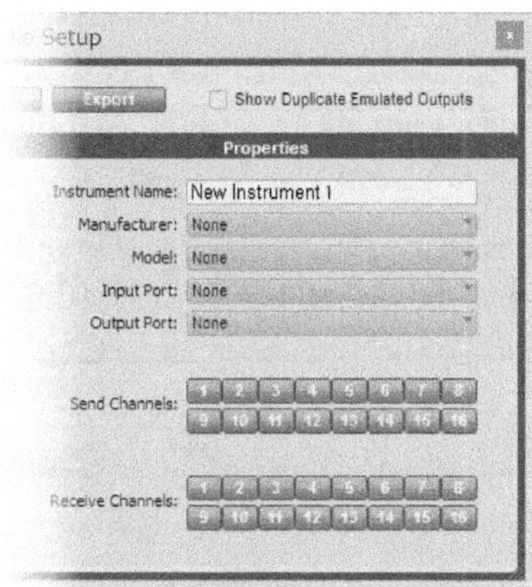

Figure 6.10 MIDI Device Properties (Windows)

3. Click the INPUT PORT down arrow. A menu will appear. Choose the appropriate MIDI IN port on your MIDI interface (the MIDI IN port that is connected to your external device).

4. Now it's time to choose how your system will *send* MIDI information to the device. Click the OUTPUT PORT down arrow. A menu will appear. Choose the appropriate MIDI OUT port on your MIDI interface (the MIDI OUT port that is connected to your external device).
5. Click the SEND CHANNELS buttons for the channels that you want to make available for your device. (Enabled channels will be colored blue.)
6. Click the RECEIVE CHANNELS buttons for the channels that you want to make available for your device. (Enabled channels will be colored blue.)

Since MIDI setups come in all shapes and sizes, it's a good general rule to start off by enabling all of the MIDI transmit and receive channels. This will give you maximum flexibility when recording and playing back MIDI (which you'll learn about later in this chapter), and you can always change the device's settings later, to better suit your individual studio layout.

7. You can repeat this process for each of the external MIDI devices in your system. When you're finished, **close** the **window**, and your settings will be applied to your system.

Creating MIDI Tracks and Instrument tracks

If there's one important thing to remember about MIDI, it's this: MIDI is not audio. MIDI isn't even audible on its own—it's a digital language that enables musical devices to communicate with each other. It's a common misconception that MIDI and audio are somehow directly related, and this misunderstanding about MIDI can cause inefficiency and frustration in getting MIDI to work the way that it should.

There are two common ways that MIDI is set up in Pro Tools: through a MIDI track/Auxiliary Input track combination, or with an Instrument track.

MIDI/Aux Track Workflow

The oldest method of setting up virtual instruments in Pro Tools is to use a MIDI track (which can record and play back MIDI data, but has no sound on its own), and an Auxiliary Input track (which cannot hold MIDI or audio clips, but *can* host a virtual instrument plug-in). Let's tackle this first:

1. Create a MIDI track and assign it a descriptive name. (Refer to Chapter 2, "Creating Projects and Tracks," if you need a refresher on how to do this.) You'll notice that the overall layout of a MIDI track is consistent with other tracks you've seen so far.

Figure 6.11 Creating a MIDI Track

2. Click on the MIDI INPUT SELECTOR. The Input menu will appear, including the following options:

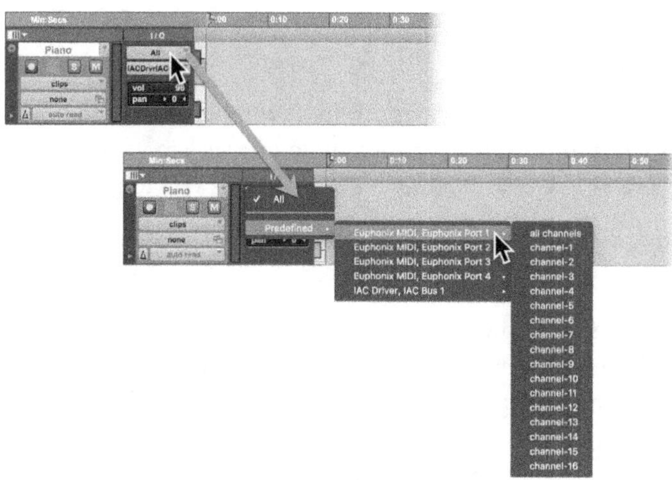

Figure 6.12 Selecting a MIDI Input

- By default, a new MIDI track will have ALL set as the input and will enable the track to accept MIDI data from any port on any channel. This is a convenient way to work if you're a single user in a multi-keyboard studio. With All selected as an input, you can play any MIDI device in your studio and have it recorded to the track, without having to change your input selection.
- Each input device you've specified in your MIDI setup will appear as an input option. You can choose a single device or even a specific MIDI channel on a given device as an input for your track. This is useful in multi-keyboard setups in which you have multiple musicians playing simultaneously. You can assign multiple tracks to accept input from specific MIDI sources, isolating each musician's performance to separate tracks.

3. Select the input that suits your situation.
4. Click on the MIDI OUTPUT SELECTOR. The Output menu will appear.
5. Select the device and MIDI channel that are routed to the device you want to use for MIDI playback on this track. If you're using external MIDI synthesizer hardware, then you'll need to set this up. If you want to use a virtual instrument, you can skip this step for now.

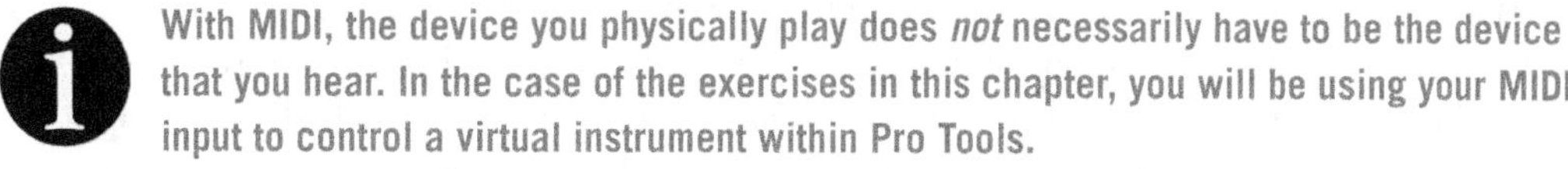

With MIDI, the device you physically play does *not* necessarily have to be the device that you hear. In the case of the exercises in this chapter, you will be using your MIDI input to control a virtual instrument within Pro Tools.

Your MIDI track is now set up to receive MIDI data from a source (for example, a MIDI controller) to a destination (for example, an external sound module or virtual instrument). The next choice to make is where that data will *go*. There are different scenarios that will involve the use of an *Auxiliary Input* track:

Even though an Aux track is an *audible* track, it isn't an *Audio* track. The main difference between the two is that an Audio track can play back clips in your session (as you've already seen), whereas an Aux track cannot. Although you technically *could* use an Audio track to monitor an external MIDI device's output, Aux tracks are generally more suited to the task, and using Aux tracks whenever possible will conserve resources, so you can get the maximum performance out of your system.

6. Create a new Stereo Aux track and assign it a descriptive name. (This is the track you'll use to hear your MIDI device.)
7. If you are using external MIDI synthesizer hardware, then you need to set up the input of the Aux track. Choose the input that corresponds to the inputs of your audio interface to which your synthesizer is attached. If you want to use a virtual instrument, you can skip this step for now.
8. Assign the output of this Aux track to the audio outputs to which your monitor speakers are connected.

At this point, you've completely configured a basic MIDI signal flow, as well as the audio signal routing that will enable you to listen to your sound-producing device. When you play your MIDI controller (with the MIDI track record armed), you will trigger your sound-producing device (in Figure 6.13, it's a device I've called "My Synth"). The synth device will respond by making sound, which you'll hear through the Aux track (in Figure 6.13, the signal coming from the synth is coming into input "1-2" and going out of the output "Built-In Output 1-2").

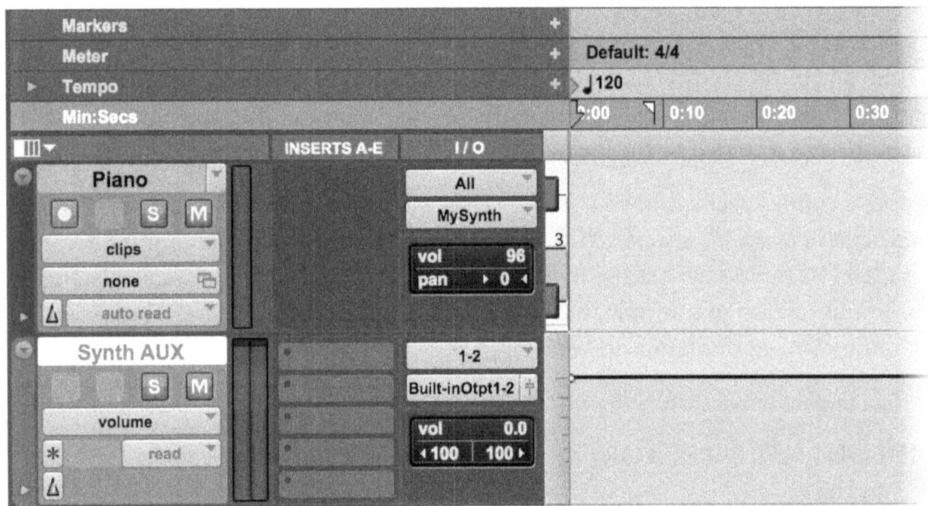

Figure 6.13 A MIDI Track Controlling and an Aux Track Monitoring a Hardware Synth Device

If you're setting up a situation that involves a hardware synthesizer module, you can now test your work: Just record-enable the MIDI track (which you learned how to do in the previous chapter), so that it will accept signal from the input source (just as you did with an audio track in the previous chapter). Playing notes on your MIDI controller should now show levels in the MIDI track's meter—that indicates that your MIDI track's input is set up correctly. If you've also correctly set your MIDI Track's output, plus the Aux track's input and output, you'll hear your synthesizer module.

Using Virtual Instruments on an Aux Track

The same MIDI track/Auxiliary Input track combination can be used if you want to use a virtual instrument rather than a hardware synthesizer to create your sounds. Here's how to do it:

1. Make sure that you're seeing one of your Inserts views (either *Inserts A-E* or *Inserts F-J*).

2. Click on any of the INSERT SELECTOR slots, as shown in Figure 6.14.

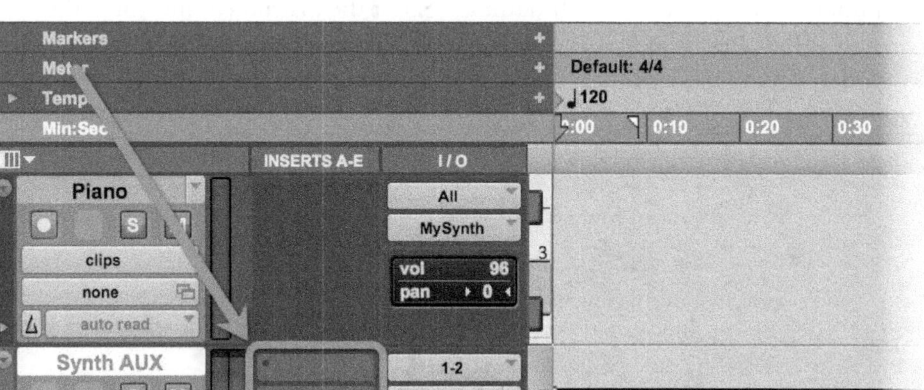

Figure 6.14 Clicking an Insert Selector

3. The first menu you'll see is the Plug-in Type Menu. Move your cursor to the MULTICHANNEL PLUG-IN item to reveal a list of different plug-in types.
4. Move your cursor to the INSTRUMENT category to reveal a list of plug-in virtual instruments.
5. Choose your desired instrument. In Figure 6.15, I've chosen XPAND!2.

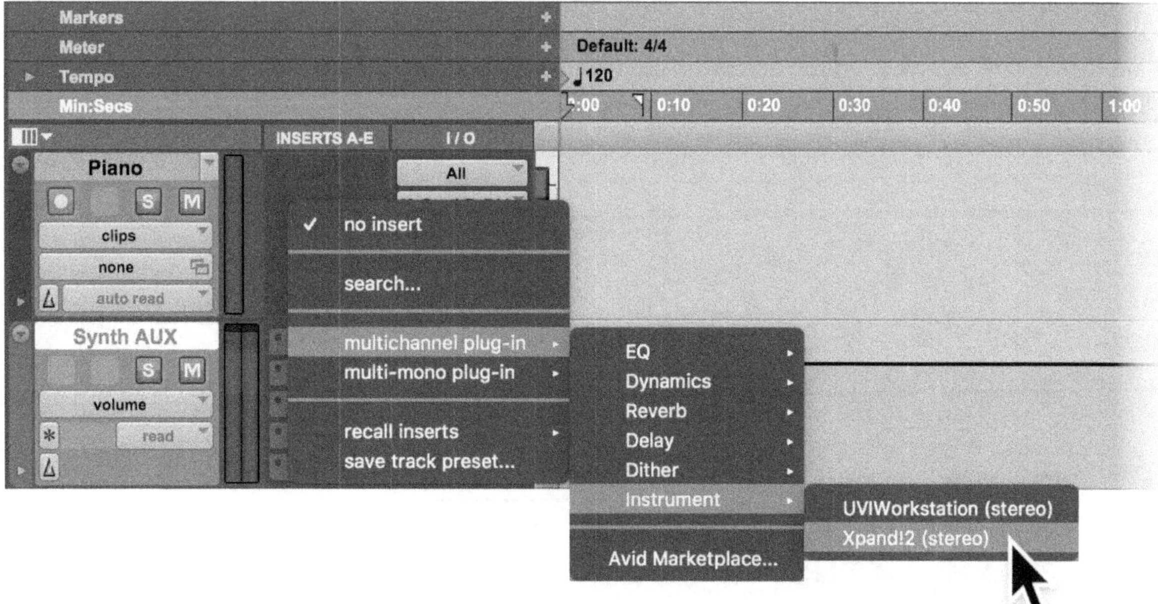

Figure 6.15 Choosing a Virtual Instrument Plug-in

6. After you've launched a virtual instrument plug-in, it will appear as an output option for your MIDI track (in addition to your physical MIDI outputs). Select the instrument including the desired MIDI channel if the plug-in supports multiple MIDI channels (not all do). As shown in Figure 6.16, I've chosen XPAND!2, MIDI channel 1.

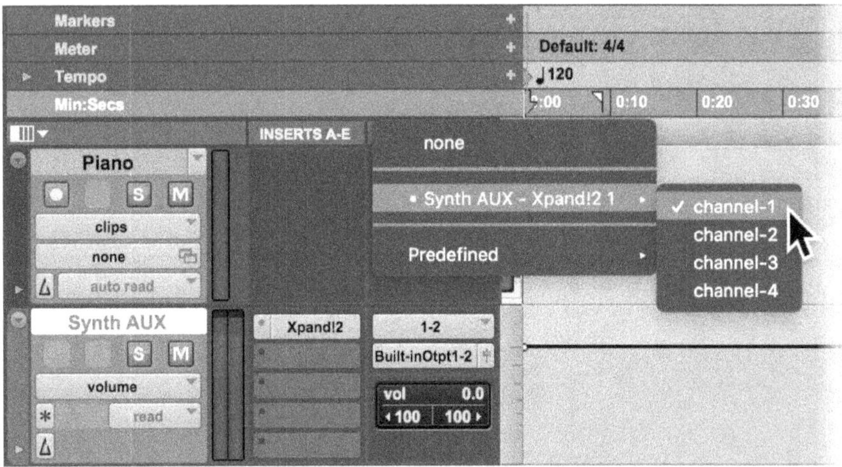

Figure 6.16 Assigning your MIDI Track's Output to the Virtual Instrument Plug-in

There are a few ways that you could test this kind of setup. For example, you could record-enable the MIDI track and play some notes. If you see the meters on the MIDI track react, then you know that you have MIDI data going to the MIDI track. That MIDI data should then go to the virtual instrument that you've chosen as the output of your MIDI track, which should respond to your MIDI data by making sound, causing the meters on the Auxiliary Input track to react.

There's another way to test your setup (which will also introduce a new bit of information to your growing Pro Tools skill set: The *Track View* selector.

1. Click the MIDI track's *Track View* selector (which will initially read "Clips"). A menu will appear.

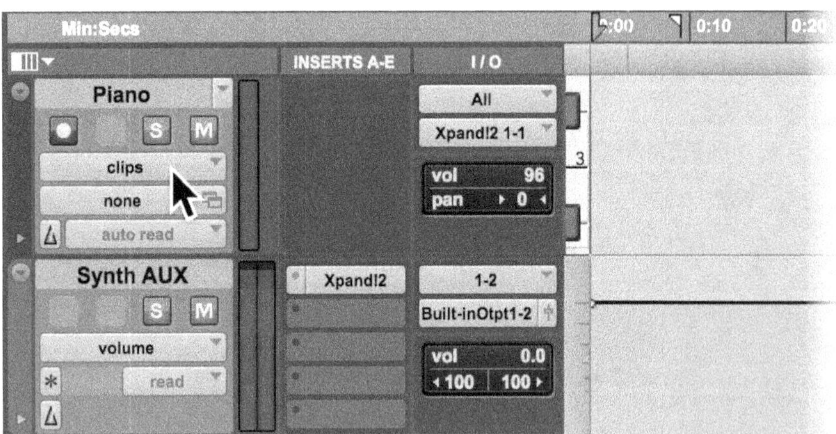

Figure 6.17 The Track View Selector

2. The Track View selector will show you the available view options for this track, with the currently active view indicated by a checkmark. To check your connection, choose NOTES from the menu.

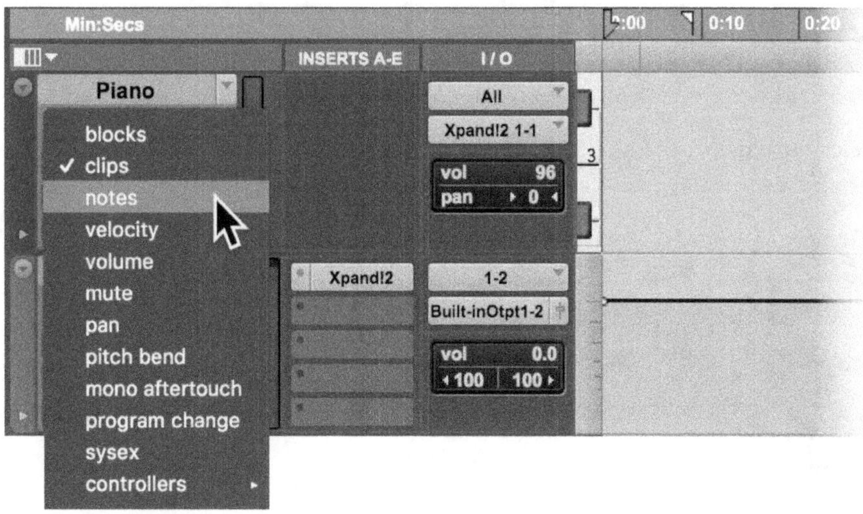

Figure 6.18 Changing to Notes View

3. Click on any note on the mini keyboard to the left of your MIDI track's playlist area. If everything is set up properly, MIDI data will be created, the data will be sent to the virtual instrument, and the instrument will sound.

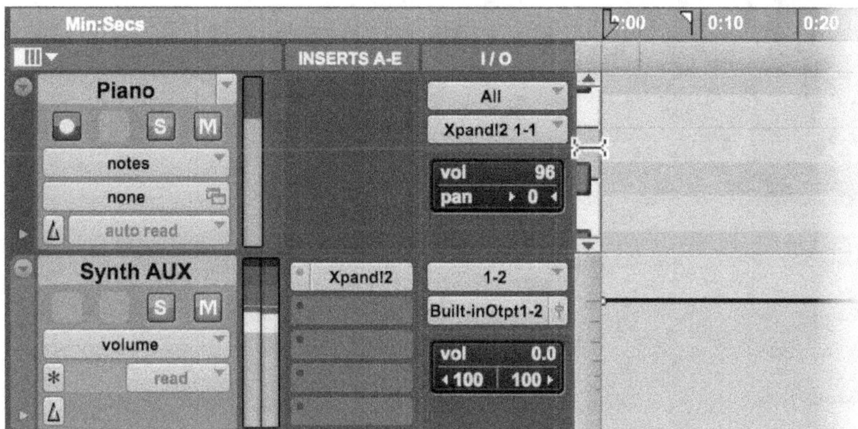

Figure 6.19 Triggering MIDI Data From the Mini Keyboard

Instrument Tracks

Instrument tracks are real timesavers for MIDI production, combining the power of a MIDI track and an Aux track in a single track:

1. Open the *New Tracks* dialog box and create a *Stereo Instrument* track. When you click CREATE, a new Instrument track will be created.

Figure 6.20 Creating a Stereo Instrument Track

2. Assign your track a descriptive name. Below the track name, you'll see some familiar-looking buttons, including *Record Enable*, *Solo*, *Mute*, and the *Track View selector*.

Figure 6.21 A New Instrument Track

3. If you're not seeing the Instrument column, click the Edit window View selector and choose Instrument. (Visible columns will be indicated by checkmarks.)

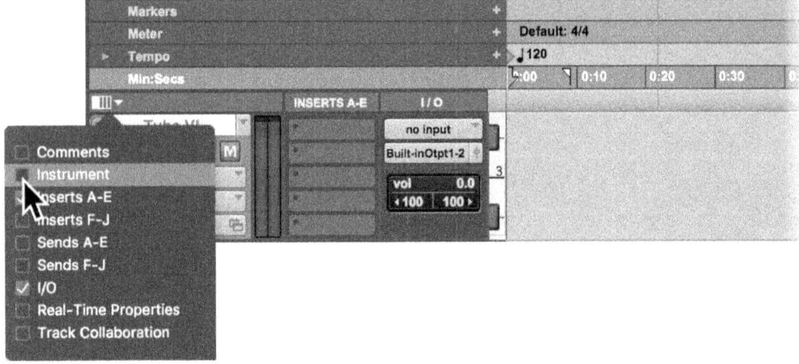

Figure 6.22 Showing the Edit Window Instrument View

4. The Instrument column mirrors the functionality of a MIDI track's I/O column, as shown in Figure 6.23.

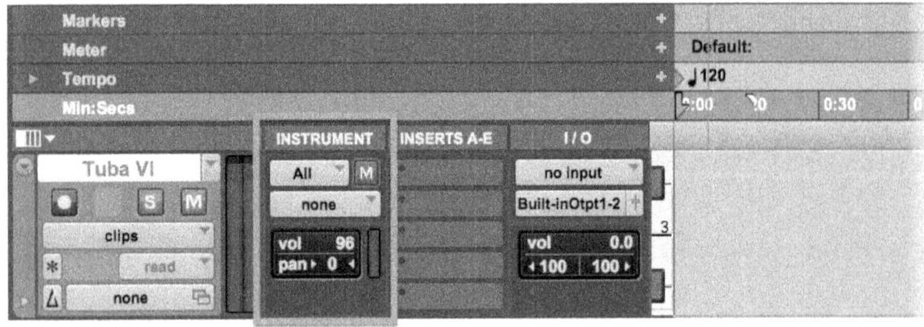

Figure 6.23 The Edit Window Instrument View

5. The controls are, from top to bottom:
   - MIDI Input selector
   - MIDI Mute button
   - MIDI Output selector
   - MIDI Volume indicator
   - MIDI Pan indicator
   - MIDI Velocity Meter
6. The Inserts column of an Instrument track functions just like the Inserts view of an Aux track. Simply **choose** the desired **virtual instrument plug-in** on this track, just as you did before with an Aux track. Your plug-in will launch, and the MIDI Output selector of the Instrument track will automatically change to match the plug-in, making an Instrument track even more convenient. If you need to change that MIDI output for any reason, you can do it easily by clicking the MIDI Output selector.

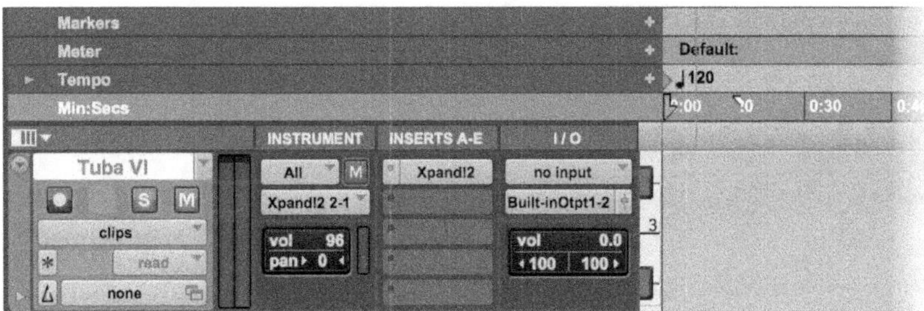

Figure 6.24 A Virtual Instrument Inserted on an Instrument Track

7. The I/O column of an Instrument track is identical to the I/O column of an Aux track, and you'll use it the same way. **Set** the **output** of the Instrument track.
8. Last but certainly not least, **adjust** your track's **output level and pan** as needed. Note that it is standard practice to control the volume level of an Instrument track from the *audio* volume fader rather than the MIDI volume fader (which is in the *Instrument* view).

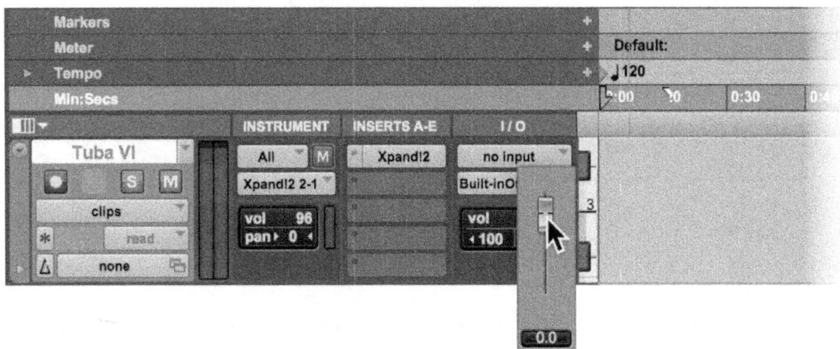

Figure 6.25 Changing an Instrument Track's Output Level

Initially, the Instrument track view will be set to Clips (similar to the MIDI track you worked with earlier), but as with a MIDI track, you can change the view to Notes and click your mini keyboard to test your setup, as you did in the previous section of this chapter.

Changing Sounds

Usually, your first step is to pick a sound that you want to use. How you do this varies slightly depending on whether you're using an external MIDI device or a virtual instrument plug-in. Let's start with the external device.

Changing Sounds on an External Device

To choose a sound for an external device, follow these steps:

1. Click on the PATCH SELECT button, as shown in Figure 6.26 (Conveniently, it's in the same position on MIDI tracks and Instrument tracks.) A dialog box containing a patch list for the MIDI device will open. Depending on the device you configured in your MIDI setup, the patch list displayed will consist of numbers and/or text names.

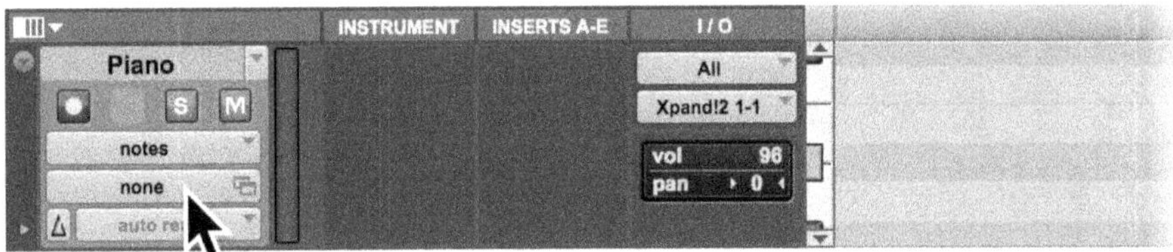

Figure 6.26 Clicking the Patch Select Button

Piano

Mode:
Bank:
Patch: 45
Controller 0:
Controller 32:

none	9	19	29	39	49	59	69	79	89	99	109	119
0	10	20	30	40	50	60	70	80	90	100	110	120
1	11	21	31	41	51	61	71	81	91	101	111	121
2	12	22	32	42	52	62	72	82	92	102	112	122
3	13	23	33	43	53	63	73	83	93	103	113	123
4	14	24	34	44	54	64	74	84	94	104	114	124
5	15	25	35	45	55	65	75	85	95	105	115	125
6	16	26	36	46	56	66	76	86	96	106	116	126
7	17	27	37	47	57	67	77	87	97	107	117	127
8	18	28	38	48	58	68	78	88	98	108	118	

Patch name file: None
Increment patch every 1 seconds

Change... Clear Cancel Done

Figure 6.27 The Patch Select Dialog Box

2. Click on the patch you want to use.
3. Click the DONE button. The dialog box will close, and the program number or name will appear on the Patch Select button.

Changing Sounds on a Virtual Instrument

If you're using a virtual instrument (such as Xpand!2), you'll need to choose a sound directly from the plug-in's window:

1. If the plug-in window isn't open already, click on the virtual instrument's Insert button. The Insert button will be highlighted, and the plug-in window will open.

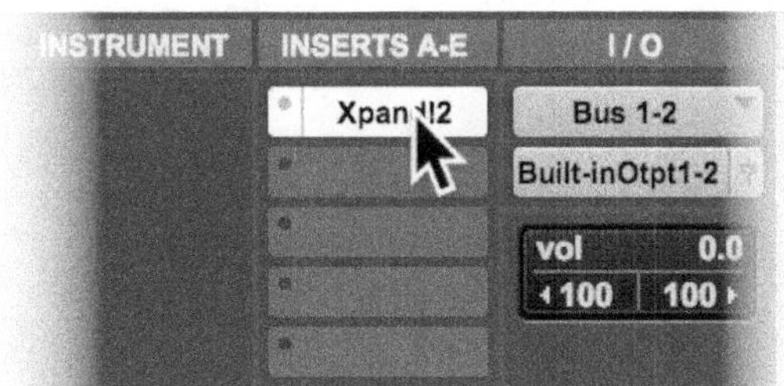

Figure 6.28 Opening a Plug-in Window

2. Click the LIBRARIAN MENU (which will display the currently active sound). A menu of available sounds will appear, sometimes nested into submenus, as shown in Figure 6.29.

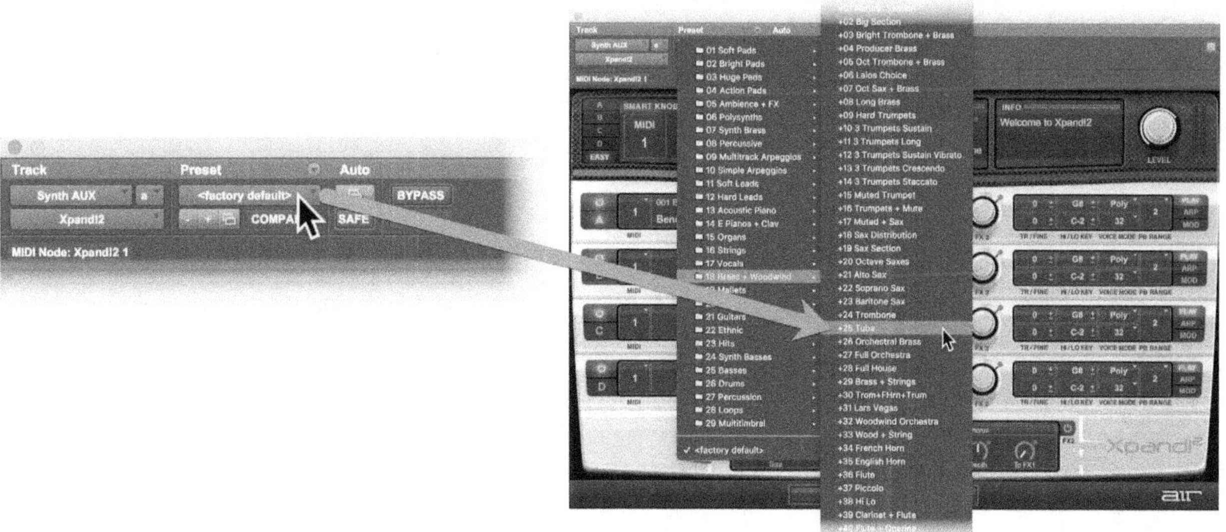

Figure 6.29 Changing a Virtual Instrument's Sound

3. Choose the desired sound from the menu. The menu will close, and your choice will be applied.

Here's an alternative method:

1. Click the PLUG-IN SETTINGS SELECT button. The plug-in settings dialog box will open.

Figure 6.30 The Plug-in Settings Select Button

2. If your plug-in presets are organized into submenus, click the Folder pop-up menu. The subfolder hierarchy will be displayed. Select the desired subfolder from the list. When you make your selection, the programs in that subfolder will be displayed in the window.

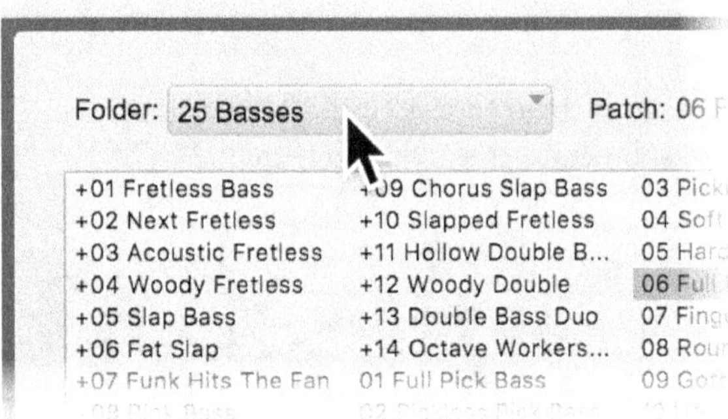

Figure 6.31 Changing Folders in the Plug-in Settings Select Dialog Box

3. Select the desired sound.
4. Click the DONE button in the lower right-hand corner of the Plug-in Settings dialog box.

If you're searching for just the right sound, the Increment Setting Every [#] Seconds check box (in the bottom-right corner of the plug-in settings dialog box) can come in handy. Just enable the feature to cycle through all the sounds automatically, allowing you to keep playing while the patches change.

Hands-On Exercise 6.1: Creating MIDI and Instrument Tracks

Let's revisit the *Mambo* song and add a little bit of MIDI to sweeten things up.

Setting Things Up

1. Create a new Project by converting the *Pro Tools First—Fundamentals of Audio Production—Chapter 6 (Mambo).ptx* session to a local Project. The session is found in the *Pro Tools First—Fundamentals of Audio Production—Chapter 6 (Mambo)* subfolder of this book's downloaded exercise material. You learned how to convert a session to a Project in Chapter 2. Choose any desired sample rate, 24-bit, and do not backup to Cloud.

Figure 6.32 The Mambo Song with an Inactive MIDI Track

Setting Up a MIDI/Aux Track Combination

The Edit window that you see in Figure 6.31 will show you an edited version of the song (the work you've done in previous chapters' exercises), plus one track that has been greyed out. Any track in Pro Tools that has this greyed-out color is missing something it needs—in this case, the track is a MIDI track that has no output.

2. Create a Stereo Auxiliary Input track, and name it *Bass VI*.

Figure 6.33 Creating an Aux Track for Your Virtual Instrument

3. Next, you'll have to launch a plug-in instrument on that track, but before you can do that, you'll need to see an *Inserts* view. Make sure that you can see the *Inserts A-E* view in the Edit window, as shown in Figure 6.34.

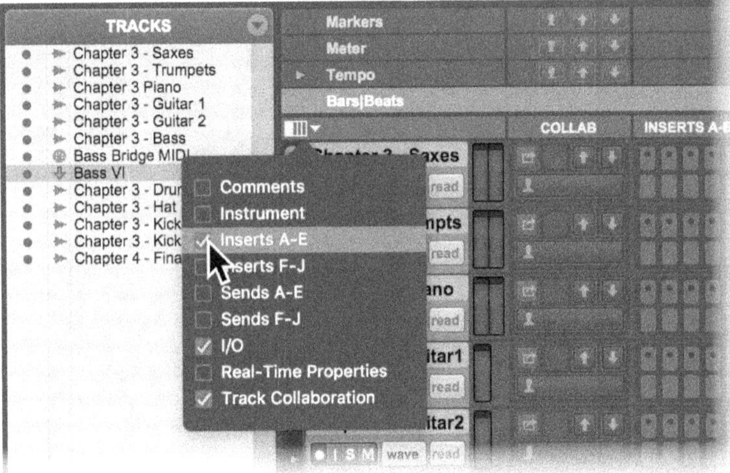

Figure 6.34 Showing the Inserts A-E View in the Edit Window

4. On the new Auxiliary Input track, launch the *Xpand!2* plug-in (MULTICHANNEL PLUG-IN>INSTRUMENT>XPAND!2).

5. In the Xpand!2 plug-in window, use any method (from the *Librarian* Menu or the *Plug-in Settings Select* button) go to the *25 Basses* category, and from there choose *06 Full Finger Bass.*

Figure 6.35 Choosing the Full Finger Bass Sound in the Xpand!2 Plug-in Window

6. Close the Xpand!2 plug-in window.
7. Now we need to route the output of the *Bass Bridge MIDI* track to the Xpand!2 plug-in (residing on the *Bass VI* Aux track). From the MIDI OUTPUT SELECTOR on the *Bass Bridge MIDI* track, choose BASS VI—XPAND!2 1>CHANNEL 1.

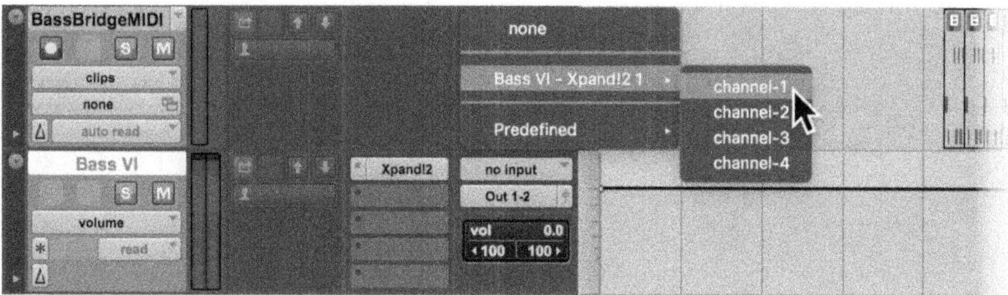

Figure 6.36 Setting the MIDI Track's Output

You'll see that your *Bass Bridge MIDI* track is no longer grey, now that it has a valid output. Now, when you play your Project, you'll hear the Xpand!2 plug-in respond to the MIDI on the *Bass Bridge MIDI* track.

Now, it's time to use your ears a bit: If you solo the *Chapter 3—Bass* audio track, the *Bass Bridge MIDI* track, and the *Bass VI* track, you can listen to the live bass compared to the MIDI bass. You can now experiment with different sounds and change the volume of the *BASS VI* track to get them to match up better. When you're done, un-solo the tracks and play your entire song. How does it sound to your ears?

Setting Up an Instrument Track

Although this song isn't complete by a long shot, it's starting to get there. Let's add a little bit of extra sweetening at the end. Instrument tracks will make it easy, and in this exercise, you'll learn a new way to set one up:

8. Inside the *Pro Tools First—Fundamentals of Audio Production—Chapter 6—MIDI For Import* folder, there is a single MIDI file, named *End Riff MIDI.mid*. Import this file into your Project (either by going to FILE>IMPORT or by dragging it into your project from a file browser window). The *MIDI Import Options* dialog box will appear.

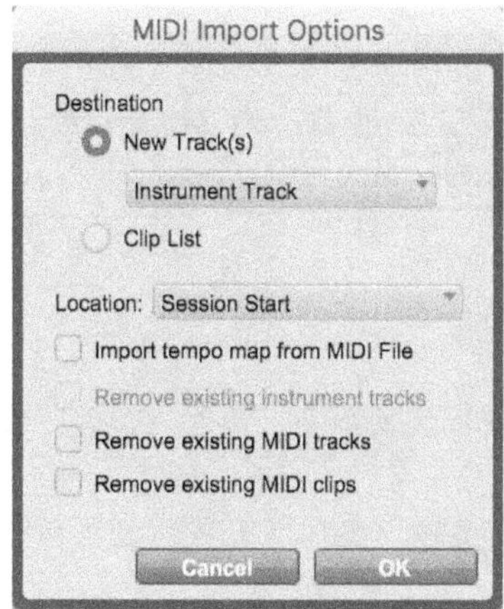

Figure 6.37 The MIDI Import Options Dialog Box

9. In the *MIDI Import Options* dialog box, you can choose whether to import the MIDI clip into an Instrument Track, MIDI Track, or to the Clip List (there isn't a Clip List in Pro Tools | First, so don't choose this). For this exercise, choose *Instrument Track*, as shown in Figure 6.38.

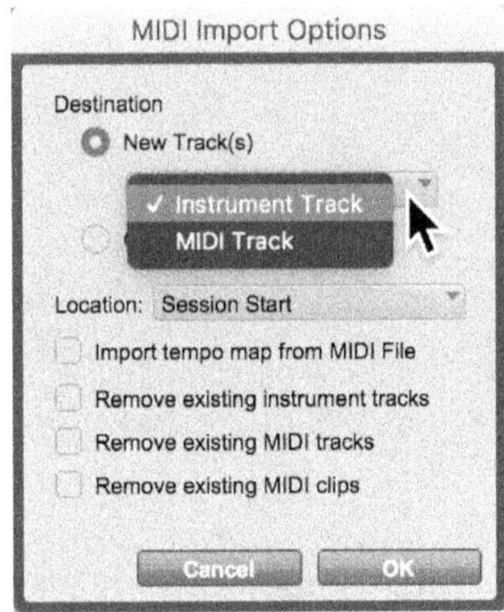

Figure 6.38 Importing to a New Instrument Track

10. On the bottom half of the *MIDI Import Options* dialog box, you can choose where you want to import the clip (*Session Start*, *Song Start*, *Selection*, or *Spot*). Choose *Session Start*.

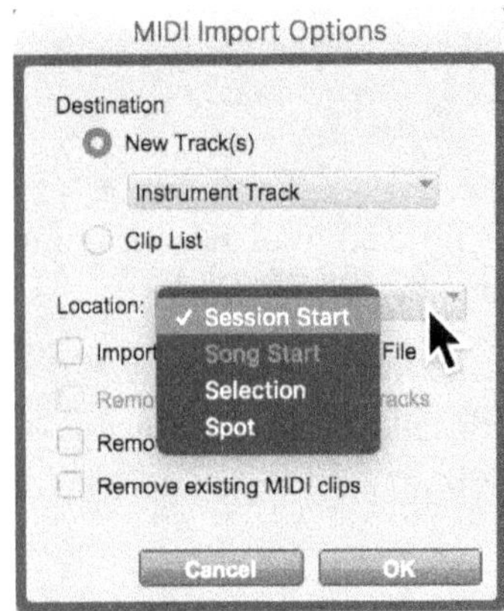

Figure 6.39 Choosing a Location for the MIDI Clip

11. Finally, you can choose whether to *Import tempo map from MIDI File*, *Remove existing Instrument tracks*, *Remove existing MIDI tracks*, and *Remove existing MIDI clips*. Leave all of these boxes unchecked, as shown in Figure 6.40.

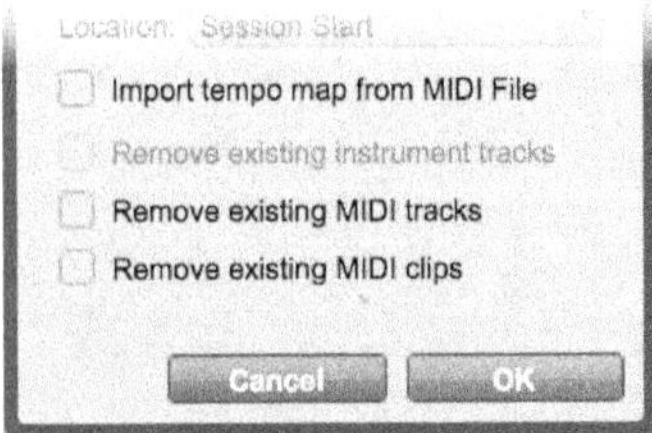

Figure 6.40 Choosing What Else to Import or Delete

12. Click the OK button at the bottom right-hand corner of the *MIDI Import Options* dialog box.
13. A new Instrument track will be created, with a single MIDI clip at the beginning of your Project's timeline, as shown in Figure 6.41.

Figure 6.41 The New Instrument Track

Workflows involve different skills. In this next section, you'll be using techniques that you've learned in previous chapters to get the job done.

14. Rename the new Instrument track (currently called *Inst 1*) to *End Sweetener VI*. You can easily do this by double-clicking the track name and renaming it from the Track Name dialog box.

Figure 6.42 Renaming the New Instrument Track

15. Now, a little housekeeping: Drag the *End Sweetener* track to the top of the Edit window (since this track relates more to the winds than it does to the bass).
16. Using the Grabber tool, drag the clip (which is currently at the beginning of your timeline) to start at bar 61 (61|1|000). You can use Grid mode or Spot mode to move this clip quickly and accurately.

17. Place copies of the clip at bars 63, 65, 67, 69, 71, 73, and 75. You can easily do this by holding the OPTION key (Mac) or ALT key (Windows) and dragging the clip while you're in Grid mode.

18. Use the Trim tool to trim the last half of the last clip on the *End Sweetener VI* track, so that the clip ends at bar 76 (76|1|000).

When you're done with your editing, the *End Sweetener VI* track should look something like this:

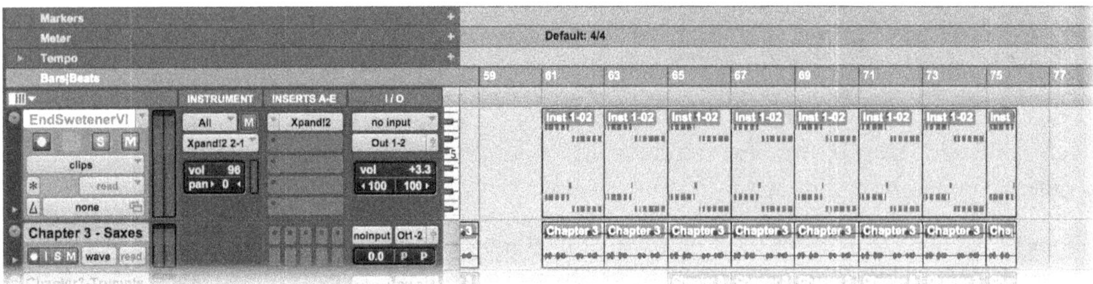

Figure 6.43 The Edited Track

19. Click any Insert selector on the *End Sweetener VI* track and launch the *Xpand!2* instrument plug-in.

20. Finally, let's change the sound: In the *08 Percussive* submenu, choose *+10 Percussive Flies.*

21. Close the Xpand!2 plug-in window

22. This next bit is usually not required, but just in case: Check the MIDI Output of the Instrument track (in the Instrument view, as shown in Figure 6.44). There are currently two Xpand!2 plug-ins in your Project. Make sure you choose the one that is on the *End Sweetener VI* track.

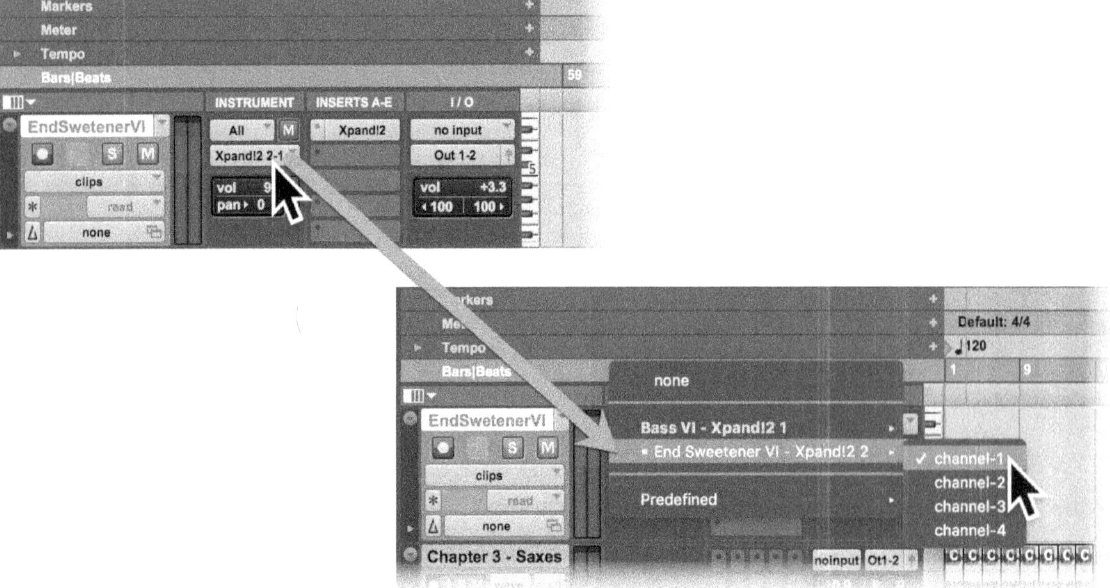

Figure 6.44 Checking the MIDI Output of the Instrument Track

Now you can test out the final tracks and change the level and sound of the *End Sweetener VI* track. Well done—this finishes the exercise (save your work before moving on)!

Time and MIDI

Early in this book, you've learned about samples and how they relate to digital audio. Audio files have a set number of samples per second, which (in a perfect world) play back perfectly every time and not change. For example, an audio file that lasts for a minute will always be one minute long (unless you time-stretch it, which you'll learn how to do in the next chapter).

Audio files are based on "real" time (hours, minutes, and seconds) and typically won't change their placement or duration based on tempo changes. MIDI, on the other hand, is entirely different—you typically *do* want your MIDI notes to change their speed, placement, and duration based on tempo. In this section, we'll look at how MIDI makes this happen.

What is a *Tick*?

If a sample is the smallest unit of time that we deal with when working with digital audio, then a *tick* is the smallest unit of time when working with MIDI. Without getting too deep into the world of music theory, *ticks* are subdivisions of quarter notes. With Pro Tools, there are 960 ticks per quarter note. Ticks are tremendously important, and the reason that we can capture the humanity of live MIDI recording.

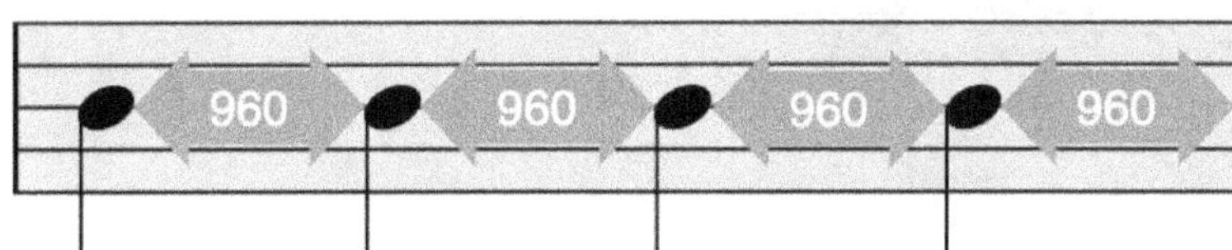

Figure 6.45 960 Ticks Per Quarter Note

Here's a scenario: Let's say that I have a piece of music in front of me, and that there are four quarter notes at bar 1, as shown in Figure 6.46:

Figure 6.46 Four Quarter Notes

Being human, I have about zero chance of playing these notes with mathematical precision. Here's how I played the notes:

- The first quarter note was close, but a little bit late compared with the perfect tempo.
- The second quarter note, I played even later (a late second beat is an essential part of many styles of music).

- Unbelievably, I played the third quarter note exactly on the beat!
- The last quarter note was played a little bit early, in relation to the click track.

So, my live performance might be represented by figure 6.47, with the red dots representing where I actually played the notes:

Figure 6.47 Where the Notes Were Actually Played

When recording, I specifically want to be able to capture the nuances of my performance as I record them. Here's how the notes might look in a MIDI or Instrument track:

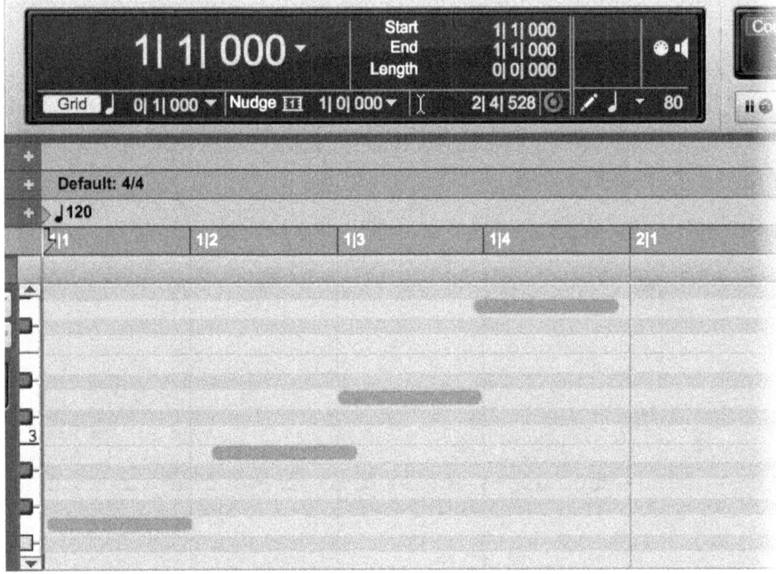

Figure 6.48 The Recorded MIDI Notes

Ticks (and because we have so many of them) will allow me to capture the human imperfection of my performance. Here's how my performance went, in ticks:

- The first note, played a little bit late, has a location of bar 1, beat 1, and *tick* 023. This is represented as **1|1|023**.

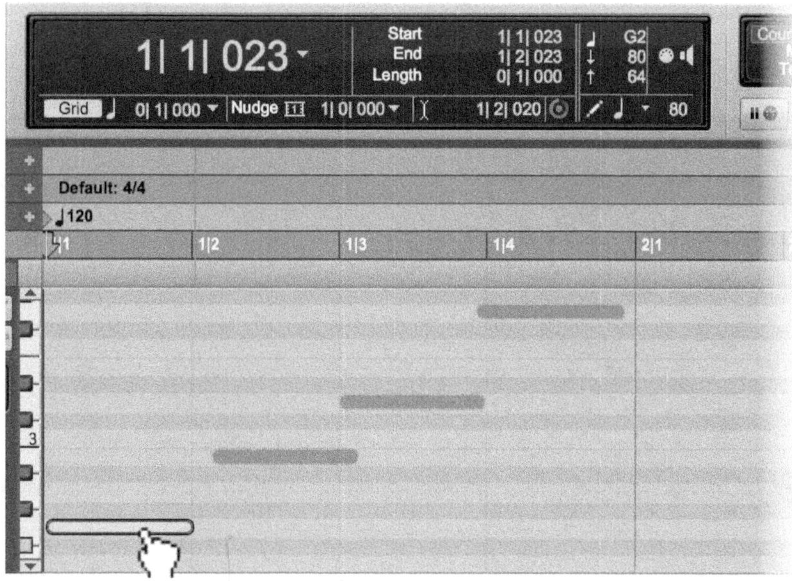

Figure 6.49 The First Note

- The second note, played later, has a location of bar 1, beat 2, and *tick* 136. This is represented as 1|2|136.

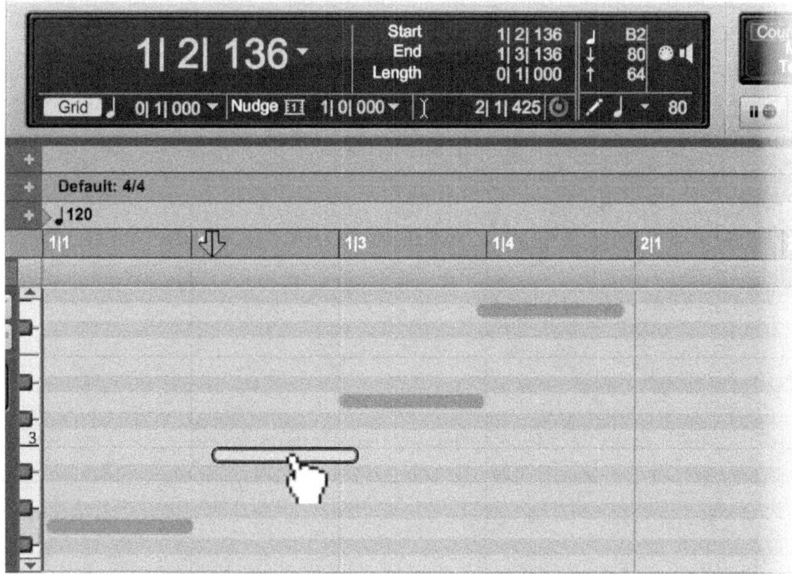

Figure 6.50 The Second Note

- The third note, played right on the beat, has a location of bar 1, beat 3, and *tick* 000. This is represented as **1|3|000**.

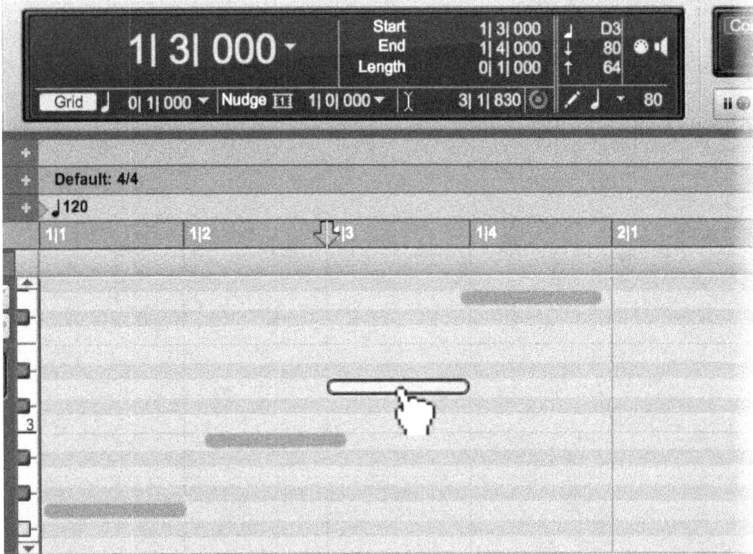

Figure 6.51 The Third Note

- The last note was played *early,* meaning it was played before the fourth beat on the timeline. Hence, it is in bar 1, beat 3 (because beat 4 hadn't happened yet), and *tick* 897. This is represented as **1|3|897**.

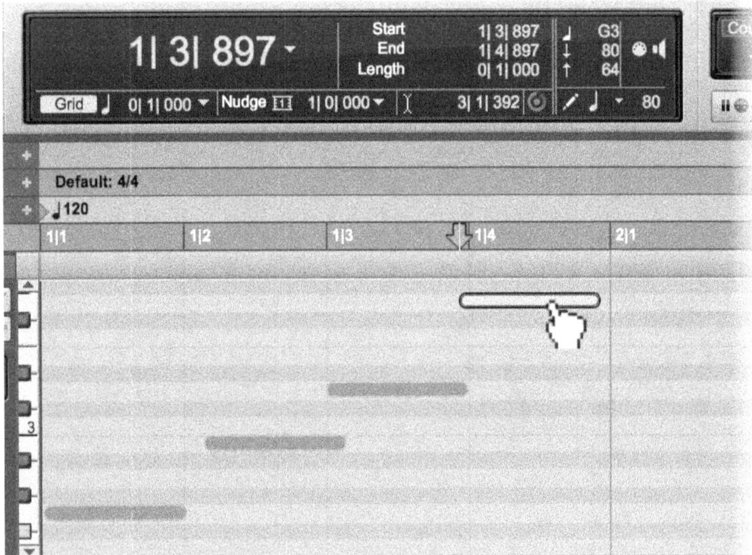

Figure 6.52 The Fourth Note

The beginnings of notes aren't the only thing that has tick-based timing; the ends of notes are also tick-based, which means that the starts, ends, and durations of the notes that you play are timed down to 1/960th of a quarter note!

Timebases and Rulers

The timing of everything on your Project's timeline is either going to be sample-based or tick-based. To best view it, is a matter of setting the right Main Time Scale in the Edit window's Main Counter.

From the Main Counter, click the disclosure triangle to the right of the main counter display to display the two choices you have in Pro Tools | First:

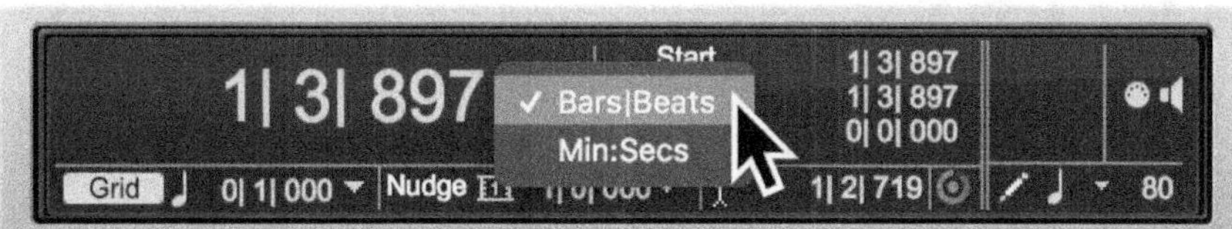

Figure 6.53 Changing your Main Time Scale

- Choose **Bars|Beats** to view the passage of time in your Project in *ticks*. The spacing of the grids will change depending upon your Project's tempo: the higher the tempo, the faster the beats (and therefore the ticks) will play, and your grid will be more narrowly spaced.
- Choose **Min:Secs** to view the passage of time in your Project in *samples*. Sample rates don't change over time; they are based on samples *per second* and will not change based on tempo.

The choice that you make will change the ruler you'll see at the bottom of the Rulers section of the Edit window:

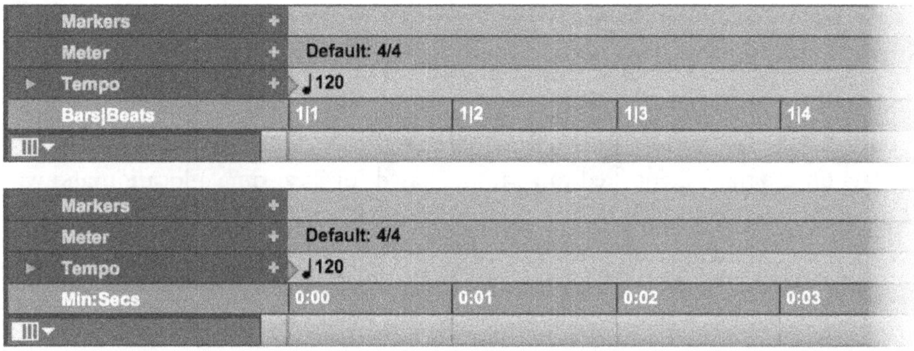

Figure 6.54 Tick-Based (Bars|Beats) and Sample-Based (Min:Secs) Rulers

Timebases and Tracks

Typically, you want your MIDI to respond to tempo and your audio not to respond to tempo. However, sometimes you want to change the way data will react to tempo changes on a given track. That's when you'll want to change a track's timebase.

By default, MIDI tracks and Instrument tracks are *tick-based*, meaning the clips, notes, and other data on the track are locked to a tick (bars, beats, and ticks) location. When tempo is changed, the data will move in sync to preserve its musical location.

A tick-based track is indicated by a green metronome icon in the lower left-hand corner of the track, as shown in Figure 6.55:

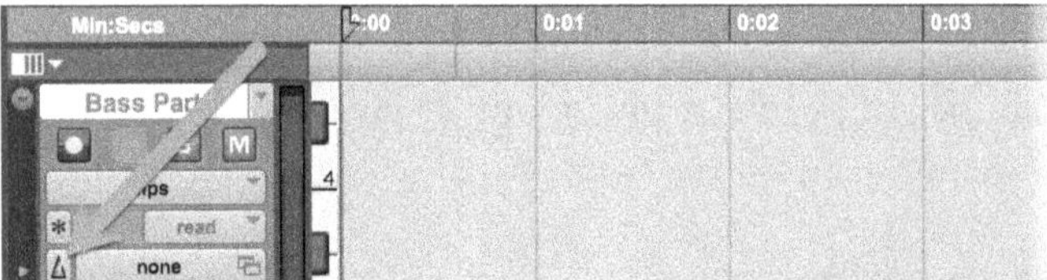

Figure 6.55 A Tick-Based Track

You can change a track from tick-based to sample-based by clicking on the track timebase icon, and choosing SAMPLES from the menu that appears:

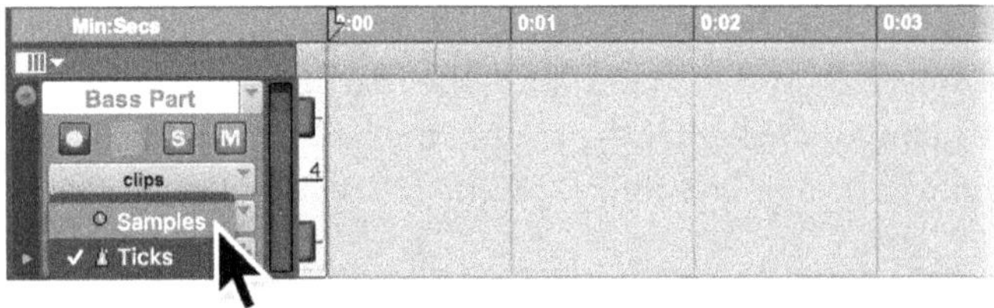

Figure 6.56 Changing a Tick-Based Track to a Sample-Based Track

When a track is set to be sample-based, clips (and in a MIDI or Instrument track's case, notes and other musical performance information) will *not* respond to tempo changes. Although this isn't commonly done when working with MIDI, there are cases when you want this kind of behavior (for example, when you're using MIDI for non-musical purposes, like triggering sound effects).

Audio tracks, Auxiliary Input tracks, and Master Fader tracks, can also be set to be sample-based, in which case the location of clips and other data on the track are locked to a sample-based (or "real-time") location and will *not* respond to tempo changes in your Project.

A sample-based track is indicated by a small blue clock icon in the lower left-hand corner of the track, as shown in Figure 6.57:

Figure 6.57 A Sample-Based Track

In Pro Tools | First, all tracks are *tick-based* by default. In Pro Tools and Pro Tools | Ultimate, however, Audio tracks, Auxiliary Input tracks, and Master Fader tracks are sample-based by default (this can be changed in Pro Tools' preferences).

Just as you can change a MIDI or Instrument track from tick-based to sample-based, you can also change an Audio (or Aux, or Master Fader) track from sample-based to tick-based. Clips and other data on a tick-based track will be locked to a tick-based location, and will change location based upon the tempo settings (and tempo changes) in your Project.

Editing MIDI

You've already learned how to use the basic Edit tools (Trim, Selector, and Grabber) with audio clips. However, because MIDI is fundamentally different than audio, there are even more editing tools available to you!

In the first exercise in this chapter, you've learned how to change your track view with the *Track View Selector*. Now let's learn how you can take your editing to the next level by changing your views.

Clips View

The basic view of a MIDI or Instrument track is the *Clips* view. When you're in Clips view, you'll see your MIDI data in clip-sized blocks, as shown in Figure 6.58:

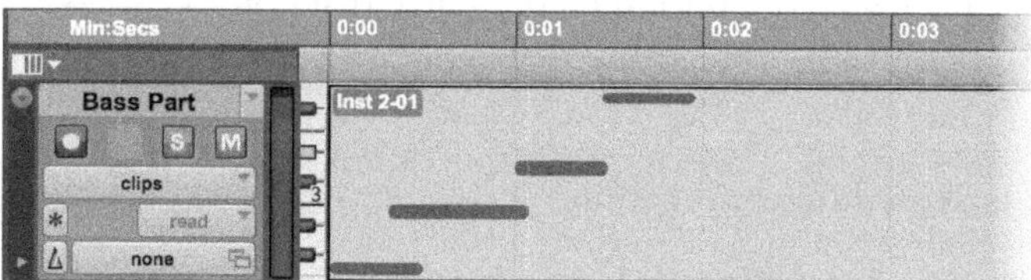

Figure 6.58 Clips View on an Instrument Track

If you need to trim, select, or move a clip, this is the view you want. In this regard, editing is very similar to the work you've already done with Audio tracks.

Notes View

Clips view is good for some kinds of work, but if you want to get specific with individual notes, it's not always the best view. Changing to *Notes* view will give you access to each individual note, so that you can change it independently of other notes.

To change the view, just click the TRACK VIEW SELECTOR, as shown in Figure 6.59:

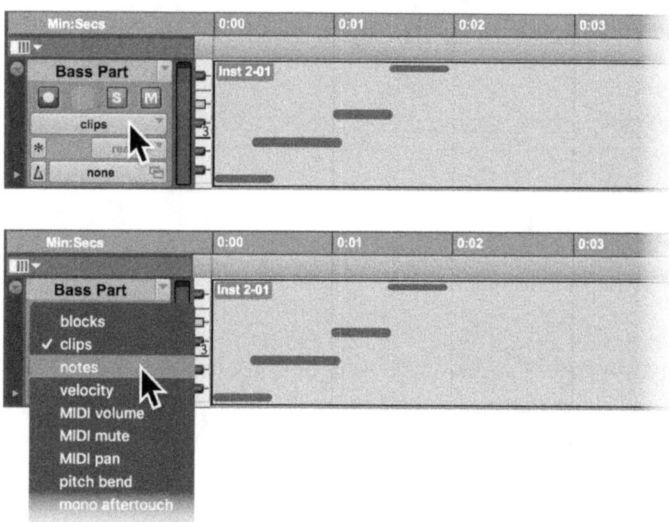

Figure 6.59 Changing the View on an Instrument Track

The menu that you'll see will vary depending on what kind of track you're working with (with the currently active view indicated by a check mark), but on any MIDI or Instrument track, you'll find *Notes* just below the *Clips* view menu item. Click NOTES, and your track view will be changed.

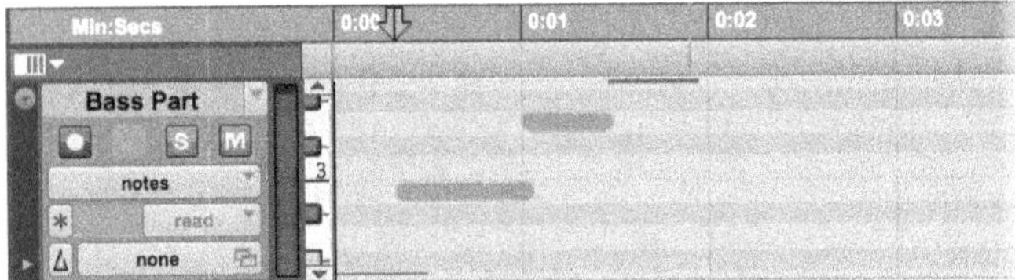

Figure 6.60 Notes View on an Instrument Track

In Figure 6.60, you'll see that the first and last of the four notes in the image are narrower, which indicates that they are out of range of the current view (in other words, below or above the note range that you can see— in Figure 6.60, it's from G#2 to D#3). You can shift the viewing range by clicking the up or down arrow icons at the top or bottom of the Mini Keyboard.

Now that you are in Notes view, your Edit tools will take on different functions:

- The **Trim tool** will now change the beginning or end of a note. Just move your cursor near the start or end of a note and drag it to the desired location. Note that these changes will depend on the currently active Edit mode (choose Slip mode for smooth dragging or choose Grid mode to have your note start or end snap to a grid)

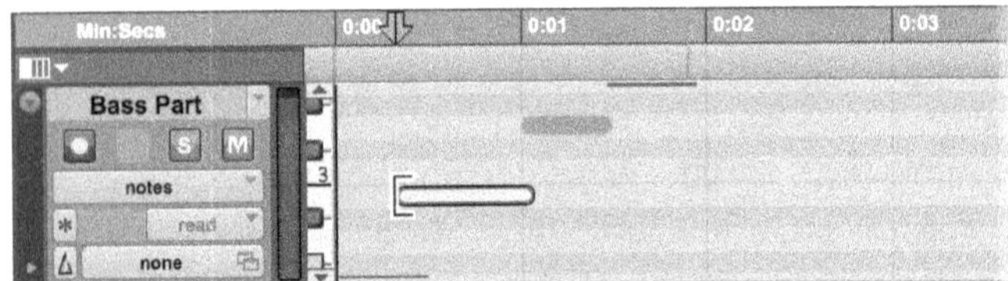

Figure 6.61 Trimming a Note with the Trim Tool

- The **Selector tool** operates a little differently than you might expect: If you create a selected area in Notes view, only the notes whose *beginning* is in your selected area will be selected (as you can see in figure 6.62).

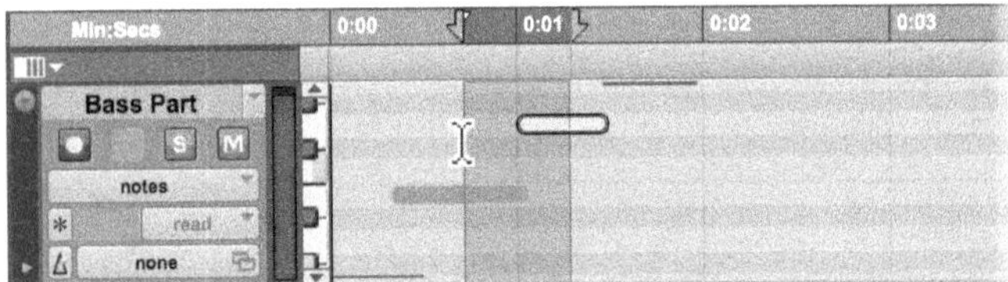

Figure 6.62 Using the Selector Tool in Notes View

- Other ways to use the **Selector tool** in Notes view: Double-clicking with the Selector tool will select the area of the clip (or space between clips) that you are clicking. Triple-clicking with the Selector tool will select all clips on the entire track.

- Clicking on a note with the **Grabber tool** will select that note. To select multiple notes, just hold the SHIFT key while clicking notes. Another way is to move your cursor to an area where there are no notes, and click and drag to create a box within which you can select a group of notes.

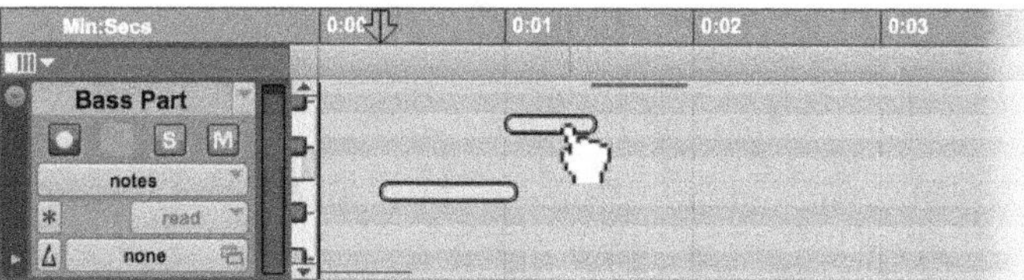

Figure 6.63 Selecting Multiple Notes by Holding the Shift Key with the Grabber Tool

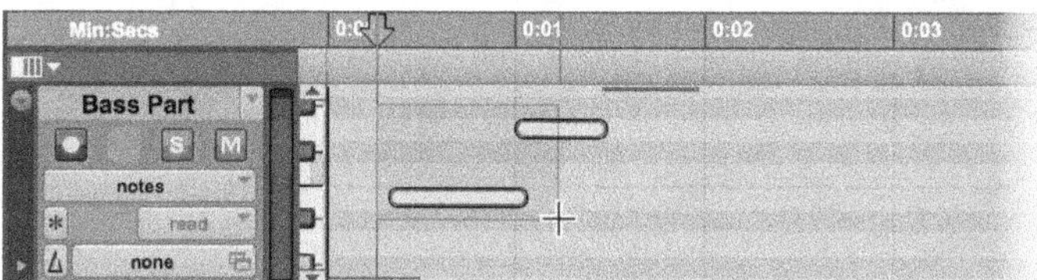

Figure 6.64 Dragging a Box to Select Multiple Notes with the Grabber Tool

As with clips, holding the OPTION key (Mac) or ALT key (Windows) will create a copy as you drag, leaving the original note(s) in position.

- Double-clicking on a note with the **Grabber tool** will delete the note.

Editing MIDI with the Pencil Tool

So far in this book, you haven't had much cause to use the Pencil tool, but in Notes view, it'll really shine! In Notes view, the Pencil tool behaves like the Smart Tool:

- Placing your cursor over the middle of a note will make the Pencil tool behave like the Grabber tool.

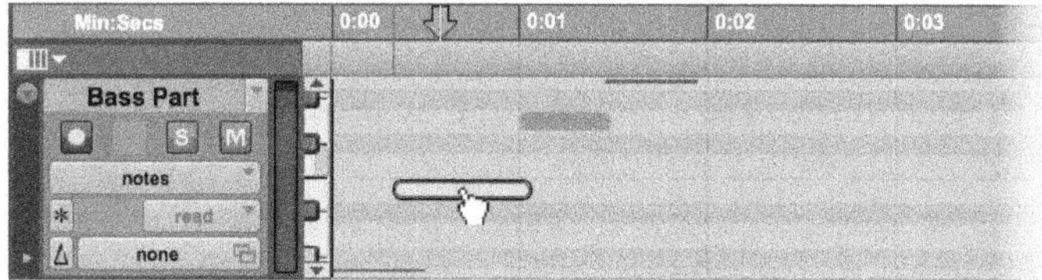

Figure 6.65 Grabbing a Note with the Pencil Tool

- Placing your cursor close to the beginning or end of a note will make the Pencil tool behave like the Trim tool.

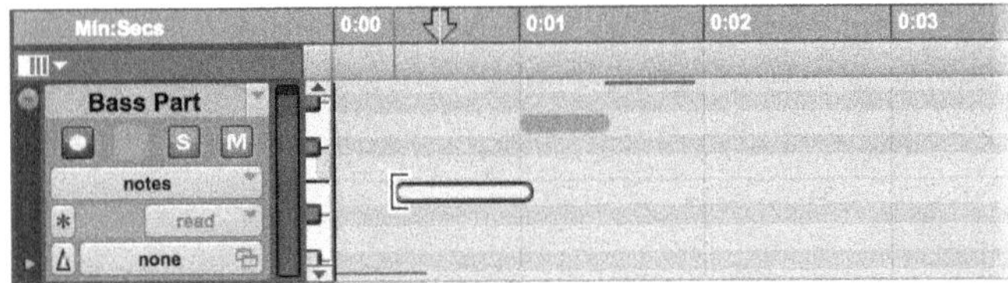

Figure 6.66 Trimming a Note with the Pencil Tool

- If you move your cursor to an area where there is no note, the Pencil tool will allow you to create a new MIDI note. Just click when you see a Pencil icon, as shown in Figure 6.67, and a new note will be created.

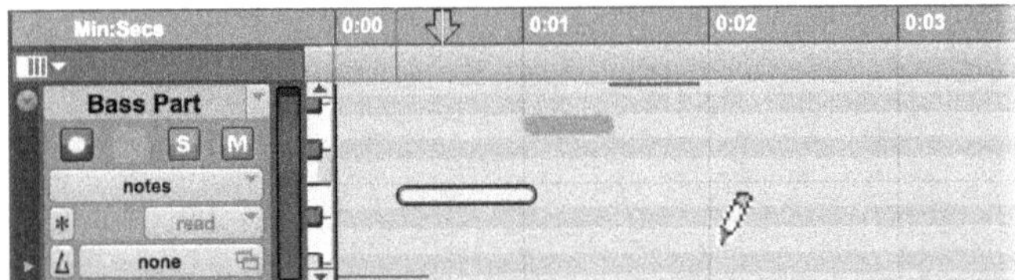

Figure 6.67 Creating a MIDI Note with a Pencil Tool

- Holding the OPTION key (Mac) or ALT key (Windows) will flip the Pencil tool to become an eraser, as shown in figure 6.68. Clicking on a note while using the eraser will delete it.

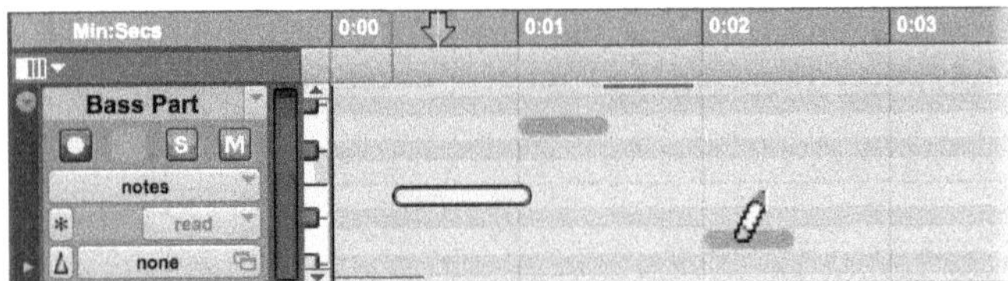

Figure 6.68 Deleting a MIDI Note with a Pencil Tool

Velocity View

MIDI velocity is a very powerful MIDI parameter that can breathe life into your MIDI projects. The good news is that it's easy to work with in Pro Tools, but first, let's discuss what exactly MIDI velocity *is*.

If you look up the word *velocity* in the dictionary, you'll see that it means "speed," and that's exactly what it means in the world of MIDI as well. Consider: You have a drummer playing real drums (not MIDI), and you tell him to play louder. How does he do that? He hits the drums with more force, of course. He strikes the drum *faster*, with more *velocity*, which changes the amplitude of the drum and the timbre of the sound (a snare drum gently tapped has a different tone than one forcefully whacked). Other instruments deal with velocity in different ways, but changes in velocity will generally result in changes in amplitude *and* tonal color.

Here's a tip: If you're trying to get your MIDI composition to sound more lifelike, and looking for a "louder" instrument, raise the velocity before you reach for the volume fader. This will give you an amplitude *and* tonal change that will more naturally emulate what "real" instruments do.

Now that you know *what* velocity is, how do you access it in Pro Tools | First?

1. Click the TRACK VIEW SELECTOR.
2. On any MIDI or Instrument track, you'll find *Velocity* just below the *Notes* view menu item. Click VELOCITY, and your track view will be changed.

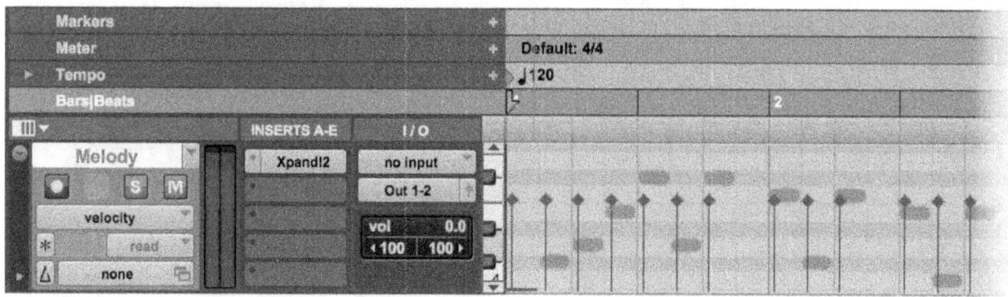

Figure 6.69 Velocity View on an Instrument Track

When you're viewing Velocity, you'll see a vertical stalk at the beginning of each note, which indicates the velocity value for that note—in other words, how *fast* you're striking the MIDI controllers key.

As with Notes view, your familiar Edit tools will take on different kinds of functions:

- If you move your **Trim tool** close to the top of one of the velocity stalks, you'll see that the Trim tool will be downward-facing, as shown in Figure 6.70. Just click and drag upward or downward to change the velocity value for that note.

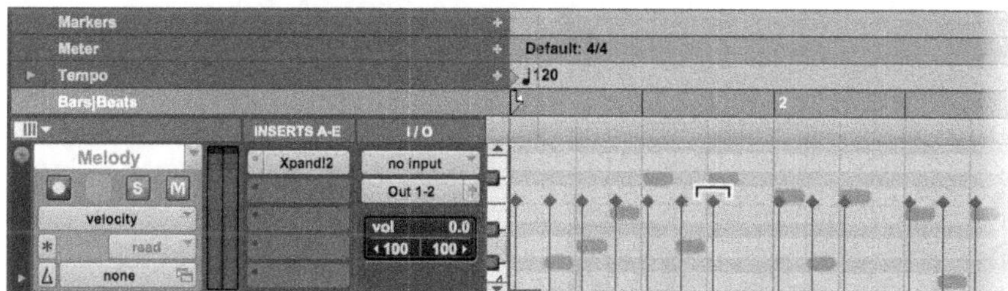

Figure 6.70 Trimming Velocity with the Trim Tool

- The **Selector tool** will allow you to select multiple velocity stalks. Dragging with the Trim tool will increase or decrease the velocity values of the selected notes.
- When using the **Grabber tool**, moving your cursor near the top of any velocity stalk will change the cursor icon to a finger, as shown in Figure 6.71. Just drag up or down to change the velocity value for that note.

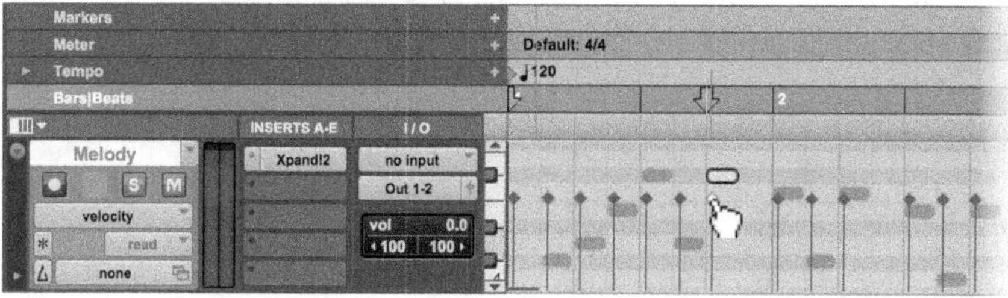

Figure 6.71 Adjusting Velocity with the Grabber Tool

- The **Pencil tool** can be quite powerful: You can click and drag it to "draw" velocity changes over multiple MIDI notes. Many musicians think of musical phrases as organic curves, with their own peaks and valleys—the Pencil tool will make it easy to draw those kinds of velocity changes.

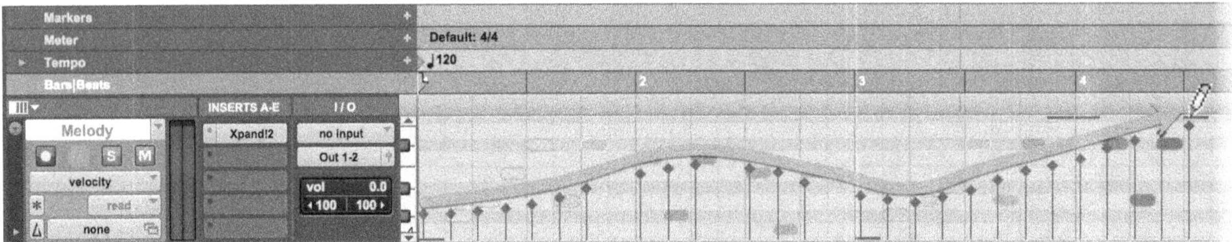

Figure 6.72 Drawing Velocity with the Pencil Tool

When drawing velocity with the Pencil tool, the shape of your "drawing" will depend upon the shape of your Pencil tool (Freehand, Line, and Triangle, and so on). As you've learned in Chapter 3, you can see a menu of the available shapes by clicking and holding on the Pencil tool.

When you're changing data like pitch and velocity, you might want to hear the changes as you make them (and sometimes you *don't*). To hear changes as you make them, just make sure that the **PLAY MIDI NOTES WHEN EDITING** button is active (when it is, it's bright green, as shown in Figure 6.73). If you don't want to hear notes as you change them, just click the button to toggle it off (dark green).

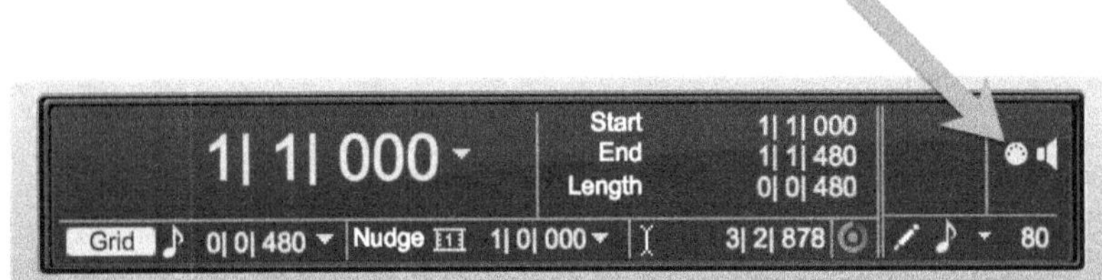

Figure 6.73 The Play MIDI Notes When Editing Button

Volume, Pan, and Continuous Controllers

There are other views that are available to you in the Track View pop-up menu—parameters like *MIDI Volume, MIDI Pan,* and *MIDI Continuous Controllers.* This kind of data is independent of note data, and changes continuously over time (hence the name *continuous* controllers). These controllers have a similar appearance and workflow, like the *Pitch Bend* parameter shown in Figure 6.74:

Figure 6.74 Viewing Pitch Bend on an Instrument Track

Here's how the Edit tools behave:

- Clicking and dragging with the **Pencil tool** will change the parameter line, according to the shape of the Pencil tool you've chosen. You'll notice that what you've drawn isn't a line, but a series of connected dots called *breakpoints*.

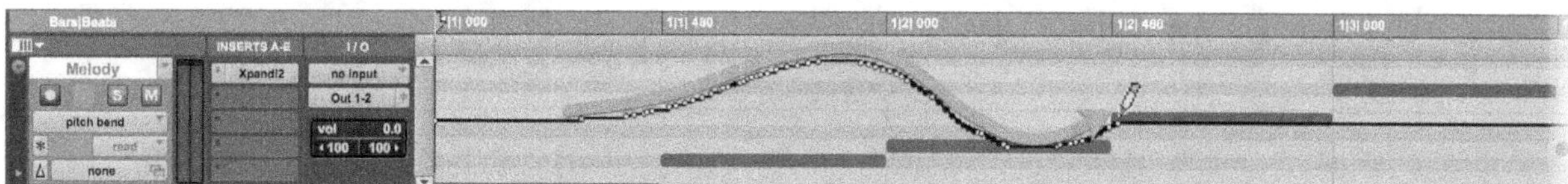

Figure 6.75 Drawing Pitch Bend with the Pencil Tool

- You can use the **Selector tool** to select a range of breakpoints, after which you can cut, copy, and paste (you can do it from the Edit menu or with shortcuts, which you will learn more about in Chapter 7).
- The **Trim tool** can be used similarly with velocity stalks—you can drag up or down to increase or decrease the value of a series of breakpoints. This works well in combination with the Selector tool: Select a range that you want to change first, and then scale it up or down with the Trim tool, as shown in Figure 6.76.

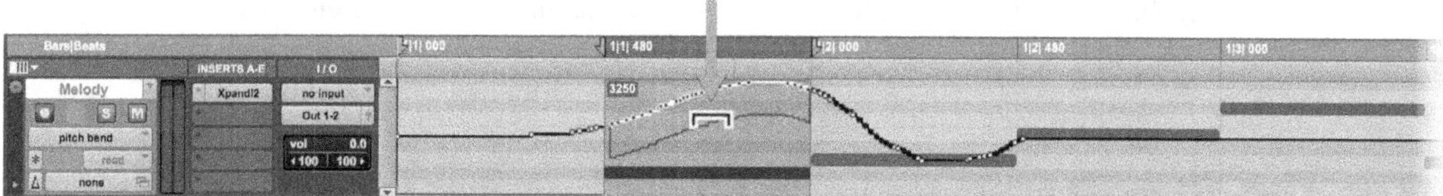

Figure 6.76 Trimming Pitch Bend with the Trim Tool

- The **Grabber tool** is your go-to for working with single breakpoints:
  - Click where there are no existing breakpoints to create a single breakpoint.

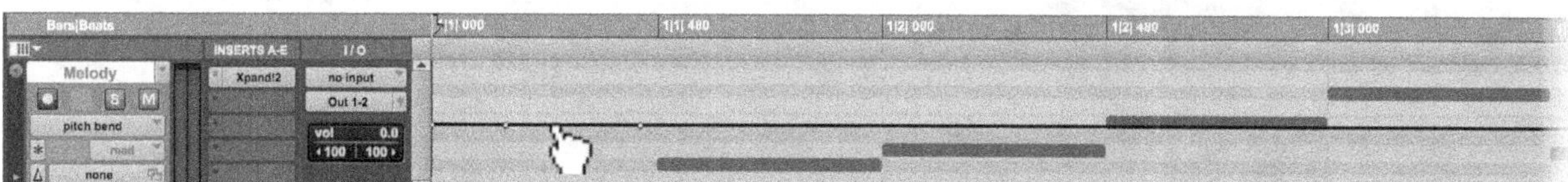

Figure 6.77 Creating a Breakpoint with the Grabber Tool

  - Click where there is an existing breakpoint to move it to a new location (left, right, up, or down).

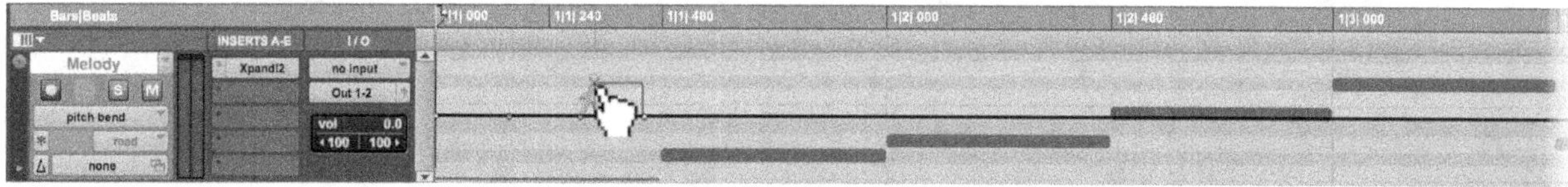

Figure 6.78 Moving a Breakpoint with the Grabber Tool

- Hold the OPTION key (Mac) or ALT key (Windows) and click on an existing breakpoint to delete it (you'll see a small minus sign beside the pointing finger icon, indicating that the breakpoint will be removed).

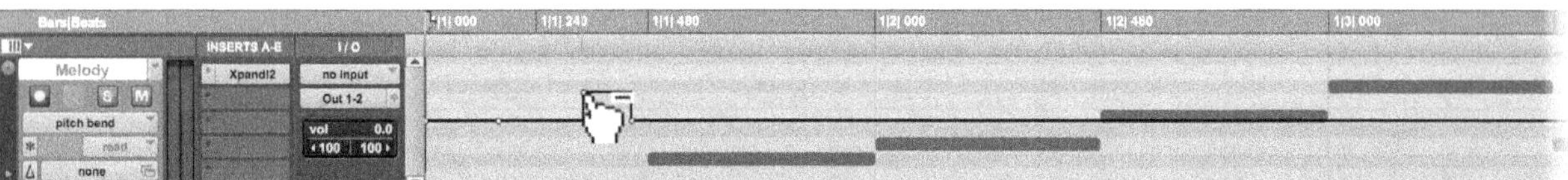

Figure 6.79 Deleting a Breakpoint with the Grabber Tool

More Ways to Work with MIDI

Now that you can get around the basics of MIDI, let's take a quick look at how you might work more deeply with MIDI data.

Working with Tempo

You've learned how to set a tempo in Chapter 5. In this chapter, you've learned how tempo affects your tick-based tracks and rulers. Here's a way to create tempo changes:

1. Click the disclosure triangle in the TEMPO ruler, revealing the *Tempo Editor*.

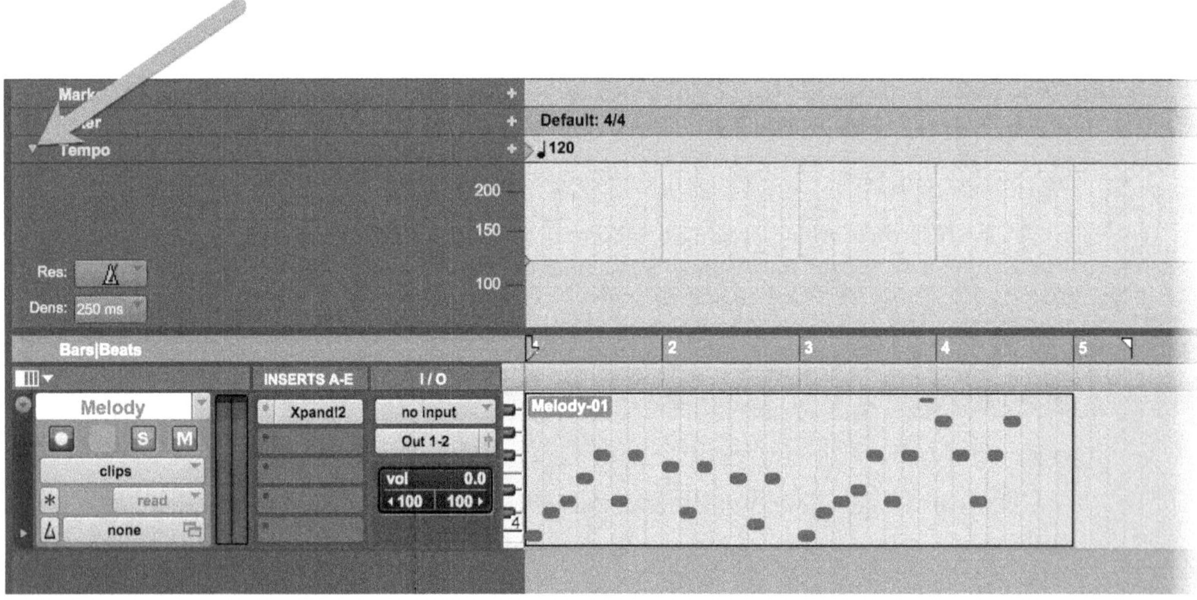

Figure 6.80 Showing the Tempo Editor

2. Using the Pencil tool, draw the tempo changes you want to use. Remember that the Pencil tool will use the shape that you've chosen in the tool (in Figure 6.81, it's the *Free Hand* shape).

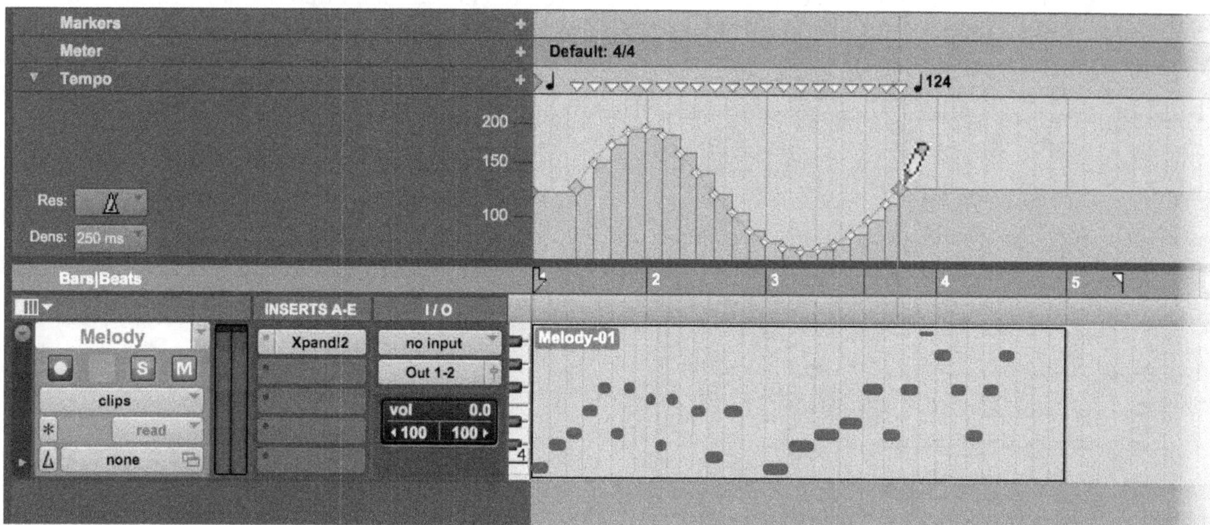

Figure 6.81 Drawing Tempo Changes with the Pencil Tool

Another way to work with time is with the *Time Operations* window.

1. From the EVENT menu, choose TIME OPERATIONS. A sub-menu will appear, with four different options:

Figure 6.82 The EVENT>TIME OPERATIONS Submenu

- **Change Meter:** This menu option will show the Time Operations/Change Meter window, as shown in Figure 6.83. You can use this window to insert a meter change at any desired location. The bottom of the window allows you to choose which tracks will be affected (tick-based rulers only, tick-based rulers and tracks, or tick-based rulers and all tracks).

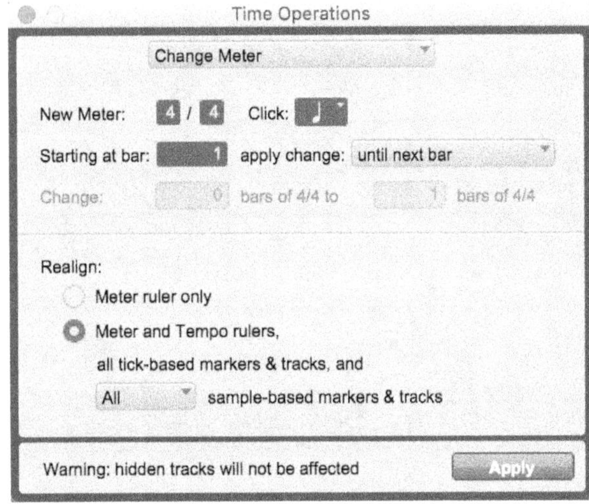

Figure 6.83 The Time Operations/Change Meter Window

- **Insert Time:** This window will allow you to add a blank area anywhere in your timeline and shift elements in your mix later after the blank area in your timeline. Do you want to add a few bars between the first and second verse and shift tempo changes, clips, and other MIDI data later in time? Insert Time will allow you to do it easily!

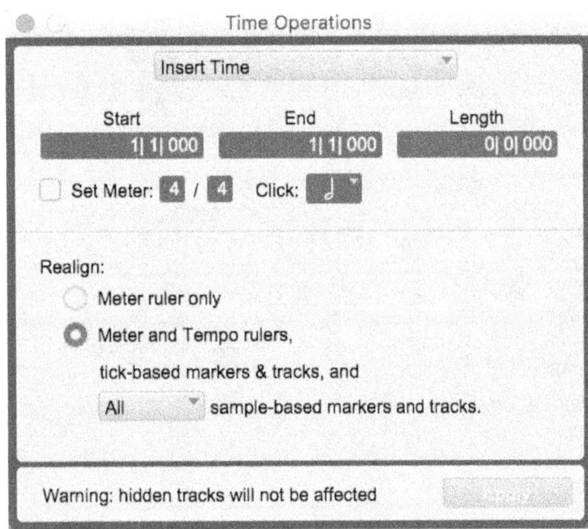

Figure 6.84 The Time Operations/Insert Time Window

- **Cut Time:** The opposite of the *Insert Time* window, *Cut Time* will allow you to remove any area from your timeline and shift anything the cut area earlier in your timeline, including tempo changes and other MIDI data.

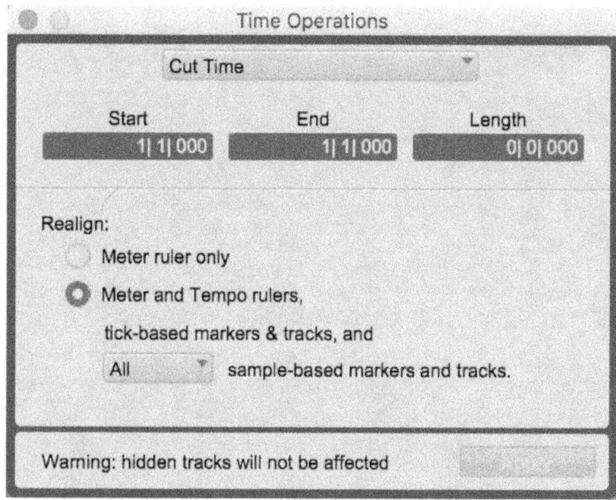

Figure 6.85 The Time Operations/Cut Time Window

- **Move Song Start:** By default, the song start (bar 1, beat 1, tick 0 or 1|1|000) is at the very beginning of your timeline (0 minutes, 0 seconds). Sometimes, though, you might want to hear something *before* 1|1|000. You can easily shift the song start from EVENT>TIME OPERATIONS>MOVE SONG START. Changing the song start will shift the MIDI data on your MIDI and Instrument track, as well as shift your tempo changes and Bars|Beats ruler.

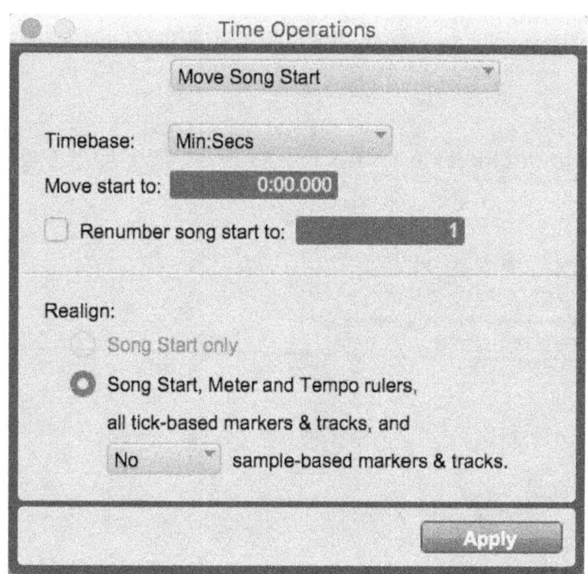

Figure 6.86 The Time Operations/Move Song Start Window

You can also manually change the song start, which is indicated by a red diamond at the beginning of the Tempo ruler. Just click and drag the song start icon to move your song start, as shown in Figure 6.87.

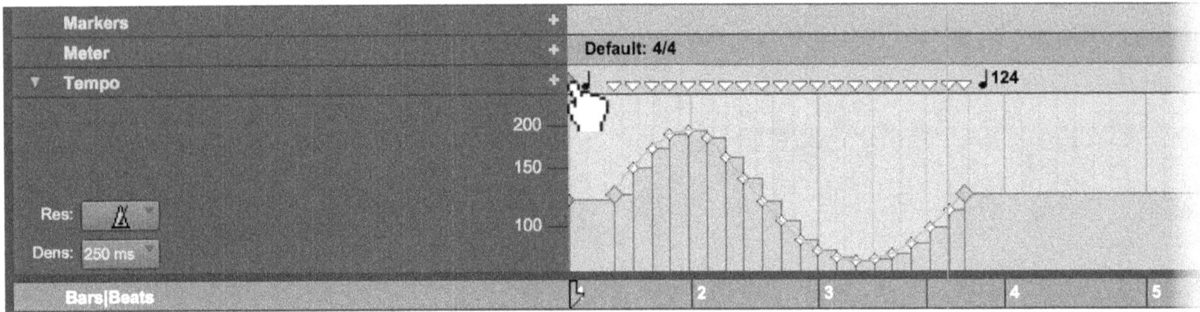

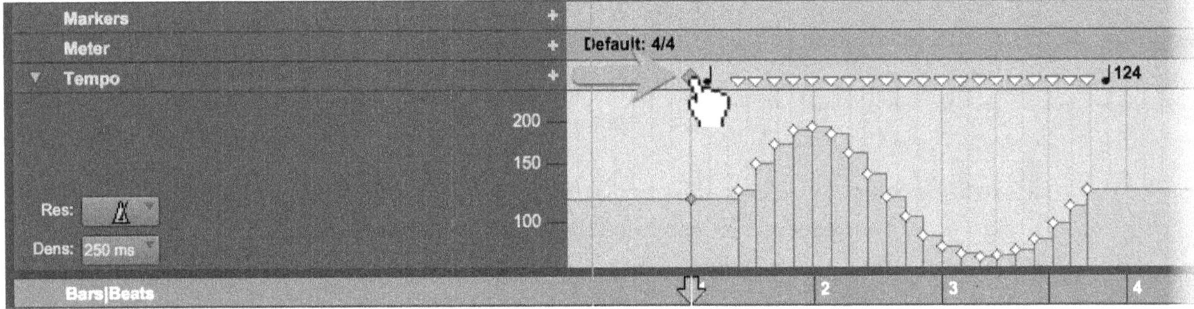

Figure 6.87 Another Way to Change the Song Start

2. In any of these windows, just click the APPLY button to make your changes.

The Event>Event Operations Window

Next on the list is the Event Operations menu, which can be found under at EVENT>EVENT OPERATIONS, as shown in Figure 6.88:

Figure 6.88 The Event>Event Operations Submenu

Most of the operations here are familiar MIDI processes:

- **Quantize:** Changes the timings of notes.
- **Change Velocity:** Changes the velocity of notes in different ways, including scaling them or randomizing their values.
- **Change Duration:** Changes the duration of notes, including removing any overlap of notes or changing the gaps between notes.
- **Transpose:** Shifts the pitch of notes
- **Select/Split Notes:** Selects or splits notes based on different criterion. Commonly used to split multiple drum notes of a drum kit to multiple MIDI tracks (each track having only one drum on it).
- **Input Quantize:** Changes the timing of all recorded notes automatically.
- **Step Input:** Allows for notes to be recorded from a MIDI controller one at a time, without having to record MIDI data in "real" time.
- **Restore Performance:** Reverts to the original performance of a selected area.
- **Flatten Performance:** "Render" a selected area. Once an area is flattened, any *Restore Performance* will go back to this flattened state.

The MIDI Editor

The MIDI Editor is the place to go if you want to get a close look at MIDI and Instrument tracks. The docked MIDI Editor is a component of your Edit window, but one you might not have seen yet. Let's take a look:

1. Click on the VIEW menu.
2. Choose the MIDI EDITOR menu item. (A checkmark will appear next to displayed elements.) The docked MIDI Editor will appear at the bottom of the Edit window.

Here's another way to show the docked MIDI Editor: Click on the small, upwards arrow in the bottom corner of the Edit window's playlist area. (Note that clicking on it can be a little tricky.) The docked MIDI Editor will appear at the bottom of the Edit window.

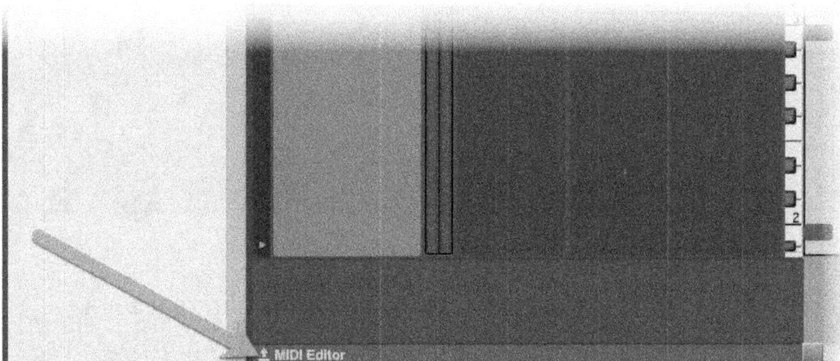

Figure 6.89 Showing the MIDI Editor

No matter which method you use to reveal it, the docked MIDI Editor will appear along the bottom of the Edit window. You can adjust its size by clicking and dragging its upper boundary. A larger MIDI Editor will give you a view of a larger range of notes, but you can also vertically zoom your MIDI with the MIDI ZOOM button in the upper right-hand corner of the MIDI Editor. If your mouse has a scroll wheel, you can use it to shift the range of viewable notes.

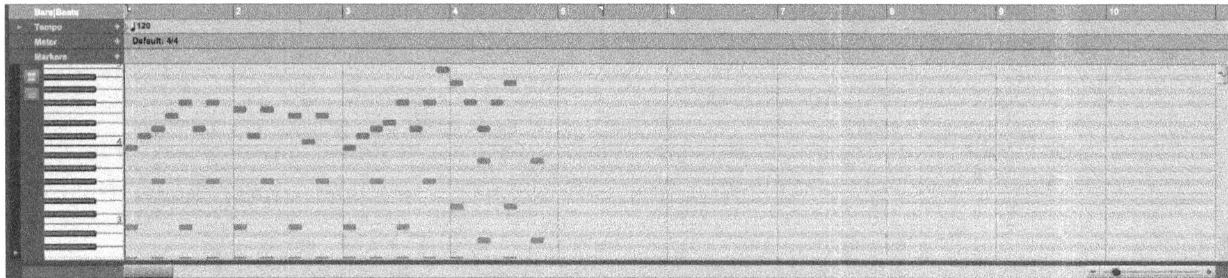

Figure 6.90 The MIDI Editor

Pro Tools | First's MIDI Editor will show MIDI data for any selected track(s), and here you see one of the key advantages of the MIDI Editor: The MIDI notes of all the shown tracks are displayed in a single environment as opposed to being separated into track rows, as they are in the normal Edit window. This enables you to work quickly and efficiently, letting you clearly see the relationships between multiple tracks.

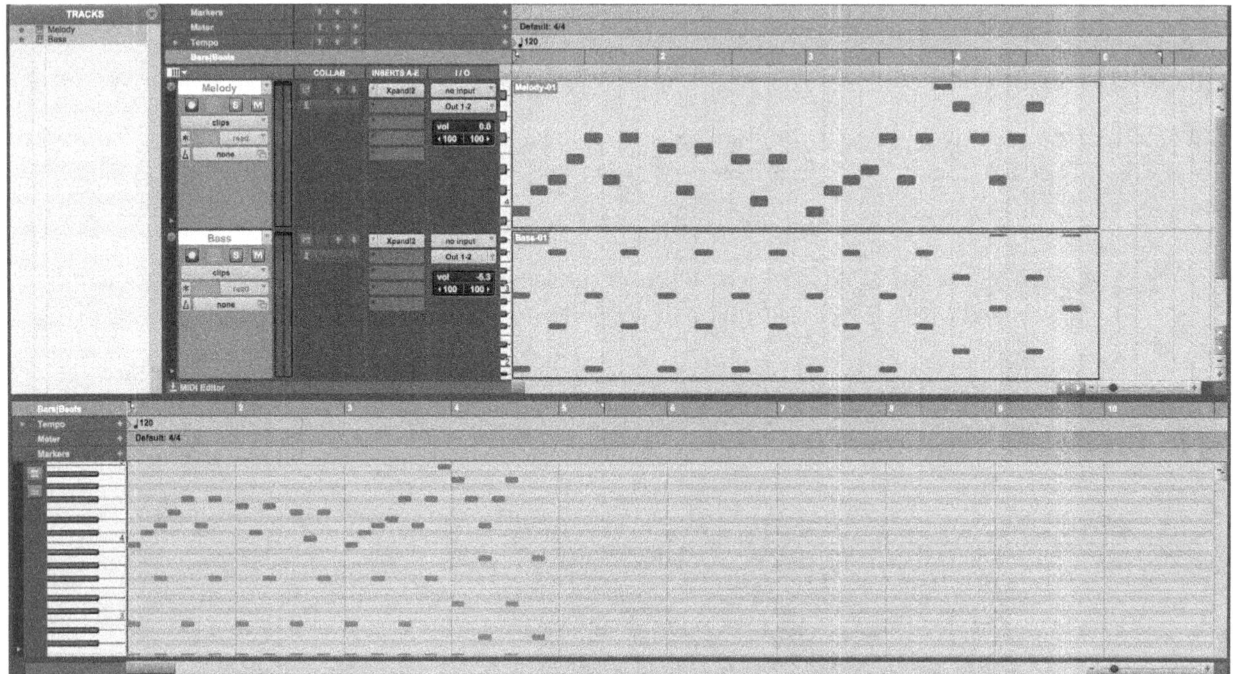

Figure 6.91 Viewing Mulitiple Tracks' MIDI in the MIDI Editor

- By default, MIDI notes shown in the MIDI Editor will follow the color of the clip they're in, in which case you'd see a number of tracks' MIDI data all in the same color. You can make your editing easier by clicking on the COLOR CODE MIDI NOTES BY TRACK button, which will automatically assign a unique color for each track's notes.

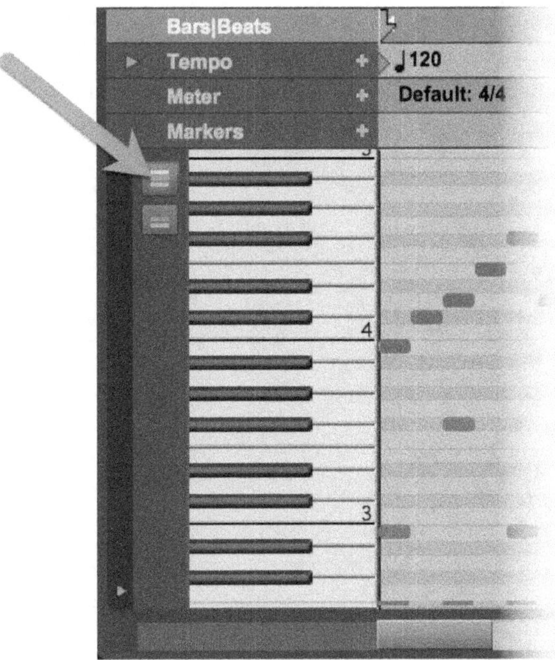

Figure 6.92 The Color Code MIDI Notes By Track Button

- You can also color-code MIDI notes by their velocity values, by clicking on the COLOR CODE MIDI NOTES BY VELOCITY button. All notes, regardless of their track, will be shown with a red color, with darker colors indicating greater velocity values.

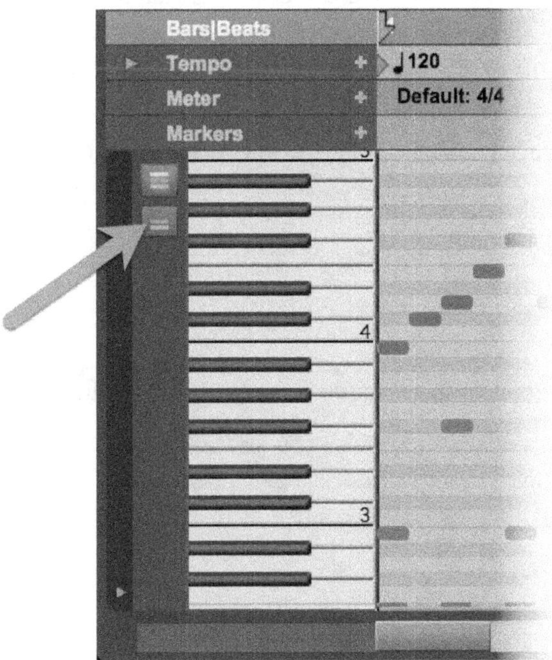

Figure 6.93 The Color Code MIDI Notes By Velocity Button

- If you click on the small triangle icon in the lower-left corner of the playlist area, you'll reveal an additional lane at the bottom of the MIDI Editor. You'll see this lane again when we talk about mixing, but in the MIDI Editor this can allow you to show or hide the notes' velocity values. Note that velocity stalks will be colored according to their corresponding notes, as shown in Figure 6.94.

Figure 6.94 Showing the Velocity Lane

Editing notes in the MIDI Editor is identical to the editing workflows covered earlier in this chapter, although in the context of the MIDI Editor, they take on a new level of usefulness. A few techniques come in particularly handy when editing notes (these work in the Edit window or the MIDI Editor, but they really shine when you're working in the MIDI Editor):

- Double-clicking on a note will delete it.
- If you're using the Grabber, Pencil, or Smart Tool, you can adjust the velocity of a note by holding down the COMMAND key (Mac) or the CTRL key (Windows), as you click and drag vertically.

Recording MIDI

The process of recording MIDI is similar to audio recording in many respects, but with some additional flexibility.

Before you start recording, you might want to set up a click track (which you learned about in Chapter 5, "Recording Audio"). Remember to click on the Metronome icon to enable your click track. Now it's time to actually record the MIDI.

Basic MIDI Recording

On a basic level, recording MIDI is the same as recording audio:

1. Click on the Track Record Enable button to arm the track (MIDI or Instrument) for recording.

2. Click on the Record Enable button in the Transport window (or in the Transport controls at the top of the Edit window).

3. Click on the Play button. Recording will begin. It operates the same as when you record audio, with pre-rolls and post-rolls. You'll play your MIDI instrument at this point, sending MIDI data to the recording track.

4. When you're finished, you'll have a clip, as you did when you recorded audio. This time, however, you'll see MIDI note data within the clip rather than audio waveforms!

MIDI Loop Recording

Loop Recording works the same when recording MIDI as it does when recording audio, creating multiple MIDI clips with each repetition of the selected area. When you're done, you'll be able to choose your takes (as well as set your match criteria) in the same way as you've previously done with audio.

Notice, though, that whenever Loop Record mode is active, there is a button in the MIDI controls that becomes greyed out: the *MIDI Merge* button.

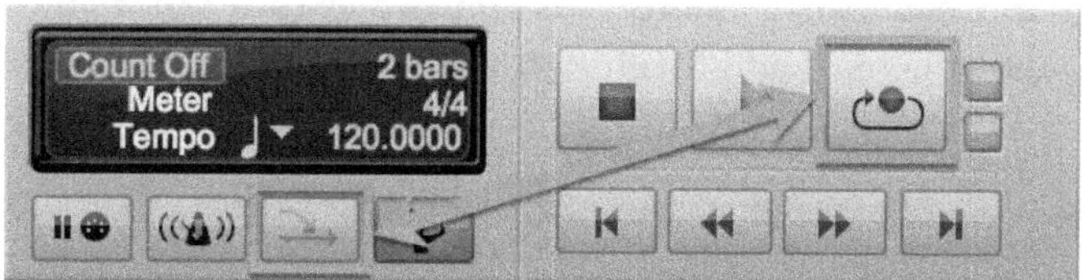

Figure 6.95 MIDI Merge Disabled

MIDI Merge Recording

When loop recording, a selected area is repeated over and over, and each time it is played, a new recorded clip is created, with each clip representing a single take. That's the way that it works with both audio and MIDI, but there's another way that you can record, called *MIDI Merge* recording.

When *MIDI Merge* is enabled, a selected area will be played, just as with Loop Record, but in this case, only a single clip is created, with each take adding more notes to the clip. The classic example of this is recording a drum kit: With MIDI Merge enabled, you can play the kick drum part first, then stack a snare drum on top of it, then put hi-hat cymbals, and so on. Although you might only play one of these drums per pass, you'll end up with a single clip that contains all of the notes that you played in each pass.

The steps for MIDI Merge mode recording are a little different than Normal or Loop Recording:

1. Enable LOOP PLAYBACK (either from the OPTIONS menu, or by right-clicking the PLAY button).

2. Make sure you're in *Normal* record (either from the OPTIONS menu, or by right-clicking the RECORD button).

3. Enable MIDI Merge by clicking the MIDI MERGE button. When enabled, the button will be blue.

When you're done, your Transport and MIDI controls should look like this:

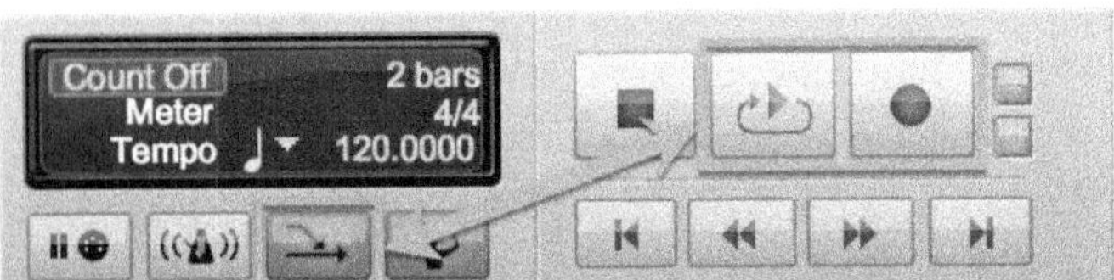

Figure 6.96 MIDI Merge and Loop Playback Enabled, Normal Record Mode

From here on, the workflow is similar to loop recording:

4. Select the area that you want to record.
5. Click on the Track Record Enable button to arm the track (MIDI or Instrument) for recording.
6. Click on the Record Enable button in the Transport window (or in the Transport controls at the top of the Edit window).
7. Click on the Play button. Recording will begin
8. With MIDI Merge recording, there's no rush, since there's no requirement to play each time your selection repeats. Whenever you *do* play, though, you'll add MIDI data to the clip.
9. When you're finished, you'll have a clip that includes all the notes (and other MIDI data) that you've played.

"Printing" MIDI

Suppose you've created a killer track using your favorite MIDI hardware, and you want to send the project to a friend, so that he can lay down tracks of his own. There's a potential problem: If your friend doesn't have the same MIDI hardware (or virtual instrument) that you have in your studio, he won't be able to hear your track the way it's meant to be heard. The solution is to "print" your MIDI instrument to an Audio track and then send your project out for collaboration.

The process of recording the output of your MIDI sound device is simple enough. You'll use a bus to connect the output of your MIDI instrument's Aux or Instrument track to the input of an Audio track to which you'll record.

1. Assign the output of your instrument's Aux or Instrument track to an available bus. (In Figure 6.97, I've chosen *Bus 1-2*.)

Figure 6.97 Selecting Bus 1-2 as an Output for an Instrument Track

2. After creating an Audio track to record to, assign the input of that track to the same bus that you chose for the output of the Aux or Instrument track (again, Bus 1-2).

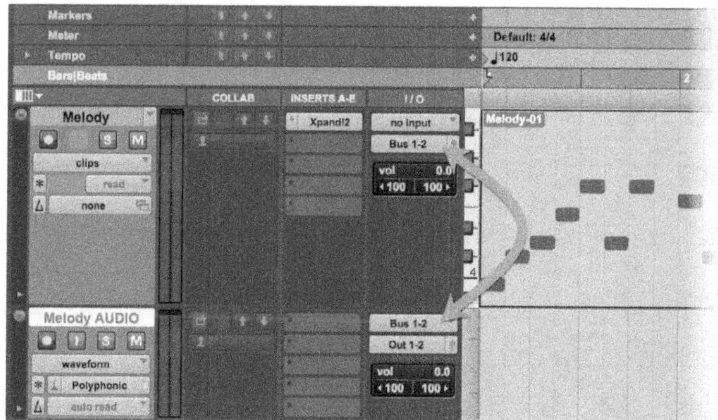

Figure 6.98 Routing Signals from an Instrument Track to an Audio Track

3. Now that you have your signals routed properly, you can record your Audio track normally (which we covered in Chapter 5). You'll see that the level meters of the two tracks are identical.

Panic!

Reality check: Sometimes, things go wrong. When working with MIDI, one of the things that can happen is a "stuck" MIDI note that never ends. When that happens, the most important thing to do is to stop the data and turn off those notes!

1. Click on the EVENT menu.
2. Choose All MIDI Notes Off—quickly! A MIDI note-off command will be sent on all channels, on all ports of your MIDI interface, and through the four virtual MIDI connections.

The fastest way to trigger the All MIDI Notes Off function is to use the shortcut keys: SHIFT+COMMAND+. (period) on Mac and SHIFT+CTRL+. (period) on Windows.

Hands-On Exercise 6.2: Editing MIDI

I've done a fair amount of arranging for other producers, fleshing out their song ideas into finished instrumental projects. In this kind of work, it's not unusual for MIDI song ideas to be very rough, often created with the Pencil tool (as opposed to being performed live). In addition to creating new musical parts, I often need to edit the songwriter's MIDI to a more refined state.

This chapter's final exercise will give you a sense of the kinds of editing that you might do when tweaking a MIDI part, including a new trick!

The melody in this exercise is probably familiar to you: Edvard Grieg's *In the Hall of the Mountain King*. The two tracks in the Project were sloppily created with the Pencil tool.

Setting Up

1. Create a new Project by converting the *Pro Tools First—Fundamentals of Audio Production—Chapter 6 (Mountain King).ptx* session to a local Project. The session is found in the *Pro Tools First—Fundamentals of Audio Production—Chapter 6 (Mountain King)* subfolder of this book's downloaded exercise material. Choose any desired sample rate, 24-bit, and do not backup to Cloud.

Creating MIDI Data with the Pencil Tool

If you're familiar at all with this melody, you'll notice right off the bat that there is a note missing!

2. Change the *Melody* track to *Notes* view.
3. Using the Pencil tool, add an F#4 at 3|3|000.

When you're done, your melody should look like this:

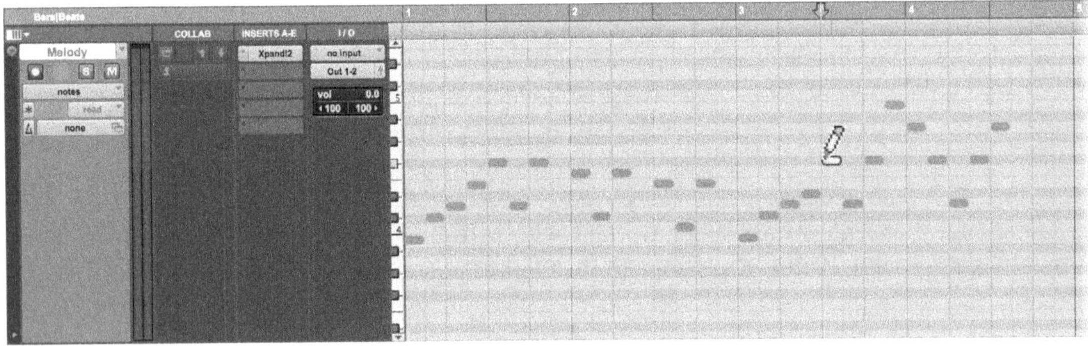

Figure 6.99 Adding a New Note

Editing Pitch

The note just before the one you created (the note at 3|2|480) is the wrong pitch.

4. Make sure that you're in Grid mode (since the timing of the note isn't a problem).
5. Using the Grabber tool or the Pencil tool, raise the note by one half step from its original pitch of D#4 to E4.

When you're done, your melody should look like this:

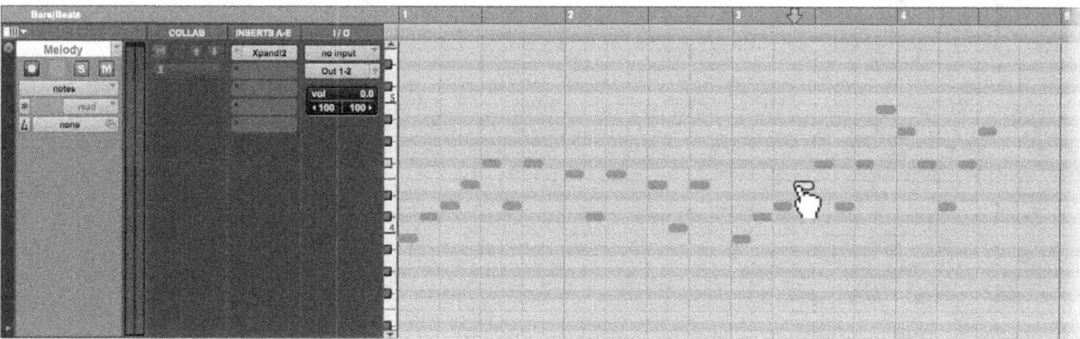

Figure 6.100 Fixing a Wrong Note

Editing Duration

Since this was all created with the Pencil tool, you'll see that all the notes' durations are identical. To be truer to the musical style, all the notes *except the last one* should be shorter, and the last note should be a little bit longer.

Here's something we haven't specifically covered so far in this chapter: Tools like the Trim tool will apply to multiple selected notes. This will make the job quick and easy!

6. Change to Slip mode.
7. This next step is optional, but let's do this as efficiently as possible: Activate the Smart Tool.
8. With the Smart Tool (or the Grabber tool, if you really don't want to use the Smart Tool), start in an area where there are no notes and draw a box that includes all of the notes, except the last note (as shown in Figure 6.101).

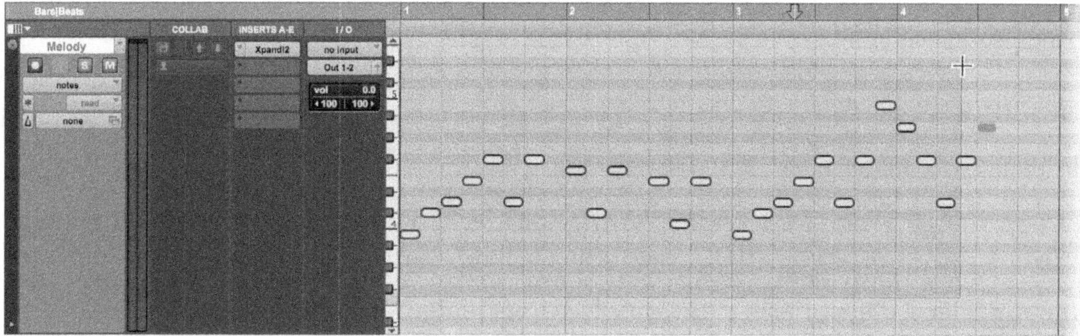

Figure 6.101 Selecting Multiple Notes

9. Still using the Smart Tool (or changing to the Trim tool, if you don't want to use the Smart Tool), trim one of the selected notes to decrease its duration to make the note shorter. Note that *all* selected notes will similarly change.
10. In music, there are no right answers. Use your ears to choose what sounds best to you. This will probably be a trial and error process, so experiment!

For whatever it's worth, here's what sounds good to me:

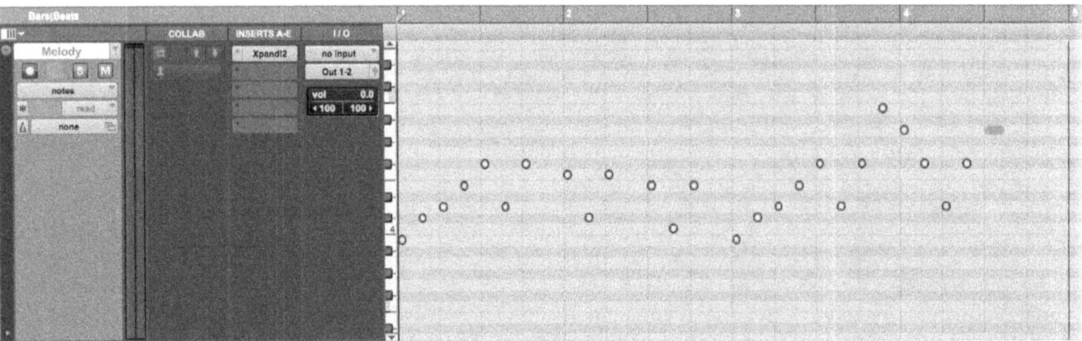

Figure 6.102 Shortening the Notes

Now, let's lengthen the last note a bit:

11. Using the Smart Tool (or Trim tool), extend the end of the last note. Here again, let your ears be your guide.

Here's where I ended up:

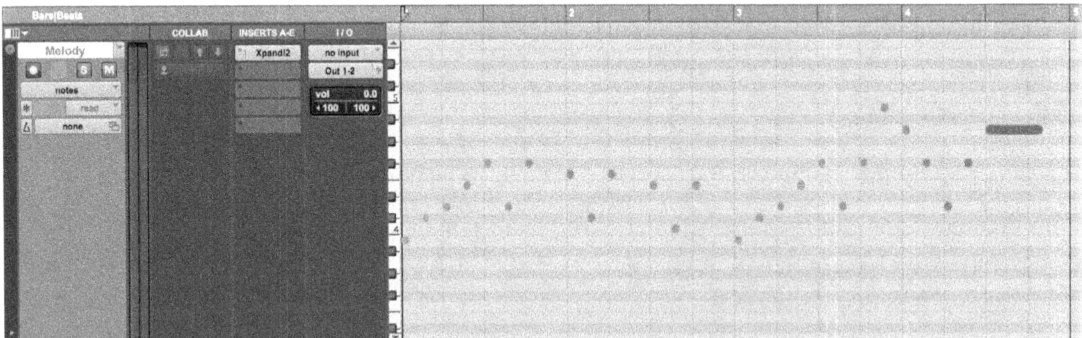

Figure 6.103 Lengthening the Last Note

Changing Velocity

Now, let's make the tracks a bit more musical through the use of velocity.

12. Change the view of the *Melody* track to *Velocity*. You'll see that all of the velocity stalks are the same height, which is typical with MIDI created with the Pencil tool.
13. There are a lot of different ways to change velocity, but to get a smooth phrase going, let's use

the Pencil tool in Free Hand mode. Draw velocity that will support the playing of the phrase by dragging left to right (or right to left).

14. Yet again, use your ears as a guide. Here's what I came up with:

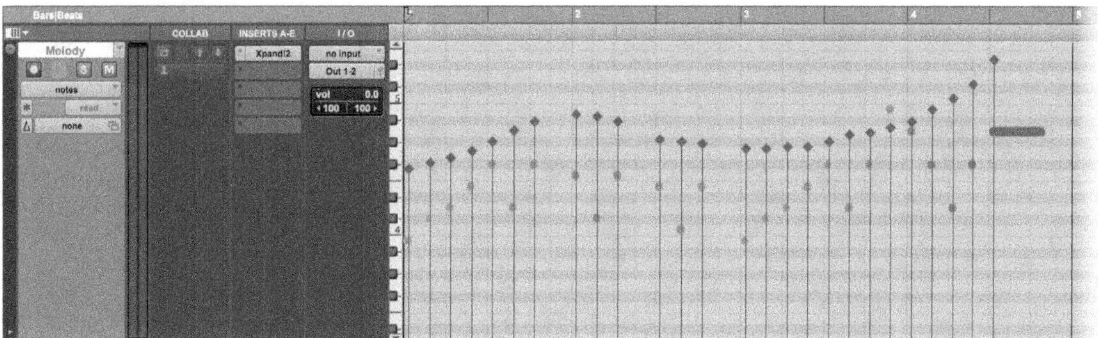

Figure 6.104 Velocity Changes to the Melody Track

To finish up the chapter, let's fix the *Bass* track:

15. Solo the *Bass* track.
16. Change the *Bass* track's view to *Velocity*.
17. The track is a series of notes played on beats 1, 2, 3, and 4. The notes are doubled in octaves. What I want to do first is raise the velocity on all the notes on beats 1 and 3, so that they're nice and strong.
18. Now, to accentuate the strength of beats 1 and 3, *decrease* the velocity on all notes on beats 2 and 4.

Use your own ears to choose what works best for you. Figure 6.105 shows what I wound up with. Note that there is a small amount of randomness in velocity (just as with a live musician), and that I increased it a little bit in bar 4 compared to the previous 3 bars, in order to build some excitement at the end of the phrase.

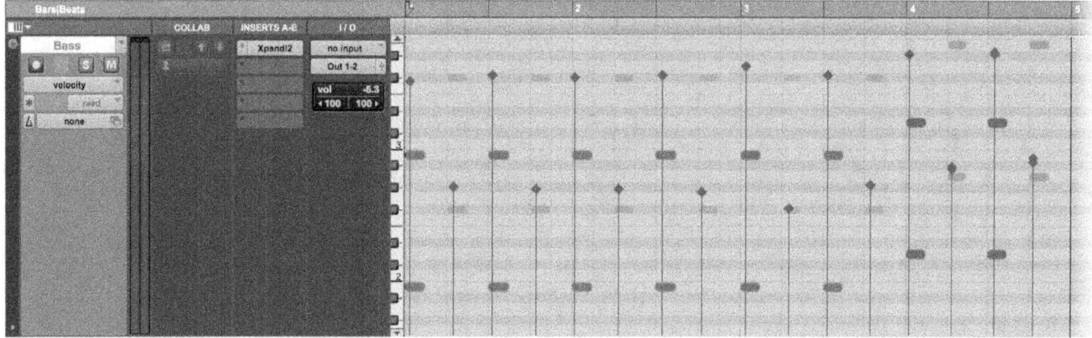

Figure 6.105 Velocity Changes on the Bass Track

Now that you've changed your velocity so that each part sounds good, just un-solo the *Bass* track, so that you can hear both parts together. You're now ready to use your tracks' volume output to mix the volume levels of the two tracks, which you'll learn more in Chapter 8. This concludes this chapter's hands-on exercises (make sure to save your work!).

Review Questions

1. What does MIDI stand for?

2. True or False? MIDI on its own makes no sound.

3. How many channels of information are supported by the MIDI protocol?

4. What is a MIDI track? What is an Instrument Track? How are the two track types different?

5. What is a *tick*?

6. How many ticks are there per quarter note in Pro Tools?

7. What kind of editing can you do in Clips view? Notes view? Velocity view?

8. How does the Pencil tool behave when working with MIDI in *Notes* view?

9. What is velocity?

10. What is the difference between MIDI Loop Record mode and MIDI Merge mode recording?

CHAPTER 7

Taking Your Editing to the Next Level

You've already learned the basics of DAWs, how to navigate Pro Tools easily and efficiently, how to import and record audio, perform basic editing, and work with MIDI. You've covered an inpressive amount of ground, so take pride in that.

Before we move on to mixing, the last major part of production, let's take a deeper look at editing. Here's the secret to becoming a strong editor: You'll do simple things (you've done them already in Chapter 4), but you'll do them many *many* times in an editing session. Efficiency is the name of the game–the faster and easier you work, the more work you'll get done, and at a higher quality.

This chapter isn't so much a discussion of new editing concepts as much as a grab-bag of new ways to work, boosting your editing power!

Media Used: ***Pro Tools First—Fundamentals of Audio Production—Chapter 7 (Mini-Gauntlet.ptx)***

Duration: 45 minutes

GOALS

- **Work with multiple tracks**
- **Learn new ways to trim clips**
- **Position precisely with *Nudge***
- **Add fades to your tracks**
- **Share your edited tracks with others using Pro Tools | First's Collaboration tools**

Managing Multiple Tracks

In Chapter 4, you've learned how to make selections on multiple tracks, which is a powerful way to work. Here are other ways to work with multiple tracks.

Selecting Tracks

You already know that you can select a track. To review, here are the different ways:

- Click on the track name in the Edit window.
- Click on the track name in the Mix window (at the bottom of the channel strip).
- Click on the track name in the Tracks List (in either the Edit window or Mix window).

Here's how you can select multiple tracks:

- To select a range of tracks, click on the first track name, press and hold the SHIFT key, and click the last track name in the range.

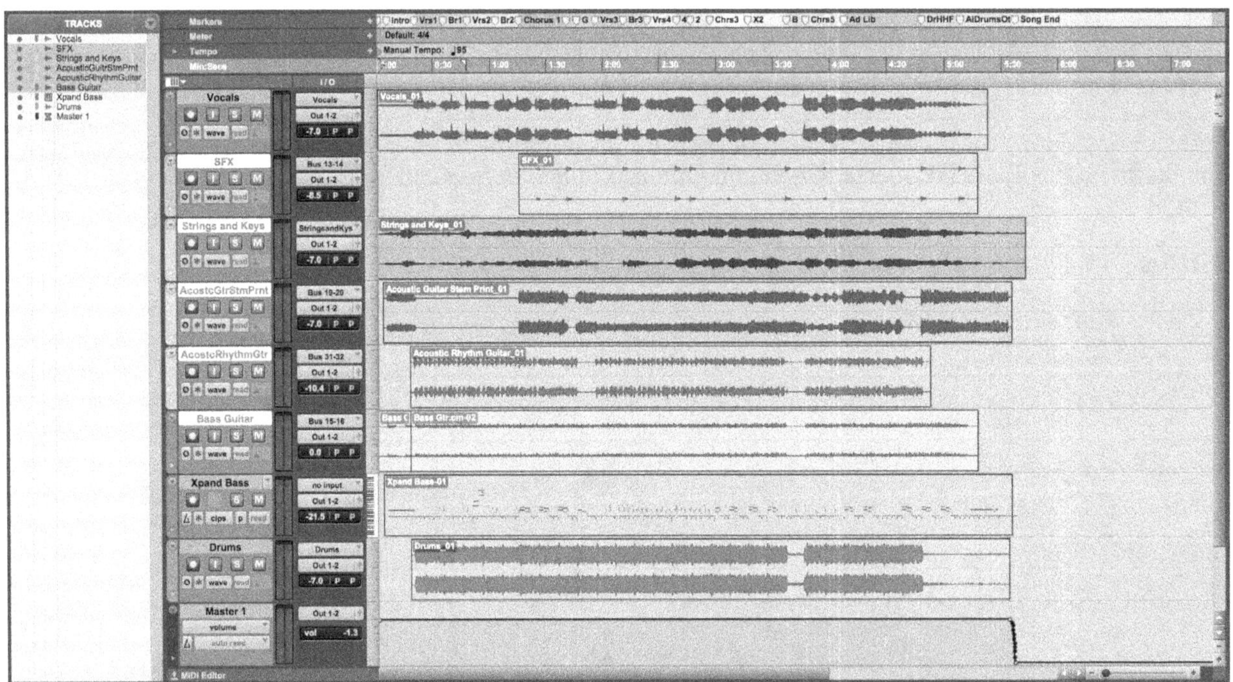

Figure 7.1 Selecting a Range of Tracks

- To individually select (or deselect) multiple tracks, press and hold the COMMAND key (Mac) or CTRL key (Windows), and click the track name of the tracks that you want to select (or deselect).

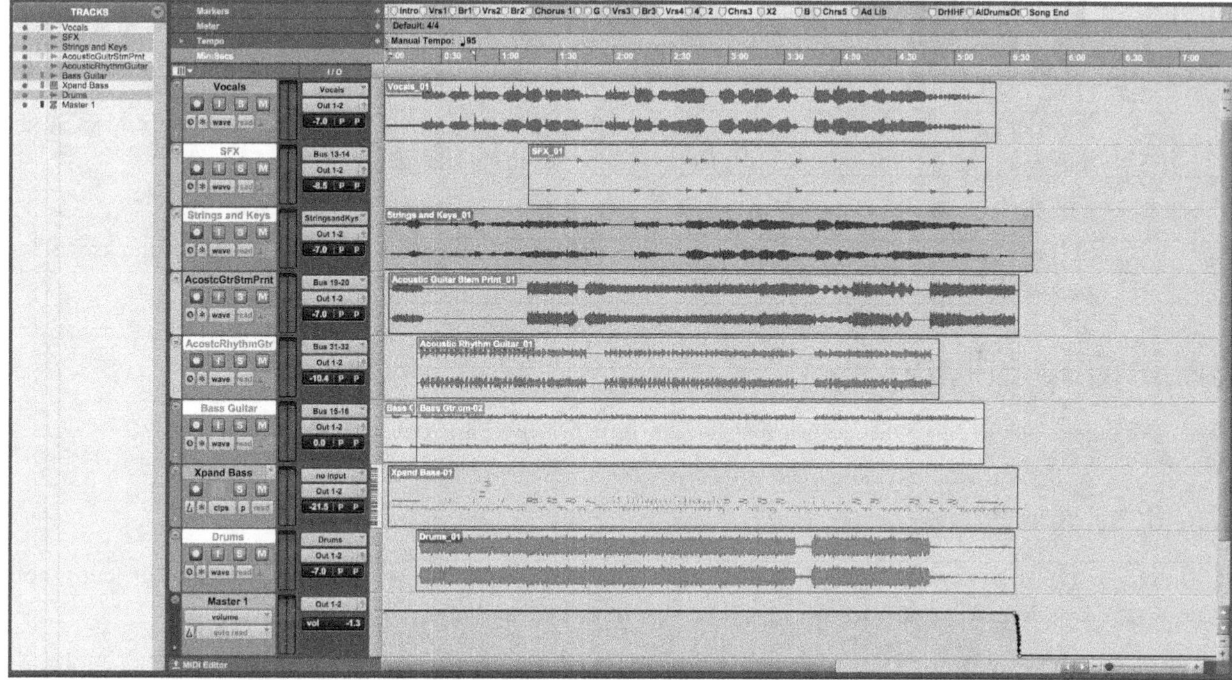

Figure 7.2 Selecting/Deselecting Tracks Individually

- To select *all* tracks, press and hold the OPTION key (Mac) or ALT key (Windows) and select any unselected track. All tracks will be selected. You can use the same process to deselect tracks: Hold the OPTION key (Mac) or ALT key (Windows) and select any selected track to unselect them all.

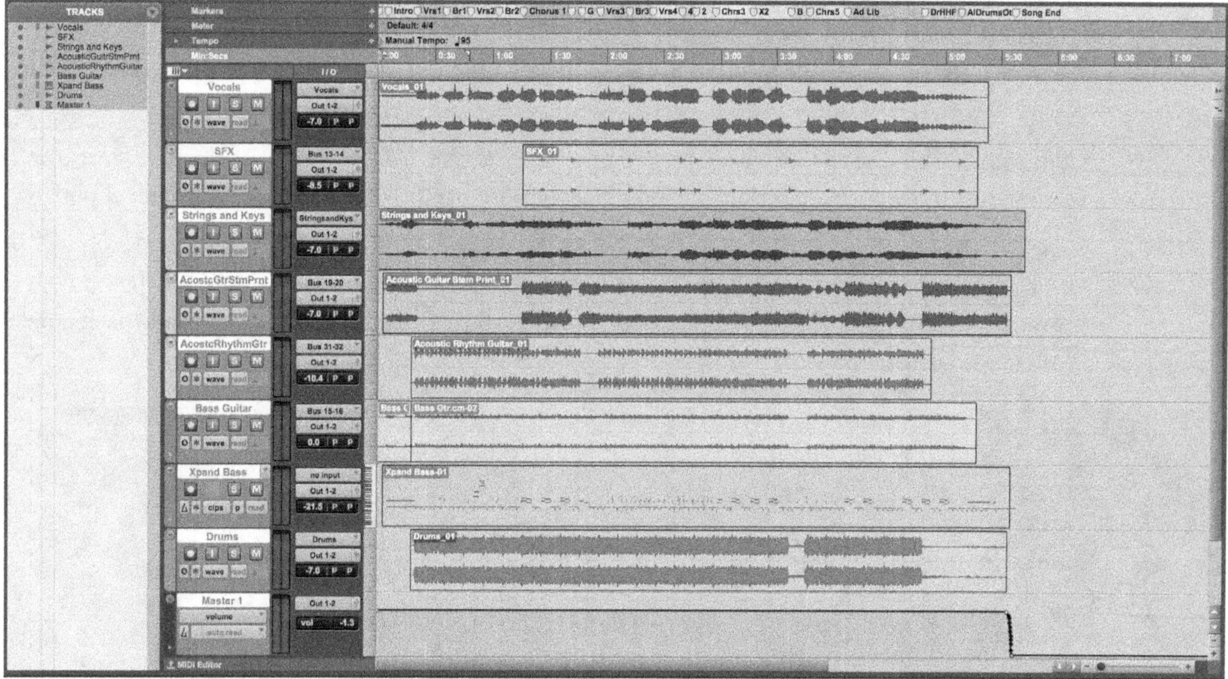

Figure 7.3 Selecting All Tracks

Changing Multiple Tracks

Now, let's say that you want to change a setting on multiple tracks (for example, change an input or output). Easy!

- In order to make a change to *all* tracks, hold the OPTION key (Mac) or ALT key (Windows) and make the change on any track. All tracks will be similarly changed.
- In order to make a change to *all selected* tracks, hold the SHIFT+OPTION key (Mac) or SHIFT+ALT key (Windows) and make the change on any selected track. All selected tracks will be similarly changed.

Basic Clip Editing

Next, let's take a look at how you can work with clips, starting with basic cut, copy, and paste.

Cut, Copy, and Paste

If you've ever typed an email or used any kind of text-based application, you'll understand how cut, copy, and paste works. Let's look at these how these processes work in Pro Tools.

- When you **Cut** a selected area, it will be removed from your timeline and put onto a data clipboard for pasting later. This includes any empty areas and clips in that selected area. For example, Figure 7.4 shows a selected area that starts and ends with an empty area, with two clips in between. *All* this will be deleted from the timeline and put into the clipboard.

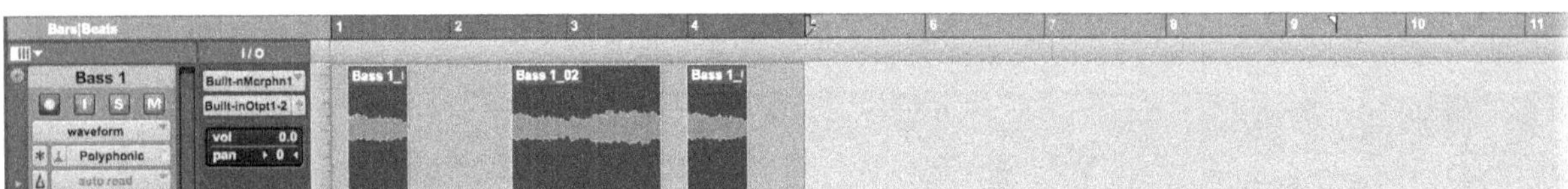

Figure 7.4 Ready To Cut Bars 1-5

- **Copy** works the same as *Cut,* but it does not remove the selected area from the timeline. Just like when you cut, the entire selection (including any empty parts) will be added to the data clipboard.
- **Paste** will deposit the data from the clipboard to the timeline of the destination track. The selection in the clipboard will be pasted at the current timeline position. For example, if you copy measures 1-5 from a track (adding that data to the clipboard), and then move your playback cursor to measure 7, the pasted area would be from 7-11, as shown in Figure 7.5.

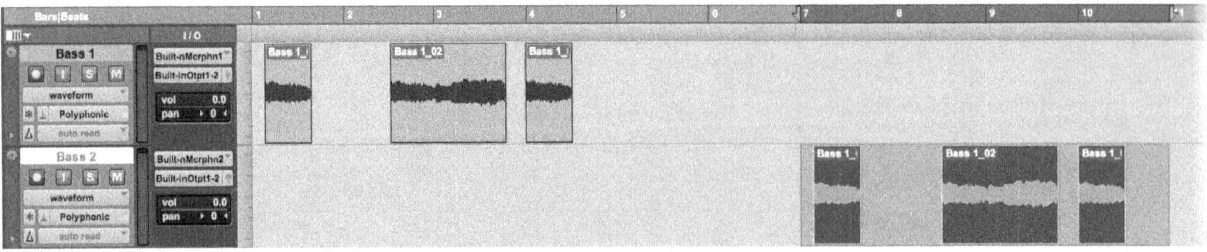

Figure 7.5 Copying Bars 1-5 on One Track and Pasting it to Bars 7-11 on Another Track

Clearing

In addition to cutting, you have the ability to *Clear* clips, which will remove them from the timeline, but will *not* put them onto a clipboard. Put another way, if you cut a selection from your timeline, you can paste it elsewhere —you can't do that if you *clear* a selection.

Here are a couple of ways to *clear* a selection from your timeline:

- From the EDIT menu, choose CLEAR.
- Shortcut: COMMAND+B (Mac) or CTRL+B (Windows).

Duplicating

In many editing situations, you'll want to repeat a clip, like a measure of drums that you want to use over many measures. Of course, you *could* just OPTION-drag (Mac) or ALT-drag (Windows) the same clip onto a track over and over (like you did earlier in this book) to create a looping phrase, but that can get really boring very quickly. *Duplicating* and *Repeating* are two ways to get the job done quicker.

Duplicating a clip will create a copy of a clip or selection and place it immediately after the original:

1. Select the clip or area that you want to duplicate (either by single-clicking with the Grabber tool or by double-clicking with the Selector tool).
2. Click on the EDIT menu.
3. Click on DUPLICATE. A duplicate of the selected clip (or area) will appear immediately after the selection.

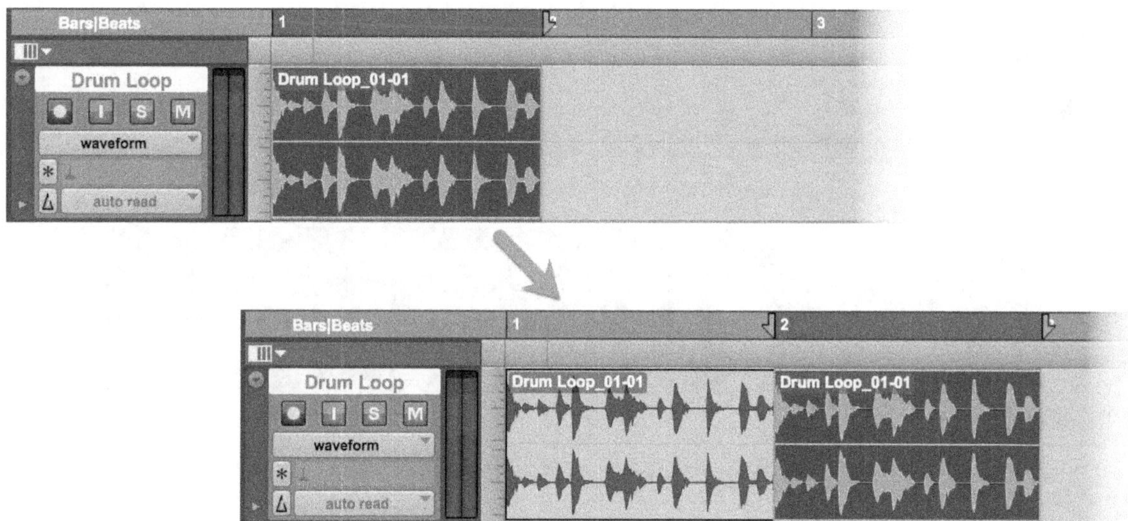

Figure 7.6 Duplicating a Clip

The shortcut for Duplicate is COMMAND+D (Mac) or CTRL+D (Windows).

Repeating

Duplicating a clip is a one-off operation —creating a duplicate of a selected clip, for example, will create a single new clip immediately after the selected clip. Although you *could* do multiple duplications, *Repeating* a clip might be a better way to go: You can create multiple repetitions in one quick process.

1. Select the clip or area that you want to repeat (either by single-clicking with the Grabber tool or by double-clicking with the Selector tool).
2. Click on the EDIT menu.
3. Click on REPEAT. The Repeat dialog box will open.

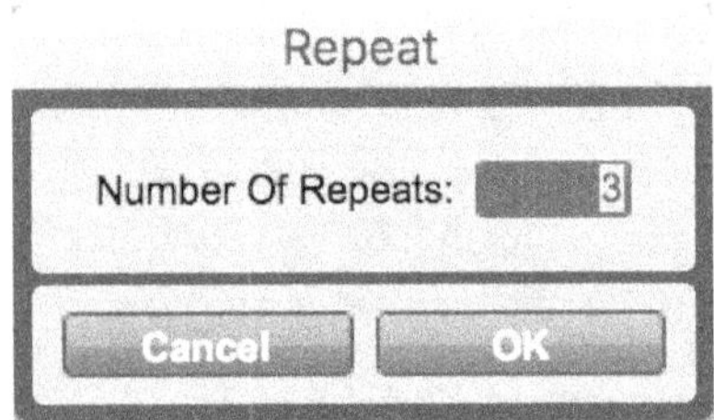

Figure 7.7 Choosing the Number of Repeats

4. Type the number of times you want the clip to repeat (excluding the original) in the *Number of Repeats* text box. In this case, I'll type 3.
5. Click on the OK button. The selected clip will be repeated the specified number of times, just as if you had used the Duplicate command multiple times.

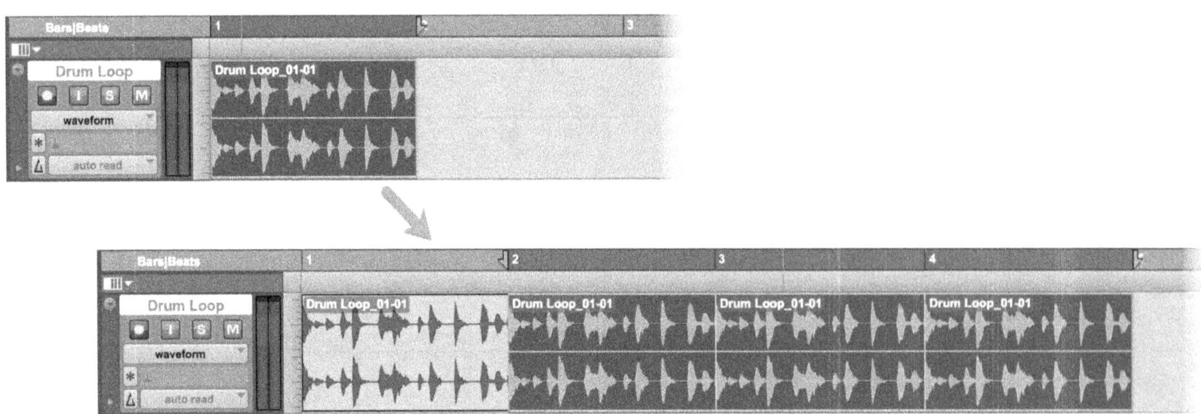

Figure 7.8 Repeated Clip

The shortcut for Repeat is OPTION+R (Mac) or ALT+R (Windows).

Constraining Motion with the CONTROL/START Key

The CONTROL key (Mac) or START key (Windows) is a very handy modifier key that can help you in a few ways to constrain the motion of a clip.

First, you can use this key to make sure that as you drag a clip vertically (from one track to another), it's timing won't change:

1. Select the clip that you want to move.
2. Holding the CONTROL key (Mac) or START key (Windows), vertically drag the clip (with the Grabber tool or Smart Tool in Grabber tool mode). You'll see that as you drag, the clip will not move left or right (earlier or later in time).

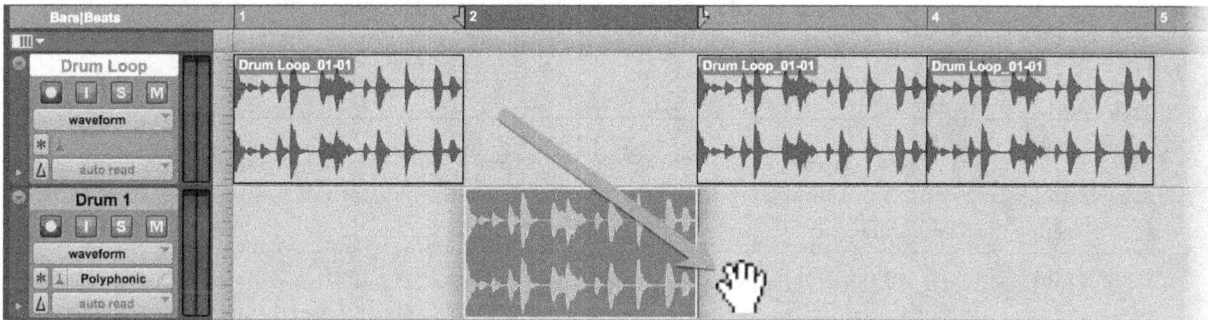

Figure 7.9 Dragging a clip holding CONTROL/START, Constraining Motion (Even If the Cursor Moves)

You can also use this modifier to immediately move a clip to your current playback cursor position:

1. Using the Selector tool, click on the desired destination location for your clip (when you click, the playback cursor will move to that location).

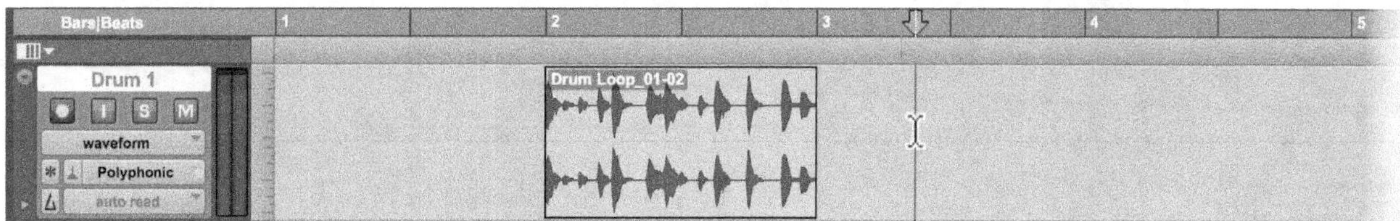

Figure 7.10 Selecting a Destination Position with the Selector Tool

2. Holding the CONTROL key (Mac) or START key (Windows), click on the clip with the Grabber tool (or the Smart Tool in Grabber tool mode). The clip will immediately jump to start at the location of your playback cursor.

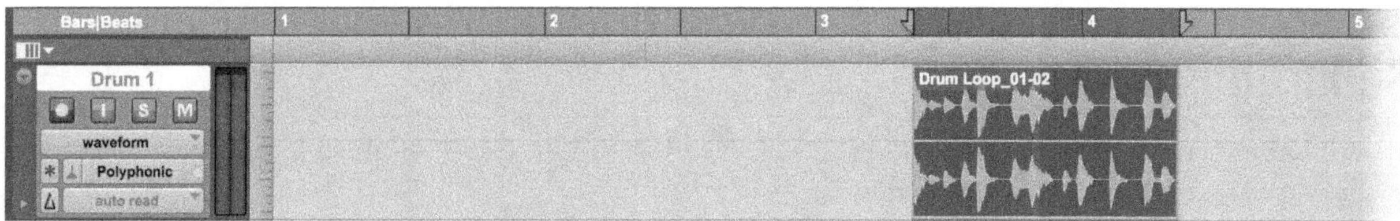

Figure 7.11 Moving a Clip to the Playback Cursor by Holding the CONTROL/START key and Clicking with the Grabber Tool

You can use this same logic to perfectly align one clip with another:

1. Select the clip that you want to align to (in other words, the clip that will not be moved). When you select the clip, the area selected in the ruler will also be selected, with the playback cursor at the beginning of the selected area.

Figure 7.12 Selecting the Clip to Align To

2. Holding the CONTROL key (Mac) or START key (Windows), click on the clip that you want to move with the Grabber tool (or the Smart Tool in Grabber tool mode). The clip will immediately jump to start at the location of your playback cursor, which is aligned with the beginning of the ruler's selected area.

Figure 7.13 Two Clips Aligned

Separating Clips

In addition to cutting, copying, and pasting clips, you'll want to split clips—breaking a clip into two or more smaller clips. There are a few ways to do this:

Basic Separate

Separating a clip is easy:

1. Using the Selector tool, select an area or click once to move the playback cursor to the location where you want to make the separation.
2. Click on the EDIT menu.
3. Move your cursor to SEPARATE CLIP. A submenu will appear.
4. Choose AT SELECTION. Depending on what you've selected, you'll get one of two results:
   - If you've clicked at a specific point (with no area selected), your clip will be split into two smaller clips, as shown in Figure 7.14.

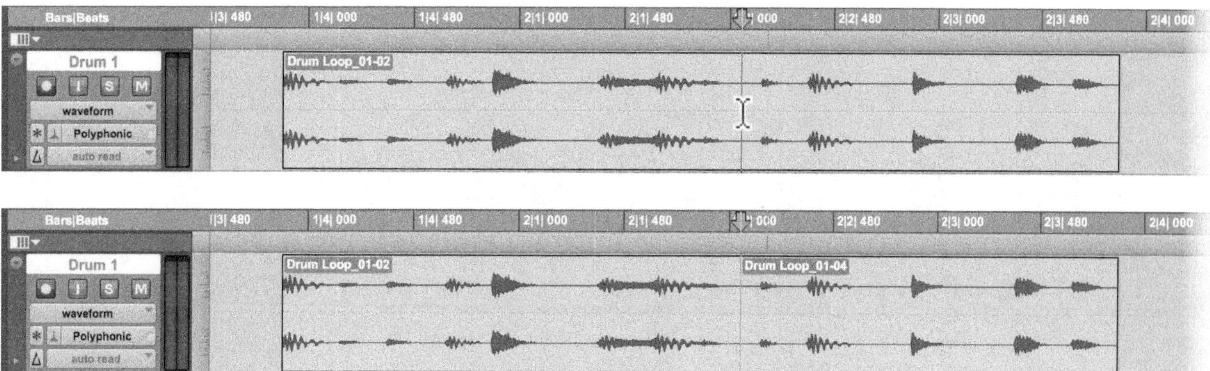

Figure 7.14 An Unconsolidated Selection (Top), and After Consolidation (Bottom)

   - If you've selected an area, your clip will be split into three smaller clips—one clip before your selection starts, one clip after your selection ends, and one clip that represents your selected area.

Figure 7.15 Selecting a Point on the Timeline (Top), and Separated Clips (Bottom)

The shortcut for *Separate>At Selection* is COMMAND+E (Mac) or CTRL+E (Windows).

There's an old rule among editors when separating (or trimming) a clip: Because all naturally occurring audio waveforms begin from a zero-voltage level (silence) with a compression phase, always cut your clips at the zero-crossing line, with the waveform ascending (as shown in Figure 7.16).

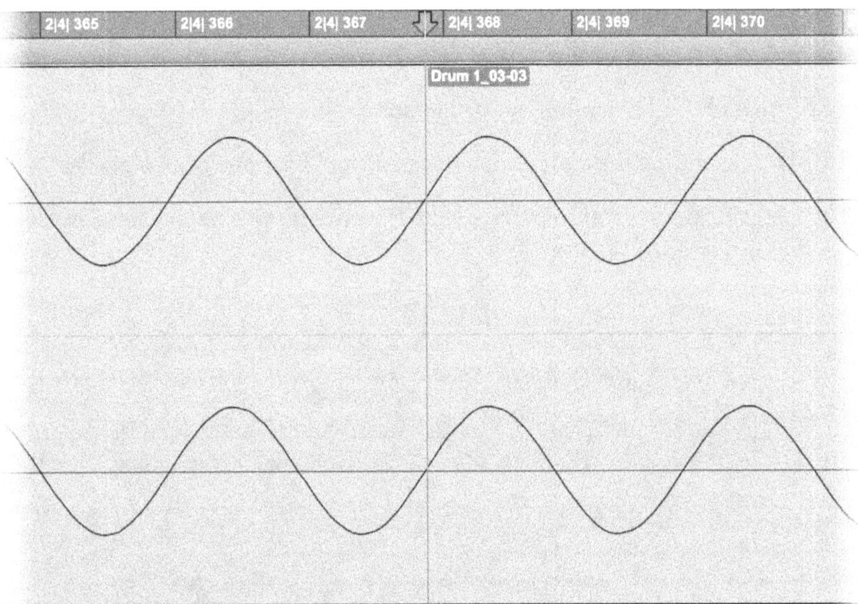

Figure 7.16 Selecting an Area on the Timeline (Top), and Separated Clips (Bottom)

This is a good habit to get into and ensures that you won't hear any unwanted clicks and pops, and that your sound will behave in a natural manner.

Separate at Grid

Here's a useful variation on the basic separation workflow that will create separate clips at each grid line.

1. Set your Grid value at the interval at which you want to make separations.
2. Select an area where you want to make grid-line separations.

Figure 7.17 Cutting on the Zero-Volt Line, with the Waveform Ascending

3. Click on the EDIT menu.
4. Move your cursor to SEPARATE CLIP. A submenu will appear.
5. Choose ON GRID. The *Pre-Separate Amount* dialog box will appear.

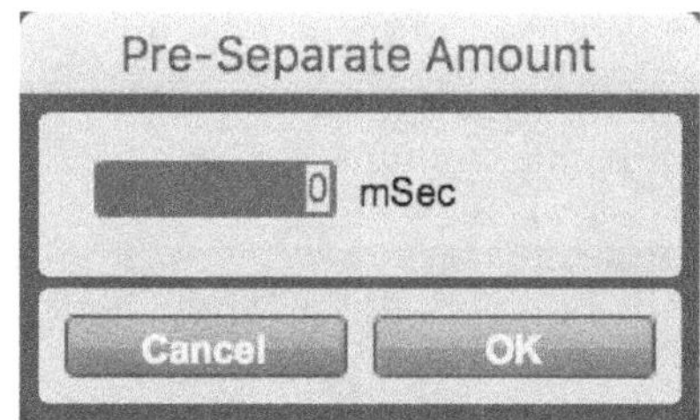

Figure 7.18 Selecting an Area

6. Any value in the pre-separate amount will shift your separations earlier in time. For example, if you have a pre-separate value of 3 milliseconds (mSec), then separations will be made 3 milliseconds before each grid line. If you want the separations to be made precisely on each grid line, leave the value at 0.
7. Click the OK button, and your separations will be made.

Here's an example of what you might end up with. In Figure 7.19, I've set my grid value to sixteenth notes (240 ticks). Within the selected area, there are separations at each grid line.

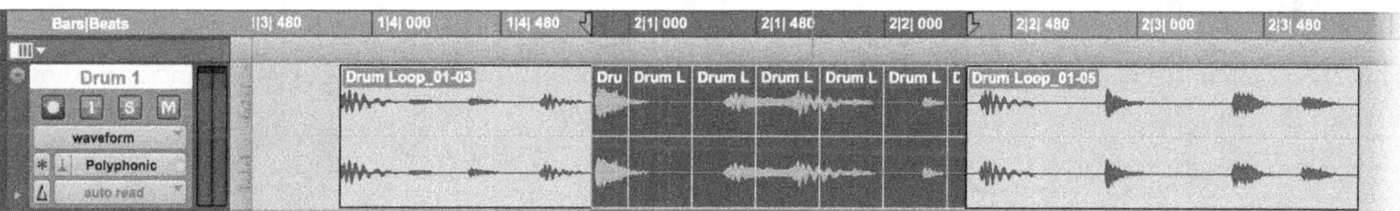

Figure 7.19 Setting a Pre-Separate Amount

Separate at Transient

A variation on *Separate>On Grid*, this is a handy little feature that creates a new clip boundary at each detected transient.

Simply put, a *transient* is a rapid increase in amplitude (loudness) often found at the beginning of a percussive waveform, such as a pick or a hammer hitting a string, or a drumstick hitting the head of a drum. Different types of instruments have different kinds of transients, but they tend to be good visual cues when editing, indicating the beginnings of notes (or words, in the case of a vocal track).

1. Select an area where you want to make transient separations.
2. Click on the EDIT menu.
3. Move your cursor to SEPARATE CLIP. The Separate Clip submenu will appear.
4. Choose AT TRANSIENTS. The *Pre-Separate Amount* dialog box will open.
5. Here again, setting any value above zero in the Pre-Separate Amount dialog box will add padding to the clips you are about to create. The greater the value, the farther ahead of each transient the separations will be. To separate clips exactly at the beginning of each transient, choose 0. When you're finished, click on the OK button.

Again, you'll see your clip immediately separated into a number of clips. The placement of the clip boundaries will be a little different from when you separated at each grid line. This time, you'll see that your clip has been separated at each transient (or just ahead of the transient, if you entered a Pre-Separate amount).

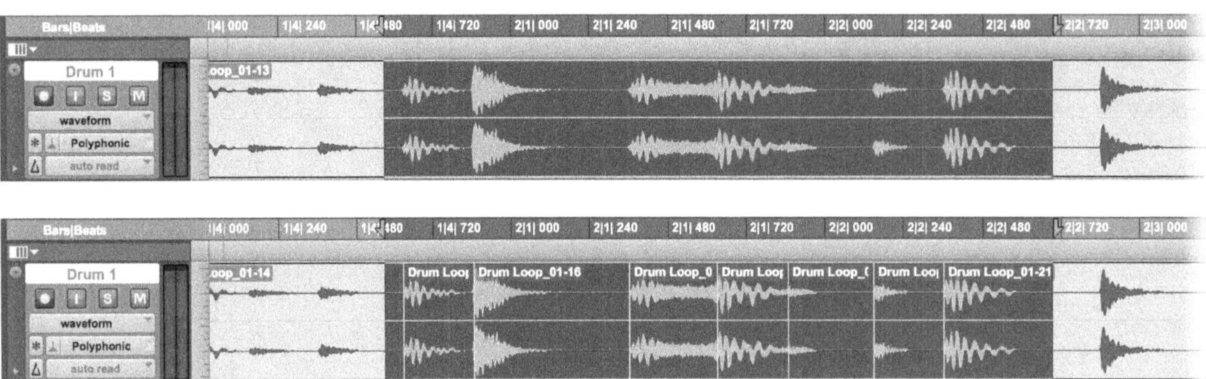

Figure 7.20 The Result of Separating on Grid

Heal Separation

What if you separated a clip, or deleted a section in the middle of a clip, and then changed your mind and wanted to rejoin the clip? That's what *Heal Separation* will enable you to do:

1. Select an area where you want to remove separations.
2. Click on the EDIT menu.
3. Move your cursor to HEAL SEPARATION.

Here's what will happen: Any separations within the selected area will be removed.

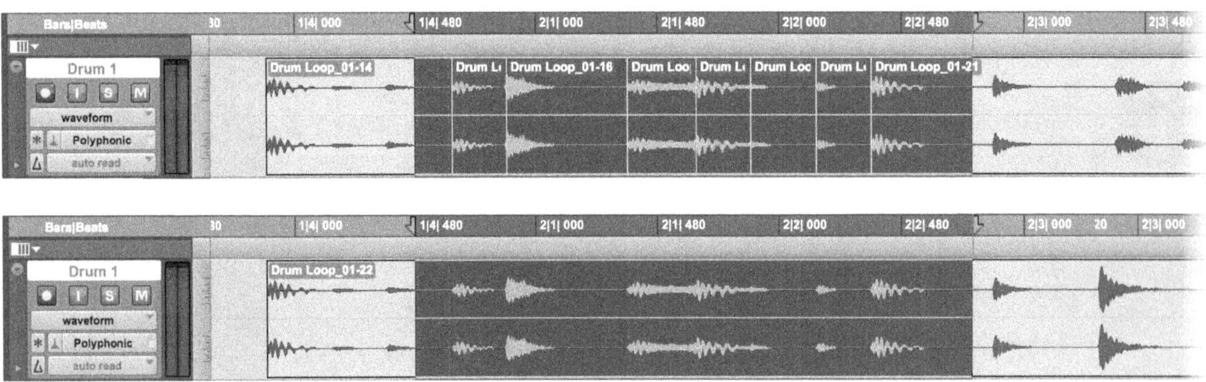

Figure 7.21 Separating at Transients (Before and After)

You can only heal a separation if all the clips involved haven't been moved in relation to each other. For example, if you split a clip into two smaller clips, and then move one of the smaller clips, you'll no longer be able to heal that separation.

The shortcut for Heal Separation is COMMAND+H (Mac) or CTRL+H (Windows).

Consolidating Clips

As you progress in an editing session, you'll tend to accumulate more and more clips as you cut, copy, paste, and move clips on your timeline. At some point, the sheer number of clips on a track will become a nuisance, and you'll want to combine some clips into a new, single clip. That's when you'll need to *consolidate* clips.

You can think of Pro Tools' *Consolidate* feature as rendering a number of clips (audio or MIDI) into a single clip (and in the case of audio, as a single new audio *file*). Here's how it works:

1. Select the area that you want to consolidate (even completely empty areas can be consolidated).
2. From the EDIT menu, choose CONSOLIDATE CLIP.

The shortcut for *Consolidate* is SHIFT+OPTION+3 (Mac) or SHIFT+ALT+3 (Windows).

Here's what you'll get: In the area that you've selected, instead of multiple clips and spaces, you'll see a single clip. The spaces between the clips have been "rendered" as silence, as shown in Figure 7.22.

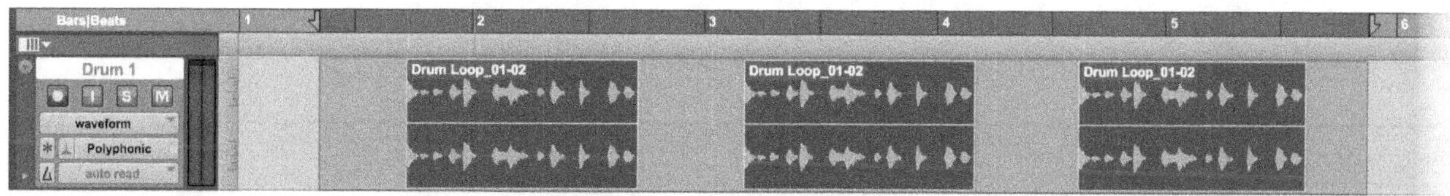

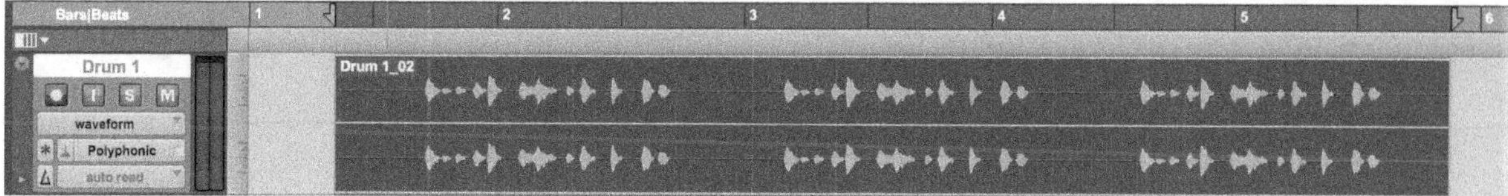

Figure 7.22 Heal Separation (Before and After)

Trimming Clips

You've learned how to use the Trim tool at a basic level. Here are more ways to trim clips.

Trimming with Shortcuts

In many cases, the quickest way to trim a clip doesn't involve the Trim tool at all!

Trimming from the Beginning of a Clip

Here's an easy way to trim the beginning of your clip, using the Selector tool and shortcuts.

1. Using the Selector tool (or the Smart Tool in Selector tool mode), place your playback cursor at the point where you want the clip to start.
2. Press the A key.

OR

2. Press OPTION+SHIFT+7 (Mac) or ALT+SHIFT+7 (Windows)

OR

2. Click on the EDIT Menu.
3. Move your cursor to TRIM CLIP. The *Trim Clip* submenu will appear.
4. Choose START TO INSERTION.

Editors do a lot of clip trimming, so learning one of the shortcut-based workflows is recommended. No matter which method you choose though, here's what you'll get: The area from the original beginning of the clip will be removed from the track, establishing a new clip start at the position where your playback cursor has been set.

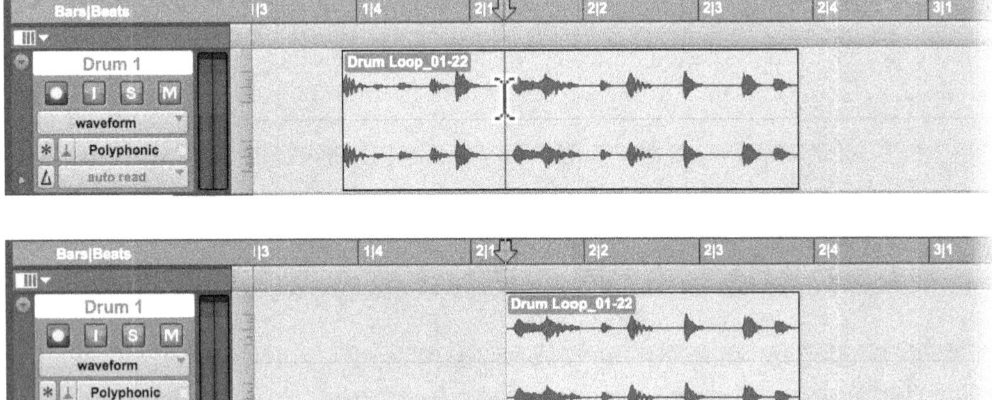

Figure 7.23 Trim Start To Insertion (Before and After)

Trimming from the End of a Clip

A mirror of the previous workflow, here's an easy way to trim the end of your clip, using the Selector tool and shortcuts.

1. Using the Selector tool (or the Smart Tool in Selector tool mode), place your playback cursor at the point where you want the clip to end.
2. Press the S key.

OR

2. Press OPTION+SHIFT+8 (Mac) or ALT+SHIFT+8 (Windows)

OR

2. Click on the EDIT Menu.
3. Move your cursor to TRIM CLIP. The *Trim Clip* submenu will appear.
4. Choose END TO INSERTION.

The area from the original end of the clip will be removed from the track, establishing a new clip end at the position where your playback cursor has been set.

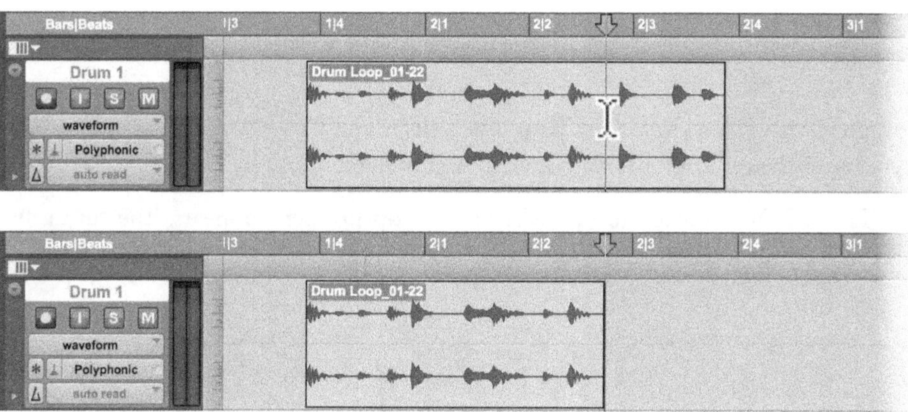

Figure 7.24 Trim End to Insertion (Before and After)

Trimming to Selection

Here's a way to trim a clip's start *and* end, effectively trimming a clip to a selected area in the same way you might crop a picture.

1. Using the Selector tool (or the Smart Tool in Selector tool mode), select the area of a clip that you want to *keep* on your timeline.
2. Press COMMAND+T (Mac) or CTRL+T (Windows)

OR

2. Click on the EDIT Menu.
3. Move your cursor to TRIM CLIP. The *Trim Clip* submenu will appear.
4. Choose TO SELECTION.

You'll see that in this case, any unselected part of the clip has been removed from the timeline, leaving only the selected area.

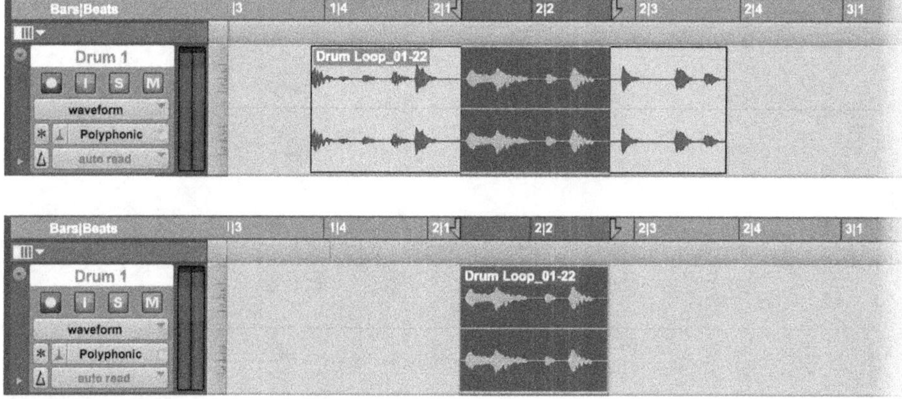

Figure 7.25 Trim To Selection (Before and After)

Trim Tool Variations

Let's go back to the Trim tool, and its two variations—*TCE Trim* and *Loop Trim*.

TCE

First on the list is the Time Compression/Expansion (TCE) Trim tool. This useful variation of the standard Trim tool enables you to stretch or compress the duration of an audio clip without changing the pitch.

1. Click and hold the TRIM TOOL button until the Trim tool pop-up menu appears. The currently selected version of the Trim tool will be indicated by a checkmark.

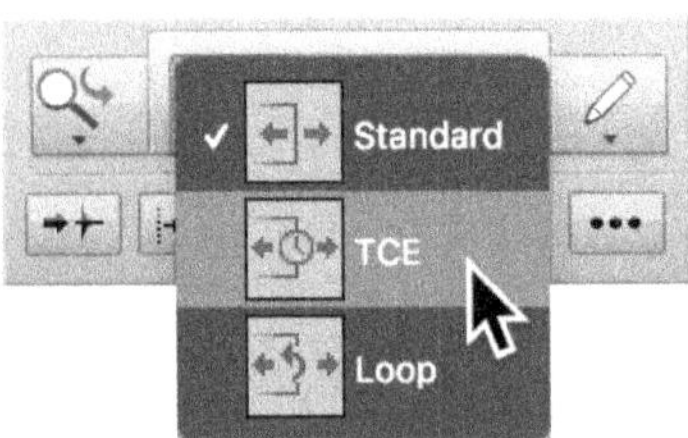

Figure 7.26 Changing Trim Tools

2. Choose TCE. The TCE Trim tool will become the active tool. The icon for the Trim tool will change to reflect the currently active version of the tool.

Figure 7.27 The TCE Trim Tool

3. Click and hold the boundary that you want to adjust.

4. Drag the boundary left or right, just as if you were using the standard Trim tool.

When you release the mouse button, a new audio clip will be created with a different duration from the original clip, but with its pitch unchanged. Figure 7.28 shows two 1-bar drum beats on two separate tracks, with the top track's beat at a faster tempo, and hence a shorter clip. After using the TCE Trim tool, they are now in the same tempo.

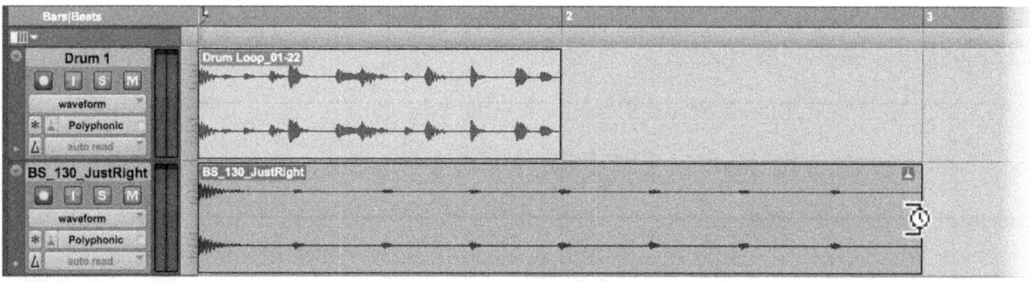

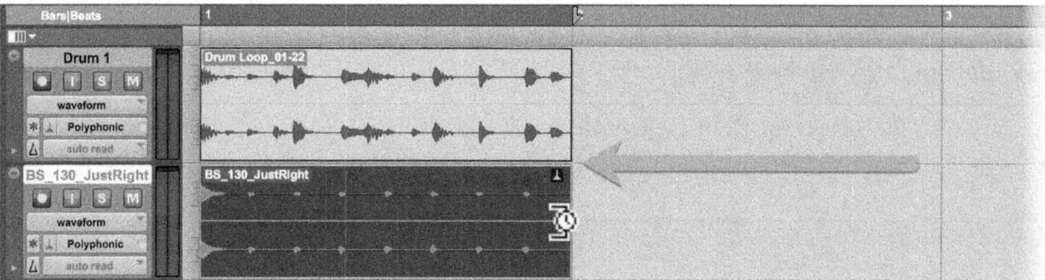

Figure 7.28 Using the TCE Trim Tool (Before and After)

The TCE Trim tool is really useful in Grid mode. Suppose you've imported a drum loop that doesn't match the tempo of the rest of your project (as is the case in the exercise session). Just make sure your grids are a musical unit and use the TCE Trim tool. The edges of the clip will snap to the nearest grid point when released, and you'll be right in tempo!

Clip Looping and the Loop Trim Tool

Clip Looping takes the convenience of the *Duplicate* and *Repeat* edit processes one step further. The ability to loop clips is very useful when you're working with repetitious material, such as drum beats. Here's how it works.

1. Select the clip you want to loop.
2. Click on the CLIP menu.
3. Choose LOOP. The *Clip Looping* dialog box will open. You have several choices when it comes to how you want your clip to loop. You can:

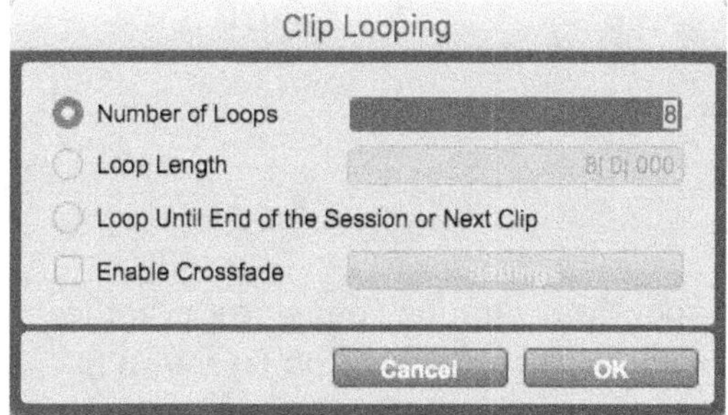

Figure 7.29 The Clip Looping Dialog Box

- Choose the Number of Loops (repetitions) you want your clip to have. This number includes the original instance of the clip.
- Specify a Loop Length (based on the Time Scale) that you want to fill with these loops.
- Loop until the End of the Session or until the Next Clip (whichever comes first).
- Check the Enable Crossfade check box to create crossfades between each loop iteration. When this check box is checked, you can adjust the crossfade curve by clicking on the Settings button (we'll explore fades later in this chapter).

4. Once you've chosen how you want your clip to loop, just click on the OK button. The dialog box will close, and your clip will be looped.

In this example, I've chosen to loop this clip eight times, and here's the result. This looped clip object functions in many ways like a single unit and can be moved and edited with great flexibility.

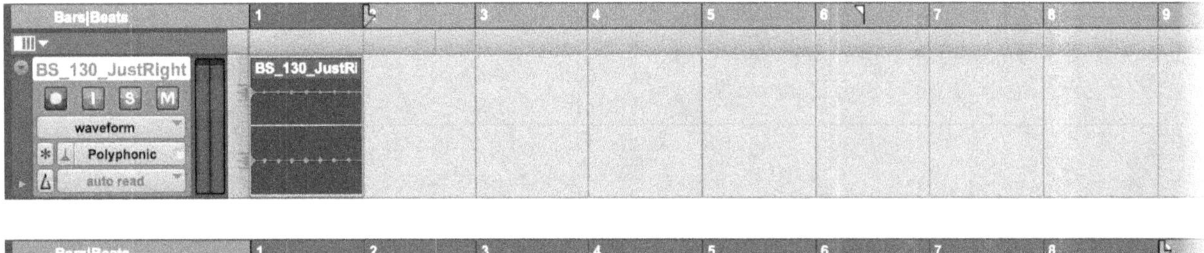

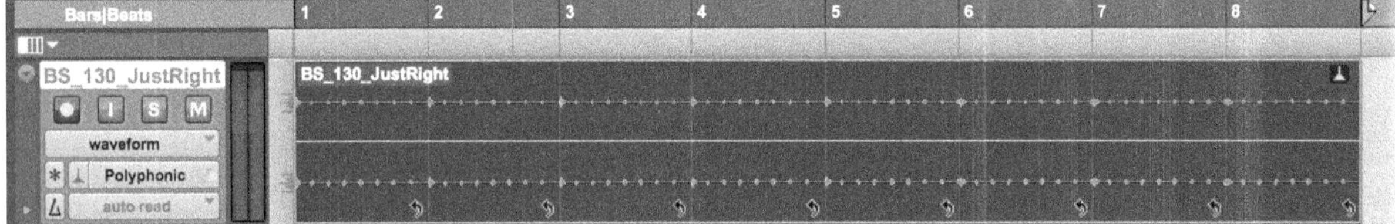

Figure 7.30 A Clip Looped Eght Times

As if clip looping wasn't easy enough already, the Loop Trim tool will give you even more functionality. For example, you can use the Loop Trim tool to quickly create just the right amount of looping.

1. Click and hold the Trim tool button until the Trim tool pop-up menu appears. The currently selected version of the Trim tool will be indicated with a checkmark.
2. Choose LOOP to change to the Loop Trim tool. The icon for the Trim tool will change to reflect the currently active version of the tool.

Figure 7.31 The Loop Trim Tool

3. Cursor placement is important to make the Loop Trim tool work: Position your cursor near the top half of a clip boundary until you see the Trim tool with the curved arrow icon (as shown in Figure 7.32).

Figure 7.32 The Loop Trim Tool Cursor

4. You can drag either the left or the right boundary to loop forward or backward. When you've got the duration you want, release the mouse, and you'll have your new looped clip.

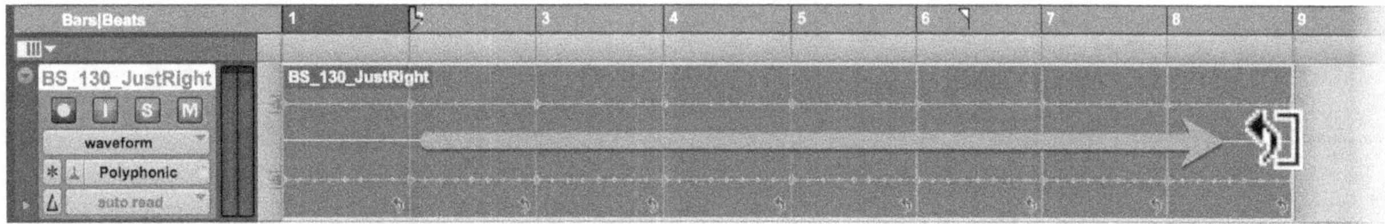

Figure 7.33 Creating a Looped Clip with the Loop Trim Tool

Nudging

Moving clips in large increments is easy, but it's tricky to move them in surgically fine small bits. That's when you'll want to stop dragging a clip and start Nudging.

First, though, you'll have to choose a Nudge value. Setting up your Nudge value is nearly identical to setting up your Grid value (which you've learned in Chapter 4):

1. Click on the down arrow to the right of the Nudge value. The Nudge pop-up menu will appear.

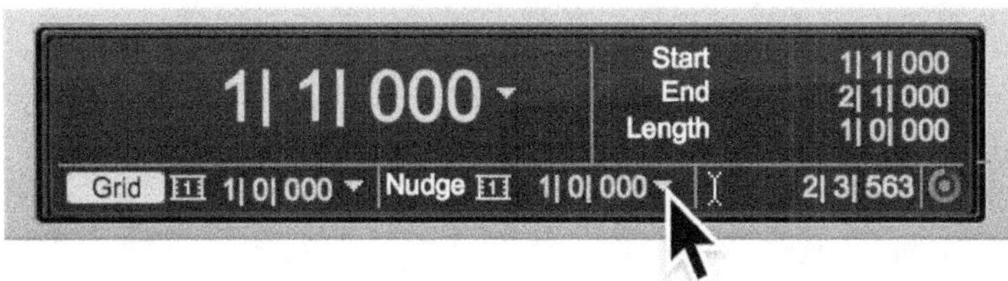

Figure 7.34 Getting Ready to Change Your Nudge Value

2. Select the Time Scale with which you want to nudge your clip. The currently chosen Time Scale will be indicated by a checkmark. (In this image, Bars|Beats is chosen, which is well suited for music projects.) Based on the Time Scale you choose, the options at the top of the list will change.

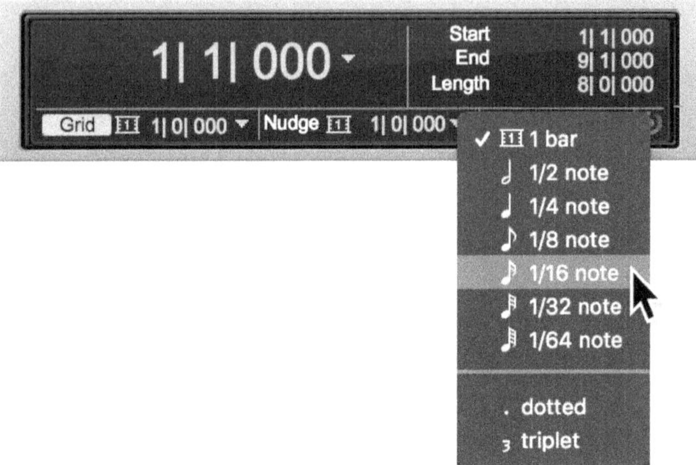

Figure 7.35 Changing the Nudge Value from One Bar to One Sixteenth Note

3. Select the increment by which you want to nudge your clip. The currently chosen increment will be indicated by a checkmark.

Once you have the nudge value you want, using the feature is very straightforward.

4. Select the clip(s) you want to move.
5. Press the plus (+) key on your keyboard's numeric keypad to move your selected clip(s) later in time (to the right) by the nudge amount.

OR

5. Press the minus (-) key on your keyboard's numeric keypad to move your selected clip(s) earlier in time (to the left) by the nudge amount.

Holding down the OPTION key (Mac) or ALT key (Windows) while pressing the plus or minus key will nudge only the left boundary of a clip. Holding down the COMMAND key (Mac) or CTRL key (Windows) while pressing the plus or minus key will nudge only the right boundary. Holding down the SHIFT key while pressing the plus or minus key will move only the selection range and leave the selected clip in its original position. (If you want to get creative, you can add the previous modifiers to the Shift key and nudge just the beginning or end of the selected range).

If you don't have a numeric keypad on your computer, you can still nudge, up to a point. Pressing the COMMA (,) key will nudge earlier in time, while the PERIOD (.) key will nudge later. Modifier keys don't work with this method of nudging, so nudging only the beginning or end of a clip isn't possible with these keys.

Fades

Fade-ins and fade-outs are used to gradually transition into or out of a clip. Additionally, you can create *crossfades* between clips to make a smooth transition from one clip to another. The topic of fades, since they change the level of clips over time, overlaps on the larger topic of mixing (which you'll explore in the next chapter), but you'll also create fades in the editing process. Let's tackle it now.

Fades are nothing new in the world of DAWs, but Pro Tools makes fades easy to create and tweak. You can even use the Smart Tool to create them!

Creating a Fade-in or Fade-out

Everybody has heard fade-ins used on a mix, such as when a song starts from a silent beginning and gets gradually louder until it reaches its running volume. A fade-out is just the opposite, with the sound getting progressively softer until it reaches silence.

In Pro Tools, you can create a fade-in or fade-out for an individual clip *within* a mix as well. Here's how:

1. Using the Selector tool (or the Selector mode of the Smart Tool), select the area of a clip that you want to turn into a fade-in or fade-out.

If you want to create a fade-in, it's important to make sure your selection starts *at* or *before* the clip begins, and that it ends where you want the fade-in to end. If you want to create a fade-out, it's important to start your selected area where you want the fade-out to start, and then end your selection at or after the clip ends. If you don't select at least to the beginning (or end) of a clip boundary, Pro Tools will get confused about what you want to do. In these cases, if you go to the EDIT menu and select FADES, the CREATE option will be greyed out and unavailable.

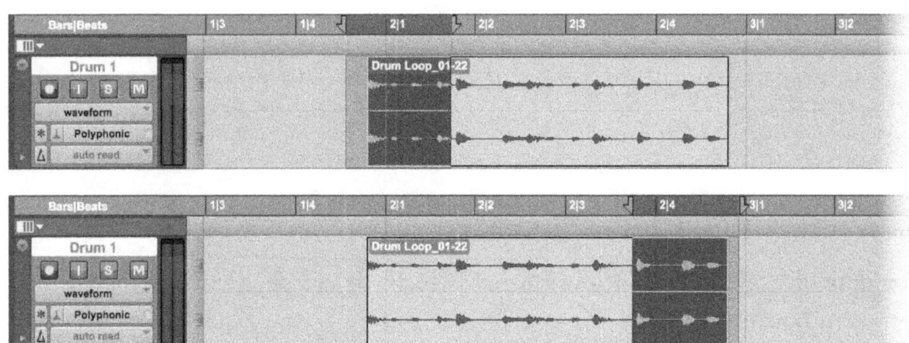

Figure 7.36 Selecting an Area for a Fade-In (Top) or Fade-Out (Bottom)

2. Click on the EDIT menu.
3. Move the cursor to FADES. The FADES submenu will appear.
4. Choose CREATE.

The shortcut to create a Fade is COMMAND+F (Mac) or CTRL+F (Windows).

5. The FADES dialog box will open. The curves shown in the Fades dialog box will be different depending on whether you're creating a fade-in or fade-out, but the controls are the same:

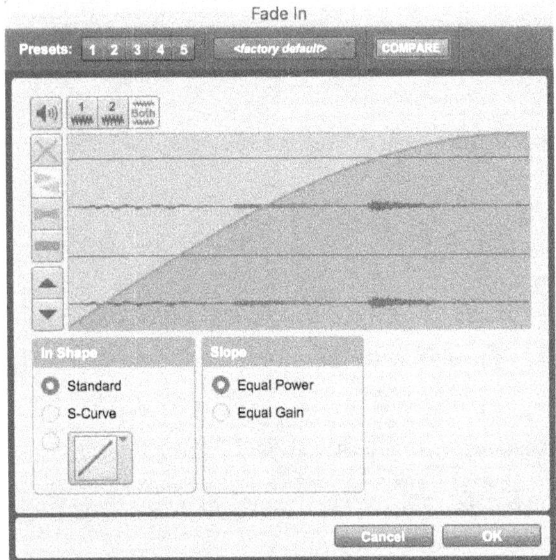

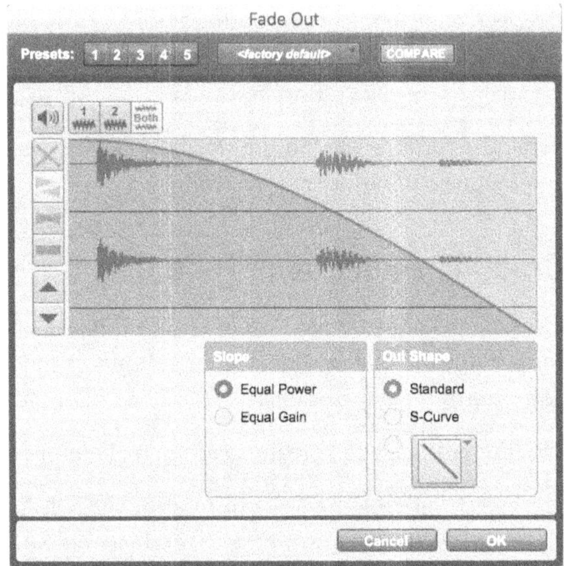

Figure 7.37 The Fade-In and Fade-Out Dialog Boxes

- On the left of the waveform display, you'll see four buttons that will allow you to view that waveform in a number of different ways (or not view it at all, which happens if you click the top of the four buttons). These options won't affect your view much when dealing with a simple fade-in or fade-out, but they will give you more useful options when working with crossfades.

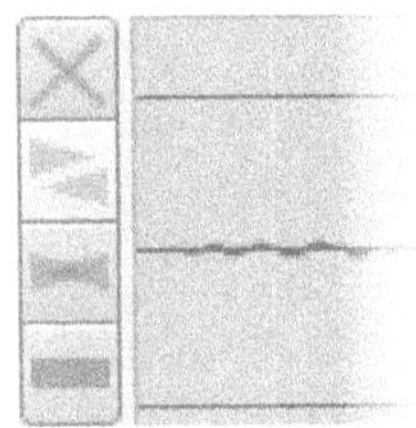

Figure 7.38 Waveform View Buttons

- Below the view options, you'll see two arrow buttons, which you can click to vertically zoom your waveform up or down.

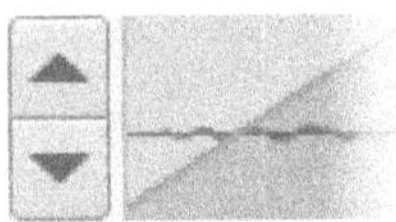

Figure 7.39 Waveform Vertical Zoom Buttons

- The *In Shape* section of the Fade-In dialog box and the *Out Shape* of the Fade-Out dialog box enable you to control the contour of your fade. Here, you have three main options:

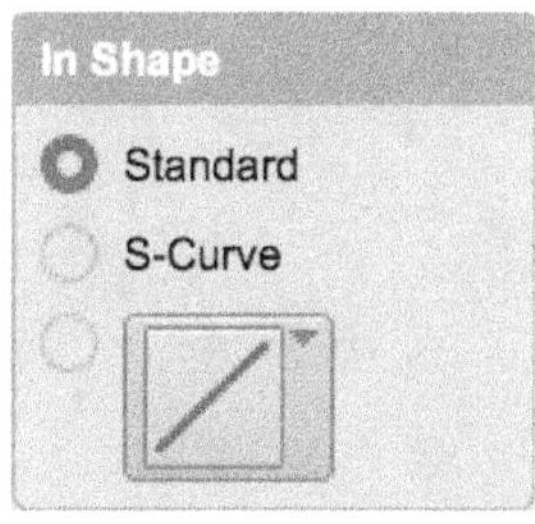

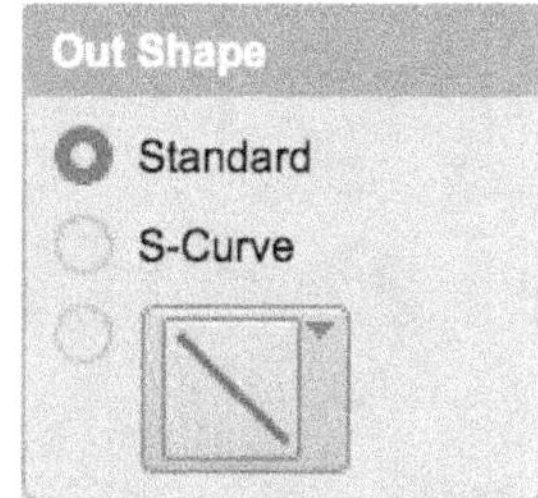

Figure 7.40 In Shape and Out Shape Sections

- Click on the STANDARD option button in the Shape section to select a basic linear fade or logarithmic curve for the new fade. (This will depend on what you choose in the Slope section, which you'll delve into during the discussion on crossfades.)
- Click on the S-Curve option button in the Shape section to select an S curve for the new fade.
- Click on the Preset Curve option button to use a standard fade curve chosen from a menu.
- If you've chosen the Preset Curve Option button, you'll have a few preset curves to choose from:

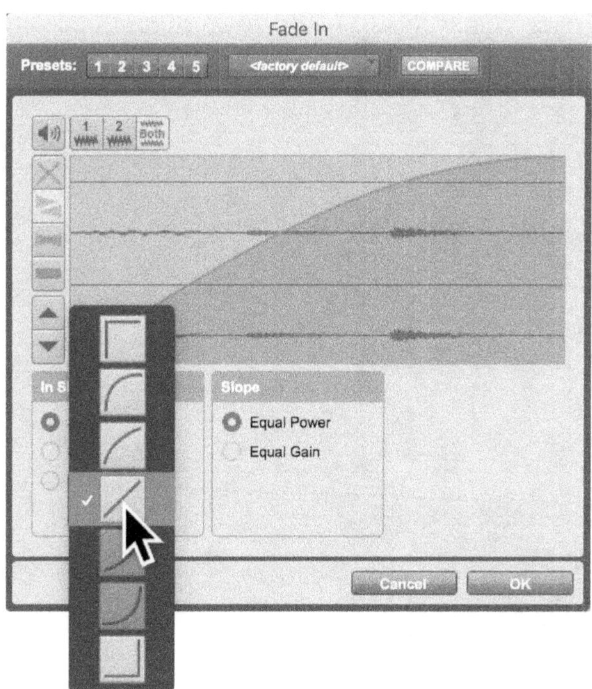

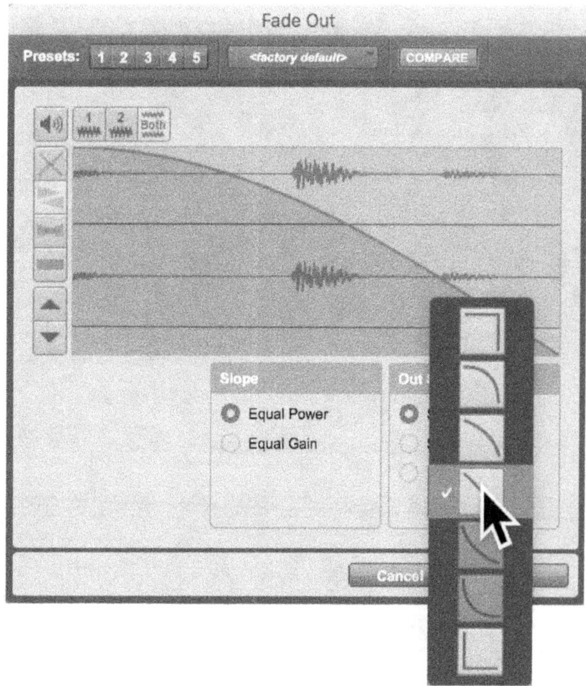

Figure 7.41 Fade Shape Presets

6. Once you've chosen the basic shape of your curve, you can further adjust it by clicking and dragging on the fade curve line. The line will change in response to your movements, and the waveform view will adjust accordingly.

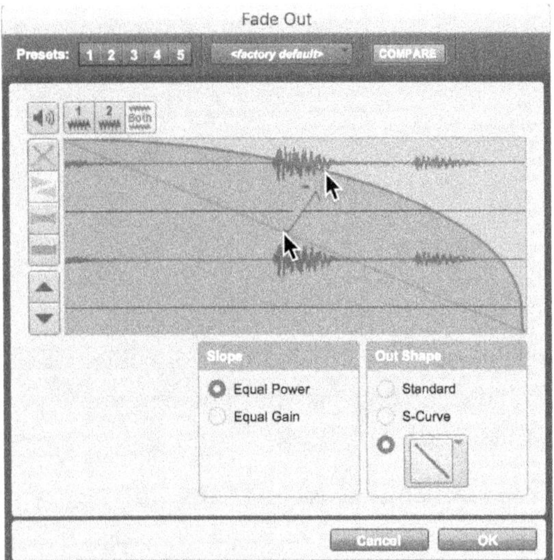

Figure 7.42 Changing the Shape of a Fade by Dragging the Curve

7. Once you have the fade curve you want, click on the OK button. The Fades dialog box will close.

If you're creating a fade-in at the beginning of the clip, you'll now see a new fade shown with an ascending line, indicating that it is a fade-in, as well as showing the fade-in's curve.

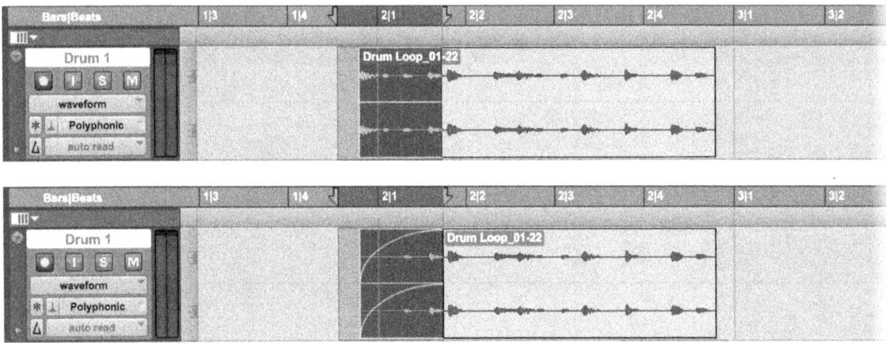

Figure 7.43 A Selected Area and the Fade-In Result

Here's what a fade-out looks like:

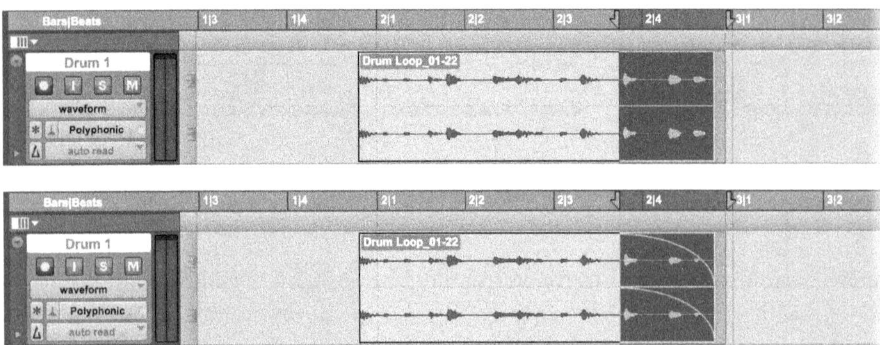

Figure 7.44 A Selected Area and the Fade-Out Result

Often, when creating a fade, it's useful to audition the sound of the fade before you create it. In the Fades dialog box, you'll see a small button in the upper-left corner (shown here) that will do just that. Click the button to hear the effect of the fade curve on the audio clip. You won't hear any other tracks in your project; just the fade that you're creating.

Figure 7.45 The Fade Dialog Box Audition Button

Creating a Crossfade

A *crossfade* is a simultaneous fading out of one sound while another sound fades in, creating a smooth transition from one sound to the other. Here's how to create a crossfade between two overlapping clips:

1. Select an area of two overlapping clips that you want to become a crossfade.

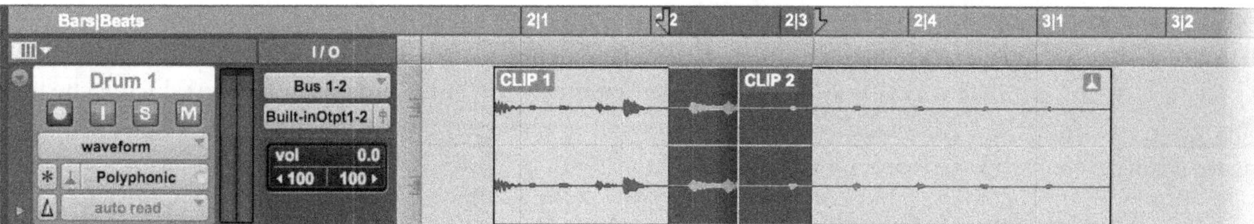

Figure 7.46 Selecting an Area for a Crossfade

2. Click on the EDIT menu.
3. Move the cursor to FADES. The Fades submenu will appear.
4. Choose CREATE. The *Crossfade* dialog box will open.

The shortcut to create a Crossfade is COMMAND+F (Mac) or CTRL+F (Windows).

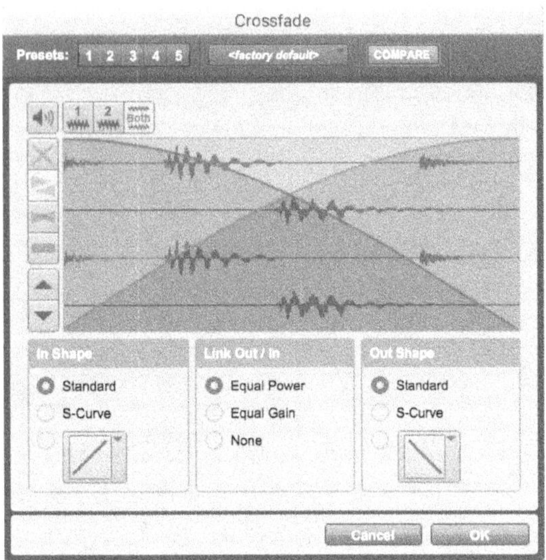

Figure 7.47 The Crossfade Dialog Box

As you saw when working with fade-ins, the display buttons to the left of the waveform display will allow you to choose the view that works best. When working with crossfades, the differences between these views are more evident than when working with fade-ins or fade-outs. (Tip: The second and third waveform display buttons are commonly used for this sort of work.)

5. Set up the fade-in portion of *your* crossfade the same way you would a standalone fade-in.
6. Set up the fade-out portion of the crossfade the same way you would a standalone fade-out.
7. Drag the crossing point of *your* crossfade earlier or later, depending on your preference for this particular crossfade.

You'll notice that the fade-in and fade-out curves are linked. Changes made to either curve will affect the other. Let's take a look at the different fade-linking options. (Let your ears be your ultimate guide as to which is the best in any given situation.) The *Link Out/In* section enables you to change the way in which gain is treated as your clips crossfade. Here, you have three options:

- **Equal Power:** This linking option will compensate for the volume drop that sometimes occur when significantly different waveforms are combined by boosting the midpoint of the fade curves. It is usually heard as a smooth transition between dissimilar clips.

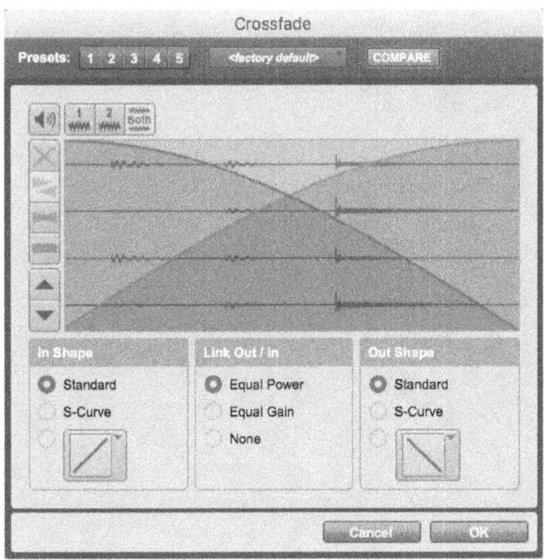

Figure 7.48 A Crossfade Showing Linking set to Equal Power

- **Equal Gain:** When you select this as a linking option, the midpoint of the fade curves will not be boosted in any way. When you are crossfading identical or very similar audio, this linking will often give you the desired smooth transition from clip to clip.

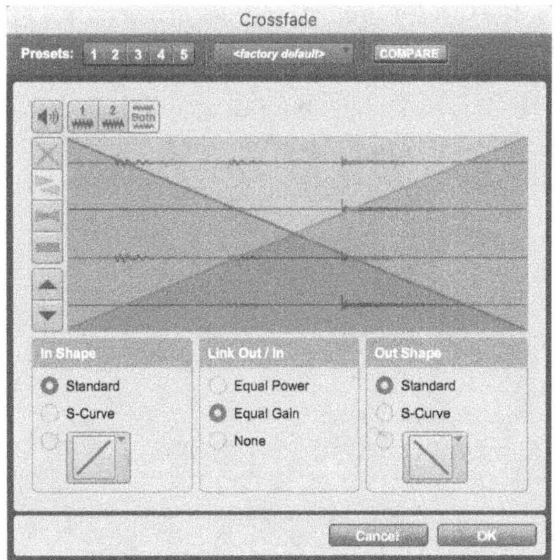

Figure 7.49 A Crossfade Showing Linking set to Equal Gain

- **None:** This option (available only when crossfading) will enable you to change one half of a crossfade without changing the other half. Although it's the least commonly used of all the linking options, it will give you a degree of flexibility that the other linking options don't provide. When linking is set to *None*, you can adjust the shape, beginning, and end of either curve independently. Just click on the small black handle at the beginning or end of a fade curve and drag it to the desired position.

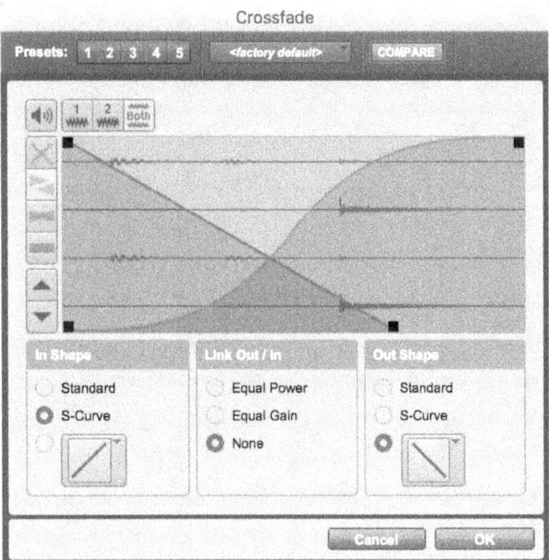

Figure 7.50 A Crossfade Showing Linking set to None

Although the *None* link mode might not be the most commonly used mode of crossfading, it is the preferred choice if you need a specific nonlinear transition.

8. Once you're happy with your crossfade's settings, click the OK button in the Fades dialog box.
9. Usually at this point, a crossfade will be created, but if there's not enough overlapping audio in both clips, you'll see a message as shown in Figure 7.51. This isn't a bug, but just a notification giving you the choice of either skipping the crossfade, or letting Pro Tools adjust the fade's boundaries to give you the largest possible area of crossfade.

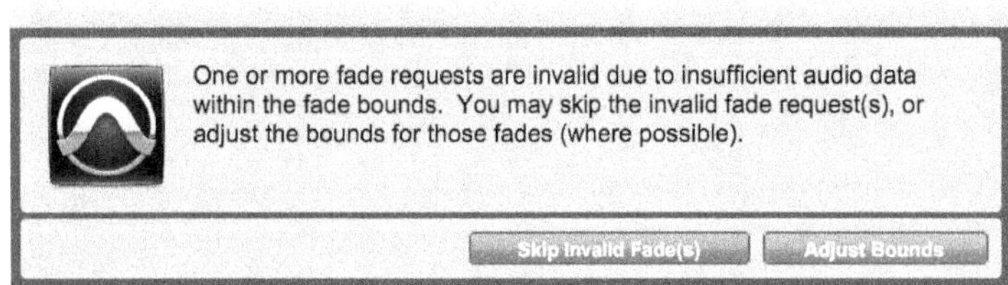

Figure 7.51 The Invalid Fades Dialog Box

Creating Fades with Shortcuts

Earlier in this chapter, you learned how to trim a clip's start or end to the location of the playback cursor. Here's a similar workflow to create a *fade* to the cursor location.

Let's start with creating a fade-in:

1. Using the Selector tool (or the Smart Tool in Selector tool mode), place your playback cursor at the point where you want a fade-in to end.
2. Press the D key.

OR

2. Press CONTROL+D (Mac) or START+D (Windows).

And here's how to create a fade-out:

1. Using the Selector tool (or the Smart Tool in Selector tool mode), place your playback cursor at the point where you want a fade-out to begin.
2. Press the G key.

OR

2. Press CONTROL+G (Mac) or START+G (Windows).

Finally, here's how to create a crossfade:

1. Using the Selector tool (or the Smart Tool in Selector tool mode), select an area of two overlapping clips that you want to become a crossfade.
2. Press the F key.

Creating Fades with The Smart Tool

In addition to the triple benefit of the Trim, Selector, and Grabber tools that you get with the Smart Tool, you can also quickly create fade-ins, fade-outs, and even crossfades!

- **Fade-in:** If you move your cursor to the upper-left corner of an audio clip, the cursor will change to a small square with an ascending diagonal line through it (looking like a fade-in line). Just click and drag your cursor to the right to quickly create a fade-in. Release the mouse button at the point where you want your fade-in to end, and the fade will be created.

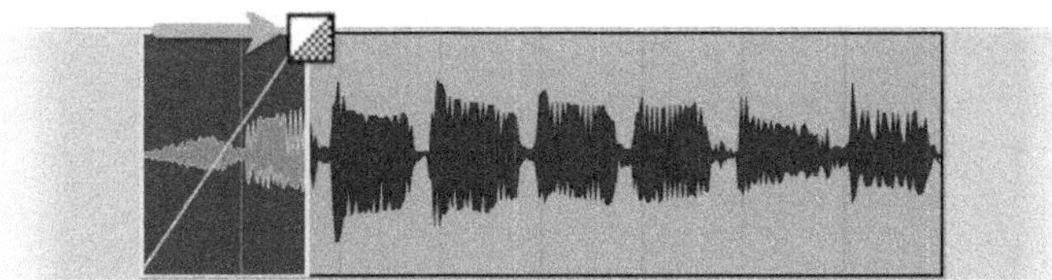

Figure 7.52 Creating a Fade-In with the Smart Tool

- **Fade-out:** If you move your cursor to the upper-right corner of a clip, the cursor will change to a small square with a descending diagonal line through it (looking like a fade-out line). Just click and drag your cursor to the left to quickly create a fade-out. Release the mouse button at the point where you want your fade-out to begin.

Figure 7.53 Creating a Fade-Out with the Smart Tool

- **Crossfade:** If you move your cursor to the bottom corners of two adjacent or overlapping clips, the cursor will change to a small square with two diagonal lines through it (looking like a crossfade). Just click and drag your cursor to the left or right to quickly create a crossfade. Release the mouse button at the point where you want your crossfade to begin or end. Your crossfade will be created and centered on the clips' boundaries.

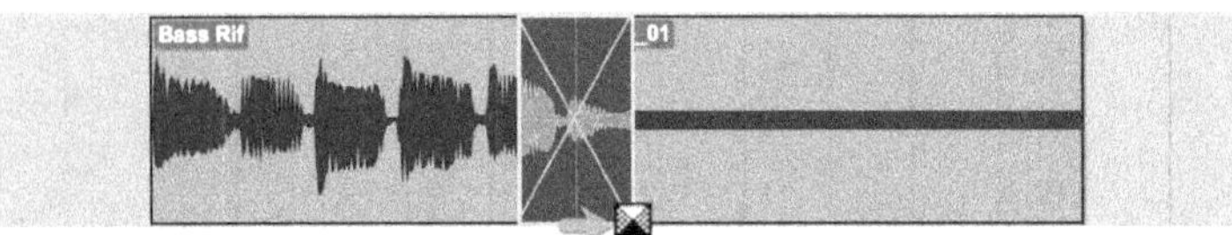

Figure 7.54 Creating a Crossfade with the Smart Tool

You'll notice that when you create a fade or crossfade using the Smart Tool, the Fades dialog box does not appear. If you want to change your fade, you'll need to edit it.

Editing Fades

If you create a fade-in in your Project and later decide that you want to change its contour, there are a few ways to do it:

- Just double-click on the fade with the Grabber tool. The Fades dialog box will open again, so you can adjust the individual fade.
- Right-click a fade (or a selection that has fades in it) that you want to change. In the menu that appears, there is a FADES submenu, and from there, you can change the shape of the fade.

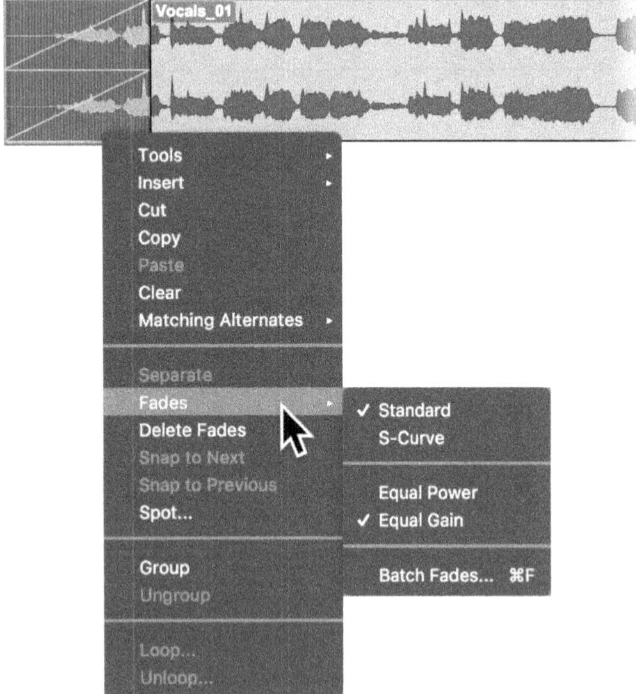

Figure 7.55 Right-Clicking a Fade

- Here's a cool way to change the shape of a fade: Move your cursor over the middle of the fade curve line of a fade. When the cursor shape changes to a fade icon, as shown in Figure 7.56, click and drag the curve to the desired shape (as you drag, the fade curve will be highlighted in yellow).

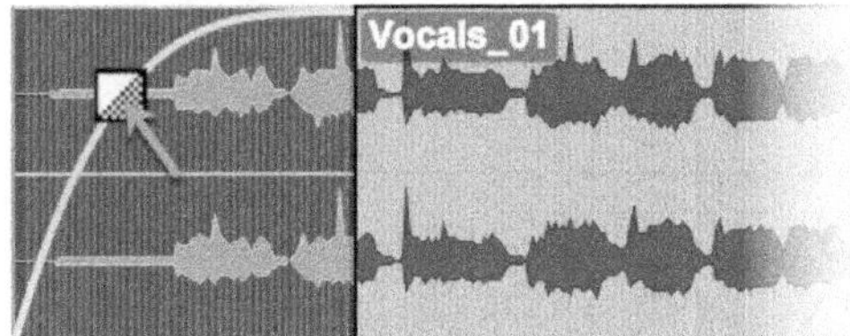

Figure 7.56 Dragging a Fade Curve

Here are some other ways to change a fade:

- Click and drag a fade with the Grabber tool to change the position of the fade. Note that as you drag the fade, you are fading (in or out) different pieces of audio.

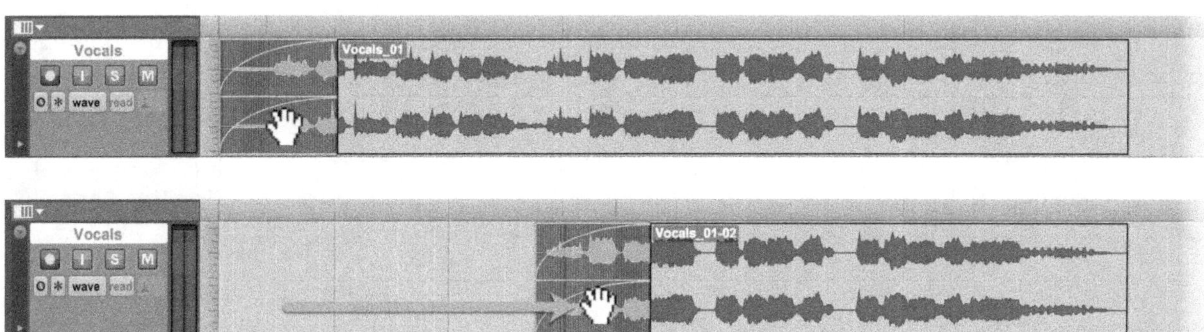

Figure 7.57 Moving a Fade with the Grabber Tool

- Use the Trim tool to change the duration of a fade by clicking on either the beginning or end of the fade and dragging, just as you would do with an audio clip.

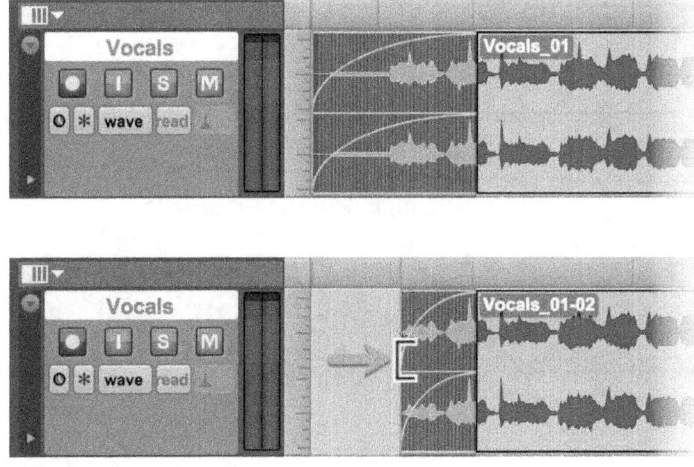

Figure 7.58 Trimming a Fade

Deleting Fades

Deleting fades is easy:

- Select the fade that you want to delete and press the DELETE key. The fade will be removed, and the original (non-faded audio) will remain.

OR

- Right-click a fade (or a selection that has fades in it) that you want to delete. In the menu that appears, choose the DELETE FADES menu item, which will delete the fade (or delete multiple fades, if you're *right-clicking* on a selection that has multiple fades in it).
- Another easy way to delete multiple fades: Select a fade (or make a selection that includes multiple fades). From the EDIT MENU, choose FADES. In the fades submenu, choose DELETE.

Batch Fades

As we've discussed back in Chapter 4 and also touched on earlier in this chapter, when cutting or trimming a clip, it's important to cut on the zero-volt line with the waveform ascending to avoid clicks and other unnatural behaviors. In reality though, there's not always enough time to do that kind of detailed work in high-pressure situations. What to do?

The thing about fades is that they either start or end at a point of silence, and silence is zero volts. This means that when you create a fade (fade-in, fade-out, or crossfade), you're *creating* a zero-volt start or end.

Here's a situation where using fades lets me work quicker: Figure 7.59 shows a few cut pieces of dialog. Since I needed to work *fast*, I didn't zoom in on each clip boundary to make sure that I was cutting on the zero-volt line. The risk, of course, is that there might be clicks and pops in the track, which is completely unacceptable!

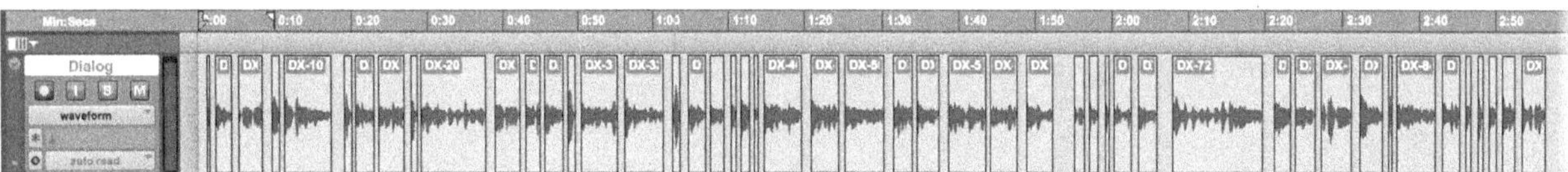

Figure 7.59 A Lot of Clips to Fade!

My workflow workaround would be to create fade-ins, fade-outs, and crossfades at all the appropriate boundaries, but it's time-consuming to create them individually. Not to worry, though—*Batch Fades* to the rescue!

1. Select an area that includes all the clips that you want to fade-in, fade-out, or crossfade.

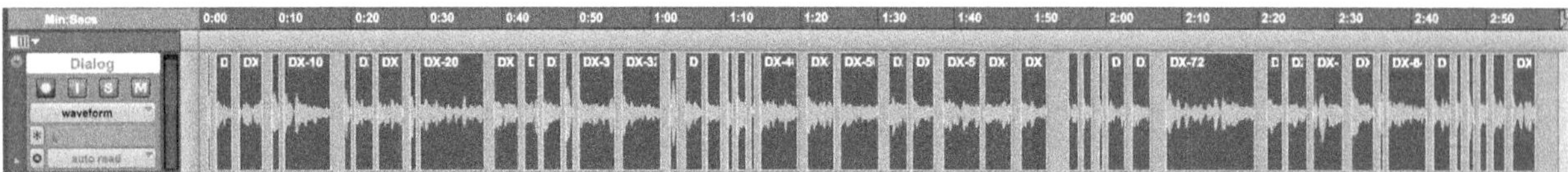

Figure 7.60 Selecting Clips for Batch Fadin

2. Click on the EDIT menu.
3. Move the cursor to FADES. The Fades submenu will appear.

4. Choose CREATE. The *Batch Fades* dialog box will open.

The shortcut to create Batch Fades is COMMAND+F (Mac) or CTRL+F (Windows)

The *Batch Fades* dialog box is the combination of a fade-in, a fade-out, and a crossfade dialog box. This will cover all the possible fades that could be created in your selected area.

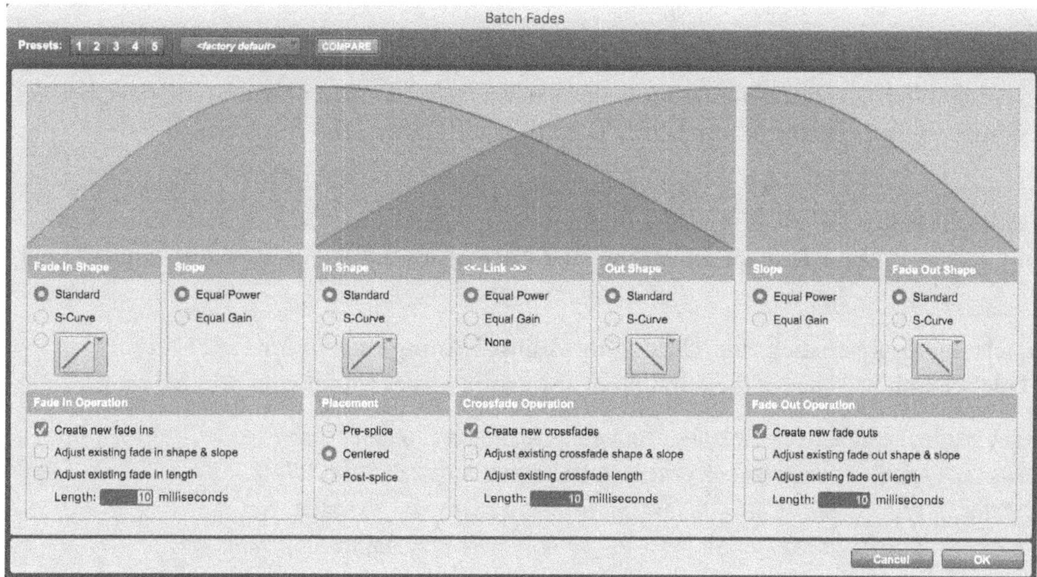

Figure 7.61 The Batch Fades Dialog Box

The top part of the *Batch Fades* dialog box will allow you to choose different curves for your different kinds of fades/crossfades. This works like other fade dialog boxes you've learned about previously in this chapter.

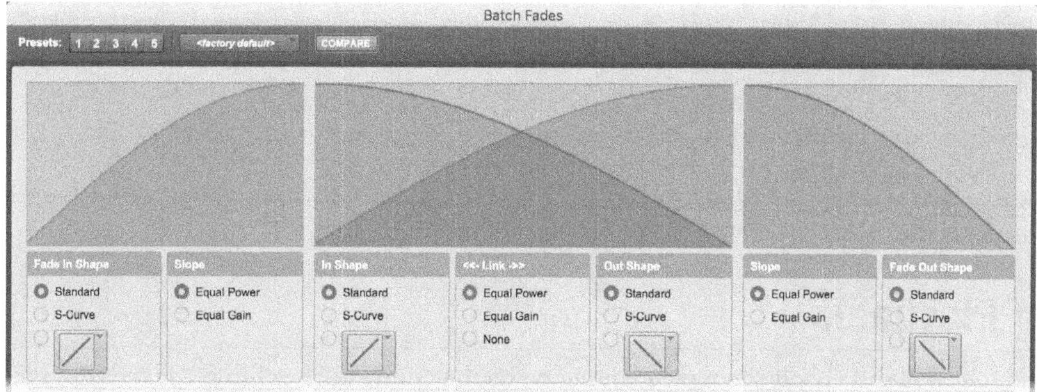

Figure 7.62 The Top Section of the Batch Fades Dialog Box

The bottom section of the *Batch Fades* dialog box is new, though, and covers aspects of the fade creation that applies specifically to this kind of workflow:

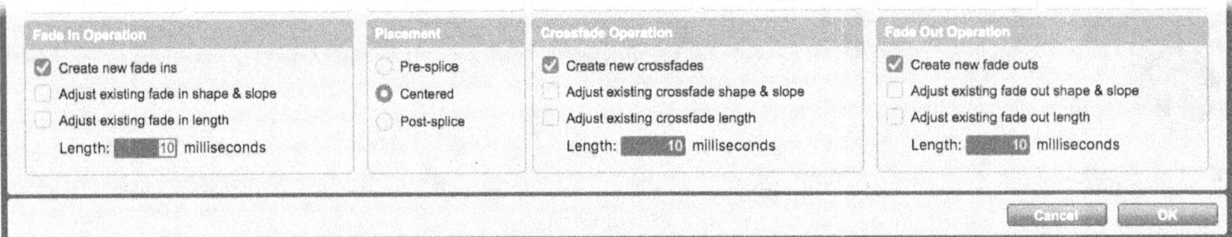

Figure 7.63 The Bottom Section of the Batch Fades Dialog Box

- The **Create New Fade Ins** (or **Fade Outs** or **Crossfades**) will allow you choose what batch fades will be created. For example, if you want to create new batch fade-ins and batch fade-outs, but *not* batch crossfades, you can uncheck the CREATE NEW CROSSFADES check box.
- Often, you'll have existing fades in your selected area—the question is whether you want your batch fades to change those existing fades or not. Clicking the **Adjust Existing Fade In** (or **Fade Out** or **Crossfade**) **Shape & Slope** will change the shape of any existing fades within your selected area.
- Again, relating to any existing fade, clicking the **Adjust Existing Fade In** (or **Fade Out** or **Crossfade**) **Length** will change the duration of any existing fades within your selected area.

If you want your existing fades to remain completely unchanged, uncheck *both* the *Adjust Existing Fade In* (or *Fade Out* or *Crossfade*) *Shape & Slope and* the *Adjust Existing Fade In* (or *Fade Out* or *Crossfade*) *Length* check boxes. For example, Figure 7.64 shows the correct settings for all pre-existing fade-outs to remain unchanged.

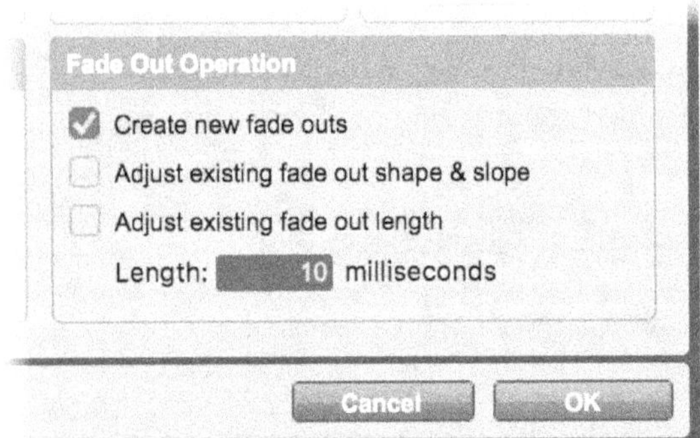

Figure 7.64 The Settings You Need to Make Sure No Existing Fade-Outs will be Changed

Controlling Playback

Using shortcuts and tools will certainly increase your editing power, but you'll still need to get *to* the clips that you want to change. Here are some ways to navigate your project more efficiently.

Scrolling Options

Your *scrolling* will determine how your Edit window will react as your playback cursor moves along the timeline during playback:

1. From the OPTIONS menu, go to the EDIT WINDOW SCROLLING menu item. The Edit Window Scrolling submenu will appear.

Figure 7.65 The Options>Edit Window Scrolling Submenu

2. In the Edit Window Scrolling submenu, you have four choices (the currently active mode is indicated by a checkmark):

   - **No Scrolling:** The time you see in the Edit window will not change in response to the playback of your Project. As your Project plays, your playback cursor will move out of your Edit window when it reaches the rightmost side of the Edit Window. When playback is stopped, the view of your Project's timeline will not change.

   - **After Playback:** This mode works much the same as *No Scrolling*, with the playback cursor moving off the Edit window once it reaches the rightmost side. The difference is that when playback stops, the view of your Project's timeline will jump to the point where playback was stopped.

   - **Page:** When this scrolling option is selected, the playback cursor will move from left to right in the Edit window, just as with the first two scrolling modes. When the cursor reaches the rightmost side, though, the timeline being shown will shift later, with the playback cursor continuing from leftmost side of the Edit window until it again reaches the right side, when the timeline will again shift.

   - **Continuous:** This mode looks and acts a bit differently than the rest. When this scrolling option is selected, the playback cursor will *not* move—your timeline *will*. The playback cursor will be anchored to the center of Edit window, with the timeline smoothly scrolling beneath it. Although this mode uses a bit more CPU than the other modes, *Continuous* scrolling will show you what's coming next on your timeline, which is a very convenient way to work in some situations.

Take note when using Continuous scrolling: When you're starting playback from the beginning of your Project's timeline (since the playback cursor is in the middle of the Edit window), you'll see a grey area prior to the start of the Project, as shown in Figure 7.66. It's neither a bug nor should it cause any concern: Once you start playback, you'll see your clips start scrolling as your playback cursor remains stationary.

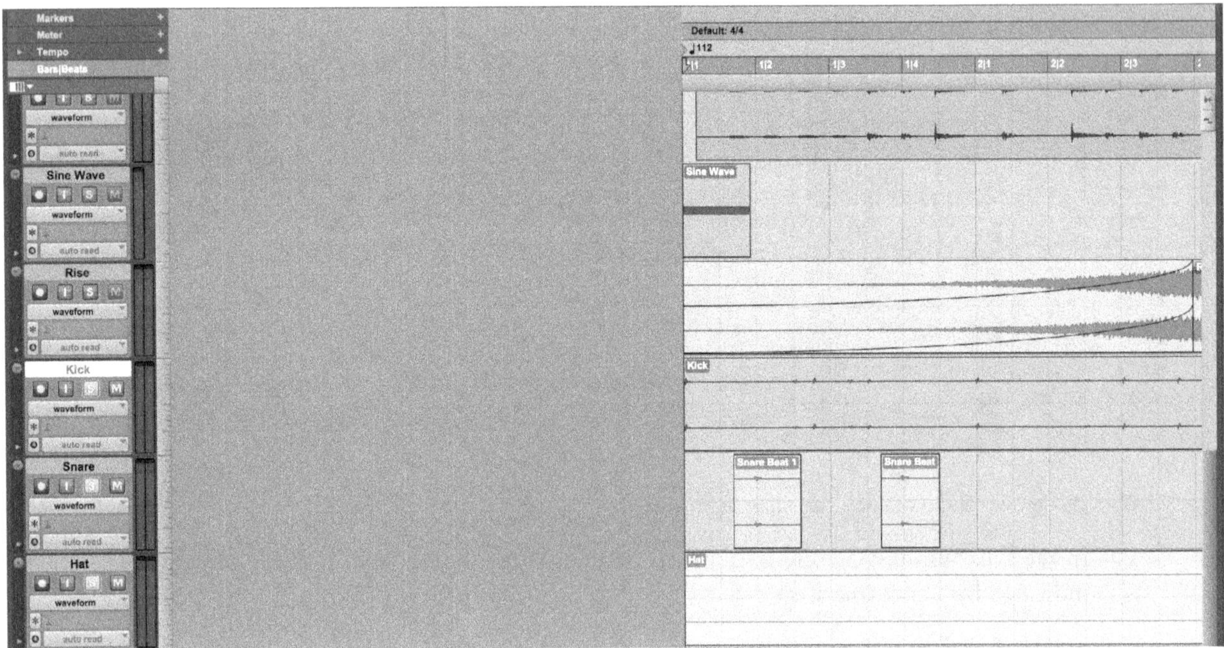

Figure 7.66 Playing from the Start of Your Project with Continuous Scrolling Selected

Insertion Follows Playback

Consider this scenario: You selected a nice, loopable selection. You wisely put yourself into Loop Playback mode to hear your selection in the proper context. Sounds great, doesn't it? Then you click on the STOP button, and the selection goes away! Is this a bug within Pro Tools? Nope—it's the effect of a mode of operation called *Insertion Follows Playback*, which you can set in the software in several ways. You want to enable or disable this mode to fit your circumstance, but it's important to understand how it works first, so you'll know when to use it.

First, let's cover the different ways to activate or deactivate *Insertion Follows Playback*:

1. Press the N key.

OR

1. Click the INSERTION FOLLOWS PLAYBACK button. When enabled, the button will be blue, as shown in Figure 7.67.

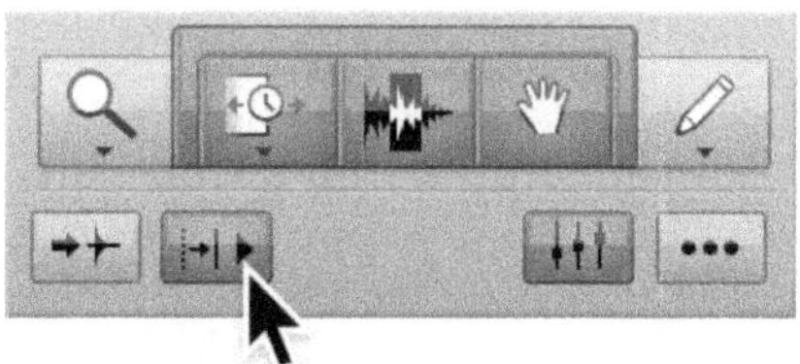

Figure 7.67 Insertion Follows Playback (Enabled)

OR

1. Click on the OPTIONS menu.
2. Choose INSERTION FOLLOWS PLAYBACK. When enabled, there will be a checkmark next to the menu item.

Here's how your Pro Tools Project will behave, depending upon whether Insertion Follows Playback is on or off:

- **ON:** Playback will begin wherever the timeline insertion is set. When playback is stopped, the timeline insertion will stay at the point where playback ended. When you start again, playback will pick up where you left off. If you have a selected area in your timeline, that selection will be lost when you click on the STOP button.
- **OFF:** Playback will begin wherever the timeline insertion is set. When playback stops in this mode, the timeline insertion jumps back to where it was originally set. When you start playback again, it will start from this original position. If you have a selected area in your timeline, that selection will be maintained when you click on the Stop button, making this the ideal mode for editing loopable selections.

When it comes to *Insertion Follows Playback*, there's no right or wrong setting. It really depends on what you're doing at the moment, and choosing the setting that will let you work faster!

Using the Tab Key

The TAB key is not only a great way to navigate your Project, but also a great editing tool!

The Tab key can be set up to operate in one of two different modes: standard and *Tab to Transients*.

Basic Tabbing

We'll look at the most basic mode first, so we need to make sure that the Tab to Transients mode is *disabled*:

1. Press COMMAND+OPTION+TAB (Mac) or CTRL+ALT+TAB (Windows) to toggle the *Tab to Transients* feature on and off.

OR

1. Immediately below the Zoomer tool in the Edit tools section, you'll find the TAB TO TRANSIENTS button. When enabled, this button is colored blue. Because you want this mode to be disabled for now, make sure the TAB TO TRANSIENTS button is toggled off and is shown in a basic grey color.

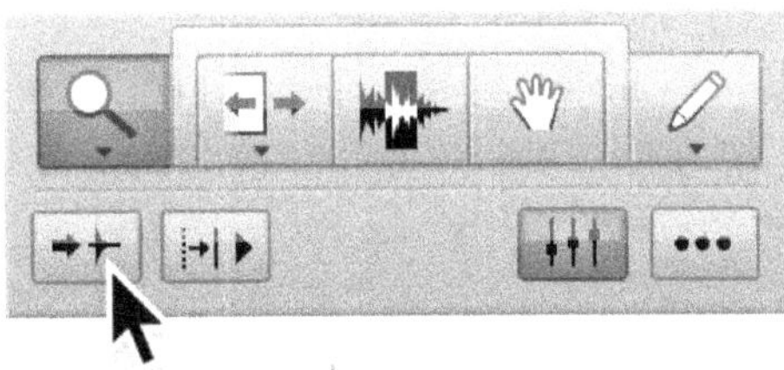

Figure 7.68 Tab To Transients (Disabled)

OR

1. Click on the OPTIONS menu.
2. In the OPTIONS menu, you'll find TAB TO TRANSIENT. When enabled, there will be a checkmark next to the menu item. Since you want to disable this mode for now, make sure that there's no checkmark by that menu item (if there is, just click TAB TO TRANSIENT to remove the checkmark and disable the feature).

Now that Tab to Transient has been disabled, let's see how the TAB key behaves normally.

1. Using the Selector tool, click on a track with several clips, before a given clip. The timeline insertion will appear wherever you click.

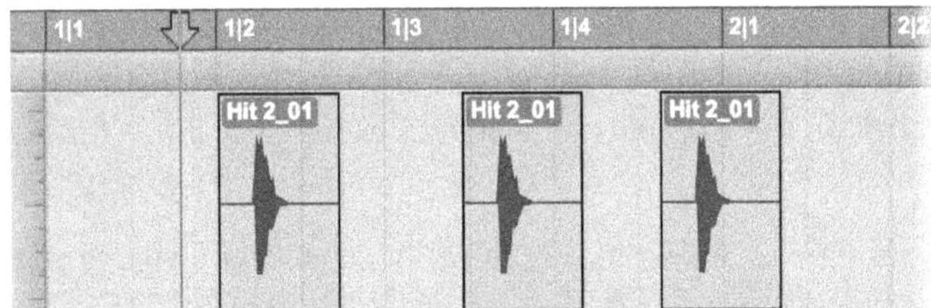

Figure 7.69 The Playback Cursor Positioned Before a Clip

2. Press the TAB key. The timeline insertion will move to the next clip boundary (in this case, the start of a clip). Each time you press the Tab key, the timeline insertion will move accordingly to the next clip boundary (moving from left to right).

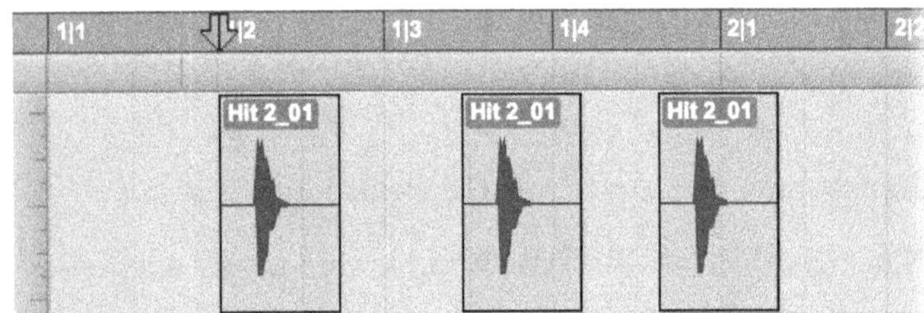

Figure 7.70 After Pressing the TAB key Once

Here's a twist on using the TAB key: Hold the OPTION key (Mac) or CTRL key (Windows) while you press the Tab key to move the timeline insertion to the previous clip boundary (moving right to left).

Tab to Transients

With Tab to Transients enabled, the Tab key will continue to jump to clip boundaries, but it will also stop at each transient.

The first step in the process is to turn *Tab to Transients* on:

- The TAB TO TRANSIENTS button will let you know if it's enabled or disabled. When enabled, this button will be colored blue. If the button is disabled (the color will be a basic grey), just click on the Tab to Transients button to turn it on.

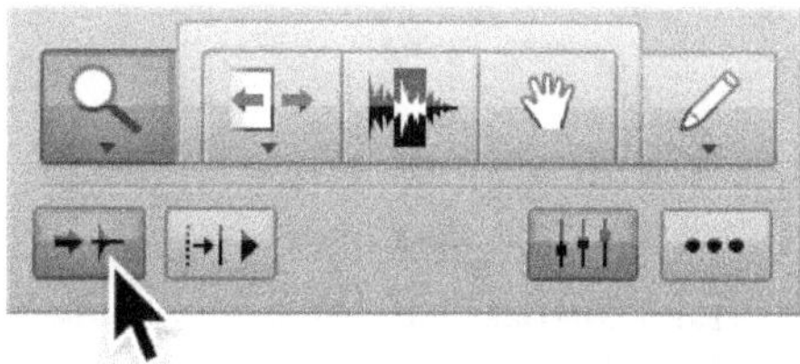

Figure 7.71 Tab to Transients Button (Enabled)

- You can also check Tab to Transient's status in the OPTIONS menu. When active, there will be a checkmark next to the TAB TO TRANSIENT menu item. Just click TAB TO TRANSIENT to activate or deactivate the feature.

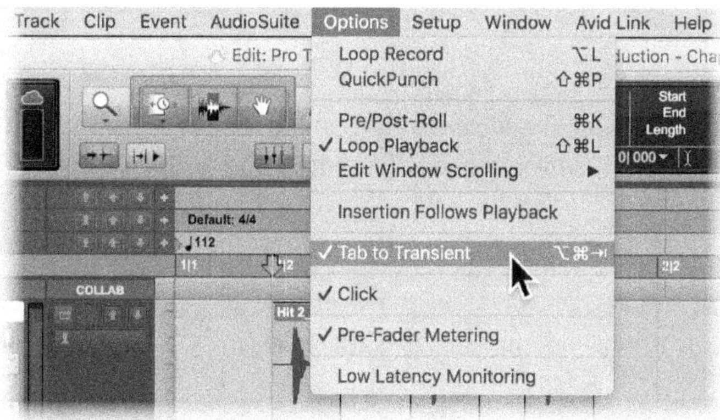

Figure 7.72 Options>Tab to Transient (Enabled)

Here's how the TAB key behaves with *Tab to Transients* enabled:

1. Using the Selector tool, click on a track with several clips, before a given clip. The timeline insertion will appear wherever you click.

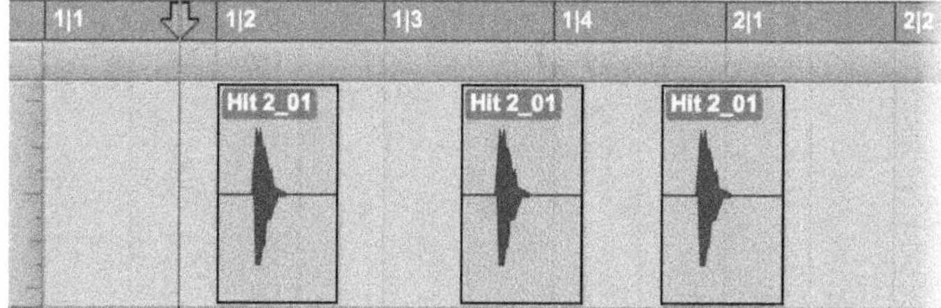

Figure 7.73 The Playback Cursor Positioned Before a Clip

2. Press the TAB key. The timeline insertion will immediately jump to the start of the clip. Regardless of whether Tab to Transients is enabled or disabled, the Tab key can always be used to quickly move to clip boundaries (start or end).

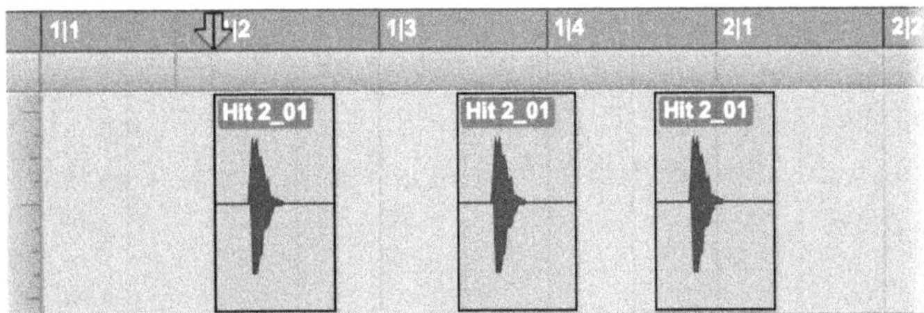

Figure 7.74 After Pressing the TAB key Once

3. Press the Tab key again. This time, instead of moving directly to the next clip boundary (as would be the case if *Tab to Transients* was not active), the timeline insertion will jump from transient to transient. This is a fantastic way to locate drum hits and other transient-based audio.

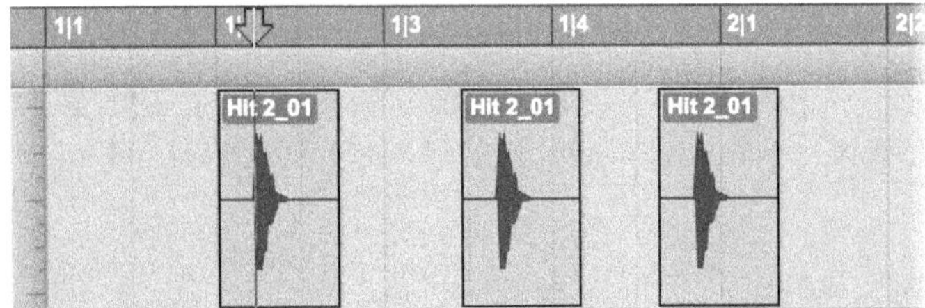

Figure 7.75 After Pressing the TAB key Twice

Here again, holding the **OPTION** key (Mac) or **CTRL** key (Windows) while you press the Tab key will move the timeline insertion to the previous transient (moving right to left).

You can use the Tab key to navigate on MIDI-based tracks (MIDI or Instrument) as well. When *Tab to Transients* is inactive, the **TAB** key will work just the same as with audio clips. However, when *Tab to Transients* is enabled, the tab key will also move from note to note.

Making Selections While Tabbing

If you want to make a selection while moving with the TAB key (with *Tab to Transients* on *or* off), just hold down the SHIFT key as you tab. This is a quick and effective way to select clips (or the space between clips), and with *Tab to Transients* on, is also a great way of chopping up drum tracks into loopable segments. Let's take a look at that workflow:

1. If *Tab to Transients* isn't already enabled, click on the TAB TO TRANSIENTS button. When enabled, it will be colored blue.

2. Use the Selector tool to set a timeline insertion a little before the transient at which you want to start your selection.

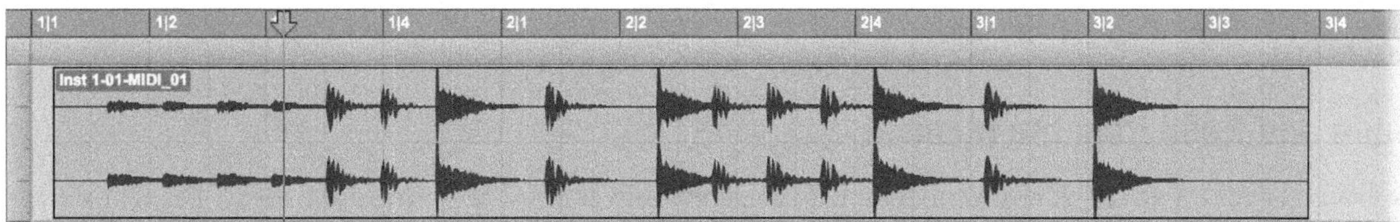

Figure 7.76 The Playback Cursor Positioned Before a Transient

3. Press the TAB key once. The timeline insertion will jump to the next transient (where you want to begin your selection).

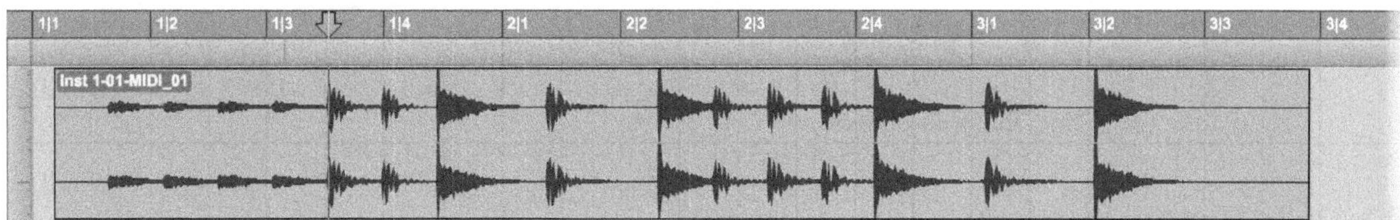

Figure 7.77 After Pressing the TAB key Once

4. Press and hold the SHIFT key and press the TAB key. As you've seen before, the timeline insertion will jump from transient to transient each time you press the TAB key, but the addition of the SHIFT key will cause a selection to be made in the process.

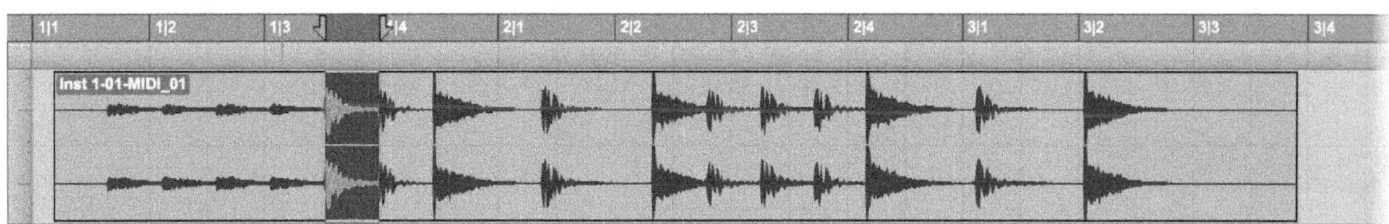

Figure 7.78 After Pressing SHIFT+TAB Once

5. When you reach the end of your desired selection, stop pressing the Tab key. Now you've made a selection based on Pro Tools' analysis of the transients, which can help you find the right start and end points quickly and accurately!

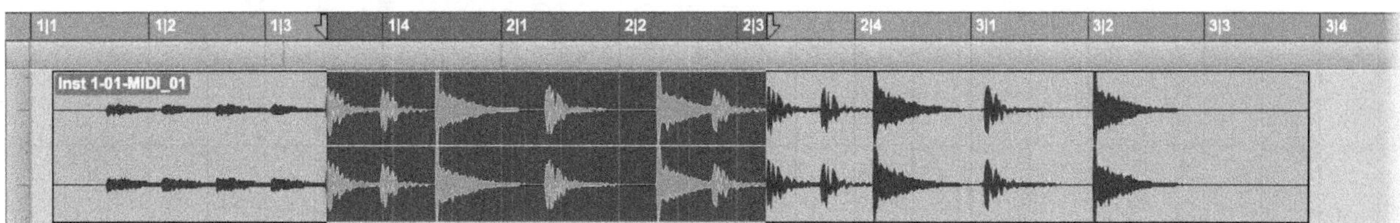

Figure 7.79 The Selected Measure of Drums

When You Make Mistakes . . .

When you edit, you will, from time to time, make a mistake or do something that you want to undo. Pro Tools gives you a number of ways to do this:

Undo and Redo from the Menu

Probably the most traditional way to undo or redo an action is to access it from the EDIT menu, like many other programs:

- To undo the last thing you've done, go to the EDIT menu and choose UNDO (at the top of the Edit menu). The Undo menu item will let you know which operation is most recent. If you recently nudged a clip, it'll read UNDO CLIP NUDGE.
- If you've undone something, and want to redo it, just go to the EDIT menu and choose REDO (right under the Undo menu item). Just like the Undo menu item, the Redo menu item will include the action that will be redone.

The Undo History Window

Using Undo or Redo from the Edit menu is great for undoing (or redoing) one thing at a time, but audio production is a progressive process, and you'll often need to undo a sequence of edits. For those situations, the Undo History window comes in handy.

1. Click on the WINDOW menu.
2. Choose UNDO HISTORY. The *Undo History* window will appear.

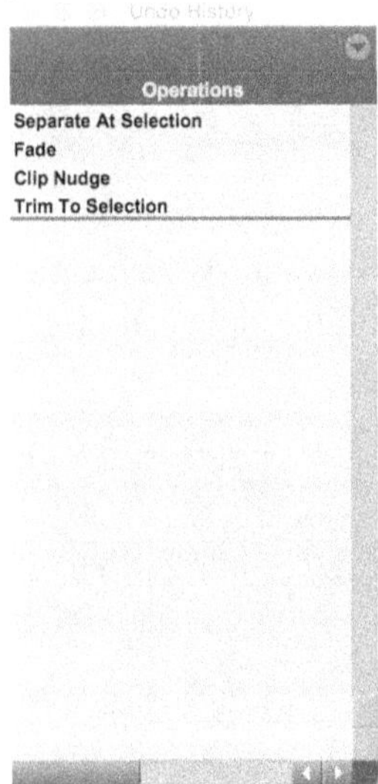

Figure 7.80 The Undo History Window

The Undo History window lists the actions you've taken in the order they were done, with the most recent change at the bottom of the list. For example, in Figure 7.80, I first separated a clip, then created a fade, nudged a clip, and finally trimmed a clip to a selected area.

You can easily undo multiple edits at once by clicking on the list item just below the last edit that you want to keep. For example, if I click on CLIP NUDGE as shown in Figure 7.81, the clip nudge and all edits after that will be undone.

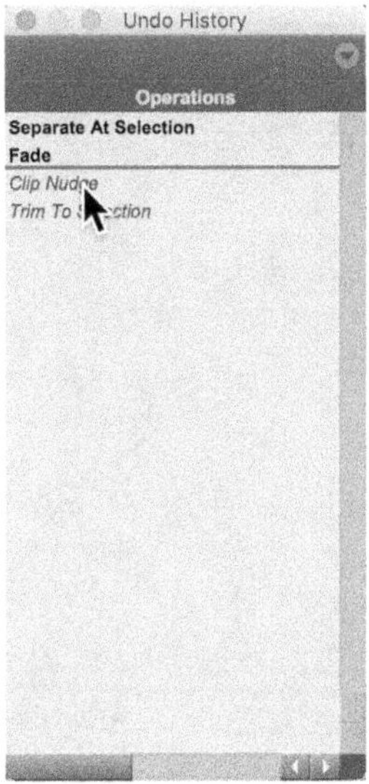

Figure 7.81 Undoing Multiple Operations

You can also redo multiple changes with a single click: Just click the last undone change that you want to keep. As shown in Figure 7.82, I clicked on TRIM TO SELECTION, which redoes all changes up to and including the one that I clicked.

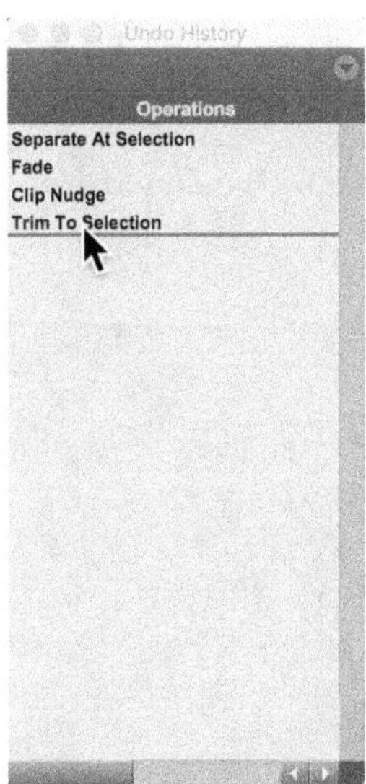

Figure 7.82 Redoing Multple Operations

Levels of Undo

It's worth noting that the list of actions that can be undone or redone in Pro Tools is not infinite. The maximum number of changes that can be undone is 64. You will know you've reached the limit when you see the top item in the Undo History window colored red. In Figure 7.83, since I had nudged a clip so many times, the first thing I had done (a clip separation) dropped off of my Undo Queue, and the oldest edit that I can undo now is a fade.

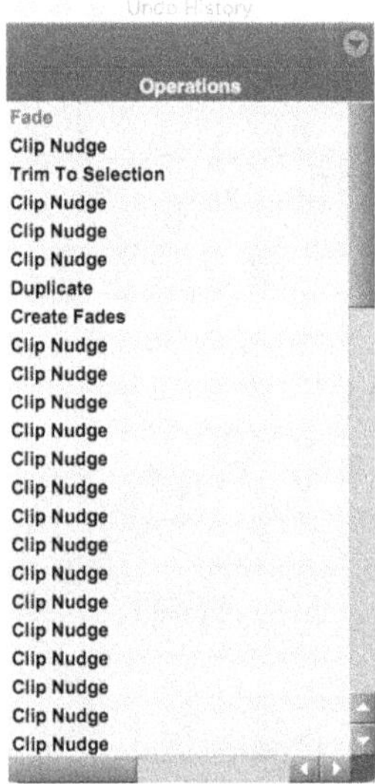

Figure 7.83 Hitting the Maximum Undo Limit

Things that Cannot be Undone

In all levels of Pro Tools, from Pro Tools | First all the way up to Pro Tools | Ultimate, there are a few things that cannot be undone. Moreover, these things that cannot be undone will also clear your undo history, so take care!

In the case of Pro Tools | First, there is only one action you'll likely do that will potentially cause this kind of problem: deleting a track. Here's a sequence of events to illustrate the point:

1. I've opened a project with a few tracks and clips. You'll see from the Undo History window that I haven't done any edits so far.

Figure 7.84 Before Editing

2. I'll make a few changes on a few different tracks. Note that as I make changes, they are listed in the Undo History window as the *Undo Queue*.

Figure 7.85 After Editing

3. Next, I'll delete a track. This can be any kind of track, even a track with no clips. In this case, I'll delete the *Vocals* track.

Figure 7.86 Deleting the Vocal Track

4. You will see now that the deleted track is gone, and my Undo Queue has been cleared (indicated by the blank Undo History window). This means that not only is the deletion of the track not undo-able, but nothing that I've done before deleting this track can be undone!

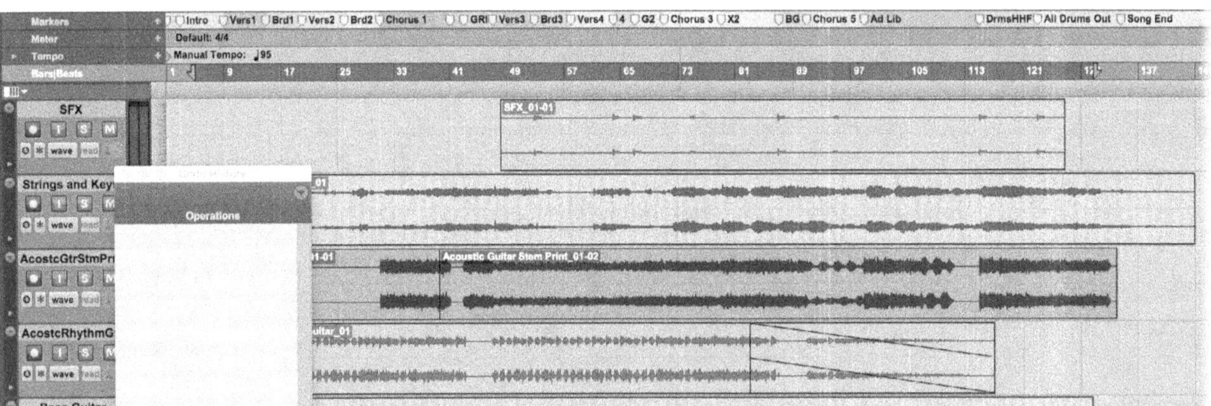

Figure 7.87 The Undo Queue Cleared!

Revert to Saved

Sometimes, your editing can go wrong to the point that it's just quicker to close the Project, reopen it, and start again. Here's a quick way to do it:

1. Click on the FILE menu.

2. Choose REVERT TO SAVED. A confirmation dialog box will appear.

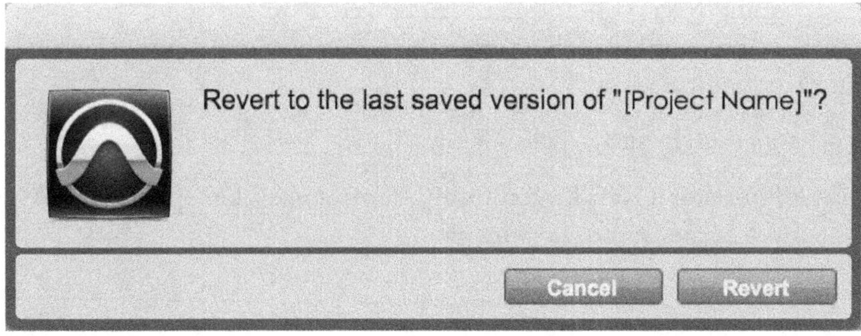

Figure 7.88 The Revert To Saved Dialog Box

3. Click the REVERT button. Your Project will close and reopen in its last saved state.

Restore Last Selection

Let's say that you've made the *perfect* selection, but you inadvertently clicked elsewhere on your timeline and lost it. Using EDIT>UNDO won't bring it back, but there's another way to recover it.

1. Click on the EDIT menu.
2. Choose RESTORE LAST SELECTION. Your previous selected point or area will be restored.

The shortcut for *Restore Last Selection* is OPTION+COMMAND+Z (Mac) or ALT+CTRL+Z (Windows).

By virtue of the way that it functions, the *Restore Last Selection* feature is a great way to toggle between two selected areas. If you select one area, and then another, repeatedly restoring last selections will effectively toggle between the two selections. If you want to compare two sections of your Project, this is a great way to do it!

Collaboration

You've learned how to create a Project, import audio, record, edit, and work with MIDI. You've really come a long way in a short time. Now you might be thinking about working with other Pro Tools users collaboratively and making the most of different artistic input.

There are different ways people work collaboratively, like sharing Projects through file-sharing platforms like Dropbox or rendering individual tracks and sending them as audio files to collaborators. They all work fine up to a point, but they have limitations, especially when you're working with several collaborators. Many people working on different Project files can be a logistical nightmare. Let's look at Pro Tools' built-in *Collaboration Tools* and see how you can use them to share your work with others, without ever having to leave your Project!

Creating a Collaborative Project

Up to this point, we've been working with local Projects that have not been backed up to the cloud. That means all the media that your Project uses is on your computer's hard drive only. This is fine if you're working alone, but for collaborative work, your Project must be cloud-based.

There are two ways you can create a Project that can be shared collaboratively:

1. **If you're creating a new blank Project or a New Project from a Template**, click the BACKUP TO CLOUD check box at the bottom of the Dashboard window.

Figure 7.89 Creating a Cloud-Based Project from the Dashboard Window

2. **If you're creating a Project from a Session**, click the COLLABORATION AND CLOUD BACKUP radio button.

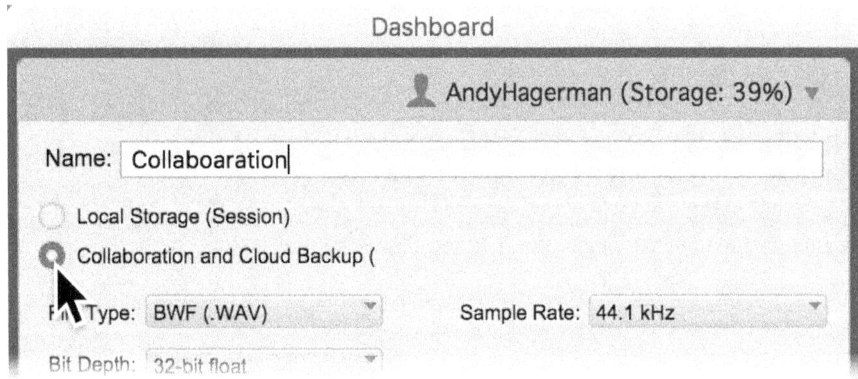

Figure 7.90 Creating a Collaboaration and Cloud Backup Project from a Session

If you've done it right, you'll see the *Global Track Collaboration tools* in their active state, as shown in Figure 7.91:

Figure 7.91 Active Collaboration Tools

Adding Collaborators

Before you can make the most of Pro Tools' Collaboration tools, you'll need to have someone to collaborate *with*. The place to start is the *Artist Chat* window.

You can show the Artist Chat window in a few different ways.

1. Click the SHOW ARTIST CHAT button in the Global Track Collaboration tools section of the Edit window.

Figure 7.92 The Show Artist Chat Button

OR

1. Press COMMAND+SHIFT+= (Mac) or CTRL+SHIFT+= (Windows)

OR

1. Click on the WINDOW menu.
2. Choose ARTIST CHAT.

The *Artist Chat* window enables you to add contacts, share projects, and of course, chat with your contacts. Let's start by using it to add a contact:

3. Click the CONTACTS category in the upper left-hand side of the Artist Chat window. In this view, you'll see two tabs: *My Contacts* and *Add Contacts*. The *My Contacts* tab (shown in Figure 7.93) will show you a list of all your current contacts: people you can currently chat with and you could invite to collaborate on a Project.

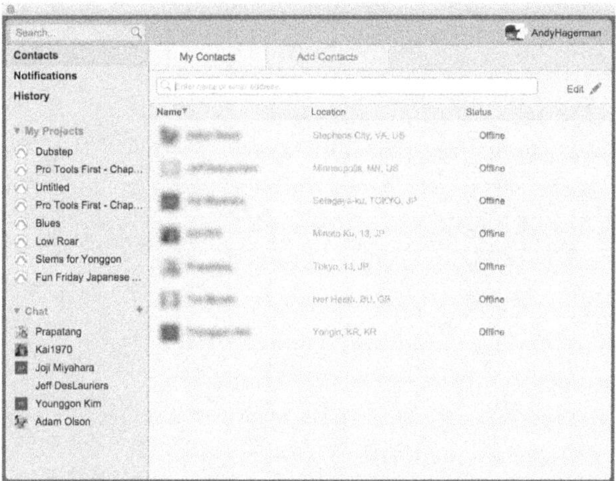

Figure 7.93 The Artist Chat Window

4. If the person you want to collaborate with isn't listed in the *My Contacts* tab (and if you're just starting out, that tab will be empty), you'll need to add them. Click the ADD CONTACTS tab.

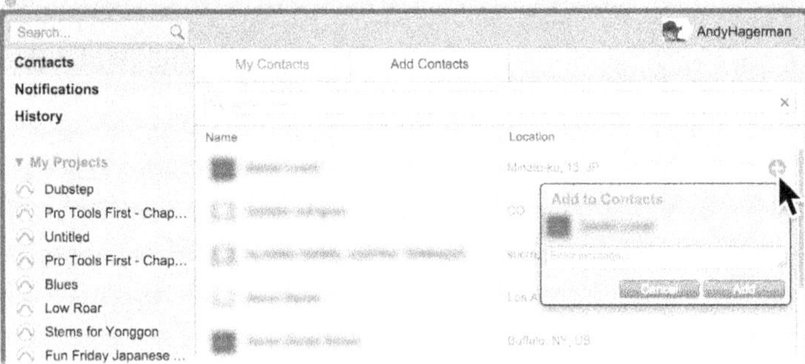

Figure 7.94 Adding a Contact

5. In the SEARCH field, type a name or email address that you want to search, then click the RETURN key (Mac) or ENTER key (Windows). The main part of the window will populate with results of your search.

6. Move your cursor to the search result that you want to add. At the right-hand side of the row you'll see an ADD (+) button appear.

7. Click the ADD button to open the ADD TO CONTACTS dialog box. You can type a message to be sent (optional), or just click the ADD button to send an invitation to the person.

Once the recipient of your invitation accepts, they will be added to your list of contacts, and from then on, you can chat with them and invite them to collaborate on Projects.

At the bottom left of the Artist Chat window is a list of your most recent chats, and a NEW CHAT (+) button immediately to the right of the word "Chat", which will let you start a new chat with any member(s) of your contacts list.

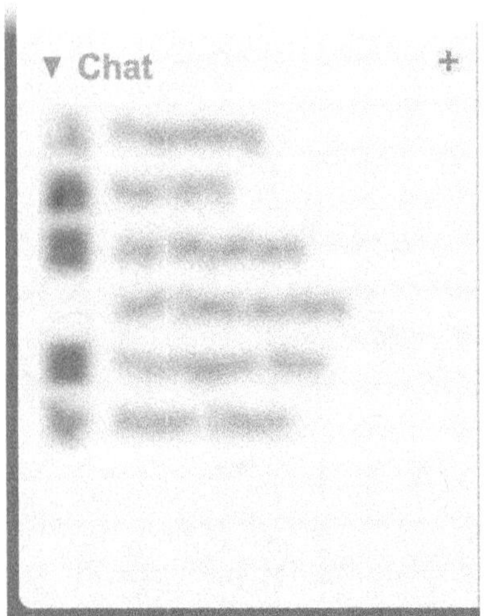

Figure 7.95 The Chat History List of the Artist Chat Window

Now that you've added the people you need to your *contacts*, you can invite them to collaborate on your cloud-based Projects. Here again, there are a couple of different ways that you can do it:

1. **If you want to invite a contact to collaborate on the currently open Project**, you can click the INVITE USER button in the Global Track Collaboration tools section of the Edit window (If you hover your cursor over the button, you'll see that it is described as *Invite another user to the project*).

Figure 7.96 The Invite User Button

OR

1. **You can invite a contact to collaborate with any cloud-based Project** by selecting it from the *My Projects* list in the Artist Chat window.

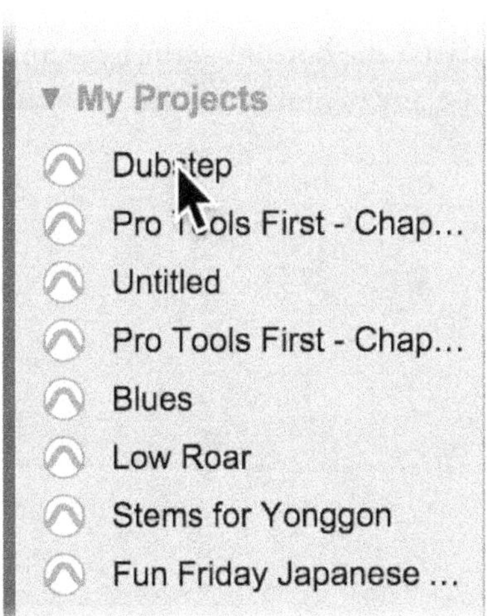

Figure 7.97 Selecting a Project in the Artist Chat Window

2. Click the INVITE CONTACTS TO COLLABORATE icon.

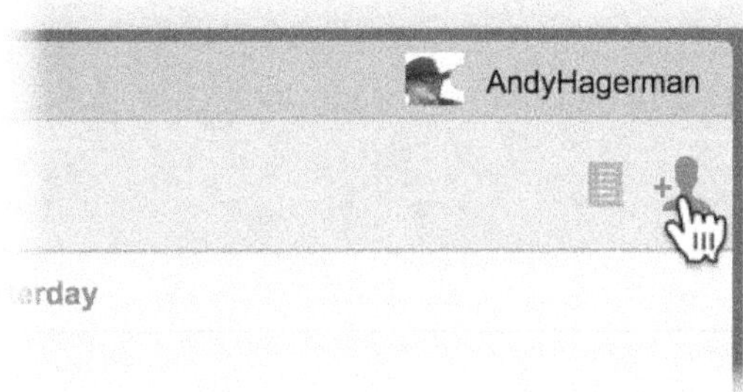

Figure 7.98 Adding a Collaborator to the Selected Project

Either method will open the *Invite Contacts to Collaborate* dialog box, as shown in Figure 7.99. The box will show you a list of all of your contacts, with a check box by each name. Just click the check box next to the name(s) of the contact(s) that you want to invite, type a message (optional), and click the ADD button. An invitation will be sent to your contact, inviting them to work with you on the Project.

On the recipient's side, they will receive your invitation in the *Notifications* section of the Artist Chat window. When there is a pending request, there will be a number by the *Notifications* category in the Artist Chat window.

In this example, I've been invited to work on a Project called "Punk Rock" by my friend, Prapatang. I'll just click the green checkmark button, and I've joined the Project.

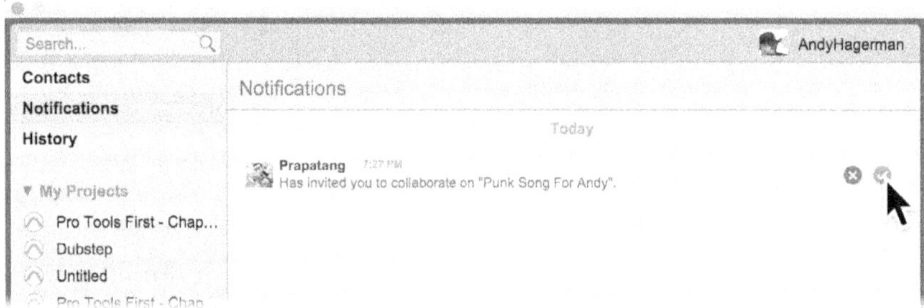

Figure 7.99 Accepting an Invitation to Collaborate in the Artist Chat Window

You can also join a Project from the Avid Link application. In the *Projects* category (at the bottom of the left-hand side of the window), you can see a list of all your Projects. At the top of the list are any invitations—just click the ACCEPT button to join the Project.

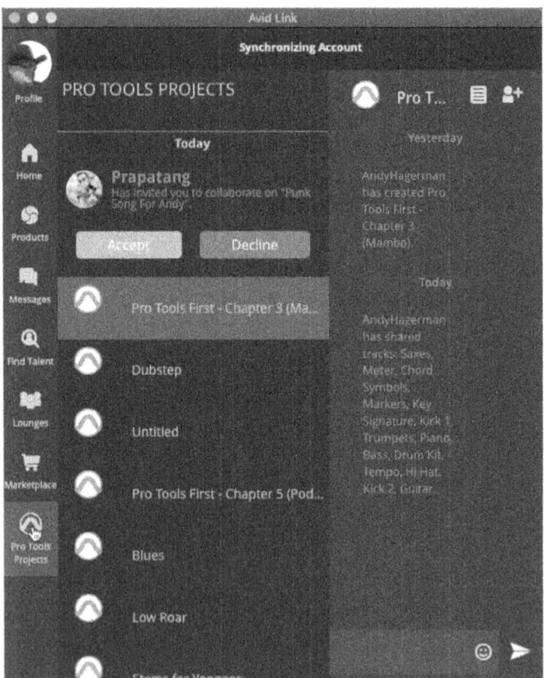

Figure 7.100 Accepting an Invitation to Collaborate in Avid Link

Collaboration Tools and Workflows

You can do different things with the Collaboration tools. The overarching theme of these is that you have a great degree of manual control if you want it, but you can also automate elements of your workflow if that works better for you.

Many of the workflows that we'll discuss here will involve not only the Global Track Collaboration tools in your Edit window's toolbar, but also the *Track Collaboration view* in the Edit or Mix window (the COLLAB column or row). Here's a general rule: The Collaboration tools at the top of the Edit window are global controls, and the buttons in the Track Collaboration view in the Edit or Mix window will allow you to make changes on a track-by-track basis.

Figure 7.101 The Edit Window Collaboration View

Although much of your collaborative work will be done from the Edit window, you'll also want to have some degree of access from the Mix window as well. The same track-specific collaborative tools that you have in the Edit window are mirrored in the Mix window, and they can be shown or hidden as you've learned in Chapter 2.

Figure 7.102 The Mix Window Collaboration View

Downloading Shared Tracks

If you've been invited to collaborate on a Project, it's quite common that the Project owner would share some tracks with you. This is indicated in a few ways:

- The *Download All Shared Tracks* button will be colored green, indicating that there are tracks that have been shared, but not downloaded.

Figure 7.103 The Download All Shared Tracks Button, Indicating that there are Tracks to be Downloaded

- In the Tracks List, you'll see small cloud icons to the left of a track's name, indicating that it has been shared with you, but not yet downloaded.

To download the shared track, click the DOWNLOAD ALL SHARED TRACKS button. All the currently shared tracks will be downloaded. If in the future, additional tracks are shared with you (which is quite likely in normal collaborative situations), the button will turn green again, indicating that there are new tracks that have been shared with you, but not downloaded.

Though collaboration in Pro Tools | First is similar to Pro Tools and Pro Tools | Ultimate in many ways, there is one significant difference: In Pro Tools and Pro Tools | Ultimate, not all tracks must be shared. For example, if I'm working on multiple drum tracks, I might not want to share all of them with all of my collaborators, choosing instead to mix them down to a single stereo track (commonly called a *stem*), just to make the workflow easier for everyone.

This selective track sharing is not available in Pro Tools | First. For simplicity's sake, all tracks in your Pro Tools | First Project are always shared.

Uploading Changes

During collaborative workflows, you'll make changes to tracks (those you share and those that are shared with you). Sometimes you'll want to share these changes; sometimes not. Still, no matter what your collaborative situation demands, Pro Tools can accommodate it.

Let's start by looking at a single track. Figure 7.104 shows the *Bass.01* track as it was shared with me.

Figure 7.104 The Shared Bass.01 Track

I think we need a fade-in at the beginning. Notice that as soon as I make any changes on the track, the upward-facing arrow button (called the *Upload Track Changes* button) in the COLLAB column turns green. This indicates that there are changes for this track that I could choose to share. You'll also see my name immediately under the Upload Track Changes button, indicating that I have taken ownership of the track.

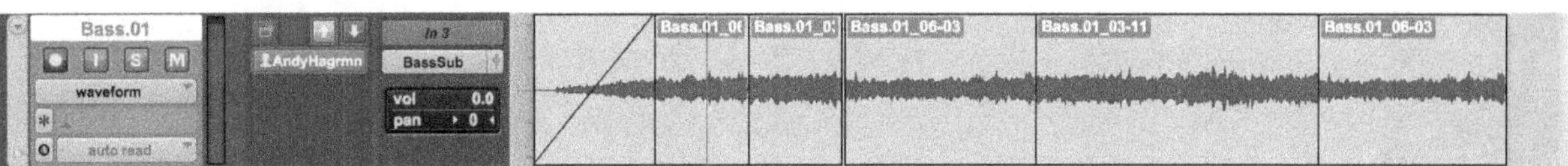

Figure 7.105 The Changed Bass.01 Track

You'll notice that at the same time, the *Upload All New Changes* button has turned green, indicating that there are changes in the Project that I could choose to share.

Figure 7.106 The Green Upload All New Changes Button, Indicating that there are Changes that May Be Uploaded

As you continue working on different tracks, you'll see the green Upload Track Changes arrows appear on all the tracks upon which you make changes. Figure 7.107, for example, indicates that I've made changes on the *GTR-Dis*, *GTR-Cln*, and *Bass.01.* tracks.

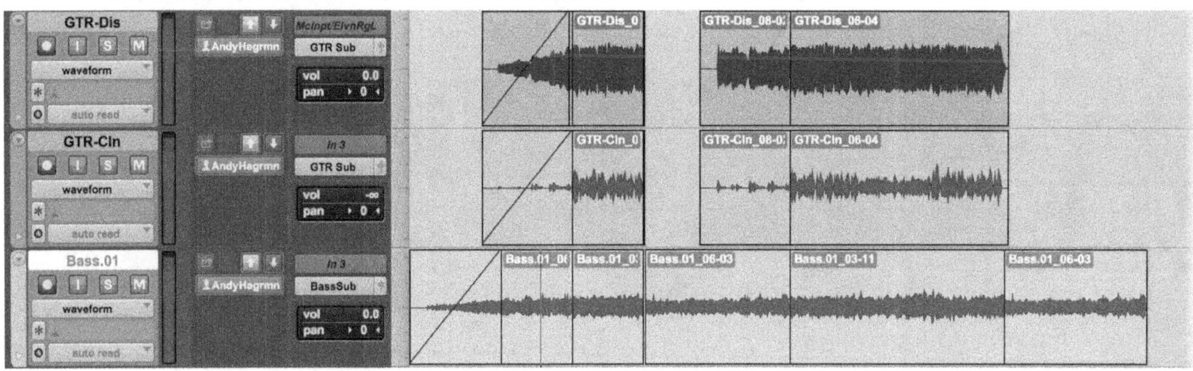

Figure 7.107 Shareable Changes Made on Multiple Tracks

There are a few ways that you can manage your changes collaboratively:

- **To upload changes on a track-by-track basis**, click the green UPLOAD TRACK CHANGES button.

Figure 7.108 Sharing Changes on a Track

- **To upload all changes in your Project**, click the UPLOAD ALL NEW CHANGES button.

Figure 7.109 Sharing All Changes in a Project

If you don't like the changes you've made on a track, one way to undo them is to right-click the green Upload Track Changes button, and choose ABANDON CHANGES from the menu that appears, as shown in Figure 7.110. You can also decide not to upload any of your changes by right-clicking the Upload All New Changes button and clicking ABANDON CHANGES.

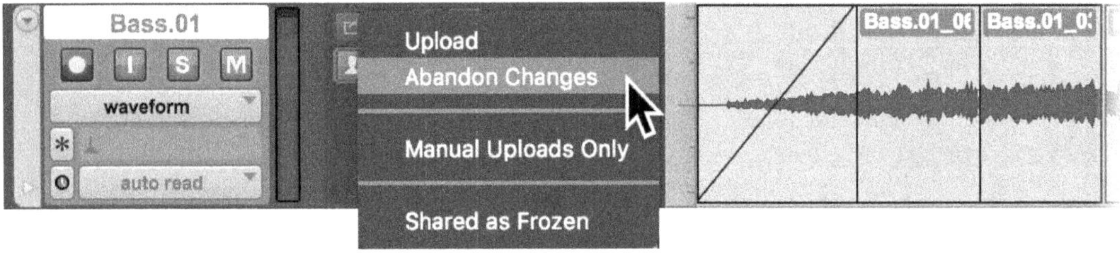

Figure 7.110 Abandoning Changes on a Track

Downloading Changes

Of course, while you make changes to some tracks, your collaborators would also be working on other tracks. They can also share their changes with you, and the workflow for downloading changes is essentially the mirror image of the workflow for uploading changes.

When a shared change is available for download on a track, you'll see it indicated in the COLLAB column with a green downward-facing arrow (called the *Download Track Changes*) button.

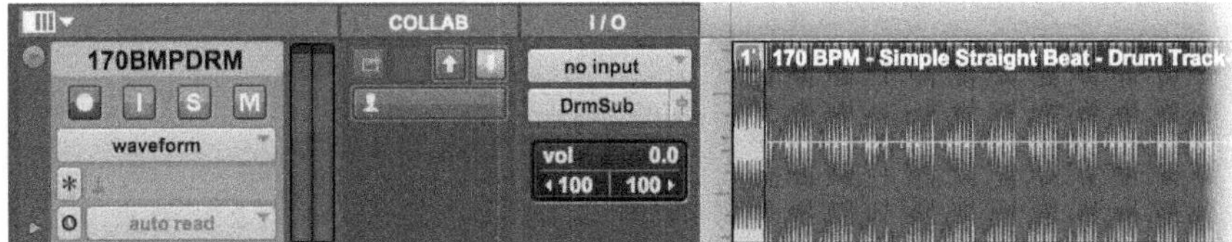

Figure 7.111 Changes available for Download on a Track

You'll also see that the DOWNLOAD ALL NEW CHANGES button has turned green, indicating that there are changes in your Project that you could accept and download.

Figure 7.112 The Green Download All New Changes Button, Indicating that there are Changes that May Be Downloaded

Just like uploading changes that you make, you have a number of options when downloading changes made by your collaborators:

- **To download changes on a track-by-track basis**, click the green DOWNLOAD TRACK CHANGES button.

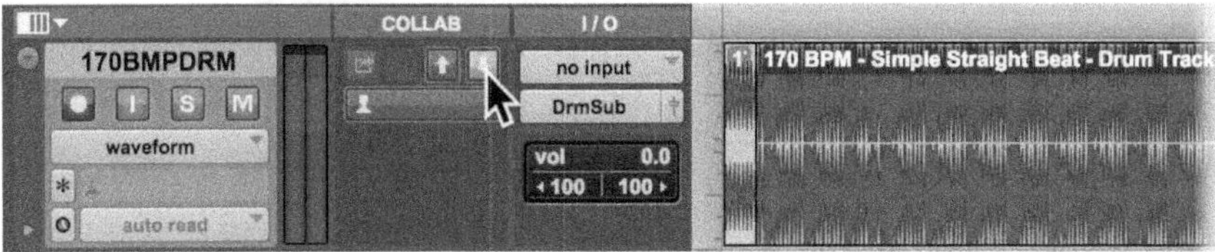

Figure 7.113 Downloading Changes on a Track

- **To download all changes in your Project**, click the DOWNLOAD ALL NEW CHANGES button.

Figure 7.114 Downloading All Changes in a Project

Hands-On Exercise 7.1: Mini-Gauntlet

Speed and accuracy are the measure of a great editor. The faster and more accurately you can get the job done, the better you are as an editor. Up to this chapter, the hands-on exercises in this book have dealt with some common workflow examples, albeit at a basic level. Since this chapter is about improving and refining the editing part of your work, that's what this exercise will address as well.

As mentioned, Avid has three levels of official certification: *User*, *Operator*, and *Expert*. The exams become more difficult as the levels increase, and the Expert exam is *tough*. At the Expert level, there's a hands-on test that we at Avid call "The Gauntlet," where the tester tells the student what to do, and the student must accomplish it (often limited to using shortcuts). If they don't get it done perfectly within 5 seconds, they lose points. Sufficeth to say, when you meet an Avid Certified Expert, you're meeting someone who really knows their stuff!

This hands-on exercise isn't a test, but it is a challenge: How fast can you get things done, and still do exactly what's being asked in each step? In this chapter, many topics that were covered showing different ways to get the job done. Go through this exercise trying out different methods, and try to improve your time!

Setting Up

1. Create a new Project by converting the *Pro Tools First - Fundamentals of Audio Production - Chapter 7 (Gauntlet).ptx* session to a local Project. The session is found in the *Pro Tools First - Fundamentals of Audio Production - Chapter 7 (Gauntlet)* subfolder of this book's downloaded exercise material. You've learned how to convert a session to a Project in Chapter 2. Choose any desired sample rate, 24-bit, and do not Backup to Cloud.

Selecting Tracks

2. Change the output of all tracks *at the same time* to an output that can be heard on your system.
3. Select *Track 1*, *Track 3*, and *Track 5* only.
4. Mute only the selected tracks *at the same time*.

TCE, Repeat, and Loop

5. Solo only the *TCE* and *Loop* tracks.
6. On the *TCE* track, stretch the clip at the beginning, so that it is exactly 1 measure.
7. Repeat or Duplicate the stretched clip on the *TCE* track 7 times, so that there is a total of 8 measures of drums on the track.
8. Loop the clip on the *Loop* track, so that there's a total of 8 measures of audio on that track.

When you're done, the two tracks should look like this:

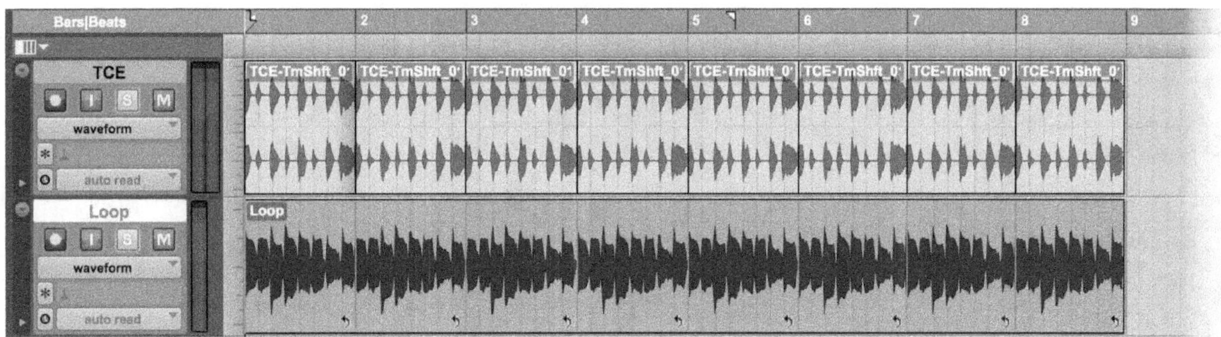

Figure 7.115 8 Measures of Drums

Trimming and Aligning

9. Solo only tracks *Hit 1* and *Hit 2*.
10. On the *Hit 1* track, trim the beginning of the clip, so that it begins exactly at the beginning of the clip's transient.
11. Align the beginning of the clip on the *Hit 2* track, so that it aligns with the beginning of the (newly trimmed) clip on the *Hit 1* track.

When you're done, your tracks should look like this:

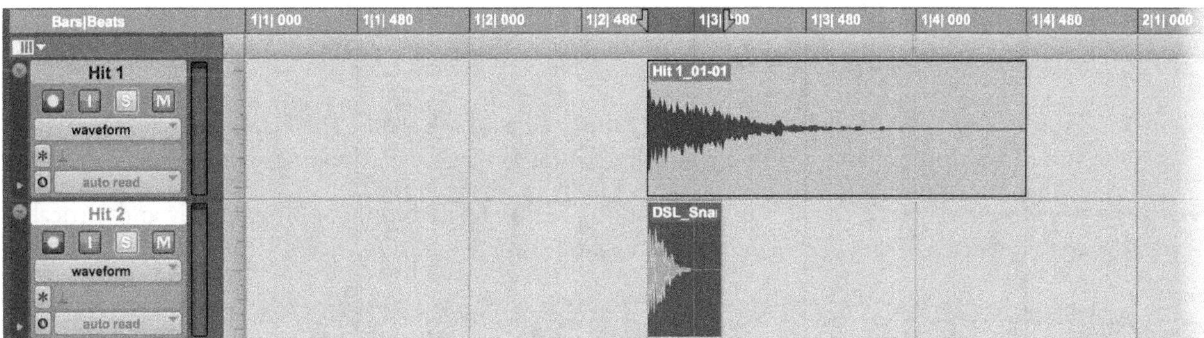

Figure 7.116 Aligned Clips

Next, let's trim a bar to just a measure of loopable drums:

12. Solo only the *Just 1 Bar* track.
13. Using Tab to Transients, select only one measure (Here's a hint: Each bar starts with two kick drum hits).
14. Trim your clip to the selection.

There are a number of ways to do this. Here's one way your track might look:

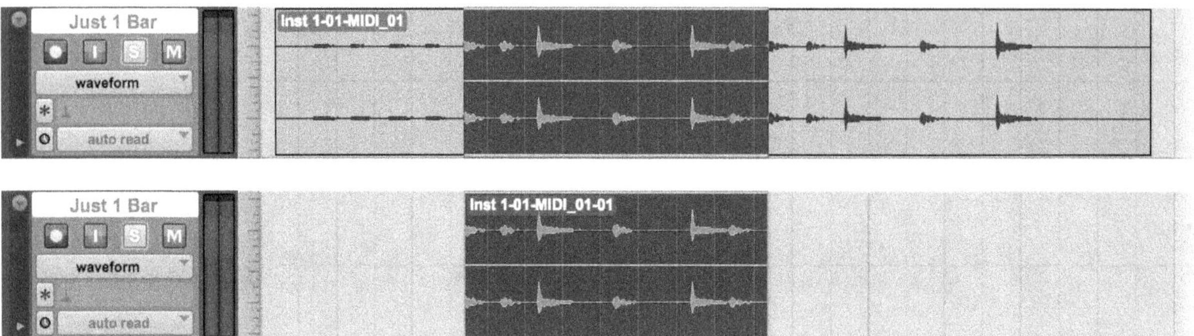

Figure 7.117 One Measure of Drums (Before and After)

15. To test your work, play the newly-trimmed clip with loop playback enabled. If it plays back smoothly and in tempo, you've done it right!

Separating Clips

Sine waves are notoriously unforgiving when it comes to editing. Your next step is to take a sine wave clip and trim it so that it loops perfectly.

16. Make sure that Loop Playback is enabled.
17. Make sure that Slip Mode is enabled
18. Solo only the *Sine Wave* track.
19. Select the *Sine Wave* clip.
20. Play the clip back. You'll hear a click every time the playback loops. This is because the clip's start and/or end isn't cut on the zero-crossing line with the waveform ascending.
21. Move your playback cursor near the beginning of the clip and zoom in (horizontally and vertically, so that you can clearly see the waveform, as shown in Figure 7.121).

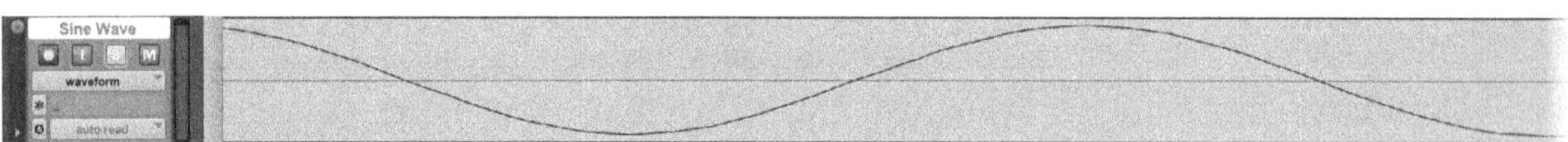

Figure 7.118 Zoomed In on a Sine Wave

22. Near the beginning of the clip, select a point at the zero-volt line with the waveform *ascending*.

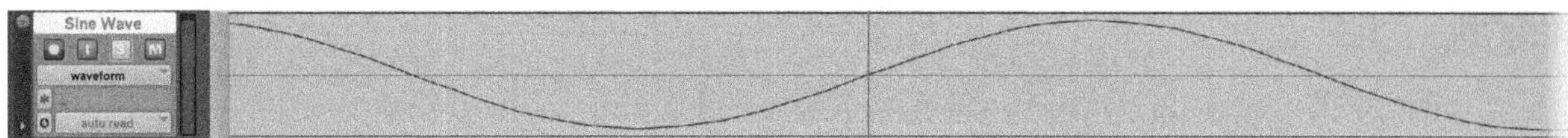

Figure 7.119 Selecting a Point to Trim To

23. Trim the start of the clip to the insertion point.

Figure 7.120 Trim Start to Insertion

24. Zoom out so that you can see the entire clip, and then move your cursor near the end of the clip.
25. Zoom in (horizontally and vertically), so that you can clearly see the waveform.
26. Select a point at the zero-volt line with the waveform ascending.
27. Trim the end of the clip to the insertion point.
28. Finally, it's time to check your work: Duplicate or repeat the *newly-trimmed* clip, so that there are a number of clips back-to-back-to-back. Play the block of repetitions. If you hear no clicks and the level meter is steady, you've done it!

Creating Fades

29. Solo only the *Rise* track.

If you play the clip on the *Rise* track, you'll hear that it starts out loud, and the audio cuts out abruptly. Let's sculpt this clip a bit with fades.

30. Using the Smart Tool, create a long fade-in, so that the volume increases as the pitch rises. The fade should end when the pitch stops rising (use the Smart Tool in Trim tool mode to adjust the end of the fade to get the timing right).
31. Still using the Smart Tool, create a fade-out that begins shortly after the pitch stops rising.
32. Change the curve shape of the fade-in to be a gentle exponential curve.
33. Change the shape of the fade-out to create a more drastic exponential shape.

Let your ears be your guide, but your final clip might look a bit like this:

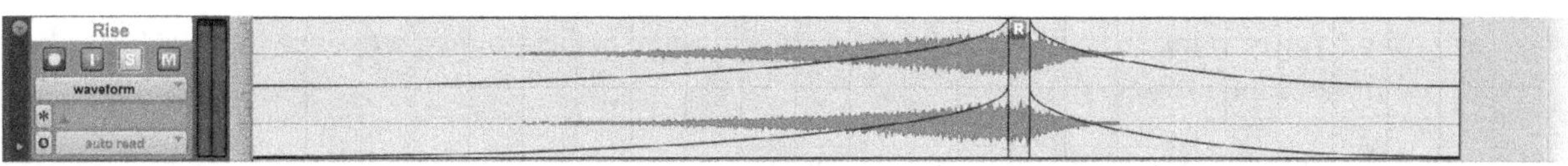

Figure 7.121 Fades on the Rise Sound Effect

Nudging

The last thing you'll need to do is nudge a snare drum part so that it sits in the groove.

When it comes to many styles of music, mathematically perfect timing isn't artistically correct. One example of this is found in some funk or R&B grooves, where the snare drum is played a bit late compared with perfect timing. Musicians often call this "laying back."

The last three tracks in your hands-on exercise are *Kick*, *Snare*, and *Hat* (hi-hat cymbal), and while you'll see that the kick and hi-hat are long, complete clips, the clips on the snare track represent only the first two hits (on bar 1, beats 2 and 4).

34. Solo only the *Kick*, *Snare*, and *Hat* tracks.
35. Change your Main Counter's Time Scale to Bars and Beats (Bars|Beats). This will change the available Nudge and Grid values.
36. Make sure that you're in Grid mode, and that your Grid value is a musical value (bar, quarter note, eighth note, and so on.)
37. On any of the three tracks, select exactly (and only) the first bar. Grid mode will help you do this.

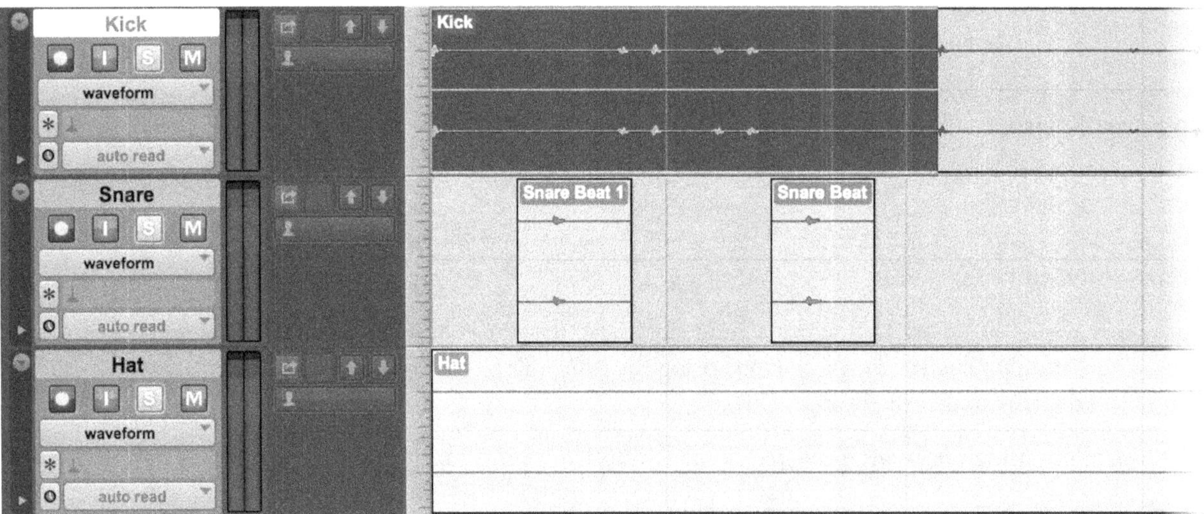

Figure 7.122 Selecting One Measure

38. Change your Main Counter's Time Scale to Minutes and Seconds (Min:Secs). This will change the available Nudge values.
39. Since you're going to be moving the snare clips in very small amounts, set your Nudge value to be 1 millisecond (1msec).
40. Make sure that you're in Loop Playback mode.
41. Play the tracks. You should hear only the first bar of only the *Kick*, *Snare*, and *Hat* tracks. Once you've confirmed this, stop playback.

Here's the problem: The snare is a bit too early, and the style of the music requires that it should lay back a bit. We're not talking about large differences in time here, though, so dragging these clips around with the Grabber tool isn't a great way to fix it.

The order of the steps here is important, so take a second to read these next steps before you take them:

42. Start Loop Playback.
43. *Without stopping playback*, select the two snare clips (selecting both because you'll be nudging both). The Grabber tool (or the Smart Tool in Grabber Tools mode) is a good way to do this. Note that making this new selection doesn't change playback *as long as you don't stop playback*.

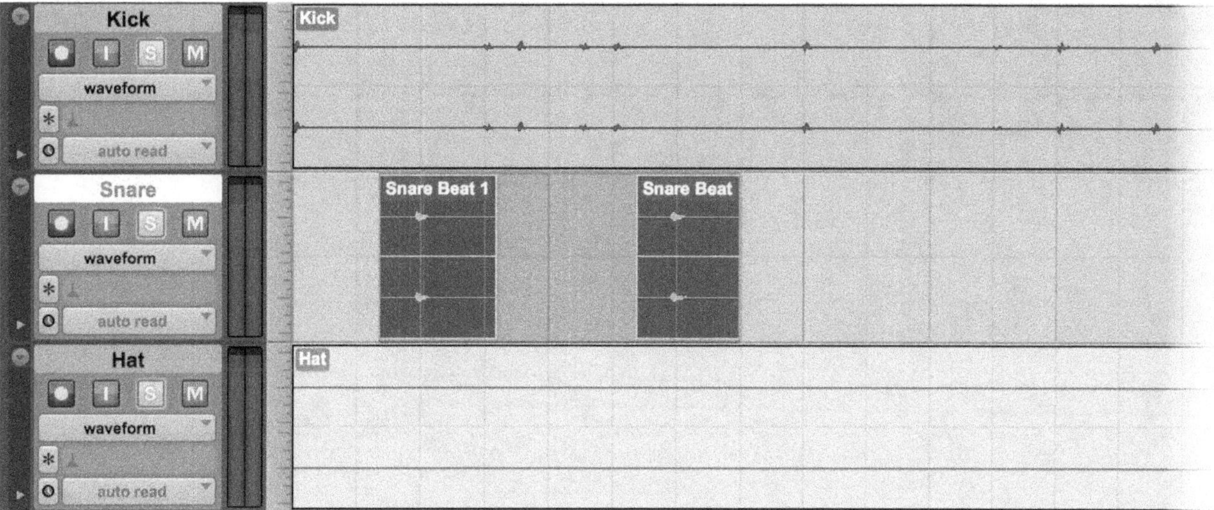

Figure 7.123 Selecting the Two Snare Hits

44. Start nudging the clips later in time, taking a moment to listen to the very subtle effect of the relationship of the timing of the snare hits to the rest of the drums. At some point, you'll have gone too far, and will notice that the snares are clearly laying back too much. At that point, start nudging the clips forward in time, until the groove sounds good to you.

Once you've got the snare hits where you want them, you'll need to repeat them to fill the rest of the drums. Here's one way to do it.

45. Change your Main Counter's Time Scale to Bars|Beats.
46. Make sure that your Grid value is set to a musical value (one bar works well here).
47. Make sure that you're in Grid Mode.
48. On the *Snare* track, select the first bar.
49. OPTIONAL: Consolidate the selection. While this isn't strictly necessary, it'll make the snare hits easier to move.
50. Repeat, Duplicate, or Loop the clip so that it covers the entire drum beat.

When you're done, your tracks should look something like this:

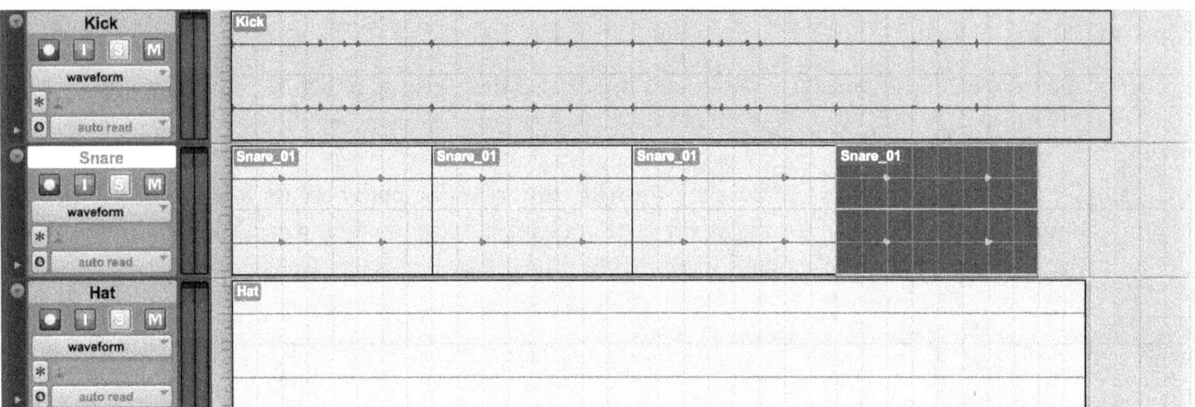

Figure 7.124 The Finished Drums

If it does, you're done—congratulations. As always, save your work before moving on!

Review Questions

1. What modifier key will enable you to change *all* tracks simultaneously? Which one will enable you to change all *selected* tracks?

2. What is the shortcut for *Duplicating* a clip? What's the shortcut for *Repeating*?

3. How can you quickly align the beginning of a clip to the playback cursor position?

4. What is the shortcut for *Consolidating* a selection?

5. What is the shortcut for trimming a clip to a selected area?

6. What are the shortcuts for nudging a clip?

7. How can a fade be created with the Smart Tool?

8. What is the difference between *equal power* and *equal gain* crossfading?

9. True or False? All changes made in Pro Tools can be undone by going to the EDIT menu and choosing UNDO.

10. What is the shortcut to *Restore Last Selection*?

CHAPTER 8

Getting Started with Mixing

Mixing—it's a *big* topic. It's big because it's generally at the end of the production process and represents the culmination of all the composition, recording, and editing. It's big because there are numerous schools of thought in mixing, including various techniques, tips, and tricks debated vigorously among professionals. It's also vast because it's *nuanced;* even the tiniest tweak can make or break a mix, and the process requires the careful execution of a series of small steps.

At its core, mixing is the combination of individual elements (such as vocal tracks, bass tracks, sound effects tracks, and so on) into a final product that can be heard by the audience. This goes beyond simply mashing tracks together—care must be taken to make sure that these elements work well collectively, sculpting individual sounds to create a harmonious whole. Within this definition is a multitude of details, and the art of mixing is a pursuit that takes massive dedication.

But don't be discouraged. Despite its rigorous demands, mixing is also a heck of a lot of fun, and one of the parts of production where your artistic vision can really shine. And even though mixing techniques and approaches may vary, its fundamental rules are consistent and simple enough for you to get started quickly.

Media Used: ***Pro Tools First—Fundamentals of Audio Production—Chapter 8 (Low Roar Tracks).ptx***

Duration: 45 minutes

GOALS

- **Understand mixing signal flow in Pro Tools**
- **Learn how to create a "static" mix**
- **Understand mix *automation***
- **Organize your mix with *subgroups***
- **Create a simple final mix**

What is Mixing?

At its most basic level, mixing is the combination of different simultaneous audio elements (different sounds heard at the same time) into a cohesive whole. There are a lot of ways that we can achieve that cohesion. Here are just a few:

- First, we manage the **levels** of different tracks with each other, so that they are appropriately loud in relation to each other, making choices on which sounds should be more prominent. For example, in a normal movie, the single most important element is the dialog. If any other sounds are so loud that what's being said can't be heard, the mixer needs to lower those other sounds, raise the dialog, or a bit of both.
- We also need to make sure that sounds can be clearly heard (even sounds that are relatively quiet in the mix). To do this, we'll use tools that will allow us to change the **timbre** of the sound. A classic example is a song that has kick drum and bass: Both instruments have strong frequency content in the same range and can obscure each other. Through tonal shaping tools like *equalization* (EQ), we can carve out frequencies in one or both of the tracks, allowing them to coexist in a way both musical parts can be clearly heard.
- Next, mixers will commonly add ambient effects like reverb and delay, to give a sense of **space** to the mix. This is especially important if the original recordings were made in sonically dead recording studios. Through careful use of ambient effects, you can create the illusion of depth to your mix.
- Some **styles** of music (and film) have trademark sounds, and many of these iconic sounds are part of the mixing process. For example, reggae music typically has more reverb and delay than would normally be found in a typical physical space, and the liberal use of those effects is completely appropriate in such cases. However, that treatment would be completely inappropriate for a string quartet playing a Bach chorale! It is important for mix engineers to thoroughly understand the stylistic requirements of the work to be done, and their mix choices should support the artists' vision.

Multitrack recording became popular in the '60s, and with that technology came the need to blend individual recorded tracks. In the early days, the idea of a dedicated mixing engineer wasn't yet common—typically, the same person who recorded the music would do the mixing as well. As mixing tools and effects evolved, though, mixing as a job in and of itself became more common. By the '80s, famous mix engineers like Dave Pensado, Chris Lord-Alge, and Bob Clearmountain started making names for themselves due to their iconic mixes.

Before the digital audio revolution, the mixing tools of the trade were large analog mixing consoles. Hardware effects modules (typically mounted in racks) were used for effects, like reverbs and delays. There were—and still are—pros and cons for using analog hardware for mixing, but it can't be ignored that the price of building even a modest mixing studio was out of reach for most people.

The advent of DAWs changed all that. Now, the power of yesterday's million-dollar facility is right there in your computer, and more! The mixing power in the modern DAW (and in particular Pro Tools, the industry's favorite) has allowed for professional work to be done entirely within the computer at a fraction of the cost of building a studio!

Which brings us to two different ways of approaching mixing: *outside the box* and *inside the box.*

When you hear people talking about mixing *outside the box*, they're referring to mixing outside of a computer. In these situations, audio is typically recorded into a DAW (like Pro Tools), where it is also edited, and perhaps even mixed to some degree. The outputs of each track would be routed out of the computer (through many channels of output from the computer's audio interface) into an analog mixing console where the majority of the mixing is done (usually in conjunction with hardware effect devices). The output of the console is then usually recorded back to a DAW as a single final mix.

On the other hand, mixing *inside the box* means that you're recording, editing, and mixing all within a DAW. Not only the levels will be adjusted inside the DAW—plug-in effects within the DAW itself will be used. The only outputs that the computer (the *box*) needs are the outputs going to the monitor speakers for the mix engineer to hear—all other routing can occur within the DAW itself.

There's lively discussion (and I'm being polite here) within the professional community regarding the virtues of mixing outside versus inside the box. Both sides have valid points, but for the end user, it all boils down to this essential truth: Great work is being done using both methods, and people should follow the path that best enables them to realize their creative vision.

For the purposes of this book, we'll focus on mixing inside the box using Pro Tools | First. The concepts you'll learn here are applicable to a wide range of mixing scenarios, and many will apply equally to outside-the-box mixing.

Careers in Mixing: An Interview with Scott Weber

These days, nearly all audio production work involves some degree of mixing, and there are quite a few different career opportunities open to students interested in pursuing a career as a mix engineer. Different kinds of mixing require different technical (and personal) skills, depending on different factors. For example, a person who mixes a couple of tracks for a podcast is going to call on different skills than someone who works with hundreds of tracks in the high-pressure world of audio for film and television.

Enter Scott Weber: Scott is a veteran in the field of sound and has worked on shows like *Lost* (for which he won an Emmy Award), *Person of Interest*, and *Westworld*. This kind of work is among the most challenging for a mixer, and requires not only that the mix sound great, but that it conforms to different international standards and formats. I sat down with Scott to chat about what it takes to make it as a mixer:

AH: Scott, what was your first big mixing job?

SW: My first big television show was *Lost*. Before that, I was a sound supervisor and mixer at Disney Studios. I mixed foreign versions of shows and various TV projects, but nothing on the scale of *Lost*. We had no idea how epic the series would become.

When we started the show over 15 years ago, mixing was much different. We were still using the traditional mixing console, with Pro Tools used mainly as a playback system to feed into the console [mixing "outside the box"]. Our tracks were limited by the amount of inputs we had on the console and the amount of I/O we had on the Pro Tools systems. Needless to say, we did not have enough inputs to handle all the tracks that were needed.

We developed a hybrid system of mixing in order to handle all of the tracks. The channels we could not fit through the console, we mixed in the box in Pro Tools. When season 3 of *Lost* started, we replaced our analog console with an ICON D-Control [Avid mixing desk, shown in Figure 8.1], allowing everything to be mixed in the box. At that time, the HD TDM systems could only handle 192 active tracks in one session. Due to the large number of tracks we were using, we had to use 6 Pro Tools systems that fed into a central recorder. For our final season, we got the new HDX systems, allowing us to handle higher track counts.

AH: How has the mixing world changed since then?

SW: We saw a huge evolution in technology since the beginning of *Lost* (2004) until its end (2010). It evolved from traditional mixing (using large consoles and lots of physical inputs/outboard gear) to mixing everything in the box. Today, we can often do the job on a single computer. The need for large studios with elaborate machine rooms and lots of equipment has diminished.

The collaboration between the sound editor and the sound mixer has evolved into a continuous work flow. The editor used to deliver unprocessed, edited tracks to the stage for the mix to begin. Today, the processing and balancing begins during editorial and is a continuation on the mix stage.

Also, the method of delivering the final product has changed dramatically. We used to layback the print master to a physical video master [record the final audio to a video tape]. During the first few seasons of *Lost*, they would take that master and beam in over a satellite for the east coast feed. Today, most "laybacks" are the creation of digital sound files that are delivered electronically.

AH: One of the kinds of work you've done is a job called a re-recording mixer, which might be a new term to people just starting out. Can you tell us a little bit about what a re-recording mixer does, and why it's called "re-recording"?

SW: In the old days of post-production mixing, the original recorded sound was mixed together with the sound effects and music from playback machines and then printed [recorded] to a recording machine, with all the mixed elements combined together to make a "print master," This was known as re-recording. The process involved winding back the source machine, playing them back together and punching into the master recorder, which was was why it was called re-recording. While we still do the same thing today to some degree, we are more often laying down the masters after we have automated our mix in Pro Tools. In many cases it is not necessary to record the master in a real time pass, since it can be done as an off-line process or "Bounce to Disc."

AH: For new students just getting started with audio production, what are the key technical skills they should focus on first?

SW: First, learn and know Pro Tools. Beyond Pro Tools, always be a student of sound. Keep up with current technology. Go to trade shows and participate in forums. Read articles and watch videos. Never stop learning. Be well-rounded. If you want to become an editor, learn to cut dialog, sound effects, and music (everything). Be willing to take a job in the business even if it is not exactly what you are interested in doing at the time. Interfacing with professionals in the industry, where you can observe and learn is far more valuable than the perfect job that you think you are waiting for.

AH: This is a question I've asked everyone: What kind of personal traits do you think are necessary to be a successful mixer, aside from the technical skills?

SW: Technical knowledge is important, and you certainly must refine your skills, so you can do the job, but your people skills are just as important. Do not forget that the client is always right (even if you think you are/or really are). Never argue with them and be willing to do whatever they ask you to do without complaining, even if you think your idea is better. Be calm and cheerful. Leave your personal problems at the door and be professional. When you are working on a project, it deserves your full attention and must be your top priority. Clients do not want to know about other projects you are working on: they should feel that their job is your #1 priority. Take the time to do the job right and do not take shortcuts. Take pride in the work you do and make it the best it can be!

Figure 8.1 Scott Weber on the Job Mixing Westworld (Season One).

AH: Pro Tools, of course, is very popular all around, but it's especially popular with mixers. What about Pro Tools that makes it *your* choice?

SW: Besides it being the industry standard for most professional sound work, it is the complete audio tool from start to finish. Pro Tools allows you to record, edit, mix, process the sound, and create your masters [final mixes], all without leaving the box. It can be as simple as recording and editing a single voice-over track on a laptop, to handling full theatrical sound mixes with hundreds of tracks on a large mixing surface in a theater. Signal processing and manipulation can all be automated and stored to be recalled and used again. Pro Tools can be used with dozens of interfaces and mixing surfaces or none at all. There is really no end to the flexibility and possibilities of Pro Tools for sound production. When I am mixing in Pro Tools, I can rely on it to be consistent and to help me achieve the results I expect.

AH: Thanks a lot, Scott. I really appreciate your time. Any final inspirational words?

SW: Never limit yourself! When I started in the sound business, I wanted to specifically record and mix music. As I accepted various opportunities throughout my career, I decided to keep an open mind, a mindset which led me to a variety of jobs such as music production, sound editorial, sound design, production mixing, foley mixing, foreign mixing, post production mixing, live mixing, and concert recording. Be willing to think outside the box and be diverse in your skill set/work experience. It will keep you busy and also make your life and career much more interesting and exciting.

Mixing and Mastering

When you're mixing a song, a few things define the process. First, you're dealing with individual elements of your project in fine details, such as different volume levels of multiple tracks and clips and the settings of specific effects. Secondly, you'll (ideally) mix in a room that is a good sonic space, so that you can clearly hear all of the detail of the sound. Professional mixing rooms, built with sound treatment, are specifically designed for that purpose to make sure your mix is sonically accurate. The final output of the mixing stage is creating a file that could be played outside the studio by anyone, like a stereo mix of a song (which in your DAW would be comprised of several individual tracks).

In many kinds of work (particularly music projects), there is a final stage called *mastering*. People think of mastering and mixing as being related phases of production, and they are, up to a point: Once a final mix (or what the mixer *thinks* is final), a mixed-down file—typically a stereo file—is sent to a mastering engineer, whose goal is to "polish" the mix and make it sound as good as possible using tools and techniques that you normally would *not* use during the mixing process.

Mastering is an important part of the production process in many different ways. If you're mastering your own mixes, it's a chance to stop mixing and focus on improving your "final" mix. When you're mixing your multi-track project, you're focusing on fine details, but in the mastering phase, you're able to take a step back and consider the entire project in a way that you might not during the mixing phase. Because there are certain things that can't be changed in mastering, like tempo and individual track levels, attention is often drawn to aspects of the overall track that weren't noticed before.

Another important function of mastering is to make sure that the song sounds as good as it possibly can be, in as wide a variety of listening environments as possible. There are limits, of course; for example, your song won't sound the same over cheap headphones compared with professional studio monitor speakers. However, those differences can be reduced in different ways, and it is the job of the mastering engineer to make the most of the final mix, so that it can be fully enjoyed on many different playback devices.

These days, mastering tools have gotten inexpensive enough that many producers also master their own mixes. Personally speaking, if my project's budget allows it, I'll definitely opt to use a dedicated mastering engineer: I know that someone who has devoted their professional life to mastering mixes will be able to bring things out of my track that I can't, even if we have the same tools. Also, it's always great to get a second set of ears to listen and have someone bring their deep understanding of genre to my work.

A deep discussion of mastering is beyond the scope of this book, but many topics you'll learn during our discussion of mixing can be used when mastering a final mix. If you are going to master your own tracks, here are a few tips:

- **Take some time off.** Give yourself a few days—or better yet, a few weeks if you can—between when you think your mix is done and when you come back to master the final mix. You'll be surprised at what you'll hear after some time away from the project, details you didn't hear while you were in the thick of mixing.
- **Listen and study.** One of the things that professional mastering engineers usually bring to a project is a deep understanding of different musical styles, and the sonic aspects that define them. If you're going to master your own mixes, it's important that you listen critically to other music in the style of the project that you're mastering. If you can take time away from your mix before mastering, immersing yourself in critical listening of other songs is a great way to prepare for mastering.
- **Compare.** Periodically jump between the mastered version of your song and your original final mix. Are the changes you're making improving the song or not? On occasions when I have to master my own mixes, I always have one track that is the final mix, unmastered, which will normally be muted. I'll use this track as a reference track, and every so often, I'll solo it to compare what I'm doing as a mastering engineer to what I did as a mix engineer.
- **Small Moves.** When a mastering engineer gets a mix, that mix represents what the mixing engineer considers to be their "final" mix. The changes that you make to this mix should be very nuanced, as mastering is a subtle and profound part of the production process.
- **Louder isn't necessarily better.** During mastering, certain dynamic effects (such as compressors and limiters, which you'll learn more about in Chapter 9) are used, which tend to raise the amplitude of the track being affected. We often perceive these changes as improvements just because they're louder. It's important to watch the levels on the mastered track and compare them to the levels on the unmastered reference track to make sure that they are as similar as possible. That way, when

you compare your mastered track to your reference track, you're making that a fair comparison. You might want your track to be louder, but you also want to make it *better*.

- **Compare different playback devices.** Listen to your final mix and mastered tracks on headphones, in the car, and on your TV. The more environments you can hear your work in will help you understand how to make your masters sound as good as possible in a wide range of listening environments.

Bob Katz is one of the world's most sought-after mastering engineers, whose technical and artistic expertise is matched only by his generosity in sharing what he knows. His website, Digital Domain (www.digido.com) is a great place to learn more about the mastering engineer's world, as well as a great source of information on a wide range of audio and music production topics.

Signal Flow, Signal Flow, Signal Flow

There's a joke that I heard years ago: "What are the three most important things in mixing? Signal flow, signal flow, and signal flow." It's funny, but it's true: When you talk about mixing, you're essentially talking about signal flow. The more complex your mix gets, the more complex signal routing can be, but even the most complex mixes can be reduced to a few simple elements. Signal flow in Pro Tools is very straightforward and consistent. Let's take a look at the signal flow of an audio track:

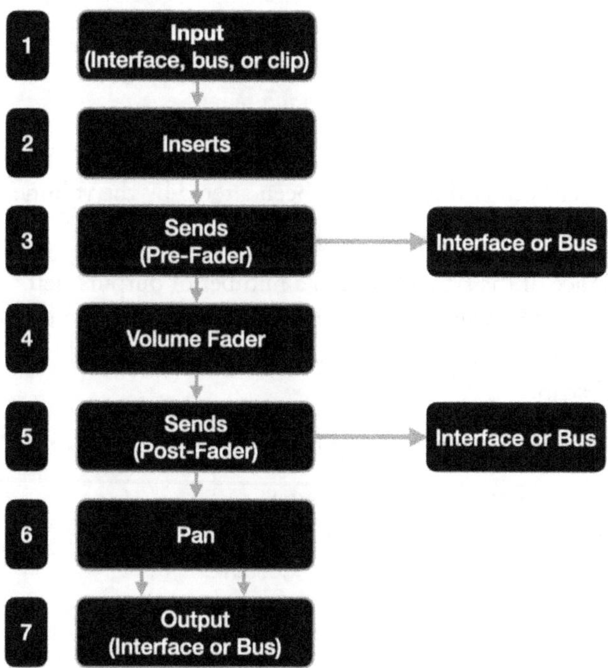

Figure 8.2 Audio Track Signal Flow (Mono Audio Track)

1. **Input.** On an Audio or Aux track, input can be from an interface input or a bus. Also, Audio tracks can contain audio clips. If an audio track is only playing back clips that are already on the track, they do not require any interface or bus input. Clips on an audio track function as an input.

You'll learn more about busses later in this chapter. For now, think of an interface input as a signal coming from outside of Pro Tools (like a recording instrument), and think of a bus as a signal routed from one track in Pro Tools to another track, completely within the Pro Tools environment.

There are a few plug-ins that have their own outputs, which can be routed to the input of a track. These plug-ins aren't part of Pro Tools I First's included plug-ins, so for this book, we'll limit our discussion to interface inputs and bus inputs.

2. **Inserts.** Inserts are most commonly used as holders for effects. For example, if a plug-in effect is placed on an insert, the entire signal of the track would be routed through that effect before passing on to the next step in the track's signal flow.

You'll learn more about how to use inserts in Chapter 9.

3. **Sends** (Pre-Fader). A send makes a copy of the signal to be routed to another destination. A pre-fader send makes that copy before the signal hits your volume fader. The destination of this send can be an interface output or a bus.
4. **Volume** (Fader). This is where you control the output volume of the track.

Remember that the Volume fader on a track *only* controls the output of that track, meaning that the fader has absolutely no effect on the *input* coming to the track. If you're bringing audio into a track (either by recording or internal routing), and you see your levels clipping, turn down the level of the signal source. Changing the fader on a destination track will not fix level clipping.

5. **Sends** (Post-Fader). This kind of send makes a copy *after* the signal has been altered by the volume fader. As with a pre-fader send, the destination can be an interface output or a bus.
6. **Pan.** Next is panning, which controls the balance of the signal between a number of outputs (left and right, in the case of a stereo mix). This is how you can create a stereo mix of several mono or stereo tracks. If, on the other hand, you route your track to a single output, no pan slider will be needed, and you won't see one in the channel strip.
7. **Output**. After all these stages, the signal goes out of an interface output or bus.

Technically, outputs don't go *directly* to an interface output or a bus. The output of a track or send goes to something commonly referred to as a *mix engine*. A DAWs mix engine is designed to collect (or *aggregate*) multiple individual signals and combine them as necessary for routing to an output. The mix engine allows us to assign multiple tracks to the same output, and still hear all of them.

The layout of a channel in the Mix window doesn't exactly follow this signal flow from top to bottom.

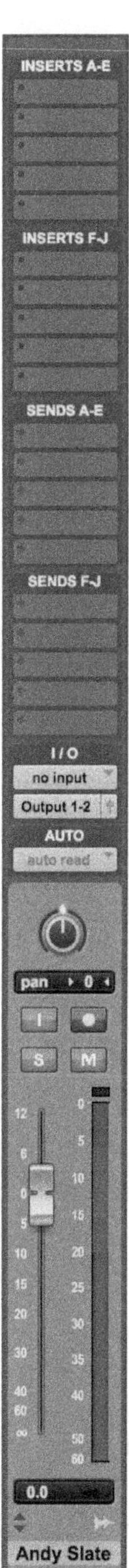

Figure 8.3 A Mix Window Channel Strip

Let's take a look at the layout of an audio track in the Mix window from a signal flow point of view:

The I/O view of the Mix window allows you to choose the *input* (the first step in the signal flow chain) and the *output* (the last step). Following analog mixing conventions, the input selector is above the output selector, as shown in Figure 8.4.

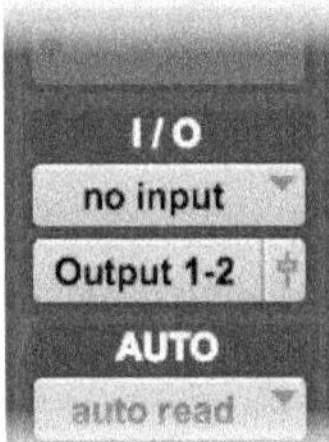

Figure 8.4 The I/O View of the Mix Window

After the input stage are the *Inserts*. In each Pro Tools audio track, you have 10 insert slots, broken up into two banks of 5—*Inserts A-E* and *Inserts F-J*—which can be individually shown or hidden. In Figure 8.5, Insert A has an EQ, followed by a Compressor on insert B. If the order was reversed (Compressor followed by an EQ), the track would sound different.

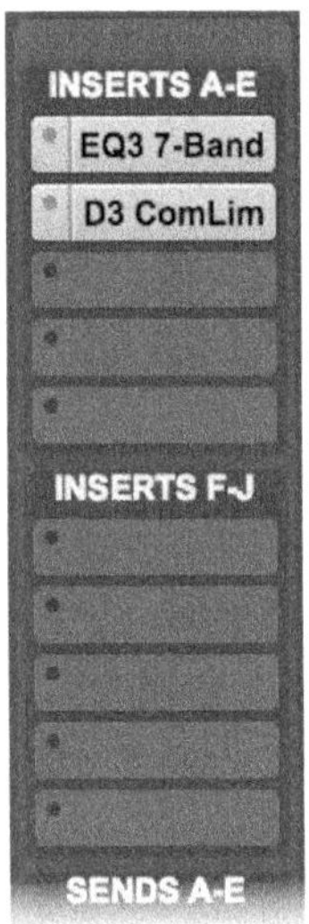

Figure 8.5 The Inserts View of the Mix Window

This is important to remember: Inserts are processed in *series*, meaning the signal from the input (or a clip) goes first to any plug-in inserted into slot A and is processed by it. Then, the resultant signal will go to any plug-in inserted into slot B, which is then processed by that plug-in before being sent to slot C, and so on. This is important—changing the order of effects can give you different results.

The *Sends* view looks a bit like the Inserts view, with 10 send slots separated into two banks of 5 each. Sends, unlike Inserts, aren't processed in series, so the order of the sends won't change the sound of the track in any way. They can be individually set up as either being *pre-fader* sends (which in the order of signal flow comes immediately after the inserts) or *post-fader* sends (immediately after the volume fader).

You can easily identify pre- and post-fader sends in the Mix window: Post-fader sends (the default type when you create a new send) is indicated by a grey *Send Selector*. Pre-fader sends are indicated by a blue Send Selector. Figure 8.6, for example, shows a post-fader send routed to Bus 1-2, and a pre-fader send routed to Bus 3-4.

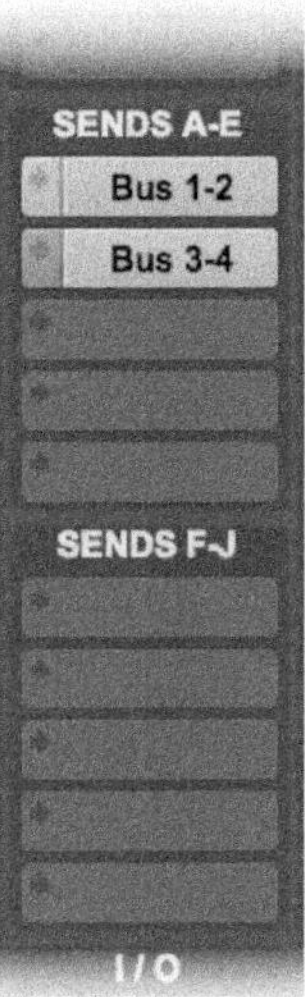

Figure 8.6 The Sends View of the Mix Window

The Volume fader (which in the order of signal flow comes after the pre-fader sends and before post-fader sends) allows you to raise or lower the volume of a track. Following normal mixing console conventions, when you create a new track, the Volume fader is set to 0 dB, commonly called *unity*. You can raise the level of a track by 12 dB, or reduce it to silence, indicated by an infinity sign (∞).

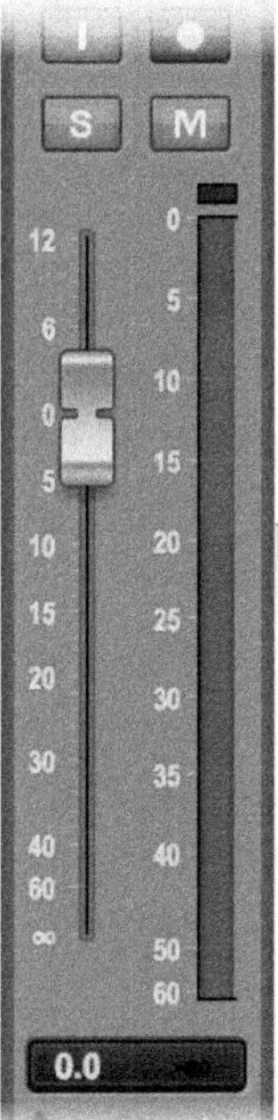

Figure 8.7 The Volume Fader of the Mix Window

The small rectangular area below the fader is the Volume indicator, which displays the Volume fader level (in Figure 8.7, the level is set to 0 dB, or unity). To the immediate left of your Volume fader you'll see your level meter, giving you important visual feedback about the output of the track. Above the fader are buttons that will allow you to enable or disable *TrackInput*, *Record Enable*, *Solo*, and *Mute*.

Finally, the last step before output, the Pan control (located above the Volume fader) will enable you to position your track spatially. In the most basic stereo mix situation, it will allow you to balance the signal between the left and right speakers. Below the Pan control(s) is a small rectangular area that will display your pan value. In Figure 8.8, the pan is set at a value of 0, meaning the signal is positioned exactly in the center in your mix. The range of panning is from 100 Left to 100 Right.

Figure 8.8 The Pan Knob of the Mix Window

If you understand the signal flow of an audio track, and how it relates to the layout of the Mix window, you've accomplished quite a lot! The signal flow of an Auxiliary Input track is identical to that of an Audio track, except that a clip cannot be an input for an Aux track (since Aux tracks cannot hold audio clips). You also understand the signal flow of an Instrument track, since an Instrument track is the combination of a MIDI track (which has no audio signal flow) and an Auxiliary Track. In fact, the only track type that is significantly different is a Master Fader track, which we'll discuss later in this chapter.

The First Step: A "Static" Mix

A *Static* mix is the simplest kind of mix, where the settings of the volume fader and pan knobs (and plug-in effects, which we'll talk about later) don't move. Static mixes are rarely final mixes, but they're often a great place to start. Creating a good-sounding static mix provides a strong foundation for later tweaking and saves a lot of time in the long run.

Setting Up a Static Mix

The steps for setting up a static mix are:

1. Confirm that the **output** of your tracks is set correctly, so that you can hear each one. If you're in doubt whether you're hearing a given track, it's a good idea to solo that track to make sure it's audible.
2. If your Audio tracks are playing back tracks, they'll not be record-enabled, and therefore their **input** setting will not impact that track. You'll learn about how to use Auxiliary Input tracks

to organize your tracks, and the inputs on those tracks *is* significant. If your project is using subgroups (which you'll learn about later in this chapter), check to make sure that their inputs *and* outputs are set correctly.

3. Later in this chapter. you'll learn about something called mix *automation*, which will enable you to have your controls move on their own during playback. For a static mix, make sure your faders *won't* move unexpectedly, so turn your automation *off*. Click the AUTOMATION MODE SELECTOR (which will read *Off*, *Read*, *Touch*, *Latch*, or *Write*), and choose OFF from the menu.

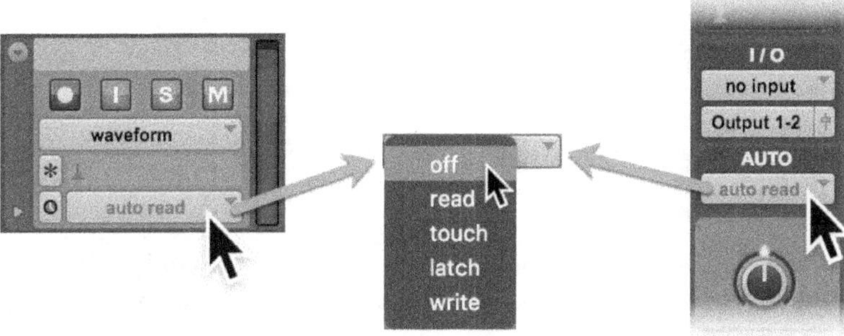

Figure 8.9 Changing the Automation Mode to OFF from the Edit or Mix Window

Volume

It is important to adjust the volume when you're working on your static mix so that the relative levels of the different tracks sounds good. Adjusting the Volume fader works pretty much like you would expect—just click and drag up or down to change the volume level.

Here are some tips when adjusting your levels:

- To quickly reset your volume levels to unity on main faders or send faders (which you'll learn more in Chapter 10), hold the OPTION key (Mac) or ALT key (Windows) and click the fader. The fader will jump back to 0 dB.
- If you're a very specific mixer (like myself), you'll find that there will be some volume settings that you can't access. As you normally drag a fader, you'll see that the settings will change in .2-.3 dB steps. That's because you're working in *coarse resolution* (the normal mode of operation with faders). You can move in fine resolution (.1 dB steps) by holding the COMMAND key (Mac) or the CTRL key (Windows), while clicking and dragging.

Many other controls work in coarse resolution as a default (like panning and many plug-in parameters). The COMMAND/CTRL modifier method works for those as well.

- You can mix from the Edit window. Just click and hold on the VOLUME INDICATOR, and a small fader will appear, as shown in Figure 8.10. This fader is a bit small to do any fine tuning (unless you're holding down COMMAND/CTRL for fine resolution movement), but it's a quick way to make volume changes from the Edit window.

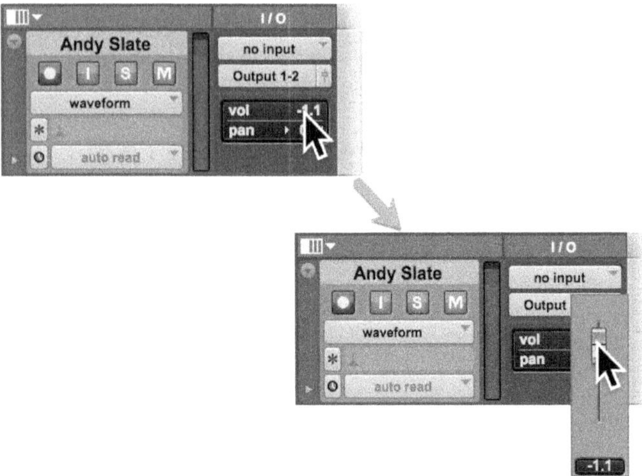

Figure 8.10 A Way to Control Volume from the Edit Window

- There's one more way to access your volume controls, from either the Mix or Edit window: The *Output Window*. You'll find the Output window button to the immediate right of the Output Path selector of either the Mix or Edit window. Clicking this button will reveal the Output window, which will give you *Output path selectors*, *Automation selector*, *Pan controls*, *Solo*, *Mute*, and the *Volume fader*. It will also display pan linking controls on stereo tracks, which we'll discuss in the next section of this chapter. This window might be a bit redundant when working in the Mix window, but it can be very useful when you're mixing from the Edit window.

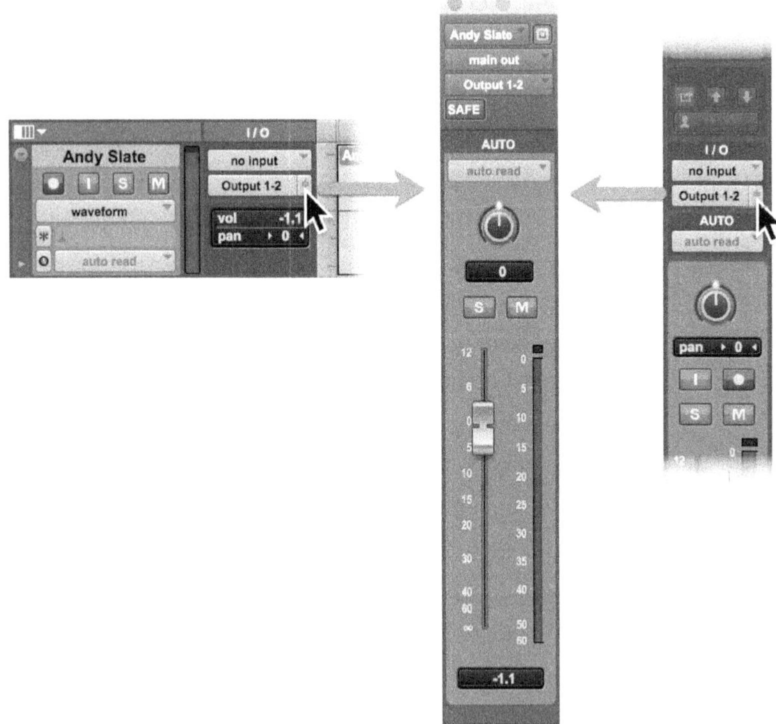

Figure 8.11 Opening the Output Window from the Edit Window or Mix Window

By default, if you have an Output window open already and you click on the Output window button for another track, that currently open Output window will change to show the values for the *newly-clicked* track. In other words, by default, you'll only have one Output window open at a time. If you want to open multiple Output windows, just hold the SHIFT key as you click on additional Output window buttons, and new additional windows will appear.

Pan

Along with volume, positioning the various elements of your mix with panning is an important part of your first static mix. Think of it this way: When you hear a live group performing a song, or a group of people having a conversation, they are not occupying the same space, but rather have their own individual positions in relation to you, the listener. That's essentially what we want to do when we pan: to create a sonic landscape with different elements placed in different locations. Not only does it reinforce a sense of realism, but it also allows for the different elements to be heard as clearly as possible.

When it comes to mixing, there are few absolute rules, but numerous traditional setups. Here are some when it comes to panning:

- Lead Vocals, Bass, Kick drums, and often Snare drums are commonly panned dead center.
- In audio for video, dialog is commonly panned dead center (even if the speaker on screen is not standing dead center). However, this doesn't always apply to off-screen dialog—panning often comes from whichever side the off-screen speaker is.
- Drum kits (except the Kick drum and sometimes the Snare) are panned either from the drummer's perspective or the audience's perspective. For example, if panning from the drummer's perspective, the hi-hat would be panned to the left, but if panning from the audience's perspective, it'd be panned to the right.
- Other instruments are panned off-center, in order to give sonic space to the critical lead vocal, kick, snare and bass. There are few established traditions when it comes to these instruments, so experiment!
- You'll often use a Master Fader to view the total output of your tracks. Watch the meters on your left and right side and try to keep them generally in the same range. If your left side's meter is significantly louder than your right side's meter, your mix will sound lopsided.
- If you've done some rough volume level setting before your panning, you might want to re-evaluate your volume choices after you're done panning. A track's level—both actual and perceived—can change based upon its position.

Stereo Track Panning and Pan Linking

On a mono track, you'll see only a single pan knob, which will allow you to allocate the single signal to the left and right channel. For a *stereo* track, you'll have two pan knobs, and you can position each signal (nominally the left and right side of the stereo track) individually to the two-channel output.

For example, Figure 8.12 shows a stereo track with the left side panned *hard left* (100% of the signal coming out of the left speaker) and the right side panned *hard right* (100% of the signal coming out of the right speaker). This will give maximum width to the track.

Figure 8.12 Hard Panning on a Stereo Track

Figure 8.13 shows the exact opposite: The left side is panned *hard right* (100% of the signal coming out of the right speaker) and the right side panned *hard left* (100% of the signal coming out of the left speaker). This will give maximum width to the track, but the image will be reversed. You could use this method to invert the image of a drum kit track from the drummer's perspective to the audience's perspective and vice versa.

Figure 8.13 Hard Inverse Panning on a Stereo Track

Here's an example where the left side of the track is panned to the left and the right side of the track is panned to the right, but neither goes all the way. This setup will give some stereo width, but without going to extremes. In my personal work as an arranger, I use this for individual string sections (violins, violas, celli, and basses), so that they each have some stereo width, but still occupy roughly the positions that they would on an orchestral stage.

Figure 8.14 Positioning a Stereo track Within a Limited Areaw

You have additional control over these two pan controls, but you'll only see them in the Output window:

- The *Link* button will appear orange-colored when active (as shown in Figure 8.15). When it is active, any change you make on one side will be similarly made on other side. This is a relative change, so only the tracks position on the stereo landscape will change, not the stereo width of your track.

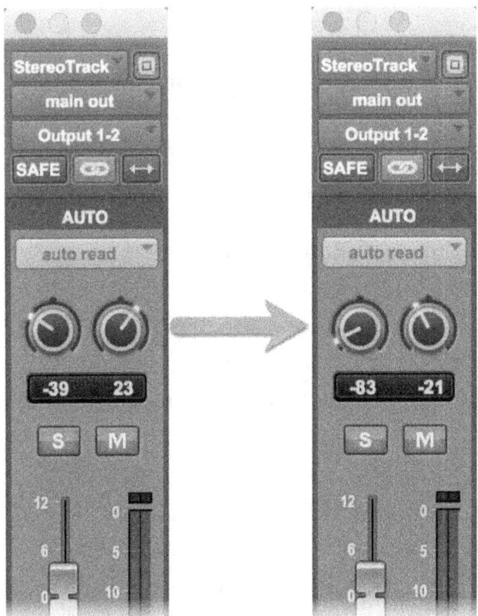

Figure 8.15 Pan Linking

- Immediately to the right of the Link button is the *Inverse Pan* button. It won't do anything on its own, but when used in combination with the *Link* feature, any change made on one side of the track will inversely be made on the other side of the track. This is quite effective on some sounds (I've used it with electronic musical styles), where you can get a very complex stereo sound to collapse and then invert.

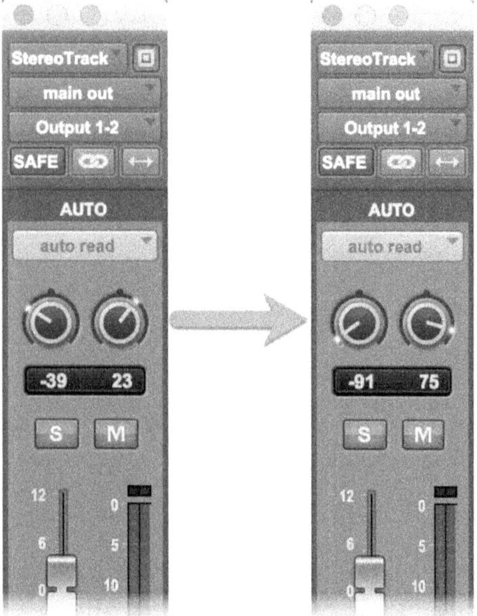

Figure 8.16 Inverse Pan Linking

Approaches on How to Create a Static Mix

They say that "rules are made to be broken", and that is never truer than when you're mixing. Some of the most famous mixes in the world have been made using the most unconventional techniques. That being said, some common traditions have evolved over time precisely because they tend to work in most cases, and rules are always best learnt before broken.

As a point of personal privilege though, I will say this: Try to never go into a mixing session without having a clear idea of what your final product will sound like. Picture in your mind what you want your mix (music or otherwise) to sound like and keep that vision throughout the entire process. It's a common mistake to simply start moving faders and pan knobs without any clear ideas, hoping that something will sound good, but more often than not this approach only confuses and frustrates the artistic concept that should be driving the project.

So, with that in mind, here are a few common approaches when creating a static mix.

- **Make the Most of Each Track:** One approach is to listen to only one family of instrument—drums, perhaps—and make sure it sounds as good as possible before moving on to other elements. This is certainly a valid way of working, but be aware that if every element of your mix is *huge*, they'll all compete, and the mix might suffer as a result.
- **Work Up From the Bottom:** If you consider that some of the most important elements of the song are the lower instruments (kick drum and bass), one approach is to start bringing up elements

from the bottom up, making sure that the drums and the bass sound good together, before adding on other elements. This can work well for some styles of music, particularly for styles that are dependent on a strong beat.

- **Work From the Most Important Part:** This method works well for me personally: I identify the most important part of the song (or the most important part of a section of a song), and then make sure it sounds exactly the way that I want. Then, I slowly bring in other elements, making sure that they don't overshadow the part that I've decided is the most important element of my mix.
- **Create a Landscape:** One great way to solidify your concept of how you want your final product to sound is to *draw* it. Figure 8.17 shows a sample of a diagram that you could use (you can find other chart styles in the internet). This chart represents an overhead view of your mix, with the listener's position indicated by a red symbol at the bottom. The concentric circles indicate the perceived distance from the listener (in this chart, the darker circles are farther away). Just write down the names of the different sonic elements in the position and distance that you envision them. Taking a bit of time to think about the kind of sonic landscape you want to create and sketching it out can be a very useful exercise!

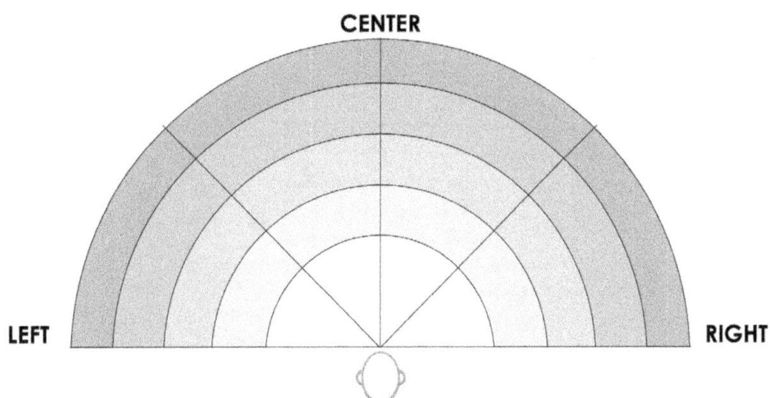

Figure 8.17 A Sample of a Mix Panning Chart

- **Check Your Mix in Mono:** One of my very good friends, Fabrizio Angelini, an audio teacher in Rome, is very fond of telling me, jokingly: "The future is mono." He might be kidding around, but periodically checking your mix in mono is a great way to see if your levels are correct. Many interfaces have a button on them especially for this purpose.

Watch Out for Levels!

When it comes to audio, especially digital audio, more is not always better. One very important rule of mixing "in the box" is: *Avoid clipping.* But what exactly *is* clipping?

When it comes to digital audio, the maximum voltage that can be captured or reproduced is a series of digital "1s"—if your project is a 16-bit project, that would be 16 "1s", and 24 "1s" for 24-bit. Since our digital dynamic scale measures amplitude from 0 dB downward, in either case, that value would be -0 dB. In the digital world, there is no amplitude level that can be recorded or reproduced greater than -0 dB.

When you look at your meters, if your level ever gets above -0 dB, a red clip indicator will appear, as shown in Figure 8.18. This is an indication that your original signal cannot be preserved, and you should reduce the level of your tracks (or plug-in).

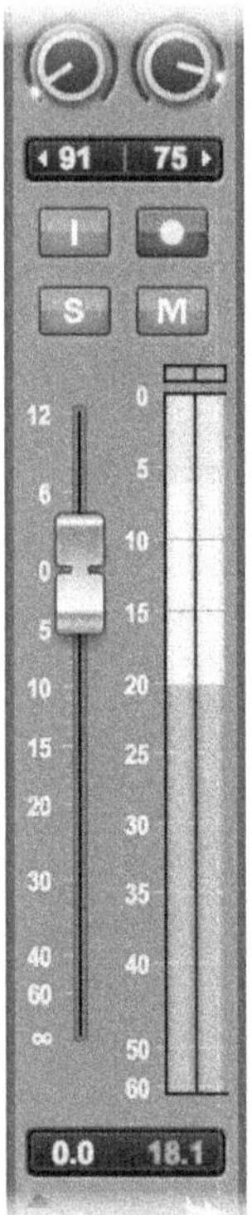

Figure 8.18 Clipping!

So far, we haven't discussed plug-in processing on your inserts, but we will tackle that in the next chapter. In a track, all metering is shown *after* the changes on any of your inserts. For example, if you have an EQ (Equalization) plug-in that boosts the signal to the point of clipping, that will show on the track's meters, and should be addressed.

In some tracks, you'll notice that the clip light isn't red, but yellow instead. A clip indicator is red when clipping happens at an input or output converter (your audio interface). If the clip indicator is yellow, it's a warning that the signal exceeds -0 dB in the internal mixer and can clip at the converters or when writing to disk. Both kinds of clipping should be avoided.

Pre-fader vs. Post-fader Metering

There are two different ways that you can view your meters: *Pre-Fader* or *Post-Fader*. Changing from one mode to another is easily done:

1. Click on the OPTIONS menu.

2. By default, *Pre-Fader Metering* is enabled (indicated by a checkmark, as shown in Figure 8.19). Click on PRE-FADER METERING to uncheck it and effectively change your view to *Post-Fader Metering*.

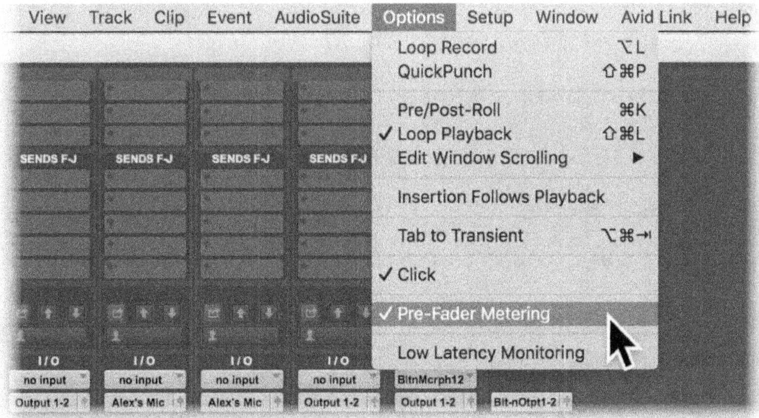

Figure 8.19 Pre-Fader Metering (Enabled)

Here's how your levels will appear in either of the modes:

- **Pre-Fader Metering:** When Pre-Fader Metering is enabled, the meters of your tracks will show the levels *after* the insert stage, but *before* your main fader. Any level change created by any inserts on your tracks will be shown in the meter, but any changes that you make with your fader will have no effect on your metering. This mode of metering (Pro Tools' default) is useful in showing if your signal is clipping as a result of effects on your inserts.
- **Post-Fader Metering:** When Pre-Fader Metering is *disabled*, your meters will show the level of your tracks *after* your main fader (and also after the inserts). In this case, any changes that you make to your fader *will* affect the metering that you see on that track. The advantage of this metering choice is that it gives a clear visual feedback on the relative output levels of your tracks.

Hands-On Exercise 8.1: A Static Mix

The exercises in this chapter will be a little different from the exercises in previous chapters. In this chapter, the directions will be simpler and less specific, allowing you to explore different approaches to mixing. See what works best for you!

Getting Started

The project that you'll be using in this chapter is the same *Low Roar* song that you heard in Chapter 1, but with more individual tracks.

1. Create a new Project by converting the *Pro Tools First—Fundamentals of Audio Production—Chapter 8 (Low Roar Tracks).ptx* session to a local Project. The session is found in the *Pro Tools First—Fundamentals of Audio Production—Chapter 8 (Low Roar Tracks)* subfolder of this book's downloaded exercise material. Choose any desired sample rate, 24-bit, and do not Backup to Cloud.

The tracks are roughly grouped as follows:

- Three Vocal Tracks (Yellow)—*Lead Vocal (Dry), Background Vocals (Dry)*, and *Mangled Vox Print*
- One Effects Track (Green)—*SFX*
- Two Guitar Tracks (Teal)—*Acoustic Guitar Stem Print* and *Acoustic Rhythm Guitar*
- Four Tracks of Percussive Sounds (Blue)—*Bells Stem, Dulcimer, Glockenspiel, Sitar*
- Three Tracks of String Sounds (Purple)—*Strings Stem Print, High Strings, Xpand Low End String*
- Two Tracks of Bass (Pink)—*Bass Gtr* and *Xpand Bass*
- Six Tracks of Drums (Red)—*Break.02, Crash, Live Drums, Hat-Tamb Stem, Rimshot*, and *Kick Stem*

Figure 8.20 Tracks in the Edit Window

Show A Mixing Environment

You've been working in the Edit window up to this point. Now, let's get comfortable with the Mix window.

2. Switch your view to the Mix Window.
3. There are a lot of elements being shown, most of which you don't need in this initial phase of mixing. Change your Mix window view so that you're only seeing the *I/O* and *Comments* views.

4. In the Edit window, it's easy to see your position and control playback, but that's not as easy when you're working in the Mix window. Show the Transport window and move it into a convenient area of your desktop. (You should have some empty space at the bottom of the Mix window, as shown in Figure 8.21).

Figure 8.21 The Mix Window Ready to Go!

5. There are no plug-in effects in this project (other than virtual instruments), so you can safely turn off *Pre-Fader Metering* if you prefer.

Create a Static Mix

You now have a project that has all tracks at unity, with all mono tracks panned to the center, and with all stereo tracks panned hard left and hard right. This is a very common setup when starting a mixing session.

6. Now, your job is to do a rough static mix. You must limit your adjustments only to volume and pan adjustments of the tracks already in the project—you'll learn how to work with other mixing tools like effects later. You can choose any method you like, but here are some things you might want to keep in mind during the process:

   - If you want to listen to a section of the song repeatedly, select an area on the timeline (in the Edit window) and put yourself into *Loop Playback*. You'll probably want to jump back into the Mix window to do your mixing, however.

If you're going to loop a selection, you might want to start and stop playback without losing that selected area (and thereby having to go back into the Edit window to re-select it. To make sure that you won't lose your selected area when you stop playback, make sure that *Insertion Follows Playback* is *disabled.*

- Use your *Solo* and *Mute* buttons to hear tracks by themselves or your entire mix without a track.
- As you position tracks, re-check their volume setting to make sure that they still work for you. When adjusting panning on the stereo tracks, also listen for tonal changes—as you narrow the stereo width of some tracks, the timbre can subtly change.
- Don't forget your *Comments* view. This is a great way to write notes within Pro Tools about individual tracks.
- Remember that static mixes are *very* rarely the final mix. You'll find that different sections really should be mixed differently. Don't worry—try to get the best-sounding mix overall, and you'll learn how to tweak individual sections later in this chapter.
- This might sound goofy, but from time to time, *close your eyes.* Listen critically, and let your ears guide you even if your eyes tell you that you're going too far! If it sounds right, it *is* right.
- If your audio interface has a *Mono* button, press it from time to time and see how your mix (especially the relative levels of tracks) changes when you listen to it as a mono mix. For many kinds of work, mixes are done with *mono compatibility* in mind. Mix engineers make sure that their stereo mixes still sound as good as possible on mono playback devices, knowing that the mixes will be played on one-channel playback devices.

7. This is a simple exercise in terms of steps, but take as much time as you can to make different changes and see what happens. Do the changes you make produce the result you expected? When the mix sounds good, save your work.

Controlling Your Mix: Subgroups and Master Faders

After trying to create a static mix by altering individual tracks, you probably think that there *must* be a better way of controlling multiple tracks at the same time. You're right—there are a few ways to do it, each with its own advantages. As with everything regarding mixing, if you keep the signal flow in mind, you can increase your mixing power with minimal effort.

Getting Organized: Subgroups

When mixing a number of related tracks (for example, a number of drum tracks that comprise a drum kit), you might start off getting the relative levels of all the tracks just right, only to find out that you have to change them *all,* after adding more tracks to your mix later on! It would be great if there was an easy way to control the levels of multiple tracks with a *single* track. For this, subgroups are the solution to your problem.

What is a subgroup? Simply put, a *subgroup* is an arrangement whereby the output of a number of tracks is routed to the input of a single track (usually a stereo Auxiliary Input track). This has the effect of funneling the audio through this single track (often referred to as a *subgroup master*), making levels and effects easier to manage.

Creating a subgroup is easy, as long as you think of the process in terms of *signal flow*. Just by way of example, I'll demonstrate the creation of a subgroup of all the drums (which you'll do in the next hands-on exercise):

1. Create an Auxiliary Input track to be your subgroup master—the track that will control the level of the other tracks. In the majority of cases, this will be a stereo Aux track, which is what I'll create in this case. I'll name my track *Drum SUB.*

2. Because I'll be using internal routing in this sort of situation, and busses are used for internal routing, I'll choose an available bus for the input of the subgroup master. (In this image, I've chosen Bus 1-2.)

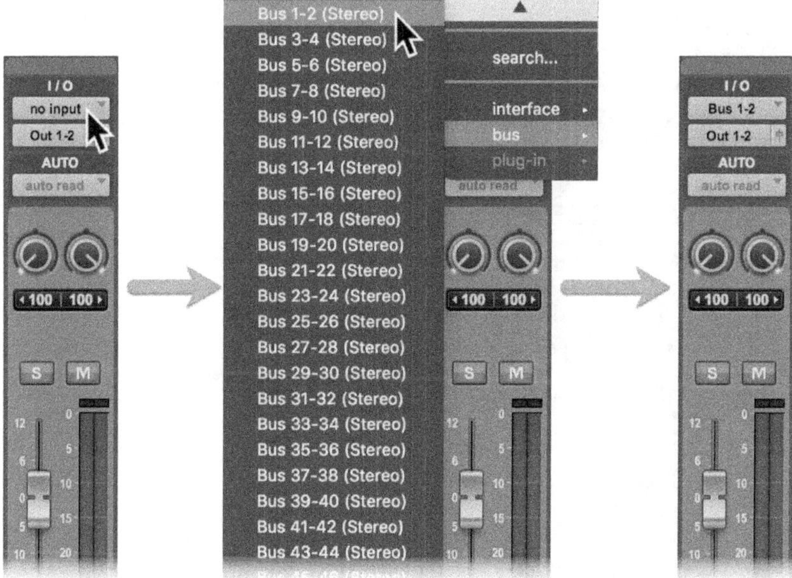

Figure 8.22 Assigning a Bus as an Input for the Subgroup Master

3. Assign the outputs of the tracks to be subgrouped (in this example, I've chosen all the drum tracks in this project) to the same bus you've chosen for the input of your subgroup master.

Figure 8.23 Assigning the Same Bus as Outputs for the Subgroup Member Tracks

Earlier in this book, you learned that the **OPTION** key (Mac) or **ALT** key (Windows) is an easy way to make changes to all the tracks in your project, and that **SHIFT+OPTION** (Mac) or **SHIFT+ALT** (Windows) will make changes to all *selected* tracks. This is a great shortcut to use when assigning a number of tracks to the same bus.

Your subgroup master track's fader is now in control of the overall volume of your subgrouped tracks. In this example, as I adjust the *Drum SUB* track's fader, the relative blend of the drums remains consistent, and the subgroup master controls the overall output. The metering of the subgroup master track (*Drum SUB* in this case) will show the total output of all the member tracks, as shown in Figure 8.24.

Figure 8.24 The Finished Drum Subgroup

In addition to making levels more manageable, subgroups can also help you work more efficiently with plug-ins. For example, if you want to apply a compressor to your drums (a very common thing to do, which you'll learn more about in the next chapter), you *could* instantiate a compressor on an insert of each of the tracks. That, however, would be unwieldy to work with and wasteful of your limited processing resources. Instead, just insert *one* compressor effect on the subgroup master. There's only one plug-in to adjust, and it's a thrifty use of your CPU!

Solo Safe

When you solo a track, all other tracks will be muted, including the Aux track functioning as your subgroup master. That means that if you want to hear just a single drum (Kick drum, for example) pressed that track's SOLO button, you would hear nothing, since the Aux track to which the Kick is routed (the *Drum Sub* track in my example) becomes muted. Of course, you can always solo that subgroup Aux track, but that can be a time-consuming annoyance. Pro Tools allows you to *solo-safe* a track, meaning it won't be muted even if other tracks are soloed.

To solo-safe a track, just hold down the COMMAND key (Mac) or CTRL (Windows) key, and click on the Solo button on the track you want to solo-safe.

When a track is in a solo-safe state, the SOLO button will be greyed-out, as shown in Figure 8.25.

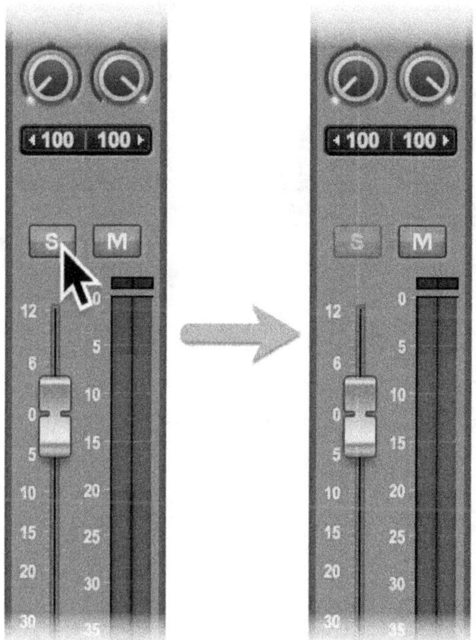

Figure 8.25 Solo-Safeing a Track (COMMAND/CTRL-click)

Just the act of creating subgroups will change the way you approach your mix. With this added control, you'll find that it's easy to get the relative levels of each of your grouped tracks (like drums, vocals, and so on) and then mix them all together. This brings us to a new term: *Stems.* In many work situations, subgroups are referred to as stems, particularly in post-production (video) circles. When you hear terms like "dialog stem" or "music stem," they're talking about a subgroup (or a track that is a mix-down of that subgroup).

Creating a Subgroup of Subgroups: the "Main SUB"

Any discussion of Mixing will have some degree of personal opinion built-in to it, so here's a common technique that I employ when routing my signals:

1. First, I'll often color-code my tracks by their type for easy identification, as shown in Figure 8.26 (and as you saw in the previous hands-on exercise project).

Figure 8.26 Color-Coded Tracks

2. I'll create subgroups of all my related tracks, like *vocals*, *drums*, and *guitars* for music projects or *dialog*, *effects*, and *music* for post-production video projects. Each subgroup would use different busses as their internal routing. Here's a flow-chart view of how the signal might be routed in a music project.

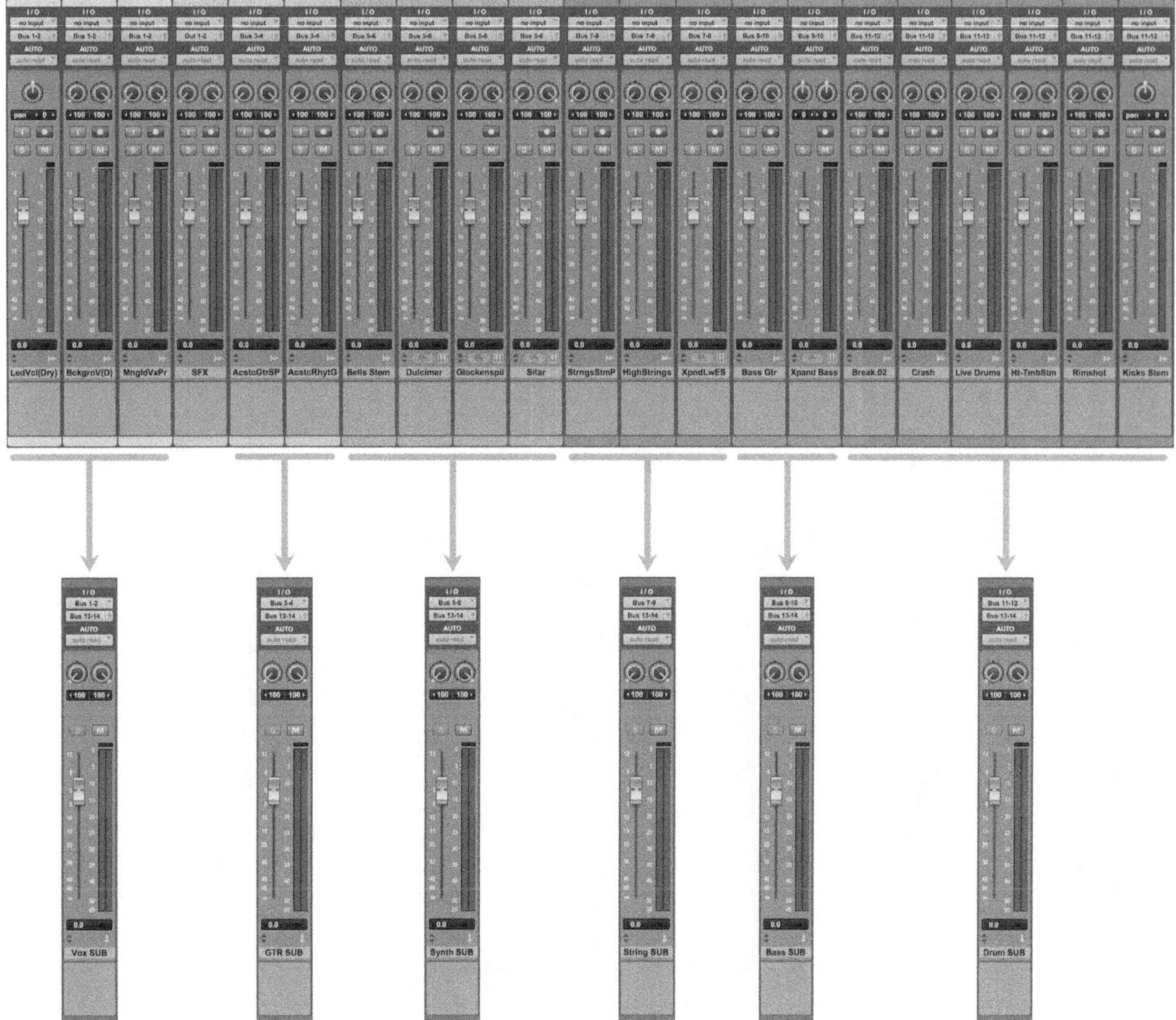

Figure 8.27 Track Outputs Assigned to Subgroup Masters

3. Then, I will make a *subgroup* of my *subgroups*. Each of the subgroups (or *stems*) outputs would be assigned to the same bus (a bus not used for any of the other subgroups).

4. I'll create a new Auxiliary Input track (which I typically name MAIN SUB), assign the inputs to the same bus, and solo safe the track.

5. Finally, if there are any tracks that aren't assigned to any subgroups, their output should be assigned to the same bus I'm using as the input of the Main Sub track. All tracks should be routed to the Main Sub track, either directly, or indirectly through a subgroup.

Figure 8.28 shows the final signal flow I've used in many of my projects. Tracks are subgrouped, and the outputs of the subgroups (as well as the outputs of any non-subgrouped tracks) are routed to an additional subgroup, to a track that I call *Main SUB*.

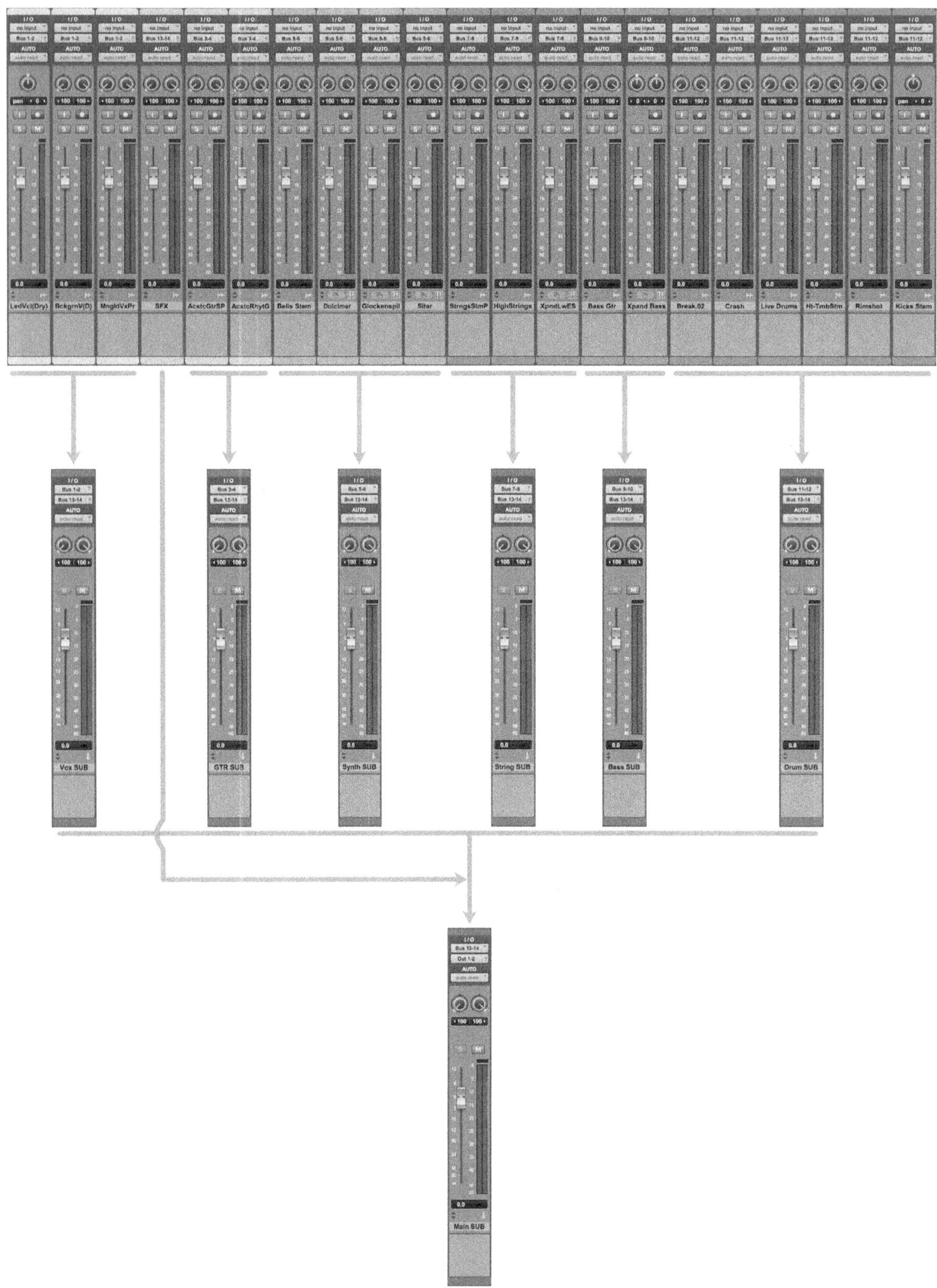

Figure 8.28 Complete Subgroup Routing

Let's stop and think about the signal flow in this kind of setup:

- On each individual track (that *isn't* a subgroup), you've got inserts that will allow you to place effects on the individual track *pre-fader*. That means that you can change the tonal color of the track, and then scale the track's output with the Volume fader without changing the timbre.
- The outputs of related tracks are routed to the inputs of subgroup masters. These are usually Auxiliary Input tracks, and any changes made to the Volume fader will change the cumulative output of all the subgroup members. Here again, the inserts are all pre-fader. This means that you can change the tonal qualities of a number of tracks (the members of the subgroup) and then scale the output of the subgroup with a single fader, without changing the timbre of the group.
- The outputs of the subgroup masters (and the outputs of any non-subgrouped tracks) are routed to the input of an additional subgroup master (which I typically call my *Main SUB*). Changes made to the Volume fader of this track will change the total output of the entire project. Since this is also an Auxiliary Input track, inserts are pre-fader, meaning that you can change the output level of the mix without changing the tonal quality of the mix.

Master Fader Tracks

There's one more track type left for you to explore: The *Master Fader* track. Although it looks similar to an Audio or Aux track, its function is substantially different from anything you've seen up to this point. A Master Fader track is a way to control output, and it is commonly used to control the output of an interface channel (although it can also be used to control the output of busses in more complex mix situations). With this simple but powerful track, you can control the entire level of your project.

Master Fader Signal Flow

As with everything related to mixing, if you understand the signal flow behind Master Fader tracks, you're going to be able to use it most effectively. Here's the signal flow of a Master Fader track:

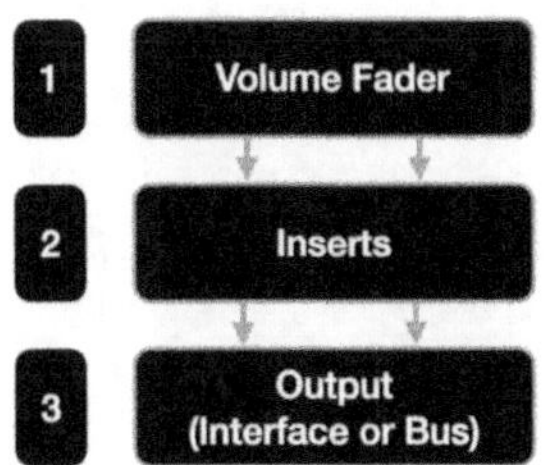

Figure 8.29 Master Fader Track Signal Flow (Stereo Master FaderTrack)

1. **Volume** (Fader). This is where you control the output volume of the output path selected for the Master Fader. This is the *first* stage in signal flow.
2. **Inserts.** Like other tracks, one hundred percent of your signal passes through your insert, and plug-ins on inserts are processed in series. *Unlike* other tracks, all the inserts on a Master Fader are *post-fader*, meaning that the changes that you make to the Volume fader will change the incoming level going to the inserts, potentially altering the tone of the final output.
3. **Output**. After all these stages, the signal goes out of an interface output or bus.

Setting Up a Master Fader Track

First things first: You need to *create* a Master Fader track before you can use it!

1. Using any of the techniques you've learned in Chapter 2, create a stereo Master Fader track. (You'll find Master Fader listed in the Track Type menu, as shown in Figure 8.30.) The new Master Fader track will be created after the last selected track in your project.

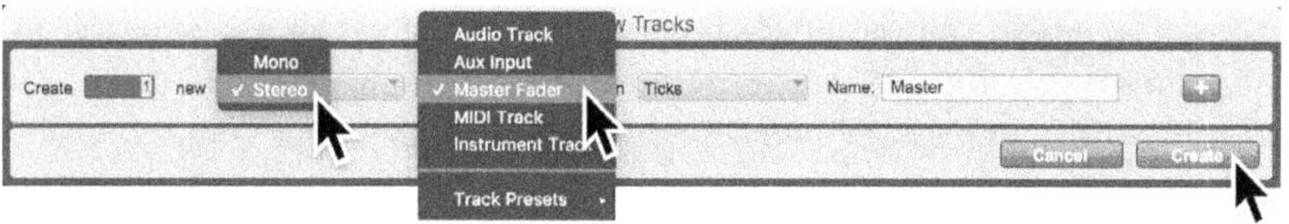

Figure 8.30 Creating a Stereo Master Fader

A Master Fader track might look like any other track, but don't be fooled—it's significantly different!

Figure 8.31 A Master Fader Track in the Mix Window

- You'll notice that the area on the channel strip that would normally display an Input Path selector is conspicuously blank. That's because there is no input on a Master Fader track; it is only a way to control an output.
- Notice also that there are no sends on a Master Fader track.
- If you take a look at a Master Fader track in the Edit window, you'll see that you can't place clips on this track. In this regard, it's similar to an Aux track.

2. Click on the OUTPUT PATH SELECTOR and select the interface output you're using to listen to your mix (if it's not already displayed on the selector). With this output selected, the Master Fader track is in its common role of controlling the output of your entire mix.

Using a Master Fader Track

There are two defining characteristics of Master Faders: They only control the level of an *output*, and their inserts are *post-fader*. This makes the Master Fader great for some things, but terrible for others. Here are some mix tips for your Master Faders:

- **Controlling total output levels of your Mix:** The most common traditional use of a Master Fader is to control the level of your entire project. Having a single Master Fader with the output assigned to the output path routed to your main monitor speakers is an easy way to take control of the total output of your mix.
- **Controlling the output of Subgroups:** With Pro Tools | First, you have up to 4 Master Faders that you can create, and any of those Master Fader tracks can be assigned to any output, whether internal or external. Let's assume that one of your Master Fader tracks is already assigned to the output going to your monitor speakers—that means you have three more Master Faders that you could assign to things, like *busses*.
- **Here's a Scenario:** Let's assume that your vocals are all assigned to a bus (let's say Bus 1-2), which is also the input of an Auxiliary Input Track functioning as a subgroup master. Let's further say that the levels of the individual vocal tracks are too high, and that the subgroup Aux track is clipping as a result. You *could* bring the levels of all the vocal tracks down, but that might take too much time. Instead, you could create a new Master Fader track assigned to Bus 1-2, and that would change the levels coming from the vocal tracks before they get to the input of the Auxiliary Input track. Remember, a Master Fader track only controls the levels of an *output.*
- **Post-Fader Inserts:** Let's talk about *mastering*: There are many different approaches to mastering your mixes, but many of them break the process into two parts: making sure the *tone* of the mix is right and making sure that the final *levels* are right. You recently learned how to create subgroups; The *Main SUB* track (the subgroup of your subgroups) is a great place to fine-tune the tone of your mix, given that the Auxiliary Input track's fader is *post*-insert. If you want to manage the final output levels with plug-ins (for example, with *Limiter* plug-ins, which you'll learn about in the next chapter), you'll want those plug-ins to be the last thing you want in your signal flow. Putting that final Limiter plug-in is best done on a Master Fader track, since the inserts on a Master Fader are *post*-fader. *Dither* is another effect best placed on a Master Fader's *post*-fader inserts.

Master Faders and Dither

In the realm of mastering, there is a process called *dither*—it's something that many audio professionals have heard of, but surprisingly few can tell you what it is and when to use it. Since it's specifically related to Master Fader tracks, let's cover it now:

In overly simplistic terms, *dither* is a very low-level noise that is added to digital audio to offset some of the negative effects of reducing bit depth. For example: If you're working on a 24-bit project, but you need to create a 16-bit file for an audio CD, you can improve the quality of your audio by instantiating a dither plug-in on a Master Fader track.

Dither should be considered only when the final product needs to be at a lesser bit depth than the original project. For example, if you have a 24-bit project and must make a 16-bit final mix, you should absolutely add dither. If, however, your final mix is to remain 24-bit, you shouldn't use it. Sample rates and file formats have no bearing on dither.

1. On an insert on the Master Fader track, select a dither plug-in (in this example, I've chosen POW-r Dither) from the Multichannel Plug-In menu. The plug-in's window will appear. (Tip: I usually put this plug-in on the last insert, in case I want to add any other plug-ins to the Master Fader—it's important that dither is the last process in your mix.)

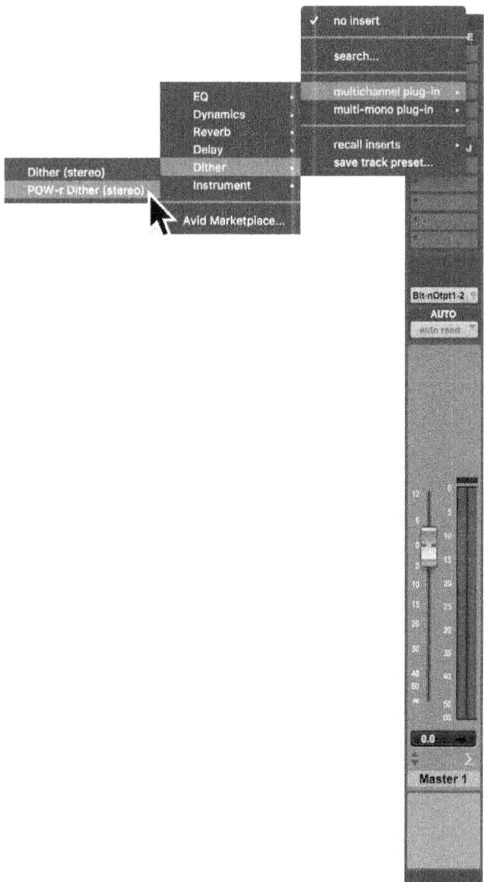

Figure 8.32 Inserting POW-R Dither on a Master Fader Track

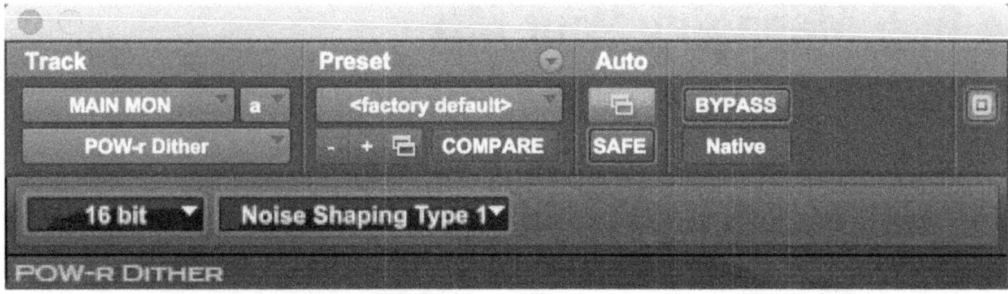

Figure 8.33 The POW-R Dither Plug-in

2. Click on the BIT RESOLUTION pop-up menu (the box in the lower left-hand corner of the plug-in window, which by default reads "16 bit") and choose the final resolution for your mix from the list that will appear. For example, if you want to make a Red Book audio CD of your mix (assuming that your project was at 24 or 32 bits), you would choose the 16-bit option.
3. Next to the bit resolution is the *Noise Shaping Type* pop-up menu. Noise shaping can help make dither "noise" even less audible than it normally is. Click on the NOISE SHAPING button and select a noise-shaping type from the list.

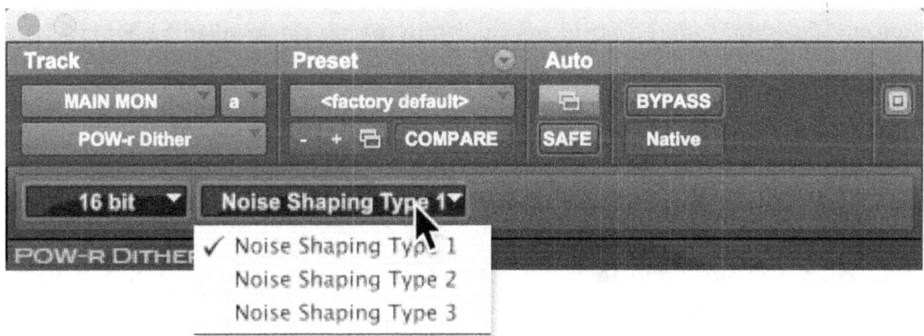

Figure 8.34 Choosing a Noise Shaping Type

The differences between the different kinds of noise shaping are very subtle, but there are some recommended guidelines:

- **Type 1:** Technically, this noise-shaping type doesn't have any noise shaping and will not impact the frequency balance of your mix. It is generally recommended for a low dynamic range (meaning that the difference between the loud sounds and the softer sounds is small), like pop or rock music.
- **Type 2:** This mode *does* employ a degree of noise shaping and is generally recommended for spoken word-based audio.
- **Type 3:** This mode employs more aggressive noise shaping and is recommended for music with a large dynamic range. It's most commonly used in orchestral music, but I've also found that it works well for other styles like traditional jazz and other more dynamic music styles.

4. When it comes to noise shaping types, there's no right answer. Listen to different mixes with different noise shaping later to determine which one is best for you.

Hands-On Exercise 8.2: Managing Your Mix

Now you're going to take your static mix to the next level with subgroups and Master Faders!

Getting Started

1. Open the project that you created in the previous Hands-On Exercise. The project represents a basic static mix.

Organize Tracks into Subgroups

2. Create subgroups of the following Tracks:
   - *Lead Vocal (Dry)*, *Background Vocals (Dry)*, and *Mangled Vox Print* into a subgroup master track called VOX SUB, using Bus 1-2
   - *Acoustic Guitar Stem Print* and *Acoustic Rhythm Guitar* into a subgroup master track called GTR SUB, using Bus 3-4
   - *Bells Stem*, *Dulcimer*, *Glockenspiel*, and *Sitar* into a subgroup master track called SYNTH SUB, using Bus 5-6
   - *Strings Stem Print*, *High Strings*, *Xpand Low End String* into a subgroup master track called STRING SUB, using Bus 7-8
   - *Bass Gtr* and *Xpand Bass* into a subgroup master track called BASS SUB, using Bus 9-10
   - *Break.02*, *Crash*, *Live Drums*, *Hat-Tamb Stem*, *Rimshot*, and *Kick Stem* into a subgroup master track called DRUM SUB, using Bus 11-12
3. Solo-safe all the subgroup master tracks.

Create a MAIN SUB

4. Create a stereo Auxiliary Input track named *MAIN SUB*. Assign the input of the track to be Bus 13-14, and the output to be the outputs connected to your monitor speakers.
5. Create a subgroup of the of the following tracks:
   - VOX SUB
   - SFX
   - GTR SUB
   - SYNTH SUB
   - STRING SUB
   - BASS SUB
   - DRUM SUB

Create a Master Fader

6. Create a stereo Master Fader named *Main MON*, with the output assigned to the outputs connected to your monitor speakers.

Figure 8.35 shows how your Mix window might look, with all the subgrouping and Master Fader completed.

Figure 8.35 Subgroups and Master Fader Setup Finished

Improve Your Static Mix

You've now just radically changed the control you have over your tracks.

7. Now you have the ability to tweak the levels of the tracks within your subgroups to make sure that their blend and position are what you want.
8. Mix your subgroup master tracks (your *stems*) to get a much quicker and better result than you could with the previous hands-on exercise. If you find that you're clipping any of your subgroups, you have three more Master Fader tracks you can add to help control the levels of those bus outputs.
9. If, as you refine your static mix, you find that your overall output is too loud or too soft, you can adjust your total output with the *Main SUB or Main MON* tracks. Just remember that it is very important to make sure you are not seeing any clip lights in your mix.
10. When you are happy with your improved static mix, you're done—make sure you save your project before we move on!

Mix Automation

Up to now, you've been creating static mixes—mixes in which none of the controls (volume and panning in our case) move over time. The limitation of static mixes is that the best settings for one part of your project might not be the right mix choices for other sections. You've been forced to compromise and choose the best settings for the project overall, but probably not the best for any given section. This is all going to change as you learn about *Mix Automation.*

Mix automation refers to the ability to change aspects of your mix (such as volume, for example) over time and to have those changes written to your project. Once those changes have been written, they can be adjusted and played back automatically (hence the term *automation*), giving you the ability to control multiple parameters in real time as your project plays. Automation is one of the coolest things about mixing in a DAW, and in my opinion, nothing beats Pro Tools' automation features.

Before we start dealing with mix automation, let's cover some basic terminology. Audio and MIDI data are *recorded*, but automation is *written*. When your project *plays* back, the written automation can be *read*. This might seem like a matter of semantics at this point, but it'll help keep things clear as you work with automation (and these are the standard industry terms).

Viewing Automation

Though you'll do much of your mixing work in the Mix window, there are still times when you will want to go to the Edit window during the mixing process. Viewing automation is one of those occasions, and the Edit window will not only show you a visual representation of the different movements of your mix controls, but will also let you edit them easily.

In Chapter 6, when we discussed MIDI, you learned how to change your track view from clips to notes, and then to velocity and continuous controllers. That's exactly where you'll go to view different mix automation. Let's start with an example of how you could see the volume automation on a track:

1. First, you'll need to be looking at the Edit window, so if you're still in the Mix window, you should change to the Edit window now.
2. On the track whose automation you want to see, click the TRACK VIEW SELECTOR (which on an audio track reads "Waveform" by default, and on an Auxiliary Input or Master Fader track reads "Volume" by default). Clicking this selector will reveal a menu, as shown in Figure 8.36.

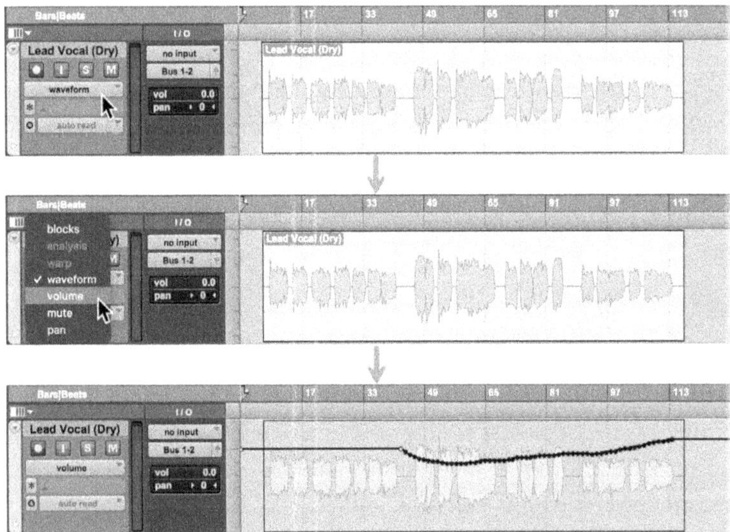

Figure 8.36 Changing Track View to Show Volume Automation

3. Select the desired view from the menu (in this case, I'll choose VOLUME). Your track's display will change accordingly

In Figure 8.36, you'll see the result of changing your track's view. Now, instead of seeing your clips on the track's timeline, you'll see a line called an *automation playlist.* In this case, it's the volume automation playlist. In this example, the fader will be static until around measure 43, when it will lower slightly and then rise again until the end of the clip.

Automation Lanes

One limitation of changing your track view is that if you're viewing an automation playlist, you won't be able to edit your clips (though the clips are visible behind the automation playlist, they are inaccessible). There is another way to view automation that will allow you to also see your clips view:

1. Click on the SHOW/HIDE AUTOMATION LANES button to reveal (or hide) a track's additional lanes.

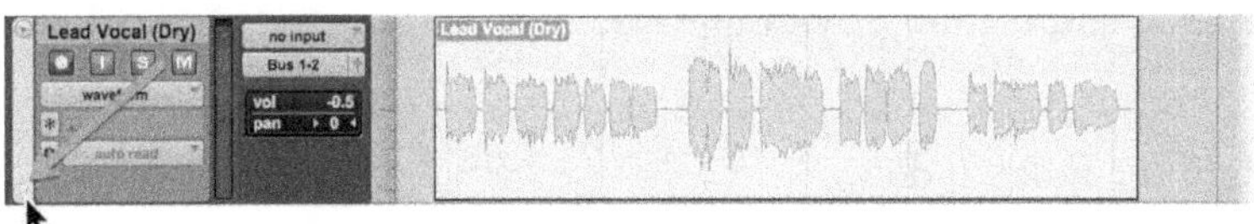

Figure 8.37 Showing an Automation Lane

2. Choosing a lane's view is very similar to what you've done using the Track View selector. Just click on the LANE VIEW SELECTOR and choose the desired automation type from the list. As with the main Track View selector, the currently visible automation type is indicated by a checkmark and will be shown in the Lane View selector itself.

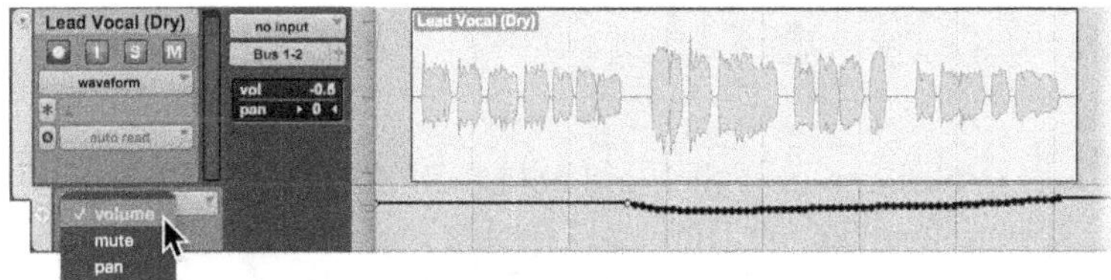

Figure 8.38 The Automation Lane View Selector

3. You can add an automation lane by clicking on the ADD LANE button, which is indicated by a plus (+) icon. To remove one, click on the REMOVE LANE button, shown as a minus (-) icon.

Figure 8.39 Adding or Removing Automation Lanes

On MIDI tracks, you can use automation lanes to view all kinds of MIDI data, including Continuous Controller (CC) data. On Instrument tracks, you can use lanes to view not only MIDI data, but also the same automation data that you'd see on an Audio or Aux track.

Editing Automation

By default, all automation playlists begin as a straight line (meaning that the mix parameter being shown will not move). Perhaps the easiest way to get started with automation is to use editing tools, which you're already familiar with:

Automation and the Pencil Tool

One of the most straightforward ways to change an automation playlist line is to draw mix automation with the Pencil tool.

1. If you're not already there, switch to the Edit window.
2. Click on the TRACK VIEW (or AUTOMATION LANE VIEW) selector of the track you want to work with and choose the data you want to edit. (In this example, I've chosen to view volume automation on the *Lead Vocal (Dry)* track)

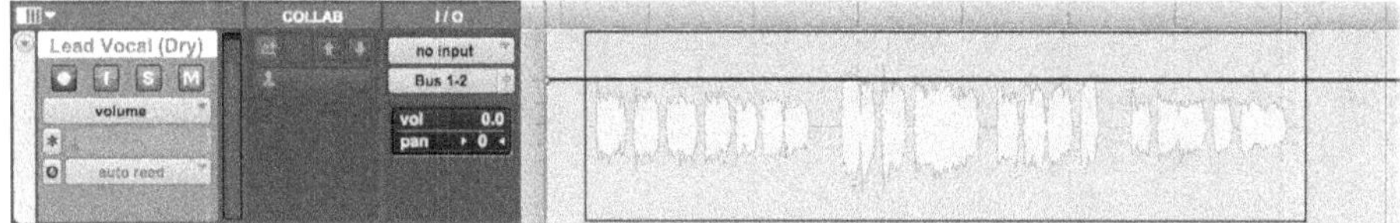

Figure 8.40 A Flat Volume Automation Playlist

3. To view the different drawing options available to you, click and hold the PENCIL TOOL icon. The Pencil tool pop-up menu will appear. Just like the Trim and Grabber tools, the Pencil tool has some useful variations. For this example, let's stick with the default Free Hand shape.

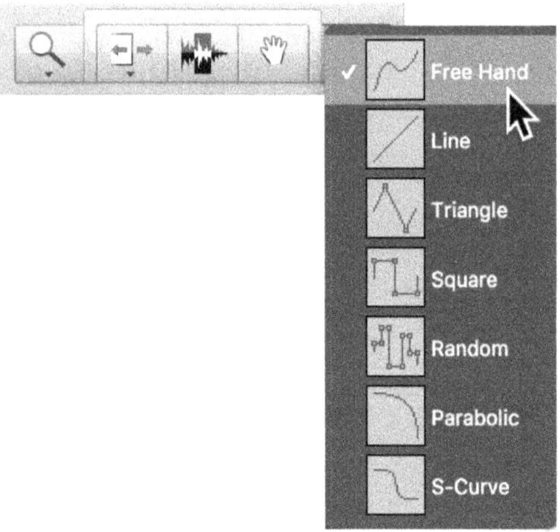

Figure 8.41 Choosing the Freehand Shape of the Pencil Tool

4. Click and hold your cursor (which will appear as a pencil icon) at the point at which you want to begin writing new automation.
5. Drag the mouse to the place where you want to stop writing new automation. The Pencil tool will progressively write over any pre-existing automation (if you're writing new automation on a track that you haven't worked on before, the pre-existing automation is a straight line).

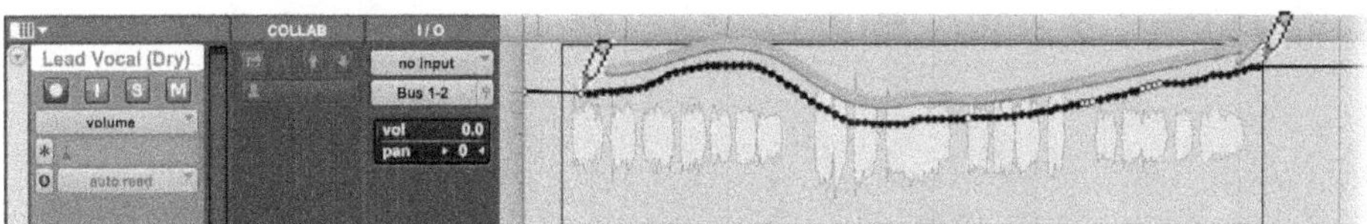

Figure 8.42 Drawing New Volume Automation

6. Release the mouse button. Your new automation will be written.

The Pencil tool's Free Hand shape is well-suited to many kinds of work, but perhaps not the best choice for other kinds of automation changes. Want a smooth transition from one parameter value to another (like a smooth increase in volume, for example)? The Line shape of the Pencil tool makes it easy.

There are other useful Pencil shapes as well. Let's try writing some pan automation on the track that ping-pongs from left to right:

1. Click and hold the PENCIL TOOL. Again, the Pencil tool options will appear.
2. This time click on the TRIANGLE shape.

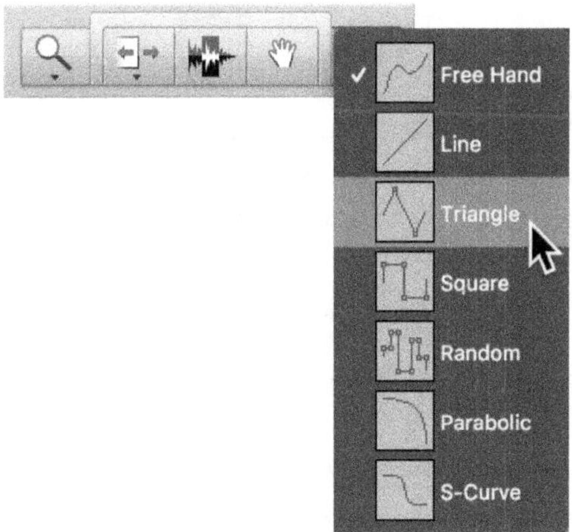

Figure 8.43 Choosing the Triangle Shape of the Pencil Tool

3. When you're dealing with the Triangle, Square, or Random Pencil tool options, the Grid value will determine the frequency of the automation changes (even if you're not in Grid mode). In this case, to pan from side to side every measure, choose *1 bar* as the Grid value, as shown here.

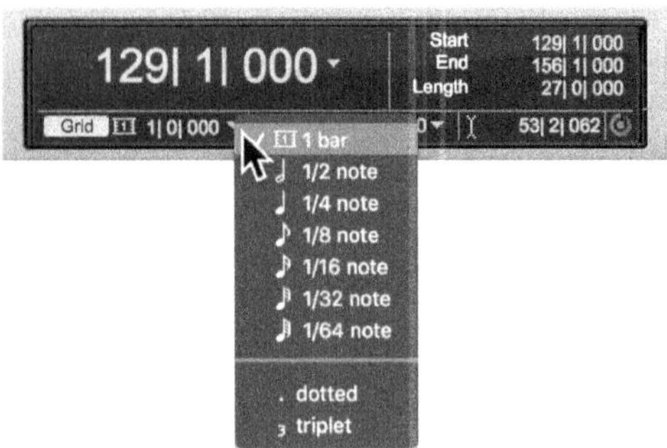

Figure 8.44 Choosing a One Bar Grid

4. You can only draw automation of the view that you're currently looking at. Since this will be pan automation, choose PAN from the Track View selector.

Figure 8.45 Changing the Track View to Pan

5. Click and hold your cursor (which will appear as a pencil icon) at the point at which you want to begin writing new automation. This time, as you drag horizontally, a triangle wave will be drawn across the track. The speed of your panning will be determined by your Grid value. (In my case, it's one measure.) You can change the height of the wave by moving your mouse vertically as you drag. In the case of pan automation, a higher and lower triangle wave will translate into a more extreme pan from left to right.

6. When you're finished, release the mouse button. The pan automation will be written to your track. Figure 8.46 shows the track panning first to the left, and then to the right, with the duration of each directional change being one measure.

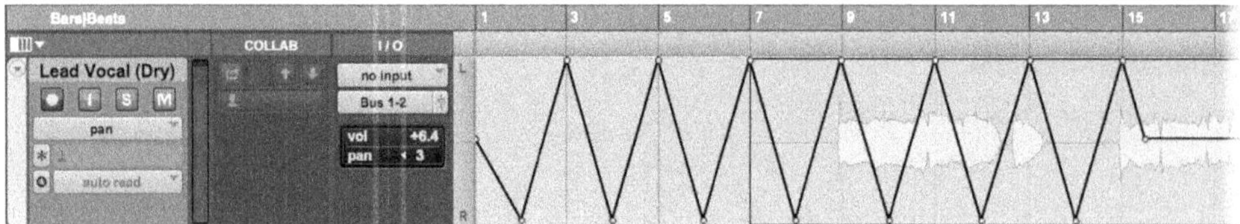

Figure 8.46 Pan Automation, Oscillating Between the Left and Right Speakers

Although a triangle wave can be drawn in any of the Edit modes, if you want the apex of the triangle wave to fall on a grid line, you must be in Grid mode.

Automation and the Trim Tool

When the Trim tool is moved into a selected area of automation, it will be shown as downward-facing, enabling you to drag your mouse up and down to increase or decrease the level of the automation in that selected area (while maintaining the shape of the automation line). Though this isn't commonly used with Pan automation, it's a great way to raise or lower a section of volume automation, while leaving the shape of the trimmed automation intact:

The workflow described here will involve both the Selector tool and the Trim tool. If you want to work even more efficiently, this can be done with the Smart Tool, which will change behavior based on your cursor's position within a track.

1. Using the Selector tool, select the area that you want to change (if you're using the Smart Tool, position your cursor at the bottom half of the track).
2. Change to the Trim tool (or if you're using the Smart Tool, move your cursor toward the top of the track, until the cursor changes).
3. Move the Trim tool into the selected area. The Trim tool will be shown downward-facing, indicating that it's ready to change your automation.

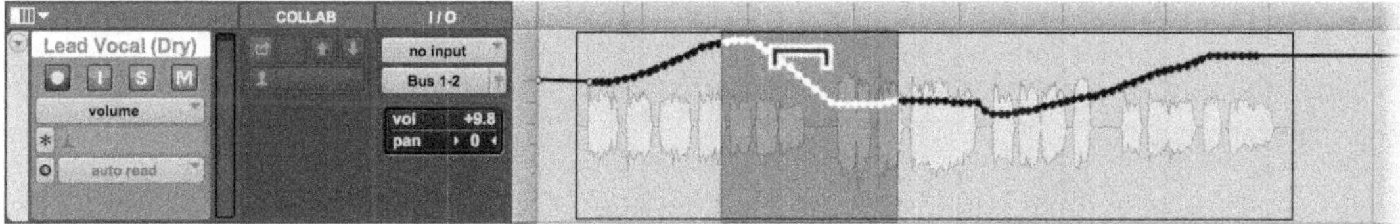

Figure 8.47 Ready to Trim Volume Automation

Click and drag your mouse up or down to adjust your automation proportionally.

Release the mouse button. The automation will be proportionally changed in the selected area.

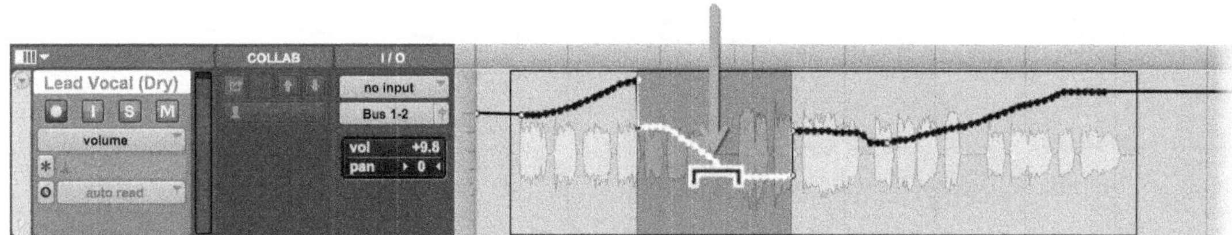

Figure 8.48 The Trimmed Automation

Note that when you use the Trim tool to change volume automation, there will be a small box at the top of the selected area that will not only show you the level of your new automation, but also a *delta* value (indicated by a triangle, the Greek letter for *delta*) when adjusting volume. This delta value lets you know the amount of change you're applying.

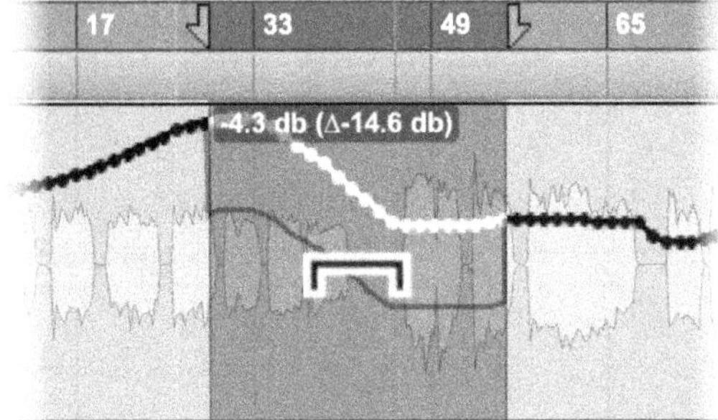

Figure 8.49 During the Process Of Trimming Automation, Showing the Delta Value

Automation and the Grabber Tool

You may have noticed that your automation line is composed of a number of small dots. These dots are called automation *breakpoints*, which define the shape of your automation playlist line. The Grabber tool is quite handy at working with these individual breakpoints. Here's how you can use it to create, modify, and delete automation breakpoints.

- To create an automation breakpoint where one doesn't currently exist: Using the Grabber tool, click on the point in time in the track where you want it to be.
- To change the time or value of an existing automation breakpoint, click and drag the breakpoint to the desired location.
- To delete an existing automation breakpoint, hold down the Option (Mac) or Alt (Windows) key and click it. The cursor will be shown as a pointing hand with a minus (-) sign next to it.

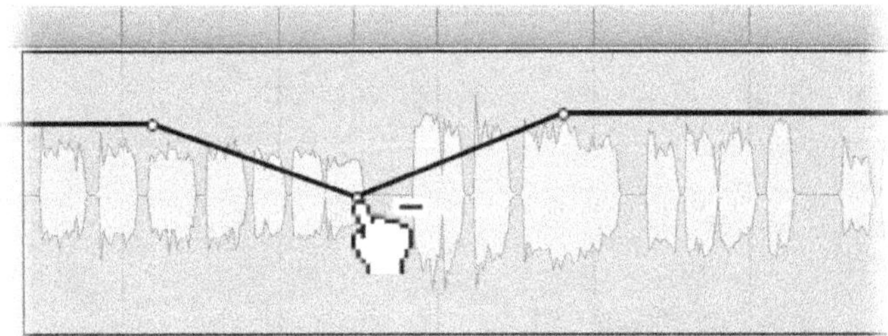
Figure 8.50 Deleting an Automation Breakpoint with the Grabber Tool

Automation Modes

In addition to creating automation with the Edit tools, you can capture your adjustments of faders, pan knobs, and other controls as your project plays. In fact, in many mixing situations, this "live" writing of automation movement is the first step after creating a static mix, and the written automation is then adjusted with editing tools.

Pro Tools | First has five automation modes, which determine the way your fader, pan, mute, send, and plug-in parameters will be written. Each automation mode is unique to fit a wide variety of mixing workflows. Understanding the distinction between these modes is the best way to choose when and how to use them.

Choosing an Automation Mode

You can choose automation modes on a track-by-track basis:

1. In the Mix or Edit window, click on the AUTOMATION MODE selector on the track that you want to automate (which by default will be say "Auto Read" or "Read" depending on track height). A menu of the five automation modes of Pro Tools will appear:

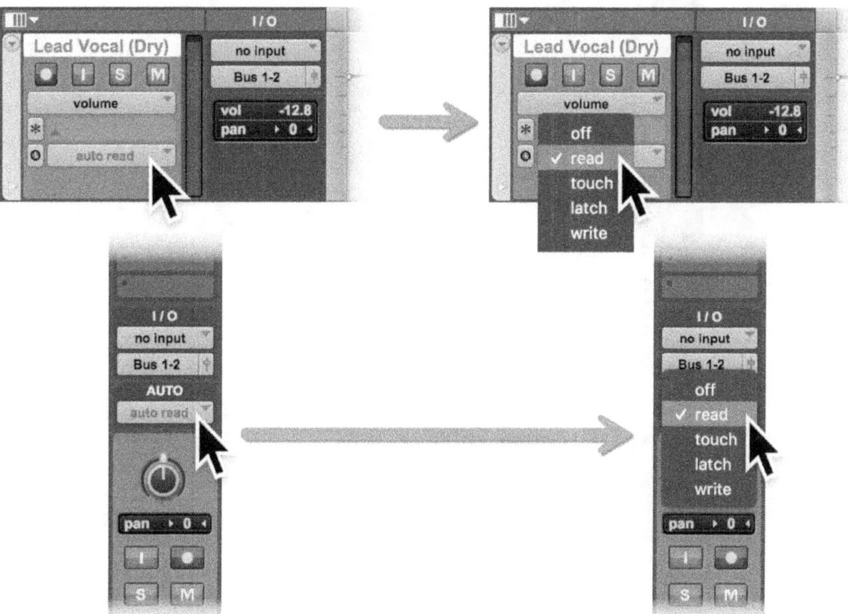

Figure 8.51 Changing Automation Modes in the Edit and Mix windows

- **Off:** Using this mode, automation will neither be written nor played back. This is a good way to suspend automation on a track that has automation.
- **Read:** Automation cannot be written in this mode, but previously written automation will be played back. Use this mode to play back your automated tracks without running the risk of overwriting that automation.
- **Touch:** The track will read previously written automation until a parameter is touched (clicked with your mouse or using a control surface), at which time automation will be written for that parameter. When the parameter is released, it will return to its previously written automation.
- **Latch:** This mode is similar to Touch. Only when a parameter is touched will automation be written. When the parameter is released in Latch mode, however, it will remain at the last value and continue to write automation at that position until you stop playback.
- **Write:** In this mode, automation will be written on all enabled parameters, regardless of whether the parameter is being touched.

2. Choose the desired automation mode from the menu.

But which automation mode is the right one? That depends on what you want to do with the track:

Read and Off

By default, *Auto Read* mode is the active mode on any new track. Read mode does what its name implies: With this mode selected, any written automation will be read during playback. For example, if a volume automation line goes downward over time, the fader will move accordingly.

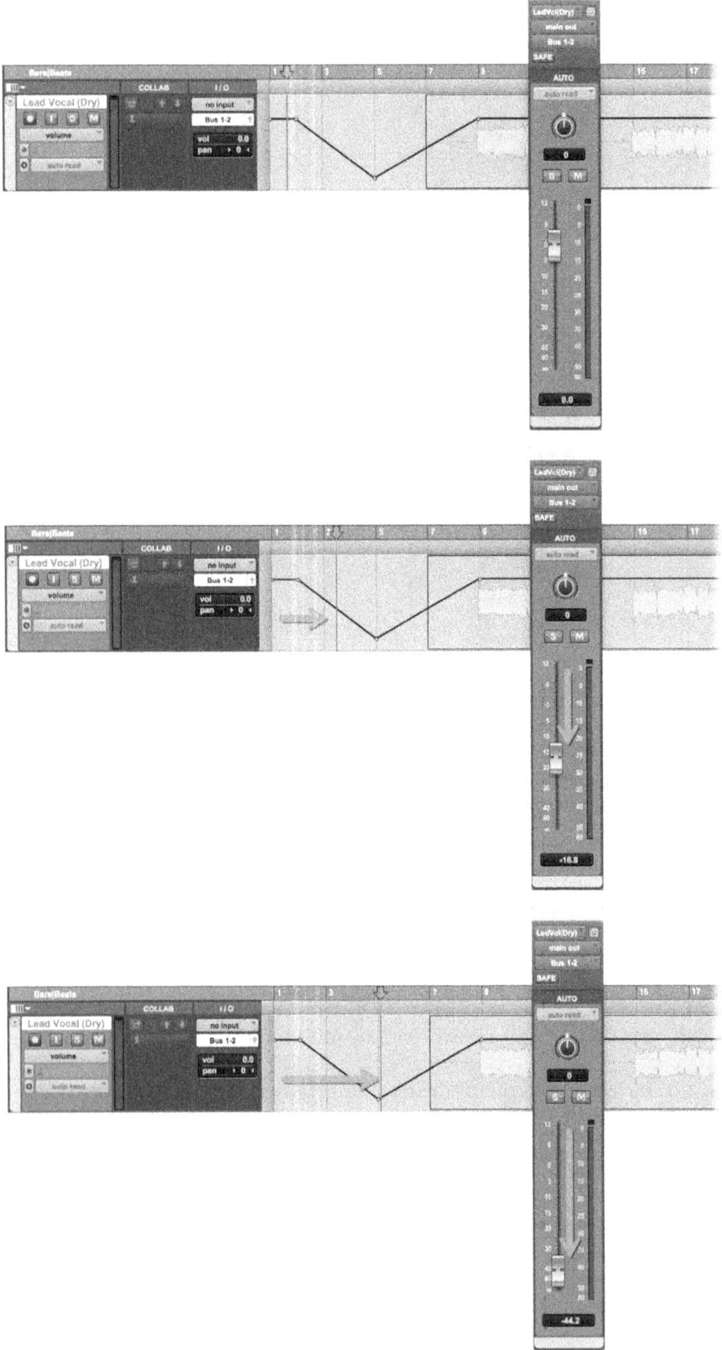

Figure 8.52 Volume Automation in Read Mode

One point about Read mode: When a track is created, the automation playlist line is flat, as you've seen previously in this chapter. In these cases, where there is only one automation breakpoint at the beginning of the track, the fader will not read any automation (since there is not enough automation to be read). The fader will stay wherever you position it.

Auto Read is a good choice if you have finished your automation work on the track and you just want it to read your automation. With this mode selected, even if you touch a fader during playback accidentally, you will not write any new automation data.

Auto Off is another automation mode that is aptly named for its purpose. When a track's automation mode is set to *Auto Off*, no automation data will be read as your project plays, even if there is automation on the track. With this mode selected, you will see a blue line (called the *Composite Playlist*) indicating the current level of the parameter.

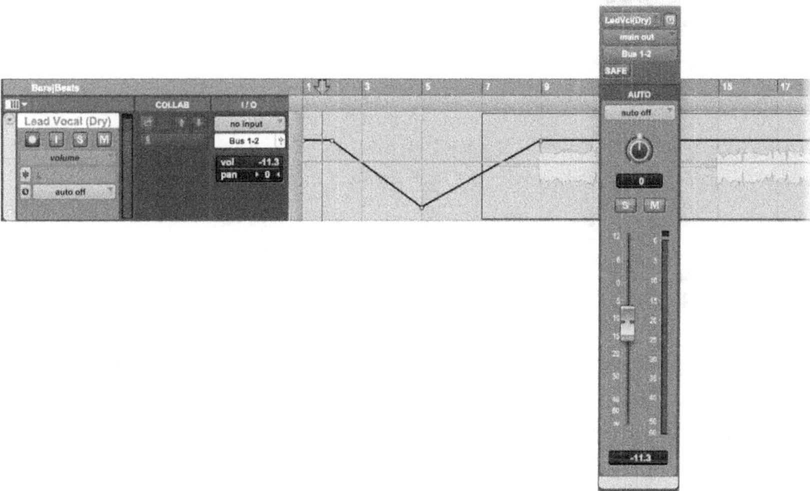

Figure 8.53 Volume Automation in Off Mode

You'll use *Auto Off* mode when you want to temporarily turn off the motion of parameters on a track. It's commonly used when you want to compare a simpler, non-automating track to a more complex track with changing mix parameters.

Touch and Latch

You'll hear *Auto Touch* and *Auto Latch* collectively referred to as the *update modes* because they're well-suited for spot-checking sections of your mix and replacing older automation with something new. They're also very commonly used for writing new automation on a track.

Auto Touch and *Auto Latch* work nearly identically, with the only difference at the end of the workflow:

1. Select TOUCH or LATCH automation mode from the Automation Mode selector.
2. Play your project. As long as you don't click on any parameters, your automation will be read back, and the appropriate controls will follow the existing automation line (in Figure 8.54, a straight line).

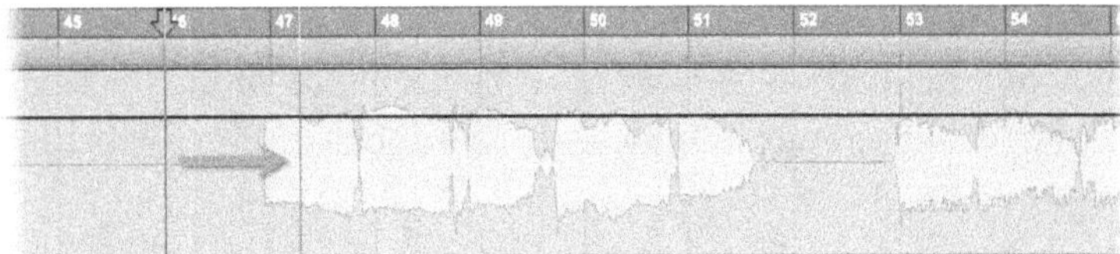

Figure 8.54 Starting in Touch or Latch Mode (Reading Pre-existing Automation)

3. When you want to make a change in your automation, just **click** on the appropriate **control** and **adjust it**. You'll see that as you move the control (in this case, a volume fader), a new automation playlist line will be written, colored red.

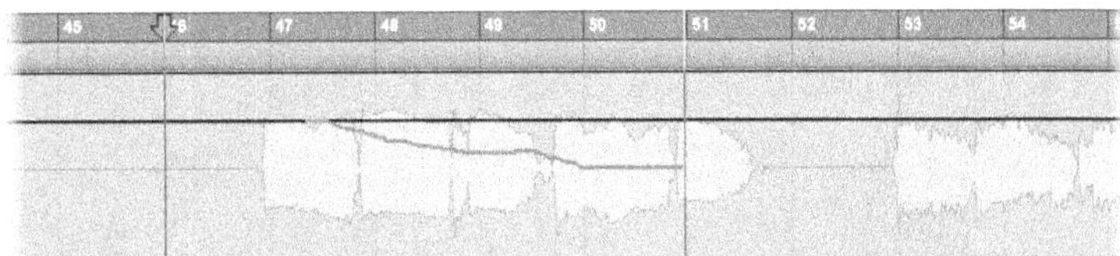

Figure 8.55 Writing New Automation (Touch or Latch Mode)

You might have noticed that the track's Automation Mode selector also turned red as soon as you moved the volume fader. What's up with that? The track's Automation Mode selector will turn red when any kind of automation data is being written to it.

Here's where the difference comes in. When you release your mouse button and your control over that mix parameter:

4. If using ***Auto Touch*** mode, your mix parameter will quickly return to the previously written automation and continue reading that preexisting automation until playback is stopped. In Figure 8.56, I released the fader in the middle of bar 51.

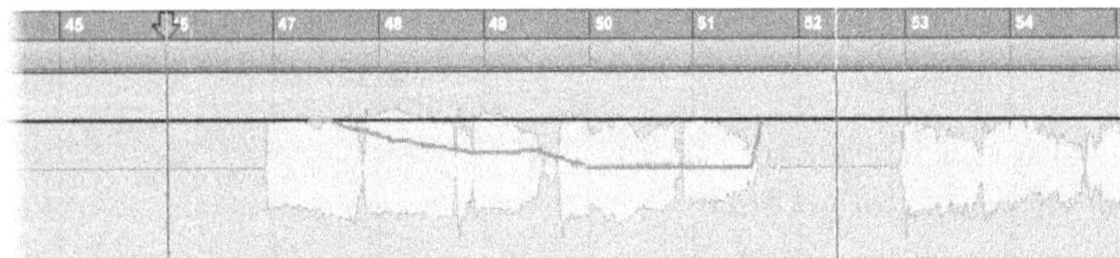

Figure 8.56 After Releasing the Fader in Touch Mode

5. If using ***Auto Latch*** mode, your mix parameter will stay at the value where you released your mouse and continue writing automation at that level until playback is stopped. In Figure 8.57, I released the fader in the middle of bar 51.

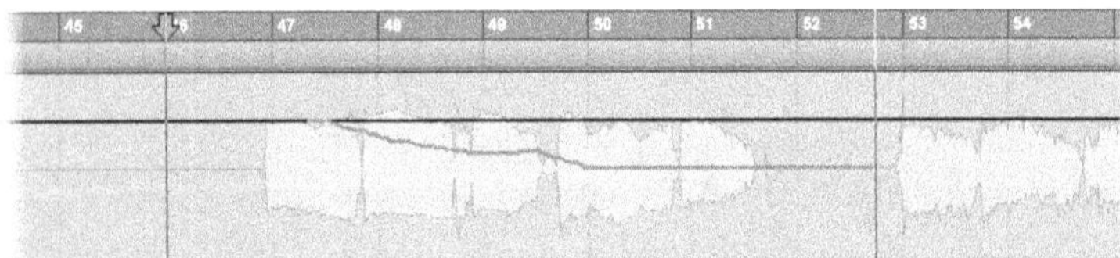

Figure 8.57 After Releasing the Fader in Latch Mode

Both of these modes are used in a variety of situations, mostly to fine-tune static mixes, adding nuanced human control over the parameters over time.

Write

Since it's already been established that automation is written (as opposed to *recorded*), you might assume that *Auto Write* is the best mode to use when starting your mix. However, this mode is actually the *least* used by many mix engineers.!

Let's take a look at an automation workflow using Auto Write mode to change the volume of a track.

1. Select WRITE automation mode from the Automation Mode selector.

Figure 8.58 Selecting Write Mode

You might have noticed that the track's Automation Mode selector turned red as soon as you changed your automation mode to Write. This indicates one of the unique behaviors of this mode—it begins writing automation as soon as playback starts.

2. Using the Selector tool, move your playback cursor to the point at which you want to start writing automation.

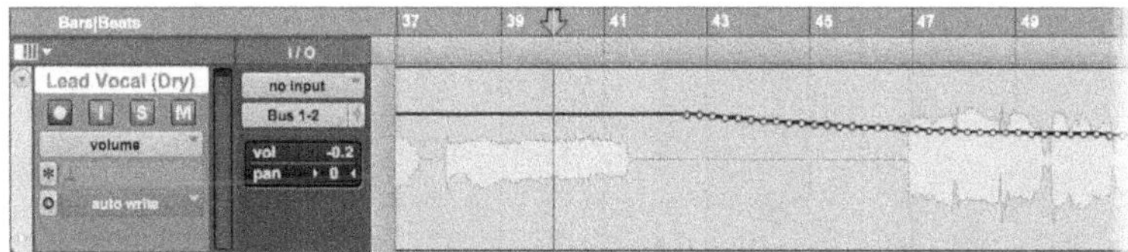

Figure 8.59 Moving the Playback Cursor to the Point where Writing will Begin

3. Change your mix parameter (in this case, volume) to the value that you want to have when writing begins.

4. Start playback. Automation will be written for all parameters that can be automated (volume, pan, mute, sends, and plugin parameters). As your automation is being written, you will see the data represented as a red line in the track's automation playlist. Initially, the automation data written will be the level of the mix parameter before playback began, but you can change this during playback (similar to how you would use Touch or Latch modes).

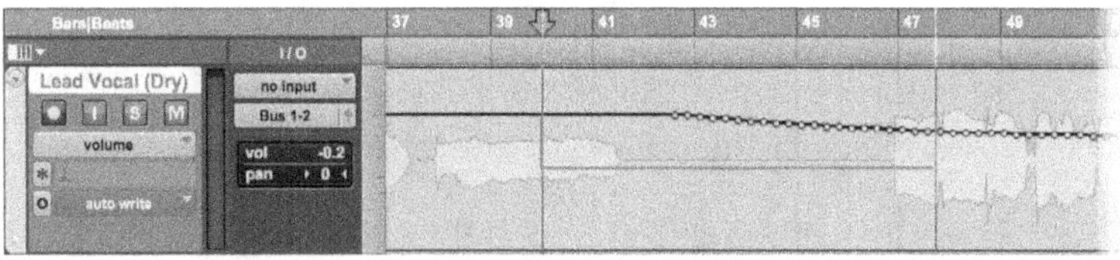

Figure 8.60 Writing New Automation (Write Mode)

5. When you're finished writing automation, stop your project's playback.

When you stop playback, you'll see that the volume line has changed shape to match the fader moves that you performed during playback. As soon as playback stopped, the automation stopped as well. However—and this is important—when you're using Write mode, you are also writing automation on other parameters, even if you didn't touch any other controls! For example, if there happened to be any pan automation in the section you were playing back, it would be overwritten, even though you weren't viewing the automation playlist or touching the parameter.

The strength of Write mode is that it writes on all enabled automation parameters (volume, pan, sends, and plug-in parameters), whether you touched those parameters or not. That makes it a choice for many for first passes at automation, but rarely beyond that. To tweak individual parameters, you'll use Touch and Latch modes.

You'll notice that after using Write mode (setting the automation mode to Write, starting playback, and then stopping), you'll see that the automation mode will automatically change to *Auto Latch*.

Creating a Mixdown

When you're working with a Pro Tools project, you're in a multitrack environment. Even though you may be listening through stereo monitor speakers, you're actually hearing many component tracks, artfully combined by Pro Tools' software mix engine. From a production standpoint, it's a very cool way to work, but if you want to hear your song *outside* the Pro Tools environment, you'll have to render the mix down to a format compatible with the outside world.

There are three common ways that a mixdown is created: *External Layback*, *Bounce to Track*, and *Bounce to Disk*. Although this book (and arguably the majority of workflows) will focus on bouncing to disk, it's good to understand all the different ways that a final product is created.

External Layback

One of the oldest ways of creating a final product (often called a final *deliverable*) is to record the output of Pro Tools' audio outputs to an external recording device. Prior to the digital audio revolution of the '80s and '90s, the output of a mixed-down multitrack tape would be recorded to another tape recorder. These days, external layback is still used in some post-production (video) workflows, where the mixed-down output of Pro Tools is routed to the analog input of a videotape recorder, although more rarely now as digital video is becoming the worldwide standard.

Bounce to Track

Bouncing to track (often called an *Internal Bounce*) follows the same kind of logic of subgroups—the routing of multiple tracks to another track within the Pro Tools software. Earlier in this chapter, you created subgroups of all the related tracks, and created a *Main SUB* and Master Fader. You could easily set up an internal bounce by changing the output of the *Main SUB* and Master Fader track to an unused bus, and then create another audio track with the same bus set as the input. Once that's done, just record to that new track using a normal recording workflow. What you'll get is a clip on that track that sounds like the entire mix, and you can then export that clip as a file.

There are pros and cons to this kind of workflow. On the plus side, many Pro Tools users like to have a mixdown track in their project from an organizational perspective. Having the clip in your project makes it easy to double-check the mix. However, there are some down sides: First, you cannot create a mixdown at a different sample rate than your project. Also, an internal bounce workflow will use an audio track, and with Pro Tools | First, there are limits on the number of audio tracks you can create.

Bounce to Disk

The last method—*Bounce to Disk*—is the most popular way of mixing down a session or project. This method has several advantages: First, it will not require you to create any new tracks or do any special routing of your audio signals. Secondly, you can do an *offline* (faster than real time) mixdown, and mix a long project in a short time. This method will also allow you to easily change sample rates and file formats, so even if your project has a high sample rate and bit-depth, you can create a final file in a format that any audio player can play back.

In *Pro Tools | First*, this method of mixdown is called *Export Audio Mix*, but this term is not commonly used in the larger Pro Tools community. For the purposes of this chapter, both *Bounce to Disk* and *Export Audio Mix* are synonymous.

You don't have to go far in an internet search to find spirited discussions on which is better, bounce to track or Bounce to Disk. The truth is, many years ago, there *was* a difference in the audio engine used when you did an internal bounce and when you bounced to disk, but even then the differences were so subtle that they were barely audible, and it was a matter of opinion about which was "better." Since Pro Tools became a 64-bit application in mid-2013, those differences no longer exist—both *bounce* to track and Bounce to Disk will give the same result.

Bouncing to disk is a simple process, but an important one that demands attention to detail, so I'll go over each step carefully. Here's how to go about bouncing to disk, so you can create a file that you can play on any device.

1. Using the Selector tool, select the area of your project you want to bounce to disk in the timeline ruler. (In this example, I'll select from the beginning of my project to the end of my Master Fader track's fade-out.)
2. Click on the FILE menu.
3. Choose EXPORT. A submenu will be displayed.
4. Choose AUDIO MIX. The *Export Audio Mix* dialog box will appear.

Figure 8.61 Opening the Export Audio Mix Dialog Box

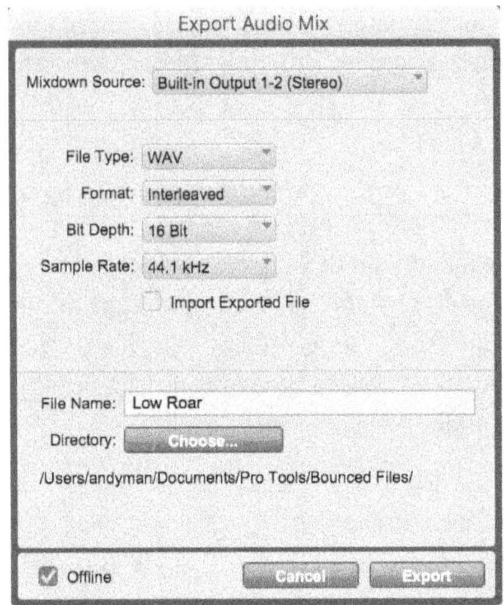

Figure 8.62 The Export Audio Mix Dialog Box

The shortcut for opening the Export Audio Mix dialog box is COMMAND+OPTION+B (Mac) or CTRL+ALT+B (Windows).

At the top of the Export Audio Mix dialog box, you'll see the *Mixdown Source* selector. (The currently selected source will be displayed.) To change the source, click on the Mixdown Source selector and select the output path you're using to listen to your mix. (In this case, I want to choose the *Built-In output 1-2*, because that's the path that is connected to my monitor speakers.)

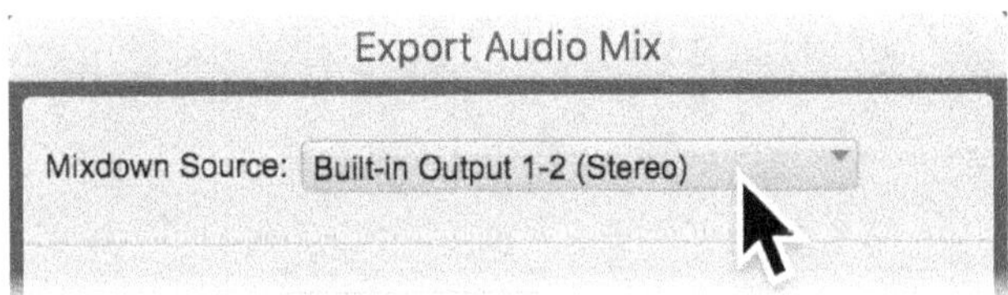

Figure 8.63 The Mixdown Source Selector

If you export your mix and later find that your mixdown is a silent audio file, you probably chose the wrong mixdown source.

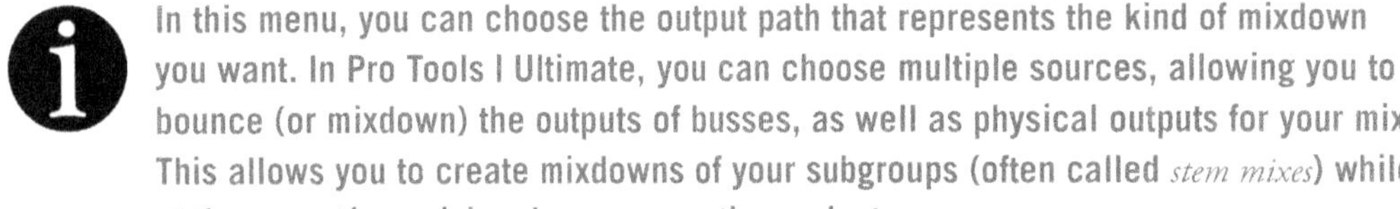

In this menu, you can choose the output path that represents the kind of mixdown you want. In Pro Tools I Ultimate, you can choose multiple sources, allowing you to bounce (or mixdown) the outputs of busses, as well as physical outputs for your mix. This allows you to create mixdowns of your subgroups (often called *stem mixes*) while at the same time mixing down your entire project.

5. The *File Type* selector will display the type of file you will be creating. (In this example, you'll be creating a WAV file.) If you want to change the file type, just click on the FILE TYPE selector and choose the desired type from the list of available file types (WAV or AIFF).

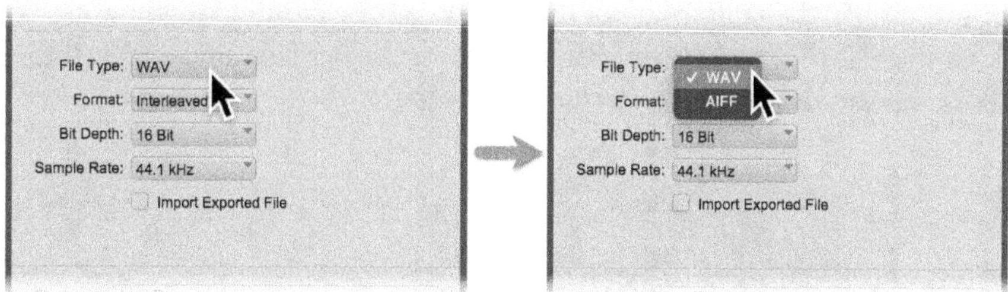

Figure 8.64 Choosing a Mixdown File Type

6. The *Format* selector will display the channel format of the file(s) you will be creating with your mixdown. If you want to change the format, just click on the FORMAT selector and choose the desired format from the list. The choices are as follows:

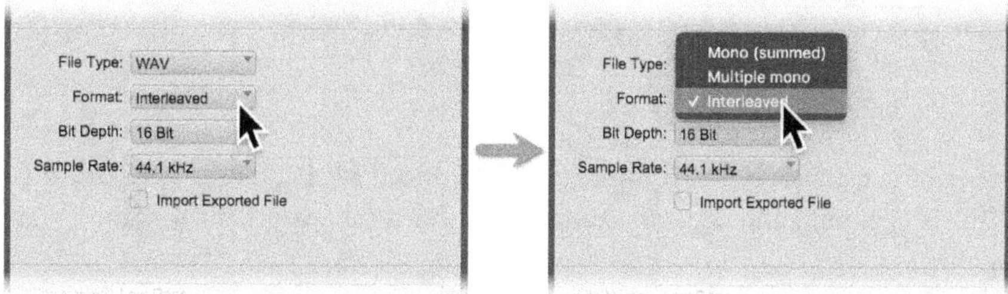

Figure 8.65 Choosing a Mixdown Format

- **Mono (Summed):** With this option selected, your project will be mixed down to a single mono file (even if it's a stereo project). If you're working on a stereo project, the left and right channels of the mix are combined into a single channel.
- **Multiple Mono:** When this is chosen, your stereo mix will be output to a pair of mono files: one for the left channel (with a .L after the filename) and one for the right (with a .R after the filename). This is particularly useful for bounces that you intend to import into another Pro Tools project or session.
- **Interleaved:** Your mix will be rendered to a single stereo file. The single file will have left and right channels.

7. The *Bit Depth* selector will display the bit depth of the file you will be creating. To change the bit depth, click on the BIT DEPTH selector and choose the desired setting from a list of available resolutions. (16-bit, 24-bit, or 32-bit float).

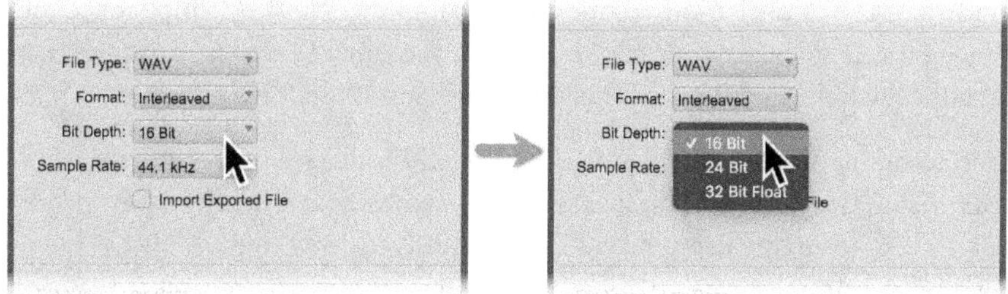

Figure 8.66 Choosing a Mixdown File Bit-Depth

8. The *Sample Rate* selector will display the sample rate of the file you will be creating. If you want to change the setting, click on the SAMPLE RATE selector and choose the desired sample rate (the list of available sample rates will vary based upon your audio interface).

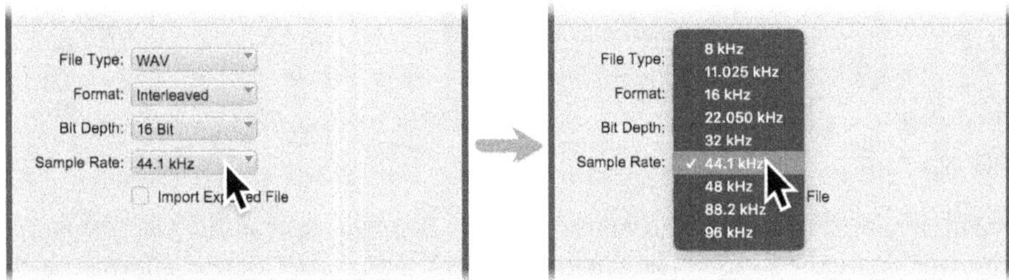

Figure 8.67 Choosing a Mixdown File Sample Rate

In this example, I'm going to export my mix to a format called *Red Book.* Audio CDs introduced this standard. For red book audio, the bit depth should be set to 16, the sample rate should be 44.1 kHz, and the format should be interleaved.

9. Clicking the Import After Bounce check box will import your bounced file back into your project on a new Audio track. This is optional, and only an available option if the export is the same sample rate as the project.
10. Type a descriptive FILE NAME for your exported file.
11. Click the Directory CHOOSE button to choose the destination location for your bounced file. If you do not choose a specific location for the file, the last used location will be the destination for the *newly-created* mixdown file, shown directly below the directory Choose button.

On a Mac, the default location for bounced files is /Users/[username]/Documents/Pro Tools/Bounced Files. On a Windows computer, it's C:\[username]\My Documents\Pro Tools\Bounced Files.

At this point, it should be emphasized how important it is to know exactly where and under what name your mixdown file is saved. You can save your bounced file anywhere you choose in your system, but with this great power comes the responsibility of using it wisely. Make sure you can find your files when you need them!

Ironically, perhaps the biggest new feature in Pro Tools is also one of the smallest check boxes. In older versions of Pro Tools, all mixdowns (external layback, bounce to track, or Bounce to Disk) were done in real time. If you had a 20-minute television show soundtrack, the bounce took 20 minutes to complete. Now, by simply checking one box in the Bounce dialog box, you'll be able to create your final bounce just as quickly as your computer can process the file. (The rapidity of the bounce will depend on the power of your computer's CPU.)

Changing your bounce from real-time to offline is very easy: Click the OFFLINE check box in the lower left-hand corner of the Export Audio Mix dialog box (this feature is enabled by default). The quality of an offline bounce and a real-time bounce is identical, so for many users, an offline bounce is the way to go.

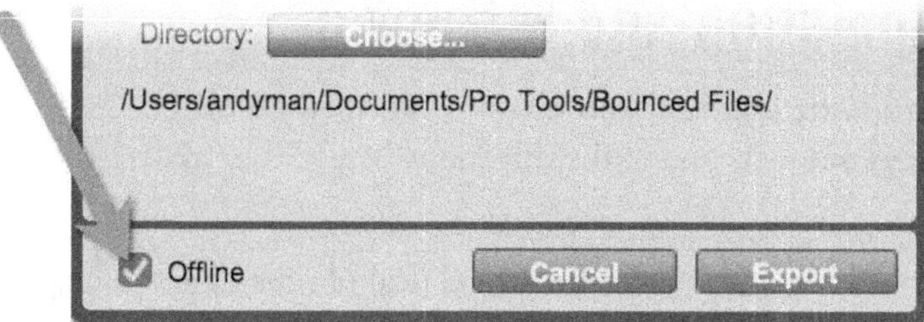

Figure 8.68 The Offline Check Box

There are certain cases in which an offline bounce is not possible:

- If hardware effects are used (as opposed to plug-ins)
- If external MIDI sound devices are being used

12. Click the EXPORT button (in the lower right-hand corner of the Export Audio Mix dialog box) to begin your mixdown.

After you click the Export button, your mixdown will begin. Depending on whether you have the *Offline* check box checked or not, you'll see one of two different behaviors.

- If the Offline box is *unchecked*, your project will play in real time. You'll see a countdown window indicating your mixdown's remaining time.

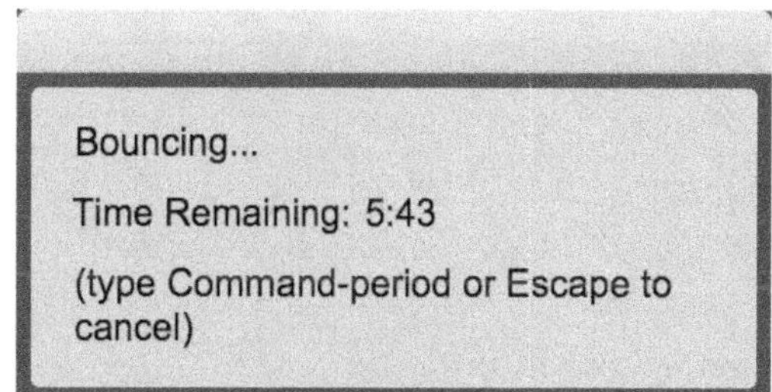

Figure 8.69 A Real-Time Bounce

- If the Offline box is *checked*, you'll see a progress indicator of your bounce. The number in parentheses to the right of the window indicates how quickly your mix is rendering compared to a real-time bounce.

Figure 8.70 An Offline Bounce

When you're done, a new file (or files, if you're exporting multiple mono files) will be created in the location that you designated in the Export Audio Mix dialog box.

Hands-On Exercise 8.3: Automation and Mixdown

In this chapter's last exercise, you'll start with your static mix, add automation, and then export that mix as an audio file. Since you've already created a mix that is uniquely yours, the directions here will be general steps for taking it to the next level.

This section will start getting into the minutiae of your mix and can take a good deal of time to get just right. If you're using this book as a part of a structured course, make sure that you understand how much time you have for each section of the exercise, and that at some point, you'll need to move on to the next section. If you're using this book on your own, you have the luxury of time and can devote as much of it as you like to each task.

If you're preparing for a professional career, take this famous quote (attributed to Leonardo Da Vinci) to heart: "Art is never finished, only abandoned." In the professional world, where deadlines are ever-present, the ability to manage one's time and focus on the most important parts first (knowing there might not be enough time to get to everything) is the mark of a good professional. As you experiment in this chapter, check yourself: What takes up most of your time, and what is the most effective in your mixing? As you grow in experience, you'll become better at time management, and here's a great place to start.

Getting Started

1. Open the project that you created in the previous Hands-On Exercise. The project represents a basic static mix, with subgroups and a master fader.

Automating by Section

To start out, you'll create rough automation for different sections of the song:

2. Make sure that all your tracks are in *Auto Read* mode.
3. Make sure that all your tracks are showing volume automation playlists.
4. Make sure that you are in *Loop Playback* mode.
5. You'll want some space to work, so change all of your track heights to *Medium* or larger.
6. Listen to your mix to determine its structure and make note of the locations where those sections begin and end.
7. One by one, select sections that you want to adjust from the timeline. This will ensure that all tracks have selections in them, as shown in Figure 8.71. It is important that these selections are accurate, so make sure you play each selection to check it before proceeding (HINT: Grid mode will make this selection process easier).

Figure 8.71 Selecting a Section of the Song (Verse 1)

8. Use the Trim tool to adjust relative volume levels as your project plays.
9. Repeat steps 6 and 7 for all the relevant sections of your song. When you're done, your project's mix will change as it plays. Now each section can have its own static mix.

Tweaking with Tools

Next, use Edit tools to make smaller changes within sections:

10. Listen critically to individual sections (this may require listening several times), making notes as to small parts (words of the vocal track, for example) that should be changed).
11. Consider which of the changes can be made with Edit tools, and which should be written "live" using the automation modes (which you'll do in the next section).
12. Using the Pencil, Trim, and Grabber tools, make the appropriate adjustments to the individual sections of the song.

Tweaking with Live Automation

After changing your automation with the various Edit tools at your disposal, it is likely that there are some sections that the tools couldn't properly fix. At this point, the personal touch is needed, and that's where you'll start moving controls manually using Pro Tools' automation modes.

13. Listen critically again to each section of your mix (isolating tracks with solo and mute as needed) to determine small parts of the mix that need to have live automation written on them.
14. Using the automation modes (Touch, Latch, and Write), write new automation as needed (NOTE: The modes that you'll most likely want to use are Touch and Latch, but not Write, as Write mode will overwrite automation on that track even when a control isn't touched.).

Exporting Your Mix

To end the exercise (and this chapter), you'll export your mix in Red Book audio format.

15. First, you'll need to make a selection. Start playback from somewhere close to the end of the song (in this case around measure 120). Watching the meter in the Edit window's toolbar, note the position where the meter drops to silence.
16. Select an area on the timeline from the beginning of the project's timeline to the point at which the meter drops to silence.
17. Do an *offline* Audio Mix Export with the following settings:
    - Mixdown Source: The output path attached to your monitor speakers
    - File Type: WAV
    - Format: Interleaved
    - Bit Depth: 16
    - Sample Rate: 44.1 kHz
    - Name and location can be anything you choose, but you must be able to quickly find the file.
18. Once finished, locate the file and preview it (in any application) to ensure that it has been correctly exported. If it has, you're done—save your work, and congratulations!

Review Questions

1. After the input of an Audio or Aux track, what is the next step in the signal flow?

2. What is the difference between a pre-fader send and a post-fader send?

3. True or False? Sends are processed in series (meaning that the level of send A will affect the level of send B, and so on).

4. What is a "static" mix?

5. What is the shortcut to move a fader in fine resolution (.1 dB increments)?

6. What is the difference between pan linking and pan inverse linking?

7. What is a subgroup?

8. What is the difference in signal flow between an Audio Track and a Master Fader?

9. What is the difference between *Auto-Touch* and *Auto-Latch* mode?

10. What is the first step in creating a mixdown?

CHAPTER 9

Getting Started with Plug-ins

So far, you've mixed using volume and pan controls. You've adjusted the amplitude and positions of your tracks, but you haven't changed the tone or timbre of individual tracks or subgroups. To do that, you'll need to start using effects.

When people talk about effects (whether hardware devices or the plug-in type that we'll discuss in this chapter), it's common to divide them into different types. Some people divide them into families like *dynamic-based* (effects that change the amplitude of a sound) and *time-based* (effects that change their duration), while others might divide them into types like *filters*, *spectral effects* and more. Some plug-in effects even defy categorization!

In the last two chapters of the book, we'll divide effects into *two* types: Effects that are entirely applied to a sound, and effects that you'll want to blend a changed sound with the original unprocessed sound. In this chapter, we'll address plug-ins that change the entire sound of a track.

Media Used: ***Pro Tools First—Fundamentals of Audio Production—Chapter 9 (EQ).ptx, Pro Tools First—Fundamentals of Audio Production—Chapter 9 (Dynamics).ptx, Pro Tools First—Fundamentals of Audio Production—Chapter 9 (Low Roar).ptx***

Duration: 45 minutes

GOALS

- **Understand the different types of inserts**
- **Understand the difference between real-time and file-based effects**
- **Understand how to use an EQ (Equalization) plug-in effect**
- **Understand Compressors and Expanders, and how to use them in your mix**
- **Learn how to automate plug-in parameters**

More Mixing = More Signal Flow

In Chapter 8, you learned a bit about signal flow on Audio, Aux, Instrument, and Master Fader tracks. Let's dig deeper into *Inserts.*

What is an *Insert*?

The term *insert* has its origin in the early days of analog mixing desks and was used so that the audio engineer could add an external processing device (in those days, this would be a hardware unit) into the signal chain. The location of these insert points varied from model to model; sometimes after the built-in microphone preamps, while others were after the built-in EQ (meaning equalization, which we'll discuss later in this chapter).

The purpose of these inserts was to introduce a process to the signal chain of a channel that wasn't already built-in. For example, mixing desks didn't have compressor units, and so to add one into a track, an insert was the easy solution. The signal flow on that track might go something like *Input* > *EQ* > ***Inserted Compressor*** > *Fader* > *Pan* > *Output.* In this case, a cable would be plugged into the insert's output (usually called an *insert send*) to the reverb unit's input, and then the reverb's output would be plugged into the console's insert input (called an *insert return*). Inserts weren't required, and if a particular effect wasn't needed (in this example, a compressor), it simply wouldn't be plugged in.

Insert structures could be quite complex, with a console's send going to multiple devices in series before the signal returned to the mixing desk. For example, a mixing desk's insert send might go into a chorus' input, with its output going into a compressor's input, and the compressor's output then going back to the desk. These were all physical connections, and the order of these connections was significant–a track that went into a chorus followed by a compressor would sound differently than one going into a compressor and then a chorus.

With the advent of DAWs, inserts (and sends, which we'll discuss in more detail in Chapter 10) have been virtualized to a large degree, but the fundamental logic behind them is quite the same as in the early days of analog mixing desks. Let's now see how inserts are created and used within the Pro Tools environment.

Using Inserts in Pro Tools

Using inserts in Pro Tools is a powerful and easy way to take control of your mix. Let's take a look at the basic usage of plug-in inserts:

Instantiating a Plug-in on an Insert

As you learned in Chapter 8, Pro Tools has 10 inserts, which are always present in an Audio, Aux, Instrument, or Master Fader track, even if there are no plug-ins occupying them. When we populate an insert position with a plug-in, we use the term *instantiate.* Here's how to instantiate a plug-in on a mono audio track.

- Before you can instantiate a plug-in on an insert, you have to be able to see the inserts Views. In the Edit or Mix window, make sure you're seeing Inserts A-E and/or Inserts F-J (you can show or hide these from the View menu or from the Mix window View selector, shown in Figure 9.1.

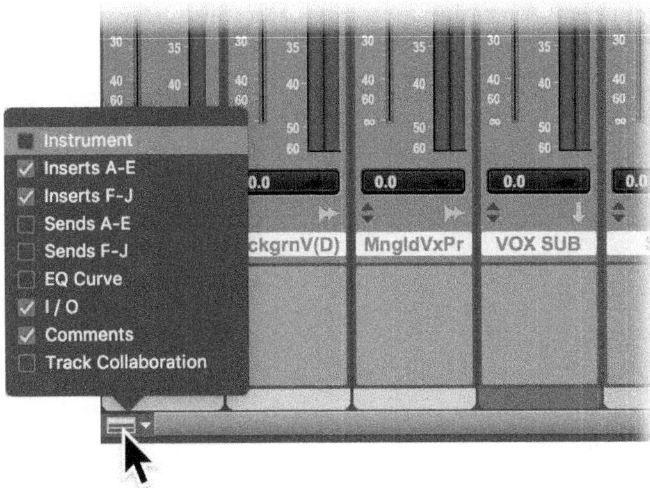

Figure 9.1 Showing Inserts in the Mix Window

- Click the INSERT SELECTOR upon which you want to instantiate your plug-in. This doesn't need to be the first insert. The Insert selector menu will appear.

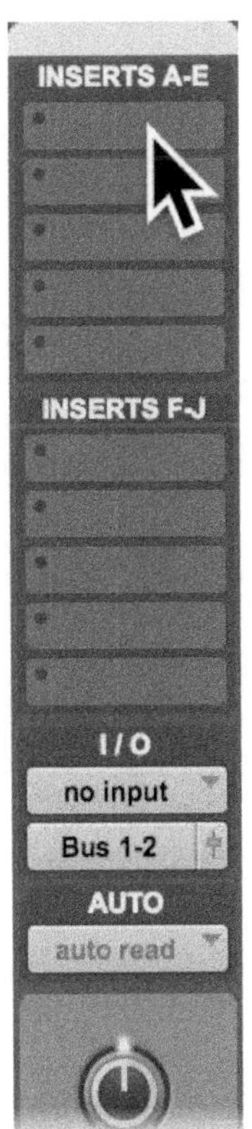

Figure 9.2 Ready to Insert a Plug-in

- Move your cursor over the PLUG-IN menu item. A list of plug-in categories will appear.

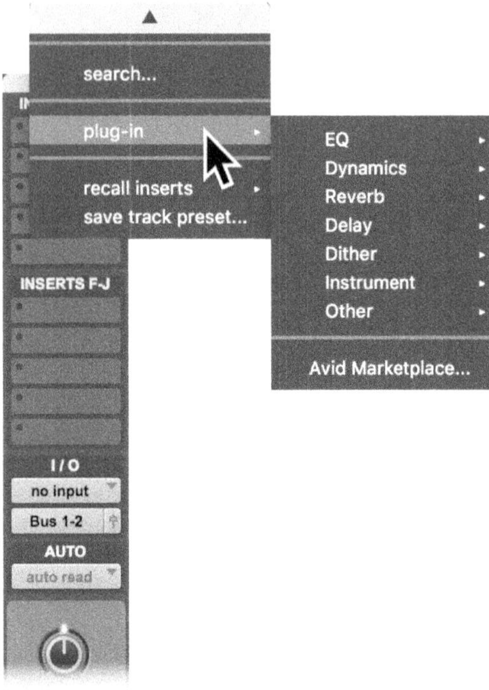

Figure 9.3 Revealing the Plug-in Menu

- Move your cursor over the desired category of effect (in this case, I'll choose EQ). A submenu will appear, showing all the specific plug-ins of that type.

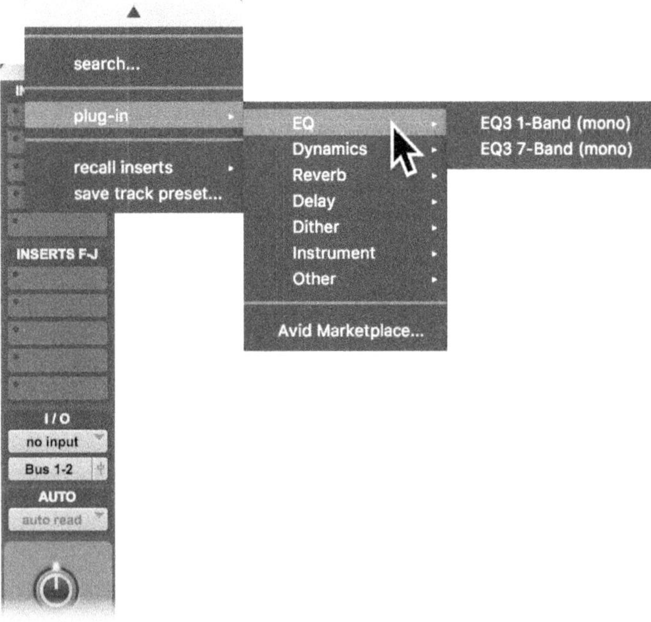

Figure 9.4 Revealing the Available EQ Plug-ins

- Click on the desired plug-in. The plug-in's window will appear. (In this image, I've chosen the *EQ3 7-Band* plug-in)

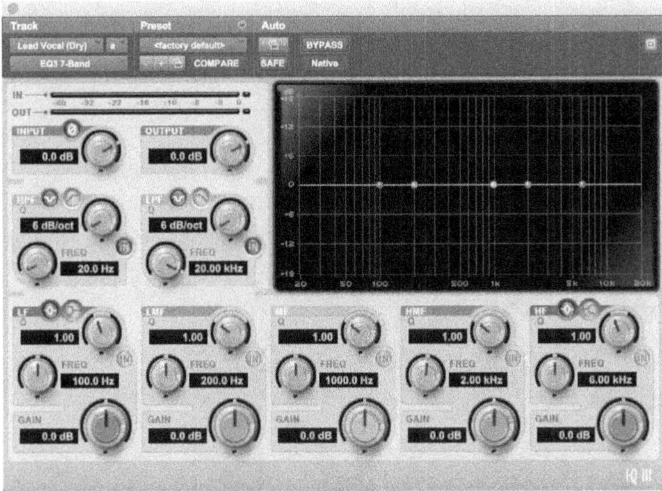

Figure 9.5 The EQ3 7-Band Plug-in

In your project, you can have several inserts on several tracks, and it might be hard to know which insert's window is open. Fortunately, Pro Tools provides a visual cue: When an insert's window is open, the Insert Assignment is colored white. When the window is not open, it is colored grey.

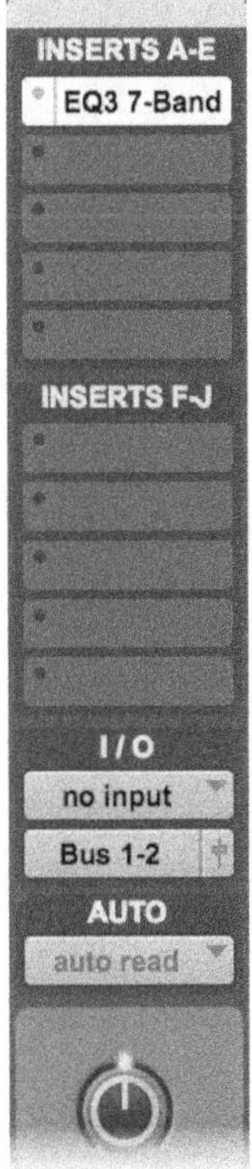

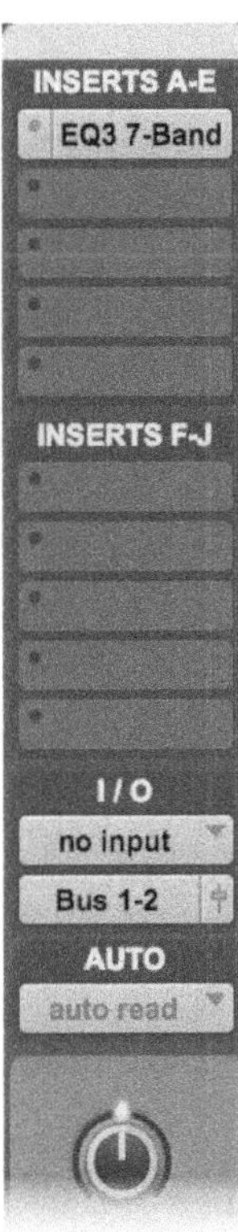

Figure 9.6 An Insert with the Corresponding Window Open (Left) and Closed (Right)

To open an insert's plug-in window, simply click on the desired INSERT ASSIGNMENT button. By default, if a plug-in window is already open, the newly-clicked plug-in will replace the previous one in the same window. If you want multiple windows open simultaneously, there are two ways to do it:

- Before opening an additional window, click the TARGET BUTTON of the plug-in window(s) that you want to remain visible. This will change the target button from red to grey, as shown in Figure 9.7. Any plug-in windows with an active (red) target button will be replaced by any *newly-clicked* insert assignment button.

Figure 9.7 A Plug-in's Target Button Active (Left) and inactive (Right)

OR

- Hold the SHIFT key as you click the insert assignment button of the plug-in that you want to add to your view. The new plug-in will appear without affecting any previously visible plug-ins.

When using Pro Tools | First, your inserts are limited to plug-ins only, but with Pro Tools and Pro Tools | Ultimate, there's another kind of insert, called an *I/O* insert, which behaves similarly to inserts on analog consoles, allowing users to incorporate external hardware effects to their "in the box" mixes. An in-depth discussion of I/O inserts and how to use them are in the Pro Tools 101 course and other courses in the Avid Learning Series curriculum.

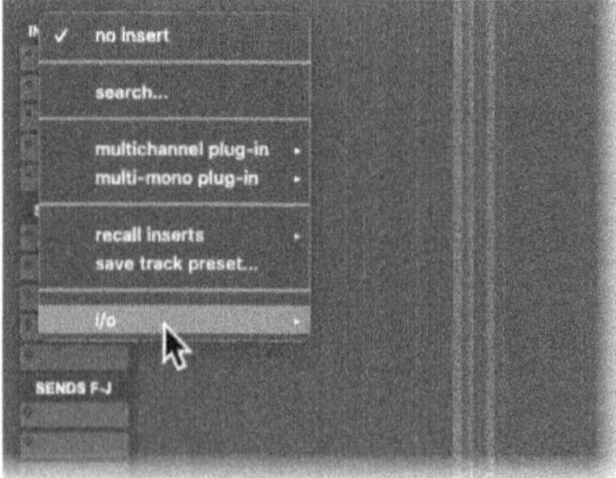

Figure 9.8 An I/O Insert in Pro Tools | Ultimate

Moving Inserts

As mentioned, inserts are processed in series, from insert A through insert J (top to bottom). The order of your plug-ins can have a profound effect on the result that you hear. The good news is that re-ordering your plug-ins is easy:

- Click and drag the insert that you want to move from its original position to wherever you want it to be. As you drag the insert, a yellow box will indicate where it would be repositioned. For example, in Figure 9.9, I'm reorganizing plug-ins from EQ>Compressor to Compressor>EQ.

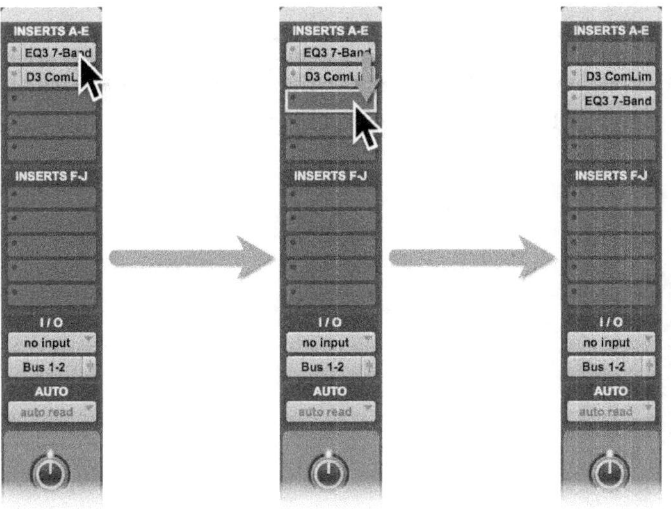

Figure 9.9 Reordering Inserts

- You can make a copy while dragging as well. Just hold the OPTION key (Mac) or ALT key (Windows) while dragging a plug-in, and a copy will be deposited in the new location, leaving the original plug-in unchanged.

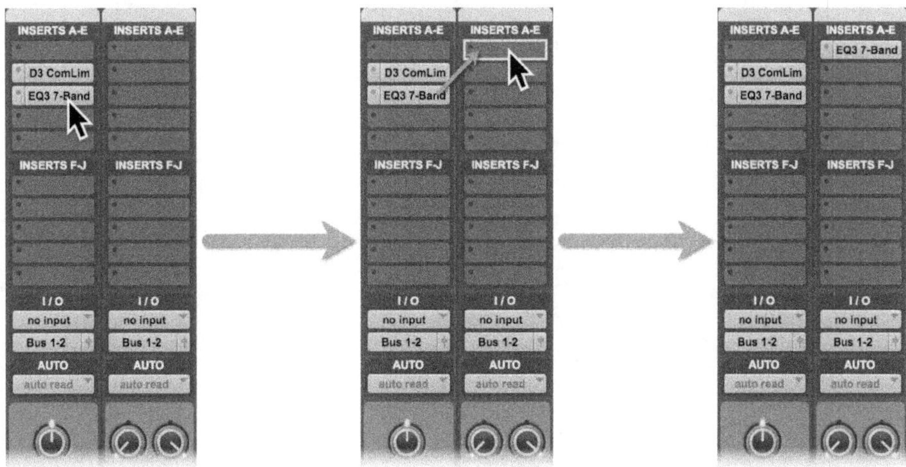

Figure 9.10 Copying an insert

Bypassing, Deactivating, and *Removing* Inserts

In addition to being moved, inserts can also be *bypassed* or *deactivated.*

Bypassing Inserts

A *bypassed* insert will allow for signal to pass through it unchanged. For example, if you have an EQ plug-in that radically changes a sound, but you want to temporarily hear the unprocessed original sound, you can bypass it. Another advantage of bypassing is that it can be automated in the same way that you've automated volume and pan in Chapter 8.

Here are ways that a plug-in effect on an insert can be bypassed:

- In the plug-in window, click the BYPASS button located in the upper right-hand area of the plug-in window. When active, the bypass button will be orange, as shown in Figure 9.11.

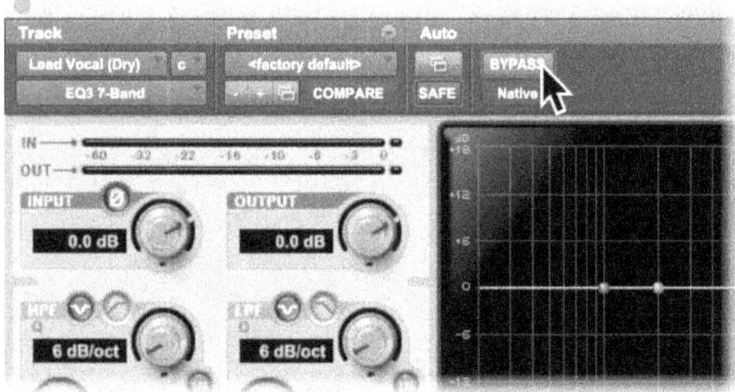

Figure 9.11 Bypassing an Insert from the Plug-in Window

- Right-click the INSERT ASSIGNMENT button for the plug-in that you want to bypass. A menu will appear, as shown in Figure 9.12. Choose BYPASS from the menu. When bypassed, you'll see a checkmark next to the menu item.

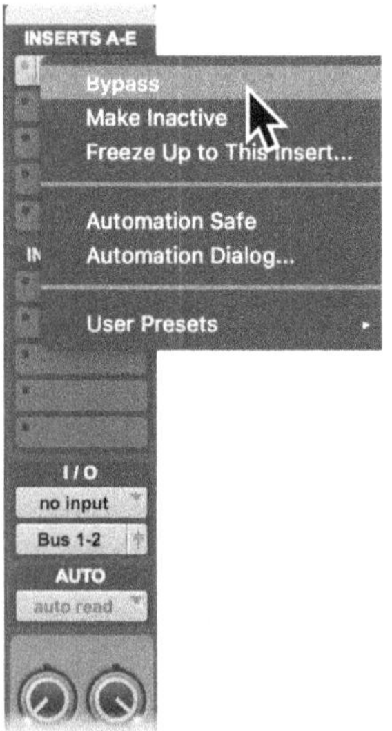

Figure 9.12 Bypassing an Insert by Right-Clicking

- Hold the COMMAND key (Mac) or the CTRL key (Windows) and click the INSERT ASSIGNMENT button for the plug-in that you want to bypass.

When a plug-in is bypassed, its Insert assignment button will appear blue (dark blue, as shown in Figure 9.13, if the corresponding plug-in window is closed, or light blue if the plug-in window is open).

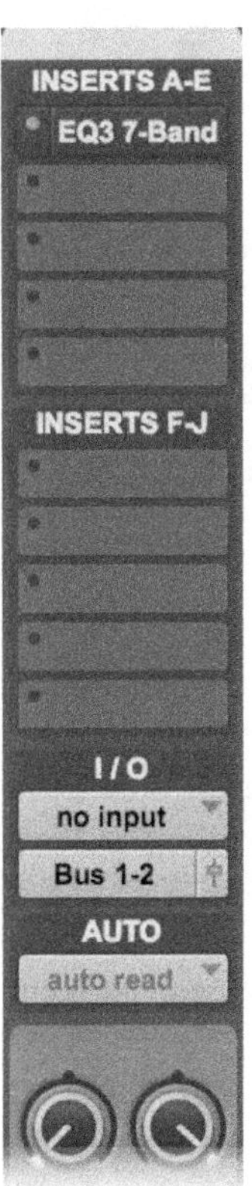

Figure 9.13 A Bypassed Insert

Deactivating Inserts

A *bypassed* insert will still be active, meaning that it will still draw upon your computer's processing power. To go one step further, you can make an insert inactive: the insert will stop processing audio and will *not* draw on computer resources. However, if you decide you want that plug-in back in your mix, you can make it active and it'll come back exactly as it was before. Unlike bypassing, making a plug-in inactive or active is not automatable.

Here's how to make a plug-in inactive:

- Right-click the INSERT ASSIGNMENT button for the plug-in that you want to deactivate. A menu will appear, as shown in Figure 9.14. Choose MAKE INACTIVE from the menu. When inactive, you'll see a checkmark next to the menu item.

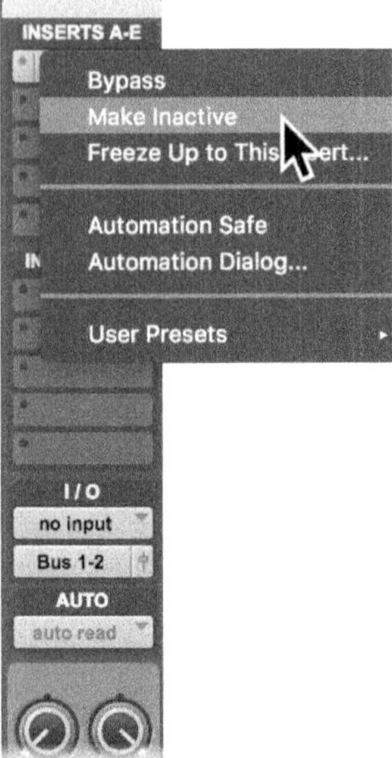

Figure 9.14 Making an Insert Inactive by Right-Clicking

- Hold the COMMAND+CONTROL key (Mac) or the CTRL+START key (Windows) and click the INSERT ASSIGNMENT button for the plug-in that you want to make inactive.

When inactive, an insert assignment button will appear greyed out with the name of the plug-in in *italic* font, as shown in Figure 9.15.

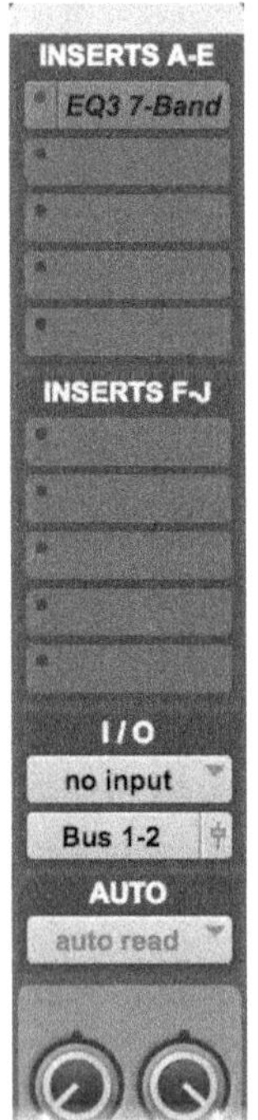

Figure 9.15 An Inactive Insert

Removing Inserts

Like deleting tracks, removing an insert is not undoable, and further will clear the entire Undo History of your Project (meaning you'll not be able to undo anything you did before removing the insert). For that reason, it's a good general rule to make a plug-in inactive rather than remove it. However, if you need to remove the insert, here's a way to do it.

1. Click the INSERT SELECTOR for the plug-in that you want to remove. This is the small dot to the left of the plug-in name, and where you'd go to change or instantiate a plug-in. The Insert selector menu will appear, as you've seen before in this chapter.

Figure 9.16 Clicking the Insert Selector

2. At the top of the menu, choose NO INSERT. Your insert will be removed.

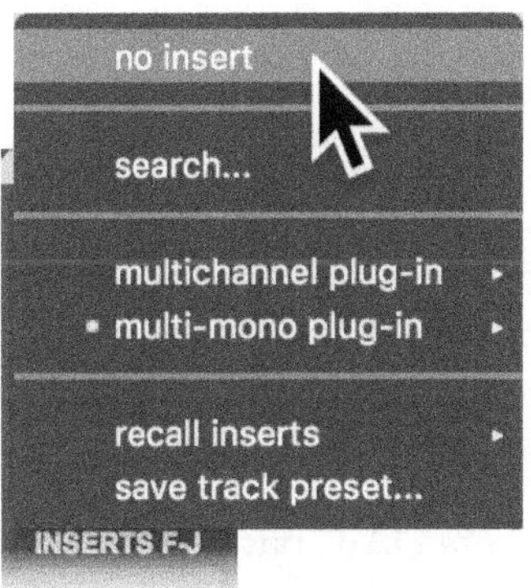

Figure 9.17 Removing a Plug-in from an Insert

Inserts on Master Faders

In Chapter 8, we've discussed how signal flow on Audio Tracks (and on Aux or Instrument tracks as well) is different from Master Fader tracks. Perhaps the biggest difference is that on Audio/Aux/Instrument tracks, inserts are *pre-fader*, and on Master Faders, they are *post-fader*. Both have a direct bearing on what we'll be doing in this chapter.

In this chapter, we'll discuss dynamic effects, especially *compressors* and *expanders,* that can add punch and power to your mix or help you manage levels, depending on how you use them:

- On **Audio/Aux/Instrument tracks**, since their inserts are pre-fader, the signal that is coming through the input will go through the inserts before they go to the volume faders. If you're using compressors or expanders to beef up a track or a subgroup, the incoming signal will go through the effects *first*, changing the sound, and then the faders on the track will allow you to change the output level *without* changing the sonic qualities of the track.
- **Master Fader tracks**, since their insets are post-fader, they are well-suited for plug-ins that manage levels. With Master Faders, the fader is the first step in the signal flow, followed by the inserts, which means the fader levels *will* affect the level of the signals being fed into any insert processing. In particular, there is a variant of a compressor plug-in, called a *limiter* that is used to prevent a signal level from exceeding a preset amount–this is commonly instantiated on a Master Fader track's inserts.

Plug-ins

Even if you don't know what a plug-in is, you've probably used one before. A *plug-in* is a bit of computer code that adds functionality to a program. It isn't a program, so it can't be run independently from its host software. However, when a *plug-in* is added (or plugged in) to the software where it is designed to operate, it can add features and possibilities that the host application on its own doesn't provide. Many applications use plug-ins, from word processors and web browsers, to virtually every DAW on the market. In the DAW world, plug-ins initially replaced hardware effects and instruments, and have since become more complex and loaded with exotic features.

Plug-in Formats

There are different types of plug-ins supported by different DAWs. The three major types are VST, AU, and AAX:

- **VST (Virtual Studio Technology):** Introduced by Steinberg, this format is widely supported by host DAWs, like Cubase, Studio One, and Ableton Live. Currently, there are multiple flavors of VST, including VST 2 and VST 3. This format is particularly popular with freeware developers and virtual instrument (called VSTi) plug-ins.
- **AU (Audio Units):** AU plug-ins are designed for use with Apple's *Logic Pro* DAW, but it is supported by other DAWs as well. One notable limitation of AU plug-ins is that it's only available on a Mac operating system. There's little difference between an AU plug-in and it's VST counterpart, and many AU plug-ins are simply modified VST plug-ins.
- **AAX (Avid Audio eXtensions):** AAX plug-ins are the only type supported by Pro Tools and operates on both Mac and Windows systems. Avid works in close partnership with third-party AAX plug-in developers to ensure that they adhere to high performance standards. Of particular note, AAX plug-ins will report their latency (the time it takes for them to process the incoming signal), so that Pro Tools can compensate for that latency, ensuring that processed signals are sample-accurate throughout your mix.

Plug-ins on Multichannel Tracks

The steps to instantiate a plug-in shown earlier in this chapter were done on a *mono* track. As you might expect, the plug-in on that track would process a single stream of audio coming from the track's input or from the preceding insert(s). On a multichannel track (for example, a stereo track in Pro Tools | First), you have some additional channel options:

1. On a stereo track (any stereo track will show the same behavior, but in this case, I'm instantiating a compressor plug-in on a stereo audio track), click the INSERT SELECTOR for the insert slot into which you want to instantiate the plug-in.
2. The Insert selector menu will appear. On a multichannel track, you have the option of opening a *Multichannel Plug-in* or a *Multi-Mono Plug-in.*

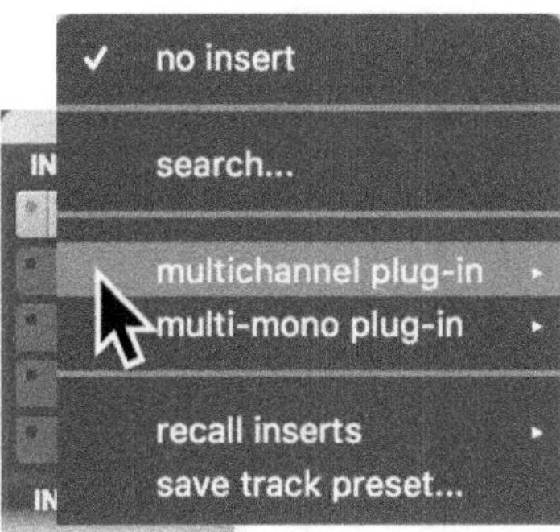

Figure 9.18 The Insert Selector Menu on a Multichannel Track

Here's the difference between a *Multichannel Plug-in* or a *Multi-Mono Plug-in*:

- A **multichannel plug-in** is a single plug-in that processes multiple audio streams within a single plug-in window. Changes you make in this plug-in window will be applied to both streams (left and right) of the track.
- On the other hand, when you choose a **multi-mono plug-in** on a stereo track, the mono plug-in you select will be opened twice, although only one plug-in window will be shown. Multi-mono plug-ins do offer the unique ability to process each channel independently *or* together.

Using Multi-Mono Plug-ins

By default, multi-mono plug-ins behave like multichannel plug-ins, processing multiple audio streams identically, but you don't *have* to work that way. Multi-mono plug-ins include controls that are not found in mono or multichannel plug-in windows.

The *Master Link* button is unique to multi-mono plug-ins. When linking is active (the button will appear blue, as in Figure 9.19), all channels of the multi-mono plug-in will share the same parameter settings–changes made to the left side will be mirrored in the right side. When linking is disabled, the Master Link button will be grey, and both sides will be independently configurable, enabling you to set different settings for them.

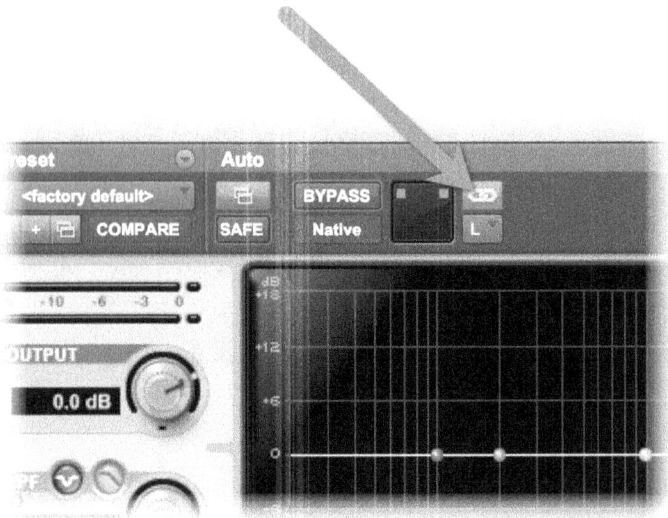

Figure 9.19 The Link Button on a Multi-Mono Plug-in (Active)

The *Channel Selector* (immediately below the Master Link button) indicates the channel of the multi-mono plug-in you're presently viewing (something that's really only necessary to change when linking is disabled). Just click on this selector to reveal a list of available channels you can choose from. (In this example, clicking on the Channel selector will enable you to switch from the left channel to the right channel.). The currently shown channel is indicated with a check mark.

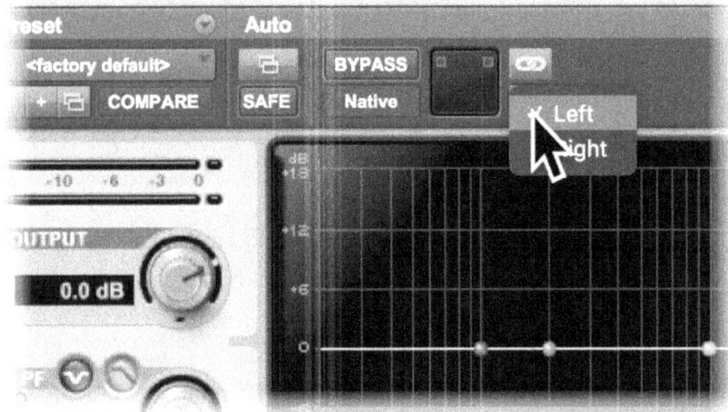

Figure 9.20 Choosing a Channel on an Unlinked Multi-Mono Plug-in

If you unlink a multi-mono effect and later choose to relink, the Relink dialog box will appear, as shown in Figure 9.21. When relinking a multi-mono plug-in, you need to choose one channel's parameters to be applied to all channels.

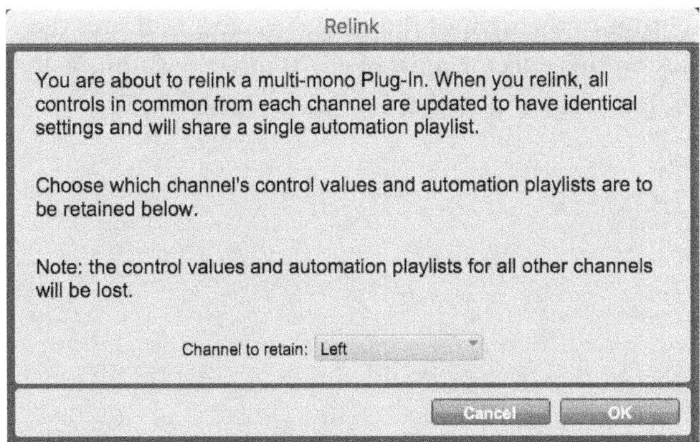

Figure 9.21 The Relink Dialog Box

Since both mono channels share the same window, by default, you'll only see one channel at a time when working with multi-mono plug-ins. Wouldn't it be cool to be able to open multiple windows and see both channels' information at the same time? Hold the OPTION key (Mac) or ALT key (Windows) and click the CHANNEL SELECTOR. A separate plug-in window will open per channel!

Getting Around the Plug-in Window

With the wide range of plug-ins available to you in Pro Tools | First (and far more in Pro Tools and Pro Tools | Ultimate), you won't probably be surprised to learn that the plug-in windows can vary based on their parameters and features. However, there are some very important controls common to all plug-in windows:

- The *Track Selector* will show you the track you're currently working with. In order to quickly jump to an insert on another track, click the TRACK SELECTOR to display a list of available tracks in your project. From this list, you can select another track and instantly open a plug-in window for that track.

Figure 9.22 The Track Selector

- The *Insert Position Selector* (a small lettered button to the right of the Track Selector) indicates the position of the insert on the track. If you click on this selector, a list of all 10 insert positions will appear. From this list, you can select any position and jump to that insert immediately.

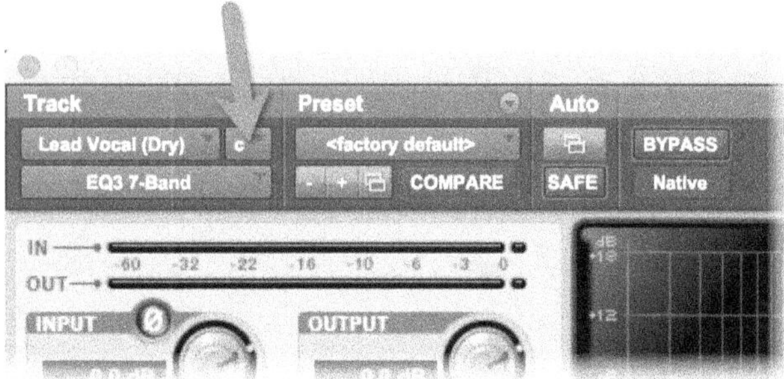

Figure 9.23 The Insert Position Selector

- Immediately below the Track Selector and Insert selector is the *Plug-In Selector* (which shows you the plug-in you're using). Clicking this selector will reveal a plug-in menu, from which you can select a different effect without closing the plug-in window. If you want to replace one plug-in with another, here's a great place to do that.

Figure 9.24 The Plug-in Selector

- Most plug-ins have several *presets*–pre-programmed settings in the plug-in that are suited for different situations (or are good starting points). Click the LIBRARIAN MENU to see a list of available presets.

Figure 9.25 The Librarian Menu

- Below the Librarian menu, you'll see a small minus (-) and plus (+) button. These are the *Previous Setting* and *Next Setting* buttons respectively. Clicking these buttons will go to the previous or next settings in the Librarian menu with a single click. This is useful if you're playing your track and browsing presets to see what works best.

Figure 9.26 The Previous Setting and Next Setting Buttons

- Click on the PLUG-IN SETTINGS SELECT button to reveal the Plug-In Settings dialog box.

Figure 9.27 The Plug-in Settings Button

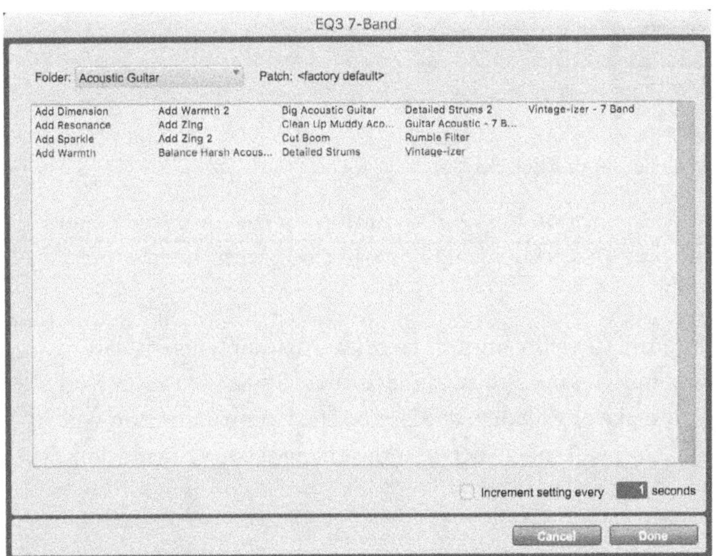

Figure 9.28 The Plug-in Settings Dialog Box

The Plug-in Settings dialog box is a very useful way to see your presets. Let's take a quick look:

- Click on the FOLDER SELECTOR to reveal a list of all preset folders for that plug-in. From there, click on the desired folder to display the presets in the dialog box's main area.

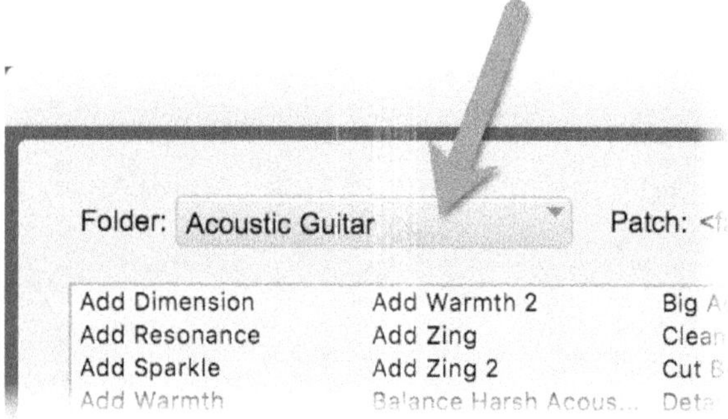

Figure 9.29 The Folder Selector in the Plug-in Settings Dialog Box

- In the main section of the Plug-in Settings dialog box, click on the desired preset, and your settings will be immediately applied.
- Click on the INCREMENT SETTING EVERY [#] SECONDS check box to automatically cycle through the available presets according to the value entered in the Seconds field. (In this image, presets will change every second.) This is a handy way to preview effect settings while your project plays, especially when there is a large number of presets to choose from.

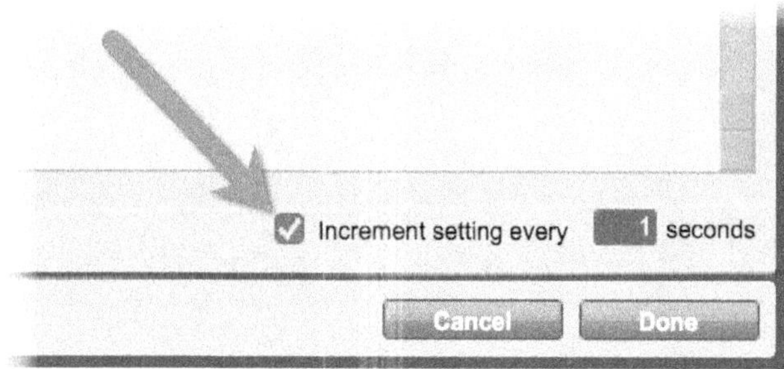

Figure 9.30 Changing Presets Automatically in the Plug-in Settings Dialog Box

- When you settle on the desired preset, click on the DONE button (in the lower right-hand corner of the dialog box), and the plug-in setting dialog box will close, with the new preset applied.

- Back in the plug-in window, you'll find the *Compare* button. Here's a situation where it will come in handy: You've chosen a preset, but you need to tweak it further to suit your mix (rarely is a preset a perfect fix). As soon as you make any change to a preset, the Compare button will turn blue. Clicking the COMPARE button will toggle between the changes you've made and the original preset.

Figure 9.31 The Compare Button

- The last preset-related component of the plug-in window is the Plug-in Settings menu, shown in Figure 3.32. Clicking the round menu button will reveal of list of preset-related functions, allowing you to create, change, and copy your plug-in settings.

Figure 9.32 The Plug-in Settings Menu

Actually, there's a way to change a plug-in's presets without even opening the plug-in window: Just right-click on the corresponding insert assignment button, and choose a preset from the USER PRESETS submenu, as shown in Figure 3.33.

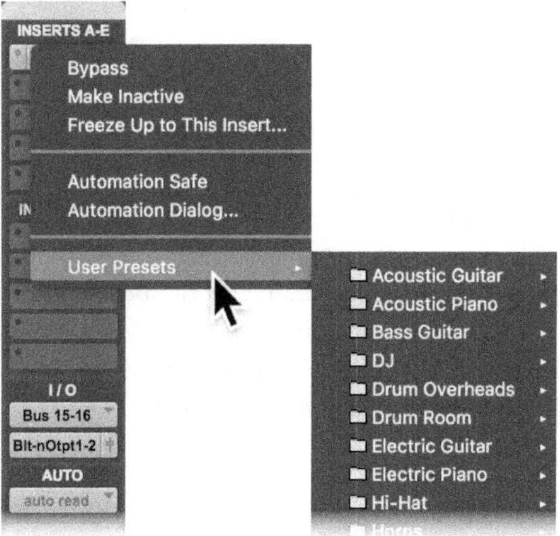

Figure 9.33 Changing Presets by Right-Clicking

To the right of the preset controls is the *Plug-In Automation Enable* button, and below that is the *Automation Safe* button. We'll talk about those features and how to automate your plug-ins' parameters in the next section of this chapter.

Figure 9.34 Automation Enable Button and Automation Safe Button

Finally, the *Bypass* button (which you already know), and below it, the word "Native". This signifies that the plug-in is a *native* plug-in, meaning that it is being processed by the host computer's CPU. Native plug-ins are the only type available in Pro Tools | First or Pro Tools system, but when using Pro Tools | Ultimate, you have the ability to use dedicated DSP chips to power a plug-in, in which case the word shown would be "DSP", signifying the fact.

Figure 9.35 The Bypass Button and Native Indicator

Automating Plug-in Parameters

In Chapter 8, you learned how to automate mix parameters like volume and pan. Now, you'll take automation into the world of plug-ins: Virtually every knob or button of a plug-in can be automated, enabling you to change tonal color, ambience, and more!

Because of the very large numbers of parameters that some plug-in effects contain, parameters can be selectively enabled or disabled for automation–enabled parameters can be automated, but not disabled ones. In Pro Tools | First, by default, all plug-in parameters are enabled, but in Pro Tools and Pro Tools | Ultimate, the default is for them not to be enabled. There are two ways to enable and disable parameters to suit your workflow:

Enabling and Disabling Plug-in Parameters for Automation: Method One

1. Click on the AUTOMATION ENABLE button. The Plug-In Automation dialog box will open.

Figure 9.36 The Automation Enable Button

The Plug-In Automation dialog box is organized with the list of disabled parameters on the left side of the window and the enabled parameters on the right. By default, in Pro Tools | First, all of your plug-in parameters will be on the right-hand side.

2. Click on an effects parameter(s) that you want to disable for automation. Holding down the SHIFT key will allow you to select a range of parameters and holding the COMMAND key (Mac) or CTRL key (Windows) will allow you to select multiple parameters one at a time.

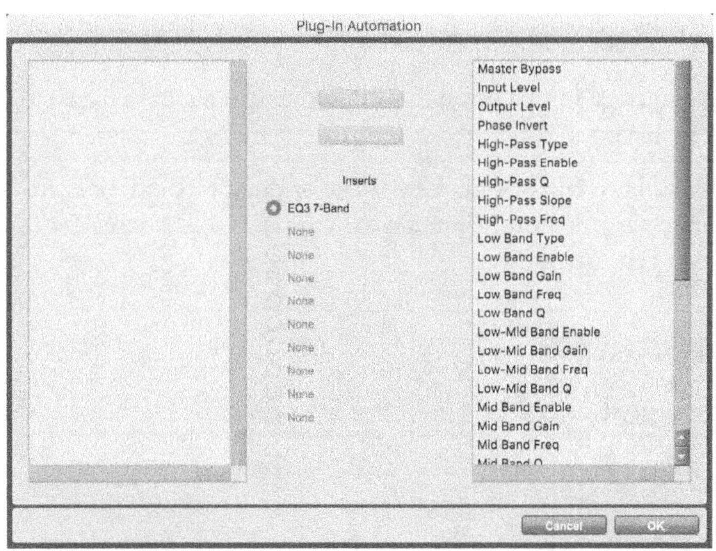

Figure 9.37 The Plug-In Automation Dialog Box

3. Click on the REMOVE button. The selected parameter(s) will move from the right-hand list to the left-hand list.

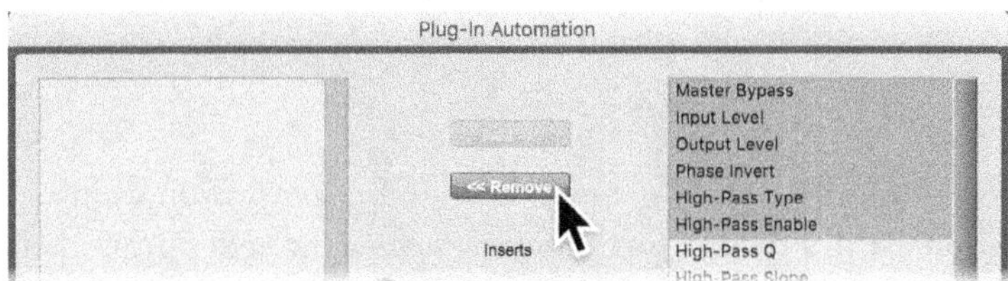

Figure 9.38 Removing an Enabled Parameter

4. Conversely, you can select any disabled parameters from the left-hand list and enable them by clicking the ADD button.

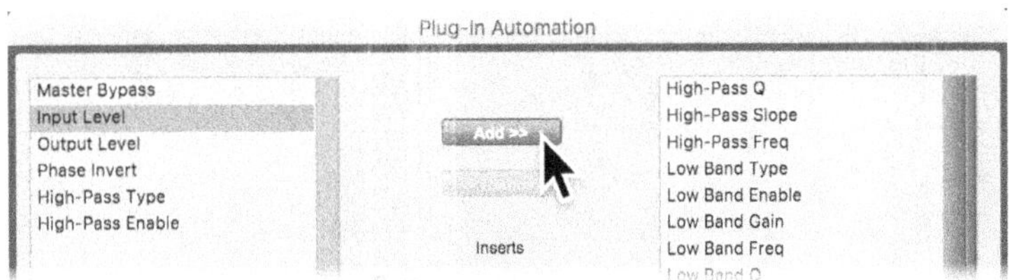

Figure 9.39 Adding a Disabled Parameter

5. When you're finished, click on the OK button.

Here's a quick way to disable or enable *all* the parameters on a specific plug-in: Press and hold the CONTROL+OPTION+COMMAND keys (Mac) or the CTRL+START+ALT keys (Windows) and click on the plug-in window's PLUG-IN AUTOMATION ENABLE button. This will alternately disable or enable all the parameters for the plug-in.

Enabling and Disabling Plug-in Parameters for Automation: Method Two

Here's another way to disable or enable plug-in parameters: In this example, I'll show how to disable a parameter for automation, since by default they are already enabled:

1. Press and hold the CONTROL+OPTION+COMMAND keys (Mac) or the CTRL+START+ALT keys (Windows) and click on the parameter you want to automate (in this case, I'll choose *Mid Band Freq*). A menu will appear, giving you two options.

Figure 9.40 Another Way to Disable or Enable a Parameter for Automation

2. Click on DISABLE AUTOMATION FOR <PARAMETER NAME> to immediately disable the parameter for automation.

OR

2. Click on OPEN PLUG-IN AUTOMATION DIALOG to open the Plug-In Automation dialog box that you saw in the previous section. At this point, you can follow steps 2 through 5 from the "Method One" section.

Parameters enabled for automation will be indicated visually, sometimes as an outline, a box, or as in this image, a small light beneath the parameter. When you're in Auto Touch, Auto Latch, or Auto Write mode, you'll see a red indicator accompanying each enabled parameter. When working in Auto Off or Auto Read mode, there will be no indicator.

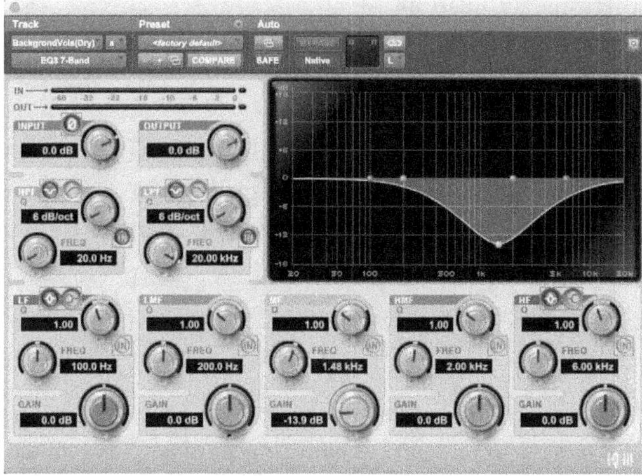

Figure 9.41 All of this Plug-in's Parameters are Enabled, Except One—Can You Find It?

Writing Plug-In Automation

Plug-in automation is largely similar to any other kind of automation, but before we close this discussion, let's take a quick look at how you can view plug-in automation data.

Once a parameter is enabled for automation, the plug-in and parameter will appear as an option when you click the TRACK VIEW SELECTOR. Just choose the desired plug-in (which will reveal a submenu) and then choose the specific parameter that you want to view. (This can be shown in track lanes as well.)

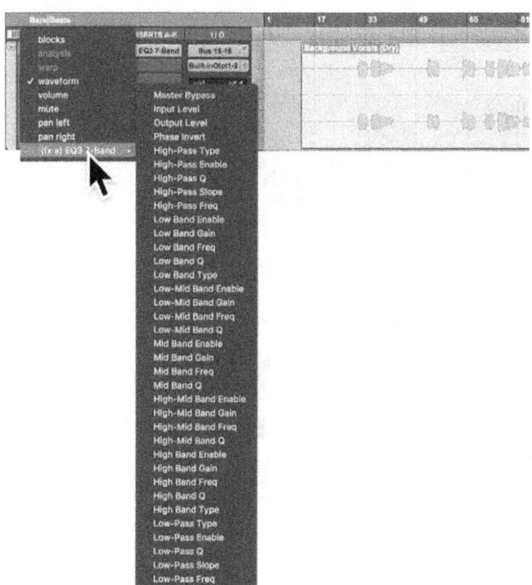

Figure 9.42 Viewing a Plug-in Parameter

In Figure 9.42, you'll see the parameter menu for the 7-band EQ plug-in I've used as an example in this chapter. It's a fairly long list and might be a bit unwieldy to navigate – one reason that you might want to disable any parameters that you don't want to work with.

From this point on, plug-in automation is identical to other kinds of automation: Choose your automation mode, begin playback, and change the parameter to start writing automation!

Another Way to Work: AudioSuite

So far, we've dealt with plug-in effects that change the sound of a track in *real time*—the signal coming into the track (either from an input or clips on that track) is unaffected (or "dry") until the signal reaches the insert with the plug-in effect on it. Because these effects process the signal in real time, the sound will change with the changing of the effect's parameters, which can be automated.

Some effects, though, can't be done in real time (like reversing a sound), so we need a different kind of effect. *AudioSuite* plug-ins can meet these needs, and then some!

Generally speaking, AudioSuite plug-ins are the most basic of Pro Tools effects. These are *file-based* plug-ins, meaning that they work directly on files, and processing is *not* done in real time as your project plays. That means AudioSuite plug-ins cannot be automated in your Pro Tools project. It also means these plug-ins won't consume your project's valuable real-time resources, making AudioSuite plug-ins well worth exploring. Here's how they work:

1. Select the clip or area that you want to process.
2. Click on the AUDIOSUITE menu. A list of plug-in categories will appear.
3. Choose the desired category of effect. A submenu will appear, showing all the plug-ins of that type. In this demonstration, I'll choose the REVERB category.
4. Choose the desired plug-in (in this case, I'll choose *D-Verb*). The plug-in's window will appear.

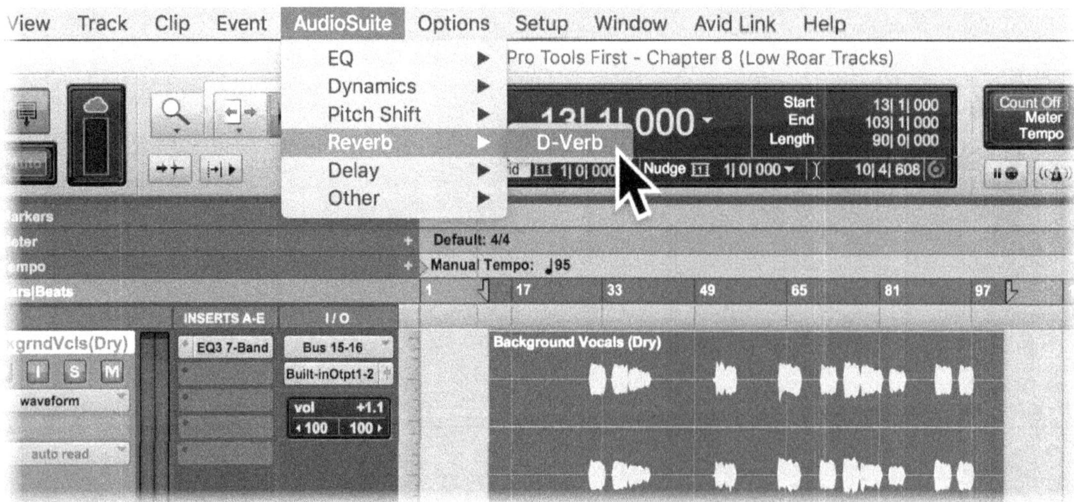

Figure 9.43 Choosing an AudioSuite Plug-in

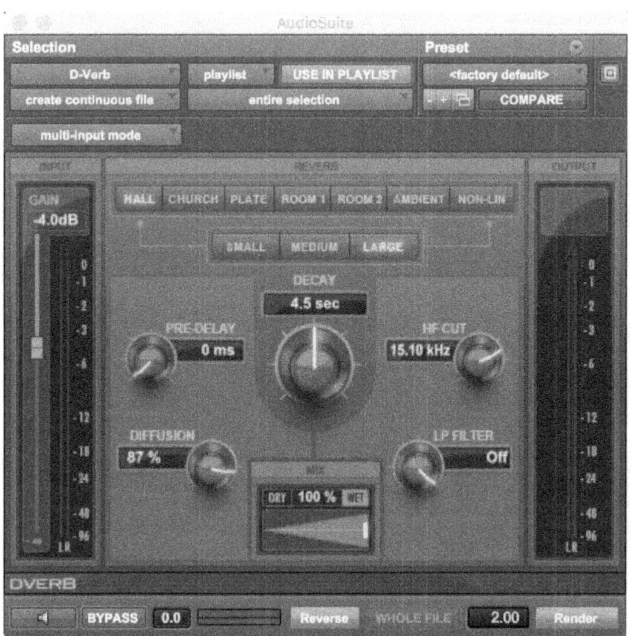

Figure 9.44 A D-Verb AudioSuite Plug-in Window

5. Adjust the parameters in the plug-in window's main section. These parameters vary from plug-in to plug-in. Since AudioSuite plug-ins don't operate in real time, you won't be able to hear them as your project plays. To hear what your settings have done to the sound of the clip(s), click the PREVIEW button (in the lower left-hand corner of the window). Next to that button is a *Bypass* button that will allow you to hear the original (unprocessed) clip, and to its right, you have volume control (just click and hold on the PREVIEW VOLUME field and a fader will appear, as shown in Figure 9.45.)

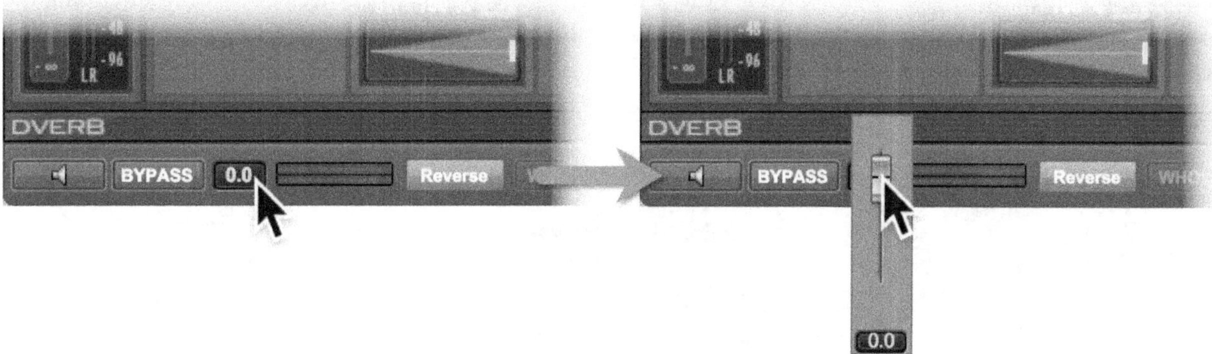

Figure 9.45 Previewing in the AudioSuite Window

Most, but not all, AudioSuite plug-in windows include preview controls.

6. Click on the RENDER button to apply your effect.

Figure 9.46 Rendering an AudioSuite Process

After you've applied an AudioSuite plug-in to a clip, you'll notice that the clip's name has changed to reflect the AudioSuite process that has been applied. For example, Figure 9.47 shows a clip—previously named *Background Vocals (Dry)*—renamed with a *DVerb* suffix, indicating that a D-Verb AudioSuite plug-in was applied.

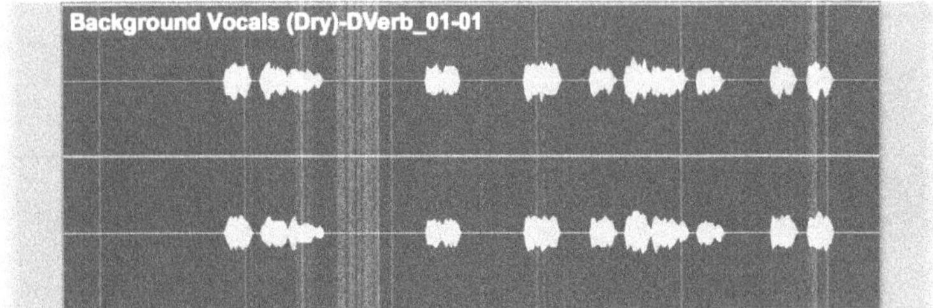

Figure 9.47 A Processed Clip

Getting Around the AudioSuite Plug-in Window

Although different AudioSuite plug-ins differ in appearance and parameters, they all share some common elements:

In the upper-left corner of the AudioSuite window, you'll find the *Plug-In Selector* (which displays the name of the current plug-in, such as D-Verb). Clicking this selector will enable you to change effects without closing the window. Just click on the selector, and a list of AudioSuite plug-ins will appear, identical to the list you saw when you clicked the AudioSuite menu.

Figure 9.48 AudioSuite Plug-In Selector

Clicking on the *Selection Reference* selector (which reads "Playlist" in Figure 9.49) enables the user to determine what will be processed.

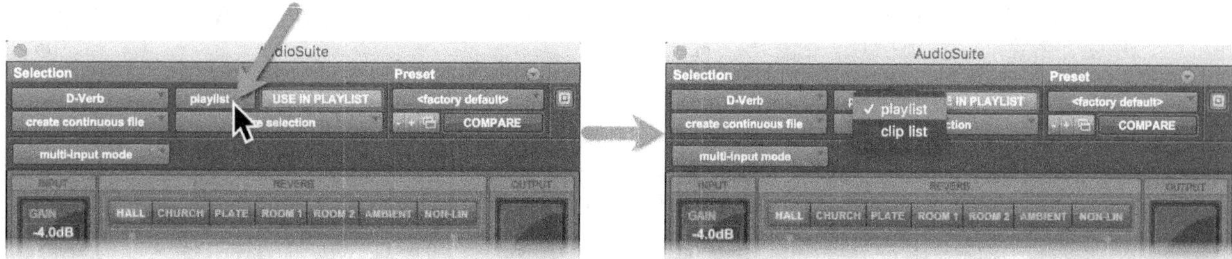

Figure 9.49 AudioSuite Selection Reference Pop-up Menu

A menu with two options will appear:

- **Playlist:** When Playlist is selected, the plug-in will process the selected area in your track(s).
- **Clip List:** Choosing the Clip List option directs the plug-in to process the currently selected clips in the Clips list.

Since Pro Tools I First doesn't have a Clips List, this option is only relevant in Pro Tools and Pro Tools I Ultimate setups.

The *Use In Playlist* button will indicate whether the processed clip will be used on your track or not. When the button is blue, the processed clip will appear on the track—if it is grey, it will only appear in the Clips List.

Figure 9.50 The Use In Playlist Button

Again, since Pro Tools I First doesn't have a Clip List, this option is only relevant in Pro Tools and Pro Tools I Ultimate setups. If you want to be able to use your processed clip in your track, the *Use In Playlist* button should be blue.

In the upper right-hand corner of the AudioSuite window is a preset management section that is identical to the real-time plug-ins controls that we've discussed earlier in this chapter.

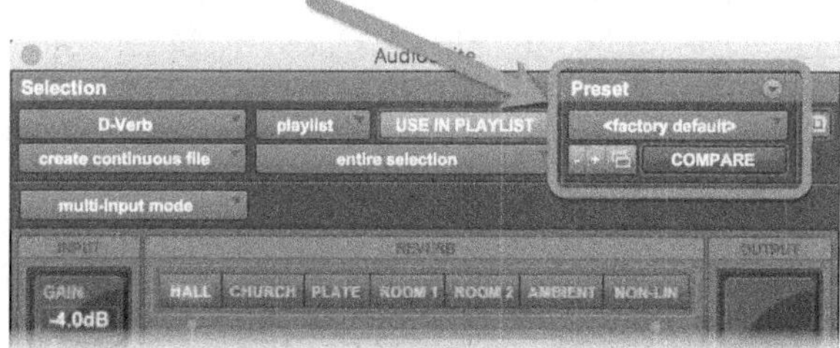

Figure 9.51 The AudioSuite Preset Controls Section

Click on the PROCESSING OUTPUT MODE selector to how audio will be processed. A menu will appear, showing three different processing options:

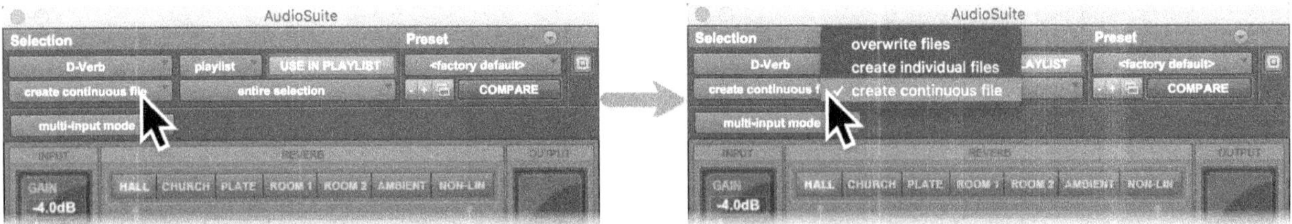

Figure 9.52 The AudioSuite Processing Output Mode Selector

- **Overwrite Files:** With this option chosen, the selected audio file(s) will be processed directly and *destructively*. This means that your original file will be permanently changed.
- **Create Individual Files:** This mode is *nondestructive* and will create separate audio files for each selected clip. If multiple clips are selected, multiple files will be created.
- **Create Continuous File:** This mode is also nondestructive, but in this case, it will create a *single* new audio file, regardless of the number of clips selected.

The PROCESSING INPUT MODE selector (which reads "Entire Selection" in Figure 9.53) enables you to determine how your clips will be analyzed prior to processing. When you click on the selector, a menu will appear, showing two options:

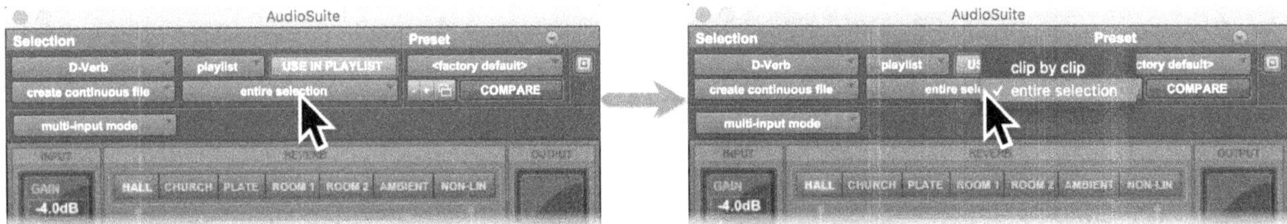

Figure 9.53 The AudioSuite Processing Input Mode Selector

- **Clip by Clip:** With this option chosen, each selected clip will be individually analyzed and processed.
- **Entire Selection:** All selected clips will be analyzed prior to being processed.

Reverse Effects

AudioSuite plug-ins are especially good for doing things that are impossible to do in real time, like reversing a sound. The *Reverse* AudioSuite plug-in is one of the most popular of the AudioSuite plug-ins, used in combination with several other effects to create interesting sounds. One of the iconic effects done using the reverse plug-in is a reverse *reverb* (you'll learn more about how to use reverb in a traditional way in Chapter 10).

To create a reverse reverb effect:

1. Select a clip that you want to process.
2. Reverse it (with an AudioSuite plug-in).

3. Apply an AudioSuite reverb.
4. Reverse it again.

Because Reverse is used frequently with reverbs and delays, Pro Tools has made it even easier. At the bottom of AudioSuite reverb and delay plug-in windows, you'll see the *Reverse* button.

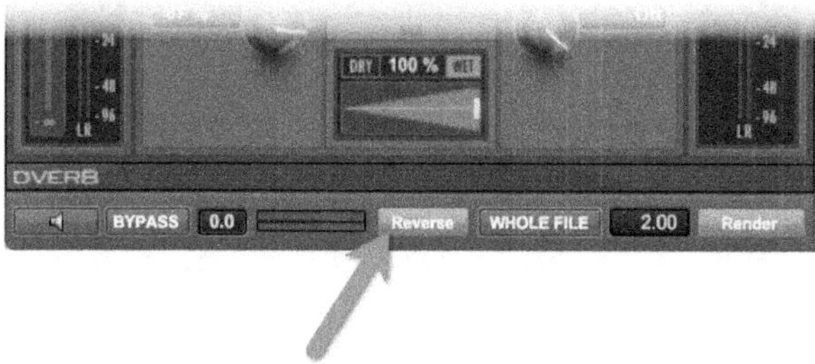

Figure 9.54 AudioSuite D-Verb's Reverse Button

This button enables you to complete an entire workflow with a single click: First, the selected area will be reversed. Next, the plug-in (Reverb or Delay) will be applied to that selection. Then, the selected area will be reversed *again*. Give it a try, and you'll immediately recognize the result!

Handles

In older versions of Pro Tools, AudioSuite processes were applied only to the selected area or clips, and hence you couldn't use the Trim tool to expand the clip's boundaries. This also presented certain limitations when crossfading clips created by AudioSuite processing.

In more recent versions of Pro Tools (starting in 2011), the problem is addressed through the addition of *handles*—additional processed audio beyond the selected area. This means that, although your timeline's clip will still be the same length as your selected area, you can now trim the clip out or crossfade the clip.

There are two ways to control the handles created by an AudioSuite plug-in:

- By default, a two-second handle will be appended to the beginning and end of the rendered file, but you can change that value to anything you like. Just click on the handle value you wish to change (as shown in Figure 9.55) and type the desired value in seconds (up to one minute). For example, if you chose to stay with the default handle length of 2 seconds, you could trim out the beginning and/or end of the clip by a maximum of 2 seconds.

Figure 9.55 A Two-Second Handle

- If you're working with a trimmed or separated clip, you might want to go ahead and apply the AudioSuite process to the entire file associated with the clip. This will create a new processed file that is equal in length to the original whole file. To do this, click on the Whole File button. (When active, the button will appear blue.)

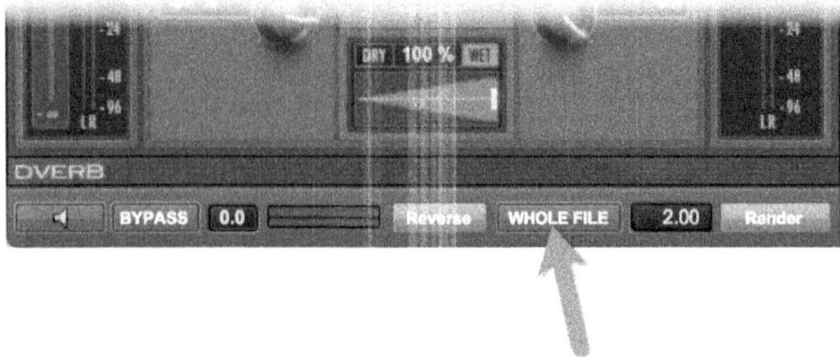

Figure 9.56 Processing the Whole File

Key Effect #1: EQ

Now that you understand inserts and plug-in effects and how to instantiate them in Pro Tools, let's talk about some of the most important mixing effects in the mixer's bag of tricks, and how to use them, starting with *equalization (EQ)*.

Chances are you've already used an EQ when you've adjusted the tone controls on an audio playback device. When using an EQ, you have direct controls over parameters like bass (low frequencies) and treble (high frequencies). Further, EQ controls are commonly available in preset configurations, like *Jazz*, *Spoken Word*, and *Dance*.

An EQ allows the user to adjust the relative amplitude of frequency ranges within a single audio stream. Do you have a vocal performance that sounds too nasal? Easily fixed—just identify the offending high frequency and reduce it *without affecting other frequencies within the sound*. Want to add more low frequency power to a kick drum? Just boost the low frequencies without touching the highs.

EQ Types

In the early days, EQs used to be hardware devices. Although they have been largely replaced by software effects, there are still studios worldwide that use hardware EQs. Regardless of their configuration, EQs have two types that are commonly used in audio production:

- **Graphic EQ:** A graphic equalizer divides the frequency range into a series of *bands*, with the number of bands varying based on the model of the EQ. The user can then raise or lower the level of these individual bands via a series of small faders, as shown in Figure 9.57. Graphic EQs are quite easy to use and provide a good view of the adjustments you're making to the sound. However, its bands are fixed, and sometimes it doesn't provide enough flexibility.

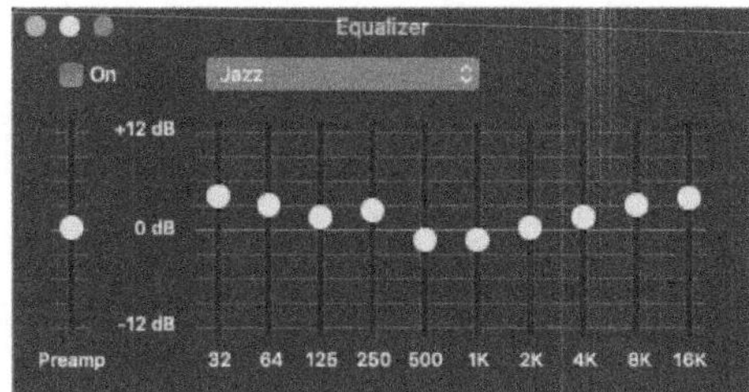

Figure 9.57 A Simple Graphic EQ

- **Parametric EQ:** A parametric equalizer typically has fewer knobs and sliders, but it gives you more control. Parametric EQs feature a number of bands (like the 7-Band EQ Plug-in shown in Figure 9.58), each of which the user can adjust in terms of *frequency*, *amplitude*, and *bandwidth* (or "Q"). (We'll focus on this type in this chapter.) Although it might not be as intuitive as a graphic EQ, you'll have much more control of the sound using parametric EQ, being able to zero in on the exact frequencies that you want to change.

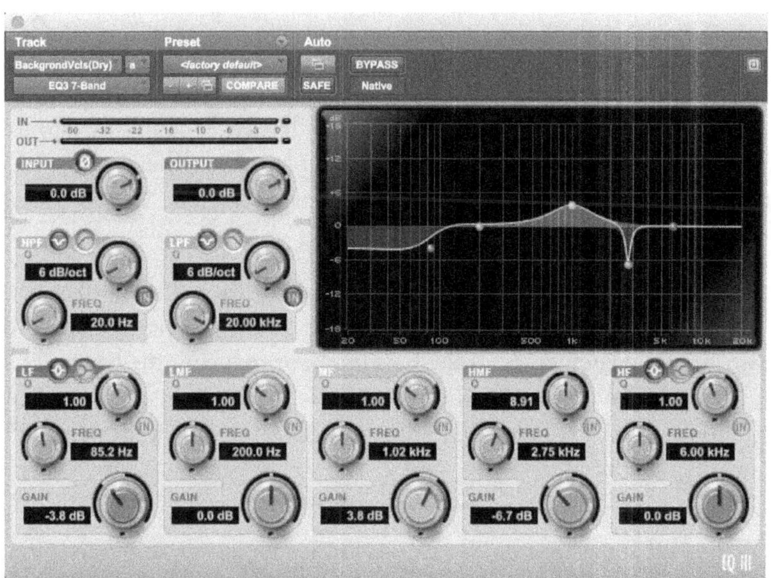

Figure 9.58 Avid's EQ3 7-Band EQ

Using EQ

In the Pro Tools environment, you'll use EQ to shape the tone of your individual tracks, allowing them to better fit together, and allowing the parts that need to stand out to do so without simply relying on volume and pan.

EQs, like many effects, can be used in many ways, and mixing is often a process of making educated guesses and experimenting. That said, there are some traditional roles that equalization can play:

Tonal Control

When you listen to a live performance of an acoustic instrument (let's say, a vocalist), you're hearing the instrument in all its natural glory. When you record it into a DAW like Pro Tools, EQ will enable you to cut the parts of the sound that you don't like and/or boost the parts that you like. Let's say the singer was too close to the microphone and has too much low frequency content as a result of the proximity effect (which you learned about in Chapter 5)—No problem;, just reduce the lows a bit. Let's say there's a bit of a nasal quality you don't care for somewhere in the higher frequencies—a parametric EQ will let you easily zero in on the offending frequency range and reduce it to the point where the sound is more pleasing. With a little practice, you'll be able to bring out the best qualities of each track using EQ.

You can go further and create different special effects with EQ. A common approach is to reduce the low end of background vocals and pan them away from the center of the mix; this can give it an airy quality (especially when combined with reverberation, which you'll learn more about in Chapter 10). Want a track to sound like it's coming through a phone? Just cut the low frequencies and high frequencies, so that you only have the mid frequencies, imitating the frequency output range of these devices.

Mix Cohesion

Try as you might, volume and pan settings alone will not do the job in having all the different elements of your mix clearly heard. Often, the problem stems from competing frequencies between multiple tracks. That's where EQ comes in handy, allowing you to sculpt the tonal qualities of a track, so that it fits within the mix like a puzzle piece.

Here's a classic example: Both kick drum and bass are low-frequency instruments. Let's say, you used EQ to bring out the best in each track, and they sound *fantastic* when you solo them. However, when you put them together, your kick and bass tracks become indistinct (or "muddy" in audio parlance). At this point, you need to remove the altercation, either by reducing the kick drum's frequency range in the bass track, or reducing the bass track's frequency range in the kick track (which one that you do depends on the situation, so use your ears). This sort of carving out of space in the frequency spectrum is not limited to kick and drum tracks, and– you'll do this in all kinds of tracks and subgroups as well.

Additive EQ vs. Subtractive EQ

EQs can be used to boost or cut individual frequency ranges (bands) on your tracks. Knowing whether to boost or cut is important. There are two ways you can go: *Additive* or *Subtractive*:

- **Additive EQ** is an approach where the desirable frequencies are boosted. If you have a specific band that captures the best character of a sound, find that frequency and raise the level of that band. Although this is an intuitive way to work, if you have a signal that already has a fairly high level, boosting frequencies can easily cause it to clip.
- With **subtractive EQ**, instead of boosting the "good" frequencies, you cut the "bad" ones. This is the more popular approach these days for two reasons: First, if you have a loud signal, cutting frequencies won't cause it to clip. Also, cutting unnecessary frequencies tends to reduce unwanted noise. (Here's a tip: Noise may be barely audible on one track, but it can quickly accumulate when you add noisy tracks together!)

You don't have to commit yourself to one approach or another. In professional workflows, even mixers who prefer subtractive EQ will boost frequencies when it's needed. If it sounds good, it *is* good!

The EQ Plug-in Window

Avid's EQ3 7-Band EQ is a great example of a parametric EQ. Understanding the parameters of this plug-in's window will allow you to understand virtually every EQ.

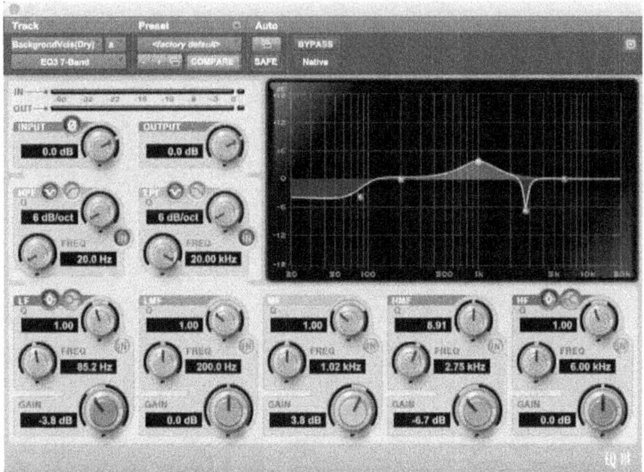

Figure 9.59 Avid's EQ3 7-Band EQ

Input and Output Meters

In the upper left-hand corner of the plug-in window, you'll see input level meters and output level meters, which will help you view the incoming and outgoing signal. To the far right of these meters are clip indicators—if they turn red, that means your signal is too loud and might sound distorted. Below those meters are two knobs, which will allow you to raise or lower these levels.

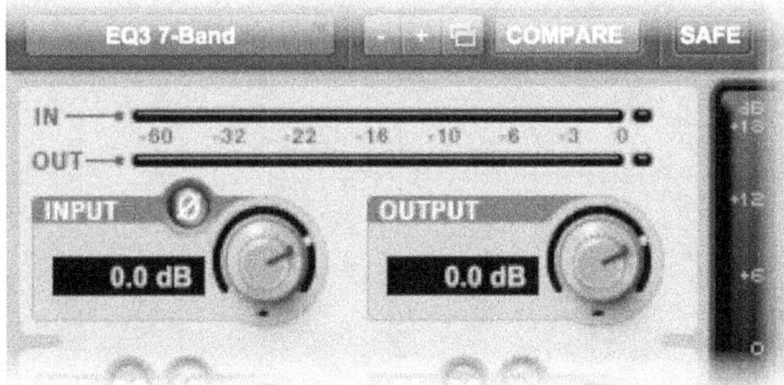

Figure 9.60 Input and Output Meters and Controls

Assuming that your track isn't clipping as a result of a previous insert, you typically don't need to adjust the input levels. If you're boosting a frequency (additive EQ), and you find that your output meter is clipping, you can lower the output level and fix the problem.

You'll also see an odd-looking symbol, which is a stylized version of the Greek letter *Theta*. You'll see this button (called the *Phase Invert* button) on many different plug-ins, but they all do the same thing: Clicking this button will invert the phase of the audio, turning compression phases to rarefaction and vice versa. When active, the button will appear blue, as shown in Figure 9.61.

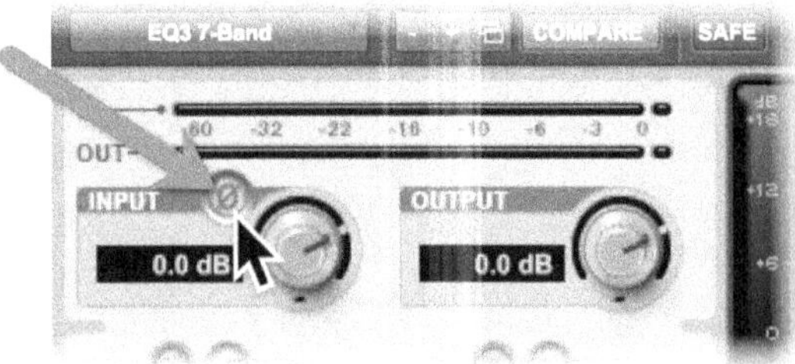

Figure 9.61 Inverting Phase

The primary use for phase inversion is to compensate for phase problems that arise during the recording process.

Bands

Different EQ plug-ins have different number of bands. The EQ3 7-Band EQ has seven bands:

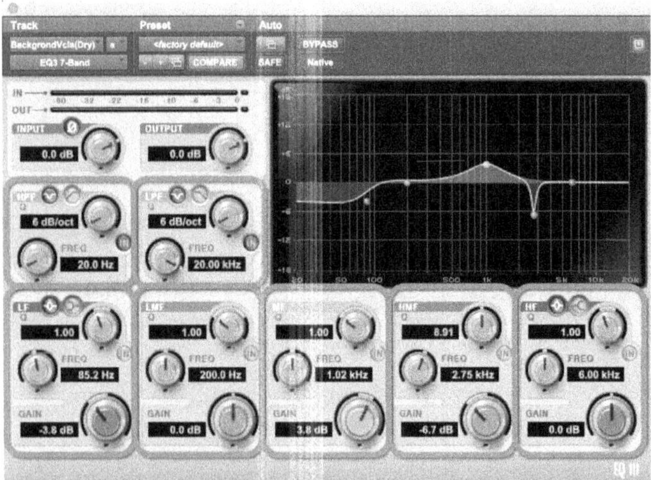

Figure 9.62 The Plug-in's 7 Bands

- High Pass Filter (HPF)
- Low Pass Filter (LPF)
- Low Frequency (LF)
- Low Mid Frequency (LMF)
- Mid Frequency (MF)
- High Mid Frequency (HMF)
- High Frequency (HF)

As you can see, there's a good bit of similarity in the controls of the different bands. Let's take a look at the Mid Frequency band as an example.

Each band can be enabled or disabled with the *Band Enable* button, shown in Figure 9.63. It's a simple but useful control, enabling you to compare the sound with or without that particular band's changes.

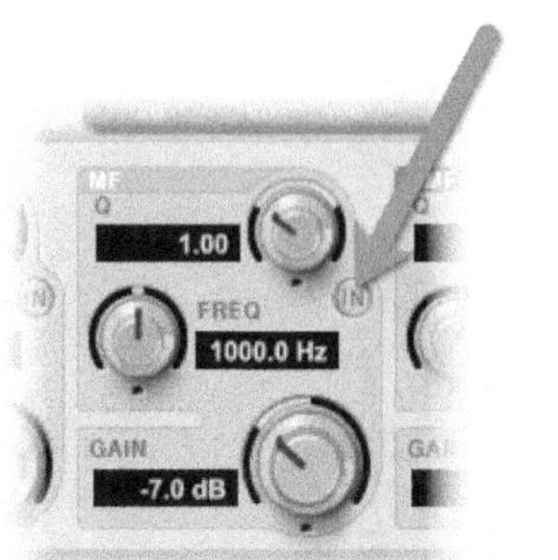

Figure 9.63 The Band Enable Button

The *Frequency* control allows you to choose the center frequency of the band controls. The different bands have different ranges (for example, the mid frequency band can be set anywhere between 124 Hz and 5 kHz). In Figure 9.64, you'll see that the changes you make to the settings are reflected in the frequency graph as a small dot (color-coded to match the corresponding band).

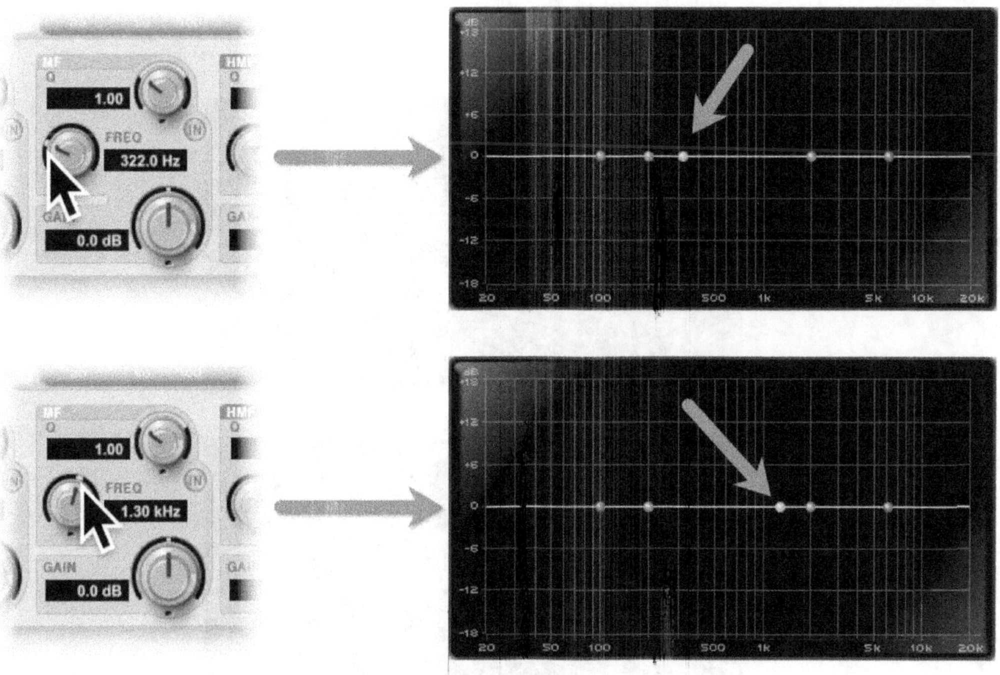

Figure 9.64 Changing Frequency

The *Gain* control enables you to boost or cut frequencies. With the EQ3 7-Band EQ plug-in, you can boost or cut by 18 dB.

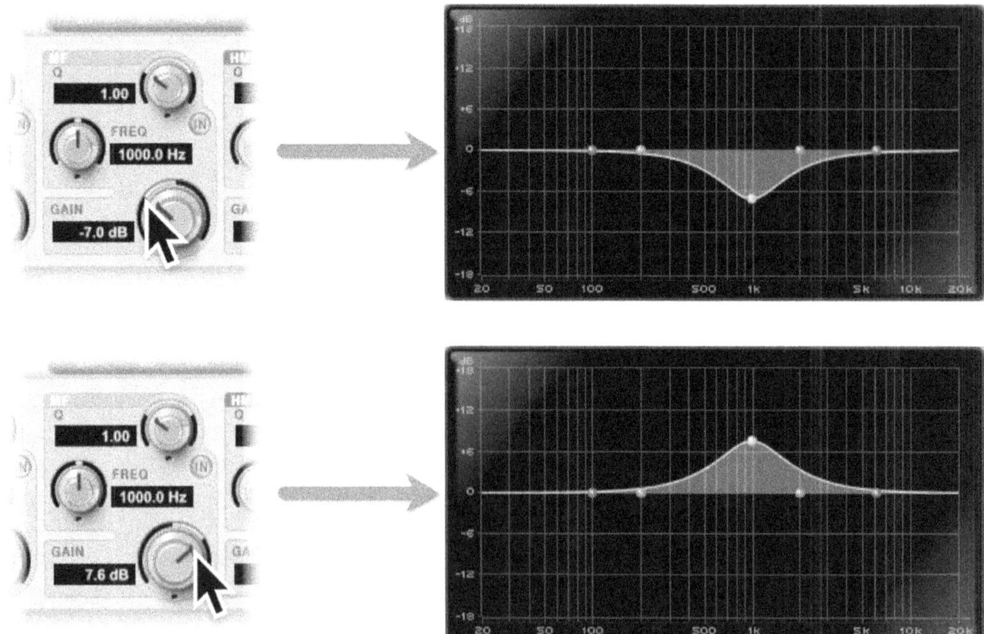

Figure 9.65 Changing Gain

The *Q* control allows you to choose how wide the band is (with the *frequency* setting representing the frequency at the center of the band. Using this control takes a little getting used to: Turning the knob clockwise to 12 o'clock, with a value of 10, will give you the narrowest bandwidth. Turning the knob counterclockwise from this position will broaden the bandwidth with a minimum value of .10.

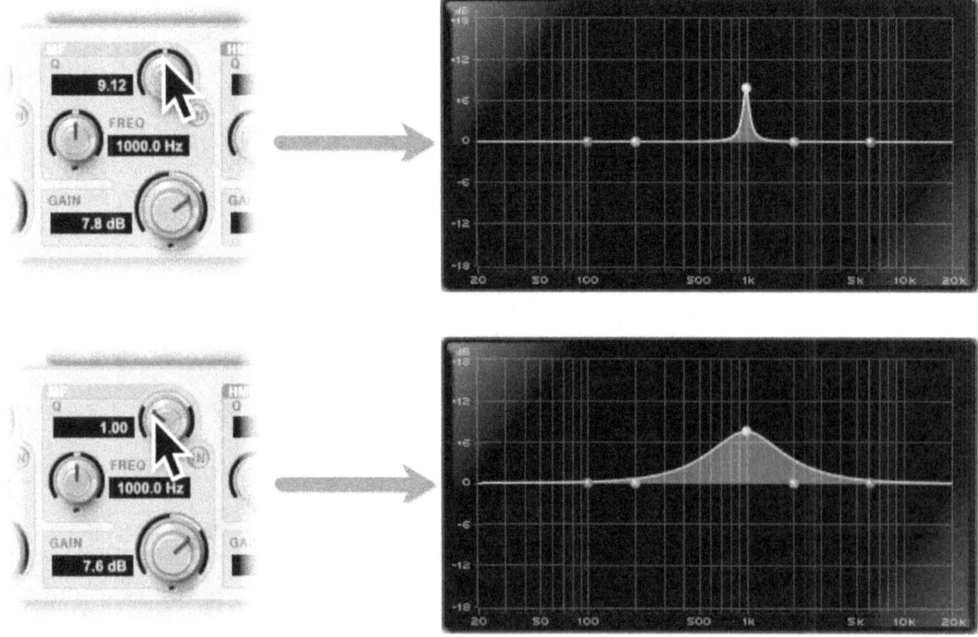

Figure 9.66 Changing Q

In the case of the Low Frequency and High Frequency bands, you have the choice between having a *shelf* shape or a *peak* shape:

- Choosing the **peak** option (by clicking the PEAK button, which will appear blue when active), will cause the band to function similarly to the mid band, with the band centered around the frequency and the bandwidth controlled by the Q setting.
- Choosing the **shelf** option (by clicking the SHELF button, which will appear blue when active, will cause the band to extend to higher frequencies (with a high shelf chosen in the HF band) or lower frequencies (with a low shelf chosen in the LF band), as shown in Figure 9.67.

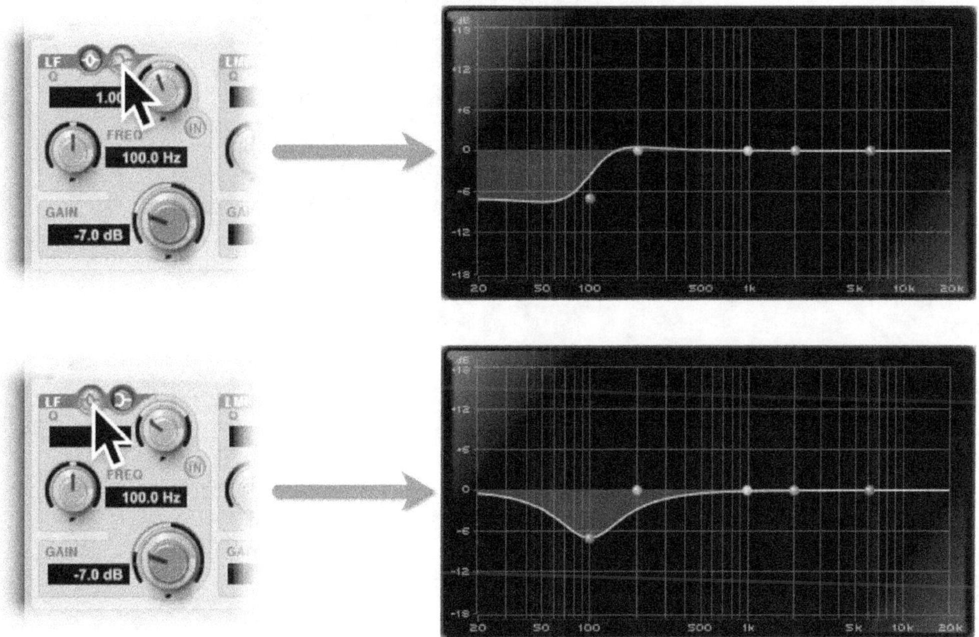

Figure 9.67 Shelf (Top) and Peak (Bottom) Modes for the Low Frequency Band

High Pass and Low Pass Filters

When you use EQ in a subtractive way, one of the common first steps is to cut out low and high frequencies that aren't part of the sound that you want. This is where the High Pass Filter (HPF) and Low Pass Filter (LPF) will help out. The High Pass Filter cuts the low frequencies out of a signal, allowing the high frequencies to "pass" through, and the Low Pass Filter does the opposite, cutting high frequencies.

The High Pass Filter (HPF) and Low Pass Filter (LPF) operate a little differently than the other bands. Let's take a look:

The first thing that you'll notice is that, by default, these two bands are not enabled. If you want to use them, you'll need to activate them manually.

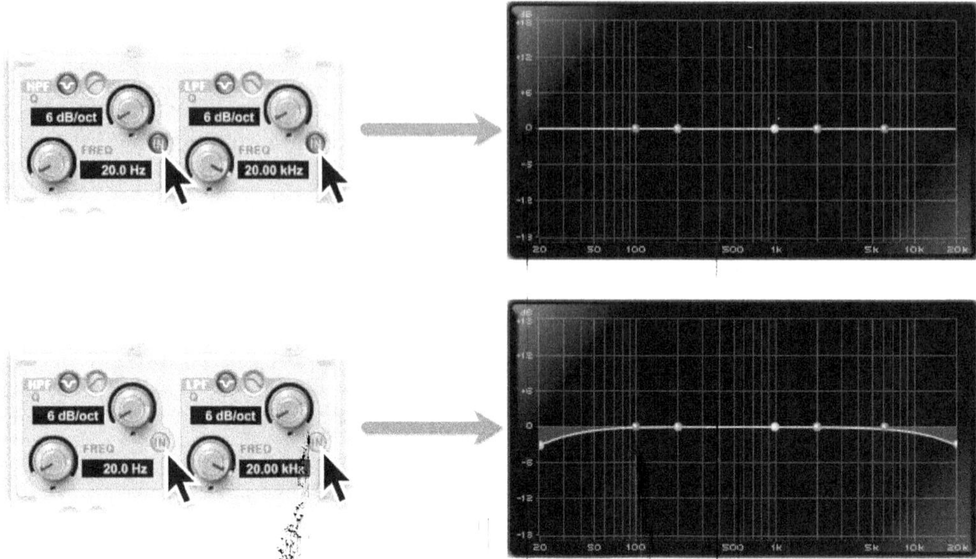

Figure 9.68 Activating the High Pass and Low Pass Filters

There are two modes of operation for these bands: *Pass Filter* and *Notch EQ*. By default, they are set as pass filters, so let's look at them first.

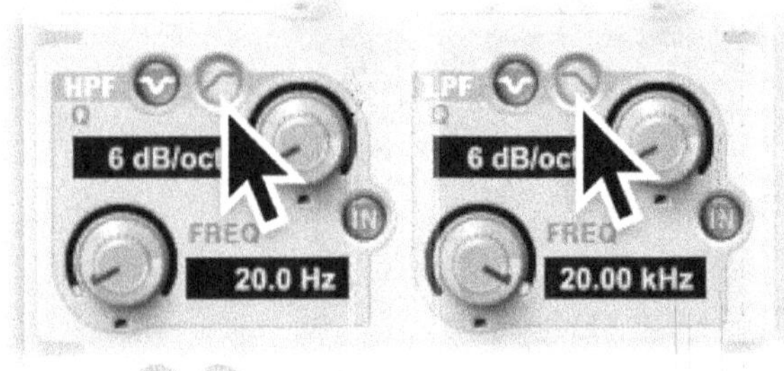

Figure 9.69 High Pass and Low Pass Filter Mode

- Like the other bands, the *Frequency* parameter allows you to choose the center frequency of the filter.
- One important difference is that these will *cut* low or high frequencies, as opposed to the shelving controls of the LF and HF bands. This cut can either be gradual or aggressive and is determined by your settings in the *Q* parameter. The higher the value, the steeper the slope of the filter.

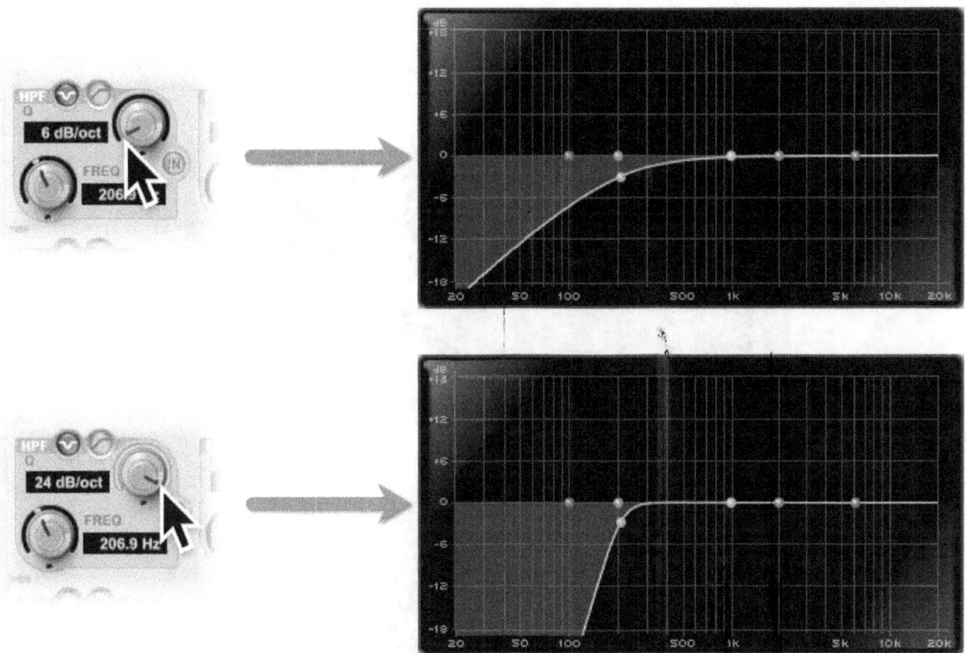

Figure 9.70 Changing Q on a High Pass Filter

These two filters are quite powerful, and there are many mixers (myself included) who typically start their EQing with filters. In the case of vocal tracks, for example, there's usually a bit of low frequency sound that is not voice-related but comes as a by-product of the recording environment. Although this might be barely audible when you solo individual tracks, when you listen to multiple tracks, this unneeded noise will accumulate, and can make your mix muddy. Thankfully, it's easy to fix:

1. Solo the track and adjust the output level if needed, so that it can be heard clearly.
2. In the case of a vocal track, the first thing to do will be to activate the HPF band and set a moderate curve (to start with, I'd recommend the Q knob to be at 12 o'clock). Move the frequency setting to the lowest level.
3. Gradually raise the frequency value and listen carefully to the tone of the track. Stop as soon as you hear a change in the sound of the audio (in the case of a vocal, as soon as I hear the vocalist's low end start to weaken, I'll stop raising the frequency).
4. After this point, it's a bit of tweaking to get the result you want. Sometimes you'll lower the frequency a bit, so that you don't hear any important change in the track, and other times you'll want to change the shape of the curve with the *Q* parameter, or a bit of both. Using the *Bypass* button will help you compare.

Sometimes you'll repeat these steps with the low pass filter (LPF); other times, you won't. Often, I'll want to have the vocal part include all the high-frequency content possible, as this is its natural position in the mix. For kick drums or bass, on the other hand, I'll frequently cut any unnecessary high frequencies, so that they don't accumulate and compete with other elements of the mix. The goal with this workflow is the same in any case—not to change the quality of the sound in any significant way, but to trim away unneeded frequencies. After that, you can sculpt the tone of the sound with the other five bands.

The other mode for these filters is called *Notch*. When you choose this (by clicking the NOTCH EQ button, which will then turn blue), the HPF will change into a low frequency notch, and the LPF will turn into a high frequency notch, as shown in Figure 9.71.

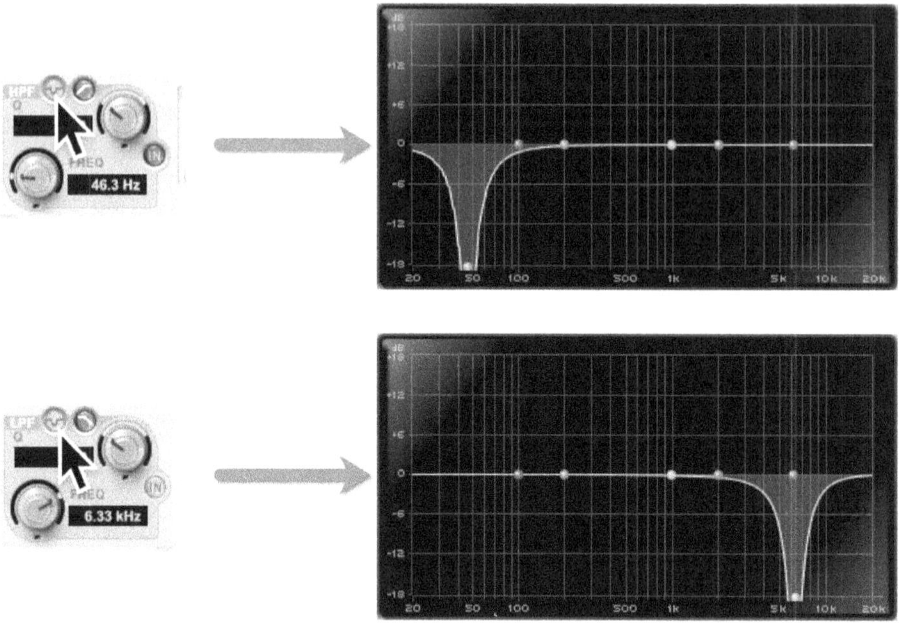

Figure 9.71 Low Frequency Notch (Top) and High Frequency Notch (Bottom)

Think of a notch filter as being similar to reducing the gain on other bands, but in a more extreme way. The *frequency* parameter will allow you to choose the center of the notch, and the *Q* will allow you to choose its width, as shown in Figure 9.72.

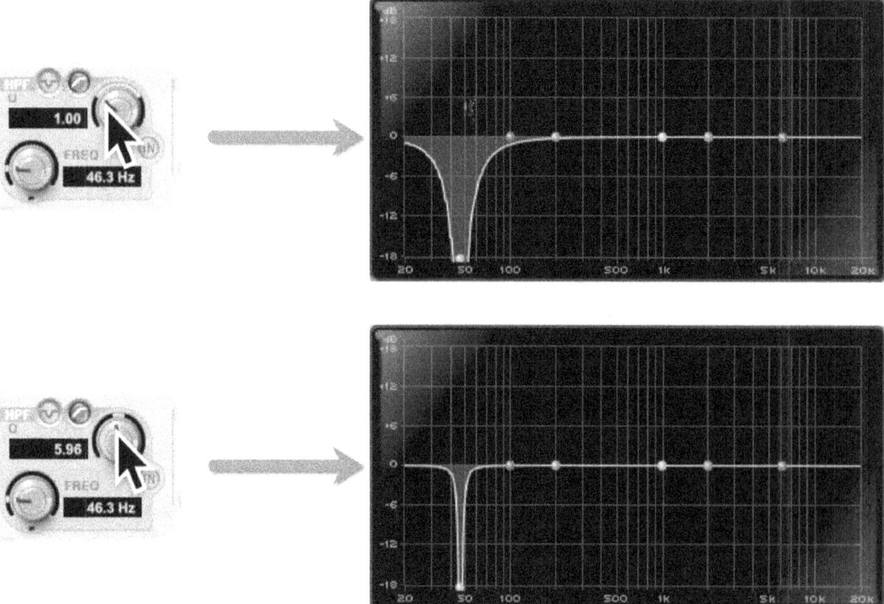

Figure 9.72 Changing Q on a Low Frequency Notch

In general, the high and low pass filters are used more frequently than notches, but notches are very useful in surgically removing problems. One classic example is the hum that can be recorded when equipment isn't properly electrically grounded (this frequency will vary by country, but will be either 50 Hz or 60 Hz). A notch filter will do the job nicely, allowing you to remove the hum with minimal damage to the rest of the track's sound.

You've probably noticed that as you change knob parameters for different bands, correspondingly colored dots (called *control* points) will move in the EQ plug-in's graph section. Instead of moving knobs, you can click and drag the dots to change the frequency and gain of the band. Going one step further, if you hold down the CONTROL key (Mac) or START key (Windows) and click and drag up or down on one of these dots, you can change the band's Q.

The 1-Band EQ

In addition to the 7-band EQ, you've got a 1-band EQ as well. With only a single band, you might think it's not particularly useful, but it's actually quite handy for some tasks, especially for high or low pass filtering. Its features and user interface are similar to the 7-band EQ, but simplified.

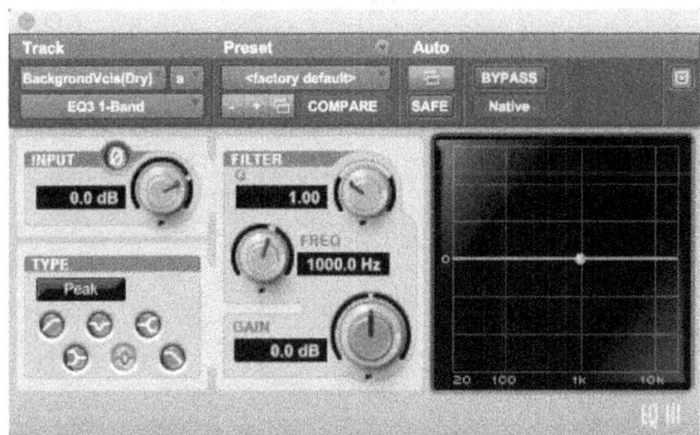

Figure 9.73 Avid's EQ3 1-Band EQ

- You'll notice that at the top of the window, you have input gain control, but not output control. Here, as with the 7-band EQ, you can invert phase.
- The Filter section in the center of the plug-in window is similar to band controls for the 7-band EQ plug-in, which includes Frequency, Gain, and *Q* controls.
- You'll notice that the EQ graph display has been reduced in size and has only one control point dot. As with the 7-band EQ version, you can drag this dot to any desired position.

The single band of this plug-in can serve all of the individual functions of its 7-band counterpart. You can choose the function in the lower left-hand area of the window. As shown in Figure 9.74, in the top row, from left to right, they are *High Pass Filter*, *Notch*, and *High Shelf*. The low row, from left to right, are *Low Shelf*, *Peak*, and *Low Pass Filter*. The active mode will be colored blue, and its name will be displayed above the buttons.

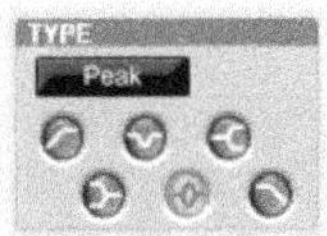

Figure 9.74 The Different Modes of the 1-Band EQ Plug-In

Finding Frequencies

We've already discussed using the filters and notches as EQ utilities to get started and fix specific recorded problems in the sound. Beyond that, you'll want to find good frequencies and boost them (additive EQ) or find bad frequencies and cut them (subtractive EQ).

You could try randomly turning knobs or dragging dots, but you'll quickly find that this is far from efficient and gets you nowhere fast. There are a couple methods of finding your frequencies that will serve you much better!

Sweeping

The first method, called *sweeping*, is the most traditional, dating back to the early days of EQs: Just for the sake of demonstration, I'll describe it in the context of subtractive equalization (finding a bad frequency so you can cut it), but you can also use this method for additive equalization.

1. Raise the gain of a band that you want to sweep. The idea here is to raise it by a good amount, to exaggerate the effect of the EQ. The band that you want to raise the gain on depends on the range of the sound that you want to change: For example, if it's the nasal quality of a vocal, it would be one of the higher bands; if it's the thump of a kick drum, it'd be one of the lower ones.

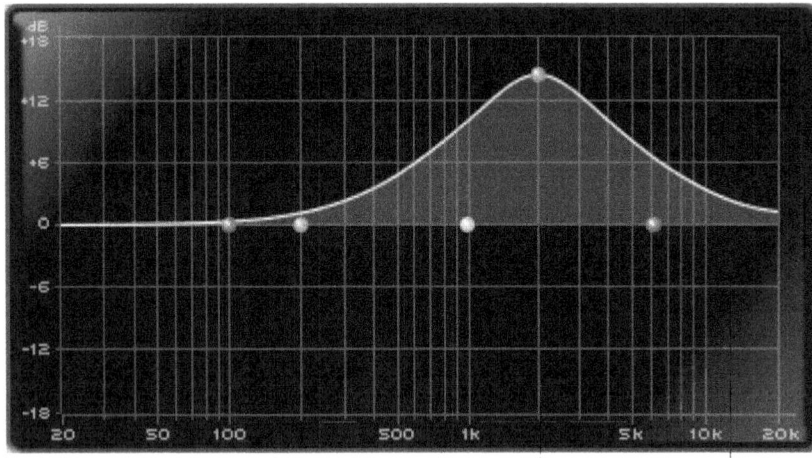

Figure 9.75 Boosting a Band

2. For this workflow, you'll want to start with a narrow bandwidth, so set the *Q* accordingly.

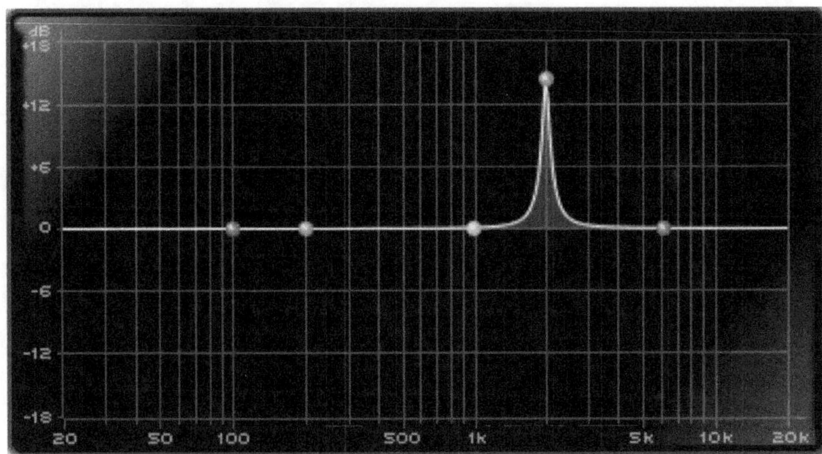

Figure 9.76 Narrowing the Band

3. Once that's done, start playback (usually with the track soloed), and slowly change the frequency value of the band that you want to change. As you do it, you'll hear that range of frequencies greatly exaggerated. Once your sound gets *worse* (since in this case, we're looking for a bad sound to cut), you've found your offending frequency center.

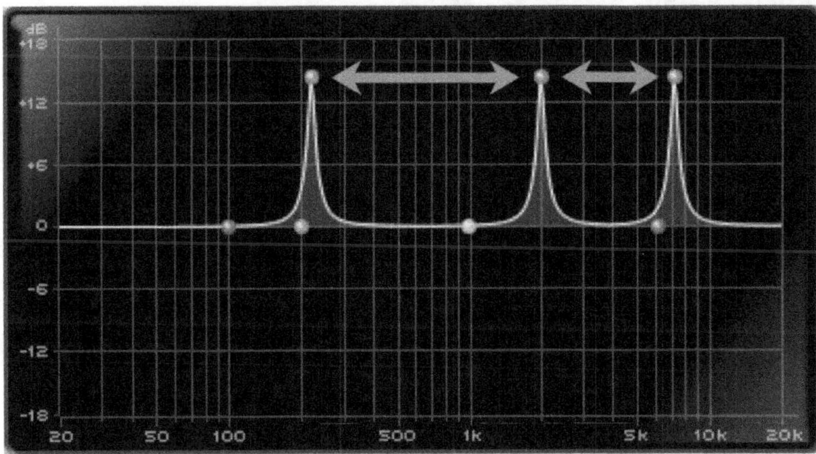

Figure 9.77 Sweeping the Band

From then on, it's pretty simple: Reduce the gain so that instead of boosting the unwanted frequencies, you're cutting them. You'll probably want to adjust the width of the Q as well.

There are a couple of inherent problems with this workflow though: First, if you have a loud sound and boost a frequency range, you run the risk of clipping the track, and hearing a distorted sound isn't going to help you at all. Secondly, and more deviously, as you sweep your frequency, your brain will naturally try to adapt to it, and after a while you'll start to lose your ability to judge the right frequency.

There *must* be a better way . . .

Soloing the Band

Avid has put a great feature in their EQ plug-ins, which makes finding the frequencies you want *much* easier. It's called *Band Pass Mode*, and features like it can be found in many (but not all) EQ plug-ins.

Not only is this a better way to work in terms of quality; it's easier too, if you know the trick!

1. Start playback (usually with the track soloed).
2. Holding down SHIFT+CONTROL (Mac) or SHIFT+START (Windows), move any parameter on the band that you want to use. You'll immediately see your EQ graph change, similar to Figure 9.78:

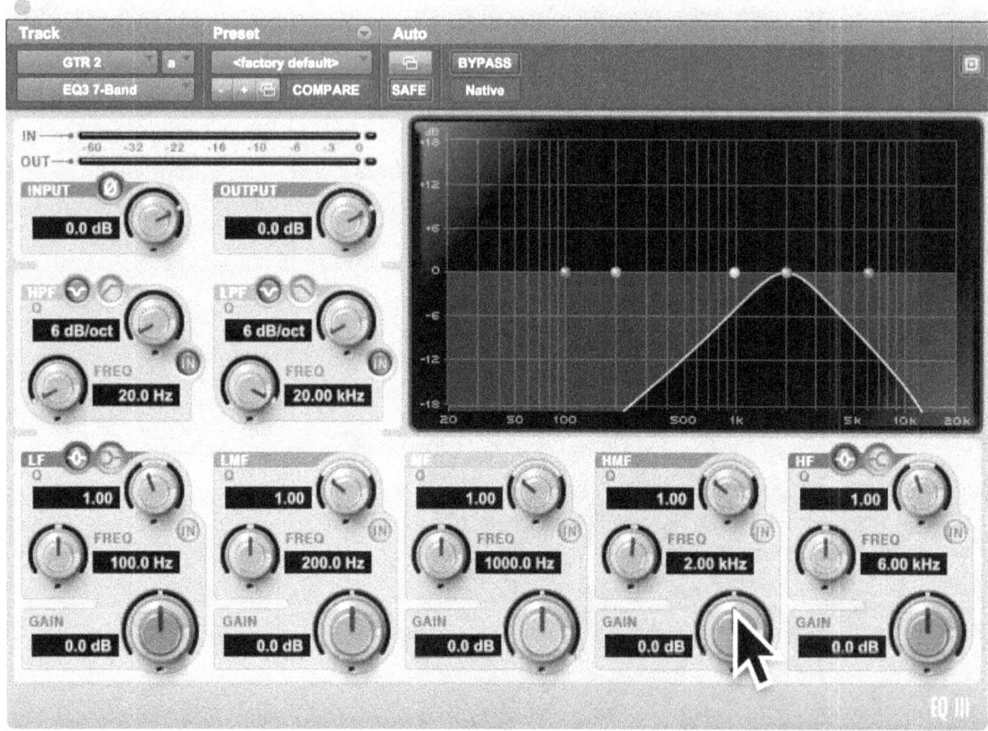

Figure 9.78 Soloing the High Mid Frequency Band

As long as you hold down these keys, you will only hear the sound of the band on its own, cutting out the rest of the signal. This includes adjustments made to frequency and Q, allowing you to find the frequency you want more easily than traditional sweeping. As soon as you release the keys, you can then adjust the gain to suit the needs of the track.

Hands-On Exercise 9.1: EQ Practice

When mixing, setting volume levels and panning will only get you partway there. Let's take a look at a simple scenario where a bit of EQ can make a big difference.

Setting Up

1. Create a new Project by converting the *Pro Tools First—Fundamentals of Audio Production—Chapter 9 (EQ).ptx* session to a local Project. The session is found in the *Pro Tools First—Fundamentals of Audio Production—Chapter 9 (EQ)* subfolder of this book's downloaded exercise material. Choose any desired sample rate, 24-bit, and do not Backup to Cloud.
2. Once you've opened the project, listen to it. You can see that it's pretty simple: a drum loop, a couple of guitars (note the panning and subgrouping), and a bass. At this point, instead of being a passive listener, become an active critic. Here are some questions you should be thinking about:
    - Which of the elements is the most important?
    - Listening to each track separately, what is the most important sonic aspect of the sound? What about the tone do you like and what would you like to change?
    - Listening to each track (separately and together), which ones are most important in the low frequencies? The middle frequencies? The high end?

Bear in mind that there are no hard and fast rules when it comes to EQ, but there *are* tried and true traditions. Here are a few things you might want to do in order to bring out the best in your mix.

Taming the Bass

One thing often overlooked by folks who are new to mixing is that low-pitched sounds (like a bass), even if they're playing a low note, can have a lot of high-frequency content in their sound, due to their *overtones* (a topic beyond the scope of this book, but worth looking into for the aspiring mixer). Sometimes these higher-frequency components of the track are desirable, but they can also compete with other more important parts of the mix. In this case, I want to get rid of some of those higher frequencies, and to do that, I'll start out with a 1-Band EQ.

3. Instantiate an EQ3 1-Band EQ plug-in on the first insert of the *Bass* track.
4. Choose the *Low Pass* type.

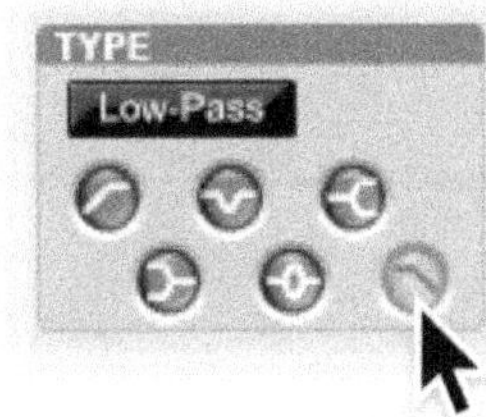

Figure 9.79 Changing to a Low Pass Filter

5. Set the *Frequency* parameter to its highest value.
6. Solo the *Bass* track and start playback.
7. As your bass track plays, gradually lower the *Frequency* parameter, taking note of how the feel of the bass track changes as high frequencies are removed.

8. You'll hear that the bass part smooths out a bit as high frequencies are cut, but if you go too far, it'll cease to sound like a real bass. Here's where it comes down to a matter of taste, so experiment with different frequencies *and* different filter values. Here's what I came up with:

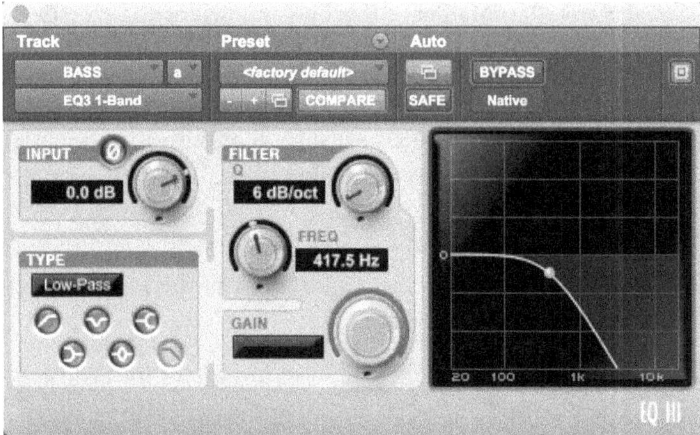

Figure 9.80 Settings for the Bass Track

You'll notice that by cutting some of the unwanted higher frequencies, it's easier to hear a bit more punch in the bass. You'll also notice that your output level has decreased (because you're removing energy as you're cutting frequencies). This will allow you to bring up the fader on the track, adding more punch to the project as a whole.

Emphasizing Kick and Snare

When it comes to drum loops, you'll often find that while the loop sounds fine on its own, when it's in the mix with other tracks, you wish you could bring up one or two of the drums, but not the others. But it's all on only one track, so that's *impossible*, right?

9. Solo the *Drum Beat* track, so that you can hear it clearly.
10. Instantiate a multichannel EQ3 7-Band EQ plug in on the first insert of the *Drum Beat* track.
11. If it's not already, set the Low Frequency (LF) band to *Low Shelf* mode.

Figure 9.81 Enabling the Low Shelf

12. Soloing the band, holding the SHIFT+CONTROL keys (Mac) or the SHIFT+START keys (Windows), change the *Frequency* and *Q* settings, so that you can hear the punch of the Kick drum, but as little of the other drums as possible (you won't be able to remove them completely, but that's not a problem).

13. Increase the gain of the LF band to a point where the kick is more prominent. You might notice that the clip light of the *Out* meter turns red, but we'll tackle that in a bit.

Next, let's see if we can emphasize the hit of the snare:

14. Soloing the Low Mid Frequency (LMF) band, change the *Frequency* and *Q* settings, so that you can hear the hit of the snare drum but as little of the other drums as possible (you won't be able to remove them completely, but that's not a problem). In the case of the snare drum, you'll notice that as you change frequency and Q, you'll change the character of the snare drum and its perceived size. When you find the kind of snare sound you like, you're done and ready to move on.

15. Increase the gain of the LMF band to a point where the Snare is more prominent. At this point, you can change the gain of the LF and LMF bands to get a good punchy kick and a strong snare in relation to the rest of the kit. For what it's worth, here are my settings:

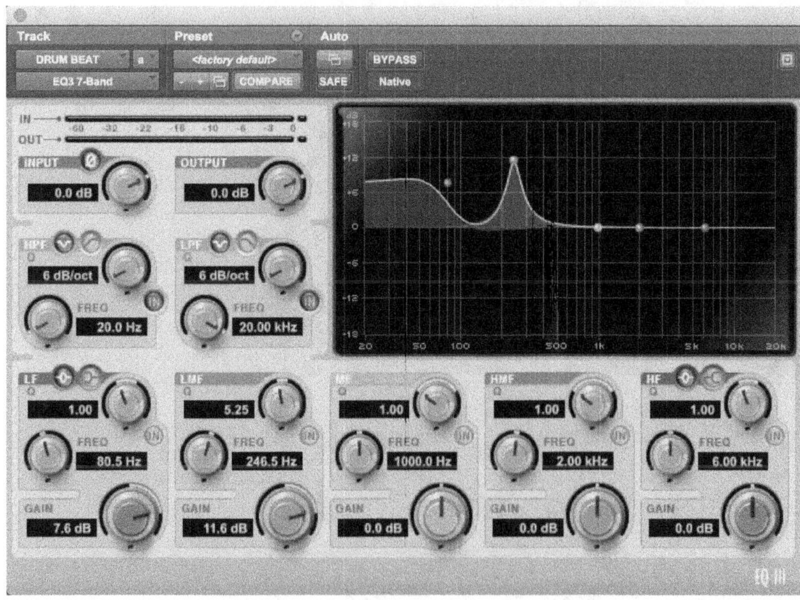

Figure 9.82 Settings for the Drum Beat Track

Since you're boosting frequencies (additive EQ), you're running into a common problem—clipping on the output side of the plug-in. This is easily fixed:

16. Reduce the *Output* of the plug-in until clip light no longer illuminates (NOTE: Once a clip occurs, the clip indicator will remain red until the clip light is *cleared*. You can do this by clicking on the clip indicator).

Sculpting the Guitars

If you listen to the two guitar tracks individually, you'll find that they are different parts. *GTR 1* is a chunky rhythm guitar track, and *GTR 2* plays a higher-pitched riff. They are both separated by panning already, but let's sculpt the sound of each guitar, so that both can be clearly heard. To do this, we'll need to do a bit of subtractive EQ, followed by some additive EQ.

17. On each track, instantiate an EQ3 7-Band plug-in on an insert.

18. Soloing each track individually, enable the High Pass Filter (HPF) and reduce or remove all of the unimportant low frequencies. Since the *GTR 1* track is filling a rhythm guitar role, you might want to keep more of the low end in that track than in the *GTR 2* track.

Listening to the two parts, you'll need to make a choice about which part is more important to the mix. This is ultimately a matter of subjective preference, but to me, the *GTR 2* track is more interesting, so I'll start there.

19. On the *GTR 2* track, solo the HMF band and find the frequency range where the guitar riff is strongest. Boost that band to bring out that part of the sound. You might also want to add a little bit of an HF shelf. Here's what sounds good to my ear:

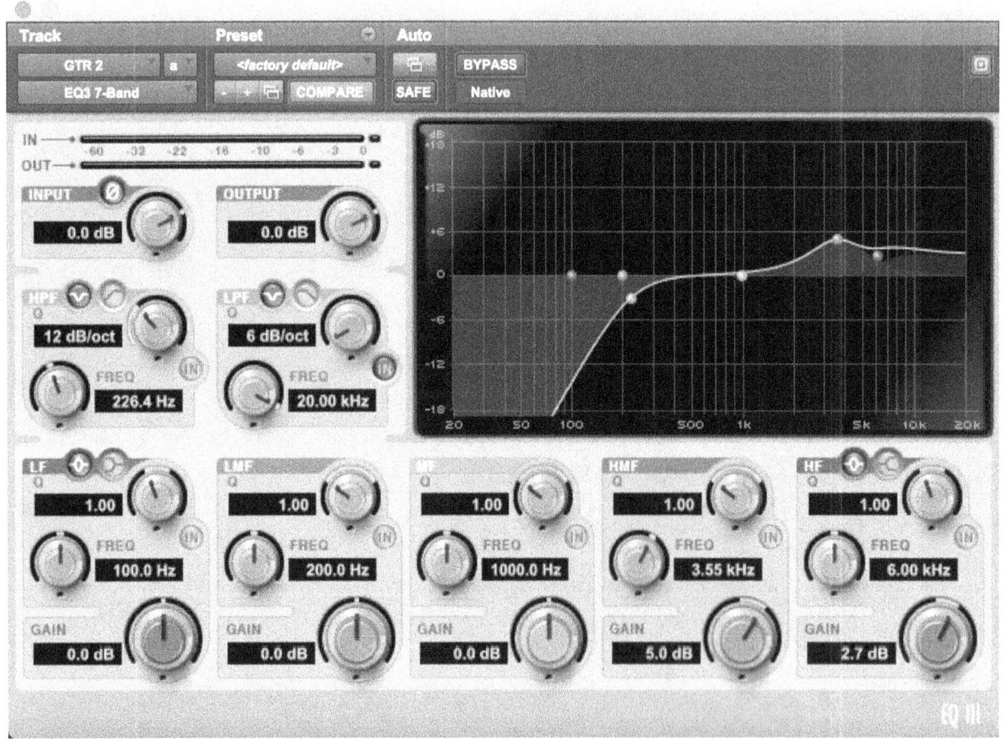

Figure 9.83 My EQ on the GTR 2 Track

20. On the *GTR 1* track, solo the MF band and find the frequency (and Q) that best brings out the rhythmic articulations of the track. Raise the gain on that band to bring out that quality of the track.

21. To my ear, the *GTR 2* track is more important than the *GTR 1* track. To make sure that the riff of the *GTR 2* track can be clearly heard, on the *GTR 1* track, I'll set the HF band to be a high frequency shelf and decrease the gain to give some sonic space for the *GTR 2* track. Here's what I wound up with for the *GTR 1* track:

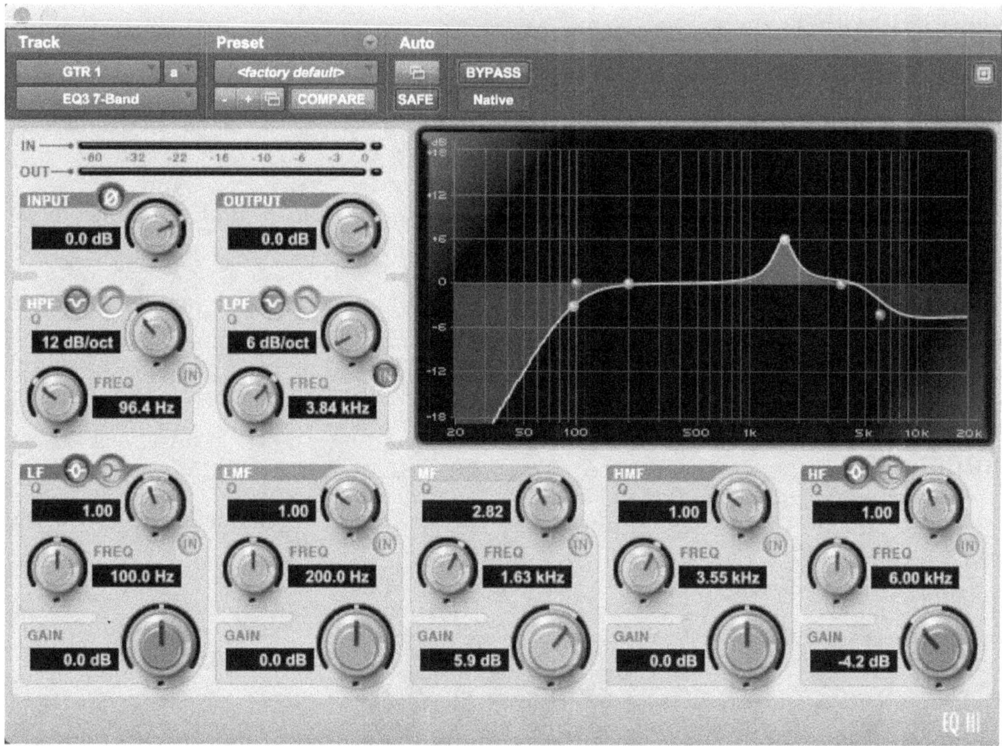

Figure 9.84 My EQ on the GTR 1 Track

Finishing Up

When you boost or cut frequencies with an EQ, you're adding or removing power from the track, so the levels will naturally change. Just as importantly, but more subtly, the tonal changes of the tracks will allow them to fit together in a different way. For both these reasons, you'll usually want to adjust your levels after EQing.

22. Change your volume levels to rebalance the track to suit your taste. When it sounds good, you're done—make sure to save your work before we move on!

Key Effect #2: Compression

Compression is an effect that can be a very powerful tool for the mixing engineer, but it can easily cause problems if it's not used with care. In this section, we'll talk about what a compressor does, the various parameters included in a basic compressor, and how it's used in mixing.

What is a *Compressor*?

The word *compress* means to *squeeze* or to reduce by means of pressure. In a nutshell, that's precisely what a compressor does: reduces (squeezes) the dynamic range of a track (the difference between the tracks loudest and softest sounds) by a means of pressure (called attenuation, which we'll discuss in more detail in a bit).

Compressors are used in a variety of ways in mixing:

- To manage the levels of a track, so that the levels are more consistent.
- To emphasize the beginnings of a sound. A compressor is often used to add "punch" to drums and other instruments with a strong initial attack.
- To enhance an entire mix, making it louder and more "radio-ready." A little bit of compression on a Main SUB track can go a long way to solidifying a mix.

There are two ways that a compressor can decrease the difference between loud sounds and quieter sounds: It can make the loud sounds quieter (called *downward* compression) or it can make quieter sounds louder (called upward compression). Downward compression is the more common type, which we'll focus on here.

Compression Parameters

Avid's *Dyn3 Compressor/Limiter* is a great example of a compressor. Going through its parameters will show you how a compressor works:

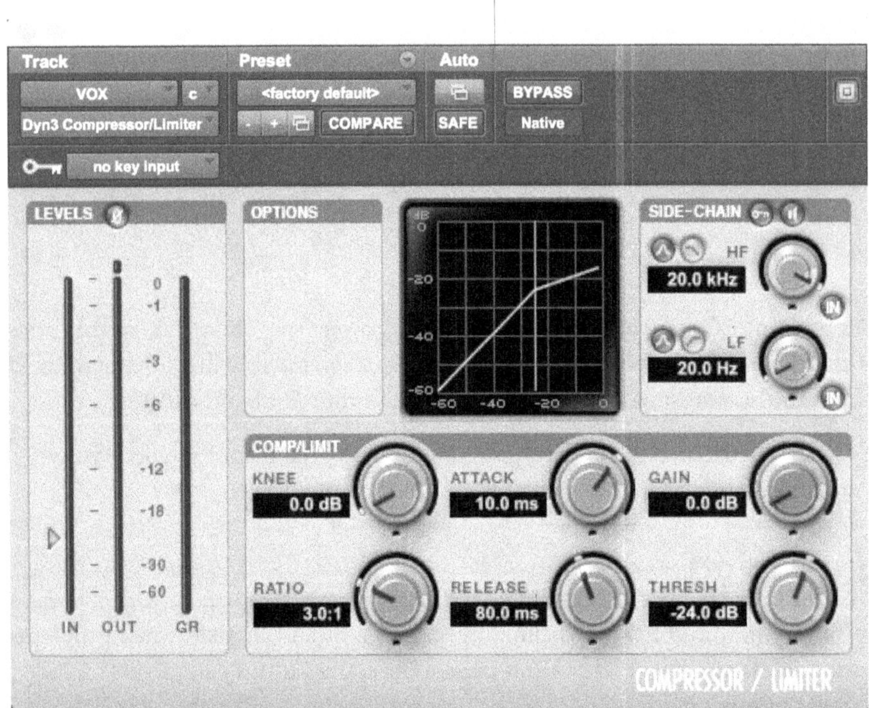

Figure 9.85 Avid's Dyn3 Compressor/Limiter Plug-in

Understanding the Compressor Graph

In the center of the *Dyn3 Compressor/Limiter* plug-in window, you'll see a graph with a roughly diagonal line. This graph can give you valuable visual feedback (you'll find similar sections in other compressor plug-in windows) but can be a little confusing. Here's how it works:

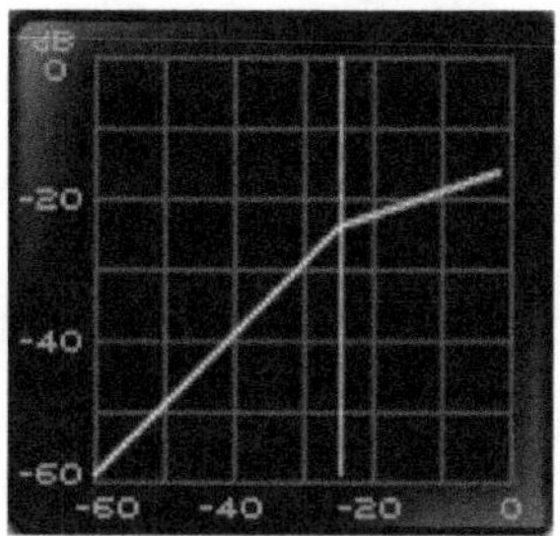

Figure 9.86 The Dyn3 Compressor/Limiter Graph

- The bottom (x) axis corresponds to the incoming signal—the sound coming *into* the compressor.
- The left side (y) axis corresponds to the outgoing signal—the sound coming *out* of the compressor.
- The diagonal white line and the vertical orange line indicates parameters that you'll learn more about next.
- A small square indicates the current level of the signal.

Let's take a look at a couple of examples. Figure 9.87 shows a signal going into the compressor at a level of -40 dB and coming out of the compressor unchanged at -40 dB.

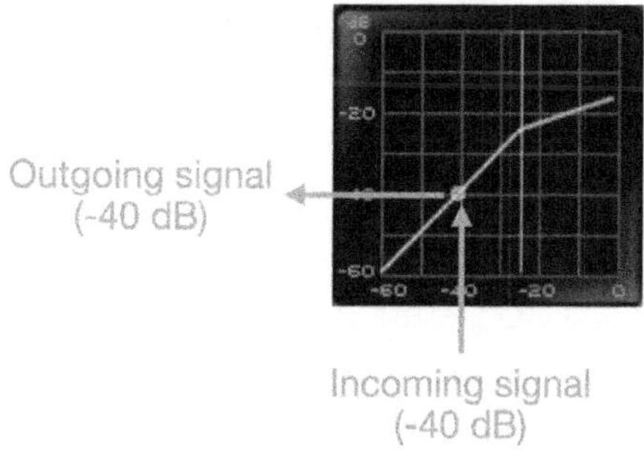

Figure 9.87 An incoming and Outgoing Signal of -40 dB

Figure 9.88 shows a signal going into the compressor at a level of about -10 dB and coming out of the compressor at roughly -20 dB. In this case, the outgoing sound is reduced in level (called *attenuation* or *gain reduction*), indicated by the square icon colored red.

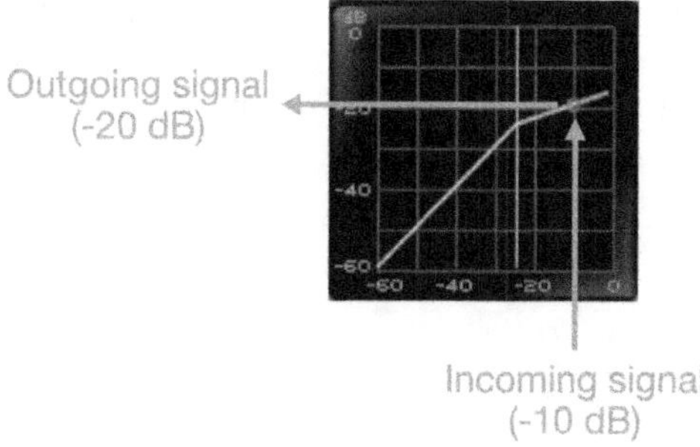

Figure 9.88 An Incoming Signal of -10 dB and an Outgoing Signal of -20 dB

Threshold

Everything that a compressor does centers around a *threshold,* which is a decibel (dB) level that you can set, below which the signal will not be affected, but above which will be attenuated (made quieter).

Figure 9.89 shows the threshold value at its highest level (-0 dB). This is indicated in the Compressor's graph section as an orange line at the far right of the graph. In this example, only signals that are louder than -0 dB would be attenuated. Since no sound can be above -0 dB, the entire signal would pass through the compressor unchanged. The level of the signal is indicated by the small white square.

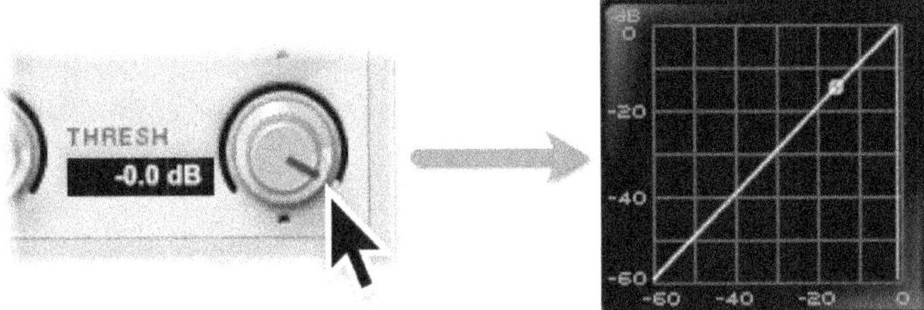

Figure 9.89 The Compressor with the Threshold Set at the Higest Value

Figure 9.90 shows a threshold value of -20 dB. You'll see that the orange threshold indicator line has moved to the left. All the levels below -20 dB (to the left of the line) will remain unaffected, but anytime the amplitude exceeds the threshold (indicated by the red square to the right of the threshold indicator) the level of the signal will be decreased, or *attenuated.*

Figure 9.90 A threshold of -20 dB

Ratio

But how *much* will a signal be attenuated when it exceeds the threshold? That depends on the *Ratio* setting.

In the *Dyn3 Compressor/Limiter* plug-in, the lowest ratio setting is 1.0:1; in other words, a one-to-one ratio, which would result in no attenuation.

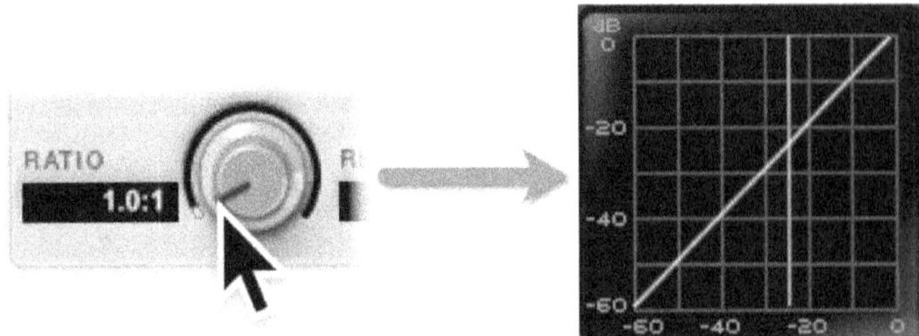

Figure 9.91 A 1.0:1 Ratio

If, for example, the ratio was 2.0:1 or two-to-one, any signal that exceeded the threshold would be cut in half. If a signal exceeded the threshold by 2 dB, it'd be attenuated down to 1 dB. A signal that was 1 dB over the threshold would be attenuated down by .5 dB and so on. Here's what a 2.0:1 ratio looks like on the plug-in graph:

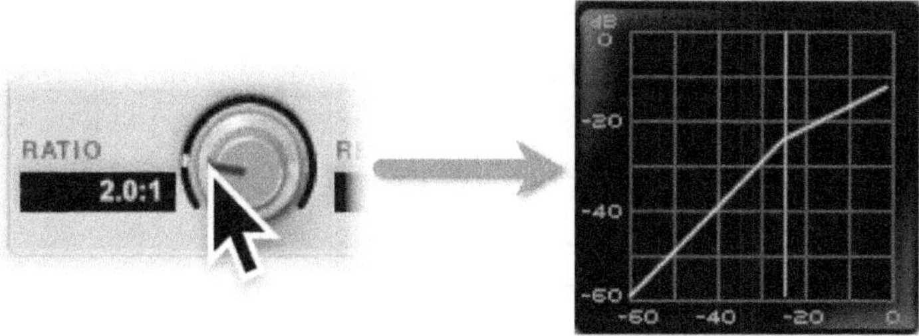

Figure 9.92 A 2.0:1 Ratio

The whole idea of attenuating signals above the threshold by a ratio (as opposed to a fixed amount) might seem strange at first, but it's the right way to go: Compressing with a ratio preserves the contours of the original signal while making sure that the attenuated signal never goes below the threshold value. As your threshold value gets higher, the line to the right of the threshold will become flatter, and amplitudes that cross the threshold will be reduced by a higher value.

Attack Time and Release Time

The *Attack* and *Release* parameters are often overlooked or misunderstood, but these two parameters are absolutely critical to understand if you want to make the most of compressors.

Here's an example that will show what these two parameters will do: Figure 9.93 shows a sine wave that starts out at -20 dB and then jumps up to -3 dB.

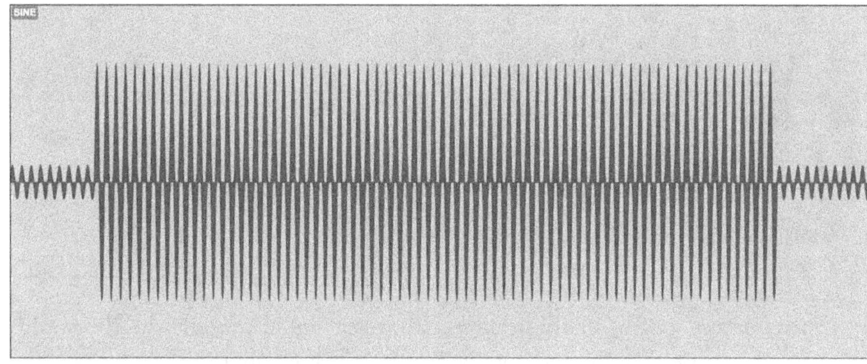

Figure 9.93 The Original Sine Wave Clip

In the compressor plug-in on the track, I've set the *threshold* to be -13 dB, and the *ratio* to be 2.0:1, just to keep the math simple.

With these settings, we can infer the following:

- When the level of the signal is at -20 dB, the signal won't be affected, since the level is below the threshold.

- When the level of the signal is at -3 dB, the signal *will* be affected, since the level is above the threshold (in this case, by 10 dB).
- Because the ratio of the compressor is 2.0:1, the difference between the original signal and the attenuated signal will be halved, with the louder sound being brought down by 5 dB to -8 dB.

Let's see what happens with a quick attack time. I'll set the value to its lowest, which in this plug-in is an attack time of 10 microseconds. Figure 9.94 is a rendering of what you'll hear. As you can see, the gain reduction is virtually instantaneous (when you're using a real-time effect, you will hear a change, but the clips on your track won't change appearance).

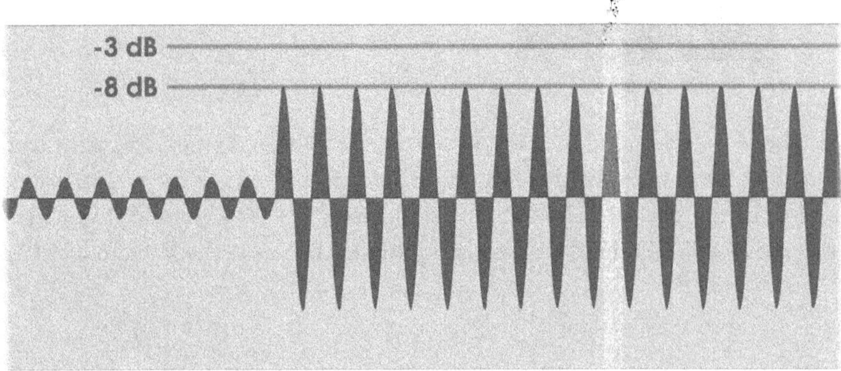

Figure 9.94 Compressing with a Fast Attack

Next, I'll increase the attack time to 4 milliseconds. Here's what I'll get:

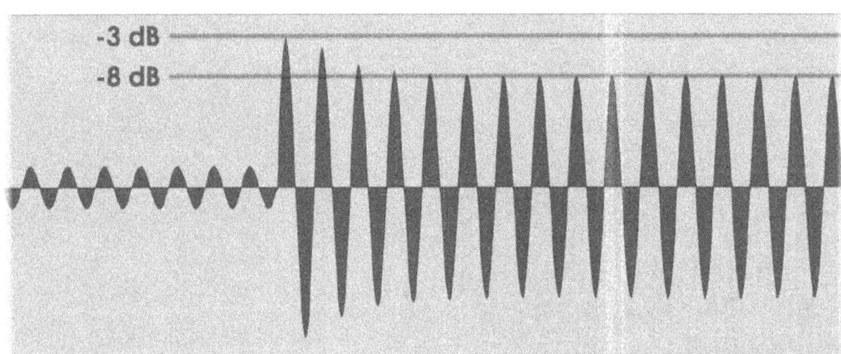

Figure 9.95 Compressing with a Slower Attack

You'll see that in either situation, the attenuation begins at the moment that the signal exceeds the threshold. In the case of a fast attack, the attenuation is immediately and totally applied. When the attack is longer, the attenuation takes some time to be applied, and will only reach the full 2.0:1 ratio after the attack time (in this case 4 milliseconds)

Your understanding of this parameter opens up a world of possibilities. Do you want to bring all the levels of a track, even the initial attack of notes? No problem—a short attack time will do the trick. Do you want to accentuate the attack of a percussive track like drums or bass? A slower attack will let more of the initial attack through and emphasize the start of individual notes, adding "punch" to the track.

If the attack time is the time that the compressor will take to fully apply the attenuation after a signal exceeds the threshold, then *release* time refers to how quickly the attenuation will *stop* after the signal goes back *below* the threshold.

To show how this works, I'll start by setting my release time to its lowest value (5 milliseconds).

Figure 9.96 shows the result (I've zoomed the waveform vertically, so that you can see it clearly). You can see a very small increase in amplitude of the waveform after the signal goes below the threshold as it comes back up to its original amplitude of -20 dB. That's the release time:

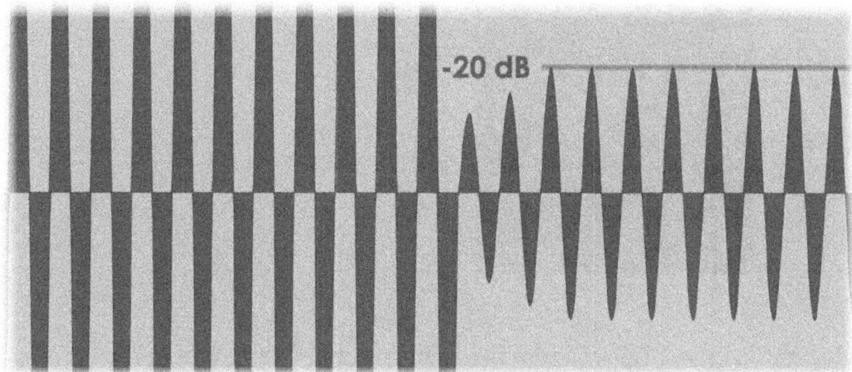

Figure 9.96 Compressing with a Fast Release

Next, I'll set the release time to be 10 milliseconds, and the result should be what you'd expect by this point—the sound eases into not being attenuated over the longer release time.

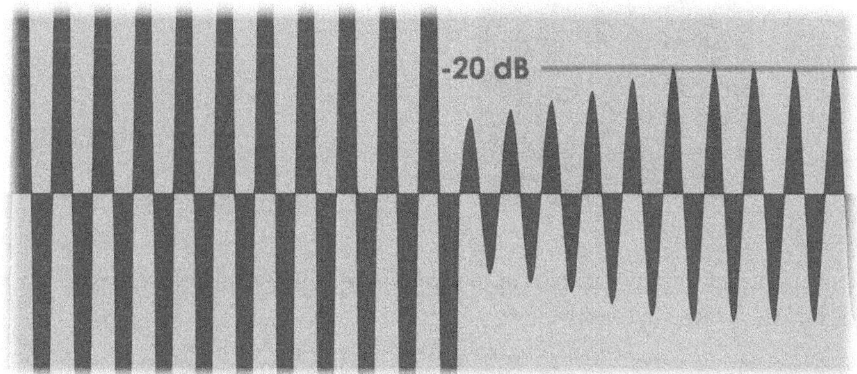

Figure 9.97 Compressing with a Slower Release

The effect of different release times is sometimes not as obvious as changes in attack times, but understanding both is crucial, especially when adding punch to a drum kit (with a slower attack)—a slow release can help preserve more of the initial impact of a drum.

Knee

Often, you will want your compressor to be a subtle effect, but especially if you have a high compression ratio setting, the attenuation can be pretty obvious. The *Knee* value can help to mask the attenuation by easing into the threshold value.

With a low value (often called a "hard" knee), the signal attenuation (commonly called *Gain Reduction*) will be applied as soon as the signal exceeds the threshold, but not before. On the *Dyn3 Compressor/Limiter* plug-in graph, it's represented like this:

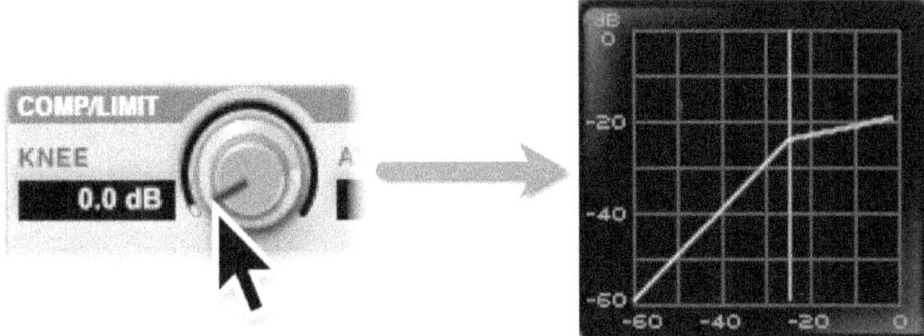

Figure 9.98 A Hard Knee

As you raise the *Knee* parameter's value, the knee will "soften," and the attenuation will be a more gradual process, beginning a bit before the signal's amplitude reaches the threshold. This is represented by a rounded curve in the plug-in graph, as shown in Figure 9.99.

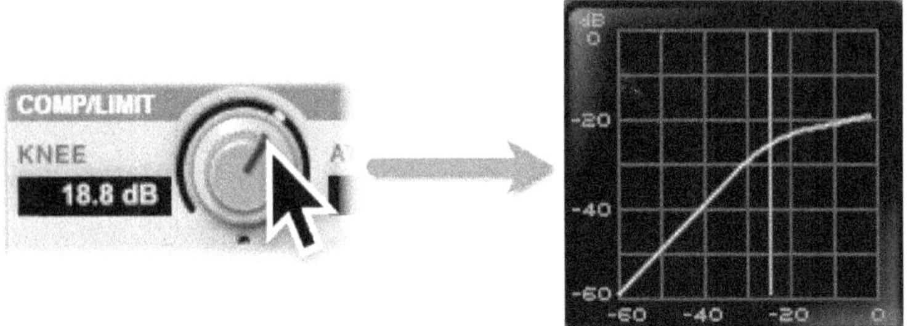

Figure 9.99 A Soft Knee

As with all aspects of mixing, different situations require different approaches, and you should always let your ears be your guide. A softer knee often results in a more natural feel.

Gain

You've learned that a compressor works by making loud sounds *softer*. Why, then, do so many audio professionals use it to make their tracks sound *bigger*? That's where something commonly called "Makeup Gain" comes in.

After compressing your signal (especially in cases of more aggressive compressing), you'll find that your track can be significantly quieter due to its lowered amplitude. Adjusting the *Gain* knob, as shown in figure 9.100, allows you to compensate (or "make up") for this decrease. This has the effect of raising the compressed dynamic range to a higher level.

Figure 9.100 Makeup Gain

Levels

On the left-hand side of the plug-in window are the level meters (with a phase invert button next to the word "levels").

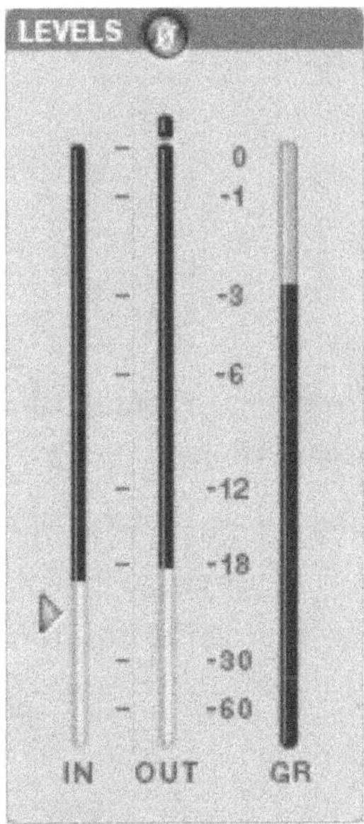

Figure 9.101 Level Meters in the Dyn3 Compressor/Limiter Plug-in

From left to right, they are:

- **Input Meter:** This shows the level coming into the plug-in. The threshold is indicated by an orange triangle (you can also click and drag this icon to change the threshold setting).
- **Output Meter:** This shows the outgoing level from the plug-in, including any makeup gain that has been applied.
- **Gain Reduction (GR):** The attenuation of levels that exceed the threshold is often called "Gain Reduction," and is shown in this meter. As you can see in Figure 9.102, when a signal is being attenuated (or the *gain* is *reduced*), you'll see this represented by a downward-moving orange indicator.

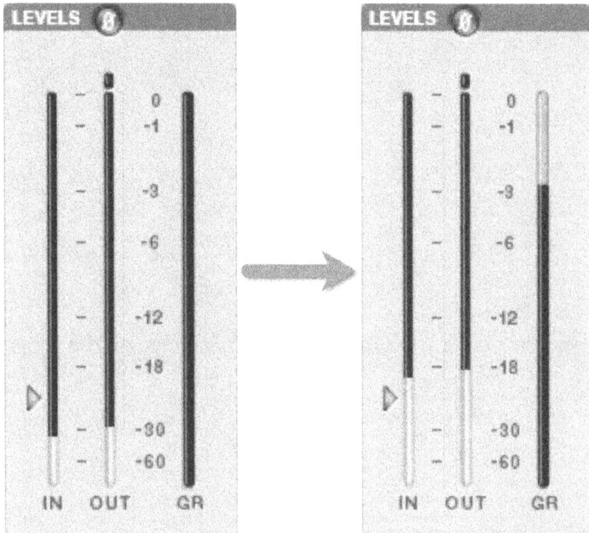

Figure 9.102 The Level Section, Showing No Attenuation (Left) and Attenuation (Right)

Side-Chain Controls

Here's another commonly overlooked and misunderstood part of a compressor—the *side-chain*. This might be confusing at first, but if you can understand this, you can make a compressor do just what you want.

Every compressor has a *side-chain,* which is the part of the compressor that controls the attenuation of the incoming signal, based on settings like threshold, ratio, attack and release times, and knee. If you were to look at the logical structure of a typical compressor, you can think of the incoming signal as splitting in two, with one signal moving to an attenuating mechanism and the other going to a *side-chain,* which controls the attenuator.

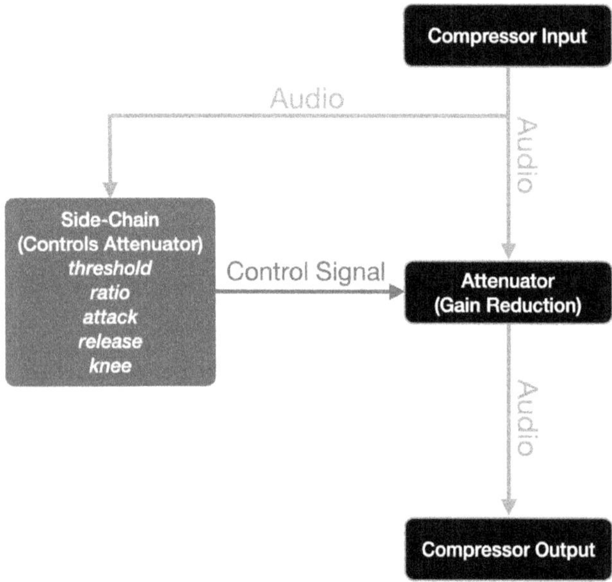

Figure 9.103 Typical Compressor Signal Flow

In many compressors, including the *Dyn3 Compressor/Limiter,* you can choose what the side-chain "hears," and therefore how it will control the attenuation of the processed signal. Think of the side-chain controls in the plug-in as being inserted between the source signal and the input of the side-chain, like this:

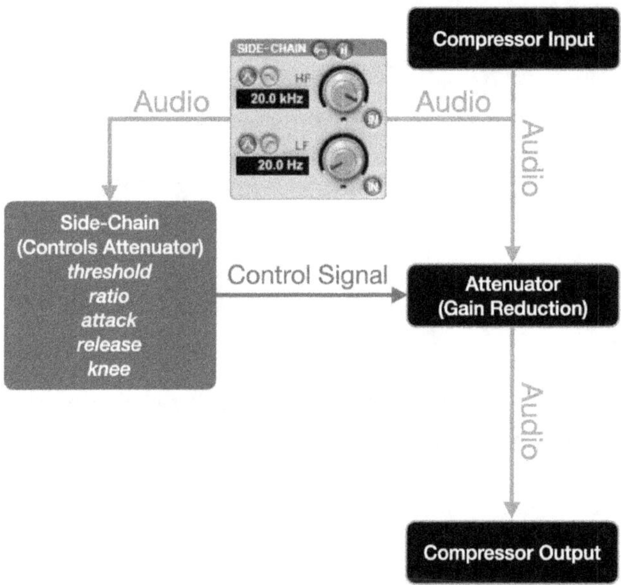

Figure 9.104 Typical Compressor Signal Flow, Showing Side-Chain Controls

The first thing that you'll see in the side-chain section are two filters: *High Frequency* (HF) and *Low Frequency* (LF). Like bands in an EQ plug-in, they can be individually enabled (with a blue IN indicator) or disabled (a grey IN indicator). Just click the IN button that corresponds with the band that you want to be active.

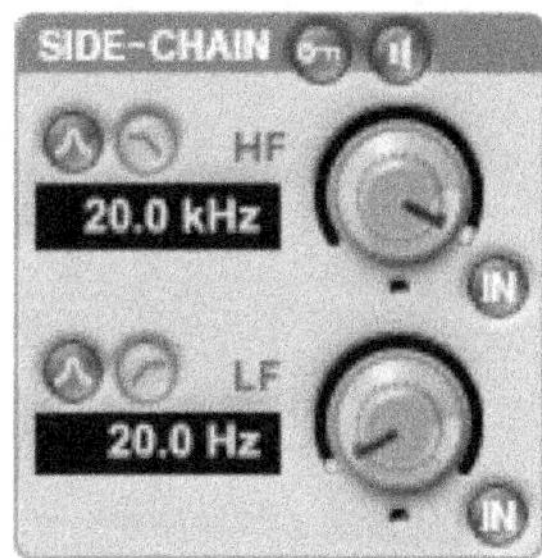

Figure 9.105 Dyn3 Compressor/Limiter Side-Chain Controls

For example, if you're using a compressor on a dance mix's main output, the compressor will tend to react strongly to the low-frequency kick drum that defines the style. The gain reduction meter will jump around, and you may hear the compressor's attack and release (something called "pumping"). If you're trying to apply a smooth gentle compression, the kick drum is definitely *not* helping and instead of making your mix sound bigger it's sounding smaller!

The solution is simple: Turn on the LF filter (as shown in Figure 9.106) and raise the frequency knob. You'll be progressively filtering out the low frequencies fed to the *side-chain* and therefore change the way it controls the attenuation of the compressor, smoothing it out. As for your low frequency instruments, since they're not "heard" by the side-chain, they won't trigger attenuation.

Figure 9.106 Filtering Low Frequencies from the Side-Chain

Sometimes it's hard to get a sense of how your changes are affecting the signal going into the side-chain, but this plug-in has you covered: Clicking the *Side-Chain Listen* button will let you hear only the signal that is fed into the side-chain.

Figure 9.107 The Side-Chain Listen Button

Finally, you'll see the *External Key* button. Clicking this will allow a signal routed from another track (a track different from the one that the compressor resides on) to control the side-chain.

Figure 9.108 The Side-Chain External Key Button

The use of external key inputs with side-chains is beyond the scope of this book, but is discussed in other books in the Avid Learning Series.

Compressors vs. Limiters

So far, we've been working with the *Dyn3 Compressor/Limiter* plug-in. What's the difference between a *compressor* and a *limiter*? With the caveat that this answer is overly simplistic, a compressor taken to the extreme becomes a limiter. As you increase the ratio, the output levels will move closer and closer to the threshold level—eventually, the ratio will become a *ceiling*, beyond which the levels will not pass. For example, if you set your ratio to 100.0:1 and the threshold to -20 dB (as shown in Figure 9.109), no level higher than -20 dB would show up on the meters. The plug-in graph would look like this:

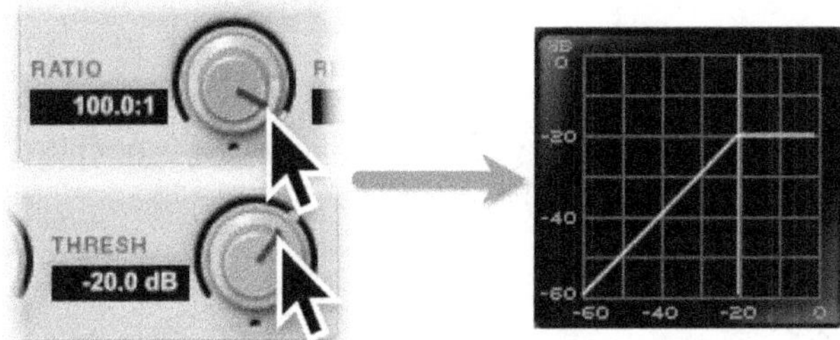

Figure 9.109 A Compressor Functioning as a Limiter

Limiters are used in all kinds of work, but they're used sparingly. In music production, it's usually reserved for the mastering phase of production. In prost-production (audio for film or video), there is no mastering process per se, but limiters are often used to make sure that levels don't exceed certain targets (these targets can vary by format or country).

Before we leave our discussion on compression, it bears mentioning that not every track (or every mastering session) needs a compressor. Compressors are often overused and can ruin a good mix quickly. Also, since the attenuation is based upon a ratio, multiple compressors *multiply* the amount of compression. If you have a 10.1:1 compressor on a track that goes to a subgroup that also has a 10.1:1 compressor, the result is *100.0:1*!

Key Effect #3: Expansion

As its name suggests, an *expander* does the opposite of what a *compressor* does. Instead of reducing the difference between the loud and quiet sound, an expander increases that difference. Surprisingly though, expanders operate in much the same way as compressors do, and what you've learned about a compressor's parameters will help you to quickly understand how to use an expander.

Just as there are upward and downward compressors, there are upward and downward expanders. An upward expander will make loud sounds louder and a downward expander will make quiet sounds quieter. Just as downward compression is more common, downward expansion is the more commonly-used type.

Avid's *Dyn3 Expander/Gate* is a great example of a downward expander:

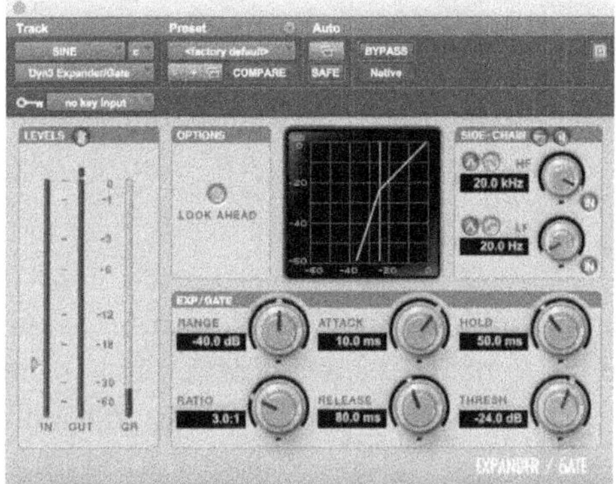

Figure 9.110 Avid's Dyn3 Expander/Gate Plug-in

Expanders are used in a variety of ways in mixing:

- Decreasing ambient noise
- Reducing "bleed" (when a microphone picks up other instruments than the one that it is intended for, like a snare drum being "heard" by a kick drum microphone)
- Emphasizing attacks by de-emphasizing the decay of a sound
- Shortening a reverb by reducing amplitude of the end of the reverb (the "tail")

Expander Parameters

The expander plug-in window looks like its compressor counterpart, and in many ways, it operates similarly, We can go through many of these parameters quite quickly.

Threshold and Ratio

The *Threshold* and *Ratio* parameters of an expander operate like a compressor's threshold and ratio, but in reverse: When an incoming signal goes *below* the threshold level, it is attenuated downward according to the ratio settings. Like a compressor, when the ratio is set to its lowest setting (1.0:1) there will be no attenuation, and as the level is increased, the amount of attenuation will increase accordingly.

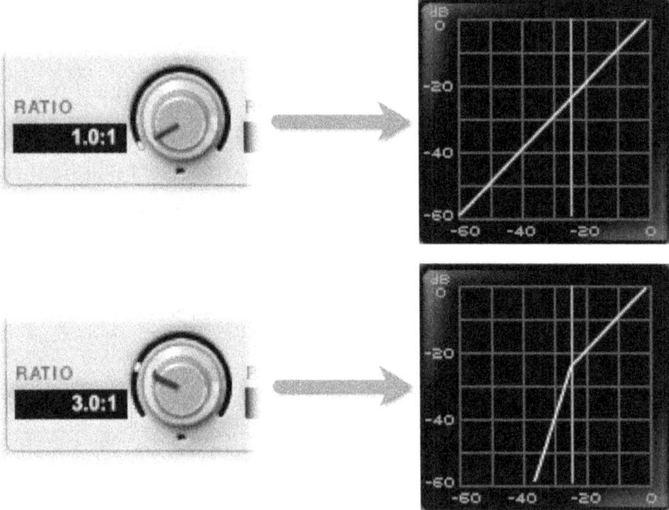

Figure 9.111 Changing the Ratio Value on an Expander

Attack and Release

Here again, these parameters operate just like a compressor's but in reverse: The *Attack* setting will determine how long it takes for the expander to fully stop attenuating the signal once the signal goes above the threshold. The *Release* setting will determine how long it takes for the expander to fully reach full attenuation (based on the ratio setting) once the signal goes *below* the threshold.

Levels

The levels section of the *Dyn3 Expander/Gate* is identical to the levels section of *Dyn3 Compressor/Limiter* plug-in. The only significant difference in what you'll see is the *GR* (Gain Reduction) meter, which will be *greater* as the signal gets *quieter*.

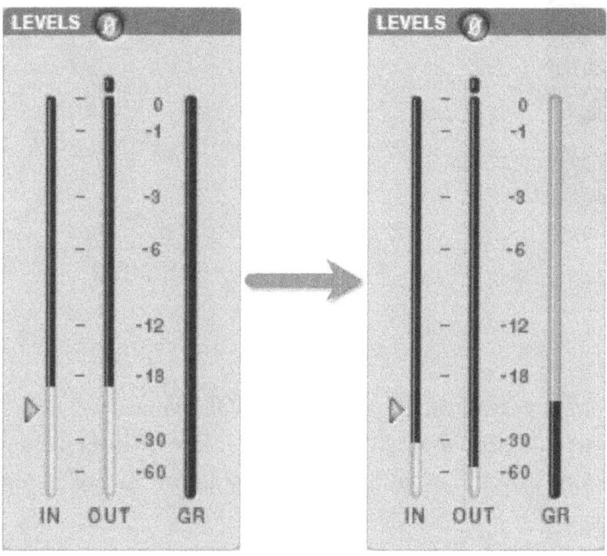

Figure 9.112 The Levels Section, Showing No Attenuation (Left) and Attenuation (Right)

Range is a parameter that *isn't* also in the Compressor plug-in and needs a little bit of explanation. Let's review what we know so far: When a signal falls below the *threshold,* it will be attenuated downward (the gain is reduced) by the *ratio* amount, and the speed of that attenuation is controlled by the *attack* and *release* parameters. *Range* allows you to set the "floor" of the expander, or the maximum amount of gain reduction (not as a ratio, but as a Decibel value).

Here's a common scenario where you'd change the range: Let's say that you're recording some spoken word (for a podcast or perhaps a video project) in a room that has some ambient noise (maybe a fan or an air conditioner—quiet, but ever-present). You can use an expander to get rid of that ambient noise when there's no talking, since the ambient noise is well below the words being spoken. However, there's a problem: You want to start attenuating quickly after you're done talking (so you'll use a relatively high ratio and fast attack time), but if you cut out the ambient sound completely, it'd sound conspicuous and unnatural. For example, this setting will make the track sound as if the air conditioner is turning on and off along with the speaking:

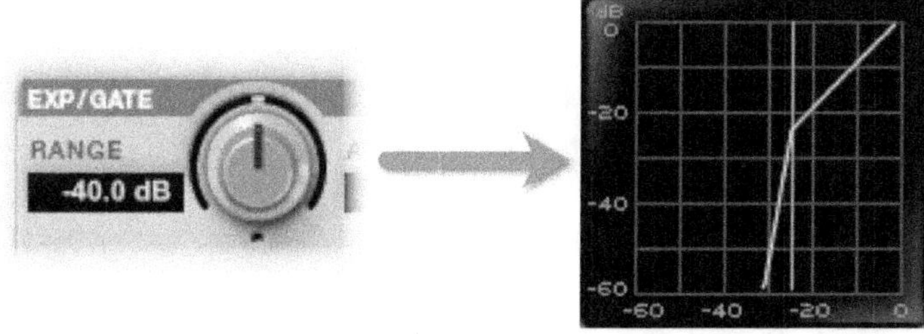

Figure 9.113 A Default -40 dB Range Setting

Changing the *range* can help: As you raise the value from its default setting (-40 dB), you'll see that the graph changes. Figure 9.114 shows an aggressive ratio (as indicated by the sharp initial drop below the threshold), but a reduced range—it will reduce the sound, but by no more than 10 decibels, so that the soft background noise is deemphasized rather than being completely removed.

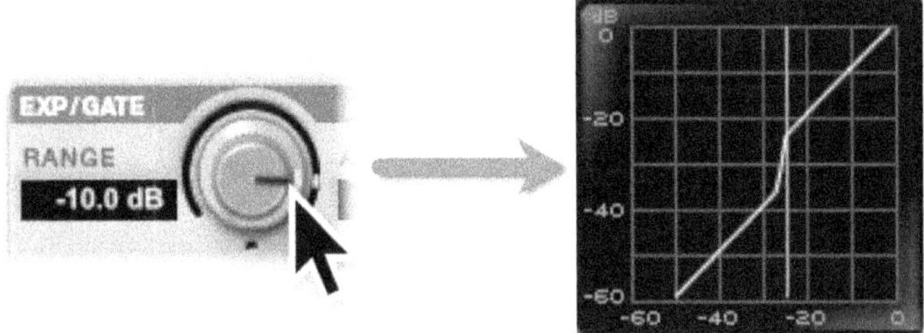

Figure 9.114 Reducing the Range to -10 dB

Hold

Here's another parameter that isn't part of a compressor but *is* part of an expander: The *Hold* parameter allows you to determine the amount of time the expander will wait before attenuating a signal, after it drops below the threshold. Hold times are sometimes increased in order to stop the expander from attenuating and releasing rapidly (something that is commonly referred to as "chatter").

Figure 9.115 The Hold Parameter

Look Ahead

Look Ahead is a feature that you'll find on many (but not all) expanders, and some compressors/limiters as well. This is an option that can be turned on or off.

Figure 9.116 Look Ahead Enabled

Normally, an expander will only react when the amplitude of a signal crosses the threshold (in either direction). For example, attenuation will stop only at the point where the signal's amplitude goes above the threshold. Even with short attack values though, this can cut off the beginnings of sounds. Activating *Look Ahead* will cause attenuation to begin earlier than it normally would—in the case of the *Dyn3 Expander/Gate* plug-in, it'll begin 2 milliseconds earlier. This is useful to activate for sounds with important transients (like drums), so that the initial part of the sound isn't lost.

The Expansion Process

Now that you understand the basic controls of an expander, here's how it works, step-by-step (for the purposes of clarity, let's assume that *Look Ahead* is *disabled*):

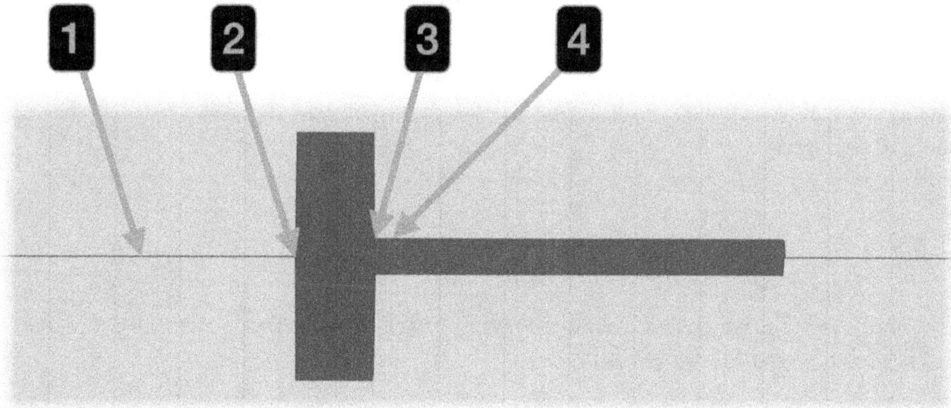

Figure 9.117 The Expansion Process

1. Prior to encountering a signal, there is silence, which is below the threshold. Therefore, the attenuation will be full (the expander will be "closed").
2. Once a signal exceeds the threshold, the attenuation will stop (the expander will "open"), allowing the sound to be heard. The speed of this opening is determined by the *Attack* setting.
3. Once the signal drops below the threshold, the expander will *not attenuate* (stay "open") for the amount of time set in the *Hold* parameter.
4. After the hold, the expander will attenuate ("close"). The speed of this attenuation is determined by the *Release* setting, and the maximum amount of attenuation is determined by the *Range* setting.

Expanders vs. Gates

Just as a compressor taken to the extreme becomes a limiter, an *Expander* taken to the extreme becomes a *Gate*. A maximum ratio setting (100.0:1) will not allow any sounds with an amplitude below the threshold to be heard. Like limiters, a gate is typically less used in mixing than an expander, but there are situations (and styles of music) for which it is used, particularly on drums (in the '80s, gated snare drums—often with longer hold times—were an iconic sound).

Hands-On Exercise 9.2: Dynamics Practice

To finish this chapter, let's take a look at some common mix problems and how they can be fixed with Compressors and Expanders.

Setting Up

1. Create a new Project by converting the *Pro Tools First—Fundamentals of Audio Production—Chapter 9 (Dynamics).ptx* session to a local Project. The session is found in the *Pro Tools First—Fundamentals of Audio Production—Chapter 9 (Dynamics)* subfolder of this book's downloaded exercise material. Choose any desired sample rate, 24-bit, and do not Backup to Cloud.

In this exercise, you'll see a number of individual drum tracks (*Kick*, *Snare*, and *Hat*), plus a few stereo tracks that are part of the drum kit: The *Overheads* track are from a pair of microphones that were placed above the drum set. The *Room* track was from a pair of microphones that were placed a bit further away in the room. The *Talkback* track was recorded through the recording console's talkback microphone (an old technique that can be used to bring some extra attack to the drums).

Fixing the Kick

If you solo the *Kick* track, you'll see that we have a classic recording problem—the kick microphone picked up some of the snare drum. Let's use an expander to get rid of it.

2. Solo the *Kick* track, so that you can hear it clearly.
3. Instantiate the *Dyn3 Expander/Gate* plug-in on the *Kick* track.
4. Adjust the threshold, Ratio, and attack and release times to remove the snare drum from the Kick track. You'll want to keep the initial attacks, so you want the shortest attack time possible, and to enable *Look-Ahead*. You'll find that by adjusting the release time, you can tighten up the kick sound so that it doesn't ring for quite so long. (Note: A quicker release time will cut out more of the snare, but too fast a release can start to shorten the kick drum too much.) Here's what I settled on:

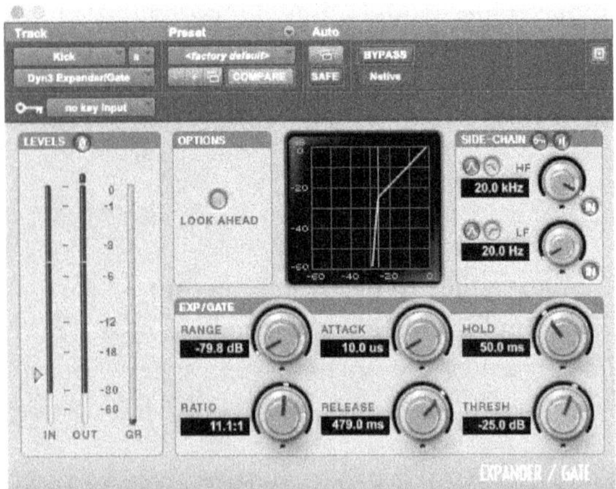

Figure 9.118 My Expander Settings for the Kick Track

Taming the Bass

One of the problems with slap bass parts is that the levels tend to jump around quite a bit. Let's use a little bit of compression to make the *Bass* track a bit more manageable.

5. Solo the *Bass* track, so that you can hear it clearly.
6. Instantiate the *Dyn3 Compressor/Limiter* plug-in on the *Bass* track.
7. Just like you did with the Kick track with an Expander, adjust the Threshold and Ratio to make sure that you're slightly attenuating most of the notes (and the louder notes will be more attenuated). Use the attack time to slightly soften the attacks (but not too much), so that you get a nice smooth part that works well with the drums. A little gentle compression will go a long way with this part.
8. Use the *Gain* parameter to bring up the output of the track. (Take care to avoid clipping in the output meter. Remember that you must click the clip indicators to reset them.) Here are the settings that I chose, but let your ears be your guide!

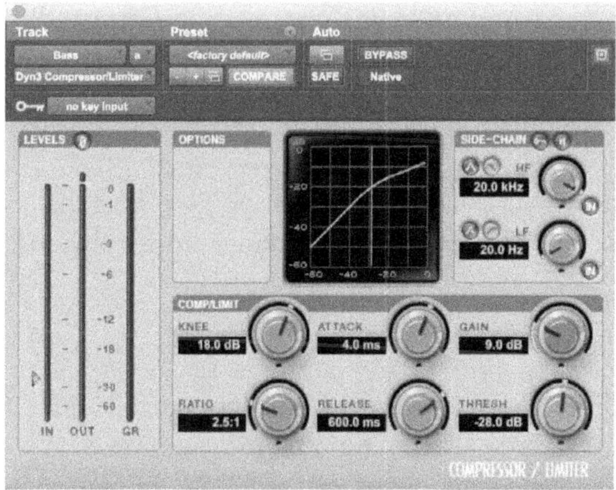

Figure 9.119 My Compressor Settings for the Bass Track

Adding Punch to the Drums

You'll see that the drum tracks have been set up with their outputs routed to the *Drum SUB* Aux track. Let's use that routing to our advantage and apply some compression to the entire drum kit with just one plug-in!

9. Mute the *Bass* track, so that all you can hear is the drum kit.
10. Instantiate the *Dyn3 Compressor/Limiter* plug-in on any insert of the *Drum SUB* track.
11. By now, you are getting a sense as to how the controls will affect the sound. The goal here is to apply gentle compression to the drum kit and make sure that the attack of the drums can clearly be heard (which means a longer attack time on the compressor). Use make up gain to bring the levels up. Here's what sounded good on my system:

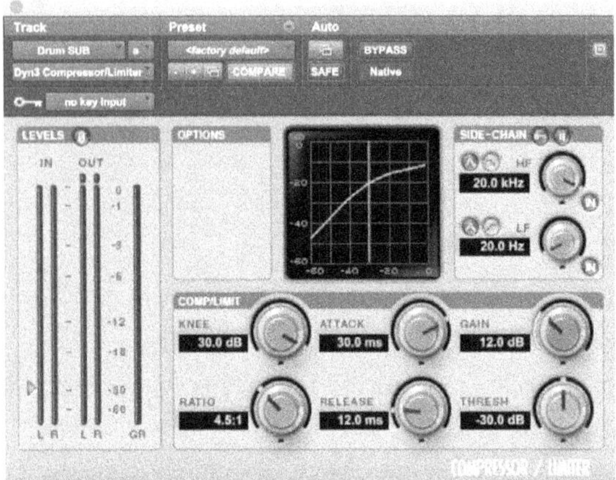

Figure 9.120 My Compressor Settings for the Drum SUB Track

Reducing Ambient Noise

For the last thing in this project, we need to deemphasize the background noise in a podcast. The *Podcast* track is one half of a discussion (done by my good friend Alex Brooke, who has already contributed some materials to this book). The problem is that there is an air conditioner running in the background. We want to decrease the level whenever he's not talking, but not cut it out completely.

12. Solo the *Podcast* track, so that you can hear it clearly. When you play the track, you can hear the air conditioner in the background. It's not so much a problem when he's speaking, but it's obvious when he's not.
13. Instantiate a *Dyn3 Expander/Gate* plug-in on any insert of the *Podcast* track.
14. The goal here is to make sure that the beginnings of his words are clearly heard (fast attack) and that the signal is reduced quickly after he's done talking (fast release), but that the sound isn't completely cut out (increase the *Range* value). With a little work, you'll find that you can make a significant different—Here's what works for me:

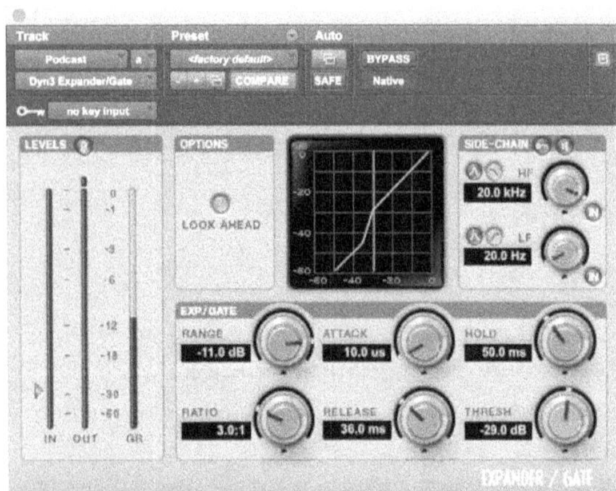

Figure 9.121 My Expander Settings for the Podcast Track

Experimentation

The two exercises in this chapter took a look at EQ and Dynamics effects in isolation, but of course, in any mix you'll use both (for example, a bass track might be both EQed and Compressed).

15. Go back to the *Low Roar* project that you used in Chapter 8. Alternately, you can create a new Project by converting the *Pro Tools First—Fundamentals of Audio Production—Chapter 9 (Low Roar).ptx* session to a local Project. The session is found in the *Pro Tools First—Fundamentals of Audio Production—Chapter 9 (Low Roar)* subfolder of this book's downloaded exercise material.
16. Take what you've learned in this chapter to take the mix to the next level. Here are some things you might want to do:
    - On the *Lead Vocal (Dry)* track, use a high pass filter to remove unwanted low frequencies, and add brightness with a high shelf at about 7 kHz.
    - Also on the *Lead Vocal (Dry)* track, make the levels a bit more manageable with some compression, with a threshold around -35 dB.
    - On the *Background Vocals (Dry)* track, cut more of the lows and boost the HMF band at about 3.5 kHz. A little bit of compression (not much) will help here as well.
    - On the *Synth Stem* track, a bit of compression with a soft knee and a low threshold will help the bells stand out.
    - On the *Bass Sub* track, a very gentle high pass filter will make room in the low frequencies for the drums.
    - On the *Rimshot* track, the woodiness of the track is around 125 Hz (in the LMF band). Boost that a little to bring out the best in that track. The levels jump around a little bit on this track as well, so some compression (with a threshold at around -30 dB) might help—not too much, though!
    - Don't forget the *Main SUB* track. A very subtle low shelf boost and high shelf boost might help the mix. The main vocal also sits at around 2 kHz, so boosting those frequencies (in the HMF band) with a broad Q will bring out the vocal. It doesn't have to be much. Here's what I used:

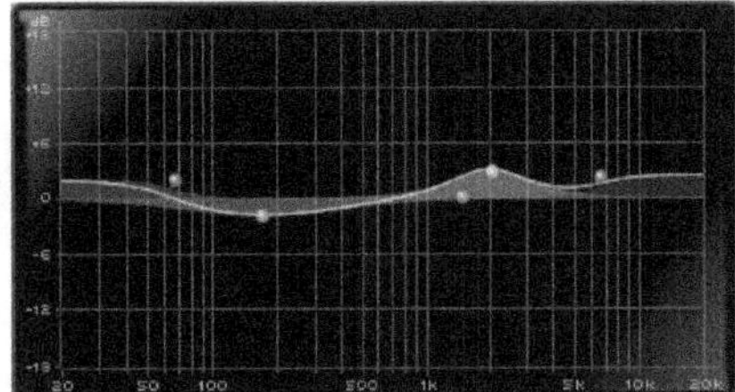

Figure 9.122 My EQ Curve on the Main SUB Track

    - On the *Main MON* Master Fader track: On the first insert, instantiate a compressor plug-in and set it up as a limiter with a threshold of about -5 dB, with a fast attack and release. Use make-up gain to bring the signal up, but make sure that it doesn't clip.
17. Experiment with the mix and learn how to get the sound that's in your mind to come out of the speakers. Before you're ready to move on, make sure you save your work!

Review Questions

1. In this chapter, we've covered three ways to bypass a plug-in. What were they?
2. How can a plug-in be copied as it's dragged from one insert to another?
3. True or False? On a multi-mono plug-in, changes made to the left channel will always be also applied to the right channel.
4. What is the difference between a graphic EQ and a parametric EQ?
5. On an EQ plug-in, what does the *Q* parameter control?
6. In this chapter, we've covered two ways to find frequencies using an EQ. One of them was the "sweeping" technique. What was the other way?
7. If a compressor makes loud sounds softer, what does an *expander* do?
8. What does the threshold determine on a compressor? What does it determine on an expander?
9. What does the *Attack* time and *Release* time control on a compressor? On an expander?
10. What does the Side-Chain do? What do the Side-Chain controls of the Compressor or Expander plug-in control?

CHAPTER 10

Adding Ambience to your Mix

You've learned how to use basic mix controls, like volume and pan, to get started with a mix, as well as how to shape the sound with EQ and dynamic effects, like compressors and expanders. Now it's time to add a sense of space to your mixes through effects like *reverb* and *delay*!

Media Used: *Pro Tools First—Fundamentals of Audio Production—Chapter 10 (Low Roar Tracks).ptx*

Duration: 45 minutes

GOALS

- How to use sends for time-based effects
- How to use sends for headphone mixes
- Understand Reverb, and how to add ambience to your mix
- Understand Delay, and how to add more interest to your projects

More Signal Flow with Sends

As mentioned earlier in this book, there are some effects that will change the total sound of a track (like EQ and Dynamic effects), which you learned about in Chapter 9. There are other effects, particularly *time-based* effects (like reverbs and delays) that you will want to blend the original "dry" signal with the effected signal. To get this done, you'll want to use *sends*.

Sends and Returns

The term "Send" can be traced back to early analog mixing boards. When people talk about using sends, they also often refer to something called a "return". Although sends and returns are used differently in Pro Tools (and most DAWs), going through the signal flow of an analog board is a good place to start.

Let's say that you have a mixing board with 8 mono channels (8 faders), and let's further say that you have lead vocal on channel 1, and background vocals on channels 2, 3, and 4. On each channel, we have two "sends" (usually knobs) which will route a copy of the signal out of two dedicated stereo pairs of outputs (of course, different boards have different numbers of sends—this is just a simple example).

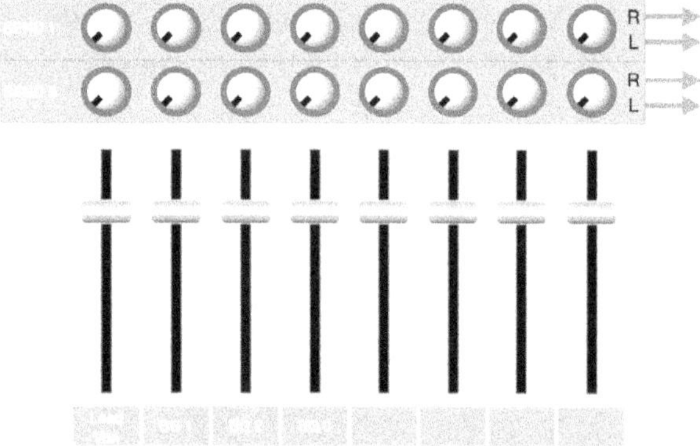

Figure 10.1 A simple Analog Mixer

I want to add reverb to my vocals, so I'll also need to have a hardware reverb unit (remember, this is an *analog* console). I will route the output of one of my available sends to the *input* of the reverb unit. Next, I'll want to be able to hear the reverb in my mix, so I'll route the *outputs* of the reverb to available tracks on the mixing board—since in this example, each channel is mono, I'll need to use two tracks to get a proper stereo signal—one for the left channel and one for the right. That's the *return*.

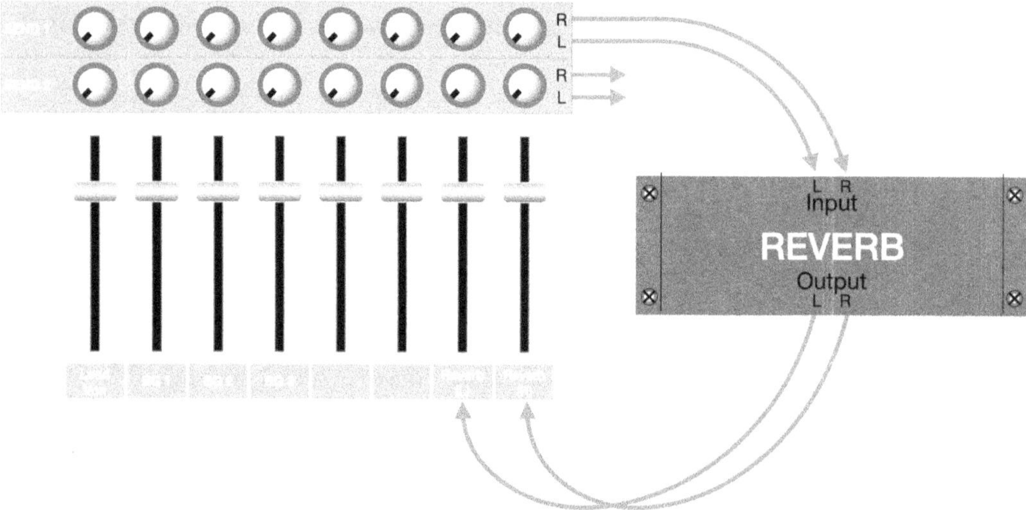

Figure 10.2 Sending to a Reverb and Returning on Available Tracks

Here's what you can do with a setup like this:

- The send controls on the individual tracks can be set individually for more or less of the track's signal to be sent to the effect. If you want more reverb on the lead vocal, just turn up the send on that track.
- The faders on the "return" tracks function as a master control over the amount of effect you'll have in your mix. In this example, changing the fader on these tracks would increase or decrease the amount of reverb.

This kind of routing is traditionally used for effects like reverbs and delays (which fall into a category called *time-based* effects). This will allow you to preserve the original tracks (the "dry" tracks) and blend them with a track (or tracks) which are the effect (the "wet" tracks). We do something quite similar in Pro Tools and other DAWs.

But *Why* Do We Do This?

A send/return setup might be the traditional way to set up reverbs and delays, but tradition for tradition's sake alone is meaningless. In a DAW like Pro Tools, why not just put individual reverb plug-ins on each track, like we did for EQs and Dynamic effects?

Actually, this routing scheme has many advantages when you're working with blended effects like reverbs and delays:

- **Mixer-Level Access:** Having reverbs and other blended effects reside on their own tracks simplifies the mixer's job. The mixer can just adjust the volume fader on the reverb track to increase or decrease the level of the effect—easy and intuitive.
- **Mix Agility:** If you've got only one reverb or delay applied to multiple tracks, and you want to make a change to the reverb settings, you only need to change *one* plug-in. If you were to put individual reverbs on each track, you'd have to change all of them individually!
- **Processing Efficiency:** When you use this kind of structure, your computer only runs a single reverb plug-in. If you were to put individual reverbs on each track that you want to process, that would increase the demands on your host computer. It might not be a huge factor with a small Pro Tools | First project, but when you start running large sessions with hundreds of tracks, it can make a significant difference.
- **Realism:** Routing multiple signals to ambient effects like reverbs mimics the way the real world works, allowing combined signals to interact within a single reverb effect, in the same way multiple performers together in a single room would. This can give you a more realistic result.

Using Sends

You've learned a little about sends in Chapter 8. Now, let's discuss how to use them.

Viewing Sends

In Chapter 2, you learned about the different Edit and Mix window *Views*—the different ways to show or hide elements of your project, like *Inserts*, *Comments*, *I/O*, and *Sends*. Before you can work with sends, you'll need to be able to see them. To review, here are a few ways that you can show or hide your sends.

- Perhaps the most straightforward way to change your Edit or Mix window Views is to go to the VIEW menu and choose EDIT WINDOW VIEWS or MIX WINDOW VIEWS. From there, you can show or hide either of the two banks of Sends (Sends A-E or Sends F-J).
- In the Edit window, click on the Edit window View selector (the small white icon at the top left corner of the tracks, as shown in Figure 10.3). Clicking this icon will reveal a list similar to the one you've seen in the VIEW menu, with columns that are shown indicated with a check mark. Any changes that you make in this list will immediately be reflected in the columns of your tracks.

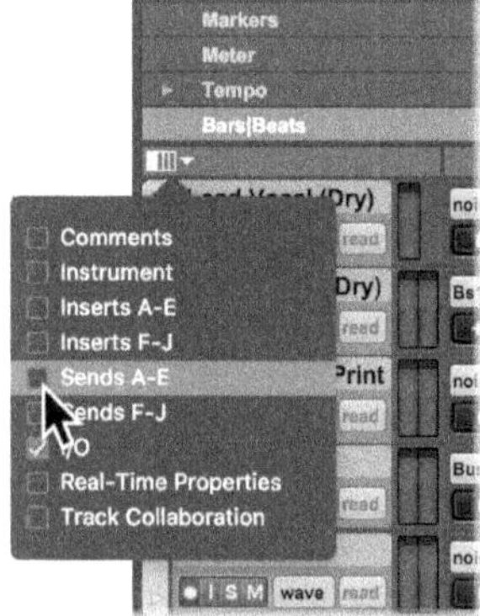

Figure 10.3 Showing Sends A-E in the Edit Window

- At the bottom left corner of the Mix window, you'll find the Mix window View selector (a small white icon), as shown in Figure 10.4. Clicking this icon will reveal a list of elements that can be shown or hidden.

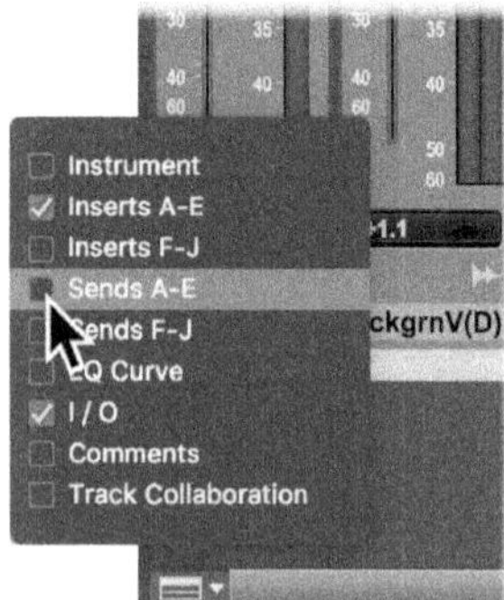

Figure 10.4 Showing Sends A-E in the Mix Window

Creating Sends and "Returns" in Pro Tools

The way that we traditionally deal with effects like reverb in Pro Tools follows the same logic as an analog mixer setup, but if you're using plug-in effects, there is no "return" per se. Here's an example of how it could be done:

In Figure 10.5, I have one lead vocal track and three background vocals. As you've learned how to do in Chapter 8, I created a vocal subgroup, which is going to a main subgroup, with a Master Fader controlling the output. I want to add a reverb.

Figure 10.5 Ready to Create Sends

1. On one of the tracks that I want to have the effect applied (in this case, a reverb), click on any available Send. A menu will appear.

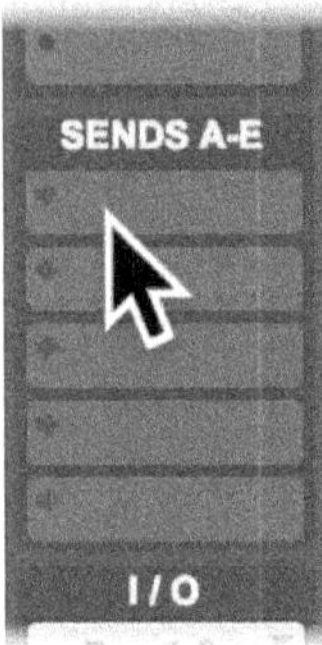

Figure 10.6 Creating a Send

2. Because I'll be routing audio from one track to another within the Pro Tools environment, you'll want to use a bus. Click on BUS in the menu of output options.

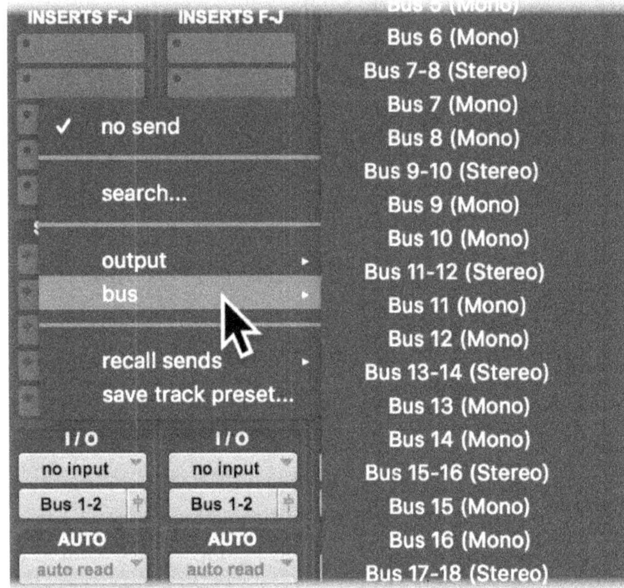

Figure 10.7 Choosing a Bus for the Send

3. I'll select an unused stereo bus for the first send. (We're using stereo buses because the signal will be sent to a stereo track.) Busses already being used in the project will be shown in a bold amber font.

4. Since I'm applying the same effect to multiple tracks, I'll need to create sends on the other tracks, assigned to the same bus that I used for the first send.

Here's what I've got so far:

Figure 10.8 Sends Created

5. Now, we need to create the Pro Tools equivalent of a "return." I'll create a stereo Aux track (which I'll name "Verb" in this case) and instantiate the time-based plug-in I want to use on any available insert on that track (in this case, D-Verb).
6. To complete the signal-routing process, I'll need to set the input of the Aux track to match the same stereo bus I chose for the other tracks' send. Like subgroup Aux tracks, I'll want to "solo safe" them, so that they don't mute when other tracks are soloed. To do this, hold the COMMAND key (Mac) or CTRL key (Windows) and click on the SOLO button.

Figure 10.9 Solo Safe-ing a Track

Here's the new routing as I see it in my Mix window, which now replicates the analog example that I outlined earlier. Now I can adjust the individual levels of each track as it is sent to the reverb plug-in (we'll discuss that in the next section).

Figure 10.10 Sends and a "Return

On the Aux track, I can adjust the volume fader to achieve the desired blend of wet and dry sounds. (The original Audio tracks are the "dry" part of the mix, and the Aux track is the "wet" part.) Since I've solo-safed my *Verb* track, soloing individual tracks won't mute the reverb. On the send's level fader, just like the track's volume fader, I can easily set it to unity by holding the OPTION key (Mac) or ALT key (Windows) and clicking on the fader (which you learned how to do back in Chapter 8).

At this point, I could change the output of the Auxiliary Input "return" track to go to the subgroup Aux track, or have it routed to the main output along with the subgroup Auxes in my project. One advantage of putting the return track within the subgroup is that changes made to the subgroup master track (in the example I showed before, the subgroup master is the "Vox SUB" track) would affect the reverb level as well as the dry levels. In other cases, having a track like my *Verb* track exist outside any subgroups allows me to more easily use it with other tracks (in this case, the instrumental tracks of the song).

Adjusting Send Parameters

When you create a send in Pro Tools, a *Send window* will appear:

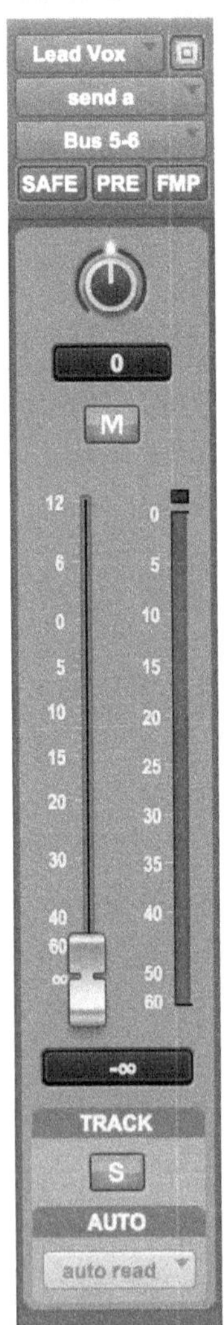

Figure 10.11 A Send Window

You'll notice that a Send window is similar to the Track Output window that you've seen in Chapter 8, with normal controls like pan and level controls. Send windows on stereo tracks, like the Track Output windows for these tracks, feature linking and inverse linking options.

As for setting the output level of a send, you can do that by adjusting the Send window's fader. Like other faders in Pro Tools, if you hold the OPTION key (Mac) or ALT key (Windows) and click the fader, you can quickly set the send's level to unity. You can open up multiple Send windows by holding the SHIFT key while clicking on Send Assignment buttons.

But there are a few things that you *haven't* seen before—aspects that are unique to sends:

Send Selector

Just like a Track Output window, the top of the Send window will display the track that the send is on, and you can change the track you're viewing by clicking the TRACK SELECTOR and selecting it from the menu. Below the Track selector is the *Send selector*, which will allow you to quickly switch between sends on that track. For example, in Figure 10.12, I have sends in position A and D. Clicking the SEND SELECTOR will reveal a list (with the currently shown send being indicated with a check mark). Just click on the desired send and the view in the window will be replaced.

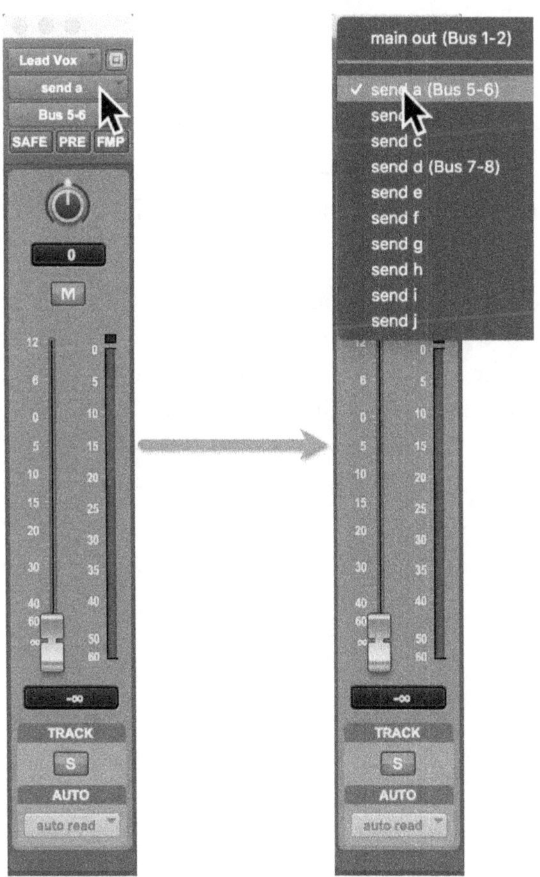

Figure 10.12 Changing Sends on a Track

Follow Main Pan

The pan controls in the Send window allow you to position the signal that is sent to the effect. Frequently, it's preferable to have the send's pan mirror the panning of the track, which is what *Follow Main Pan* does. Simply click on the FMP button in the Send window, and the send's pan will follow the panning that you choose for your track's output. You can tell whether your send is set to follow the main track panning by the lit FMP button and the greyed-out pan controls in the Send window.

Figure 10.13 Follow Main Pan (Enabled)

PRE

Sends are switchable between *pre-fader* and *post-fader*, as you've learned in Chapter 8. By default, when a send is created, it is *post-fader*, which is typically the option that you'll want for traditional effects routing. We'll talk about when you'd want to use a *pre-fader* send later in this chapter.

You can change the state of your send by clicking the PRE/POST FADER button. When the PRE button is highlighted in the Send window, the send is acting as a *pre-fader send*, meaning the output of the send will not be affected by the track's main volume fader or Mute button. When the PRE button is not highlighted (the initial state of sends in Pro Tools), the send is a *post-fader send*, and the volume fader and Mute button of the Audio track will affect the volume going out of the send.

Figure 10.14 Pre-Fader Send (Enabled)

Working with Sends

In addition to looking similar in the Mix and Edit Windows, sends and inserts share some common behavior:

- A send may be moved from one track to another (or to another position within a track), simply by clicking and dragging. As you drag the send, a yellow box will indicate where it will be dropped when the mouse is released.

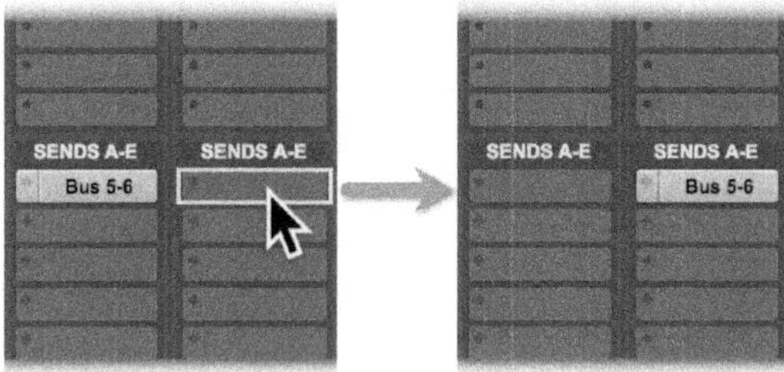

Figure 10.15 Moving a Send

- Instead of creating sends on additional tracks individually, you can also copy sends. Just hold the OPTION key (Mac) or ALT key (Windows) and drag a send from one track to another. A copy will be dragged and created when the mouse is released.

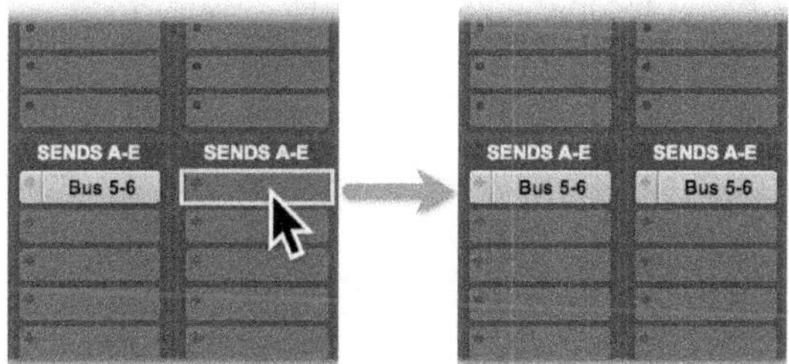

Figure 10.16 Copying a Send

- The parameters of a send (level, pan, and mute) can all be automated. Unlike plug-ins, they can't be enabled or disabled; they're always available to you. You can view send automation playlists in the Edit window from the *Track View Selector*.

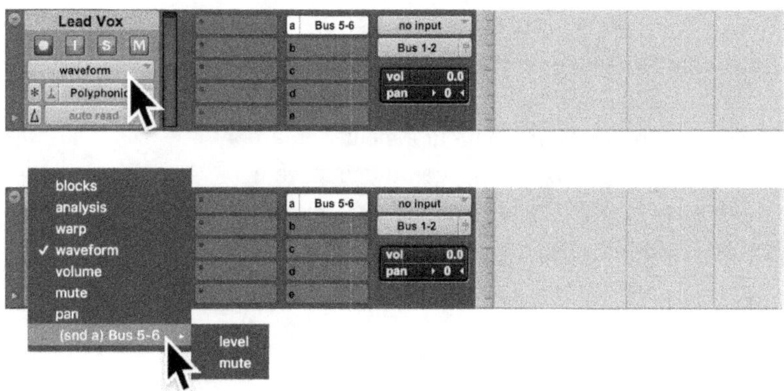

Figure 10.17 Showing Send Automation Playlists

Send outputs can be changed after they're created. As with many things in Pro Tools, there are multiple ways to do this:

- Click the SEND SELECTOR (the small section on the left of the send assignment button, as shown in figure 10.18) of the send that you want to change. A menu will appear (similar to the menu you saw when you initially created the send) allowing you to choose another output path.

Figure 10.18 The Send Selector

- In the Send window, click the OUTPUT PATH SELECTOR, and choose another output path.

Figure 10.19 The Output Path Selector in the Send Window

When you move, copy, or change the output of a send, any automation for that send will be retained. There are two caveats though: If you move a send from a stereo track to a mono track (or change the output from a stereo path to a mono path), only the left panning will be retained, and a warning dialog will appear. If you move a send from a mono track to a stereo track (or change the output from a mono path to a stereo path), *all* pan automation will be lost without warning.

Sends and Cue Mixes

When creating a send, you'll see in the menu presented that you can choose an *output* or a *bus* as a destination. So far, you've seen busses being used, since the routing is being done internally within the Pro Tools mixer.

There are a few situations that would call for an *output* as a destination. One case might be if you wanted to use a hardware reverb unit, similar to what was described at the beginning of this chapter. However, hardware effects are becoming increasingly rare in the face of improving virtual effects, and for those studios that use outboard hardware effects, they usually use something called an *I/O insert* (which isn't available in Pro Tools | First, but is covered in other books in the Avid Learning Series).

A more common case where you'd choose an *output* for your send is for creating a "cue mix," which is a headphone mix that a performer listens to while recording. This mix is different from the main mix that the engineer is hearing. Here's a common scenario: You have a guitar player and a bass player, each in separate rooms, ready to record their parts. They each have their own preference about what they want to hear in the headphones, which is different from the other performer. As a mixer, both these mixes are different from what you want to hear in the control room. Here's how you would do it (starting with the guitarist for no particular reason):

1. Create sends on all the tracks that would be included in the guitarist's cue mix (sometimes it's all the tracks, sometimes not). These will be assigned to the physical outputs connected to the guitarist's headphones.

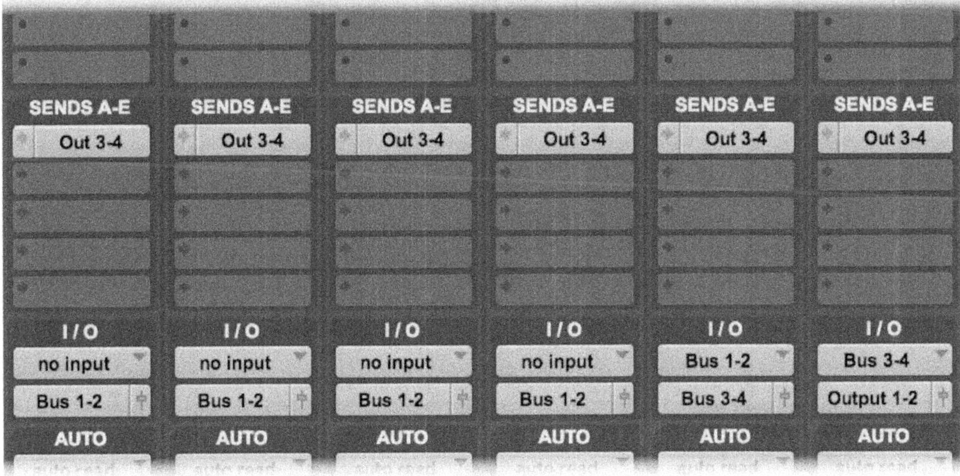

Figure 10.20 Creating the Guitarist's Cue Mix Sends

2. Next, the bass player. I'll create another row of sends and assign them to a (different) set of physical outputs, which would be the ones connected to the bassist's headphones.

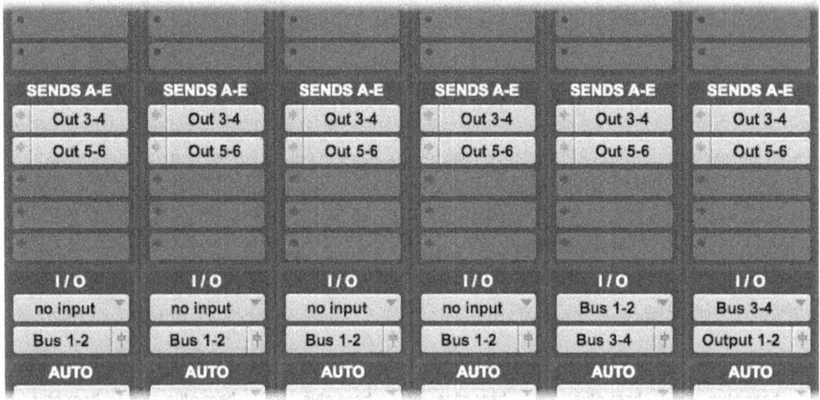

Figure 10.21 Creating the Bassist's Cue Mix Sends

In order to create cue mixes, you'll need to have an audio interface that supports more than two channels of output. If you're using your computer's built-in output, you won't have any extra outputs that you could use for cue mixes.

Here is where some modifier keys that you've learned earlier in this book can come in handy: Holding the OPTION key (Mac) or ALT key (Window) and creating a send on one track will create a send on that track and *all* other tracks. Holding the SHIFT+OPTION keys (Mac) or SHIFT+ALT keys (Windows) and creating a send on a track will create a send on that track and *all selected* tracks.

Pre-Fader vs. Post-Fader

In Chapter 8, you learned about pre-fader sends and post-fader sends, and where they fit in a track's signal flow:

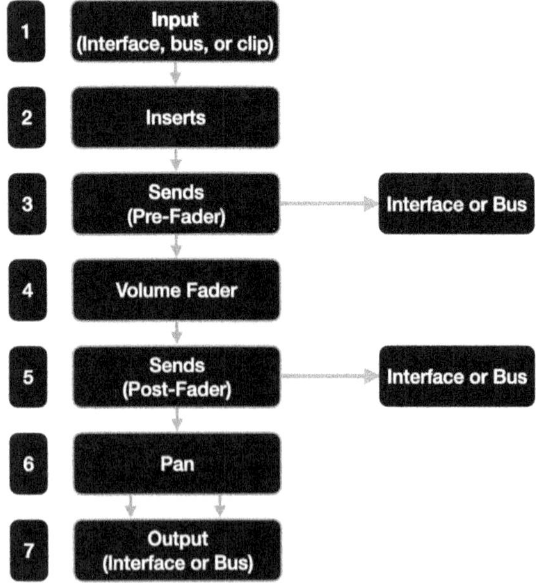

Figure 10.22 Audio/Aux/Instrument Track Signal Flow

Earlier in this chapter, we've used post-fader sends (the Pro Tools default) because when you're using sends and returns to add effects, you want your dry track's level to affect the wet track's output. This way, when you raise and lower the volume fader on the dry track, you'll raise and lower the signal being routed to the Aux, maintaining a consistent blend of wet and dry.

In the case of cue mixes, however, you'll typically use *pre-fader* sends, so that any changes you make in the control room mix won't affect either of the headphone mixes. Here are two ways to do it:

- In the Send window, click the PRE button. It will turn blue, indicating that it is now a pre-fader send.

Figure 10.23 Changing a Send to Pre-Fader in the Send Window

- Right-click any send (in the Mix or Edit window), and you'll see a menu of options. Choose PRE-FADER from the menu.

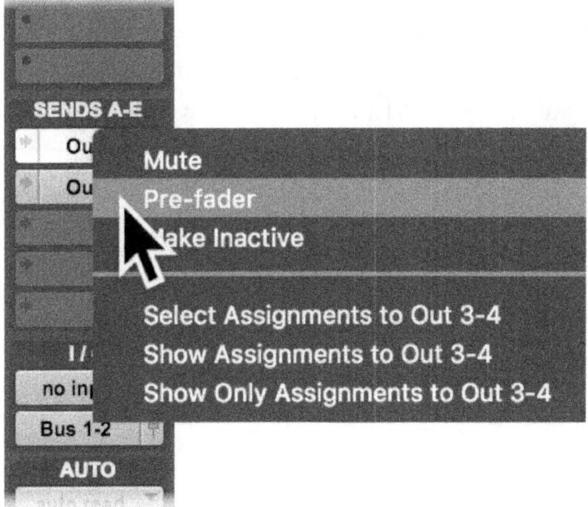

Figure 10.24 Changing a Send to Pre-Fader in the Mix Window

Sends that are pre-fader will be indicated by a blue Send selector.

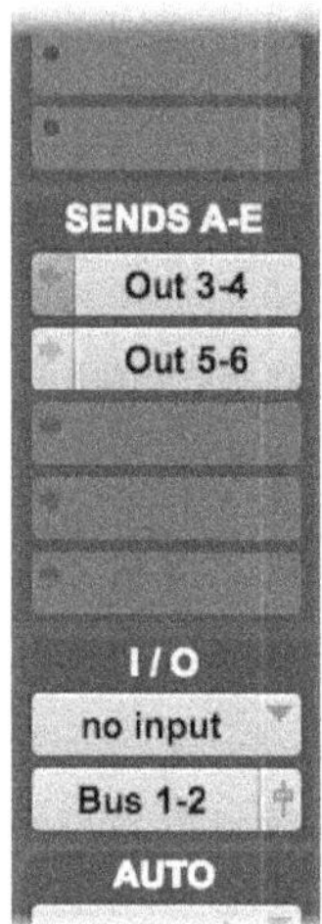

Figure 10.25 A Pre-Fader Send (Top) and a Post-Fader Send (Bottom)

Holding the OPTION key (Mac) or ALT key (Windows) and changing a track's send from pre- to post-fader will change all sends in that position on all tracks.

Pre-fader sends are mostly used in cue mixes, but not exclusively. If you're using effects and you want the wet and dry track levels to be completely independent, use a pre-fader send. Because signal will be routed to the Aux track *before* the dry track's fader, a full signal will be sent to *both* faders, allowing more flexibility with the wet and dry balance. Experiment!

Key Effect #4: Reverb

Reverberation (or *reverb* for short) is the persistence of sound after the source signal stops. How (or *if*) that sound persists is dependent on the physical space where the source of sound is, and the source's position within that space. Put into practical terms, a person speaking inside a glass box will sound different from the same person speaking in a cathedral. Moreover, the reverberant ambience that you'd hear from that person speaking in a cathedral will sound different depending on how far away from you they are.

Reverb in a mix is a great way to breathe ambient life into a project that was recorded in a dry studio situation, and the send/return setup that you learned earlier in this chapter will help you make the most of reverb in your mixes.

How Reverb Is Used in a Mix

With the qualifiers that no rules in mixing are absolute, there are a few traditional uses for reverb in a mix:

- **Mix Cohesion:** Very often, different tracks are recorded in acoustically "dead" studios—rooms specifically designed to have minimal reverberation. Of course, virtual instruments and other internally generated sounds will usually not have any reverberant qualities. Adding a reverb to a mix can place all of these instruments into a single cohesive space, adding a sense of realism to the mix.
- **Physical Space Re-Creation:** Especially for Post-Production projects, many elements (especially dialog) are re-recorded in a studio. A good post-production mixer will devote attention to choosing the right reverb—one that matches the physical space of the actor on the screen—so that the re-recorded material sonically matches the visual environment.
- **Ambient Effects:** Reverb isn't just for replicating a "real" space. Many styles of music (and sometimes in post-production as well) utilize reverb to create ambience that can't be found in the natural world.

Types of Reverb

Like other kinds of effects, reverbs come in many types. Traditionally, though, there are a few types of reverbs that you should be aware of. (Disclaimer: these descriptions contain some personal opinion.)

- **Plate:** This kind of reverb was originally a vibrating metal plate of metal with a pickup (actually it's a little more complex than that, but not much!). Plate reverbs don't sound especially "real," but they're quite dense and have a certain shimmer in the high end that works very nicely on some musical instruments.
- **Spring:** This is a variation on a plate reverb, but instead uses a vibrating spring (or multiple springs) instead. Like plate reverbs, they are a bit bright, which is perfect for some instruments (you'll find spring reverbs quite commonly used on guitars, for example).
- **Convolution:** This kind of reverb is great for replicating real spaces. The way that the reverb is created is by introducing a sound into the empty space that you want to emulate, and then recording the response to that sound. There are a few ways that this can be done: Sometimes a sine wave is played changing frequencies throughout the audible frequency range. Other times, a short sound (like a hand clap, popping balloons, or a race starter pistol [no bullets, *please*]). Once recorded, an *impulse response* is calculated, and that data is fed into the reverb. This is a great kind of reverb for replicating real spaces, and in post-production work, impulse responses are captured of location filming spaces.
- **Hall, Chamber, and Room:** You'll find these categories in many reverbs. A *Hall* emulates a concert hall, which is a very big, lush space. *Chambers* are big, but not quite as huge as halls, and so have some lushness, but a bit more clarity than a hall. *Rooms* tend to be smaller than halls or chambers and tend to feel more like "real" spaces—if you want to give your mix a sense of having *walls*, this is a good way to go.

Reverb Parameters

Avid's *D-Verb* plug-in is included with Pro Tools | First and is a popular favorite for many Pro Tools users. It's also a great example of a reverb plug-in, and its parameters can be commonly found on other reverbs.

Figure 10.26 Avid's D-Verb Plug-In

Meters

The meters in the *D-Verb* plug-in window are on either side, with the input meter on the left side and the output meter on the right. On the input meter, there is an input level control fader, which you can decrease in order to prevent clipping, or increase to raise the level of the signal to be processed.

Reverb Algorithm

In the top center of the plug-in window, you'll find seven buttons which will allow you to choose the algorithm for the reverb.

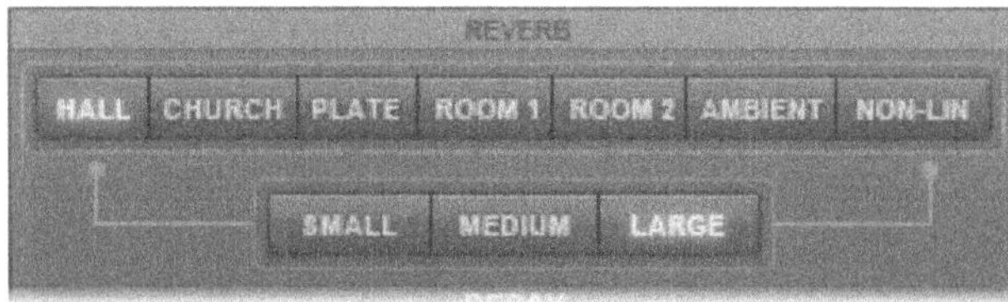

Figure 10.27 The Reverb Algorithm Controls

The types are:

- **Hall:** Concert Hall. Large and diffuse.
- **Church:** Another large diffuse space, but with slightly more solidity than *Hall.*
- **Plate:** Emulates a plate reverb.
- **Room 1**: A medium-sized room.
- **Room 2:** Smaller and brighter than *Room 1.*
- **Ambient**: A sparse, airy reverb.
- **Nonlinear**: Good for special effects and for an aggressive sound. Unlike a real reverb, this will build up gradually and end abruptly.

For each algorithm, there are *Small*, *Medium*, and *Large* options. After choosing your desired algorithm, changing these settings will change the perceived size of the space.

Decay

Imagine you're alone on the stage of a concert hall and you sing a single note. When your singing stops, you'll hear the reverb of the concert hall as the numerous reflections of your voice gradually die out. The time that it takes for this to happen is called *Decay*.

Figure 10.28 The Decay Control and Indicator

By changing the *Decay* parameter on a reverb, you can change the time that it takes for the energy of the incoming signal to decrease to silence. Be careful though, a long decay doesn't necessarily equate to a larger-feeling room. When you choose your initial algorithm and size, you'll see that the Decay parameter (and others as well) change to give you a good starting point. Changing the decay time after that can help you to fine-tune the sound of the reverb to suit your needs.

No physical space can have an infinite decay time, but that's not a problem for a plug-in. For each algorithm and size, if you increase the decay time to the maximum, you'll see "inf" in the decay parameter value, which is an *infinite* reverb that will never stop (even after you stop Pro Tools from playing, which can get maddening!). Of course, you wouldn't use this to emulate any kind of real physical space, but it can be very useful for different kinds of surreal effects.

Figure 10.29 An Infinite Reverb

Pre-Delay

Pre-Delay is a parameter that needs some explanation. Let's say you're still on that concert hall stage, and you clap your hands one time. The sound leaves your hands and radiates outward. Until that sound hits a sonically reflective wall there will be no reverb, but sound needs time to travel, and the time it takes for the sound to begin reverberating is called *pre-delay*.

Now let's say that by some magical means, you were immediately transported to another concert hall stage. This new hall is the same as the previous one in every way, except *twice as big*. That means the time it takes for your hand clap to reach a wall to reflect from is twice as long. That means a longer *pre-delay* time.

Figure 10.30 The Pre-Delay Control and Indicator

And that's just what you'll do with the *Pre-Delay* parameter in the *D-Verb* plug-in—*move walls*. A larger pre-delay value will increase the time it takes for the incoming signal to start to reverberate, simulating a larger space. Conversely, you can move walls closer to you by decreasing the pre-delay time.

Diffusion

If you think about it in physical terms, reverberation is a number of very quick echoes, and a surfaces of a space not only react to the sound it receives from the original source, but they also react to the reflections from other surfaces of the room. *Diffusion* refers to the amount of this interaction.

Figure 10.31 The Diffusion Control and Indicator

In the *D-Verb* plug-in (and most reverbs) you can control the diffusion—you'll find it just below the Pre-Delay parameter. High settings can get quite lush, but its thickness can sometimes reduce the intelligibility of words. Decreasing the diffusion can sometimes work in your favor in preserving the clarity of things like vocals (if you take this too far, reverbs sometimes take on an echo-y character).

High Frequency Cut and Low Frequency Pass Filter

On the right-hand side are two related controls: *HF (High Frequency) Cut* and *LP (Low Pass) Filter*. They work together to help you sculpt the tone of your reverb:

Figure 10.32 HF Cut and LP Filter Controls and Indicators

- **HF Cut:** This parameter controls the decay time of high frequencies in relation to the total frequency spectrum. When set lower, high frequencies will decay faster. If you experiment with this parameter, you'll find that it's easy to hear the difference. With this parameter, you can tweak how "airy" your reverb is.
- **LP Filter:** You've seen low pass filters before, in EQs and in the side-chain controls of compressors and expanders. The low-pass filter does the same thing here, cutting frequencies above the value shown to the right of the parameter knob.

Here are a couple of guidelines when it comes to managing the high frequencies of your reverb:

- Plosives (hard "P" or "B" sounds) can be jarring, and we often want to deemphasize them. Increasing the HF Cut parameter brings more brilliance to more sibilant sounds and minimizes lower frequencies (and plosives).
- People in a room tend to absorb high frequencies. If you're trying to emulate a space with a lot of people in it, decreasing the high frequency content of your reverb can help.
- Decreasing high frequencies can give a sense of a larger space (due to the fact that air tends to absorb high frequencies first, and larger spaces have more air).

Mix

We've already used the terms "dry" (the unprocessed original sound) and "wet" (the processed output of an effect). In the examples earlier in this chapter using sends and returns (even the virtual "return" in a DAW), the tracks with the sends are 100% dry, and the Aux track to which the sends are routed is 100% wet. The blend between wet and dry is done using the faders in the Pro Tools mixer.

You also have the ability to balance a wet and dry signal within the D-Verb plug-in window. Dragging the horizontal slider in the *Mix* section will allow you to control the wet and dry balance.

Figure 10.33 The Mix Control and Indicator

A recommendation: If you use the traditional send and return structure we've talked about in this chapter, you should leave this parameter *alone* (by default, it is set to 100% wet precisely because it's meant to be used in a send and return routing). However, in the (hopefully) rare cases where you want to put a reverb plug-in directly on the track you're affecting (like you would with an EQ or dynamic plug-in), you would then want to adjust this parameter to get the dry/wet balance relationship you're looking for.

Mono/Stereo

If you're using a traditional send and return routing structure, the reverb effect will reside on a stereo Aux Input track. However, if you need to place a reverb on any kind of mono track, you will find that you have *two* different D-Verbs to choose from.

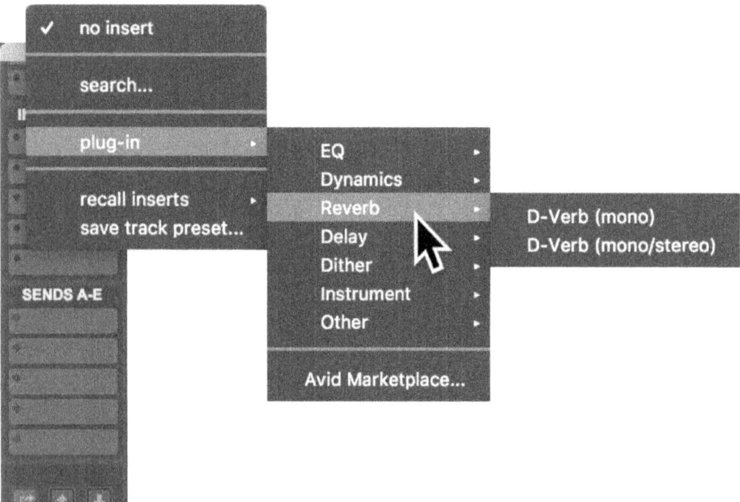

Figure 10.34 Choosing a Mono or Mono/Stereo Plug-In on a Mono Track

- **D-Verb (Mono):** This is a fully mono plug-in, with a mono input and a mono output.
- **D-Verb (Mono/Stereo):** This plug-in has a mono input (since it's instantiated on a mono track), but a *stereo* output. You'll see as soon as you instantiate this kind of plug-in on a mono track that you'll now have two output meters and the track will now behave as a stereo track would (except for any inserts prior to the mono/stereo plug-in).

Presets

So far in our discussion on effects (EQ, Compressor, and Limiter), we've focused on the parameters, and not as much on the presets that they come with. That's intentional, because with the great variety of audio that they process, presets won't be a perfect fit in most cases, and are dangerous to overly rely upon.

Reverbs are a bit different, in that they are filling a different role in your mix, replicating physical spaces or devices. You'll find that with reverbs (and delays, which we'll talk about next), the presets included are more useful. You'll want to fine-tune the effect (and you'll be glad that you understand the parameters), but often, choosing a preset is a great place to start.

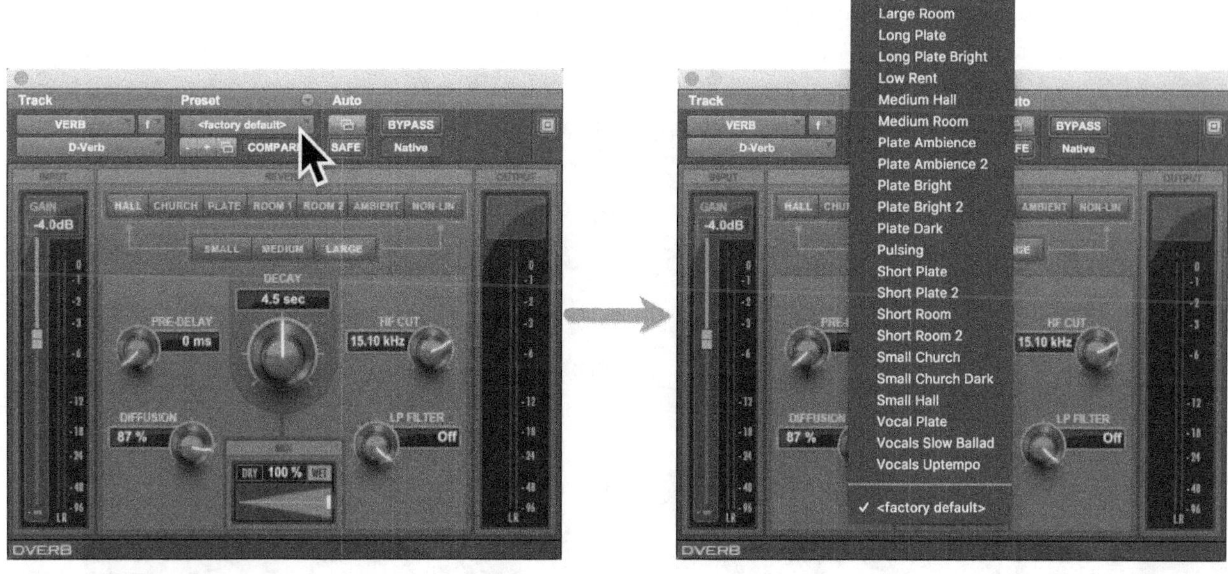

Figure 10.35 Choosing a Preset

Key Effect #5: Delay

Delay does what its name implies—it delays the incoming sound. But that's only part of the story and the name of the effect doesn't really represent how it's used in a mix. If you apply delay to the send and return structure we've talked about so far in this chapter, with the dry tracks unprocessed and the "return" track delayed, what it will sound like is an *echo*.

How Delay Is Used in a Mix

Delays are used in a variety of ways in mixing:

- **"Thickening":** A short delay can add body to an individual track or group of tracks.
- **Stereo Widening:** On a stereo track (or using a mono/stereo plug-in on a mono track), a small amount of delay on only one side can increase the perceived width of the track.
- **Ambient and Rhythmic effects:** Delays are by their nature less diffuse than reverb, which allows them to be distinctly heard. This makes them useful in reinforcing the groove of a song in ways that reverb cannot.

Unlike reverbs, which are almost always used on effects "returns" (on an Aux track that is receiving signals from sends). There are occasions where delays can be used on individual tracks directly (for example, the stereo widening of a track is typically not a blended effect). For this book, we'll focus on workflows that utilize a send and return routing, as we did with reverbs.

Delay Parameters

Avid's *Mod Delay III* plug-in is included with Pro Tools | First and is a good example of a delay. Let's go through the different parameters:

Figure 10.36 Avid's Mod Delay III Plug-In

Meters

Like the *D-Verb* plug-in, the meters in the *Mod Delay III* plug-in window are on either side, with the input meter on the left side and the output meter on the right. There are two differences: At the top of the input meter section, there is a *Phase Invert* button for each input channel. Also, the gain controls are on the output side of the plug-in.

Delay Time

The *Delay Time* parameter is very simple—it's the difference (in milliseconds) between the incoming signal and the outgoing signal. You'll see that you have two independent controls, meaning you can have a different delay time on the left and right side.

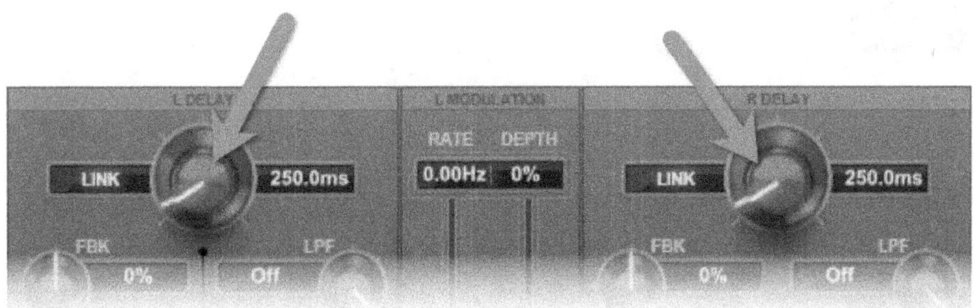

Figure 10.37 Delay Time Controls and Indicators for the Left and Right Channels

If you want to have both channels share the same delay time (and all parameters), just click either of the Link buttons.

Figure 10.38 Link Button for the Left and Right Channels

In a mono Mod Delay III plug-in window, since there are no multiple channels to link, the area to the left of the Delay Time knob will read "Mono."

Feedback

Most of the parameters on a delay are pretty straightforward, but *Feedback* requires a little bit of explanation. By default, the Mod Delay III plug-in's feedback is 0%—no feedback whatsoever. What you will hear is a single delay of the incoming sound, and when combined with the dry signal, it'll sound like a single echo.

Figure 10.39 The Feedback (FBK) Control and Indicator

If I were to increase the Feedback (FBK) parameter to 50%, here's what would happen: 50% of the delayed signal would be rerouted back (or "fed back") into the input of delay. The delay would then delay the (delayed) signal and send 50% of *that* signal (which would be 25% of the original signal) back into the input of the delay. This would go on until the level of the fed-back signal is inaudible.

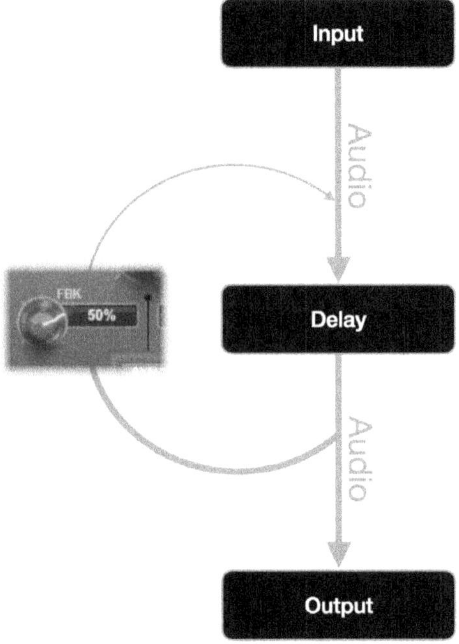

Figure 10.40 Feedback Signal Flow

Shorter feedback percentages will give you multiple delays (based on the Delay Time parameter) that die out quickly. Longer percentages will increase the number of audible repetitions of the delay—and yes, there's a 100% feedback available to you, which would be an infinite delay.

As you experiment with this parameter, you'll notice that there are positive percentages and *negative* ones. When you set your feedback to a negative percentage, the fed-back signal will be phase-inverted, which can give a more intense "flanged" sound when used with shorter delay time settings.

Low Pass Filter

Figure 10.41 Low Pass Filter (LPF) Control and Indicator

Like the reverb plug-in you saw earlier in this chapter, the Low Pass Filter (LPF) parameter allows you to cut high frequencies from the output. The maximum setting—*off*—will result in no frequencies being cut.

Musical Delay Parameters

You can easily set your delay times to follow the musical tempo and meter of a song. At the bottom of the *Mod Delay III* plug-in window are a number of parameters that will allow you to do it:

Figure 10.42 Musical Delay Parameters

- **Sync:** When the *Sync* option is enabled (the word "SYNC" will appear in orange, as shown in Figure 10.42), the musical *duration* selected below in this section will follow the tempo and meter of your project, including any tempo or meter changes as your project plays.
- **Meter:** When the Sync option is *disabled*, you can manually set a meter by clicking the appropriate field and typing the appropriate value.
- **Tempo:** Likewise, you can manually set a tempo, either by clicking in the field or typing a value or adjusting the tempo knob (to the left of the tempo value display).

When *Sync* is enabled, the *Meter* and *Tempo* fields will be greyed-out and unavailable.

- **Duration:** The duration setting allows you to select the musical values for your delay. Changing these values will correspondingly change the duration value at the top of the plug-in window. Duration values can be independently set for the left and right sides for more complex rhythmic results. Durations can include triplets and dotted note values.
- **Groove:** Changing the *groove* setting will add to the delay time (if a positive value is chosen) or subtract time (if a negative value is chosen). Positive values will result in greater spacing of the delayed sounds, and negative values will reduce their spacing (a value of 0% will follow the tempo and meter precisely). Groove is commonly used to create a "swing" effect and can be independently set on both left and right channels.

Modulation Parameters

When we use the term *modulation*, we're talking about changing some aspect of a sound (called a *carrier*) with another sound (called the "modulator"). The classic example is a vocoder, where a musical note functions as the carrier, and is acted upon by the articulation of a voice, giving the result of synthesized singing.

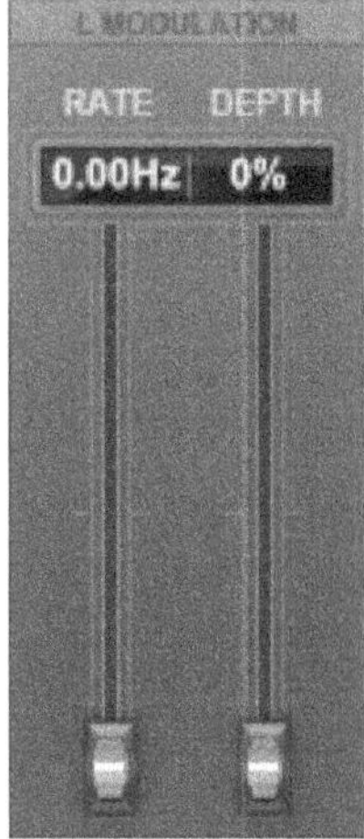

Figure 10.43 Modulation Controls and Indicators

In the *Mod Delay III* plug-in, there is a *Low Frequency Oscillator* (LFO), which is a sine wave that you can change from 0-20 Hz. This modulator acts upon the incoming signal (the carrier) to affect the pitch of the processed signal. These modulation controls are typically (but not always) used in conjunction with short delay times to achieve chorus or flanging effects. You have two different controls per channel that you can use to tweak these parameters:

- **Rate:** This parameter controls the frequency of the modulating signal. The lower the frequency, the gentler and more sweeping the effect.
- **Depth:** This parameter controls the amplitude of the modulating signal. A lower value will result in more subtle pitch variations. Larger values will make the pitch changes more obvious.

Mix

As with the D-Verb plug-in, you have the ability to balance a wet and dry signal within the *Mod Delay III* plug-in. Dragging the horizontal slider in the *Mix* section will allow you to control the wet and dry balance.

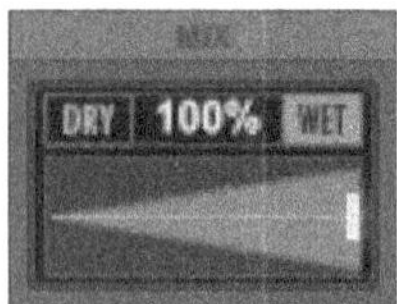

Figure 10.44 The Mix Control and Indicator

Mono/Stereo

As with the D-Verb plug-in, if you instantiate a *Mod Delay III* plug-in on a mono track, you have the option of a *Mono* or *Mono/Stereo* version of the plug-in. Choosing *Mono/Stereo* will cause the track to behave as a stereo track after the plug-in's insert.

Hands-On Exercise 10.1: Adding Ambience

For the last exercise of this book, you'll add a reverb to your *Low Roar* session, and also a neat mixing trick utilizing what you've learned about the Edit tools, sends, delays, and automation.

Setting Up

1. Open the *Low Roar* project that you started in Chapter 8 (balancing volume levels and pan) and continued working on in Chapter 9 (adding EQ and dynamic effects). Alternately, you can create a project from the *Pro Tools First—Fundamentals of Audio Production—Chapter 10 (Low Roar Tracks).ptx* session, included with the downloadable materials for this book.

Adding a Reverb

2. In the Mix window, show the *Sends A-E* View.
3. Create a send in the first send position (Send A) on the *Lead Vocal (Dry)* track, routed to an available stereo bus. If you have followed the steps outlined in Chapter 8, *Bus 15-16* should be available.
4. Create a Stereo Auxiliary Input track, named *VERB*, with an input matching the same bus that you chose for the send.
5. Assign the output of the VERB track to match the input of the Main SUB track (Bus 13-14, if you've completed the hands-on exercises from Chapter 8).
6. Solo-Safe the *Verb* track.
7. On the *Verb* track, instantiate a multichannel *D-Verb* plug-in on any available insert.

Figure 10.45 Routing a Send to a Reverb Aux Track

8. To start with, try the following reverb settings.
   - **Reverb Algorithm:** Hall (Medium)
   - **Pre-Delay:** 0 ms
   - **Decay:** 2.6 sec
   - **HF Cut:** 12.92 kHz
   - **Diffusion:** 100%
   - **LP Filter:** 12.87 kHz
   - **Mix:** 100% wet
9. On the *Lead Vocal (Dry)*, click the send assignment button in order to show the Send window for that track (if not already shown).
10. Solo the *Lead Vocal (Dry)* track, so that all you can hear is the vocal track *and* the solo-safed reverb.
11. During playback, on the *Lead Vocal (Dry)* track, raise the level of the send to add some ambience to the vocal track. Let your ears be your guide.
12. Copy the send to the *Background Vocals (Dry)* track and change the send level, so that all your vocals have the appropriate amount of reverb. Here as well, you'll want to solo your track to clearly hear the single part.
13. Un-solo the soloed tracks and begin playback. Use the fader on the *VERB* track to adjust the level of the reverb in the entire mix.

Adding a Delay

Delays are great, but long delay times can turn a track into an unrecognizable mush. Here's a way that you can take surgical control over what is delayed and what is not:

In the *Low Roar* project, I want to add something new to the second verse. In the second line of the second verse, the singer sings "Tells me what to say and to do." I want to add a trippy delay to just the word "do."

14. Create a send on the *Lead Vocal (Dry)* track in the second send position (Send B), assigned to an available stereo bus. If you're following the steps in this book, *Bus 17-18* should be available.
15. Create a new stereo Aux track, named VOX DLY. Solo-safe the track.
16. Set the input of the track to match the send that you just created. Set the output of the track to the same bus that you used for the vocal subgroup (if you're following the steps in the exercises, that should be Bus 1-2).

Figure 10.46 Routing a Send to a Delay Aux Track

Now, what we want to do is to automate the level of the send, so that only the word "do" will be sent to the *VOX DLY* track.

17. If you're looking at the Mix window, change it to the Edit window.
18. On the *Lead Vocal (Dry)* track, change the track view to (SND B) Bus [#]>LEVEL. You will now see the send level represented as a black line at the bottom of the track.

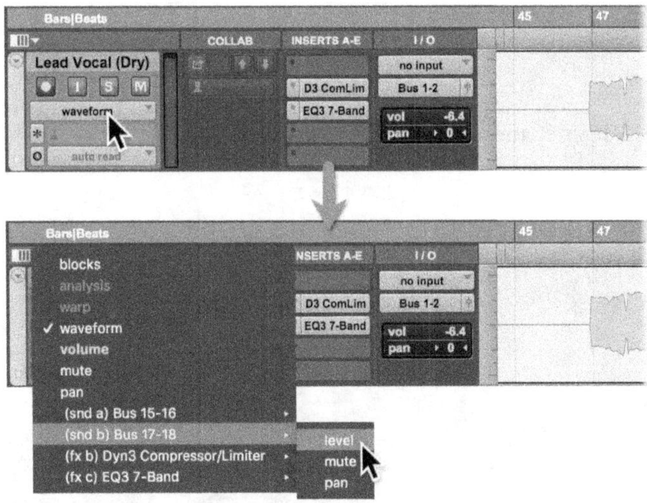

Figure 10.47 Viewing Send B's Level on the Vocal Track

19. Zoom in horizontally on the timeline, so that you can clearly see the phrase starting at bar 53.
20. Using the Selector tool, select only the word "do." (TIP: Tab to Transient will make this easy!) Make sure that you select the entire word.
21. Using the Trim tool, drag the volume line (in the selected area only), so that the send level automation only rises during the word "do." Set the level to be as close to unity (-0 dB) as possible.

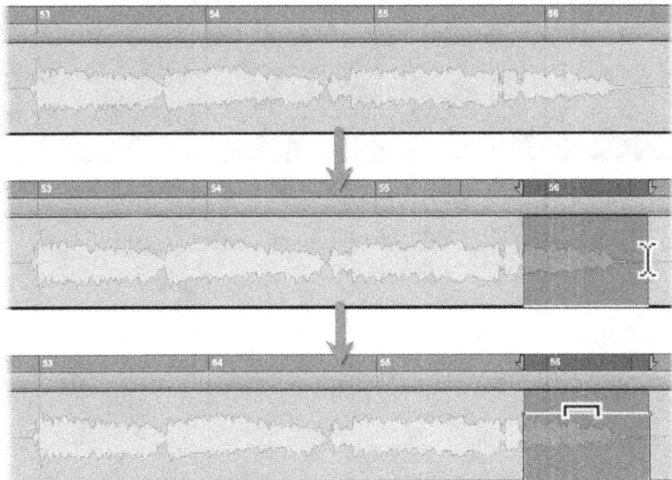

Figure 10.48 Changing Send Level Automation

Now let's have some fun and set up a Delay plug-in followed by an EQ.

22. On the *VOX DLY* track, instantiate a multichannel *Mod Delay III* plug-in in the first insert position.
23. Set up the parameters for the delay:
    - **Feedback:** 90% (for both left and right side)
    - **LPF:** Off (for both left and right side)
    - **Sync:** On
    - **Duration:** dotted quarter note on the left side, and a quarter note on the right side
    - **Groove:** 0% (for both left and right side)
    - **Mix:** 100% wet
    - **Modulation Controls:** both at 0 for both channels

Figure 10.49 Settings for the Mod Delay III Plug-In

24. On the *VOX DLY* track, instantiate a multichannel *EQ3 7-Band EQ* plug-in in the second insert position.
25. In the HPF band, make the following settings:
    - **Mode:** High Pass Filter
    - **Q:** 18 dB/Oct
    - **Frequency:** 1.00 kHz

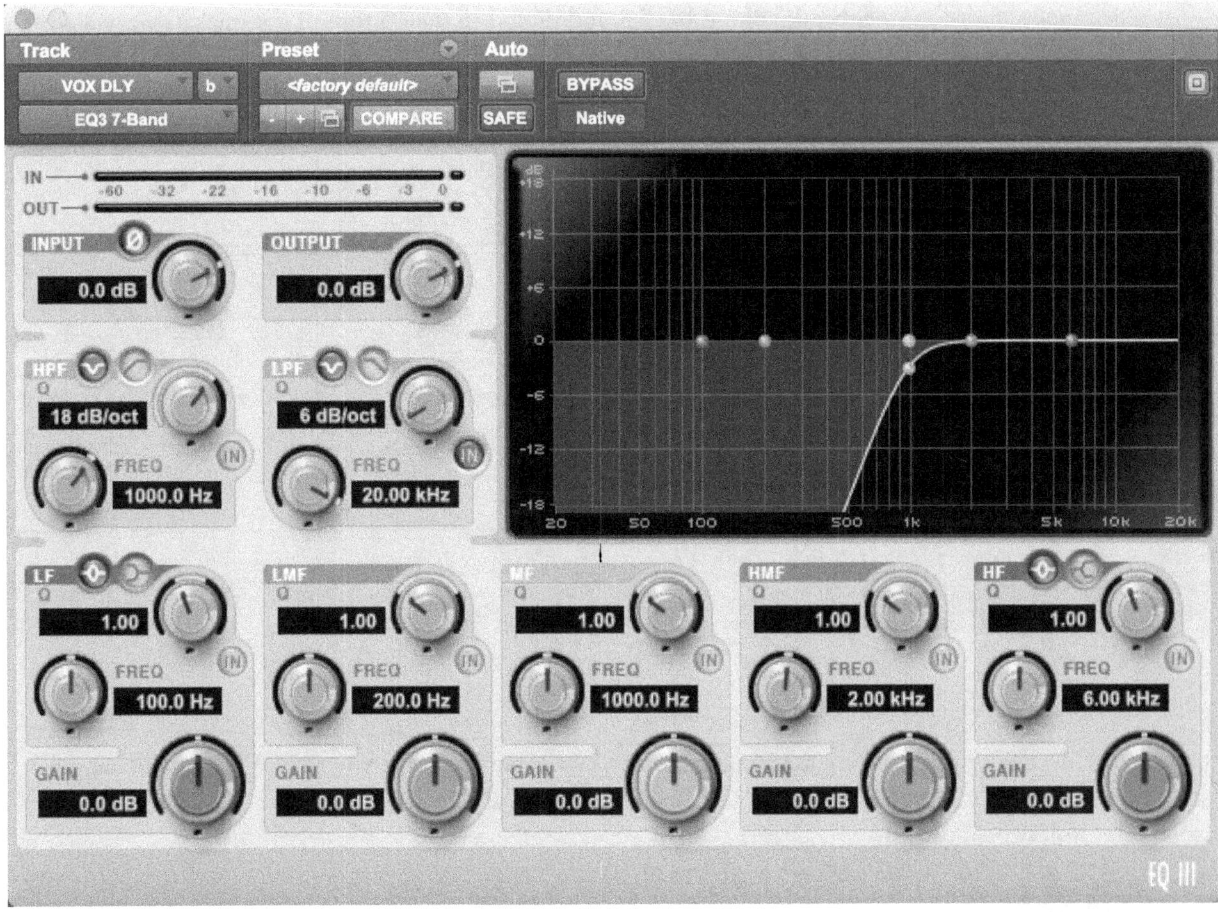

Figure 10.50 Settings for the EQ3 7-Band Plug-In

26. With *Lead Vocal (Dry)* track soloed, play the section and adjust the level of the *VOX DLY* track to get the blend that you like. Un-solo the track, so that you can hear the effect in context with the entire mix and make adjustments as needed.

> The delay and EQ settings are starting-off points. See what you think and make changes if you want!

> If you want, you could create a send on the delay track that is routed to the reverb, to give the same kind of reverb to this effect as to the rest of the vocal track. Personally, I like the contrast though!

The only problem is that with a feedback percentage of 90%, the delay will go on almost forever!

27. On the *VOX DLY* track, using the Grabber tool, create a single automation breakpoint at bar 58. (TIP: Grid mode will help you with this.)

28. Finally, create another breakpoint at bar 59, and drag it to the bottom of the track. This will create a fade out of the delayed signal.

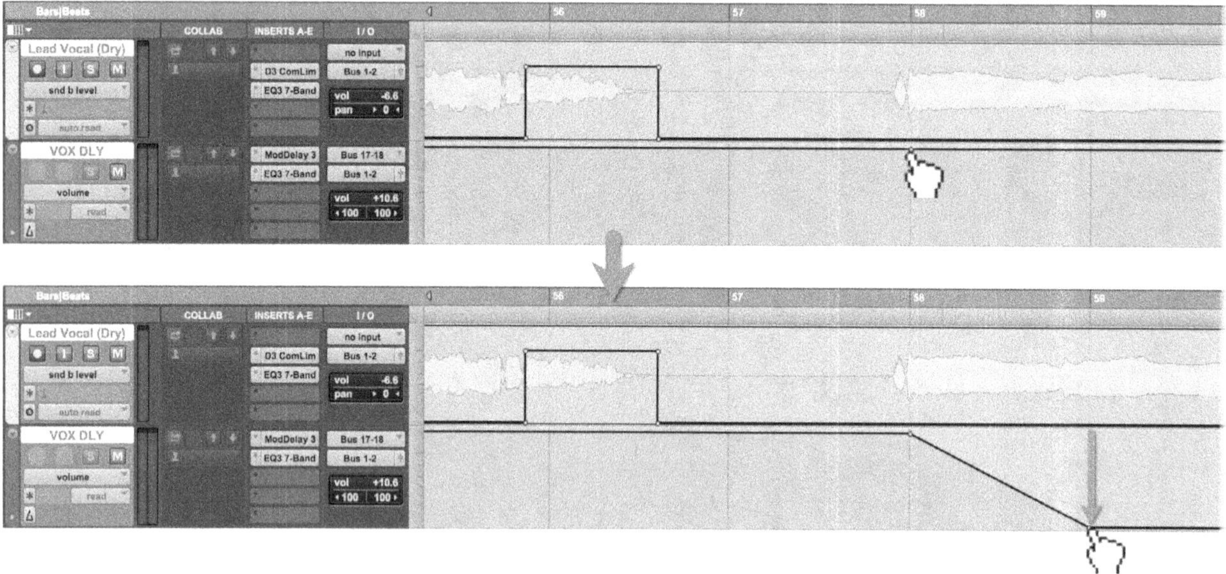

Figure 10.51 Creating a Volume Fade-out on the Vox Dly Track

29. Check your mix, making adjustments to any mix parameters that you like. When you're happy with your mix, you're done! You can export it and share it with others. Make sure to save your project first, though!

Well Done!

Congratulations, you've made it! You've covered quite a lot of ground, and the great news is that if you want, your journey is just beginning! Over time, you'll learn more about audio production, Pro Tools, and develop your own working style.

As you grow, you'll want to learn more. Fortunately, Avid has an excellent training program based on a comprehensive curriculum. With Avid's Learning Series (and with Avid's Learning Partners) you can move confidently into the larger world of professional audio production. To learn more about Avid's offerings, go to **https://www.avid.com/learn-and-support.**

At Avid, "Powering Greater Creators" is more than a slogan—it's a passion. Speaking for the whole Avid Learning team, we hope that this book has inspired you, and we wish you all the success that you wish for yourself.

Good luck!

Review Questions

1. What are the advantages of putting a blended effect (like reverb) on an Aux track with sends on the dry tracks, instead of just putting the reverb on the dry track itself?
2. How can you *solo-safe* a track?
3. What does *Follow Main Pan* mean?
4. When using a send for a cue mix, should it be *pre-* or *post-fader*?
5. When using a reverb, what does changing the *pre-delay* affect?
6. True or False? It's possible to create an *infinite* reverb in Pro Tools.
7. In a typical send and return signal routing, the *mix* setting in the plug-in window should be ______% wet.
8. In a Delay, what does the *Feedback* parameter control?
9. True or False? The Mod Delay III plug-in cannot follow your project's tempo and meter changes.
10. What aspects of a send can be automated?

www.ingramcontent.com/pod-product-compliance
Lightning Source LLC
Chambersburg PA
CBHW080531300426
44111CB00017B/2673
9781538143841